Modern Macroeconomics

Modern Macroeconomics

MICHAEL PARKIN
&
ROBIN BADE
University of Western Ontario

Philip Allan

First published 1982 by
PHILIP ALLAN PUBLISHERS LIMITED
MARKET PLACE
DEDDINGTON
OXFORD OX5 4SE

British Library Cataloguing in Publication Data

Parkin, Michael
  Modern macroeconomics.
  1. Macroeconomics.
  I. Title   II. Bade, Robin
  339'.01   HB171

  ISBN 0-86003-047-4
  ISBN 0-86003-142-X   Pbk

Set by *Sunrise Setting,* Torquay
Printed in Great Britain by Hartnoll Print Limited, Bodmin, Cornwall

To E.M. & W.P.

Contents

CLASSICAL THEORY **PART III**
THE BASIC THEORY OF INCOME, EMPLOYMENT, AND THE PRICE LEVEL

PART IV
THE KEYNESIAN THEORY OF INCOME, EMPLOYMENT, AND THE PRICE LEVEL

25. The United Kingdom's Recent Economic History: How Well is it Explained by the Neoclassical Synthesis?   358

PART V
RATIONAL EXPECTATIONS THEORY OF INCOME, EMPLOYMENT, AND THE PRICE LEVEL

26. Introduction to the Rational Expectations Theories of Income, Employment, and the Price Level   376

27. Information, Expectations, and the New Classical Theory of Aggregate Supply   381

PART VI
MACROECONOMIC POLICY

Preface

This book presents a comprehensive and up-to-date account of macroeconomics — that branch of economics which seeks to explain inflation, unemployment, interest rates, foreign exchange rates, the balance of payments, and other related phenomena. Unlike any other book currently available at this level, a considerable amount of space and attention is devoted to developments that have taken place in the subject in the past ten years. The chief of these is the incorporation into macroeconomics of the rational expectations hypothesis. The rational expectations hypothesis is explained in simple, intuitive terms, and its implications for the determination of inflation, unemployment and economic stabilisation policy are explained and analysed. The book does not only deal with the developments in macroeconomics that have taken place in the past decade. It also provides an account of the mainstream neoclassical synthesis which grew out of the Keynesian and pre-Keynesian theories. In addition, it shows how the new macroeconomics relates to these earlier approaches. The book pays careful attention to the interrelations between the domestic economy and the rest of the world — open economy macroeconomics — and to the design and conduct of macroeconomic policy.

In presenting an account of modern macroeconomics, we have attempted to avoid the extremes of dry theory and passionate policy advocacy. Theory is presented in such a way that the reader may quickly and easily see its predictive content. Those predictions are checked against the facts, revealing in the process the extent to which a theory is capable of explaining the facts as well as its main shortcomings. Policy is handled by analysing the implications of pursuing the policy recommendations of different schools of thought in such a way that the reader may clearly see why it is that different economists reach different conclusions on these important questions.

The central purpose of the book is to make modern macroeconomics accessible to beginning and intermediate students. To this end, we have used the simplest available analytical techniques, intuitive explanations and, wherever possible, illustrations drawn directly from United Kingdom macroeconomic experience. The book is pitched for the most part at a level which we hope is appropriate for university students who are in their second undergraduate year, although large parts of the book will be easily understood by beginning students; and other parts will be found useful by more advanced students who are looking for a simplified and intuitive explanation of material which is only otherwise available in journal articles. Indeed, in view of the lack of any alternative exposition (other than original research articles in learned journals) of much of the material that is presented here, the book will be found useful even by beginning graduate students who are looking for a broad

xix

overview of material which they will study in greater depth in their post-graduate courses, as well as by those whose formal study of economics was completed before the rational expectations revolution hit macroeconomics and who are now professional economists in government, industry and commerce and wish to be given a quick guided tour of this material.

The book is organised around three main themes — facts, theories and policies. The two introductory sections set out the facts that macroeconomics seeks to explain and also give an account of the ways in which macroeconomic phenomena are observed and measured. The core of the book deals with theory. It is organised around a series of progressively more comprehensive models of the economy, each of which has some merits in explaining a limited set of facts, but each of which also has some shortcomings which are highlighted. Following the development of alternative theories, macroeconomic policy — the problem of stabilising output, employment and prices — is discussed at considerable length.

Macroeconomics is a controversial subject and economists often disagree vehemently on policy issues. Despite this, there is a considerable measure of agreement on most matters. There do, however, remain crucial issues that divide economists and, although it is a slight over-simplification, it seems reasonably accurate to divide macroeconomists into two camps — Keynesians and Monetarists. One of us is widely regarded as being a Monetarist and, as a descriptive matter, neither of us can seriously quarrel about being so labelled. We have, nevertheless, tried to write a book which avoids falling into the trap of being a Monetarist tract. Some, no doubt, will conclude that we have failed. We have certainly not shied away from presenting alternative views on macroeconomic policy in the sharpest possible focus. We have attempted to do justice to the positions of each view and explain precisely what it is that each believes and why. Acceptance of the hypothesis that expectations are formed rationally is often regarded as being synonymous with Monetarism. The fact that this book, unlike any other at this level, presents an account of rational expectations (and a sympathetic one at that) will no doubt lead some to conclude that for that reason alone this book is a Monetarist tract. Such a view will be seen, on careful reflection, to be incorrect. There are rational expectations Keynesians (usually referred to as new Keynesians) as well as rational expectations Monetarists (usually referred to as new Classicals). Both of these strands in the literature are presented and explained.

This book would not have been completed without the help of a large number of people. Michael Cox (of the Virginia Polytechnic Institute) has been involved in the project from which the book has resulted since its inception and has read and commented upon substantial parts of the manuscript and provided many of the review questions. Bob Nobay (of the University of Liverpool) and our colleagues David Laidler and Stephen Margolis have provided extensive comments on various parts of the manuscript. We also benefited from the comments on some earlier drafts of what were, at the time, anonymous referees, but whom we now know to have been Brian Scarfe of the University of Alberta and James Pesando of the University of Toronto. Several generations of undergraduate students and graduate teaching assistants at the University of Western Ontario have been of considerable help in providing comments and criticisms upon various parts of the book at different stages of its development. We are especially grateful to Rosalind Wong, Monica van Huystee and David Abramson. Jane McAndrew provided expert library and clerical assistance and research assistance was provided by Kevin Dowd and Eddie McDonnell. The many drafts and revisions of this book have been typed with great skill by Marg Gower, Yvonne Adams, Leslie Farrant and Brenda Campbell. Ann Hirst has provided the speediest and most thorough copy and production editing that we have ever seen. We are immensely indebted to them all.

Although our debts to all the people named above are considerable, we owe a special debt to Michael Sumner of the University of Salford. The contribution which he has made to this book is enormous. He read the complete penultimate and final drafts with meticulous care and supplied us with the most extensive comments on both style and substance, helping us to remove both blemishes and outright errors. Whatever merit this final product has is in no small measure to be credited to him. We do, of course, absolve him, and all our other helpers, from responsibility for the errors that remain.

Michael Parkin and Robin Bade
London, Ontario
March, 1982

Part I

Introduction

1
Macroeconomic Questions

This book is going to help you get abreast of the current state of knowledge in macroeconomics. Three tasks in this introductory chapter will start you out on that process. Those tasks are to know:

A. **the questions which macroeconomics seeks to answer;**
B. **the macroeconomic policy issues on which economists disagree;** and
C. **the views of the leading 'schools of thought'.**

A. Macroeconomic Questions

Macroeconomic questions have changed over the years and have usually been motivated by a concern to understand the economic problems of the day.

(i) Inflation

The oldest macroeconomic question is, 'what determines the general level of prices?' or the very closely related question, *'what determines the rate of inflation* (or the rate of deflation)?'

Excitement over this question dates back to Greek and Roman times. The first scientific answer to the question was given in the sixteenth century by the French philosopher-economist, Jean Bodin.

Following the period of European (particularly Spanish) colonisation of the Americas and the influx into Europe of vast quantities of gold, there was a substantial rise in the general level of prices. This went on well into the early seventeenth century. There then followed a period of price stability, which in turn was followed (from about 1750 to the early nineteenth century) by further very strong inflation. In the early part of the nineteenth century, however, following the Napoleonic wars, there was a period of falling prices. At the present time, of course, and in fact since the late 1960s, prices have been rising quickly.[1]

The questions for macroeconomics are: Why have there been periods of prolonged inflation and deflation? What has caused these major movements in the general level of prices? How can we forecast future movements in their level? and How can we control inflation?

(ii)   Unemployment

The second question for macroeconomics is, '*what determines the percentage of the labour force that is unemployed?*' The earliest attempts to answer this question linked movements in unemployment with movements in inflation and sought to understand the process whereby both inflation and unemployment fluctuated in recurrent, but non-periodic cycles — *the business cycle*. (Chapter 7 gives a complete and precise definition of the business cycle.)

In the late 1920s and 1930s a high unemployment rate was established throughout Western Europe and North America which was very persistent. Unemployment hardly fell below 20 per cent for almost fifteen years in several countries. This gave rise in 1936 to one of the major contributions to modern macroeconomics — *The General Theory of Employment, Interest and Money* by John Maynard Keynes.[2] In that work, Keynes changed the focus of economists away from the hard, and at the time unyielding, question of what causes the business cycle, to the narrower and easier question of what determines the level of unemployment (and levels of other aggregates) at a particular point in time. He also elevated to a position of central importance in macroeconomics a related question, namely:

(iii)   Real National Income

'*What determines the level of real national income?*' Roughly speaking, real national income is a measure of the value of the goods and services that can be bought with the incomes of all the individuals in the economy. (Chapter 3 makes the concept of national income more precise.) Fluctuations in real national income give rise to fluctuations in the standard of living, and differences in average growth rates of real national income between countries produce large inter-country differences in living standards. Macroeconomics does *not* explain why there are persistent differences in real income growth rates between countries. It is the movements in real national income around its trend growth rate which is the concern of macroeconomics.

---

1. An excellent account of the long-term movements in prices may be found in Anna J. Schwartz (1973) Secular price change in historical perspective, *Journal of Money, Credit and Banking*, Vol. V, No. 1, Pt II, February, pp. 243–69.

2. John Maynard Keynes (1936) *The General Theory of Employment, Interest and Money*, Macmillan.

(iv) The Rate of Interest

The fourth question which macroeconomics addresses is, 'what determines the level of interest rates?' There are, of course, many rates of interest in a modern economy. In the study of macroeconomics it is customary to distinguish between *short-term* and *long-term rates of interest*. Short-term rates (or more simply, short rates) are the rates of interest paid and received on loans of a short-term or temporary nature — say, up to five years. Long rates are those on loans of more than five years — and could be on loans which run indefinitely. There is a tendency for all interest rates to move up and down together, but for short rates to fluctuate more strongly than long rates. The essential problem for macroeconomics is to understand what determines the general ups and downs in interest rates and to understand why short-term rates fluctuate more than long-term rates.

(v) Balance of Payments

and

(vi) Exchange Rate

The fifth question is, 'what determines a country's balance of payments with the rest of the world?' and a sixth, related question is, 'what determines the value of one country's currency in relation to the value of another country's currency — i.e. *what determines the exchange rate?*'

These questions have also been around for a long time. Countries have been concerned with their balance of payments for as long as there has been international trade. The Scottish philosopher, David Hume, provided the first properly worked out scientific explanation for movements in the balance of payments in the middle of the eighteenth century.[3]

Britain's Macroeconomic Questions in 1981[4]

It is evident that although some of the macroeconomic questions posed above have been more important at certain stages in history than at others, at the present time they all take on considerable importance. In 1981 Britain's inflation was 12 per cent and unemployment stood at $11\frac{1}{2}$ per cent by the end of the year. Real national income *fell* during 1980 (the latest year for which we have data) by 1.6 per cent. Interest rates were at historically high levels with long-term government bonds yielding more than 16 per cent and short-term government securities yielding 14 per cent. The balance of payments was in surplus but the foreign exchange value of the pound, having soared to around $2.40 US in 1980, fell to below $2.00 US by the end of 1981 and is apparently continuing to fall still further.

---

3. This is still a highly readable piece of work and may be found in David Hume's essay, Of the balance of trade, in *Essays: Moral, Political and Literary* (1963) Oxford University Press, pp. 316–33.

4. Good, comprehensive and up-to-date sources for facts about the macroeconomic condition of the United Kingdom are: the *Bank of England Quarterly Bulletin* (published in March, June, September and December), the *National Institute Economic Review* (published in February, May, August and November), and *Economic Trends* (HMSO) (published monthly).

Thus, at the beginning of the 1980s the macroeconomic questions for the United Kingdom are: Why is it that inflation, unemployment, and interest rates are behaving so badly? Why have we had so much inflation in recent years and why are interest rates and unemployment so unusually high? Why is real income growth so negative at the present time? Why, at the same time, do we have a balance of payments surplus and why is it that the pound has fluctuated so wildly on the foreign exchange markets?

A related, more important, and yet harder to answer set of questions is: What are the effects on these variables of the policies which the United Kingdom government might adopt? How might policy be arranged so as to achieve lower inflation, lower interest rates, lower unemployment, higher real income and a foreign exchange rate that keeps Britain's international trading activities on a competitive basis?

You will recognise these as questions which you repeatedly hear and for which most people, and certainly most journalists, TV and radio commentators, as well as politicians, appear to have answers. You are going to discover that many of the popular answers are wrong! You are also going to discover that economists often disagree with each other on the answers to these questions, particularly the policy questions.

B.   Macroeconomic Policy Issues

As you are probably aware, there is a widespread belief that the government can and should take actions designed to influence key economic variables such as inflation and unemployment. Economists do not agree on what measures will achieve the desired results. The main reason why there is disagreement is that we still lack good theories: no theory fits the facts so exactly that it is compelling. This means that we tend to subscribe to that theory which best supports our predisposition (or perhaps prejudices). The lack of a close enough correspondence between the current theories and the facts will be highlighted and emphasised throughout this book. You will come to know and understand the existing theories; you will also know the facts — both those that the theories 'fit' or explain and those that they do not. It is the as yet unexplained facts which provide much of the agenda for future research in macroeconomics.

There are two major macroeconomic policy disagreements amongst economists. The first is:

(i) Should Macroeconomic Policy be Global or Detailed?

Global policies are those which are directed at influencing the values of a small number of aggregate variables such as the money supply, the foreign exchange rate, the overall level of government expenditures, the overall level of taxes, or the size of the government's budget deficit. Those who take the view that a small number of aggregate policy instruments should be the central concern of macroeconomic policy generally believe that it is desirable to leave as much scope as possible for individual economic initiative co-ordinated through the market mechanism.

Detailed policies are directed at controlling the prices of, or other terms concerning the exchange of, a large number of specific goods and services. Such policies are too numerous to list in full. Some examples are: prices and incomes policies, which regulate the wages and prices of a large number of types of worker and individual products; minimum wage policies; interest rate ceilings or other regulations of banks and insurance companies; regional policies of the form of special subsidies to particular regions; investment incentive programs; regulation and control of private manufacturing industry; regulation of international trade by the use of tariffs and quotas; and regulation of international capital flows. Those economists (and others) who favour detailed policies generally take the view that there are a large number of important areas in which markets fail to achieve a desirable economic outcome. They believe that detailed government intervention is needed to modify the outcome of the market process.

Often the disagreement between those advocating detailed intervention and those arguing against it is not so much a disagreement about the *existence* of a problem which the free market is having trouble solving, but rather about whether or not the *government* is the appropriate agent to solve the problem.

A second disagreement concerns the question:

> (ii) (a) *Should government policy be governed by a set of* **rules which the** *government announces and commits itself to and never deviates from, or*
>
> (b) *Should government intervention be responsive to current developments in the economy; that is, should the government adjust its policies from time to time at its absolute* **discretion in the light of** *current economic events?*

Those economists favouring *rules* are not necessarily agreed upon what the rules should be. They are agreed, however, on one crucial point — that controlling an economy is fundamentally different from controlling a mechanical (or electrical, or electronic) system, such as, for example, the heating/cooling system in a building. What makes controlling the economy different is the fact that it is people who are being controlled and, unlike machines, people know that they are being controlled and are capable of learning the procedures that are being employed by the controllers — the government — and organising their affairs so as to take best advantage of the situation created by policy. A policy based on fixed rules minimises the uncertainty that people have to face, and thus enables a better economic performance.

Those who favour *discretion* argue that if new information becomes available, it is foolish not to use it. By committing itself to a set of rules, the government thereby ties its hands and bars itself from being in a position to exploit the new information.

The key difference between the *rules* and *discretion* advocates is a judgment as to whether individuals acting in their own interests, co-ordinated by markets, are capable of reacting to, and taking proper account of, new information without the need for government assistance in the matter.

In view of the major source of the disagreement on *global versus detailed* and *rules versus discretion*, you will not be surprised to be told that, on the whole, those economists who favour *global* policies also favour policy *rules*, while those who favour *detailed* policies also favour *discretionary* intervention.

C. Leading 'Schools of Thought'

Broadly speaking, economists fall into two schools of thought on macroeconomic policy. There are no widely accepted, neat labels for identifying these two schools, although the term *Monetarist* is often applied to one group, and the term *Keynesian* to the other. An alternative classification would be between those who advocate fixed rules *versus* those who favour active intervention. These alternative labels give the flavour of, but often fail to do full justice to, some of the subtleties of the distinctions between the two broad schools of thought. In this book, the terms *Monetarist* and *Keynesian* will be used to identify the two schools.[5]

(i) The Monetarist View

Monetarists prefer the government to have policies towards a limited number of *global* macroeconomic variables such as money supply growth, government expenditure, taxes, or the government deficit. They advocate the adoption of fixed *rules* for the behaviour of these variables. Thus, for example, a widely advocated rule is that the money supply should grow at a certain fixed percentage rate year in and year out. Another widely advocated rule is that the government budget should be balanced, on the average, over a period of four to five years. More strongly, some members of this group of economists advocate the introduction of a constitutional limitation on the fraction of peoples' incomes which the government may take in taxes. In any event, all policy interventions which do occur should be announced as far ahead as possible so as to enable people to take account of them in planning and ordering their own economic affairs.

The intellectual leader of this school is Milton Friedman (formally of the University of Chicago). Other members of the school are Karl Brunner (University of Rochester), Robert Lucas (University of Chicago), as well as numerous other economists in the universities, in central banks and indeed in government. Since May 1979 the government of the United Kingdom has been a self-styled Monetarist government. Whether or not it has actually been a Monetarist government is something which, in part, will be considered later in this book.

(ii) The Keynesian View

Keynesians advocate *detailed* intervention to 'fine tune' the economy in the neighbourhood of full employment and low inflation. They seek to control inflation by direct controls of wages and prices and to control unemployment by stimulating demand, using monetary and fiscal policy (the details of which will be dealt with later in this book). They would use *discretion* in seeking to stimulate the economy in a

---

5. An excellent, up-to-date, and thorough, though demanding, discussion of the identifying characteristics of the different schools may be found in Douglas D. Purvis (1980) Monetarism: a review, *The Canadian Journal of Economics,* XIII, No. 1, February, pp. 96–122. The coarse, twofold classification suggested here is qualified in many subtle ways by Purvis.

depression or holding it back in a boom, modifying their policy in the light of current, and best-available, forecasted immediate future events. In their view, policy changes are best not pre-announced, so as to deter speculation.

The intellectual leaders of this group of macroeconomists are Franco Modigliani (Massachusetts Institute of Technology) and James Tobin (Yale University). In the United Kingdom there are a number of economists who subscribe to the Keynesian view in most university departments, as well as in the Bank of England, the Treasury, and all the major political parties.

You should not form the impression that the Monetarist/Keynesian division is one that follows neat political boundaries. Although there is perhaps some tendency for there to be an association between Monetarism and conservatism, and between Keynesianism and liberalism/socialism, that association is far from perfect. Monetarists range all the way from die-hard libertarians to conventional Marxists. Keynesians perhaps don't go quite so far to the right, but they do go a long way in that direction.

The distinction between Monetarists and Keynesians can be well illustrated by a simple analogy.

An Analogy

Imagine that you are listening to an FM radio station in a crowded part of the wave band. The signals are repeatedly and randomly drifting, so that, from time to time, your station drifts out of hearing, and a neighbouring station in which you have no interest comes through loud and clear. What should you do to get a stronger and more persistent signal from the station you want to hear?

The Keynesian says,

'Hang on to the tuning knob and whenever the signal begins to fade, fiddle with the knob, attempting, as best you can, to stay with the signal.'

The Monetarist says,

'Get yourself a good quality AFC (automatic frequency control) tuner; set it on the station you wish to hear; sit back; relax, and enjoy the music. Do not fiddle with the tuner knob; your reception will not be perfect, but on the average you will not be able to do any better than the AFC.'

SUMMARY

A.   Macroeconomic Questions

There are six questions in macroeconomics. They are:
- (i)   What determines the rate of *inflation?*
- (ii)   What determines the *unemployment* rate?
- (iii) What determines the level of *real national income?*
- (iv)   What determines the rate of *interest?*
- (v)   What determines the *balance of payments?*
- (vi)   What determines the *exchange rate?*

B. Macroeconomic Policy Issues

There are two major disagreements amongst economists concerning macroeconomic policy. One concerns whether macroeconomic policy should use *global* instruments or whether it should involve *detailed* intervention in individual markets. The second concerns whether macroeconomic policy should be governed by fixed *rules* or whether policies should be varied from time to time at the *discretion* of the government in the light of current economic conditions.

C. Leading 'Schools of Thought'

There are two major schools of thought: *Monetarists,* who advocate *global* instrument setting under fixed *rules,* and *Keynesians*, who advocate *detailed* intervention in a large number of individual markets with *discretion* to vary that intervention from time to time.

Review Questions

The following statements from *The Bank of England Quarterly Bulletin* (BEQB), the *National Institute Economic Review* (NIER) and *The Economist*, all concern some aspect or other of British economic policy or economic problems: Read the statements carefully and then classify them according to whether:

(i) they deal with *macro*economic issues or not
(ii) they deal with *detailed* or *global* policy
(iii) they are talking about *rules* or *discretion* in the conduct of policy.

a. 'The principal aim of monetary policy during this period [June to August 1981] was to influence the rate of monetary expansion, primarily the growth of sterling M3, in line with the current target of 6%–10% (at an annual rate) between mid-February 1981 and mid-April 1982.' (BEQB, September 1981, p. 327)

b. 'The public sector deficit was expanded deliberately in the mid-1970s to offset the contractionary effect of the first jump in oil prices.' (BEQB, March 1981, p. 71)

c. 'Certainly since the war there has been a decline in the international importance of manufacturing in this country. There has also been a decline in the relative importance of manufacturing in our economy.' (BEQB, June 1980, p. 203)

d. 'There are those in the bleaker of our two ancient universities, and perhaps elsewhere, who argue for the erection of a general tariff wall.' (BEQB, June 1980, p. 204)

e. 'The basic paradox is that, if there were less concern to achieve rises in money wages, rises in real wages, and thus in the standard of living, might in fact be greater.' (BEQB, June 1980, p. 204)

f. 'The government has been campaigning strongly for a much reduced level of pay increases in the next pay round.' (NIER, August 1981, p. 4)

g. 'Since the price of oil is denominated in US dollars its real price relative to world prices of manufactures has risen substantially in the last three months.' (NIER, May 1981, p. 7)

h. '[N]ew expenditure plans were presented in the [...] public expenditure White Paper, *The Government's Expenditure Plans 1981–82 to 1983–84* [...], which gave new implied PSBR/GDP ratios.' (NIER, May 1981, p. 11)

i. 'Total world trade in 1982 is likely to increase in volume by about 5 per cent, with world trade in manufactures growing a little faster.' (NIER, May 1981, pp. 25–26)

j. 'Conservative Party's Blackpool conference was called to debate the public spending targets for 1982–83.' (*The Economist*, 24 October 1981, p. 51)

k. 'The 132,000 police have now got their index-linked rise of 13.2%. The 36,000 firemen have been promised that the agreement linking their pay to that of the top 25% of manual workers will be honoured.' (*The Economist*, 24 October 1981, p. 52)

l. 'The government this week agreed to sell the National Freight Company Ltd., mainly to its managers and employees, for £53.3m.' (*The Economist,* 24 October 1981, p. 54)

m. 'The [St. James's] group's forecasts suggest that the standard rate of tax could be cut to 27% in the 1983 budget.' (*The Economist,* 24 October 1981, p. 60)

n. '[M]onetary growth is forecast to overshoot slightly so as to allow some gradual fall in interest rates.' (*The Economist*, 24 October 1981, p. 60)

o. 'The mortgage rate is assumed to fall from today's 15% to about $10\frac{1}{2}$% in early 1984.' (*The Economist*, 24 October 1981, p. 60)

p.   'With this gloomy outlook for growth, unemployment goes on rising throughout 1982.' (*The Economist*, 24 October 1981, p. 61)

q.   'Lord Soames ... reaffirmed to parliament the government's determination to offer no more than 7% pay increase to the civil servants for 1981–82.' (*The Economist*, 18 April 1981, p. 53)

r.   'Sir Keith announced last July that he was splitting the old Post Office into separate posts and telecommunications corporations and ending the monopoly of both as well.' (*The Economist*, 18 April 1981, p. 56)

s.   'Lead is dead or dying out of petrol ... in America, ... and elsewhere. Now the British government is planning its demise — but a slow one.' (*The Economist*, 18 April 1981, p. 58)

t.   'Cut Concorde's costs or be prepared to kill it, said a parliamentary committee.' (*The Economist*, 18 April 1981, p. 61)

u.   '... What to do about youth unemployment. ... Mr. Jim Prior, the Employment Secretary, wants to expand the youth opportunities programme.' (*The Economist*, 18 July 1981, p. 19)

v.   'Under Mr. Walters' scheme, employers would be subsidised for each school-leaver they employed at wages of under £40 per week.' (*The Economist*, 18 July 1981, p. 20)

w.   'This week's figures for sterling M3 show monetary growth still soaring; ... But future hopes cannot wipe out a 2% jump in sterling M3 in November alone.' (*The Economist*, 13 December 1980, p. 49)

x.   'Sir Keith's suggestion is to shift the burden of gas prices more sharply onto domestic consumers.' (*The Economist*, 13 December 1980, p. 49)

y.   'Britain's money supply is still overshooting its official target — by miles. Banking figures suggest that sterling M3 rose 2% last month. Government borrowing was higher than forecast.' (*The Economist*, 13 December 1980, p. 57)

z.   'Britain's Conservative Government has been lobbied this week to support costly and bureaucratic ways of channelling investment into small business.' (*The Economist*, 18 October 1980, p. 18)

2

Britain's Macroeconomic History since 1900

Too often in the past, economists have disagreed with each other about theory while paying little or no attention to the basic questions: What are the facts? Which, if any, of the theories being advanced are capable of explaining the facts? All useful theories begin with *some* facts that it is sought to explain. Theories are, in effect, 'rigged' to explain a limited set of facts. They are subsequently tested by checking their ability to explain other facts, either not known or not explicitly taken into account, when 'rigging' the theory. The theories of macroeconomics that are presented in this book have been designed to explain some aspect or other of the facts about inflation, unemployment, real income, interest rates, the foreign exchange rate and the balance of payments. The evolution of these variables over time may be called the macroeconomic history of a country. This chapter is designed to give you a 'broad brush' picture of the macroeconomic history of Britain. It should be thought of as a first quick look at some of the facts which macroeconomics seeks to explain. It presents the facts in the most direct, uncluttered manner possible and in no way tries to begin the task of explaining the facts. The chapter will serve two main purposes. First it will provide you with some basic equipment that will enable you to reject some of the more obviously incorrect theories that you may come across. Second it will provide you with a quick reference source — especially the Appendix to this chapter and the data sources listed therein — in the event that you want to pursue a more systematic testing of macroeconomic theories.

The chapter pursues two tasks which are to enable you to know:
A.   **the main features in the evolution of the key macroeconomic variables since 1900: (i) inflation, (ii) unemployment, (iii) real income, (iv) interest rates, (v) the balance of payments, and (vi) the exchange rate;**
     and
B.   **the main macroeconomic characteristics of each decade since 1900.**

A. Evolution of the Macroeconomic Variables

(i) Inflation

Figure 2.1 shows two measures of Britain's inflation. One is the annual rate of change of an Index of Retail Prices. The other is known as the GDP Deflator. Chapter 5 will explain precisely how these inflation rates are calculated and measured. For now, it is sufficient if you think of inflation as being simply the rate at which prices, on the average, are rising. Notice that although the two measures of inflation are not identical, they do, nevertheless, tend to move up and down together. What do they tell us about Britain's inflation?

The first rather striking thing that they suggest is that Britain's inflation has been on a *rising trend* in the period since the early 1920s. In both the 1920s and 1930s there were several years in which prices were falling (inflation measured negatively). Since 1934, however, there has not been a single year in which prices fell. Further, since the early 1960s, the rate at which prices have been rising has become progressively more severe.

The second thing that we learn from the figure about Britain's inflation is that it has been erratic. There are some distinct *cycles* in the inflation rate, but the up and down movements could not be described as following a regular cycle. Before the First World War there were two distinct cycles with inflation reaching a peak in 1907 and 1912. There then followed a much longer swing with strongly rising prices during World War I and falling prices in the years of the early 20s. A more regular cyclical pattern is clear in the 30s and again in the post-World War II period.

The range of Britain's inflation experience in the 20th century is enormous. As measured by the Retail Price Index it goes from a maximum of almost 22 per cent (in 1975) to a minimum of minus 21 per cent (in 1922). As measured by the GDP Deflator, the range is from 24 per cent (1975) down to a minimum of minus 17 per cent (1921). These extreme values are clearly uncommon as you can see from the figure.

With the exception of the most recent past, the biggest bursts of inflation occurred during the war years, with World War I displaying a more severe inflation than World War II. There was also a burst of inflation in the early 1950s associated with the Korean War. The years of strongest deflation are those immediately after World War I and during the 1930s.

Aside from these extreme experiences of strongly rising or strongly falling prices, Britain's inflation rate for the most part has been moderate though by no means zero. In fact, the average inflation rate over the 80 years of this century has been slightly over 4 per cent per annum. Maintained over eighty years, this rate of inflation has increased the price level almost twenty-six fold.

Let us now turn to look at the second macroeconomic variable — the unemployment rate.

(ii) Unemployment

Figure 2.2 shows the unemployment rate in Britain since 1900. As with inflation, the precise definition of, and method of measuring, unemployment will be dealt with in Chapter 5. For the present you may think of unemployment as measuring the extent

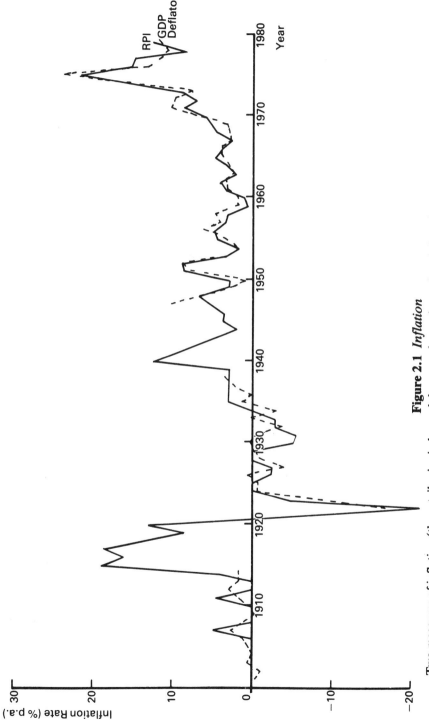

Figure 2.1 *Inflation*

Two measures of inflation (the retail price index and the gross domestic product deflator) tell broadly the same story. Prices rose at a rapid rate during World War I, again (though slightly less so) in World War II and very strongly at the end of the 1970s. Prices were falling in the years between the two World Wars. The inflation rate has cycled in a periodic fashion over the entire period since 1900, but most noticeably so in the post-war years. *Source:* Appendix to this chapter.

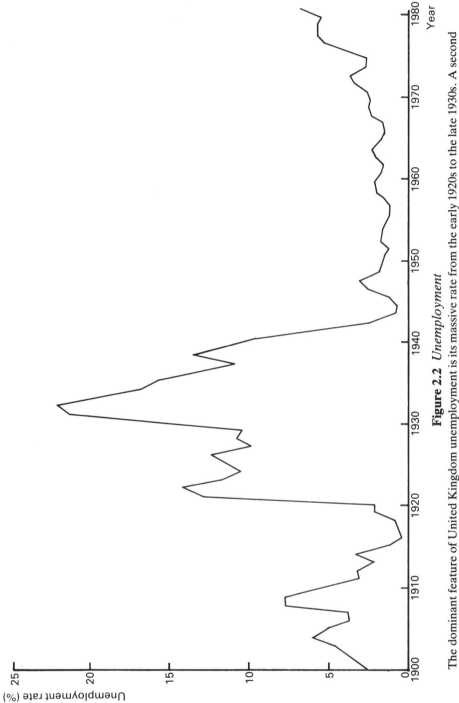

Figure 2.2 *Unemployment*

The dominant feature of United Kingdom unemployment is its massive rate from the early 1920s to the late 1930s. A second noteworthy feature is the periodic cycle. Since the early 1950s unemployment has trended upwards and strongly so in the late 1970s. *Source:* Appendix to this chapter.

to which people, who have indicated that they wish to work, are not able to find a job.

The most striking feature about the behaviour of unemployment in Britain in this century is its persistently very high level all the way from the early 1920s to the early 1940s. The second half of this period, from 1929 to the end of the 1930s, was the period known as the Great Depression — a period when the whole world economy was in a state of high unemployment. As you can see from the figure however, Britain suffered from high unemployment before the world depression of the 1930s set in.

In addition to the massive unemployment experienced during the 1920s and 1930s you will also be struck, perhaps, by the rather clear long cycles in unemployment. There seems to be a tendency for unemployment to move downwards from the beginning of the century to 1916. It then rises persistently to 1932, falls continuously until 1944, and then tends to rise in the period after 1944. Although one may describe these long swings as a long cycle, there are less than two complete such cycles and, of course, no guarantee that this long swing pattern will repeat.

Superimposed upon the long cycles in unemployment are some very distinct shorter cycles. There are many of these and it would not be instructive simply to catalogue them. You may, by carefully inspecting Figure 2.2, observe some of these shorter up and down movements that are distinctly present in the data.

The range of Britain's unemployment goes all the way from a peak of 22.1 per cent in 1932, down to a trough of less than 1 per cent during the war years of 1916 and 1944. The average unemployment rate over the entire century has been 5.5 per cent.

(iii) Real Income

There are two ways in which the evolution of real income can be examined. One fairly natural thing to do is to look at the behaviour of its *growth rate*. Another is to look at the percentage deviations of its level from trend. Let us do both of these things.

Figure 2.3 sets out the behaviour of the growth rate of real income in Britain since 1900. (We do not have data for the war years which account for the two gaps, 1914 to 1918 and 1939 to 1945.) Chapter 3 will describe exactly how the level of real income is calculated. For now you can think of it as a measure of the value of the goods and services produced in the economy each year.

The first thing that immediately strikes the eye when inspecting Figure 2.3 is the erratic nature of the path of real income growth. It seems to bounce around all over the place and, to a large degree, at random. The range of the apparently random fluctuations in real income growth seem to have narrowed slightly in the period after World War II as compared with the first four decades of the century. To some extent that is probably an illusion that arises from the fact that we are able to measure real income more accurately in recent years than we were in earlier years. It is probably not, however, entirely illusory. Certainly there were some big reductions in real income in the Great Depression years of the 1930s. Also, real income growth did become very strong in the recovery from the Great Depression as we moved towards the Second World War. There were also some fairly strong swings in real income growth in the first decade of the century. In the period since World War II the swings seem to have been less violent and have been remarkably frequent in their

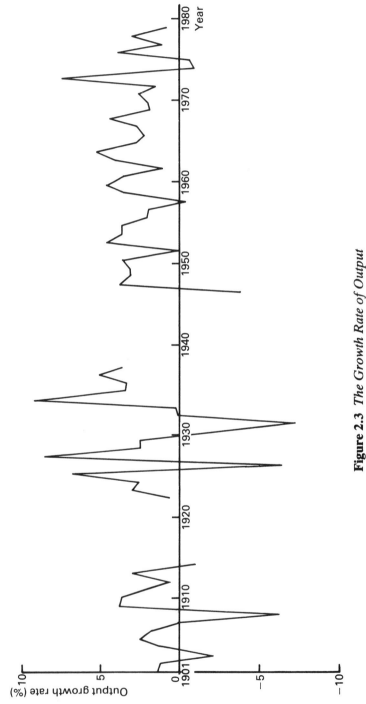

Figure 2.3 *The Growth Rate of Output*

Output growth has been quite erratic. It has usually averaged around $2\frac{1}{2}$ % per annum. The growth rate was much more variable in the early part of this century than after the Second World War. *Source:* Appendix to this chapter.

occurrence. There has been a tendency since the Second World War for real income to grow (though not by very much) every year. Exceptions were 1947, 1958, 1974–75 and 1980.

The range of real income growth has been substantial. The maximum positive growth rate was rather more than 9 per cent and occurred in the recovery from the Great Depression in 1934. The biggest fall in real income occurred in the onset of the Great Depression in 1931 when it fell by more than 7 per cent. The trend real income growth rate over the entire period since 1900 has only been 1.6 per cent per annum which implies that aggregate income has increased only some $3\frac{1}{2}$ times this century.

Before examining the deviations of real income from its trend level, it will be instructive to look at the actual level of real income graphed on a logarithmic scale in the period since 1900. This is done in Figure 2.4.

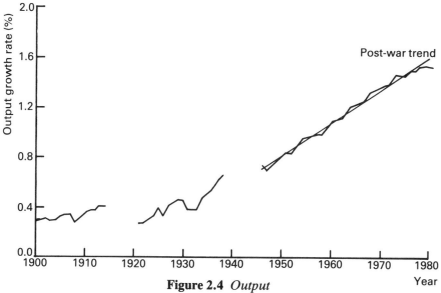

Figure 2.4 *Output*

Output is plotted on a logarithmic scale so that its growth trend is evident. The trend growth rate after World War II has been 2.6% per annum. In the early years of the decade and the 20s and early 30s, output growth was highly erratic and evidently does not fit the simple post-war trend line. A massive reduction in the country's productive potential took place in World War II. Average real growth in the inter-war years was strong but the economy was very severely depressed for most of that time. *Source:* Appendix to this chapter.

The two breaks represent the breaks in the data available to us due to the two World Wars. It is immediately obvious from inspecting Figure 2.4 that there is no single constant trend growth rate that adequately describes the path of real income in the United Kingdom over this entire eighty-year period. In the early years of the century, growth was very low on the average. During the inter-war years, the growth rate was quite high but we know that the economy was in a state of considerable depression throughout that period. In the post-war years there does appear to have been a fairly constant upward trend to real income with, of course, fluctuations around that trend. In examining the deviations of real income from trend, it seems best to focus on that post-war period.

If we pass a straight line through the level of real income (measured as a logarithm) for the post-war years, we find that the line has a constant growth rate of 2.62 per cent per annum. That line is shown in Figure 2.4 and marked post-war trend. The deviations of actual income from trend, expressed as a percentage, are shown in Figure 2.5. Evidently, according to the figures shown there, there have been a series of rather short cyclical movements in the deviation of real income from trend, with a tendency for real income to be somewhat below trend on the average during the late 1940s and 1950s all the way up to the mid-1960s. Between 1965 and 1974, real income was persistently above its post-war trend. In the final years of the 1970s and the opening of the 1980s, real income has sunk below trend.

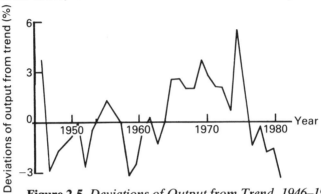

Figure 2.5 *Deviations of Output from Trend, 1946–1980*

Output fluctuations around trend in the post-war period follow a quite systematic cycle. There is a tendency for output to be below trend in the late 1940s and early 50s. Output moves above trend and remains there for the entire decade 1964–74. In the second half of the 70s real output falls below trend and increasingly so in 1980. *Source:* Appendix to this chapter.

If the trend line fitted to the post-war years was extended backwards through to the inter-war years (and you can perform such an experiment visually in Figure 2.4), it is evident that all the experience of the 1930s, depressed though the economy was, would appear to be above that trend line. Why might that be? The answer almost certainly lies in the fact that during the six years of World War II, output in the United Kingdom economy was unusually high with a very large fraction of the population entering the labour force but, it was all used in the war effort so that the stock of capital equipment available in 1939 was virtually depleted by 1946. Thus, the economy had to go through a considerable capital equipment building exercise in the post-war years, simply to get back to a level of productive potential that had been reached by the end of the 1930s.

Although it is not possible to calculate a meaningful trend for output during the earlier years of this century, it is evident from Figure 2.4 alone that the economy was severely depressed especially in the early years of the 1930s. It is also evident that the swings in economic activity prior to World War II were much stronger in amplitude than those that have occurred in the last three and a half decades.

(iv) Interest Rates

Figure 2.6 sets out the behaviour of two rates of interest. One of them is the rate on long-term government bonds and the other the rate on three-month Treasury bills. It

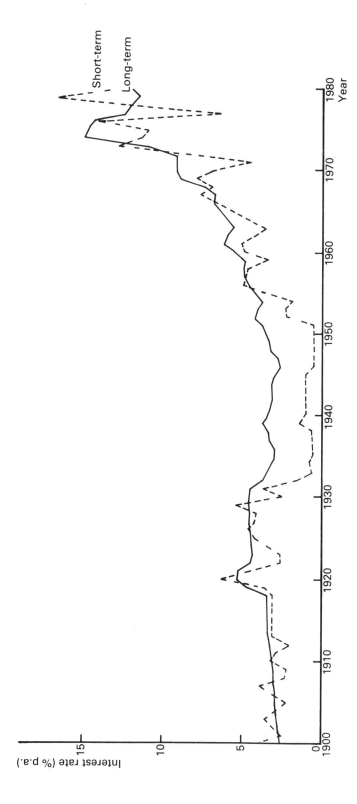

Figure 2.6 *Interest Rates: 1900–1980*

Interest rates have followed a similar path to inflation (Figure 2.1) but long-term rates have been much less volatile than inflation. Short-term rates fluctuate with greater amplitude than long-term rates. *Source:* Appendix to this chapter.

is evident that the long-term rate of interest is remarkably smooth in its movements, both in comparison with the short-term rate and with the other macroeconomic variables that we have examined. Both rates display the same long-term movements. There is a tendency for rates to rise slightly from the beginning of the century up to 1920. They then fall until the end of the Second World War, and after that, display a strongly rising trend. There are shorter cycles in the movement of both rates with the short-term rate fluctuating much more markedly than the long-term rate.

The range in interest rates is quite considerable. Long-term rates were at their lowest at the beginning of the century ($2\frac{1}{2}$ per cent) and at their highest in 1974 (14.6 per cent). Short-term rates were at their lowest during the Second World War, when they averaged $\frac{1}{2}$ per cent a year, and were at their highest in 1979, when they reached $16\frac{1}{2}$ per cent. As the 1980s began, interest rates were at a high level.

(v) The Balance of Payments

Let us now turn our attention to Britain's balance of payments. The precise way in which the balance of payments is measured will be dealt with in Chapter 6. For now you may think of it as a measure of the net payments to, or receipts from, the rest of the world by residents of Britain taken in aggregate. If, in their economic relations with the rest of the world, aggregate British sales of goods and services plus borrowing exceeds British purchases of goods and services plus lending, then the balance of payments will be in surplus. The reverse situation, in which British residents sell less than they buy and borrow less than they lend, is referred to as a deficit.

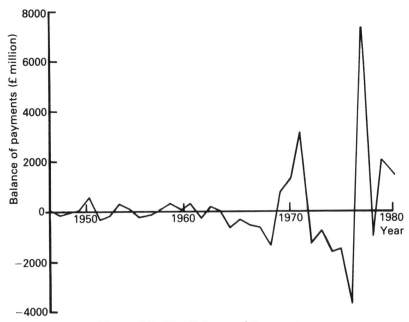

Figure 2.7 *The Balance of Payments*

Balance of payments fluctuations were mild but systematic in the 1950s and early 60s. In the late 60s and 70s the fluctuations have been quite violent. *Source:* Appendix to this chapter.

Figure 2.7 shows the post-war history of Britain's balance of payments (the history since 1946). Earlier figures are not shown because the ones that are readily available refer not to Britain alone but to the entire sterling area of which, in the period before World War II, Britain was the centre. The single most striking feature of the balance of payments, shown in Figure 2.7, is the dramatic tendency for the fluctuations in payments to get bigger. The balance of payments did fluctuate during the 1940s, 50s, and 60s, but only mildly so, compared with the swings that occurred beginning in the early 1970s. There are fairly clear cycles in the balance of payments. The range of fluctuation is at its widest in the years of the second half of the 1970s, with the biggest deficit being 3,628 million pounds in 1976 and the biggest surplus being 7,362 million pounds in 1977.

(vi) *The Exchange Rate*

The exchange rate is the value of the pound in terms of other currencies. The particular other currency chosen here to represent the foreign exchange value of the pound is the United States dollar. The history of the value of the pound measured as the number of United States dollars that would have to be paid for one pound sterling is set out in Figure 2.8. During some parts of this history, the value of the pound was *flexible* — the exchange rate was free to fluctuate, much like the prices of ordinary goods, and during other parts of the history, the pound was *fixed* — a situation in which the government pegs the exchange rate. The fixed exchange rate periods have been the most common ones. From 1900 all the way up to the end of the First World

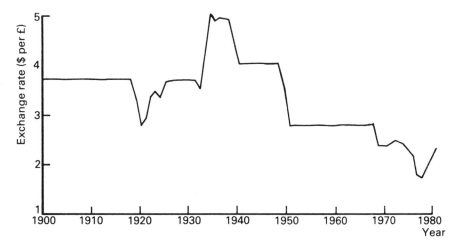

Figure 2.8 *The Exchange Rate*
The foreign exchange value of the pound was pegged at 3.70 US dollars per pound up to 1918. After World War I the pound floated and depreciated. The pre-war fixed value was restored when the pound returned to the gold standard in 1925. In 1931 the pound was floated again and its value dipped at first, but then appreciated strongly to exceed 5 US dollars briefly in 1934. Throughout World War II the value of the pound was pegged again at 4.03 US dollars. A devaluation to 2.80 US dollars occurred in 1949, but that new value was maintained until 1967 when a further devaluation took place. The exchange value of the pound floated again after 1972. *Source:* Appendix to this chapter.

War the pound was pegged at $3.70 US. During the early 1920s the pound sank in value to hit $2.78 US in 1920. From 1926 to 1931 the pre-war value of $3.70 US was restored. Then, in the 1930s the pound rose in value to exceed $5 US in 1934. By the beginning of World War II, the foreign exchange value of the pound was pegged again, this time at $4.03 US. The pound was devalued in 1949 to $2.80 US at which it was pegged by the British government until 1967 when it was devalued again this time to $2.40 US. This rate was maintained until 1971 when the foreign exchange value of the pound was allowed to find its own level. In the decade since then, the pound has fluctuated, reaching a low value of $1.74 US in 1977. From 1977 to 1980, the exchange value of the pound rose again to $2.32 US by 1980.

B. Decade Summaries

In order to present Britain's macroeconomic history in a slightly more compact manner, this section focuses on the decade averages of the variables since 1900. Those averages are set out in Table 2.1. Also, for purposes of comparison, the figures for 1980 and the average from 1900 to 1980 are presented in the last two rows of that table.

The first decade of the century is somewhat unremarkable. Prices were almost exactly stable, though unemployment was fairly high (slightly below the average for the entire eighty-year period). Output growth was very sluggish at only 0.6 per cent per annum. Interest rates were steady at below 3 per cent and the foreign exchange value of the pound was held steady at $3.70 US.

The period 1910–1920 was dominated by World War I. This was a decade of substantial inflation — 10 per cent per annum on the average — but also a decade of lower unemployment. It was a period which ended with output being hardly any different from what it had been at the beginning of the decade. Interest rates moved up slightly and the foreign exchange value of the pound remained constant.

The 1920s was a period of great economic hardship in Britain. Prices fell substantially during that decade and the unemployment rate moved up to average more than 10 per cent. Interest rates also moved up and the foreign exchange value of the pound sagged a little. Although the decade was one of severe depression, it was a decade of a slightly above average output growth. This happened because the decade both opened and closed with roughly equally severe depression, but this depression was superimposed upon a reasonably strong rising output trend.

The 1930s saw a continuation of the problems of the 1920s. Prices stopped falling and were roughly constant. Unemployment rose even further, however, to average 16 per cent for the decade as a whole. Through this decade, the output growth trend of a little over 2 per cent per annum was maintained.

Like the 1920s, the 1940s were dominated by war. In the Second World War, inflation was less severe than it had been in World War I (of the order of a half the severity). As in the previous war, unemployment fell to a very low average level. For the decade as a whole, output growth was modest compared with the more severely depressed 1920s and 1930s.

The 1950s was a decade of macroeconomic calm and solid progress. Prices rose,

Table 2.1 The Decade Averages

Period	Inflation		Unemployment	Output		Long-term Interest Rate (% pa)	Short-term Interest Rate (% pa)	Balance of Payments (£ million)	Exchange Rate ($ US per £)
	Retail Prices (% pa)	GDP Deflator (% pa)	%	Growth Rate (% pa)	Deviations from Trend (%)				
1900s	0.5	0.3	4.8	0.6	..	2.8	2.9	..	3.7
1910s	10.2	9.1[a]	2.1	−0.8[a]	..	3.4	3.0	..	3.7
1920s	−4.4	−3.4[b]	10.6	2.1[b]	..	4.6	4.2	..	3.4
1930s	1.5	−0.1[c]	16.1	2.2[c]	..	3.5	1.2	..	4.4
1940s	4.7	5.5[d]	3.0	1.5[d]	..	3.1	0.8	..	4.0
1950s	4.1	4.3	1.5	2.7	−0.74	4.3	2.9	42.1	2.8
1960s	4.0	3.7	1.9	2.9	1.39	6.5	5.7	−286.9	2.7
1970s	13.7	14.1	4.1	1.7	0.36	11.8	10.4	418.1	2.4
1980	16.5	17.4	6.8	−1.6	−7.63	11.9	13.5	1372.0	2.3
Average 1900–80	4.2	4.4	5.5	1.6	0[e]	5.1	4.0	83.8[f]	3.4

Source:　Appendix to Chapter 2

Notes:　[a]　1910–1921
　　　　　[b]　1921–1930
　　　　　[c]　1930–1938
　　　　　[d]　1938–1950
　　　　　[e]　Defined to be zero by the method of construction of the series
　　　　　[f]　1946–1980 average
　　　　　..　not available

but only by 4 per cent per annum (practically the same as the eighty year average). Unemployment was modest and averaged even less than it had done in the two war decades of the 1910s and 1940s. Output growth moved up to almost 3 per cent per annum. After being lowered in 1949, the foreign exchange value of the pound was maintained throughout the decade at its new fixed level of $2.80 US. Through this period the balance of payments behaved in an unremarkable way, fluctuating from year to year but averaging a surplus of just over £40 million per annum.

The 1960s looked very much like the 1950s. Inflation continued to average about 4 per cent per annum, unemployment remained low and output growth strong by British standards. Some signs of problems were beginning to emerge, however, with interest rates and the external aspect of the economy. In contrast to the previous decade, the balance of payments had now moved into a deficit of almost £300 million a year. The foreign exchange value of the pound was maintained until 1967 but, in that year was lowered to $2.40 US. Interest rates began to move up in quite a significant way during this decade.

The 1970s was a decade of inflation, rising unemployment and strongly rising interest rates. The average inflation rate turned out to be in the middle teens, with unemployment almost double what it had been in the 1960s. Interest rates also almost doubled from their previous decade average level. The situation that developed in the 1970s remains as a broad description of the macroeconomic condition of Britain in the opening years of the 1980s. That is a condition characterised by high inflation, high unemployment, high interest rates, and a volatile external payments position. On top of these problems is the appearance that the output growth trend has perhaps slackened off.

You have now reviewed the behaviour of the six key macroeconomic variables in Britain and have looked at the main macroeconomic characteristics of each decade during the twentieth century. Many questions will no doubt now be occurring to you:

On Inflation:

Why are there some periods when the inflation rate is very high, others when it is moderate, and yet others when prices are falling? Can the ups and downs in inflation be controlled and perhaps eliminated, or do we have to live with them? What has caused the apparent trend in Britain's inflation in recent years? Is that trend going to continue into the future? Is there anything that can be done to stop it?

We do not know the full answers to any of these questions. We know substantial parts of the answers to all of them, however, and explaining what we know constitutes one of the prime tasks of this book.

On Unemployment:

Why was there such an enormous and prolonged burst of unemployment during the 1920s and 1930s? You will discover that important though this question is, a satisfactory answer still eludes us. Part IV of the book deals with the most comprehensive and systematic attempt to answer this question and explains why we are still searching for a fully satisfactory answer. Why have there been such marked movements in unemployment, characterised by the long cycle that we identified? In particular, why has there been a tendency for unemployment to rise persistently since the early 1950s? Why does unemployment fluctuate so markedly in shorter, yet very clear, cycles? Finally, can unemployment be controlled so that the fluctuations in its rate can be removed? These questions also will occupy the centre of our attention in what follows.

On Real Income:

Why does real income grow in a cyclical but erratic fashion? Why was income so severely depressed in the 1920s and early 1930s? Why has real income deviated from its trend in the post-war period — mainly being below trend in the 1940s and 50s, above trend in the late 60s and early 70s, and severely below trend in the late 70s and early 80s? What can be done to erradicate the fluctuations in real income?

On Interest Rates:

Why are long-term interest rate movements relatively smooth? Why did interest rates gradually trend downwards through the 1920s and then gradually rise again — not so gradually in recent years? Why are the fluctuations in short-term interest rates more pronounced than those in long-term rates?

On the Balance of Payments and the Exchange Rate:

Why has Britain's balance of payments fluctuated so violently? Why have the fluctuations become bigger in more recent years? What can be done by the government to correct the balance of payments deficit and return the British economy to a condition similar to that which it experienced in the 1950s?

Why is it that sometimes the foreign exchange value of the pound has been fixed and at other times it has been allowed to fluctuate? Why has the value of the pound fallen successively in the period since World War II?

These questions concerning Britain's external macroeconomic relations will also be given prominence in what follows in this book.

It would not be sensible or useful to attempt a detailed mapping out of the specific parts of the book that deal with each of these questions. Many of the questions turn out to be intimately related to each other in a way that you will find hard to appreciate if you have little or no knowledge of macroeconomics, but that will seem obvious and natural once you have made some progress with your study of the subject. To help you see some of the connections between the questions, after explaining in more detail how the macroeconomic variables are defined, observed and measured, but before embarking upon the task of *explanation* of macroeconomic phenomena, Chapter 7 will explore some of the connections among the variables by defining and describing the business cycle. In the final section of that chapter you will have a further opportunity to return to the features of the six variables described here and to gain some further insights into the way that they behave.

SUMMARY

A. Evolution of the Macroeconomic Variables

Inflation's main feature has been a distinctly rising trend. There have also been clear but irregular cycles. The range of inflation (as measured by retail prices) runs from falling prices of 21 per cent per annum (in 1922) to rising prices of 22 per cent per annum in 1975. The average rate of inflation between 1900 and 1980 has been just over 4 per cent per annum.

Unemployment has displayed a long cyclical swing with clear shorter cycles superimposed upon that. The worst unemployment occurred during the 20 years from 1920 to 1940, with 1932 being the single worst year when unemployment was 22.1 per cent. Unemployment reached its lowest levels during World War I and World War II when it was below 1 per cent.

Real income growth has averaged just over $1\frac{1}{2}$ per cent per annum during this century. There has been a marked amount of random fluctuation in the growth rate, however, about that average. The highest growth rate ever achieved was 9.2 per cent (in 1934) as the economy was coming out of the worst of the Great Depression. The biggest drop in output occurred in 1931 when output fell by $7\frac{1}{2}$ per cent.

Interest rates have been remarkably steady through the first half of the century, but have trended upwards strongly since the middle 1950s. Long-term interest rates have a very smooth pattern, while short-term rates fluctuate more markedly.

The balance of payments has fluctuated in an increasingly volatile manner. In the early post-war years there was a modest surplus in the balance of payments. This was succeeded by years of increasing deficits through the 1960s. After 1968 fluctuations in the balance of payments have been the order of ten times the magnitude prevailing earlier.

The exchange rate has been fixed for the most part against the US dollar. It has, however, been devalued on two occasions in the post-war period. Since 1971 the foreign exchange value of the pound has been free to find its own level on the foreign exchange market.

B. Decade Summaries

The averages of the macroeconomic variables in each decade since 1900 are set out in Table 2.1 and should be studied carefully. The first decade was an unremarkable one with virtually stable prices, slow output growth and moderately high unemployment. The second decade was dominated by World War I and saw an average inflation rate of 10 per cent, lower unemployment but a poor output growth rate. Through both of these decades the pound was held at a constant level against the US dollar and interest rates were close to 3 per cent. The 1920s and 1930s were decades of severe depression with unemployment climbing to the teens and prices either steady or falling. An output growth rate in excess of 2 per cent per annum, nevertheless, was maintained throughout this period. Interest rates also remained fairly steady at between 3 and 5 per cent.

Like the 1910s, the 1940s were dominated by war and saw the inflation rate rise and unemployment fall. The 1950s was a decade of macroeconomic calm and steady progress with inflation around 4 per cent, output growing strongly above its long-term average level and unemployment being very low. Interest rates remained steady and the external payments was in surplus. The 1960s was much like the 1950s, except that interest rates started to move up and the balance of payments began to show an increasing deficit. The 1970s was a decade of inflation and high unemployment, high interest rates and volatile external payments. As the 1980s open, all the problems of the 70s remain, but if anything in accentuated form.

Appendix: Britain's Macroeconomic Variables 1900–1980

Year	Inflation		Unemployment Rate (%)	Real Income (GDP)		Interest Rates		Balance of Payments (£ million)	Exchange Rate ($US per £)
	RPI (% pa)	GDP Deflator (%pa)		Growth Rate (%pa)	Deviations From Trend (%)	Long Term (%pa)	Short Term (%pa)		
1900	0.0	0.0	2.5	0.0	—	2.5	3.9	—	3.70
1901	0.0	-0.4	3.3	1.3	—	2.6	2.4	—	3.70
1902	0.0	-1.0	4.0	1.1	—	2.6	2.9	—	3.70
1903	0.0	0.5	4.7	-2.3	—	2.7	3.4	—	3.69
1904	0.0	0.3	6.0	0.8	—	2.8	2.9	—	3.70
1905	0.0	0.3	5.0	2.4	—	2.7	2.2	—	3.69
1906	0.0	1.1	3.6	1.7	—	2.8	3.0	—	3.69
1907	4.6	2.6	3.7	0.0	—	2.9	3.7	—	3.69
1908	0.0	0.8	7.8	-6.2	—	2.9	2.2	—	3.69
1909	0.0	-0.5	7.7	3.8	—	2.9	2.1	—	3.70
1910	0.0	0.0	4.7	3.6	—	3.0	3.0	—	3.69
1911	4.4	1.9	3.0	2.3	—	3.1	2.8	—	3.69
1912	0.0	2.7	3.2	0.4	—	3.2	2.0	—	3.70
1913	0.0	1.6	2.1	2.9	—	3.3	3.0	—	3.69
1914	4.2	1.5	3.3	-1.1	—	3.3	3.0	—	3.71
1915	18.9	—	1.1	—	—	3.3	3.0	—	3.71
1916	15.9	—	0.4	—	—	3.3	3.0	—	3.71
1917	18.7	—	0.6	—	—	3.3	3.0	—	3.71
1918	13.6	—	0.8	—	—	3.3	3.0	—	3.71
1919	8.1	—	2.1	—	—	4.6	3.4	—	3.36
1920	12.8	—	2.0	—	—	5.3	6.2	—	2.78
1921	-9.0	—	12.9	—	—	5.2	4.5	—	2.92
1922	-20.9	-16.8	14.3	0.5	—	4.4	2.5	—	3.36
1923	-4.7	-8.4	11.7	2.9	—	4.3	2.6	—	3.47
1924	0.0	-0.6	10.3	2.4	—	4.3	3.3	—	3.35
1925	0.0	-0.8	11.3	6.7	—	4.4	4.0	—	3.67
1926	-2.4	0.5	12.5	-6.4	—	4.5	4.5	—	3.69
1927	-2.5	-4.1	9.7	8.4	—	4.5	4.2	—	3.69
1928	0.0	-1.1	10.8	2.3	—	4.4	4.1	—	3.69
1929	0.0	-0.1	10.4	2.4	—	4.6	5.2	—	3.69
1930	-5.2	0.1	16.0	-0.7	—	4.4	2.4	—	3.69
1931	-5.5	-0.5	21.3	-7.4	—	4.3	3.5	—	3.60
1932	-2.8	-3.7	22.1	0.0	—	3.7	1.4	—	3.50
1933	-2.9	-3.0	19.9	0.3	—	3.3	0.5	—	4.21
1934	0.0	-3.1	16.7	9.2	—	3.1	0.7	—	5.04

Year	(1)	(2)	(3)	(4)	(5)	(6)	(7)	(8)	(9)
1935	4.90	—	0.5	2.8	—	3.3	15.5	1.1	2.9
1936	4.97	—	0.5	2.9	—	3.2	13.1	0.2	2.8
1937	4.94	—	0.5	3.2	—	5.0	10.8	2.1	2.8
1938	4.89	—	0.63	3.7	—	3.3	13.5	3.1	2.7
1939	4.46	—	1.3		—		11.6		2.6
1940	4.03	—	1.0	3.4	—	—	9.7	—	12.3
1941	4.03	—	1.0	3.1	—	—	6.6	—	8.8
1942	4.03	—	1.0	3.0	—	—	2.4	—	6.1
1943	4.03	—	1.0	3.1	—	—	0.8	—	3.9
1944	4.03	—	0.8	2.9	—	—	0.7	—	1.7
1945	4.03	—	0.5	2.6	—	—	1.2	—	3.7
1946	4.03	55	0.5	2.7	3.7	—	2.5	—	3.5
1947	4.03	-159	0.5	3.2	-2.9	-4.0	3.1	10.0	5.1
1948	4.03	-64	0.5	3.3	-1.8	3.7	1.8	6.2	6.7
1949	3.68	-3			-1.3	3.0	1.6	2.8	2.9
1950	2.80	575	0.5	3.5	-0.8	3.1	1.5	0.5	2.8
1951	2.80	-334	0.5	3.7	0.05	3.5	1.2	7.2	8.5
1952	2.79	-175	2.1	4.2	-0.5	0.5	1.7	8.7	8.9
1953	2.81	296	2.3	4.0	-0.3	4.5	1.6	2.9	3.0
1954	2.81	126	1.7	3.7	1.0	3.6	1.4	1.9	1.6
1955	2.79	-229	3.9	4.1	0.6	3.9	1.1	3.4	4.4
1956	2.79	-159	4.9	4.7	0.02	1.8	1.1	6.0	4.8
1957	2.81	13	4.8	4.9	-3.2	-1.8	1.4	3.9	3.5
1958	2.80	290	4.5	4.9	-2.5	-0.4	2.0	4.6	3.1
1959		18	3.3	4.8		3.3	2.1	1.6	0.5
1960	2.80	325	4.8	5.4	-0.6	4.5	1.7	1.7	1.1
1961	2.80	-339	5.1	6.2	-0.2	3.5	1.5	3.2	3.2
1962	2.80	192	4.6	5.5	-1.4	0.9	2.0	3.3	4.1
1963	2.80	-58	3.6	6.0	-0.5	3.0	2.3	2.9	2.0
1964	2.79	-695	4.6	6.4	2.5	5.2	1.7	3.9	3.1
1965	2.79	-353	5.6	6.8	2.5	2.6	1.4	3.8	4.7
1966	2.82	-547	6.6	6.6	1.9	2.5	1.5	2.7	3.8
1967	2.39	-671	7.6	6.3	3.7	4.3	2.3	2.9	2.4
1968	2.39	-1 410	6.8	7.3	2.8	1.7	2.5	3.6	4.6
1969		687	7.8	8.8			2.4		5.2
1970	2.39	1 287	6.9	9.1	2.1	1.9	2.6	7.4	6.0
1971	2.44	3 146	4.4	9.0	2.0	2.6	3.4	10.2	8.9
1972	2.50	-1 265	8.4	9.1	0.6	1.3	3.7	9.8	7.0
1973	2.45	-771	12.8	10.8	5.4	7.3	2.6	7.6	8.7
1974	2.34	-1 646	11.3	14.6	-1.7	-0.6	2.6	15.7	14.8
1975	2.22	-1 465	10.9	14.2	-1.4	3.8	3.9	23.9	21.6
1976	1.80	-3 628	13.9	12.3	-0.2	2.0	5.3	13.0	15.2
1977	1.74	7 362	16.3	11.9	-1.8	7.9	5.7	10.6	14.7
1978	1.92	-1 126	11.9	11.3	-1.5	0.8	5.7	11.6	7.9
1979	2.12	-1 905	16.4		-3.4		5.4	17.3	12.5
1980	2.32	1 372	13.4	11.8	-7.6	-1.6	6.8	17.3	16.5

Sources and Methods:

The British Economy Key Statistics 1900–1964, published for the London and Cambridge Economic Service by the Times Publishing Company Ltd., referred to below as Key Statistics.

1. *Inflation:*

(a)*RPI* is General Index of Retail Prices all items

1900–1947: Key Statistics, Table C, p. 8.

1948–1978: *Economic Trends Annual Supplement, 1980 edition*, p. 112.

1979–1980: *Economic Trends,* June 1981, p. 42.

The figures in the table are percentage changes in the index over the previous year.

(b)*GDP Deflator* is GDP at factor cost divided by real GDP at factor cost

1900–1949: Key Statistics, Tables A and A*, pp. 4–5.

1950–1974: *Economic Trends Annual Supplement, 1980 edition*, p. 5.

1975–1980: *Economic Trends,* May 1981, pp. 6–8.

The figures in the table are percentage changes in the GDP Deflator over the previous year.

2. *Unemployment:*

1900–1949: Key Statistics, Table C, p. 8.

1950–1970: *Economic Trends Annual Supplement, 1980 edition*, p. 97.

1971–1980: *Economic Trends,* June 1981, p. 36.

The figures in the table for 1950–1970 are the ratio of unemployed excluding school leavers to the sum of employees in employment and the unemployed excluding school leavers. The figures for all other years are as published.

The figures in the table for 1971–1980 are the annual average of quarterly figures.

3. *Real Income:*

Real Income is GDP at factor cost.

1900–1950: Key Statistics, Table A, p. 5.

1950–1974: *Economic Trends Annual Supplement, 1981 edition,* p. 5.

1975–1980: *Economic Trends,* May 1981, pp. 6–8.

(a)*Growth Rate* is the percentage change in real GDP over the previous year.

(b)*Deviations from Trend* is the percentage deviation of real GDP from a logarithmic trend fitted to real GDP 1946–1980. The trend line is log (real GDP) = 9.47 + 0.026 (year – 1945) indicating a trend growth rate of real GDP of 2.6 per cent per annum.

4. *Interest Rates:*

(a)*Long-term*: interest rate on $2\frac{1}{2}$ per cent Consols

1900–1954: Key Statistics, Table G, p. 16.

1955–1979: *Economic Trends Annual Supplement, 1981 edition*, p. 194.

1980: *Financial Statistics*, Table 13.6, June 1980.

(b)*Short-term*: Treasury bill rate

1900–1954: Key Statistics, Table G, p. 16.

1955–1979: *Economic Trends Annual Supplement, 1981 edition*, p. 194.

1980: *Economic Trends,* June 1981, p. 66.

5. *Balance of Payments:*

1946–1978: *Economic Trends Annual Supplement, 1981 edition*, p. 124.

1979–1980: *Financial Statistics*, July 1981, p. 115.

The figure in the table is the negative of official financing figure.

6. *Exchange Rate:*

Annual average exchange rate between the pound sterling and the US dollar, expressed as the number of US dollars per pound.

1900–1964: Key Statistics, Table F*, p. 15.

1965–1980: *International Financial Statistics*, May 1981.

Review Questions

1. Briefly describe the history of each of the following macroeconomic variables in the United Kingdom since 1945:
    (i) inflation; (ii) unemployment; (iii) real income; (iv) interest rates; (v) balance of payments; and (vi) the exchange rate.

2. Briefly describe the history of each of the above macroeconomic variables in the United Kingdom in the 'inter-war years' — 1920 to 1940.

3. Using later editions of the sources given at the foot of the table in the Appendix to Chapter 2, update the table for each of the variables. Describe how each of these variables has evolved so far in the 1980s.

4. One of these 6 macroeconomic variables has at some time been fixed by the government. Which variable is this, and for what periods has it been fixed?

5. In which decade was inflation the United Kingdom's major macroeconomic problem? Was it associated with any other major macroeconomic problems?

6. What were the United Kingdom's major macroeconomic problems of the 1930s?

7. In which decade since 1900 has the United Kingdom suffered the highest average unemployment rate? Compare this average with that so far in the 1980s.

8. In which decade of British history since 1900 has the average long-term interest rate been highest? Compare this with the average long-term interest rate so far for the 1980s.

9. Has the United Kingdom's balance of payments, on the average, been in deficit in any decade since 1950? Would you deduce from this that the United Kingdom has had balance of payments problems?

10. Looking at decade averages of the history of the exchange rate and the balance of payments, does there appear to be a relationship between them? If so, what is that relationship?

11. What are the major economic problems of the United Kingdom in the eighties (thus far)?

12. Assume that you are employed as an economic speech writer by Mrs Thatcher. Write a short speech which argues as strongly as possible that the United Kingdom's macroeconomic performance since 1979 compares favourably with that of earlier periods and is a credit to the economic management of the government.

13. Assume that you are employed as an economic speech writer by the leader of the Labour Party. Write a short speech which argues as strongly as possible that the United Kingdom's macroeconomic performance since 1979 compares unfavourably with that of earlier periods and discredits the government's economic management.

Part II

Measuring Macroeconomic Activity

3

Aggregate Income Accounting

Aggregate income accounting is the centrepiece of Keynesian macroeconomics, and detailed descriptions of the concepts involved, the methods of measurement and sources of data are commonplace in a large number of more traditional texts. Modern macroeconomics does not neglect the aggregate income accounts. Nevertheless, it views them as just one of the inputs needed to do macroeconomic analysis. The other major inputs are the aggregate balance sheet — a statement of what people in the economy owe and own, the measurement of inflation and unemployment, and the measurement of international economic transactions. This chapter deals with aggregate income accounting; Chapter 4 with aggregate balance sheet accounting; Chapter 5 with the measurement of inflation and unemployment; and Chapter 6 with international transactions. Because it does not play the critically central role in the new theories that it plays in Keynesian theory, it is not necessary to devote the same degree of detailed attention to aggregate income accounting as was common in the past. This chapter, therefore, focuses only on those central aspects of the topic which are essential to your further understanding of modern macroeconomics. Additionally, and as a preliminary to examining aggregate income and balance sheet accounting, the important distinction between flows and stocks is highlighted. You have six specific tasks in this chapter which are to:

A. understand the distinction between flows and stocks;

B. know the definitions of: (i) output (product), income and expenditure, (ii) domestic and national, (iii) gross and net, (iv) market price and factor cost, (v) nominal and real;

C. understand the concepts of aggregate income, output (product), and expenditure;

D. know how aggregate income is measured, using: (i) the expenditure approach, (ii) the factor incomes approach, (iii) the output approach;

E. know how aggregate income in constant pounds (real) is measured; and

F. know how to read the United Kingdom's national income and expenditure accounts.

A. Flows and Stocks

A macroeconomic variable that measures a *flow* measures a rate per unit of time. In contrast, a *stock* is a value at a point in time. Examples of flows are income and expenditure. The dimension of these variables is pounds per unit of time, for example, pounds per month or pounds per year. Examples of stocks are: money in the bank, the value of a car, a house, the value of the railway carriages, trains and track owned by British Rail, the value of the telephone lines and exchange switching equipment owned by British Telecom. All these variables are measured in pounds on a given day.

Although such items as cars, houses, and physical plant and equipment are stocks, the purchase of additional equipment and the physical wearing-out of plant and equipment are flows. Stocks of physical plant and equipment are called *capital*. Additions to capital are called *investment*. The reduction in the value of equipment as a result of wear and tear and/or the passage of time is known as *depreciation*. Let us illustrate this with something concrete. Imagine that on 1 June 1981 you had a 1975 car that had a current market value of £1000. In the year from 1 June 1981 to 1 June 1982 the market value of the car fell to £800. The value of the car on the 1st of June each year is a stock. That stock has fallen from £1000 in 1981 to £800 in 1982. The depreciation (the loss in the value of the car) is a flow. That flow here is £200 per year (or, equivalently, £16.67 per month). If, in May 1982, you sold your 1975 car and replaced it with a 1978 car, the value of which is £1500, your capital stock at the end of May 1982 would, of course, be the same £1500. In that case you would have *invested* a total of £700. (The £700 is the difference between the £1500 that your newer car is worth and the £800 that your old car would have been worth, had you kept it.) The change in your capital stock from June 1981 to June 1982 is, of course, not £700 but £500. This is made up of an investment in a new car known as a *gross* investment of £700 minus the depreciation of the old car of £200. The difference between your gross investment and the depreciation of your capital is known as *net* investment.

A useful analogy to illustrate the distinction between flows and stocks is a physical one involving a bathtub, a tap, and a drain. Suppose a bathtub has some water in it, has the tap turned on, and has no plug in the plug-hole, so that water is flowing into the bathtub and flowing out of it. The water in the tub is a *stock,* the water entering the tub through the tap and the water leaving the tub through the plug-hole are *flows*. If the flow through the tap is greater than the flow through the drain, the stock will be rising. If, conversely, the flow through the drain is greater than the flow through the tap, the stock will be falling. In this example there are two flows and one stock, and the stock is determined by the flows. Suppose that the rate of outflow through the drain is a constant which cannot be controlled. The stock can be increased by opening the tap so that the inflow exceeds the outflow, and the stock can be decreased by closing the tap so that the outflow exceeds the inflow.

In terms of the capital stock, investment and depreciation concepts illustrated earlier with reference to transactions in used cars you can think of the water in the bathtub as the capital stock, the outflow through the plug-hole as depreciation, and the inflow through the tap as gross investment. The difference between the outflow and inflow is net investment, which may, of course, be positive (if the water level is rising) or negative (if the water level is falling).

Suppose, however, that we introduce a human element into the story. Imagine that someone wants to maintain the water level in the tub at a particular height. That is, they have a *desired stock* of water. If the *actual stock* exceeds the desired stock, the corrective action would be to slow down the rate of inflow. If the actual stock was less than the desired stock, the corrective action would be to speed up the rate of inflow. You can see that in this extended story, the stock determines the flow in the sense that individual actions which adjust the flow are triggered by the level of the stock. In the economic analysis which you will be doing shortly, flows (such as national income and expenditure) will be determined by stocks (such as the supply of money).

The remaining tasks in this and the next chapter are a necessary prelude to conducting such economic analyses. The rest of this chapter explains how the national income and expenditure flows are measured and Chapter 4 deals with the measurement of the stocks of assets and liabilities in the economy. Let us begin by reviewing some of the definitions of the main aggregate income and expenditure flows.

B. Some Frequently Used Terms

You have almost certainly encountered in newspapers or on television current affairs programmes, terms like 'Gross Domestic Product' or 'Gross National Income', or perhaps 'Gross National Expenditure in Constant Prices'. This section will enable you to know what these and a few other important terms mean. Following are *five* groups of words which you need to be able to distinguish from each other.

(i) Output (or Product), Income, and Expenditure

Three concepts of aggregate economic activity are commonly used. They are dealt with in some detail in Part (iii) below. For now, all that you need to know are the definitions of these terms:

Output (Product) means the value of the output of the economy.

Income   means the sum of the incomes of all the factors of production (labour, capital, and land) employed in the economy.

Expenditure   means the sum of all the *expenditures* in the economy on *final goods and services*.
(Note: See below for the distinction between expenditure on *final* goods and services and expenditure on *intermediate* goods and services.)

(ii) Domestic and National

In (i) above, the term 'the economy' is used as if it is unambiguous. However, there is ambiguity as to what is meant by 'the economy'. What is the 'British economy'? There are two possible answers. One involves the

Domestic economy, which is all economic activity taking place in the geographical domain of the United Kingdom. The other involves the

National economy, which is all economic activity of United Kingdom residents, wherever in the world they happen to perform that activity.

Thus, *domestic* output (product), income, and expenditure refer to the aggregate of output, income, and expenditure in the geographical domain of the United Kingdom.

National output (product), income, and expenditure refer to the output produced by, the income earned by, or expenditure made on, goods produced by United Kingdom residents, no matter where in the world the economic activity takes place.

The difference between these two aggregates is known as 'net property income from (or paid) abroad'. It is not large for most countries and is not large for the United Kingdom. When no special purpose is served by the distinction between the two concepts, this book will use the term *aggregate* product, income, and expenditure to refer to either or both the *national* and *domestic* concepts.

(iii) Gross and Net

Gross national (or domestic) product (or income or expenditure) means that the aggregate is measured *before* deducting the value of the assets of the economy which have been used up or *depreciated* in the production process during the year.

Net national (or domestic) product (or income or expenditure) means that the aggregate is measured *after* deducting the value of the assets of the economy which have been used up or *depreciated* in the production process during the year. Macroeconomics is concerned with explaining the overall scale of economic activity and uses the *gross* concept. The *net* concept is of use in measuring standards of living, a topic outside the scope of macroeconomics.

(iv) Market Price and Factor Cost

In most modern economies (and certainly in the United Kingdom) the government levies taxes on expenditure on some goods and subsidises others. An example of a tax on expenditure is the value added tax (VAT). An example of a subsidy is that on milk. There are two ways of measuring the *value* of a good or service. One is based on the prices paid by the final user (consumer) and is known as the *market price* valuation. The other is based on the cost of all the factors of production used in its production, including the profits made. This is known as the *factor cost* valuation. Market prices include taxes on expenditures and are net of subsidies. Factor costs exclude taxes on expenditures, but do not have subsidies netted out. The various aggregates defined above can be measured on either the *market price* or *factor cost* basis. If value added taxes rose and income taxes fell, nothing (as a first approximation) would happen to the level of employment, or aggregate output. The *market price* concept of national income, however, would rise. The *factor cost* concept would not change. Macroeconomics is concerned with measuring the scale of economic activity and, ideally, would use the *factor cost* concept. In practice, provided care is taken to interpret any large changes in indirect taxes and subsidies, the *market price* concept is used.

(v) Nominal and Real

The various aggregates defined above can be measured either in
current pounds (nominal) or in
constant pounds (real).

The *nominal* valuation uses prices of goods or factors of production prevailing in the current period to value the current period's output or expenditure. The *real* valuation uses prices of goods or factors which prevailed in a *base* period to value the current period's output or expenditure. Since macroeconomics is concerned with both the scale of real activity and with prices (and inflation), both of these concepts are of importance and will appear again later in this chapter and in Chapter 5.

It is now time to go beyond learning and remembering definitions, and to develop a deeper understanding of the central concepts of output (or product), income, and expenditure.

C. Aggregate Income, Output (Product), and Expenditure

In order to help you understand the central concepts of aggregate income, output, and expenditure it will be convenient to begin by considering an economy that is much simpler than the one in which you live. We will then successively add various features of the world until we have a picture which corresponds quite closely to the one in which we live.

(i) The Simplest Economy

Let us suppose that the economy is one which has no transactions with the rest of the world; that is, no one exports anything to foreigners or imports anything from them. No borrowing or lending takes place across the national borders, either. Indeed, no communications of any kind occur between the domestic economy and the rest of the world.

Next, suppose that there is no government; that is, no one pays taxes, all expenditures by households are voluntary, and all the goods and services which firms produce are bought by households, rather than some of them being bought by governments or their agencies.

The economy consists of just two kinds of economic institutions or *agents*; they are *households* and *firms*. A *household* is an agent which:

(a)   owns factors of production; and
(b)   buys all final consumer goods.

A *firm* is an agent which:

(a)   owns nothing;
(b)   hires factors of production from households;
(c)   sells the goods which it produces to households; and
(d)   pays any profits which it makes on its activities to households.

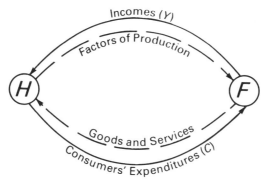

Figure 3.1 *Real and Money Flows in the Simplest Economy*

The flow of factors of production from households to firms and the flow of goods and services from firms to households (clockwise) is matched by equivalent flows of money — firms paying incomes to households and households paying firms for consumers' goods and services (anticlockwise).

This simple economy can be visualised more clearly by considering Figure 3.1. The households in this economy are represented by the circle labelled H, and the firms are represented by the circle labelled F. Two kinds of *flows* take place between households and firms. First, *real* things are supplied by households to firms and by firms to households. Second, *money* passes between households and firms in exchange for these real things. The *real flows* are shown with the dashed lines and the *money flows* are shown with the continuous lines. Households are shown as supplying factors of production to firms, and firms are shown as supplying goods and services to households. Moving in the opposite direction to these *real flows* are the *money flows*. Firms pay incomes to households, and households spend their incomes on consumer goods. The aggregate income payment will be denoted by Y and aggregate expenditure by C.

It is evident that in this simple economy the value of the incomes which households receive from firms must be equal to the value of the expenditures which households make on consumer goods. If this were not so, firms would be making either gains or losses which they would not be passing on to the households, who are the ultimate suppliers of factor services. It will also be evident that the *value* of the goods and services produced by the firms — the *value of output* of the firms — is also equal to the value of the expenditures on those goods and services by the households. In other words,

$$EXPENDITURE = INCOME = VALUE\ OF\ OUTPUT. \qquad (3.1)$$

This very simple economy, which abstracts from much of the detail of the actual world in which we live, has enabled us to establish the equality of income, expenditure, and output which follows purely from the definitions of the terms involved. We now want to go on to see that this equality also applies to the more complicated world in which we live. There are three features of the 'real world' which are not captured in the story above and in Figure 3.1. They are:

(1) Households typically do not spend all their income on consumer goods — they also save some of their income.

(2)   Governments are large (and indeed growing) institutions in the modern world which tax individual incomes and which use their tax proceeds to buy large quantities of goods and services from firms.

(3)   Economic activity is not restricted to trading with other domestic residents. International trade, travel, and capital movements are commonplace.

We will introduce these three characteristics of the world in which we live one-by-one, rather than all at once.

(ii) Savings by Households

Since households typically do not spend all their incomes on consumer goods, but also do some saving, it looks as if Figure 3.1 has a serious defect. If households save some of their incomes, then consumers' expenditures must be less than incomes, and therefore, the flow of expenditures from households to firms shown in Figure 3.1 must be smaller than the flow of incomes received by households from firms. This must mean that firms are continually short of cash, since they are paying out more than they are receiving. How does this complicating factor affect the concepts of national income, expenditure, and output and their equality?

The easiest way of dealing with this is to consider a still slightly fictitious (but less fictitious than previously) representation of the economy in which we think of there being two kinds of firms — those that produce consumer goods and those that produce buildings, plant, equipment and other durable goods — known as capital goods. (Denote consumer-goods firms by the letters F_c, and capital-goods firms by the letters F_k.) You can think of F_c firms as being, for example, those that produce food, clothing, and the thousands of commodities which households typically

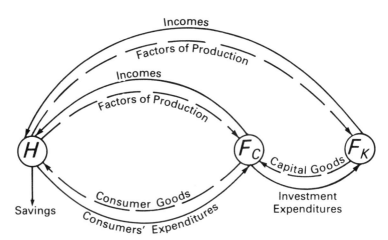

Figure 3.2 *Real and Money Flows in an Economy with Savings and Investment*
Households supply factor services to producers of consumer goods and capital goods. Consumer-goods producers supply households, and capital-goods producers supply consumer-goods producers with new equipment. These real flows are matched by equivalent money flows. Incomes are paid to households equal in value to the production of both consumer and capital goods. Households pay firms for the purchase of consumer goods and save. Firms purchasing new capital goods pay the firms producing those goods the flow of investment expenditures.

consume, and you can think of F_k firms as those that produce, for example, steel mills, motorways, generating stations, and the like. (Of course, in the real world there isn't a clean-cut, hard-and-fast division.) Figure 3.2 illustrates the real flows and the money flows between the various kinds of firms and households. Households supply factors of production to both consumer-goods and capital-goods producers. These are shown as the two continuous lines representing flows from households to the two kinds of firms. The consumer-goods producers, F_c, supply consumer goods to households, and the capital-goods producers, F_k, supply capital goods to the producers of consumer goods. (Another fiction which we will maintain is that capital-goods firms do not themselves buy capital goods. We could easily relax this, although it would make the pictorial representation of what is going on more complicated.) To summarise: the real flows in the economy are the two sets of factor services flowing from households to the two kinds of firms, and real goods flowing in the opposite directions, with capital goods flowing from capital-goods producers to consumer-goods producers, and with consumer goods flowing from consumer-goods producers to households.

The financial flows in this economy move in the opposite directions. Two kinds of firms pay incomes to households. Households make *consumer expenditures*, which represent flows of money from households to consumer-goods producers, and consumer-goods producers make *investment expenditures* by paying money to capital-goods producers in exchange for the capital goods supplied. In addition, households *save* some of their income. This is shown as the flow from households. Households' savings are not payments to either capital-goods or consumer-goods producers directly and, therefore, are not shown as a flow into either of these two institutions, but simply as a flow out of households.

In order to make the picture of the economy simpler, let us now add together the two kinds of firms (F_c and F_k) into a single, aggregate firms sector (F). This is done in Figure 3.3.

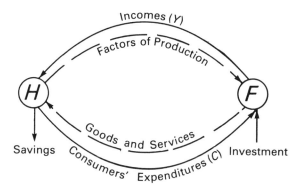

Figure 3.3 *Real and Money Flows in an Economy with Savings and Investment —*
Simplified

Consumer- and capital-goods producers are consolidated into an aggregate firms sector. Firms in total buy factor services from households in exchange for incomes. Households buy consumer goods and services in exchange for the money flow of consumers' expenditures. What households do not spend on consumer goods they save. Savings are equal in value to firms' investment expenditures.

Now, instead of having two income flows from firms to households, there is one, and this represents the sum of the two flows in Figure 3.2. Also, instead of there being two flows of factor services to firms, there is one, and this also represents the sum of the two flows shown in Figure 3.2. The expenditures by households on goods and services to firms is exactly the same as before, namely, the expenditure on consumer goods. Also, the flow of goods and services from firms to households is the same as the flow from the consumer-goods firms to households. By aggregating all the firms in the economy into a single sector, the flow of capital goods from one kind of firm to another and the flow of investment expenditures on those goods has been lost, so to speak, in the aggregation. That is, by looking only at the aggregate of firms and the transactions which they have with households, we are not able to 'see' in the picture the flow of investment expenditures between the firms and the flow of capital goods between the firms. As a substitute for this, and so that we do not forget that it is there, Figure 3.3 shows the flow of investment expenditures as a net receipt by firms.

To simplify things further and to make it easier to move on to the next two stages of complexity, Figure 3.4 reproduces Figure 3.3, but leaves out the flows of factors of production and real goods and services, showing only the *financial flows*. Also, it uses only the symbolic names for the flows rather than their full names. Let us now focus on Figure 3.4. What this figure shows us is that *Income* (Y) is paid by firms to households; households' *Consumer Expenditures*(C) are received by firms; households also *Save* (S). This latter activity simply represents the non-spending of income by households and does not represent *direct* transfers of resources to firms. In addition, firms make *Investment* (I) expenditures on new capital goods.

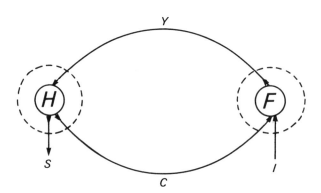

Figure 3.4 *The Money Flows in an Economy with Savings and Investment — A More Abstract Representation*
The money flows only are shown with symbols to denote: income (Y), consumers' expenditure (C), savings (S), investment (I). The broken circles around the households and firms contain arrows going to or from households and firms. An arrow leading into a sector represents a receipt. An arrow leaving a sector represents a payment. Total receipts by a sector equal total payments. Thus, for households, $Y = C + S$. For firms, $Y = C + I$. It follows directly that $S = I$.

The savings which households make out of their incomes and the investments which firms make in new capital goods clearly are in some sense related to each other. It is *capital markets* — markets in which people borrow and lend — which provide the mechanism whereby these two variables are linked. Households place their savings in various kinds of financial assets, and firms borrow in a variety of ways from households in order to undertake their investment activity. Thus, it is the capital markets — the balance sheets of households, firms, banks and other financial institutions — which provide the financial flow linkage between savings and investments.

Let us now return to Figure 3.4 and look again at the concepts of income, output, and expenditure embodied in this more complicated representation of the world.

To highlight matters, focus first of all upon the firms (the circle labelled F). Around the firms circle we have put an extra circle (dashed) which contains three arrows — two leading into the firms, and one going from the firms. Recall that everything a firm receives it also has to pay out. Firms do not own anything, and profits they make are paid out to households as factor incomes. Given this fact, it is clear that the incomes paid out by firms must be equal to the expenditures by households on consumer goods and expenditures by firms on investment goods; that is,

$$Y = C + I \tag{3.2}$$

Next, focus on households and the dashed circle surrounding them in Figure 3.4. It also has three arrows — one leading to the households, and two leading from the households. Since households must, in some way, dispose of their incomes, either by consuming or saving, it is evident that consumption plus savings (the outflows from households) must be equal to households' incomes, i.e.,

$$Y = C + S \tag{3.3}$$

Equation 3.2 above tells us that the value of all incomes in the economy is equal to the value of all expenditures. The expenditures are now broader than they were in the first example and include investment expenditures as well as consumer expenditures.

Further, just as it was in the simpler example, the value of output in the economy is also equal to income or expenditure. To see this, all you have to do is to recognise that the value of the goods and services produced is equal to the value placed upon them by the final demanders of those goods and services. That value is the value of consumer expenditures plus investment expenditures. Thus, income, expenditure, and output are again equal in this more 'realistic' representation of the world.

You must be careful to distinguish between expenditure on final goods and services, payments to factors of production, and expenditures on intermediate goods and services. These distinctions are easiest to see in this simplified economy, but apply to all the more complicated economies described below.

*Expenditure on **final** goods and services* must be distinguished from *expenditure on **intermediate** goods and services*. This distinction is most easily understood with the aid of an example. Suppose you buy a bar of chocolate from the local university store for 15p. The university store bought that chocolate bar from its wholesale supplier for 10p; the wholesaler bought it from the manufacturer for 8p; the manufacturer bought milk for 1p, cocoa beans for 1p, sugar for 1p, electricity for 2p, paid wages to its workers of 5p, and made a 2p profit which it paid to its shareholders. The total expenditures in the story of the chocolate bar are 15 + 10 + 8 + 1 + 1 + 1 + 2 + 5 + 2 = 45p. Of these 45p, only 15p represents *expenditure on final goods and services*. The rest are *expenditures on intermediate goods and services* or *payments to factors of production*. The expenditures can be classified as follows:

	Expenditure on Final Goods and Services	Factor Incomes	Expenditure on Intermediate Goods and Services
Purchase Price of Chocolate Bar	15p	–	–
Wholesaler's Selling Price	–	–	10p
Manufacturer's Selling Price	–	–	8p
Farmer's Income (Milk)	–	1p	–
Farmer's Income (Cocoa Beans)	–	1p	–
Farmer's Income (Sugar)	–	1p	–
Electricity Producers' Incomes	–	2p	–
Chocolate Producers' Wages	–	5p	–
Chocolate Producers' Profits	–	2p	–
Wholesaler's Profit	–	1p	–
Retailer's Profit	–	2p	–
Totals	15p	15p	

Notice that the first column gives the value of expenditure (*expenditure on final goods and services*) on a bar of chocolate, the second column total gives the *incomes* earned by all those who had a hand in producing the bar of chocolate, and the final column simply records some intermediate transactions. From the viewpoint of macroeconomics, these last items are irrelevant. They arise from a particular form of industrial structure and would change if the industrial structure changed. For example, if the manufacturer sold directly to the retailer (for the 10p charged by the wholesaler in the above example), the *expenditure on intermediate goods and services* would fall by 8p. However, nothing interesting would have changed. *Total expenditure on final goods and services* would still be 15p. Also, *factor incomes* would still be 15p; the profit of the wholesaler would have been eliminated and transferred to the manufacturer (by assumption in the above story). To count the *expenditure on intermediate goods and services* as well as the *expenditure on final goods and services* involves counting the same thing twice (or more than twice if there are several intermediate stages) and is known as *double counting*.

(iii) Government Expenditure and Taxes

Now let us consider a yet more complicated world; one in which government economic activity plays a role. Figure 3.5 illustrates this. In addition to households (*H*) and firms (*F*), we also have government (denoted *GOV*). Figure 3.5, which shows the relationship between households, firms, and government, is drawn on the simplified basis introduced in Figure 3.4. That is, we do not show both the real flows and the money flows. We show only the money flows. Also, we label the various flows with only their symbolic rather than their full names. There are two new symbols:

  T stands for *Taxes*, and

  G stands for *Government Expenditures on Goods and Services*.

  In this more complicated world, households receive incomes (*Y*) from firms. They

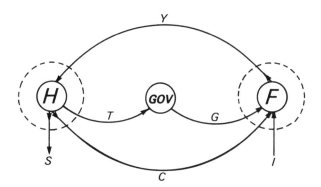

Figure 3.5 *Money Flows in an Economy with Savings, Investment, and Government Economic Activity*

Government taxes households (T) and buys goods and services produced by firms — government expenditures on goods and services (G). When these flows are added to those shown in the previous figures, the households' income and expenditure account is modified to become $Y = C + S + T$. The firms' income and expenditure account is modified to become $Y = C + I + G$. It follows directly from these last two statements that $S + T = I + G$. There is no reason why government expenditure should equal taxes. The government may run a surplus $(T > G)$ or a deficit $(T < G)$.

---

dispose of those incomes either by buying consumer goods (C), paying taxes (T), or saving (S). Firms, as before, receive households' consumption expenditures as well as investment expenditures (financed by various capital market operations). They also have receipts from the government in exchange for its purchases of goods and services (G). The government itself simply receives taxes (net of any transfers that it makes to households) and makes expenditures on goods and services.

Now, to see the National Income Accounts that emerge from this more complex view of the world, focus again, first of all, on firms and on the arrows in the broken circle surrounding firms. Notice that now firms pay out incomes (Y) and receive consumer expenditures (C), government expenditures (G), and investment expenditure (I). Since, as before, firms have no ultimate ownership of resources, everything which they receive is paid out to households. Hence,

$$Y = C + I + G \qquad\qquad (3.4)$$

Next, focus on households. They receive incomes and dispose of those incomes in the activities of consuming (C), saving (S), and paying taxes (T). Hence,

$$Y = C + S + T \qquad\qquad (3.5)$$

In this economy, expenditure is still equal to income, but expenditure now incorporates consumers' expenditures, firms' investment expenditures, and in addition, government expenditures on goods and services.

It is important that you understand that government payments to households, such as, for example, unemployment benefits, old age pensions, and the like, are *not* government expenditures on goods and services; they are simply the transfer of money from the government to households and are called *transfer payments*. You can think of these as negative taxes, so that total tax payments (denoted as T) need to be thought of as being *net* taxes, equal to the gross taxes paid minus the gross transfers from government to households.

As in the two simpler economies considered above, not only are income and expenditure equal to each other, but so also is output equal to income and expenditure. The value of the goods and services bought by households (C), firms (I), and government (G) represents the value of the goods and services produced in the economy — the output of the economy. Hence, even in this more complex economy, aggregate income, expenditure, and output are one and the same.

(iv) The Rest of the World

Now consider the final complication arising from the fact that economic agents do business with their counterparts in the rest of the world. Figure 3.6 will illustrate the story here. Now we have households (H), firms (F), government (GOV), and the rest of the world (R). All the flows are as before, except for some additional flows between the rest of the world and the domestic economy. The left-hand part of Figure 3.6 is identical to Figure 3.5 and does not need to be described again. The additional activities in Figure 3.6 are *imports and exports of goods and services*. Foreigners buy goods from the producers of goods in the domestic economy — from domestic firms — and therefore there is a flow of money from the rest of the world to the domestic firms — (EX) for exports. In addition, domestic citizens buy goods from the rest of the world, transferring money to foreigners in exchange for those goods — imports (IM). From the way the figure has been drawn, it looks as if only firms do the importing. We know, of course, that sometimes households import

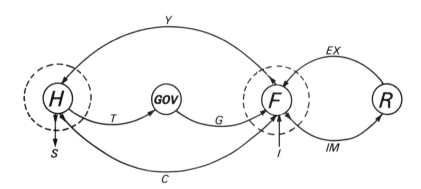

Figure 3.6 *Money Flows in an Economy with Savings, Investment, Government Economic Activity, and Transactions with the Rest of the World*

The flow transactions with the rest of the world are exports, which give rise to a receipt by the firms doing the exporting (EX), and imports, which give rise to payments by firms doing the importing (IM). These receipts and payments run between firms and the rest of the world (R). Extending the flows to include those with the rest of the world leaves the households' incomes and expenditures unchanged. They remain $Y = C + S + T$. The firms' accounts now become $Y = C + I + G + EX - IM$. It follows directly from this that $S + T + IM = I + G + EX$. There is no requirement that exports (EX) = imports (IM). There may be a trade surplus ($EX > IM$) or a trade deficit ($EX < IM$) with the rest of the world.

goods directly. This could equally be shown in the picture, but it would not add anything of substance.

Let us see how the National Income Accounts will now look in this economy. There is no change in households' behaviour. It is true that households now buy consumer goods, some of which have been imported from the rest of the world by the firms from which they buy them. However, that will not show up directly in the households' accounts. Their accounts still say that income (Y) is equal to consumption (C) plus savings (S) plus taxes (T). However, we get a slightly different picture when we look at firms. We now have two arrows leading out of the firms' circle — flows of money from firms to other agents — and four arrows flowing into firms. Firms pay factor incomes to households (Y) and pay foreigners for the value of goods and services which have been imported from them (IM). They receive from foreigners the value of exports (EX); from government the value of goods and services purchased by government (G); and from households the value of consumer goods purchased (C). There is also a net inflow of funds to finance the firms' investment expenditures (I). Thus, considering all the arrows showing flows into and out from the firms, it is clear that

$$Y = C + I + G + EX - IM \tag{3.6}$$

The items on the right-hand side of equation (3.6) are total expenditures on domestic output. Hence, the equality between income and expenditure is retained in the world pictured in Figure 3.6. Income is the flow of money from firms to households, which represents the value of the factor services supplied by households to firms. Expenditure is equal to the consumer expenditures of households (C), the value of purchases of capital equipment by firms (I), government expenditures of goods and services (G), and the net value of foreigners' expenditures on domestic output. By *net* value we mean the difference between the gross purchases by foreigners (exports) and the purchases of foreign goods by domestic citizens (imports).

The National Income Accounts reveal an additional interesting implication in this more 'realistic' picture of the world. It follows immediately from the equality between income and expenditure and the fact that income is allocated by households to consumption, savings, and taxes. If you begin by considering equations (3.5) and (3.6), it will be immediately apparent to you that

$$I + G + EX = S + T + IM \tag{3.7}$$

Now, deduct savings, taxes, and imports from both sides of this equation and rearrange the order of the terms so that we obtain:

$$(I - S) + (G - T) + (EX - IM) = 0 \tag{3.8}$$

The three terms in brackets in equation (3.8) have a very natural interpretation. The first term, $(I - S)$, is the excess of investment over savings by the private sector of the economy. The second term, $(G - T)$, is the government's budget deficit, or surplus. The third term, $(EX - IM)$, is surplus or deficit in the balance of trade with the rest of the world.

What equation (3.8) says is that the sum of these three items must always be zero. There are various alternative ways in which this could be expressed. One, which is perhaps helpful, is to notice that equation (3.8) implies that if firms are investing more than households are saving, then either it is necessary for there to be a balance of trade deficit — that is, for imports to exceed exports — so that the extra investment goods may indeed be acquired by firms, or it is going to be necessary for government expenditures to be less than taxes so that, in effect, the government is doing some of the saving which is enabling capital goods to be accumulated by firms. Another way of expressing the same thing would be to say that if the government insists on spending more than it generates in taxes — if there is a government budget deficit — then there must either be a shortfall of investment as compared with savings, or there must be a balance of trade deficit with the rest of the world to enable the government to acquire the resources in excess of the value of the taxes that it is levying.

D. Measuring Aggregate Income

(i) The Expenditure Approach

In order to measure national income (or expenditure or output), it is necessary to record and add together the appropriate flows that are taking place in the economy. The two most common methods of measuring national income will now be discussed. The first is the *expenditure approach*. You can think of the expenditure approach as an attempt by the national income statisticians to measure the total value of consumer expenditures on goods and services, firms' investment expenditures, government expenditures on goods and services, exports, and imports. When these are combined in accordance with equation (3.6), they provide one estimate of the value of national income, expenditure or output. These items can be measured with varying degrees of accuracy. Consumer expenditures are measured partly by taking surveys of what households are spending and partly by observing the value of the sales of consumer goods by producers. Government expenditures are measured directly from the accounts of government itself. Investment expenditures are measured by surveying firms' capital spending programs and inventories. Finally, foreign trade is monitored through the official documentation required to conduct that trade. Most countries have some form of control over international movements of goods and services, and in some cases, these items are subject either to restrictive quotas or tariffs. In order to implement those arrangements, governments automatically collect data on the volumes of international trade flows. Thus, by measuring these items, $C, I, G, EX,$ and IM, it is possible to obtain a measure of aggregate income, expenditure or output by using the formula

$$Y = C + I + G + EX - IM \tag{3.6}$$

By adding the values of *expenditures,* the aggregate which results will be based on *market prices* and will include *taxes on expenditures* and *subsidies.* To convert this to the *factor cost* measure needed for macroeconomic analysis, it is necessary to *deduct taxes on expenditure* and *add subsidies,* to give *aggregate income (output or expenditure) at factor cost.*

(ii) The Factor Incomes Approach

An alternative method of attempting to measure national income is to measure factor incomes directly. The major sources of such measurements are the returns which individuals and firms make to the tax-collecting branch of government — in Britain, the Inland Revenue. Since most taxes are collected as a levy on incomes earned, the reporting of those incomes for the purpose of tax calculations provides the major input for the factor incomes approach to the measurement of aggregate income. By using these sources, it is possible to arrive at an estimate of aggregate income by what is known as the *factor incomes approach*. This measure of aggregate income (output or expenditure) is automatically on a *factor cost* basis and needs no further adjustment.

(iii) The Output Approach

A third method of attempting to measure national income is to measure the value of output of each industry and then aggregate those output measures to arrive at an estimate of aggregate output. The major sources of direct measurement of output are the census of production and census of distribution. By using the data collected by these census surveys it is possible to arrive at estimates of aggregate output by what is known as the output approach. In addition to providing a third way of arriving at an estimate of aggregate economic activity, this approach also provides estimates of the output of each major sector of the economy. As you have seen earlier in this chapter, in principle, aggregate output is identical to aggregate income, which in turn is identical to aggregate expenditure. In practice, since the measurement of these variables is based on incomplete and imprecise recording of all the transactions and activities that take place, the three measures do not exactly agree. There is always a statistical discrepancy, since it is simply too costly to devote the resources that would be necessary to obtain precise values of all the variables involved.

The National Institute for Economic and Social Research publishes, in its *National Institute Economic Review,* a compromise estimate of aggregate economic activity based on all three approaches to its measurement.

E. Measuring Aggregate Income in Constant Pounds (Real)

There are two methods of measuring aggregate income (output or expenditure) in constant pounds. One of them uses the *expenditure approach* and the other the *output approach*. Both methods begin by selecting what is called a *base period*. The average level of prices prevailing in the base period is defined to be equal to 100. The expenditures and output measures derived for a particular year are revalued using the prices prevailing in the base year. The resulting expenditures and output, valued in prices prevailing in the base year, are aggregated using the same basic methods as employed to arrive at the values of national expenditure and output in terms of current pounds. The resulting aggregates provide an estimate of output and expenditure as well, of course, as an estimate of real income. At the present time, in Britain, the base year for the constant pound national income measures is 1975.

F. Reading National Income and Expenditure Accounts

The United Kingdom's aggregate income accounts are assembled by the Central Statistical Office. The annual accounts are published in *National Income and Expenditure* (known as the 'Blue Book') each year. The detailed definitions, concepts, sources and methods are described, with immense attention being paid to the intricacies involved in national accounts statistics; see *National Accounts Statistics: Sources and Methods*, Studies in Official Statistics, No. 13 (HMSO, 1968).

Reading the National Income Accounts and translating them into the aggregate concepts that you have become familiar with in the preceding parts of this chapter is a relatively straightforward business. You may, nevertheless, need some guidance in the task.

If you look at the National Income Blue Book (you will find a copy in any university library and in the business/economics section of many public libraries), the first thing that will strike you (probably with mild alarm) is the immense detail presented. There are (in the 1979 accounts) more than eighty tables covering almost one hundred pages. It is hard to know where to begin. Fortunately, for the purposes of macroeconomic analysis, a small number of summary tables in Section I of the Blue Book contain most of what is needed. Table 1.1 provides an estimate of the gross national product classified according to the expenditure approach and using both market prices and factor costs as the basis of valuation. Table 1.2 provides an estimate by the income approach, aggregating incomes over various categories. That table provides an estimate of gross national product from the income approach and shows the discrepancy (residual error) between the income and expenditure methods of measuring aggregate activity. Table 1.9 provides an estimate of gross domestic product by industry from the output approach.

Section II of the National Income Blue Book provides comparable figures to those supplied in Section I, but revalues all the items in constant 1975 prices.

Some of the more important items in the National Income Blue Book tables are brought together in Table 3.1 in a form that will enable you to see the relationships between the variables, using the concepts developed earlier in this chapter. The name (or names) of the items given in parentheses beneath each major item refer to the details contained in the Blue Book tables. There is little to be gained from committing this to memory. You may, however, find it a useful reference in the event that you want to construct your own accounts for a year, or years, other than 1979 (the example used here).

Looking at the major items in Table 3.1 you will see that consumption (C) plus investment (I) plus government expenditures (G) plus exports (EX) *less* imports (IM) add up to gross domestic product at market prices. By deducting indirect taxes less subsidies, an estimate of gross domestic product at factor cost is arrived at. Adding the net property income from abroad provides an estimate of gross national product at factor cost. The bottom of the table notes the amount of capital consumption — that is, depreciation of fixed capital — which has accrued in the year. By subtracting that amount from any of the other *gross* figures you may arrive at the corresponding *net* national or domestic product estimate either at factor cost or market price.

Table 3.1 United Kingdom's Aggregate Income, Expenditure and Product in 1979

		£ million
	CONSUMPTION (*C*) (Consumer Expenditure)	114,805
add	INVESTMENT (*I*) (Gross domestic fixed capital formation 33,646 *plus* value of physical increase in stocks and work in progress 2,760)	36,406
add	GOVERNMENT EXPENDITURE (*G*) (General Government Final Consumption)	38,316
add	EXPORTS (*EX*) (Exports of goods and services)	54,676
deduct	IMPORTS (*IM*) (Imports of goods and services)	−54,501
equals	GROSS DOMESTIC PRODUCT AT MARKET PRICES	189,702
deduct	INDIRECT TAXES *less* SUBSIDIES	−26,055
equals	GROSS DOMESTIC PRODUCT AT FACTOR COST	163,647
add	NET PROPERTY INCOME FROM ABROAD	289
equals	GROSS NATIONAL PRODUCT AT FACTOR COST	163,936
	(CAPITAL CONSUMPTION)	(22,163)

Source: *National Income and Expenditure,* Table 1.1 (HMSO, 1980).

SUMMARY

A. Flows and Stocks

A flow is a rate per unit of time, such as income per annum or expenditure per month. A stock is the value of a variable at a point in time, such as the amount of money you have in the bank on a particular day.

B. Some Frequently Used Terms

(i)   *Output (Product), Income and Expenditure*

—*output* (or *product*) is the value of the goods and services produced in the economy.
—*income* is the sum of all the incomes earned in producing the output of the economy.
—*expenditure* is the sum of all expenditures on final goods and services in the economy.

(ii)   *Domestic and National*

—*domestic* refers to an aggregation of economic activity taking place in a particular country.
—*national* refers to an aggregation of the economic activity of all residents no matter in which country the activity takes place.

(iii)   *Gross and Net*

—*gross* is *before* deducting the depreciation of assets.
—*net* is *after* deducting the depreciation of assets.

(iv)   *Market Price and Factor Cost*

—*market price* valuations are based on the prices paid by consumers and include taxes on expenditure and are net of subsidies.
—*factor cost* valuations are based on the amounts paid by consumers and include taxes on expenditures and are gross of subsidies.

C. Aggregate Income, Output (Product) and Expenditure

Aggregate income is the sum of all the incomes of all the individuals in the economy. Aggregate expenditure is the sum of all the expenditures on *final* goods and services of all the individuals in the economy. Aggregate output is the value of the *final* goods and services produced by the economy.

   The values of aggregate income, expenditure and output are equal to each other.

D. Measuring Aggregate Income

The expenditure approach to national income measurement samples the expenditures of households, firms, government, and foreigners and makes an estimate of the sum of those expenditures. From the fact that income, expenditure, and output are equal to each other, this estimate of expenditure is also an estimate of income and output.

The factor incomes approach samples the incomes of individuals and from this forms an estimate of aggregate income. From the conceptual equality of income, expenditure, and output, this provides an alternative estimate of aggregate expenditure and output as well as income.

The output approach measures the value added by each major sector of the economy and from this forms an estimate of the value of output for the economy as a whole. Again, from the conceptual equality of income, expenditure, and output, this provides yet a third estimate of aggregate expenditure and income as well as an estimate of output.

The three approaches never produce the same estimate, but provide a good approximation to the value of aggregate income, expenditure, and output.

E. Measuring Aggregate Income in Constant Pounds (Real)

To measure real income (output and expenditure) both the expenditure and output approaches are used. The final goods and services purchased in each year are valued at the prices which prevailed in the base year to arrive at an estimate of real aggregate expenditure. The value added of each industry is revalued in the prices prevailing in the base year to arrive at an estimate of real aggregate output. Both of these approaches provide alternative estimates of real aggregate income.

F. Reading National Income and Expenditure Accounts

The United Kingdom's national income and expenditure accounts (annual data) are published in August of each year by the Central Statistical Office in *National Income and Expenditure* (known more commonly as the 'Blue Book'). The key tables in that publication are Tables 1.1 (gross national product by category of expenditure), 1.2 (gross national product by category of income), 1.9 (gross domestic product by industry), and 2.1 (expenditure and output at 1975 prices). The way in which the detailed items supplied by the Central Statistical Office aggregate into the concepts employed in macroeconomics are set out in Table 3.1, and that table should be used as a reference guide.

Review Questions

1. Indicate which of the following are flows and which are stocks:
    (i)   The rate at which oil is pumped through a pipeline from a North Sea well
    (ii)   The amount of oil under the North Sea
    (iii)   Gross domestic product
    (iv)   Real national income
    (v)   The value of the airliners owned by British Airways.

2. Review the definition of each of the following terms:
    (i)   gross national product
    (ii)   gross national product at market price
    (iii)   gross national product at factor cost
    (iv)   real national income.

3. Give examples which illustrate the differences between the following terms:
    (i)   nominal and real
    (ii)   gross and net
    (iii)   national and domestic
    (iv)   factor cost and market price.

4. What are the units of measurement of (i) a nominal variable and (ii) a real variable?

5. Using the latest available volume of *National Income and Expenditure* (Central Statistical Office), calculate the latest year values of (i) aggregate income; (ii) aggregate expenditure; and (iii) aggregate output.

6. Using *National Income and Expenditure* (Central Statistical Office), calculate aggregate income for 1980, using (i) the expenditure approach, (ii) the factor incomes approach, and (iii) the output approach. Is your measure of aggregate income a gross or a net measure? What is the difference between gross aggregate income and net aggregate income in 1980?

7. Using gross aggregate income for 1980 (calculated in Question 6 above) and *National Income and Expenditure*, calculate 1980 aggregate income in constant 1975 pounds.

8. Suppose that you want to describe the pattern of aggregate output in the United Kingdom during the 1970s. Which of the following would be the best series to use, and why?
    (i)   aggregate expenditure at market prices
    (ii)   aggregate output at factor cost
    (iii)   gross domestic product in constant pounds
    (iv)   gross domestic product.
    Say exactly what *all* the faults are with the series that you would *not* use.

9. The following activities took place in an imaginary economy last year:

	£m
Wages paid to labour	800,000
Consumer expenditures	650,000
Taxes paid on wages	200,000
Government payments to support the unemployed, sick and aged	50,000
Firms' profits	200,000
Investment	250,000
Taxes paid on profits	50,000
Government purchases on goods and services	200,000
Exports	250,000

There was no property income paid to or received from non-residents.

(a) Calculate:
  (i)   gross domestic income
  (ii)   gross national expenditure
  (iii)   savings
  (iv)   imports
  (v)   the government budget surplus/deficit.
(b) What extra information do you need in order to calculate net national income?

10.   A troupe of Russian dancers tours Britain. The dancers fly to Britain on an *Aeroflot* (Soviet airline) flight at a total round trip cost of £100,000. They travel inside Britain on British Rail at a total cost of £20,000. Their hotel and food bills in Britain amount to £75,000. The receipts from ticket sales for performances of the troupe amount to £500,000. The cost of renting theatres, hiring British musicians, and advertising is £150,000. The Russian dancers' wages amount to £35,000 for the period of the visit. The dancers buy British-made souvenirs worth a total of £1000. Any profit or loss on the visit accrues to or is borne by the Soviet government. Show where each of the economic activities described here appears in the United Kingdom's National Income Accounts.

4
Aggregate Balance Sheet Accounting

This is an unusual topic to appear in an introductory macroeconomics text, and it reflects the unusual nature of the book with which you are working. Keynesian macroeconomics places a great deal of emphasis on the National Income Accounts and on aggregate income and expenditure flows, and the last chapter dealt with the concepts that lie behind that accounting framework. If you were working with a conventional Keynesian-orientated macroeconomics book, you would now be reading the first 'theory' chapter. That chapter would present a theory about how national income is determined, and the theory would be based purely on the items from national income flow accounts. It would postulate hypothetical relationships between various flows — hypotheses that one flow depends in some behavioural way on another flow — and would from that develop a predictive theory of the determination of national income.

That route is not taken here. The kind of macroeconomics that you are studying in this book is built on the presumption that the most important behavioural relationships are not only those between flows and flows, but also between flows and stocks. Accordingly, as a prelude to studying macroeconomic theory, this chapter explains the connections between the main stocks (the assets and liabilities in the economy) and also explains how those stocks are measured.

Your four tasks are to:
A. understand the meaning of 'asset', 'liability', and 'balance sheet';
B. know the definition of money and understand the nature of money;
C. know the main items in the balance sheets of households, firms, commercial banks, the central bank, government and the rest of the world;
and
D. know the main sources of information about aggregate balance sheets in the United Kingdom.

A. Asset, Liability, and Balance Sheet

(i) Asset and Liability

An *asset* is simply something which someone *owns*.
A *liability* is what someone *owes*.

There are two types of assets: *financial* and *real*. A *real asset* is concrete, tangible, a real piece of nuts and bolts. Examples of real assets are the desks and tables at which you sit and study; your stereo and records; and your car, motorcycle, etc. Other examples are motorways, steel mills, coal mines, power stations, aeroplanes.

There is one special real asset which you probably do not ordinarily think of as an asset — that is yourself (and everyone else). The value of that asset in the economy as a whole is the value of all the work that human beings are capable of doing now and in the future. The asset is called *human capital*. Of course, in societies such as our own where slavery is prohibited, it is not possible to buy and sell human capital. It is possible, however, to borrow from a bank against a promise to commit future income (i.e., human capital) to the repayment of the loan.

Financial assets are different from real assets. They are pieces of paper which constitute an asset to one economic agent and a liability to another. That is, they *define a debt relationship* between two agents. Examples of financial assets (which are also someone else's financial liabilities) are:

(a) your deposit account with (say) Barclays Bank — from your point of view that is a financial asset (you *own* the deposit) while from the point of view of Barclays Bank it is a liability (they *owe* you the deposit);

(b) an ICI bond — this is an asset to the person who owns it, but a liability to ICI shareholders;

(c) a Bank of England one-pound note — this is an asset to you, but is it anyone's liability? Yes, it is — it is a liability of the Bank of England, the central bank of this country. The Bank of England owes you one pound's worth of goods and services in exchange for that note and has to hold assets (government securities) which it could sell in order to meet its commitment. In fact, of course, since just about everyone is willing to accept your pound note in exchange for goods and services, the Bank of England never has to!

All financial assets are like the three examples just given. Each financial asset has a financial liability that goes with it. It is simply a piece of paper that specifies that someone, X, has a claim on someone else, Y; that is an asset to X and a liability to Y.

(ii) Balance Sheet

A *balance sheet* is a *statement* about what is *owned by* (is an asset of) and what is *owed by* (is a liability of) a particular individual or agency. It could be an individual like yourself or it could be an agency like the Bank of England, a commercial bank, the British government or ICI. The best way to get a feel for a balance sheet is to consider the balance sheet of an individual like yourself.

Table 4.1 sets out an example of what an individual student's balance sheet might look like. The balance sheet shown in Table 4.1 lists the *assets* in the first column and

Table 4.1 An Individual's Balance Sheet

		Assets £	Liabilities £
1.	Bank Notes and Coins	25	
2.	Deposit Account	50	
3.	National Savings Certificate	100	
4.	Bank Loan		500
5.	Visa Account		100
6.	TOTAL FINANCIAL ASSETS AND LIABILITIES	175	600
7.	Car	1000	
8.	Stereo and Records	500	
9.	TOTAL REAL ASSETS	1500	
10.	TOTAL ASSETS AND LIABILITIES	1675	600
11.	WEALTH		1075
12.	Totals	1675	1675

the *liabilities* in the second column. The assets are divided between *financial* items (in the top part of the balance sheet) and *real* items (in the bottom part of the balance sheet). The person whose balance sheet is shown here has some bank notes and coins, £25 (row 1); a deposit account, £50 (row 2); national savings certificate, £100 (row 3). These are the person's *financial assets*. There are two *financial liabilities:* a bank loan, £500 (row 4); and an outstanding balance with a credit card company, Visa, £100 (row 5). Row 6 totals the financial assets and liabilities. You will see that this person owes more (has bigger liabilities) than he owns (has assets).

The next items are *real assets*. This individual has a car worth a thousand pounds and a stereo and record collection worth £500, giving *total real assets* (row 9) of £1500. The total assets and liabilities are shown in row 10. This individual has assets of £1675 and liabilities of £600.

It is a feature of a *balance sheet* that it must *balance*! Clearly, as depicted in row 10, the assets of this individual exceed his liabilities. The amount by which the assets exceed the liabilities is £1075. This amount of money is the *wealth* of this individual. *Wealth* is defined to be a 'fictitious' liability (yes liability) and is shown in row 11 as a liability of £1075. If you add the *wealth* of the individual to the rest of his liabilities you see that total liabilities (row 12) are equal to total assets, £1675. In order to feel more comfortable with the idea of *wealth* as a liability, you may like to think of it as the amount which is owed by an individual to himself. Another equivalent way of defining *wealth* which is perhaps more appealing is simply: *Wealth* equals *Total Assets* less *Total Liabilities*. In the example:

$$\begin{aligned} \text{Total Assets} &= \text{£1675} \\ less \text{ Total Liabilities} &= \text{£ } 600 \\ equals \text{ Wealth} &= \text{£1075} \end{aligned}$$

B. Definition and the Nature of Money

Money is anything which is generally acceptable as a medium of exchange. A *medium of exchange* is anything which is acceptable in exchange for goods and services. Which precise assets constitute the medium of exchange varies from one society to another and has varied over the years. Gold has commonly served as a medium of exchange; so have silver and other metals. In some prisoner-of-war camps in World War II, cigarettes circulated as a medium of exchange. These are all examples of *commodity money.*

In modern societies money is typically a financial asset which is the financial liability of either the central bank or the commercial banks. There are two widely-used working definitions of money in the United Kingdom today. One is sometimes called *narrow money* (or *M1*) and the other *broad money* (or *£M3*).

Narrow money (or *M1*) consists of *currency in circulation plus sterling current accounts held by households and firms with commercial banks.* Notice that a cheque is not money — it is not something with which you *pay.* A cheque is simply an instruction to your bank to pay on your behalf by transferring funds from your current account to that of someone else. So it is the current account itself that is money.

Broad money (or *£M3*) consists of *M1 plus all other sterling deposits held by the government, households and firms with commercial banks.* These private sector accounts are not directly transferable from one person to another by writing a cheque, and while it is customary to think of money as including the 'money in the bank', it is important to recognise that only *M1* is money in the strict sense that it is a means of payment.

Money does not include 'plastic money' such as Visa and Access cards. These plastic cards are convenient identification tags that enable you to simultaneously create two debts. One debt is between the buyer and the credit card company, and the other debt is between the credit card company and the seller. These debts are settled when the buyer pays the credit card company and the credit card company pays the seller.

Money in the modern world stands in sharp contrast to *commodity money* in that it is simply a *financial asset* not backed by any commodities and not exchangeable by the issuer for anything other than another unit of itself. Its value arises from the fact that it is universally acceptable by all in exchange for goods and services.

C. Main Balance Sheet Items

We are going to look at the balance sheets of six agents:

Households .... *H*
Firms .... *F*
Commercial Banks .... *CB*
The Bank of England .... *B*
British Government .... *GOV*
Rest of the World .... *R*

You will identify this as an extension of the agents whose flow activities we analysed when dealing with the National Income Accounts in the previous chapter. There we examined households, firms, government and the rest of the world. We did not deal with either commercial banks or the central bank. The central bank in the United Kingdom is the Bank of England. The reason for that is that banks are not major actors in the flow of goods and services. They are, however, major actors in the monetary and balance sheet structure of the economy.

(i) Financial Assets and Liabilities

Table 4.2 records the main financial items in the balance sheets of these six agents. A (+) denotes an asset and a (−) denotes a liability.

Table 4.2 The Structure of Financial Indebtedness

ITEM	H	F	B	CB	GOV	R
Commercial Banks' Deposits with the Bank of England			+	−		
Currency (Notes and Coins)	+	+	+	−		−
Sterling Current Accounts	+	+	−		+	
Other Sterling Deposits	+	+	−			
Government Securities	+	+	+	+	−	+
Bank Loans	−	−	+			
Equities	+	−				+
Debentures	+	−				+
Foreign Securities	+	+	+			−
Foreign Exchange				+	+	−
Net Financial Assets	+	−	0	0	−	±

Notes: + Asset
         − Liability   M1 ¦ £M3 ¦ MB

(a) Commercial Bank Deposits with the Bank of England:

Commercial banks maintain current accounts just as individuals do. The banker to the commercial banks is the central bank — the Bank of England. As far as the commercial banks are concerned, their deposits with the Bank of England are like money and are part of their assets. Like notes and coins, they are a liability of the Bank of England. A commercial bank can convert its deposits with the Bank of England into notes and coins, or vice versa, as it chooses.

(b) Currency: Currency consists of all the notes and coins held by (and therefore assets of) households, firms and banks. The notes are a liability of the Bank of England, but the coin is issued by the Royal Mint, a government agency, and is therefore shown as a liability of the government.

(c) Monetary Base (MB):   All the liabilities of the Bank of England added together plus the currency liabilities of the government make up what is known as the *monetary base*. This is shown in the triangle in Table 4.2.

(d) Sterling Current Accounts: Current Accounts are accounts from which funds may be withdrawn on demand. They are liabilities of the commercial banks and assets of households, firms, and the government.

(e) Narrow Money (M1):   The total of currency held by the public and sterling current accounts held by households and firms is 'narrow money' or *M1*. The solid box shows the total of narrow money, *M1*. Notice that *M1* does not include the currency held inside the banking system, nor does it include commercial bank deposits with the Bank of England. Further, *M1* does not include the sterling current accounts in the commercial banks owned by the British Government.

(f) Other Sterling Deposits: These are all the deposits held at commercial banks which may not be withdrawn on demand without penalty. They are held by households and firms.

(g) Broad Money (£M3):   If we add the above item to *M1*, along with Government sterling current accounts, we obtain *£M3* which is shown as the broken box in Table 4.2.

(h) Government Securities: Next there is a whole class of financial assets called government securities. Very many different types of assets are in this category. Examples are: national savings certificates, marketable securities and Treasury bills. These items are a liability of the British Government and are held by (are assets of) all the other five groups. The Bank of England's government securities are the assets which provide the backing for the monetary base. In order to change the size of the monetary base and the amount of money in circulation, the Bank of England buys government securities with new money.

(i) Bank Loans: The next major item to consider in the sectoral balance sheets is bank loans. These are personal and business loans which forms an asset as far as the banks are concerned and are liabilities of the people and firms who have borrowed the money.

(j) Equities: Companies raise funds to buy capital equipment by issuing shares or debentures. Shares are known as equities. An equity holder in a firm is in fact an owner of the firm. That is, the households and foreigners that own equity shares in firms really own a share of the firm's physical capital stock. In legal terms, of course, the owner of a share in a firm can only sell the share. The owner cannot decide to sell the physical plant itself. Thus, in legal terms there is an indebtedness

between the households and foreigners who own firms and the firm itself. The firm has a liability and the households and foreigners own the corresponding asset.

(k) *Debentures*: In addition to raising capital by issuing equity shares, companies also sell bonds. Company bonds are called debentures. A debenture-holder in a company, unlike an equity holder, is not an owner of the company. Rather, such a person has simply made a loan to a company. All that the debentureholder is entitled to is the pre-agreed interest payment on the debenture. In contrast, an equity holder is entitled to any residual profits earned by the firm. In terms of the balance sheet accounting, a debenture, like an equity, appears as a liability to firms and as an asset to households and the rest of the world.

Next we come to two items which deal with further connections between the domestic economy and the rest of the world.

(l) *Foreign Securities*: There is a whole variety of securities issued by foreign governments and foreign companies which are held by British households, firms and banks.

(m) *Foreign Exchange Reserves*: The final item is the foreign exchange reserves of the country. These constitute an asset to the Bank of England and to the government, which holds (and owns) the country's foreign exchange reserves. These reserves are typically in the form of deposits and other short-term securities issued by foreign governments, central banks and commercial banks. You can think of this item as representing the United Kingdom's bank account with the rest of the world.

(ii) Net Financial Assets

If we add up all ten items in Table 4.2 we arrive at the *net financial assets* of each of the major sectors in the economy. Those for the commercial banks and for the Bank of England will approximately add up to zero, reflecting the fact that those institutions have comparatively small holdings of real assets. (They do, of course, have large *absolute* holdings of real assets. The commercial banks and the Bank of England own quite a large amount of real estate and office space. However, compared with their financial assets and liabilities, these items are relatively insignificant and, for our purposes, can be ignored.)

Typically, households and firms which together constitute what is sometimes called the *non-bank private sector,* have positive net financial assets. That is, they own financial assets in excess of the liabilities which they have issued. The government, on the other hand, typically has a net financial liability sometimes referred to as the *national debt*. The net financial asset position of the country *vis-à-vis* the rest of the world may be positive or negative. That is, the rest of the world may have a net financial claim on the United Kingdom (the United Kingdom having a net liability — referred to as a net debtor) or the United Kingdom may have a net financial claim on the rest of the world (having a net financial asset — referred to as a net creditor). As a matter of fact, the United Kingdom is a fairly sizeable net creditor.

(iii) Financial and Real Assets

Table 4.3 shows the net financial assets of the six sectors and some additional items as well. Also, that table contains an extra column which shows the economy-wide total value of each item.

Table 4.3 Financial and Real Assets

—ITEM—	SECTOR						
	H	F	B	CB	GOV	R	Economy
Net Financial Assets	+	−	0	0	−	±	0
Real Assets	+	+	0	0	+	(excluded)	Non-Human Wealth
Future Tax Liabilities	−	−			+		0
Undistributed Profits	+	−					
Human Wealth	+						Human Wealth
Wealth	+	0	0	0	0	±	Wealth

For the world as a whole, net financial assets are zero. Someone's financial asset is someone else's liability.

(a) **Real Assets:** Real assets — plant, equipment, buildings, etc. — are owned by households, firms and government. (The banks' holdings are very small in relation to the total and are ignored.) The rest of the world's holding of real assets is excluded from the table, since they do not constitute part of the economy of the country with which we are dealing.

The total of all the real assets held by households, firms, and government constitute the *non-human wealth* of the economy.

(b) **Future Tax Liabilities:** If the government has liabilities which exceed its real assets — which it typically does — then it is the households and firms which pay taxes which will be responsible for meeting those liabilities. The government will have to levy taxes on households and firms which equal in value the excess of its liabilities over its assets. This may be thought of as an implicit financial asset. It is implicit because no explicit paper claim exists to represent this item. It is an asset to the government and a liability to households and firms.

(c) **Undistributed Profits:** The government and firms are fundamentally different legal entities from households. The household (and the individuals which constitute it) are the *ultimate wealth holders*. Firms can be regarded as owing (being liable) to households the net undistributed profits from their activities. These profits (losses) are exactly equal to the difference between the firms' real assets and net financial liabilities and are shown as an asset to households and as a liability to firms. In the case of firms that have issued equity, undistributed profits are already taken into account (provided that the equity has been valued correctly). To see this, consider two firms that are identical in all respects except that one of the firms has purchased some plant equipment with undistributed profits, while another has purchased the equivalent amount of plant and equipment with the proceeds from a debenture sale. The stock market value of the equity of the firm with undistributed profits will clearly be higher than the firm that has financed some of its planned acquisitions with the proceeds of a debenture sale. For firms that do not issue equity, however, for example partnerships and other private firms, the undistributed profits need to be counted as a liability to the firm and an asset to the owner or owners of the firm, even though there is no explicit marketable security representing that asset and liability.

(d) Human Wealth: The value of the future income of the individuals in the economy constitutes the economy's *human wealth* (or human capital). This value is equal to the price that would have to be paid for a pension plan which paid each year the same amount as each individual earned.

(e) Wealth: The net value of all the real assets plus human wealth is the economy's *wealth*. This is also the same thing as the household sector's wealth. The reason why all the wealth is owned by the households is because of the implicit asset/liability items which take account of future tax liabilities and undistributed profits. Government has no wealth on its own account. It owes any excess of assets over liabilities to the households, and the households are liable for its net debts. Similarly, firms have no net wealth because they owe (are liable) to households any undistributed profits (and households have to stand any losses).

(iv) National Balance Sheets and National Income Accounts

Changes in the net financial asset position of the various sectors are related to flows in the National Income Accounts which we examined in Chapter 3. The change in the net financial assets of households and firms taken together represents the difference between savings and investment (shown in Table 4.4 as $S-I$). The reason for this is very natural. Savings constitute the difference between what is earned (the

Table 4.4 Change in Financial Assets and the National Income Flows

———ITEM———	H	F	B	CB	GOV	R
	\multicolumn{2}{c}{}				
Change in Net Financial Assets	$S-I$		0	0	$T-G$	$IM-EX$

economy's income) and what is spent on consumer goods and paid in taxes. Some of that saving is used to buy physical capital goods. That is, it is invested in real assets. That which is not invested (i.e., not used to buy real assets) is used to buy financial assets. Therefore, the change in the net financial assets of households and firms is the same thing as savings minus investment $(S-I)$.

Commercial banks and the Bank of England having zero net financial assets also, of course, have zero change in net financial assets.

The change in the government's financial assets is exactly equal to the difference between its current tax receipts and its current expenditures. Thus, we show in Table 4.4 $T-G$ as the change in net financial assets of the government.

The change in the net financial assets of the rest of the world is measured by the difference between the flow of expenditures by domestic citizens on foreign goods (imports, IM) and the flow of foreign expenditures on domestic goods (exports, EX). We show the change in net financial assets of the rest of the world as being the difference between imports and exports $(IM-EX)$.

It is evident that if we aggregate (add up) net financial assets across all the sectors, then we wind up with zero. That is, what is issued as a liability by one sector is held as an asset by another sector, or sectors. If we add up the net financial asset changes, that is, savings minus investment $(S-I)$ *plus* taxes minus government expenditure $(T-G)$ *plus* imports minus exports $(IM-EX)$, then we also always come out with zero, reflecting a fact which we discovered when examining the National Income Accounts; namely that *savings plus taxes plus imports are equal to investment plus government expenditure plus exports*.

(v) The Sectoral Balance Sheets

If you look at each column of Table 4.2 separately you will see the financial aspects of the balance sheets of each of the six sectors. Usually in macroeconomics we do not separately analyse the balance sheets of households and firms but rather aggregate them together. If we aggregate the two items *currency* and *sterling current accounts* across both households and firms (solid box), the total of those times equals the *narrow money supply, M1*. If we aggregate the three rows *currency, sterling current accounts* and *other sterling deposits with commercial banks* across households, firms and government (the dashed box), then we arrive at a total equal to the *broad money supply, £M3*. These magnitudes are of crucial importance in the subsequent analysis.

Consider next the third column of Table 4.2. This shows tha balance sheet of the commercial banks. It is clear that the commercial banks' liabilities are the deposits which they issue both in the form of current account deposits and other deposits. Their assets consist of deposits with the Bank of England, currency, government securities, bank loans to individuals and firms' and foreign securities. The commercial banks maintain a reserve of deposits with the Bank of England and currency with which to make payments to depositors wishing to withdraw their deposits and to be able to transfer deposits to accounts in other banks.

The Bank of England's balance sheet has a very simple structure. The liability of the Bank of England consists of all the notes outstanding plus the commercial banks' deposits with the Bank of England. This aggregate plus the coin is sometimes known as the *monetary base*. The assets of the Bank of England which back that monetary base are government securities and foreign exchange reserves. The Bank of England can change the volume of the *monetary base* either by buying and selling government securities or by trading in the foreign exchange market. If the Bank of England wants to *increase* the *monetary base* it will simply go into the stock market and buy government securities, paying for the securities with newly created money. It could equivalently enter the foreign exchange market buying foreign exchange, that is, buying, say, American dollars using newly created pounds. It could, of course, *reduce* the *monetary base* with the opposite operation.

The balance sheets of the government sector and the rest of the world do not in and of themselves have any intrinsic interest for our present purposes and have been presented here so that you can have a complete picture of the structure of indebtedness in the economy and the connection between changes in net financial assets and the flows in the National Income Accounts.

D. Measuring Aggregate Balance Sheets

Two agencies collect information about aggregate balance sheets in the United Kingdom — The Bank of England and the Central Statistical Office.[1]

The Bank of England collects and publishes balance sheets covering the following institutions: the Bank of England, the commercial banks, and other financial institutions and finance houses.

Balance sheet information on these institutions is published regularly in the *Bank of England Quarterly Bulletin*.

The Central Statistical Office collects data on, and regularly publishes, as part of the system of National Accounts, what are usually known as the flow of funds accounts or, to use the Central Statistical Office's own terminology, simply the Financial Accounts. On a quarterly basis, the United Kingdom Financial Accounts give information about financial flows between six sectors of the economy. The six sector classification of the economy presented in Section C above is not quite the same as the one used by the official statisticians in the United Kingdom. There is no separate Bank of England sector. It is aggregated in with the rest of the government sector to form a sector called 'public'. The firms' sector is divided into two sub-groups, 'industrial and commercial companies' and 'other financial institutions'. The remaining sectors correspond to those used in Section C above. The Financial Accounts report more than fifty different financial asset and liability categories describing the financial flows between the six sectors.

It is important to take careful note that the flow of funds or Financial Accounts, although giving information about aggregate balance sheet movements, are not themselves balance sheets. Rather, they give information about *changes* in assets and liabilities. This means that there are some valuation problems, which are potentially

1. A comprehensive account of the availability of national financial statistics is provided by the Central Statistical Office in *Financial Statistics Explanatory Handbook* (HMSO, October 1977). Also, in the introduction to that explanatory handbook there is a useful, if brief, account of the National Income Accounts as well as the Financial Accounts and the relationships between them.

difficult to solve, since the flow of funds accounts show only the values of the assets and liabilities acquired or disposed of during a particular period and do not give information about changes in values of previous and remaining outstanding stocks of assets and liabilities. The flow of funds accounts are published both in the *Bank of England Quarterly Bulletin* and in an important monthly publication, *Financial Statistics* (HMSO), on a regular basis but with a fairly considerable time lag, since the data involved are detailed and expensive to collect and process.

You will see from the above that our knowledge about aggregate balance sheets in the United Kingdom is fragmentary. From what is collected and published by the Bank of England we obtain reliable, frequent, and up-to-date information on the Bank of England itself, the commercial banks, and a small number of key financial institutions. We obtain no information, however, concerning the balance sheets of households and non-financial firms. The Financial Accounts help, to some extent, to fill that gap. The sectors of the economy whose flows of funds are recorded in the Financial Accounts are all embracing. The information processed in those accounts, however, is not really a balance sheet. It does not allow for changes in the values of outstanding stocks of assets; it merely records assets and liabilities acquired during a specific quarter and valued at the prices prevailing during that quarter.

Despite the fragmentary nature of the information on aggregate balance sheets, it turns out that we do have sufficient material to form the basis of a serious macroeconomic analysis of the determination of the key variables with which the subject is concerned. Specifically, we have good information about the money supply (variously defined) and the monetary base, the two central stocks that feature prominently in the theories of output, employment, and prices that we shall be looking at shortly.

SUMMARY

A. Asset, Liability, and Balance Sheet

An *asset* is what someone *owns*.
A *liability* is what someone *owes*.

There are two types of assets: *financial* and *real*. A financial asset is always someone else's liability. An individual's *wealth* equals *total financial and real assets* less *total liabilities*.

A *balance sheet* is a statement of *assets* and *liabilities*.

B. Definition and the Nature of Money

Money is anything which is generally acceptable as a medium of exchange. In the United Kingdom today, money is narrowly defined (*M1*) as the *sum of currency in circulation* plus *sterling current accounts held by households and firms with commercial banks*. Money is defined more broadly (*£M3*) as *M1* plus *government current accounts* plus *other sterling deposits held by households and firms with commercial banks*.

The *monetary base* is defined as the *total liabilities* of the *Bank of England* — notes and coins outstanding plus commercial banks' deposits with the Bank of England.

C. Main Balance Sheet Items

These items are summarised in Tables 4.2 and 4.3 above. The net value of financial assets in an economy is zero. The change in net financial assets of the economy equals:

	Savings minus *Investment* $(S - I)$
plus	*Taxes* minus *Government Expenditure* $(T - G)$
plus	*Imports* minus *Exports* $(IM - EX)$,

which is *always zero*.

The aggregate of *real assets* and *human wealth* is the *wealth* of the economy.

A major part of the macroeconomic analysis which we shall be doing centres on the behavioural connection between stocks and flows. In particular, it centres on the connection between the stock of money and the flows of expenditure. The theory of aggregate demand which we shall be developing shortly builds on the concepts which have been defined and on the accounting frameworks which are dealt with in this and in the previous chapter.

D. Measuring Aggregate Balance Sheets

There are two sources of information about aggregate balance sheets in the United Kingdom. The Bank of England collects and publishes information about its own balance sheet, those of the banks, and of other financial institutions. The Central Statistical Office collects information on and publishes the National Financial Accounts. These accounts give information about *changes* in stocks rather than stocks themselves and do not include information about valuation changes.

The key stock variables needed for macroeconomic analysis are those concerning the monetary base and various definitions of the aggregate stock of money, all of which are collected frequently and reported in the *Bank of England Quarterly Bulletin* as well as in the Central Statistical Office's monthly publication, *Financial Statistics*.

Review Questions

1. Which of the following are stocks and which are flows?
   (a)   a pocket calculator worth £20
   (b)   a bank deposit of £25
   (c)   the *purchase* of a pocket calculator for £20
   (d)   a car
   (e)   the labour used to make a car
   (f)   the consumption of petrol by a car
   (g)   the labour used to serve petrol
   (h)   an outstanding bank loan
   (i)   the interest paid on a bank loan.

2. Which items in a balance sheet are stocks and which are flows?

3. What is the difference between an asset and a liability?

4. Construct your own personal balance sheet. What are your total financial assets and liabilities? What are your real assets? What is your wealth?

5. Using the *Bank of England Quarterly Bulletin*, set out, for a recent date, the balance sheets of the Bank of England and of the commercial bank sector. What are the net financial assets, real assets, and wealth of the Bank of England and of the commercial banks?

6. Indicate how you would set about calculating the British national debt.

7. How would you set about calculating the British future tax liabilities? Whose liabilities are these, and why?

8. Which of the following are 'money' in the United Kingdom today?

   (i)   Visa card
   (ii) Building society deposits
   (iii) Bank of France Fr F10 notes
   (iv) Bank of England £1 notes
   (v)   Federal Reserve System (US) $1 bills
   (vi) Current accounts at commercial banks
   (vii) Deposit accounts at commercial banks
   (viii) Cheques
   (ix) Bank loans
   (x)   Bank overdrafts

9.   Using data which you will find in the *Bank of England Quarterly Bulletin*, draw a time-series graph from 1967 to the present of (i) *M1* growth rate and (ii) *£M3* growth rate. Describe these two series. Highlight when each grew the fastest and the slowest. Compare and contrast the magnitudes and the direction of change of each.

10.   What are the links between aggregate balance sheets and aggregate income accounts? In describing the links, be explicit about flows and stocks.

11.   Trace the effects of the following on the balance sheets of the six sectors of Table 4.2.
        You take a bank loan of £1000 with which you buy a new computer costing £1500 from Radio Shack in Houston, Texas. You use your deposit account to make up the difference between the bank loan and the purchase price. The Radio Shack computer is made in the US with American-made component parts.

12.   Show the effects of the above transaction on the aggregate income accounts. What are the effects on savings, investment, exports, and imports? Show the effects also on the net changes in financial assets and show that these are consistent with the aggregate income accounts.

5

Measuring Inflation and Unemployment

Inflation and unemployment are the two central variables which macroeconomic theory is designed to explain and which macroeconomic policy seeks to control. Your next tasks are to:

A. **know the definition of inflation;**
B. **understand the concept of a price index and its percentage rate of change;**
C. **know how inflation is measured in the United Kingdom;**
D. **know the definition of unemployment;**
    and
E. **know how unemployment is measured in the United Kingdom.**

A. Definition of Inflation

Inflation may be defined, if somewhat loosely, as *the percentage rate at which the general level of prices is changing.* We refer to the 'general level of prices' as the *price level.* You will notice that the dimension of inflation is the percentage rate of change per unit of time. The concept of the general level of prices is a little bit vague and we will give more precision to that term below.

Even at this level of imprecision, two aspects of the phenomenon of inflation are worth emphasising. First, it is important to notice that inflation is an ongoing process — that is, a process of prices rising on a more or less continuous basis rather than on a once-and-for-all basis.

Figure 5.1 illustrates this distinction. The *price level* is measured on the vertical axis and time measured in years on the horizontal axis. Suppose an economy started out in year 0 with a price level equal to 100. If, over the four-year period shown, the price level rose gradually and continuously (as indicated by the continuous, upward

73

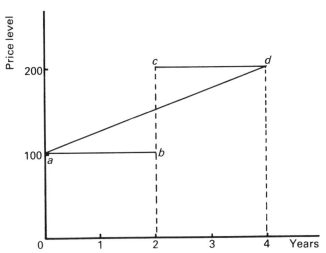

Figure 5.1 *The Distinction Between* **Inflation** *and a*
Once-and-for-all Rise *in the* **Price Level**
The economy that moves directly along the line *ad* is one which experiences inflation. The
economy that moves along the line *abcd* experiences a once-and-for-all rise in the price level in
year 2.

sloping straight line) to the level 200, then we would want to describe that four-year
period as a period of *inflation*. In contrast, suppose the economy started out at price
level 100 and had a stable level of prices, that is, with prices remaining at level 100 all
the way through the first two years. Then suppose that at the beginning of year 2
there was a sudden jump in the price level, from 100 to 200. Suppose thereafter that
prices remained at the level 200 and were stable at that level for the remaining two
years. We would not normally want to describe this second economy as having had an
inflationary four years. Indeed, prices would have been stable in that economy for
the first two years at a level of 100 and stable for the second two years at a level of 200.
It is true that the price level starts out at 100 and finishes up at 200 in both cases.
However, in the first case inflation was present in the economy throughout the four-
year period. In the second case we could think of there having been a single instant of
inflation when the price level doubled (from 100 to 200) at the beginning of year 2,
while for the rest of the four-year period the economy was characterised by stable
prices. That is, there was a *once-and-for-all* rise in the price level at the beginning of
year 2. In practice, the distinction between a once-and-for-all rise in the price level
and inflation may be somewhat blurred, for it is possible that a shock to the economy
which produces a once-and-for-all rise in prices may have effects which are somewhat
drawn out. Thus, although in principle the distinction between inflation and a once-
and-for-all rise in prices is an important one, it may in practice often be hard to
distinguish one from the other.

The second feature of the phenomenon of inflation worth emphasising at this stage
is that it is a rise in the *general* level of prices and not the rise in some particular price
or group of prices. The economy may, for example, be experiencing rapid increases
in the prices of food and yet not be undergoing inflation. The rapid increases in food
prices may be offset by rapid decreases in prices of some other commodities such as,

for example, electronic data processing equipment, TV games, fuel efficient cars, and the like. Such price movements, even though they may be very rapid and of great social consequence, are not inflation. They are changes in relative prices.

In order to give more precision to the meaning of inflation, it is now necessary to give more precision to the meaning of the term 'the general level of prices' or *price level*.

B. Price Index and Percentage Rate of Change

There can be no unique measure of the *price level*. The prices of some commodities rise faster than others, and the prices of some things even fall. Movements in the *price level* can only be calculated once we have fixed the basket of goods to which the price level refers.

A *price index* measures the amount that would have to be paid for a specific basket of goods in the *current period* compared with what would have had to be paid for that same basket in some previous period, known as the *base period*. The basket of goods used may be representative of typical consumption patterns in the base period or in the current period.

The value of the index in the *base period* is defined to be 100.

Percentage changes in the value of a price index from one year to the next measure the *rate of inflation* according to the particular index being used.

In order to gain a more concrete understanding of the ideas just set out in summary form, it will be best if we move straight to the next task and illustrate the above propositions.

C. Measuring Inflation in the United Kingdom

There are two widely used price indexes in the United Kingdom. One is known as the *General Index of Retail Prices* and the other known as the *Gross Domestic Product (GDP) Deflator*.

(i) The General Index of Retail Prices

The *General Index of Retail Prices* (which is calculated and published by the Central Statistical Office each month) is an index which attempts to measure *movements in the average level of prices of a large and representative selection of goods and services which are purchased by all types of household in the United Kingdom*.

The General Index of Retail Prices (RPI) is a weighted average of price movements of 150,000 items. The weights attached to each item are revised each

January on the basis of the most recent Family Expenditure Survey.

Each month, price statistics are collected by the local offices of the Department of Employment in more than 230 local office areas selected so as to secure an adequate representation of different localities throughout the country. The prices used are the prices actually charged in retail shops. As far as possible they relate to goods of unchanged quality at successive dates; when the quality changes, an appropriate adjustment is made. An index is calculated using the following formula:

$$RPI_t = \frac{P_1^t Q_1^0 + P_2^t Q_2^0 + \ldots + P_{150,000}^t Q_{150,000}^0}{P_1^0 Q_1^0 + P_2^0 Q_2^0 + \ldots + P_{150,000}^0 Q_{150,000}^0} \times 100$$

Although this formula looks formidable, it is in fact very simple. Let us take it piece by piece. The numerator

$$P_1^t Q_1^0 + P_2^t Q_2^0 + \ldots + P_{150,000}^t Q_{150,000}^0$$

represents the total amount of money that it would cost in month t at the prices ruling in month t to buy the bundle of commodities which is being used to weight the prices. The term P_1^t is simply the price of commodity one in month t and the number Q_1^0 is the number of units of commodity one in the basket of goods that is being valued. If we simply add up the total outlay on each commodity of the 150,000 commodities in the index, then we arrive at the number of pounds that would have to be spent to buy the basket of commodities at the prices prevailing in month t. (The dots in the middle of the expression stand for commodities 3 to 149,999.)

The denominator of the index number calculation

$$P_1^0 Q_1^0 + P_2^0 Q_2^0 + \ldots + P_{150,000}^0 Q_{150,000}^0$$

is simply the amount of money that would have had to be spent in the base period to purchase the index basket of commodities valued at the prices ruling in the base period. The term P_1^0 is the price of commodity one in the base period, period 0. So $P_1^0 Q_1^0$ is the expenditure on commodity 1 in the base period. Adding the expenditures on all 150,000 commodities gives the pound sum of money that would have had to be spent purchasing this bundle of 150,000 commodities in the base period. (The base period currently used is 1975.)

The ratio of the outlay in month t to the base period outlay, multiplied by 100, gives the index number for the General Index of Retail Prices in month t. If that index number is 100, then prices have been constant. If the index is greater than 100, prices have risen and if less than 100, prices have fallen.

Various subsidiary index numbers are available for 11 main groups and 36 sub-groups, including food; all non-food items; housing; clothing and footwear; transport and vehicles; fuel and light; durable household goods; services; tobacco; and alcoholic drink.

A detailed description of the calculation of the General Index of Retail Prices is given in *Method of Construction and Calculation of the Index of Retail Prices* (HMSO, 1967).

(ii) The GDP Deflator

The General Index of Retail Prices seeks to measure movements in the prices of a basket of goods which would be purchased by all households in the United Kingdom.

In contrast, the GDP *Deflator* seeks to measure *movements in the general level of prices of the entire basket of goods and services produced in the United Kingdom economy.*

If you think of gross domestic product, measured by the expenditure approach, as being equal to the sum of the values of all the goods and services produced, then you have the starting point for the GDP Deflator. In order to calculate the value of all the goods and services produced we have to take the quantity of each good, Q_i, and multiply it by its factor cost, P_i. We then have to add up these values over all the goods and services in the economy. This gives gross domestic product. That is,

Gross Domestic Product at Current Factor Cost $= P_1^t Q_1^t + P_2^t Q_2^t + \ldots + P_n^t Q_n^t$

The P's and Q's in this formula stand for the factor costs and quantities of the entire production of final goods and services in the economy and not simply of that typical consumer basket which was referred to in the preceding section on the General Index of Retail Prices. It will include consumer goods and services *not* bought by all types of household, as well as capital goods, goods bought by the government and goods exported to foreigners.

Another measure of gross domestic product which is of importance and interest is what is known as *gross domestic product at constant factor cost.*

Instead of measuring the value of gross domestic product by multiplying each good produced in year t by the factor cost of that good in year t, we could multiply production in year t by factor costs prevailing in some base year, call it year 0. Thus we could calculate

Gross Domestic Product at Constant Factor Cost $= P_1^0 Q_1^t + P_2^0 Q_2^t + \ldots + P_n^0 Q_n^t$

This is a measure of the value of expenditure in year t but valued at the factor costs prevailing in some base year. (Current base year is 1975.)

If we divide the *constant factor cost* GDP figure into the *current factor cost* GDP figure we obtain the GDP *Deflator*.

$$GDP\,Deflator = \frac{GDP\,at\,current\,factor\,cost}{GDP\,at\,constant\,factor\,cost}$$

The GDP Deflator is sometimes called the GDP *implicit deflator*. The deflator is *implicit* because we arrive at it from the evaluation of GDP on the basis of two alternative sets of factor costs.

The GDP Deflator differs from the General Index of Retail Prices in two important respects. First, it covers the *entire basket* of final goods and services produced in the economy rather than *only the consumption basket* of all types of household. Secondly, the weights used to construct this GDP Deflator are *current weights*. That is, current output is the basis for weighting the average of factor costs, whereas the General Index of Retail Prices uses *base period weights*.

(iii) The Percentage Rate of Change in the Price Index as a Measure of Inflation

We can now define British inflation precisely. *British inflation is the percentage rate of change over a specified unit of time (usually a year) in either the General Index of Retail Prices or the GDP Deflator.*

For example, in February 1980, the General Index of Retail Prices was 248.8. In February of the previous year, 1979, the index was 208.9. To calculate the rate of inflation as measured by the General Index of Retail Prices in the year from February 1979 to February 1980, perform the following calculation:

$$Inflation = \left(\frac{248.8 - 208.9}{208.9}\right) \times 100$$

$$= \quad 19.1 \% \text{ p.a.}$$

We could perform a similar calculation using the Gross Domestic Product Deflator.

The General Index of Retail Prices is available monthly and gives a continuous monitoring of the economy's inflation rate. It is also available reasonably soon after the end of the month. By contrast, the GDP Deflator is only available on a quarterly basis and is not available until well after the end of the quarter. Movements in the two indexes do not coincide, but are not excessively divergent. Table 5.1 lists the rate of inflation in the United Kingdom each year for the past ten years as measured by the General Index of Retail Prices (first column) and the GDP Deflator (second column).

Table 5.1 A Comparison of Inflation Rates as Measured by the General Index of Retail Prices and the GDP Deflator

Year	General Index of Retail Prices (% Change per annum)	GDP Deflator (% Change per annum)
1970	6.1	7.4
1971	9.0	10.2
1972	7.0	9.9
1973	8.7	7.7
1974	14.8	15.7
1975	21.7	23.9
1976	15.3	13.1
1977	14.7	11.5
1978	8.0	10.6
1979	12.6	11.7
1980	16.5	17.4

Sources: Appendix to Chapter 2.

We will be analysing the determination of the rate of inflation as measured by the GDP Deflator in our theoretical analysis later in this book. However, since movements in the two index numbers are broadly in line with each other you can think of the analysis as also relating to the General Index of Retail Prices for most purposes, although there may be some specific exercises for which such a presumption would not be warranted.

D. Definition of Unemployment

A person is said to be unemployed when that person is capable of and is available for work but does not have work. The number of people unemployed in an economy is the number of people whom that description fits. The unemployment rate in an economy is the number of unemployed expressed as a percentage of the total labour force. The total labour force is defined as the number of people employed, plus the number of people unemployed.

You will notice that the definition of unemployment says nothing at all about the *reasons* for unemployment. It simply defines an aggregate or a percentage rate based on an explicit and objective criterion for classifying individuals. Some economic analyses of the causes of unemployment and fluctuations in its rate use terms such as 'voluntary' and 'involuntary' to describe different types of unemployment. We shall not have any reason to use such definitions. It may be very interesting for some purposes to know whether a person is voluntarily or involuntarily unemployed. From our point of view, however, such considerations are not relevant. We are going to be concerned with an objective analysis of the factors that lead to variations in unemployment and with developing theories that will enable us to predict the consequences for unemployment of certain well-defined policies. It will not be necessary for us to enquire into the state of mind of the unemployed person concerning the voluntary or involuntary nature of the unemployment being experienced.

E. Measuring Unemployment in the United Kingdom

Unemployment figures are calculated by the Department of Employment and are published in the *Department of Employment Gazette*. Figures are provided for unemployment by region; by sex, and age; by industry; and by duration.

As already indicated, the unemployment rate represents the number of unemployed persons as a percentage of the labour force. All the unemployment figures published in the United Kingdom are based on information generated by the Department of Employment through the operation of the unemployment benefits available under the National Insurance Acts. The measured unemployment series records the number of persons registered at employment exchanges and youth employment service offices who were unemployed and capable of and available for work on a particular day on which the monthly count took place. A distinction is made in the published figures between those with no work (wholly unemployed) and those who are working shorter than normal hours, or who have been temporarily laid-off work with a clear understanding that they will shortly be returning to their previous employment (known as temporarily stopped).

No information is available concerning the wages at which a person who is capable of and available for work would be willing to work. Thus, although the measured unemployment rate shows the number of persons who have registered at an employment exchange who are capable of and available for work, there is no indication as to whether or not they are willing to work at wages that are currently available. What we really would like to know is the total number of people who are capable of, available for, and willing to work on terms and conditions currently available. There can be no presumption that the way in which unemployment is measured in the United Kingdom captures that concept.

The fact that the unemployment rate is measured on the basis of the number of persons that have registered at employment exchanges provides a further source of bias in the measurement. Many people, especially older people and married women who have opted for a more limited national insurance coverage plan, will typically enter and leave the labour force without passing through the ranks of the measured unemployed, even though, from an economic point of view, their position may be identical to an equivalent, say, prime age male who appears on the unemployment register.

It may well be that, although the absolute measurement of unemployment is distorted by both a failure to take account of the wages at which unemployed persons would be willing to work and by the failure to measure non-registered unemployed, the general cyclical movements in the unemployment rate may nevertheless provide a good indication of the direction of change in unemployment if not its precisely measured magnitude.

SUMMARY

A. Definition of Inflation

Inflation is defined as the percentage rate of change in a price index.

B. Price Index and Percentage Rate of Change

A price index is calculated by valuing a specific basket of goods at the prices prevailing in a base period and at the prices prevailing in a subsequent period. The price index is the ratio of the values of the two baskets multiplied by one hundred. The rate of inflation is measured as the percentage rate of change of the index.

C. Measuring Inflation in the United Kingdom

There are two commonly used price indexes in the United Kingdom: the General Index of Retail Prices and the GDP Deflator. The General Index of Retail Prices is based on a basket of goods and services containing 150,000 items and the weights attached to each are revised each year on the basis of the most recent Family Expenditure Survey. The GDP Deflator is calculated on the basis of the current basket of all the goods and services produced in the economy.

D. Definition of Unemployment

Unemployment is defined as the number of people capable of and willing to work and available for work, but not having work.

E. Measuring Unemployment in the United Kingdom

Unemployment is measured in the United Kingdom by counting the number of people who have registered at job centres, who are capable of work, but who do not have work. This overestimates unemployment to the extent that some people are registered as being unemployed but are not willing to work on terms and conditions currently available, and underestimates unemployment to the extent that others are available and willing to work on current terms and conditions but are not registered at a job centre.

Review Questions

1. What is inflation?

2. What are the two commonly used measures of inflation in the United Kingdom?

3. How is the General Index of Retail Prices in the United Kingdom calculated? What is the General Index of Retail Prices designed to measure?

4. Using the *Monthly Digest*, find the General Index of Retail Prices (RPI) for the period from 1966 to the present. Be sure you are consistent and collect either mid-year (June) or end-of-year (December) figures. What is the base year of the RPI that you have collected? Calculate the percentage rate of change of the RPI each year since 1966 and explain exactly what it measures.

5. What does the GDP Deflator measure and how is it calculated? Why is it called an 'implicit' deflator?

6. From the latest *National Income and Expenditure*, collect the GDP Deflator for the period from 1966 to the present. Calculate the percentage rate of change of the GDP Deflator. Explain exactly what this series measures.

7. Table 5.1 gives a comparison of inflation rates as measured by the RPI and GDP Deflator. Plot these two time-series graphs. Describe these series. Highlight the highest and lowest measures of inflation. Compare and contrast inflation as measured by these two series.

8. What is unemployment?

9. How exactly does the Department of Employment define unemployment?

10. How is unemployment in the United Kingdom measured?

11. The unemployment rate in the United Kingdom varies from region to region. Use the *Department of Employment Gazette* to collect time-series data beginning in 1967 on the unemployment rate of each region. Plot these time series as graphs. Describe, compare, and contrast them. Which regions of the United Kingdom have a higher unemployment rate than the United Kingdom average? Which have a lower unemployment rate than the United Kingdom average?

12. What are the main problems with the way in which unemployment is measured in the United Kingdom?

6

Economic Trans-
actions with the
Rest of the World

The United Kingdom economy has extensive economic links with the rest of the world. In 1980, of every pound spent in the United Kingdom on final goods and services, thirty-three pence represented the expenditures of non-residents on United Kingdom exports. Similarly, of every pound spent, thirty pence represented expenditure on imports. In the first two years of the 1970s the United Kingdom had an overall surplus on its balance of payments which amounted to almost £4,000 million. In the five years between 1972 and 1976 a deficit of almost £9,000 million was recorded. In the four years between 1977 and 1980 the United Kingdom had an overall surplus of almost £10,000 million. Over that same decade, the foreign exchange value of the pound fluctuated markedly from a high value of $2.50 US in 1972 to a low of $1.74 US by 1977. The pound climbed again to more than $2.30 US by 1980.

This chapter is going to explain the concepts of the balance of payments and the foreign exchange rate, how these magnitudes are measured and how you can obtain more detailed information on them. The chapter will take you through four tasks which are to know:

A. the definitions of the balance of payments: (i) current account; (ii) capital account; (iii) official settlements account;

B. how the United Kingdom's balance of payments accounts are measured;

C. the definitions of: (i) foreign exchange rate; (ii) fixed exchange rate; (iii) flexible exchange rate; (iv) managed (or dirty) floating exchange rate; (v) effective exchange rate; (vi) real exchange rate;
and

D. how the exchange rate is measured.

A. Balance of Payments

(i) Current Account

The current account of the balance of payments is the account in which the values of the flows of goods and services and other *current* receipts and payments between residents of the United Kingdom and residents of the rest of the world are recorded. Specifically, the current account contains the items shown in Table 6.1. (The values of the items for 1980 are given so that you may have a feel for the orders of magnitude involved.) The items recorded in the current account refer to three types of transaction. The first concerns the import and export of goods and services. The *export of goods and services* is the sum of the value of all the goods and services purchased by non-residents from residents of the United Kingdom in a given period. Examples would include the export of North Sea oil, of Scotch whisky, of Rolls Royce cars, and manufactures and raw materials in general. It would also include the export of services such as banking, insurance, and general financial services as well as shipping services. It also includes, in principle, the spending by non-residents on holidays in the United Kingdom.

Table 6.1 The Current Account 1980

		Item	£ million
	1.	Exports of Goods and Services:	62,718
less:	2.	Imports of Goods and Services:	57,816
	3.	Dividends and Interest Paid Abroad (net):	32
	4.	Unilateral Transfers Paid Abroad (net):	2,107
equals:		Current Account Balance:	2,763

Source: National Institute Economic Review, August 1981, pp. 30 & 92.

Imports of goods and services consist of purchases by United Kingdom residents of goods and services made in the rest of the world. This would include, for example, oranges from Israel, cars and television sets from Japan, cotton goods from Hong Kong and Taiwan, and in general manufactures and raw materials of all types produced outside the United Kingdom. It would also include the purchase of insurance, shipping and other general services by United Kingdom residents from residents of the rest of the world. In principle, it also includes the expenditures of United Kingdom residents when visiting other countries.

The difference between the value of exports of goods and services and imports of goods and services is usually referred to as the *trade balance*. Often, the trade balance itself is subdivided into two balances, one called the *visible trade balance* which refers to the difference between the values of the exports of goods and the imports of goods, and the *invisible balance* which refers to the difference between the value of the export and import of services. No operational significance attaches to the visible/invisible distinction.

The second class of items that appears in the current account of the balance of payments is the *dividends and interest payments* made between residents and non-residents. This is shown in Table 6.1 as a net item and, in 1980 represented net payments by residents to non-residents. The dividends and interest received from abroad are payments on investments made by residents of the United Kingdom in the rest of the world. Examples would include the dividends paid by IBM to United Kingdom stockholders and interest paid by the United States Government on United States Treasury bills held by banks and other financial institutions in London. Dividends and interest paid abroad are the payments made in respect of United Kingdom securities that have been bought by non-residents. Examples would include payments to American oil companies in connection with their investments in the North Sea oil program, or payments by the United Kingdom government of interest on Treasury bills and other government securities held by non-residents.

The final class of items is under the heading of *unilateral transfers* and this, like the previous item, is shown simply as a net figure. Unilateral transfers are payments received from or made to non-residents by residents, in effect, as gifts. The biggest single item in this category is the aid given by the United Kingdom government and private organisations to less developed countries.

The difference between the total receipts and total outlays recorded in the current account is called the *current account balance*. The current account is said to be in surplus when the receipts exceed the outlays and in deficit in the reverse situation.

It may be useful to think of an individual analogy to the country's current account balance. The exports of goods and services of a country can be thought of as being analogous to an individual's labour income. That is, from the viewpoint of the country as a whole, exports of goods and services are similar to the receipt of wages and salaries and other fees for labour services as viewed by an individual. Dividends and interest received are analogous to income from investments made by an individual, and unilateral transfers are analogous to gifts received by the individual. On the outgoing side, imports of goods and services are analogous to an individual's expenditures on consumption goods. Dividends and interest paid abroad are analogous to an individual's payment of interest on loans made to him by, for example, banks and building societies; unilateral transfers are the equivalent of gifts made by an individual to others.

Thus, for an individual, the current account balance represents the net addition to (surplus) or subtraction from (deficit) that individual's wealth. If an individual has a current account surplus he has become wealthier, in the sense that more assets have been acquired or some liabilities have been paid off. Likewise, if a country has a current account surplus, its residents in aggregate have become wealthier in the sense that their assets have increased (or their liabilities have decreased). Conversely, if a country has a current account deficit, it has become poorer in the sense that it now has fewer assets or more liabilities.

(ii) Capital Account

The capital account records the receipts from non-residents and payments made to non-residents arising from the *issuing of new debt or the repayment of old debt*. For example, the purchase by American residents of shares in British Petroleum appears as an *import of capital*. Such a transaction would therefore be recorded as a receipt in the United Kingdom's capital account. Conversely, if a United Kingdom resident bought some shares in a Japanese company, using resources that were previously invested in the United Kingdom, that transaction would be recorded in the capital account as a *capital export*.

The difference between capital imports and capital exports represents the country's *capital account balance*. In 1980, the capital account of the United Kingdom showed a deficit of £829 million. That is, in 1980, United Kingdom residents invested more in the rest of the world than non-residents invested in the United Kingdom by that amount.

Another individual analogy may be helpful. The capital account of an individual is a statement of the receipts of that individual arising from the negotiation of new loans, minus the outlays of that individual in paying off old loans. Thus, for example, if an individual negotiated a bank loan of £3,000 and a mortgage of £15,000 and repaid an outstanding credit card account for £500, that individual would have a capital account surplus of £17,500.

(iii) Official Settlements Account

The official settlements account records the net receipts and payments of *gold, international reserves,* and *foreign currency* which result from the current account and capital account transactions just described. The balance on the official settlements account is sometimes called more simply the *official settlements balance* or, by the official statisticians in the United Kingdom, the *official financing balance*. It is the change in the foreign exchange reserves of the country minus the change in official borrowing. It is, if everything is accurately measured, exactly equal to the sum of the current account balance and the capital account balance. By accounting convention, the official settlements balance is defined as the negative of the sum of the current account and capital account balance. This ensures that if the balances of all three accounts are added together, they always add to zero.

Another individual analogy might be helpful here. Suppose an individual had a current account deficit of, say, £20,000 in some particular year in which perhaps a house and some furniture and other durable goods had been bought. That is, in the particular year the individual received, from the sale of labour and in interest and dividends and gifts, £20,000 less than was spent on goods and services. Suppose, further, that the individual negotiated loans such that there was a net capital account surplus of £15,000. If the individual spent £20,000 in excess of income and received £15,000 from new loans, where did the difference of £5,000 come from? It must be the case that the individual used £5,000 of the cash balances which were previously being held. If this were not so, the individual's expenditure could not have exceeded total receipts by £5,000 which, according to the example, they did. Thus, the individual analogy of the official settlements balance is simply the change in the individual's cash balances — bank account and currency holdings.

Now that the concepts lying behind the balance of payments accounts have been described, let us turn to an examination of the United Kingdom's balance of payments accounts and see how these concepts are put into practice.

B. Measuring the United Kingdom's Balance of Payments Accounts

The United Kingdom's balance of payments are published in an annual Central Statistical Office publication called *The United Kingdom Balance of Payments* and often referred to simply as 'the Pink Book'. The accounts are also published on a quarterly basis in *Economic Trends* and *Financial Statistics*. The accounts for the years 1970–1980 are set out in Table 6.2. The first two columns show the current account and capital account balances and the fourth column snows the official settlements balance. Although the theoretical concepts of the current account, capital account, and official settlements account add up to zero, there are problems in *measuring* international transactions. In the period since 1976 those measurement problems have become quite serious. The third column of Table 6.2, headed errors and omissions, shows the extent to which the measured capital account and current account and official settlements account fail to reconcile with each other. In the published United Kingdom balance of payments accounts this item is referred to as the *balancing item*.

Table 6.2 United Kingdom Balance of Payments 1970 to 1980 (£ million)

Year	Current Account	Capital Account	Errors and Omissions	Official Settlements
1970	+ 779	+ 678	− 37	− 1420
1971	+ 1076	+ 1916	+ 279	− 3271
1972	+ 189	− 560	− 770	+ 1141
1973	− 1056	+ 107	+ 178	+ 771
1974	− 3380	+ 1520	+ 214	+ 1646
1975	− 1674	+ 132	+ 77	+ 1465
1976	− 1060	− 3093	+ 525	+ 3628
1977	− 206	+ 4434	+ 3134	− 7362
1978	+ 776	− 3817	+ 1915	+ 1126
1979	− 1425	+ 1683	+ 1647	− 1905
1980	+ 2763	− 649	− 742	− 1372

Source: Financial Statistics, July 1981, Table 11.1.

The transactions which appear in the current account are recorded mainly for the purpose of administering the customs and excise service. This activity provides the primary raw material for estimating the total volume and value of exports and imports. It is not unlikely that this is the main source of the increase in the errors and omissions in recent years. Such errors and omissions arise mainly from valuation problems. Foreign transactions may be invoiced either in sterling or in some other currency. When they are invoiced in some other currency, the precise date on which the payment is made will determine the exchange rate relevant to the transaction. When exchange rates are moving around considerably, such as they have done in recent years, imprecise knowledge of the precise timing of the transactions makes the valuation of exports and imports in sterling an approximate rather than an exact activity.

The capital account transactions in the balance of payments are recorded from a variety of sources, but mainly as a result of data collected from the banking and financial system by the Bank of England. There is by no means a complete and exact measurement of these items.

The official settlements balance is measured exactly, since it shows up in the transactions undertaken by the Bank of England. The errors and omissions in the balance of payments accounts are, therefore, entirely due to errors and omissions in the recording of the current and capital account transactions. There is no ready way in which the errors and omissions can be allocated between current and capital account activities.

Although the errors and omissions in the balance of payments accounts look very large, especially in 1977, 1978, and 1979, their magnitude in relation to the items being measured is clearly quite modest. For example, the total volume of exports and imports in 1977 was more than £65,000 million so that, even in that year in which the errors and omissions item was exceptionally large, it amounted to less than 5 per cent of the total value of trade.

After this brief review of the United Kingdom's balance of payments accounts, let us turn our attention to the exchange rate.

C. Exchange Rate Definitions

(i) Foreign Exchange Rate

A foreign exchange rate is the relative price of two national monies. It expresses the number of units of one currency which must be paid in order to acquire a unit of some other currency. There are two ways in which a relative price may be defined. It may be expressed as so many units of A per unit of B, or as so many units of B per unit of A. For example, the average exchange rate between the pound sterling (£) and the United States dollar ($) in November 1981 was $1.96 US per £1. This may be expressed equivalently as 51 pence per US dollar. It is always necessary to be precise as to which way around the exchange rate is being defined. When the *value* of a currency rises (called appreciation) the exchange rate, when expressed in units of domestic currency per unit of foreign currency, falls, but, expressed the other way around, as units of foreign currency per unit of domestic currency, the exchange rate rises. It is common in the United Kingdom to express the exchange rate as units of foreign currency per pound. It is very common (indeed, probably more common) in theoretical analysis to define the exchange rate the other way round as the number of units of domestic currency per unit of foreign currency.

(ii) Fixed Exchange Rate

A fixed exchange rate regime is one in which the central bank declares a central or *par value* at which it will maintain its currency. It also, usually, involves the central bank in declaring what is known as an *intervention band*. That is, in declaring a fixed exchange rate, the central bank announces that if the exchange rate rises above the par value by more than a certain percentage amount, then it will intervene in the foreign exchange market to prevent the rate from moving any further away from the par value. Likewise, if the rate falls below the par value by a certain percentage amount, the central bank declares that it will intervene to prevent the rate from falling any further.

In order to maintain a fixed exchange rate, the central bank *stands ready* to use its stock of foreign exchange reserves to raise or lower the quantity of money outstanding, so as to maintain its price relative to the price of some other money.

From 1945 to 1972 the Western world operated on a fixed exchange rate system sometimes called the *Bretton Woods System*. The name derives from the fact that the plan for the world monetary system, which survived for almost thirty years, was negotiated at Bretton Woods, New Hampshire, by John Maynard Keynes and William H. White. That system pegged the world's monetary system to gold. This was achieved by the United States declaring that one fine ounce of gold was worth $35 US. Each country then defined its own currency value in terms of the US dollar. The United Kingdom initially declared the value of the pound to be $4.03 US. In 1949 that value was lowered to $2.80 US. That exchange rate was maintained until November 1967 when it was lowered to $2.40 US. Minor adjustments occurred subsequently and the fixed exchange rate for sterling was abandoned on 23 June 1972 when the Bank of England announced that sterling was to be allowed to float 'as a temporary measure'.

(iii) Flexible Exchange Rate

A *flexible exchange rate* — sometimes called a *floating exchange rate* — is one which is determined by market forces. The central bank declares no target value for the exchange rate and has no direct interest in its value. The central bank holds a constant stock of foreign exchange reserves — or even a zero stock — and does not intervene in the foreign exchange market to manipulate the price of its currency. (This does not mean that the actions of the central bank do not indirectly affect the value of the exchange rate. This will become clear in Chapter 14 when we examine how the exchange rate is determined.)

(iv) Managed (or Dirty) Floating Exchange Rate

A *managed (or dirty) floating exchange rate* is one which is manipulated by the central bank, but is not necessarily being maintained at a constant rate. Usually, a dirty floating regime is one in which the central bank announces that it is floating, but does not give any indication to the market concerning the course which it would like to see the exchange rate follow. It does, however, have a view about the appropriate behaviour of the exchange rate, and it intervenes in order to achieve its desires. This method of operating the foreign exchange market is the one which gives most difficulty to speculators. They not only have to speculate on what other private individuals, on the average, will be doing, but they also have to make predictions about central bank intervention behaviour.

(v) Effective Exchange Rate

In a world in which most currencies are floating against each other so that exchange rates are varying all the time, a country does not have one exchange rate; it has as many exchange rates as there are other currencies floating against its own currency. Thus, for example, there is an exchange rate between the pound and the US dollar, the pound and the Canadian dollar, the pound and the D-mark, the pound and the yen, and so on. In order to express the value of the pound against the value of all other currencies in a single number, it is necessary to calculate an index number (analogous to the index number that measures the price level) that in some way weighs the values of the different currencies against which the value of the pound is fluctuating. Such a calculation is done to yield what is called the *effective exchange rate*. The effective exchange rate is a weighted average of the value of the pound in terms of the other major currencies of the countries with which the United Kingdom trades. The weight supplied to the values of these other currencies is based on the share of the United Kingdom's total trade with the countries in question. Thus, for example, if there were just two other currencies — call them the dollar and the yen — and just two trading partners, America and Japan, and if one-half of the trade was conducted with each of these two countries, and if further, the value of the pound rose against the value of the dollar by 10 per cent but fell by the same 10 per cent against the value of the yen, then the effective exchange rate of the pound would be constant.

(vi) Real Exchange Rate

The foreign exchange rate as it has been described in the preceding sections is a *relative* price. It is the relative price of two monies. There is another concept of the exchange rate which is useful in macroeconomic analysis and that is the *real exchange rate*. The real exchange rate is also a *relative* price. It is not, however, the relative price of two monies; rather it is the relative price of two baskets of goods, a domestic basket and a rest of the world basket. A concept of a basket of goods is simply a list of goods combined together with specified weights. The real exchange rate represents the number of baskets of domestic goods that will exchange for one basket of foreign goods. To calculate the real exchange rate it is necessary to take a specific basket of goods, value them in the prices prevailing in the rest of the world, convert those prices into domestic currency, and then compare the result with the price of that same basket of goods in the domestic economy. Clearly, there are many different examples of a real exchange rate. Attention may focus on the real exchange rate between only the goods that feature in international trade or the entire gross domestic product.

D. Measuring Exchange Rates

Foreign exchange rates are continuously varying even from minute to minute and the foreign exchange market is open, taking account of time zone differences, for practically twenty-four hours a day. Thus, in principle, an enormous amount of continuous information is generated on this particular set of prices — the relative prices of the different national monies. In effect, the recorded and reported exchange rate figures that are available to us constitute a sampling of this continuous process at a particular point in time. The Bank of England records and reports the foreign exchange value of the pound by recording the rate 'during the late afternoon' each day. The Bank of England reports in the *Bank of England Quarterly Bulletin* figures expressed as values on particular days, as well as annual averages of the exchange rate. It gives the value of the pound sterling on this basis in terms of US dollars, Belgian francs, Swiss francs, French francs, Italian lira, Netherlands guilders, Deutschemark, and Japanese yen.

The International Monetary Fund in its monthly publication, *International Financial Statistics*, provides more detail and covers the exchange rates between all currencies.

Effective exchange rates are calculated and published by the Bank of England and the International Monetary Fund. The method used by each of these institutions to calculate the effective exchange rate is essentially the same, although they differ in some details. As the Bank of England comments:

> An effective exchange rate index is a measure of the overall value of a currency against a number of other currencies relative to a certain base date. The measure depends upon which other currencies are included in the calculation and the relative importance (weight) attached to each of them. Various effective exchange rate indices can therefore be calculated for any one currency.
>
> *(Bank of England Quarterly Bulletin,* March 1981, p. 69)

The Bank of England calculates and reports effective exchange rates for the eight currencies listed above. The International Monetary Fund does the calculation for all the currencies. The weights used to calculate the effective exchange rate are derived from a statistical model called MERM (standing for Multilateral Exchange Rate Model) developed by the International Monetary Fund. The weights used in the calculation are in principle supposed to be 'such that any combination of changes in other currencies against sterling which would have the same effect on the United Kingdom trade balance as a one per cent change in sterling against each of the other currencies is reflected as a one per cent change in the index' of the effective sterling exchange rate. 'For example, the US dollar has a weight of approximately one quarter in the present calculation of the sterling effective rate: thus a one per cent depreciation of the US dollar is considered to have the same impact on the UK trade balance as a uniform appreciation of sterling of some one quarter of one per cent against all currencies in the basket' (*Bank of England Quarterly Bulletin,* March 1981, p. 69). What the Bank of England is saying in the above quotation is that it uses weights to calculate the effective exchange rate. These weights are supposed to tell us the effect of the measured change in the effective exchange rate on the country's trade balance, regardless of whether the change occurred because sterling changed its value uniformly against all other currencies or in a non-uniform way.

The effective exchange rate for sterling as calculated by the Bank of England is shown in Figure 6.1. Alongside it is also shown the value of sterling against the US dollar. Clearly these two representations of the value of the pound do not exactly coincide, but they do follow the same broad general pattern.

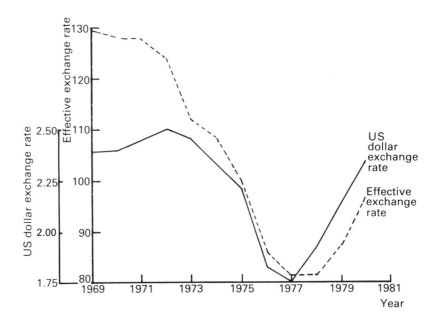

Figure 6.1 *Exchange Rates 1969–1980*

The effective exchange rate of the pound fell steadily from 1972 to 1977. It then rose, quite strongly, up to 1980. The movements in the US dollar value of the pound have been similar to the movements in the effective exchange rate.

Source: US dollar exchange rate, Appendix to Chapter 2.

Effective exchange rate, *Bank of England Quarterly Bulletin*, Vol. 17, No. 1, March 1977, pp. 46–7 and Vol. 21, No. 1, March 1981, Table 18.

SUMMARY

A. Balance of Payments

(i) The *current account* records the values of current goods and services sold by residents to non-residents and purchased by residents from non-residents, debt interest receipts and payments, and unilateral transfers received from and paid to non-residents.

(ii) The *capital account* records the receipts and payments between residents and non-residents arising from the issue of new debt or the retirement of old debt.

(iii) The *official settlements account* records the movements in foreign exchange reserves and official borrowing resulting from the net of the balances on the current and capital accounts.

B. Measuring the United Kingdom's Balance of Payments Accounts

The current account of the balance of payments is measured mainly from documentation required for customs and excise purposes. When exchange rates are fluctuating markedly, the conversion of foreign currency invoice values into sterling is only approximate and gives rise to measurement errors. The capital account transactions are recorded incompletely and also contain errors. The official settlements balance is measured exactly by the Bank of England. The difference between the measured balance on the current and capital accounts and the official settlements balance has grown in recent years.

C. Exchange Rate Definitions

(i) *Foreign exchange rate* is the relative price between two national monies.

(ii) *Fixed exchange rate* is one which takes on a value declared and maintained by the active intervention of the central bank.

(iii) *Flexible exchange rate* is one which is determined purely by market forces with no direct central bank intervention.

(iv) *Managed* (or *dirty*) *floating exchange rate* is one which is manipulated by the central bank, but not manipulated according to any pre-announced rules.

(v) *Effective exchange rate* is a weighted average of the exchange rate of one currency against a basket of other currencies.

(vi) *Real exchange rate* is the relative price of two baskets of goods, one domestic and one foreign.

D. Measuring Exchange Rates

Exchange rates are continuously varying and are measured at a specific time of the day. They are recorded and reported in the *Bank of England Quarterly Bulletin* and in *International Financial Statistics*.

Review Questions

1. Sort out the following list into four categories according to which items belong in (a) the current account, (b) the capital account, (c) the official settlements account, or (d) none of the balance of payments accounts:
   (i)   Your summer holiday expenses in Europe.
   (ii)   The British Government's receipts for the sale of bonds to Americans.
   (iii) Barclays Bank's purchase of US dollar travellers' cheques from the American Express Company.
   (iv)   The transfer by the Bank of England to the Bank of Canada of 1000 ounces of gold.
   (v)   British imports of Japanese cars.
   (vi)   United Kingdom exports of Scotch whisky.
   (vii) The takeover of a US company by a British company.
   (viii) The payment of interest on its bonds by the British Government.
   (ix)   The money taken to Canada by newly-arrived immigrants from the United Kingdom.
   (x)   Britain's aid to poor countries.

2. Using the following items and numbers, construct the balance of payments accounts of the hypothetical economy:

	£m
Capital Imports	2000
Debt Interest Received From Abroad	800
Exports of Goods and Services	1000
Capital Exports	1800
Gifts Made to Foreigners	100
Imports of Goods and Services	1100
Gifts Received from Foreigners	300
Debt Interest Paid Abroad	700
Rise in Gold and Foreign Exchange Reserves	400

   (a) What are the 'errors and omissions'?
   (b) What is the current account balance?
   (c) What is the capital account balance?
   (d) What is the balance of the official settlements account?

3. What is a foreign exchange rate?

4. What is a fixed exchange rate? How is it kept fixed?

5. What is a flexible exchange rate?

6. What is a managed floating exchange rate? How is it 'managed'?

7. What is an effective exchange rate? How is it measured?

8. What is a real exchange rate? How is it measured?

7

The Business Cycle

The final chapter of this section is different from the other four. It does not deal with the problem of measuring a single macroeconomic variable (or group of variables). Rather, it is concerned with the problem of observing and discerning patterns in the relationships between variables and in the evolution of the economic aggregates. In short, it is concerned with the *business cycle*.[1]

Until the mid-1930s, the term business cycle was used to describe the phenomenon which students of short-term movements in economic aggregates sought to explain and understand. Scholars saw their task as one of understanding the general recurrent ups and downs in economic activity *viewed as an ongoing process*. In 1936, however, with the publication by John Maynard Keynes of *The General Theory of Employment, Interest and Money,* there was a fundamental redirection of research effort. What Keynes did was to change the question which students of aggregate economic phenomena tried to answer. Instead of trying to understand the recurrent ups and downs of economic activity viewed as an ongoing process, Keynes redirected our research efforts to an apparently easier question, namely, that of the determination of output, employment, prices, interest rates, etc. *at a point in time taking the past history of the economy and expectations about the future as given.* At about the same time as Keynes's simplification enabled scholars to direct their attention to the simpler question of the determination of the aggregate economic variables at a point in time, strides were being made in the mathematical formulation and statistical testing of economic theories, notably by the Dutch economist Jan Tinbergen. As a result of the pioneering efforts of Keynes and Tinbergen, subsequent scholars were able to develop a considerably refined body of knowledge which came to be known as macroeconomics. In this new macroeconomic analysis there seemed to be no special place for business cycle theory. Indeed, as far as Keynes himself was concerned, the job of explaining what determines the values of economic variables at a moment in time is almost the same thing as explaining the business cycle (or trade cycle, as it is known in Europe). Keynes said that 'since we claim to have shown ... what determines the volume of employment at any time, it

---

1. This chapter draws heavily on, and in places will be recognised as a paraphrase of, parts of the important paper, Understanding business cycles (1977) by Robert E. Lucas Jr., in Karl Brunner and Allan H. Meltzer (eds), *Stabilization of the Domestic and International Economy,* Carnegie-Rochester Conference Series on Public Policy, Vol. 5, North-Holland Publishing Co.

follows, if we are right, that our theory must be capable of explaining the phenomena of the Trade Cycle'.[2] Further, not only did it appear that there was no need for a special theory of the business cycle, it even seemed as if the earlier attempts to find a theory of the business cycle were hopelessly muddled and confused in comparison with the clarity that had been brought to the task of understanding the determination of the aggregate economic variables at a point in time.

It was not until the early 1970s, with the seminal work of Robert E. Lucas Jr. of the University of Chicago, that attention was redirected to the problem of understanding more than what determines income, employment, prices, etc. at a point in time, given their past history. Lucas suggested that the bigger question of what determines the evolution of the aggregate economic variables over time, and viewed as a process, had to be tackled head-on if we were to develop a deep enough understanding of aggregate economic phenomena for us to be able to design policy that would stand some chance of improving matters. As Lucas saw things, and as will be elaborated more fully later in this book, the task of understanding what determines income, employment, and prices at a moment in time, given their past history, cannot be accomplished without analysing the entire ongoing cyclical process that determines these aggregate economic variables. The key reason for this is that what people do today depends on their expectations of what is going to happen in the future. To formulate an expectation of what is going to happen in the future, people have to do the best they can to assess how the economy will evolve in the future. This means that their current action will depend upon their expectations of future actions by themselves and others. Now it is evident that the only guide that is available concerning what will happen in the future is what has happened in the past. This means that if present actions depend on expectations of the future, they must also depend upon what has happened in the past. Only by analysing an entire economic process — past, present, and future — shall we be able to understand what is happening at any given moment.

The redirection of research effort in macroeconomics by Keynes was not, in our view, a blind alley. Rather, it was a necessary stage in the process of developing a satisfactory theory of the business cycle. Not until we had made a great deal of progress with the simpler question posed by Keynes were we able to go back to the harder question to which Lucas has now redirected us.

To progress through the subject matter of modern macroeconomics all the way to the new theories of business cycles will take most of the rest of this book. Not until we get to Chapter 33 will it be possible to summarise our current understanding of what determines business cycles.

In order to pave the way for that, this final chapter of Part II on 'Measuring Macroeconomic Activity' will take you through five tasks which are designed to enable you to understand what we mean by business cycles. Those tasks are to:

A. **know the definition of the business cycle;**
B. **understand the concept of autocorrelation;**
C. **understand the concept of co-movement;**
D. **know the properties of the business cycle;**
   and
E. **know the features of the United Kingdom's business cycle.**

---

2. John Maynard Keynes (1936) *The General Theory of Employment, Interest and Money*, Macmillan, p. 313.

A. The Definition of the Business Cycle

Although business cycles have been studied for well over a hundred years, it was not until the 1940s, thanks to the efforts of a group of outstanding and careful observers of cycles, working under the auspices of the National Bureau of Economic Research in New York, that a clear definition of business cycles emerged. Wesley Clare Mitchell and Arthur F. Burns (Burns subsequently became Chairman of the Board of Governors of the Federal Reserve System) defined the business cycle as follows:[3]

> Business cycles are a type of fluctuation found in the aggregate economic activity of nations that organize their work mainly in business enterprises: A cycle consists of expansions occurring at about the same time in many economic activities, followed by similarly general recessions, contractions, and revivals which merge into the expansion phase of the next cycle; this sequence of changes is recurrent but not periodic; in duration business cycles vary from more than one year to ten or twelve years; they are not divisible into shorter cycles of similar character with amplitudes approximating their own.

Let us dissect this definition a little bit. Three aspects of the definition are worth highlighting. First, let us ask, What is a business cycle a cycle *in*? The answer to that is given in the first part of the definition: the business cycle is a cycle (or fluctuation) in aggregate economic activity. Although there are several alternative ways in which 'aggregate economic activity' may be measured, the most natural comprehensive measure is the level of real income (output or expenditure) — real GDP. Such a measure summarises all the many individual producing and spending activities in the economy.

Because real GDP, on average, grows from one year to the next, in defining the cycle it is necessary to abstract from that growth trend and define the cycle as *deviations of real GDP from trend*. Table 7.1 may help to make this concept clear. Imagine an economy in which GDP grows, on average, at 4 per cent each year. If in

Table 7.1 Calculating Deviations of Real GDP from Trend

Year	Trend Value	Actual Value	Deviation from Trend
0	100.0	102.5	+ 2.5
1	104.0	105.0	+ 1.0
2	108.2	108.2	0
3	112.5	111.5	− 1.0
4	117.0	114.5	− 2.5
5	121.7	120.7	− 1.0
6	126.5	126.5	0
7	131.6	132.6	+ 1.0
8	136.9	139.4	+ 2.5
9	142.3	143.3	+ 1.0
10	148.0	148.0	0

Real GDP

3. This definition is from Arthur F. Burns and Wesley Clare Mitchell (1946) *Measuring Business Cycles*, National Bureau of Economic Research, New York, p. 3.

the first year (year 0) we call GDP 100, then the *trend values of GDP* will be those shown in the first column of numbers (notice that these numbers rise by 4 per cent each year). Suppose (purely by way of example) that the *actual values of GDP* are those shown in the second column of the table. Then the difference between the actual and trend values, the *deviation from trend*, is as shown in the final column of the table. It is the *deviation from trend* that we use to define the business cycle.

By regarding the deviations of real GDP from trend as defining the cycle, it is possible to examine the ups and downs of other aggregate variables in relation to or with *reference* to the *cycle* in real GDP. (In their pioneering work on measuring the business cycle the National Bureau of Economic Research economists referred to above developed a concept of the *reference cycle* which was somewhat more general than simply using deviations of real GDP from trend. Their methods, however, to some degree involve judgment and to describe them and fully appreciate them would divert us too far.)

The second thing to notice about the definition of the cycle is that it involves two *turning points,* an *upper* turning point and a *lower* turning point; and two *phases,* an *expansion* phase and a *contraction* phase. Figure 7.1 illustrates the hypothetical cycle of Table 7.1. The upper turning point is often referred to as the cyclical *peak* and the lower turning point as the cyclical *trough.* The movement from the peak to the trough is the contraction, and the movement from trough back to peak is the expansion. If a contraction is particularly severe it is referred to as a *recession.* Technically, a recession occurs when *real GDP falls for two successive quarters.* An even more severe contraction and prolonged trough would be known as a *depression* or if particularly severe, the prefix *great* would be attached to it.

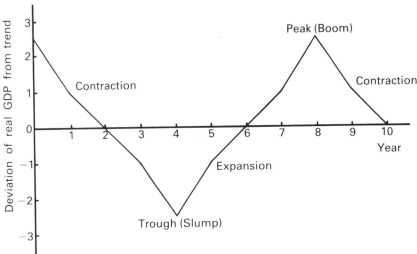

Figure 7.1 *A Hypothetical Cycle*

A cycle in the deviation of real GDP from trend begins in the contraction phase, reaches a trough (or slump), moves through an expansion to a peak (or boom) and then turns into a further contraction phase.

The picture of the cycle shown in Figure 7.1 gives just one complete up-and-down movement in the deviation of real GDP from trend.

The third feature of the definition of the business cycle emphasises the fact that cycles are not regular *periodic* ups and downs, but are *irregular* though *recurrent* ups and downs the duration of which (measured from trough to trough) could run from something slightly more than one year to as long as ten or twelve years. To see how we might characterise this in a simple way involves introducing a technical idea which will be developed in the next section of this chapter.

The fourth and final feature of the definition of the cycle given above, that 'they are not divisible into shorter cycles of similar character with amplitudes approximating their own,' is simply designed to capture the idea that the cycle is a basic unit of observation and analysis. It is not divisible into smaller similar patterns.

Let us now turn to the first of the two technical tasks that face us in this chapter.

B. Autocorrelation

This section and the next one deal with technical matters. It is nevertheless worthwhile mastering them, for they will give you a more precise, and at the same time very simple, way of viewing a process that may be used to describe the recurrent but non-periodic ups and downs in economic activity that characterise the business cycle.

It will be best if we approach the concept of *autocorrelation* gradually. Let us first understand what is meant by a *difference equation*. A *difference equation* is nothing other than a statement that tells us how some variable evolves over time. We shall only deal with the simplest kind of difference equation and even then only with an example. Let us suppose that we want to describe the evolution of real GDP over time. Let us call real GDP y. So that we are clear about the date that applies to the variable, let us denote the value of real GDP in some particular year, the tth year, as y_t. Let us suppose that real GDP in year t is always related in some way to its own value in the previous year. Never mind why this might be so for the present. Specifically, let us suppose that the following equation describes the evolution of real GDP from one year to the next.

$$y_t = 25 + \tfrac{3}{4} y_{t-1} \tag{7.1}$$

Let us first of all satisfy ourselves that we can read this equation. What it says in words is that real GDP in year $t (y_t)$ will be equal to 25, plus three-quarters of the level of real GDP in the previous year (year $t-1$), that is, (y_{t-1}). To get a feel for this, imagine that real GDP in year $t-1$ was equal to 100. You can calculate three-quarters of 100 (equals 75), add 25 to that, and the result is the value of real GDP in year t. The answer that you have obtained, of course, is that real GDP in year t will be 100. Now imagine going forward to year $t+1$. At year $t+1$ the previous year becomes year t. Since real GDP in year t is 100, in year $t+1$, by the same calculation, it will also be 100. You can quickly convince yourself that real GDP will be 100 in each and every year if the above equation is true and if real GDP in year $t-1$ was equal to 100.

Now suppose that real GDP in the previous year (y_{t-1}) was not 100 but 110. What does this imply about the value of real GDP in year t? You can calculate that answer by finding three-quarters of 110 and adding 25 to that to give you the value of GDP in year t. You should get an answer of 107.5. In the next year, year $t+1$, GDP will be 25 plus three-quarters of 107.5. This will give a level of GDP of 105.6. By repeating the calculation you will obtain for the next successive years values of 104.2, 103.2, 102.4, 101.8, 101.3, 101.0, 100.8 . . . . and, in the indefinite future, GDP will converge to the level of 100. The value of 100 is known as the *steady-state* value of GDP. It is that value which the above equation always tends towards.

You are probably now saying to yourself, 'Well that's all very simple but so what?' Clearly, GDP doesn't behave like either of these paths that have just been calculated. If GDP starts out at 100 it always stays at 100, according to the first exercise that we did, and if it starts out at something other than 100, it monotonically converges towards 100, according to the second exercise. How does this help us understand the movements of GDP such as those which occur in an actual economy like that of the United Kingdom? The answer is that, on its own, it is of no help at all. With one tiny addition, however, the first-order difference equation above (first order means that GDP today depends only on GDP yesterday) is capable of producing patterns in the evolution of GDP which are similar in character to the patterns that we observe in the data.

That simple addition is to make the difference equation above a *stochastic* difference equation. A *stochastic difference equation* is very similar to a difference equation. That is, it has all the properties of the equation that you have just looked at and become familiar with. In addition, however, it adds on to the above equation a *random* shock. In other words, instead of GDP in one year being uniquely determined, given knowledge of GDP in the previous year, there is an additional random element that will allow GDP in the current year to deviate from the prediction of the above equation by a random amount. We could write a stochastic difference equation comparable to the above equation as follows:

$$y_t = 25 + \tfrac{3}{4} y_{t-1} + e_t \tag{7.2}$$

The term e_t at the end of the equation represents a random shock. On the average it will take on the value of 0. From time to time, however, it will take on different values than 0, sometimes positive and sometimes negative.

To keep things simple and very concrete, let us generate an example of a random shock (or a series of random shocks) and then see how GDP evolves when the difference equation that describes its path is stochastically disturbed.

We have created a set of random shocks by conducting a simple experiment which you can conduct for yourself. The experiment involves rolling a die and assigning an economic shock depending on the score of the die roll. Table 7.2 sets out the way that we have converted die scores into economic shocks. You will see that if the die came up 3 or 4, we scored an economic shock of 0, so that there is a 1 in 3 chance that there is no random disturbance to the economy. If the die came up 2, we scored a negative shock of 5 (think of that as a shock that is depressing the economy), and if the die scored 1, then we gave a bigger weight to the depressing effect on the economy (-10). If the die came up 5 or 6 we scored a positive shock to the economy (a boom), assigning a shock of 5 for a die score of 5 and 10 for a die score of 6. Thus you can see that there is a 1 in 6 chance that the economy will be hit with any of $+10$, $+5$, -5, -10, and a 1 in 3 chance of no shock. The shocks, then, that will hit the economy are symmetrical and have an average value of 0 and a range of 20, ranging from $+10$ to -10. We rolled the die 30 times, and Table 7.3 records the scores of our 30 die rolls,

Table 7.2 Converting Die Scores into Economic Shocks

Die Score	Economic Shock
1	− 10
2	− 5
3	0
4	0
5	+ 5
6	+ 10

Table 7.3 Thirty Random Shocks in an Imaginary Economy

Die Roll	Die Score	Economic Shock
1	5	+ 5
2	1	− 10
3	6	+ 10
4	6	+ 10
5	4	0
6	4	0
7	6	+ 10
8	4	0
9	2	− 5
10	3	0
11	3	0
12	4	0
13	4	0
14	6	+ 10
15	5	+ 5
16	5	+ 5
17	1	− 10
18	1	− 10
19	3	0
20	2	− 5
21	3	0
22	6	+ 10
23	5	+ 5
24	6	+ 10
25	2	− 5
26	5	+ 5
27	2	− 5
28	4	0
29	1	− 10
30	5	+ 5

Table 7.4 Calculation of Evolution of GDP in an Imaginary Economy
(periods 0 to 10 only)

$y_t = 25 + \frac{3}{4} y_{t-1} + \text{shock}$			
Period	y_t	y_{t-1}	*Shock*
0	100	100	0
1	105	100	+ 5
2	94	105	− 10
3	105	94	+ 10
4	114	105	+ 10
5	111	114	0
6	108	111	0
7	116	108	+ 10
8	112	116	0
9	104	112	− 5
10	103	104	0

together with the value of the economic shock implied by the scoring scheme set out in Table 7.2. You will notice that our 30 rolls turned out to have an average value that was greater than 0 (in fact our average was +1), indicating that we rolled rather more 5's and 6's than we did 1's and 2's. Nevertheless, if we had rolled, say, 1000 times, then it is certain that our average would have been very close to 0. With the series of economic shocks shown in Table 7.3, it is now possible to see how the economy would evolve if the stochastic difference equation above describes the evolution of GDP. The calculation for the first ten values of GDP are set out in Table 7.4. The first column shows the level of GDP in year t and the second column in year $t-1$. The third column records the values of the shocks. The values of the shocks listed there are the first ten shocks from Table 7.2. Imagine that in period 0 the economy started out in its steady state with GDP equal to 100 and with GDP in the previous year equal to 100 and with no random shock. The shocks then begin. In period 1 we need to take three-quarters of the previous GDP (75) plus 25 (= 100) and then add the shock of 5 to get the value shown for GDP of 105. In period 2, period 1's GDP of 105 becomes the previous period's GDP level. To calculate period 2 GDP, we take three-quarters of 105 and add 25 to that; we then subtract the current-period shock of 10 to give a value to GDP of 94. This process is repeated throughout the table. Check that you can reproduce the figures listed in column 1 of Table 7.3 by applying the formula described above. (The figures given in the table are rounded. To calculate the correct values you should carry the unrounded figures in your calculator.)

Figure 7.2 illustrates the values of real income over the full 30-period experiment that is described in Tables 7.2 and 7.3. The graph of the ups and downs of GDP in this imaginary economy looks remarkably as if it could have been generated from

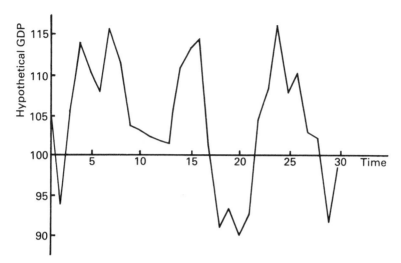

Figure 7.2 *A Hypothetical Cycle Generated by a First-Order Autocorrelation*
The simple randomly disturbed difference equation $y_t = 25 + (\frac{3}{4})y_{t-1} + e_t$ generates non-periodic but recurrent fluctuations that could easily be taken to be real world deviations of real GDP from trend.

plotting actual figures, such as those shown in Chapter 2. Notice that there is certainly a recurrent up-and-down movement, but there is no exact periodicity. The timing from the trough of observation 2 to the next trough (observation 13) is 11 periods. The next trough occurs at period 20 — a seven-period cycle. The next trough occurs at observation period 29 — a nine-period cycle. Thus, the cycle lengths in this example, as measured from trough to trough, vary from a short cycle of seven periods to a long cycle of eleven periods. Notice too that the severity of the down periods varies. The downturn that begins in period 8 continues throughout period 13 but never gets very deep. The next downturn that begins in period 17 only runs for four periods, but it goes all the way to 10 per cent below the steady state value.

The particular path of real income generated by a stochastic difference equation depends in an important way on the strength of the inertia in the process — that is, on the magnitude of the effect of previous income on current income. In our example, that effect is $\frac{3}{4}$. If, instead of current income depending on previous income with a weight of $\frac{3}{4}$, we were to lower that weight almost to zero, then real income would no longer display much systematic movement but would be purely random (completely unpredictable) like the random shocks, e_t, that are bombarding the economy. At the other extreme, if we were to raise the weight on previous income from $\frac{3}{4}$ to almost 1, then the cyclical swings in real income would be much longer. (That is, the time from the peak of one cycle to the peak of the next one would be longer.)

The key thing to take careful note of is that a very simple process, a stochastically disturbed, first-order difference equation, is capable of generating a path for a variable that is very similar in its characteristics to the recurrent but non-periodic ups and downs of real GDP and other variables over the course of the business cycle. Of course, the specific path of actual GDP movements about trend will only be capable of description by specific shocks and a specific difference equation.

You have now discovered what autocorrelation is. *Autocorrelation* simply means that *the value of some particular variable at some particular date is related to its own value at some earlier date.* In the above example, income at date t is related to income at date $t-1$. The relationship is not perfect. There is a randomness that loosens the link between income at date t and at date $t-1$. In rough terms, an autocorrelated series is one which shows systematic recurrent up-and-down movements.

It is important to realise that describing the path of GDP by a low-order stochastic difference equation is not the same thing as understanding what causes GDP movements — that is, what causes the business cycle. The description is simply a neat and convenient way of thinking about the process. It also directs our attention to potential explanations in the sense that it alerts us to the idea that we shall have to find, in any theory of the business cycle, two things;

(1)   a source of or, more generally, sources of random disturbance to the economy; and

(2)   systematic sources of inertia causing movements of GDP (and other aggregates) from one period to another to be gradual — to display autocorrelation.

Although you are now able to describe the recurrent ups and downs in real income in very simple terms, you need to be aware of some other technical language that will help you to talk about broader aspects of the business cycle. That is the next task.

C. Co-Movement

In fully characterising business cycles it is going to be necessary to talk about the way in which different variables move in relation to each other. That is, we shall want to be able to say how employment and unemployment, prices and wages, money and interest rates all move in relationship to the movements in real income. We shall want to be able to characterise the *co-movements* of various pairwise combinations of variables.

There are three types of co-movements which are found in economic series. First, there are *procyclical co-movements*. A procyclical co-movement is a movement in a variable that has broadly the same cyclical pattern as the variable with which it is being compared, and tends to rise when the reference variable rises and to fall when the reference variable falls. Since the reference variable for the business cycle is deviations of GDP from trend, procyclical variables are those which rise as GDP rises above trend and fall as GDP falls below trend.

Usually, variables do not exactly move in a procyclical manner. They tend to either *lead* or *lag* the reference variable. Figure 7.3 illustrates leading and lagging procyclical variables. Suppose that the curve labelled (*a*) represents the cycle in real GDP. Then the line (*b*) would represent a variable that leads the cycle, and (*c*) would represent a variable that lags the cycle. Both variables are generally procyclical. That is, they generally move up with income and down with income, but they don't move at exactly the same time.

The second type of co-movement is a *countercyclical co-movement* which Figure 7.4 illustrates. If (*a*) is the path of real GDP again, then (*d*) would be the path of a variable which moves countercyclically.

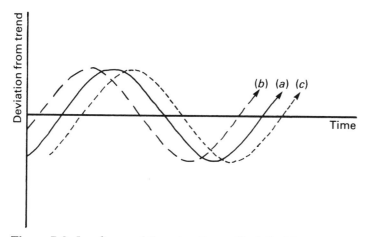

Figure 7.3 *Leading and Lagging Procyclical Co-Movements*
The three series plotted here have procyclical co-movements. If (*a*) describes the reference cycle of real income deviations from trend, then the variable (*b*) leads the cycle in income, and the variable (*c*) lags that cycle.

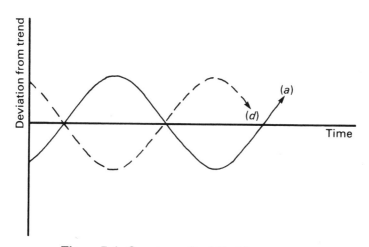

Figure 7.4 *Countercyclical Co-Movements*
The variable marked (*d*) displays perfect countercyclical co-movement with the variable marked (*a*).

You will recognise that there is a potential element of ambiguity as to whether a variable is countercyclical or procyclical, if it leads or lags the reference variable by too much. You could, as a matter of description, regard a variable that is exactly countercyclical as one that is procyclical but lagged by half a cycle. That would seem to be using language in an awkward way, however. We don't think of leads and lags as being as big as half a cycle.

The third feature of co-movement has to do with the degree of closeness of the relationship between one variable and another. In Figures 7.3 and 7.4 the variables illustrated move in a manner that has what is technically known as *perfect coherence*. To make more sense of the notion of coherence, consider Figure 7.5. Again the line

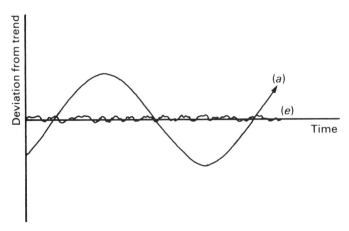

Figure 7.5 *Coherence*

All the series shown in Figures 7.3 and 7.4 have perfect coherence. The variable graphed as (*e*) in this figure is an example of low coherence. There is no association between the movement in the variable (*e*) and the reference variable (*a*).

---

marked (*a*) is the path of real GDP. The line marked (*e*) is a purely random line with no systematic cycle in it whatsoever. It would be said that there is no coherence between (*a*) and (*e*). In other words, (*e*) does not possess any cyclical characteristics that match the cycle in (*a*). In the real world, of course, we would rarely see anything as extreme as the perfect coherence of Figures 7.3 and 7.4 or the total lack of coherence that we see in Figure 7.5. Rather, there would be some intermediate degree of coherence. In loose terms, we talk about a high degree of coherence as indicating a high degree of *conformity* between the cycles in two variables. They need not turn at the same time, they may be pro- or countercyclical, they may lead or lag.

This completes the language of describing business cycles, and it is now possible to go on to this chapter's more substantive tasks of which the next one is to characterise the business cycle more fully.

D. Properties of the Business Cycle

The properties of the business cycle may now be set out more precisely, using the technical language that has been introduced to you in the previous two sections.

The first feature of business cycles has to do with the movements in the deviations of real GDP from trend. 'Technically, movements about trend in gross national product in any country can be well described by a stochastically disturbed difference equation of very low order' (of 'first order' in the above example). 'These movements do not exhibit uniformity of either period or amplitude, which is to say, they do not resemble the deterministic wave motions which sometimes arise in the natural sciences.'[4]

---

4. Robert E. Lucas Jr., Understanding business cycles, op. cit., p. 9.

The second feature of business cycles has to do with the co-movements between the various aggregates.

> [The chief] regularities which are observed are in the co-movements between different aggregate time series.
>   The principal among these are the following:
>   (i)   Output movements across broadly defined sectors of the economy move together ...
>   (ii)   Production of durable goods exhibits much greater amplitude than production of non-durables.
>   (iii) Production and prices of agricultural goods and natural resources have lower than average conformity.
>   (iv)   Business profits show high conformity and much greater amplitude than other series.
>   (v)   Prices generally are procyclical.
>   (vi)   Short-term interest rates are procyclical; long-term rates slightly so.
>   (vii) Monetary aggregates and velocity measures are procyclical.[5]

For the purpose of what will follow in this book, where the primary emphasis is on economic aggregates, we shall be concerned with five features of the cycle selected from those set out above. First, we shall be concerned with understanding why it is that movements in real GDP can be described by a 'stochastically disturbed difference equation' of first (or other low) order. Secondly, we shall be concerned with understanding why fluctuations in the output of durable goods exhibit greater amplitude than those of non-durables; thirdly, why prices are generally procyclical; fourthly, why interest rates are procyclical; and fifthly, why the monetary aggregates and velocity measures of money are procyclical.

These are the central features of the business cycle which macroeconomics seeks to understand. In addition, implicit in the characterisation, but needing to be made explicit, we shall be concerned with explaining why unemployment is countercyclical and unemployment procyclical. If unemployment is countercyclical and prices (inflation) procyclical, there will, in general, be a negative relationship between inflation and unemployment. We shall also seek to understand that stylised feature of the business cycle.

Before moving to begin these tasks, let us look at some of the stylised facts about the United Kingdom's business cycle.

E. The United Kingdom's Business Cycle

(i) The Movements of Real GDP About Trend

You have already discovered in Chapter 2 that real GDP (real income) in the United Kingdom has grown at an average rate of 2.6 per cent over the period between 1946 and 1980. The deviations of real GDP about that trend were set out in Figure 2.5 (Chapter 2). As we noted in Chapter 2, there was a tendency for the deviations of real GDP from trend to fluctuate in a series of very short cycles and also for there to be a tendency for the deviations to be negative during the 1950s and first half of the 1960s,

---

5. Robert E. Lucas Jr., Understanding business cycles, op. cit., p. 9 with slight adjustments.

positive during the second half of the 1960s and early 1970s, and then negative again in the latter part of the 1970s. Can those movements be described by a simple first-order difference equation disturbed by a random error such as that explained earlier in this chapter? In fact they can. They are well described by the following equation:[6]

$$(y_t - y_t^*) = -0.1 + 0.63 \, (y_{t-1} - y_{t-1}^*) + e_t \qquad\qquad (7.3)$$

The way to read this is as follows: y_t represents real GDP in year t; y_t^* represents the trend value of real GDP in year t; thus $(y_t - y_t^*)$ simply represents the deviation of real GDP from trend in year t. The same variable with the subscript $t-1$ represents deviations from trend in the previous year. As before, e_t represents a random disturbance. Notice that equation (7.3) is very similar, even in the magnitude of the coefficient, to the one that we used as an example in Section B above. It says that real GDP will deviate from its trend value by 0.63 of its previous deviation plus a random disturbance (minus a small adjustment 0.1 which, except for getting the arithmetic straight, may be ignored for present purposes).

In interpreting equation (7.3), recall that you discovered, in Section B above, that this way of looking at the movements of GDP simply involves breaking the actual movement into two components, (i) a source of (or, more generally, sources of) random disturbance to the economy, and (ii) systematic sources of inertia. In the above equation, the inertia is represented by the term $-0.1 + 0.63 \, (y_{t-1} - y_{t-1}^*)$ and the sources of random disturbance in any one year are represented by the term e_t. To give you a better feel for what has been going on, Figure 7.6 plots the deviations of real GDP from trend and its two components, the systematic source of inertia and the random component. In Figure 7.6, Frame (a) shows the deviations of real GDP from trend. (Notice that these are exactly the same as the deviations plotted in Figure 2.5 above.) This cycle in real GDP is decomposed into its inertia element (Frame (b)) and its purely random element (Frame (c)). From the method of constructing this graph, the random disturbances in Frame (c) add up to zero. They have, however, on occasion been very large positive numbers (for example, 1973 was +5.14) and, somewhat more frequently, have been large negative numbers (for example, −5.17 in 1947 and −5.34 in 1980). Most of the time these shocks have been small, generally less than 2 per cent. These shocks impact upon the economy to produce the cycle in real GDP described by equation (7.3) and plotted in Frame (a). Let us consider a particular year in greater detail. The year 1973 serves well to illustrate what is going on. In 1972 real GDP was very close to its trend value. (Actually it exceeded trend by about 0.7 per cent). In the absence of any random shock, real GDP would have deviated from trend in 1973 by approximately 0.3 per cent (the previous year's deviation multiplied by 0.63 and reduced by the constant in the equation (−0.1)). In 1973, however, according to Frame (c), there was a massive positive random shock of 5.14 per cent of GDP which hit the economy. Thus, in Frame (a) the actual deviation

---

6. Equation (7.3) and Figure 7.6 were constructed in the following way. First, deviations of real GDP from trend were calculated by fitting a trend line to real GDP between 1946 and 1980. The deviations were then analysed to determine the degree of autocorrelation, and it was discovered that, although not quite a perfectly satisfactory relationship, the relationship shown as equation (7.1) in the text could be regarded as a useful approximate description of the data. The random shock charted in Frame (c) of Figure 7.6 is simply the calculated residual movements in real GDP about its trend not accounted for by the previous year's value of that variable.

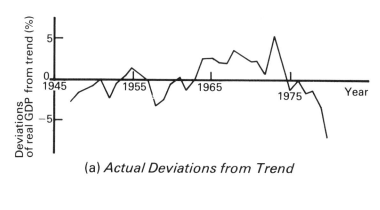

(a) *Actual Deviations from Trend*

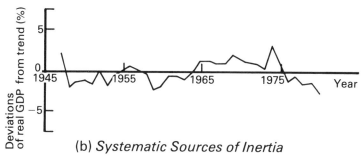

(b) *Systematic Sources of Inertia*

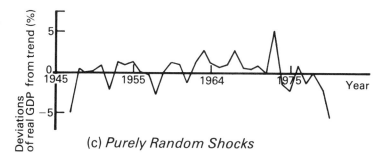

(c) *Purely Random Shocks*

Figure 7.6 *Random and Systematic Components of Deviations of Real GDP from Trend*

Frame (a) shows the deviations of real GDP from trend. These are broken into a systematic part, Frame (b), and a purely random element, Frame (c). The random disturbances are generally small but, on three occasions (1947, 1973, and 1980) were more than 5 per cent in absolute value. The random fluctuations (Frame (c)) when added to the systematic sources of inertia (Frame (b)), give the actual deviations (Frame (a)).

Source: Appendix to Chapter 2.

of GDP from trend is the sum of the shock and the small amount of inertia left over from the previous year. The figures for each year in Figure 7.6 can be interpreted in this way.

It cannot be emphasised sufficiently that what we are doing in this exercise is *describing* the movement of GDP. We are not *explaining* it. The exercise does, however, provide us with a valuable way of thinking about what has been happening. The economy is bombarded by shocks as described in Frame (c) and those shocks affect the level of output (and other variables as well) in a manner which looks much less random than the shocks themselves. As a matter of description, we can translate the random shocks into a more systematic up-and-down movement of output by the device of describing output as following a first-order difference equation which is stochastically (randomly) disturbed. The next task is to try and understand what has caused the shocks shown in Frame (c) and what gives rise to the translation of those shocks into movements of output and other variables, and what the sources giving rise to inertia described in Frame (b), in fact, are.

(ii) The Production of Durables and Non-Durables

The second feature of the business cycle that was identified in Section D above, was the tendency for the production of durables (investment goods) to fluctuate with greater amplitude than the production of non-durables (consumer goods and services). This general feature of the business cycle is very evident in the United Kingdom data as Figure 7.7 shows. Frame (a), which illustrates the movements in non-durables, shows fluctuations generally falling inside the range of plus or minus 5 per cent. In contrast, the production of durables (shown in Frame (b)) on occasion has fluctuated by as much as 20 per cent above trend and more than 30 per cent below trend. There are some interesting differences in the nature of the fluctuations of these two series. Also, very clearly, there has been a tendency for longer term movements in these two variables to run against each other, durables being above trend in the 1960s, with non-durables being below trend through that period. At the end of the 1970s, durables are below trend and non-durables above trend, a pattern that also was prevalent in the early 1950s.

(iii) Output and Unemployment

A further general feature of the business cycle that was identified in Section D above was the tendency for output and employment to move together or, equivalently, for output and unemployment to move in opposite directions from each other. A useful way of exploring the co-movements among variables is to plot one variable against another in the same diagram. Figure 7.8 does this for unemployment and deviations of real GDP from trend. To be sure that you know how to read Figure 7.8, consider the point marked 80. This is in the bottom right-hand corner of the figure. It represents the observation for the year 1980. In that year, unemployment was 6.8 per cent (which you can read off on the horizontal axis of the diagram), and real GDP was 7.6 per cent below trend (−7.6, which you can read off on the vertical axis of the diagram). Evidently, there is a clear tendency for unemployment to move in the opposite direction to deviations of output from trend. The relationship is by no

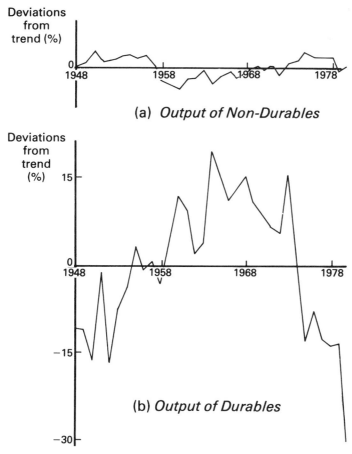

Figure 7.7 *Cycles in Non-Durables and Durables*

The fluctuations around trend in the production of non-durables (Frame (a)) is modest compared with that of durables (Frame (b)). The cycles in durables and non-durables are quite different from each other, durables tending to be above trend when non-durables are below trend and *vice versa*.

Source: Output of durables is the sum of durable household goods, cars and motor bikes, gross domestic fixed capital formation and value of physical increase in stocks and work in progress. Output of non-durables is gross domestic product at factor cost less output of durables.

Economic Trends Annual Supplement 1981 edition, No. 6, HMSO, London, 1981, Tables 14, 28.
Economic Trends, No. 336, October 1981, Tables 8, 10.

means perfect, but is nevertheless very distinct. It is evident from the figure that there has been a tendency for the relationship to drift to the right over the post-war years. Abstracting from this rightward drift, it is evident that there is a clear systematic tendency for unemployment to move countercyclically with reference to deviations of output from trend.

(iv) Price Movements

A general feature of the business cycle is that prices move procyclically. This means

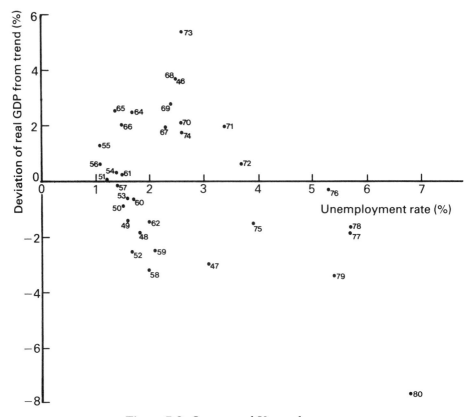

Figure 7.8 *Output and Unemployment*

When output rises above trend, unemployment tends to fall and when output falls below trend, unemployment tends to rise. There has been a tendency though for unemployment to drift upwards independently of output, i.e. for the relationship between unemployment and output fluctuations to move to the right. *Source:* Appendix to Chapter 2.

that inflation rates are strongest when output is above trend and weakest when output is below trend. Equivalently, we could expect to find a negative association between inflation movements and unemployment movements. That is, when unemployment is at its lowest, inflation should generally be at its highest. Viewing the procyclical nature of inflation as a countercyclical relation between inflation and unemployment enables us to focus on a relationship known as the Phillips curve (named after the New Zealand economist, A.W. Phillips, who developed this relationship).[7]

Figures 7.9 and 7.10 show the co-movements of inflation and unemployment in the United Kingdom between 1900 and 1938 in the first figure and 1946 and 1980 in the second figure. (The reason for plotting these on two separate figures is that the range of variation in the inter-war years is so gigantic that the actual variation in the post-

---

7. Phillips' original contribution is A.W. Phillips (1958) The relation between unemployment and the rate of change of money wage rates in the United Kingdom, 1861–1957, *Economica*, Vol. 25, November, pp. 283–99.

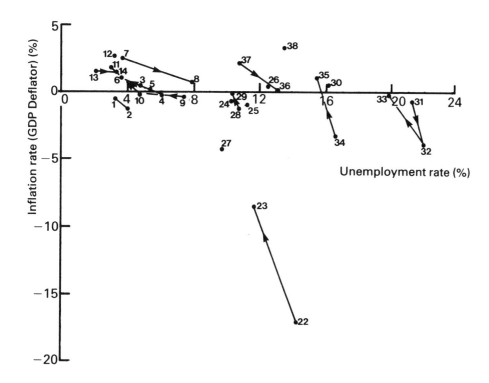

Figure 7.9 *Co-movements of Inflation and Unemployment, 1901–1938*
On the average, in two years out of three, inflation and unemployment move in opposite directions (shown by the arrowed line). On the remaining occasions, unemployment and inflation move in the same direction as each other. *Source:* Appendix to Chapter 2.

war years would be lost in the corner of the diagram if we were to plot everything on the scale shown in Figure 7.9.)

Notice that there is, from time to time, a clear tendency for inflation and unemployment to move in opposite directions. This is visible in the diagrams on all the occasions where the points describing two or more consecutive years have been joined together with a line and an arrow indicating the direction of movement of the economy. Careful inspection of Figures 7.9 and 7.10 shows that approximately two-thirds of the time there is a negative co-movement between inflation and unemployment. For the other one-third of the time, the two variables move in the same direction. What these figures show most vividly is that there is no single simple relationship that characterises all the co-movements of inflation and unemployment. The Phillips relation in the United Kingdom data raises questions about both the sources of the negative co-movements between inflation and unemployment and the sizeable positive co-movements which have occurred from time to time. It will be necessary for us to try to understand why this complicated pattern of co-movements in inflation and unemployment has arisen.

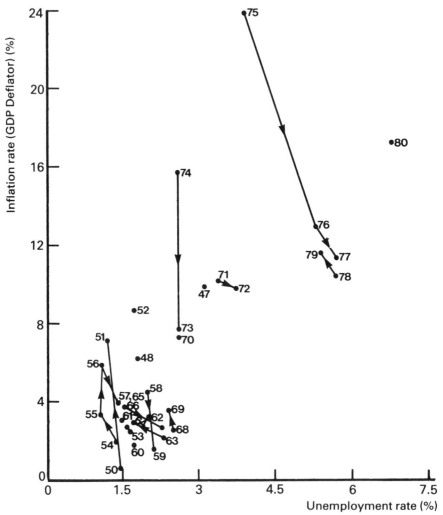

Figure 7.10 *Co-movements of Inflation and Unemployment, 1947–1980*

Like the earlier period, on the average, in two years out of three, unemployment and inflation have moved in the opposite directions to each other (shown by the arrowed lines). There have been some sizeable and important positive co-movements between the two variables however, especially between 1969–1970, 1974–1975, and 1979–1980. *Source:* Appendix to Chapter 2.

(v) Interest Rates

The general description of the business cycle included the proposition that interest rates are procyclical with short rates fluctuating more than long rates. A useful way of looking at the cyclical nature of interest rates is to examine how they move with inflation. Since we know that inflation is generally procyclical, then, if interest rates and inflation move together, we shall know that interest rates are also procyclical. Figure 7.11 shows the relationship between short-term interest rates and inflation in the United Kingdom. The generally procyclical nature of short-term interest rates is strongly seen in this figure. You can see that although there is not a perfect

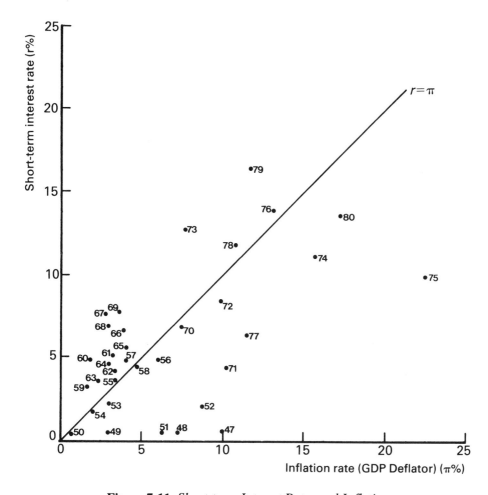

Figure 7.11 *Short-term Interest Rates and Inflation*
There is a general, positive co-movement between short-term interest rates and inflation. The
relationship between the two variables is far from perfect. Interest rates do not fluctuate as
much as inflation does. *Source:* Appendix to Chapter 2.

relationship between interest rates and the inflation rate, there is nevertheless a very
striking tendency for these two variables to move in the same direction as each other.
This feature of interest rates and inflation rates moving together is a further stylised
fact for which our theories are necessarily going to have to be able to account.

There is no need to examine separately the movements of long-term interest rates.
You know from Figure 2.5 that long-term interest rates are much smoother than
short-term rates. You also know that there is a general tendency for long-term rates
to move in the same broad direction as short-term rates. It immediately follows that
the United Kingdom's long-term interest rates do have the general characteristic that
they are procyclical, but only slightly so.

These, then, are the major features of the United Kingdom's business cycle which
macroeconomic theory seeks to explain. The rest of this book is concerned with that
task of explanation.

SUMMARY

A. The Definition of the Business Cycle

Business cycles are recurrent but non-periodic fluctuations in aggregate economic activity as measured by fluctuations in real GDP around its trend.

B. Autocorrelation

Autocorrelation is a technical term which means that the value of some variable is related to itself at some earlier date (or dates). An autocorrelated variable is described by a difference equation which is stochastically or randomly disturbed.

C. Co-Movement

The term co-movement is used in the description of the movement of one variable in relation to another. Co-movements may be procyclical, in which case two variables move up and down together, or countercyclical, in which case two variables move in opposite directions to each other. Co-movement may display high coherence, in which case two variables move together in a very close manner, or low coherence, in which case the variables do not move closely in sympathy with each other.

D. Properties of the Business Cycle

Movements in real GDP about trend are well-described by a simple difference equation which is stochastically disturbed. In general, employment, prices and interest rates are procyclical. Unemployment is countercyclical.

E. The United Kingdom's Business Cycle

The general features of the business cycle set out above apply precisely to the United Kingdom case, with the important observation that movements in inflation, while generally procyclical, are not universally so. There are important co-movements of inflation and unemployment which do not fit a simple pattern.

Review Questions

1. What are business cycles cycles *in*?

2. Describe the different phases of a cycle.

3. What is a 'recession'?

4. Are all business cycles the same length? If not, why do we use the term cycle to describe the phenomenon of non-periodic economic fluctuations?

5. What is a difference equation? Can a difference equation describe the path followed by deviations of real GDP from trend?

6. Explain how random shocks combine with inertia to describe recurrent but non-periodic up-and-down movements in economic activity.

7. Reinforce your understanding of the concept of autocorrelation by conducting the following experiments:
    (a) using the same 'economic shocks' as set out in Table 7.3, generate a path for real income if it is described by the processes

    (i) $y_t = 90 + 0.1\, y_{t-1} + e_t$

    and

    (ii) $y_t = 1 + 0.99\, y_{t-1} + e_t$

    (b) compare the paths of y_t in (i) and (ii) above with each other and with that derived in the text using equation (7.2). How do the paths differ? What do you learn from this experiment?

8. What is meant by the term co-movement?

9. What is meant by the term coherence?

10. Try to think of examples (not necessarily economic) of:
    (a) procyclical co-movements which have
         (i) high coherence
         (ii) low coherence
    (b) countercyclical co-movements which have
         (i) high coherence
         (ii) low coherence.

11. Describe the general character of business cycles.

12. How might the deviation of real GDP from trend in the United Kingdom be described in the period 1948–1979?

13. What have been the co-movements between GDP and inflation, unemployment, and interest rates in the period since 1948?

Part III

The Basic Theory of Income, Employment, and the Price Level

8

Introduction to the Basic Model

You have now reviewed: a) the questions which macroeconomics seeks to answer; b) the main facts about the evolution of the key macroeconomic variables in the United Kingdom since 1900; c) the way in which macroeconomic variables are measured; and d) how it is possible to characterise the ups and downs of economic activity and the co-movements among the variables as business cycles.

It is now time to move on to the more challenging problem of explaining macroeconomic phenomena — macroeconomic theory.

The next three chapters develop the simplest available model — what we will call the *basic model* — for the determination of real income, the level of employment, and the price level.[1] Chapters 12 and 13 show how unemployment and inflation are explained by the basic model. Chapter 14 introduces the complications arising from international economic relations, showing how shocks arising in the rest of the world affect the domestic economy and also analysing the determination of the balance of payments and the exchange rate. Chapter 15 reveals the extent to which the basic model can and cannot explain recent macroeconomic history in the United Kingdom. You will discover that the explanation given by the basic model is not a completely satisfactory one. There are, however, good reasons for starting out with the basic model even though it turns out to be not entirely satisfactory in all respects.

A. Why Study the Basic Model?

The first reason for studying *the basic model* is that some of its ingredients are present

---

1. What we are calling the basic model is usually called the classical model. The most comprehensive scholarly treatment of this body of analysis is Don Patinkin (1965) *Money, Interest and Prices,* 2nd edn, Harper and Row. Chapters I to XII of that work are *the* authoritative statement on this body of analysis.

in the more complex and satisfactory model which you will study later (in Parts IV and V). That is, it will not be necessary to unlearn as wrong, things which you are learning in this simplest of frameworks. On the contrary, you will be able to see exactly in what special circumstances this simplest theory yields useful predictions.

A second reason for studying the basic model is that it turns out to be possible to understand some of the reasons why unemployment exists and why its rate varies. Indeed, it is also possible to understand why unemployment has increased so strongly in the United Kingdom over recent years.

Thirdly, and this is of vital importance, the basic model will enable you to see the important distinction between inflation as an ongoing process and a rise in the price level as a once-and-for-all affair and to see what can and what cannot cause inflation. There is a great deal of popular mythology to the effect that inflation is the result of all kinds of social pressures, emanating in particular from the behaviour of trade unions. You will be able to see with the aid of the basic model that is shortly to be developed that this popular mythology is misleading and wrong.

Fourthly, when extended to deal with the interactions between the domestic economy and the rest of the world, the basic model provides strong insights into how the balance of payments and the foreign exchange rate are determined.

B. Weaknesses of the Basic Model

The main areas in which the basic model is deficient arise from its inability to explain the *business cycle*, and its difficulty in coping with the facts of the Great Depression. You will see later the attempts that have been made to modify the basic model to remedy these deficiencies.

SUMMARY

A. Why Study the Basic Model?

You are studying the *basic model* for four reasons:
  (i)   its *ingredients* are present in *more complex* and satisfactory models;
  (ii) it shows *why unemployment exists* and some of the reasons *why its rate varies;*
  (iii) it enables you to distinguish between *inflation* and a *once-and-for-all rise* in the *price level* and understand the *causes* of *inflation;*
  (iv) it enables you to understand how the *balance of payments* and the *exchange rate* are determined.

B. Weaknesses of the Basic Model

The basic model is unable to explain the *business cycle* and *persistent depression.*

Review Questions

1.   In economics we use a model as a means of explaining some economic phenomenon. Why do we use a model in macroeconomics?

2.   How would you determine the strengths and weaknesses of a model?

3.   What are the strengths and weaknesses of the basic model?

9

Aggregate Supply and the Labour Market

The main objective of this chapter is to enable you to understand what determines the aggregate supply of goods and services in the short run. Three tasks will enable you to achieve that objective. Those tasks are to understand:

A. **the concept of the short-run aggregate production function;**
B. **the working of a competitive aggregate labour market;** and
C. **the concept of the aggregate supply curve.**

A. Short-Run Aggregate Production Function

A useful starting point in explaining the concept of the *short-run aggregate production function* is with the production function of an individual producer. A *production function* is simply a statement about the maximum output that can be produced with a given list of inputs, and more than that, a statement of how that maximum level of output will vary as the inputs themselves are varied.

The maximum output of some particular good that can be produced will depend on the amount of capital employed, the state of technology, the amount of land resources used, and the number and skill of the workers employed.

In the *long run* all the inputs used in a production process can be varied. Capital equipment can be purchased, technology can be changed, land use can be modified, and workers can acquire new skills.

In the *short run* however, these four factors which affect the maximum output that

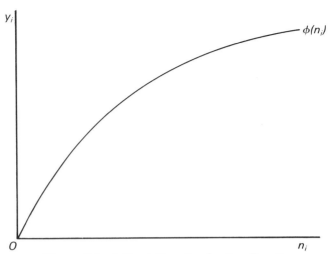

Figure 9.1 *A Short-Run Production Function*

The curve shows the maximum attainable output level as the level of labour input is varied.
The application of more units of labour always produces more units of output. Each additional
unit of labour produces less additional output than the previous unit did — there is diminishing
marginal product.

---

can be produced are relatively hard to change. They are, of course, changing
gradually over time and are the source of the long-term growth trend in output. At
any given moment, however, they may, as a useful approximation, be treated as
fixed. The input which can be varied quickly, and whose variations give rise to
fluctuations in output around its trend, is the quantity of labour employed. *The short-
run production function shows the relationship between the maximum amount of
output that can be produced as the quantity of labour employed is varied, while
holding constant the other inputs into the production process.*

The properties of the short-run production function are most easily described by
plotting a specific example. This is done in Figure 9.1.

The label on the curve, $\phi(n_i)$, is just a shorthand way of saying that output (y_i)
depends on (or is a function of) the amount of labour employed (n_i). The short-run
production function depicted in Figure 9.1 reflects a near universal technological
fact: that as the number employed is increased, so the output of the marginal worker
— *marginal product* — declines.

So far you have reviewed the short-run production function analysis which is used
in microeconomic theory to develop the theory of costs and supply in the competitive
industry, or to develop a theory of costs and profit-maximising price and output
behaviour in a monopolistic industry. It is possible, however, to use this
microeconomic production function analysis to derive an *aggregate* short-run
production function. The *aggregate short-run production function* relates the
aggregate *output* to the total *number* of workers *employed*. (Recall from Chapter 3
that aggregate output is equal to real expenditure and real income.)

Define *output* as y, and also define the *number employed* as n. Then, the aggregate
short-run production function which we could write as

$$y = \phi(n) \tag{9.1}$$

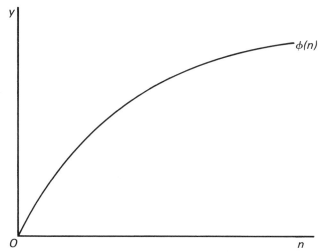

Figure 9.2 *The Aggregate Short-Run Production Function*
The relationship between aggregate output — GDP — y and aggregate labour input n will have the same shape as an individual firm's short-run production function provided either that relative prices do not change 'too much' or that different industries' shares in total output remain 'fairly constant'.

---

shows how the maximum value of y that can be produced varies as n is varied. It will look like the short-run production function for an individual product depicted in Figure 9.1 and is shown in Figure 9.2.

It cannot be guaranteed that an aggregate short-run production function will be well-defined, nor can it be guaranteed that it will have exactly the same properties as an individual product short-run production function. Two alternative conditions, however, make it possible to use the concept of the *aggregate* short-run production function as an operational tool: first, the relative constancy of relative prices; and secondly, the relative constancy of the values of the different goods produced as a proportion of aggregate output. These conditions make the concept of aggregate output sufficiently unambiguous to be useful.

Although it is possible to aggregate commodities by converting them into constant pound values, it seems perhaps less obvious that labour can be aggregated into a single, aggregate labour input figure. That is what economists do, however, when performing this kind of analysis. Brain surgeons and bus drivers are added together (typically as equal quantities of labour) to arrive at the total volume of employment, n. Again, provided the proportions of different types of labour in the aggregate labour force are relatively constant, this aggregation will not be wildly misleading.

There is another problem you should take note of concerning the labour input. It concerns the role of 'hours per worker' in the definition of the labour input. Normally, labour is measured in terms of *man-hours*. Three people each working for 4 hours a day should be able to produce a similar total output to two people working 6 hours a day each. Macroeconomics is more concerned with explaining variations in the *number* of people *employed* than with explaining the average number of *hours* worked *per worker*. As the economy goes through a cycle of activity from boom to slump it may be that output drops by, say, 10 per cent. That output drop could be accommodated by a cut of 10 per cent in the average hours worked by each worker with no one becoming fully unemployed. Typically, however, that does not happen. Average hours per worker employed remain relatively constant, while the number of workers employed declines. It is possible to develop an explanation as to why it is that employment rather than average hours per worker varies with the level of economic activity. Rather than pursue such an explanation we are simply going to assume that each worker works a fairly constant average number of hours and, as economic activity varies, so the number of workers employed varies. The variable n will therefore, throughout this book, be taken to mean the number of workers employed. It will reflect the number of man-hours employed, provided the number of hours per man is constant, which we will assume to be the case.

This completes the definition of the short-run aggregate production function.

B. Competitive Aggregate Labour Market

(i) The Demand for Labour

First consider the demand side of the labour market. Competitive firms will demand labour and produce output up to the point at which the price of their output (P_i) is equal to the marginal cost of its production (MC_i). That is,

$$P_i = MC_i \tag{9.2}$$

If this condition is satisfied, then the firm is making maximum profit (provided, of course, that the marginal cost curve is rising at this point).

Marginal cost is easy to calculate. Recall that in the short run the only input which can vary is labour. The cost of hiring one extra worker is equal to the money wage per worker (W_i). However, the money wage is not the marginal cost. The amount produced by the marginal worker is known as the *marginal product* (MP_i). The marginal cost is the cost of the marginal worker (W_i) divided by the output which that marginal worker can produce (MP_i). That is,

$$MC_i = \frac{W_i}{MP_i} \tag{9.3}$$

Now, replacing the marginal cost in equation (9.3) with price from equation (9.2), it is clear that

$$P_i = \frac{W_i}{MP_i} \tag{9.4}$$

If we divide both sides of this equation by P_i and multiply both sides by MP_i we obtain

$$MP_i = \frac{W_i}{P_i} \tag{9.5}$$

Equation (9.5) says that the marginal product in some particular industry (i) will be equal to the money wage in that industry (W_i) divided by the price of the output of that industry (P_i). To see how this condition leads directly to the demand for labour

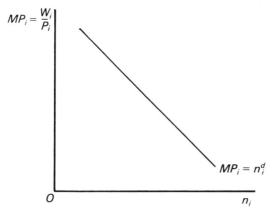

Figure 9.3 *The Marginal Product Curve — The Demand for Labour in a Competitive Industry*

Marginal product declines as labour input increases. Profits are maximised when the marginal product MP is equal to the real wage (W/P). The marginal product curve and the demand for labour curve in a competitive industry are, therefore, the same curve.

---

function, consider Figure 9.3, which plots the marginal product of labour in the ith industry against the number of workers employed in that industry.

You have seen that a condition for profit maximising (equation 9.5) is that the marginal product of labour in the industry must equal the ratio of the money wage to the price level. This ratio is the *real wage*. You can therefore equivalently measure the real wage on the vertical axis of Figure 9.3. The marginal product curve then automatically becomes the demand for labour curve when thought of as being drawn against the real wage.

If you take an average of real wages across all industries in the economy and aggregate all labour inputs across all industries in the economy, then you obtain the economy-wide demand for labour function or the *aggregate labour demand function*, as shown in Figure 9.4.

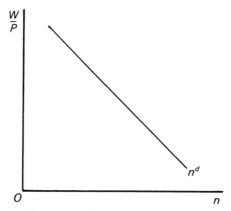

Figure 9.4 *The Demand for Labour*

The demand for labour in the economy as a whole is obtained by aggregating the demand for labour in all the individual industries. Like the industry demand curves, it will be a downward sloping function of the real wage.

A Digression on Monopoly

You may be thinking that the analysis just presented is fine for a competitive industry, but not for monopoly. You may also have been taught that we simply *know* that there are no competitive industries in the actual world. If so, you will be regarding the preceding analysis as being about as useful for the task in hand as the flat earth theory would be for charting an air route from London to Tokyo! Leaving aside the deep question of whether or not it is possible simply to know whether or not competitive industries exist, it is perhaps of some interest to notice that for the task at hand, it simply doesn't matter whether the economy is competitive or monopolistic. To see this, consider how the analysis would apply to a monopolist.

Now in order to maximise profits, a monopolist will set marginal cost equal, not to price, but to marginal revenue (MR_i). That is

$$MC_i = MR_i \tag{9.6}$$

Just as in the case of the competitive firm, the monopolist's marginal cost will be equal to the wage rate divided by the marginal product of labour; that is

$$MC_i = \frac{W_i}{MP_i} \tag{9.3}$$

The monopolist's marginal revenue will be related to price by the formula

$$MR_i = (1 + \frac{1}{\eta})P_i, \qquad \eta < -1 \tag{9.7}$$

where η is the elasticity[1] of the monopolist's demand curve. To get a feel for how the relationship between marginal revenue and price (equation 9.7) works, notice that if the elasticity of demand, η, was infinite, then MR_i would equal P_i. This, of course, is exactly the case of perfect competition. If η was equal to -1, a unit elastic or rectangular hyperbola demand curve, the monopolist's marginal revenue would be zero, and the monopolist would not be maximising profits.

In general, the monopolist's marginal revenue will be less than price, but a stable fraction of the price.

Using equations (9.7) and (9.3) in (9.6) enables us to obtain

$$(1 + \frac{1}{\eta})P_i = \frac{W_i}{MP_i} \tag{9.8}$$

Proceeding as we did in the case of the competitive firm, dividing both sides of (9.8) by P_i and multiplying both sides by MP_i, we obtain:

$$(1 + \frac{1}{\eta})MP_i = \frac{W_i}{P_i} \tag{9.9}$$

This says that some fraction (the fraction $[1 + (1/\eta)]$ of the marginal product of the monopolistic firm) will be equal to the real wage. The monopolist's demand for labour will therefore be *less* than that of a competitive producer (assuming that they have identical production functions) but will still have the crucial property that, as

---

1. A note at the end of this chapter (page 134) reviews the concept of elasticity and explains how equation (9.7) is derived.

the real wage rises, so the demand for labour falls. By aggregating across all producers, whether competitive or monopolistic, we shall still end up with an aggregate demand for labour that looks like that shown in Figure 9.4.

(ii) The Supply of Labour

Consider next the supply of labour. In the theory of household behaviour the utility maximising decisions of households lead to the prediction that as the real wage increases, an individual household will seek to supply more hours of labour, up to some maximum. Thereafter, as the real wage rises, so the number of hours supplied begins to decline, since a higher income would usually imply that a household would want to consume more leisure along with other goods.

Thus, the supply of hours per individual household would be represented by a supply curve which increases with real wages up to some maximum and then begins to fall off.

For our purposes, however, we are interested in developing a theory of the aggregate supply, not of hours per worker, but of the number of workers. In effect, we are interested in analysing the outcome of an all-or-nothing choice. That is, the potential worker has to evaluate how much utility would be derived from not working and compare that with the utility that would be derived from working for a fixed number of hours per week. If the utility from working exceeds that from not working, the individual will make the decision to be in the labour force and therefore be part of the labour supply. In general, as the real wage rises, so more and more people will evaluate the prospect of working as yielding more utility than the prospect of not working. Let us suppose that is the case and that as a consequence the aggregate supply of labour increases as the real wage increases. Figure 9.5 shows such a relation.

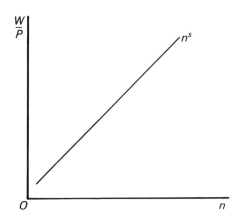

Figure 9.5 *The Supply of Labour*

Households choose whether to enter the labour force by comparing the utility they would get from working a fixed number of hours at a certain wage rate with the utility they would derive from taking leisure. The higher the real wage, the larger is the number of households who will regard working as yielding superior utility to consuming leisure. Thus, the supply of labour will rise as the real wage rises.

(iii) Competitive Equilibrium

Next consider the competitive equilibrium in the labour market. Figure 9.6 brings together the demand curve from Figure 9.4 and the supply curve from Figure 9.5. It is supposed that the economy generates sufficient information about supply and demand in the labour market for the real wage *quickly* to achieve a *market clearing* or *equilibrium* value. The economy therefore, on the average, settles down at the real wage $(W/P)^*$, and at the level of employment n^*. (Of course, the real wage is the ratio of the money wage rate to the price level, and it is the money wage which will adjust in the labour market to ensure that, for a given price level, the equilibrium real wage is attained.)

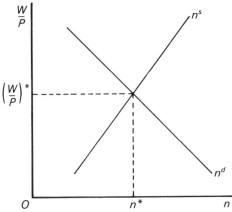

Figure 9.6 *Labour Market Equilibrium*

The labour market is in equilibrium when households are maximising utility (are on their supply curve) and firms are maximising profits (are on their demand curve). The only such point is where the supply and demand curves cut at the real wage $(W/P)^*$ and the employment level n^*.

___

The assumption that the equilibrium real wage is *quickly* achieved is a crucial one for keeping the analysis simple. The presumption is that, even though it takes time to attain equilibrium, that time is insignificantly short, relative to the length of time for which the equilibrium prevails. This would mean that although we might observe an actual economy that is not in an equilibrium, as depicted in Figure 9.5, that economy would be heading for such an equilibrium and, if we blinked, by the time we opened our eyes again the economy would have settled into such an equilibrium.

We have now determined the real wage and the level of employment at their equilibrium values. You can think of the employment level as the aggregate *number employed* in the economy. You can think of the real wage as the economy's *average real wage*. Individuals' real wages will be highly variable, depending on individual skills and other factors. If relative wages are fairly stable, however, movements in the average real wage in the economy will also reflect movements in each individual's real wage.

The way in which the analysis has been developed has ignored the phenomenon of *unemployment*. That is not to say that unemployment cannot exist in this model. It is simply to say that at the present time we are not discussing the implications of the model for the rate of unemployment. This will be taken up later at some length in

Chapter 12. Further, monopolistic elements in the labour market, such as, for example, the operation of labour unions, have been ignored. This, too, will be dealt with in Chapter 12.

C. Aggregate Supply Curve

First, a definition of the aggregate supply curve: *the aggregate supply curve shows the amount of output which the economy will supply at each different price level*, given that *firms are maximising profits, households are maximising utility, and the labour market is in equilibrium*. It is a curve which is drawn in a diagram with the *price level* on one axis and *output* on the other.

To derive the *aggregate supply curve* it is necessary to bring together the two components of analysis developed above, namely, the short-run production function and the competitive equilibrium in the labour market. This is done in Figure 9.7. Your first quick glance at Figure 9.7 may be offputting and may give you the impression that the analysis on which you are about to embark is going to be very difficult. Fortunately such a first impression would be wrong! The analysis illustrated by Figure 9.7 is actually quite easy, provided you take it step by step.

The first step is to notice that there are four parts to Figure 9.7. The first part, Frame (a), is nothing other than Figure 9.6, which you have just been studying. It shows a labour market in competitive equilibrium with the real wage equal to $(W/P)^*$ and the level of employment, n^*.

The second part of the figure, Frame (b), is exactly the same as Figure 9.2, namely, a short-run production function. Notice that the horizontal axes of Frames (a) and (b) both measure the same thing — the volume of employment. Adopt the convention that the units of measurement are the same on both horizontal axes. That being the case, you can immediately read off from the horizontal axis of Frame (b) the same equilibrium level of employment, n^*, as is determined in Frame (a). The dotted line and arrow indicate this.

With the level of employment equal to n^*, the short-run production function in Frame (b) determines the level of output y^* as shown on the vertical axis of Frame (b).

So far, you have used Frames (a) and (b) to determine the equilibrium values of the real wage, the level of employment, and the level of output.

To complete the derivation of the aggregate supply curve, the question that has to be answered is, How does the equilibrium level of output vary as the price level varies? The answer to this question (and the aggregate supply curve) will be discovered in Frame (c). This part of the figure measures the price level on the vertical axis and the level of output on the horizontal axis. Notice that the vertical axis of Frame (b) and the horizontal axis of Frame (c) measure the same thing — output. The top-right part of the diagram has output on both axes and a 45° line. It is just a pictorial device to enable you to read off from the horizontal axis of Frame (c) the same quantity as is shown on the vertical axis of Frame (b). (Notice, by the way, that the vertical axis of Frame (c) *does not* measure the same thing as the vertical axis of Frame (a) — there are no arrowed lines going from Frame (c) directly to Frame (a). The arrows (and the analysis) start in Frame (a) and go clockwise to finish in Frame (c).)

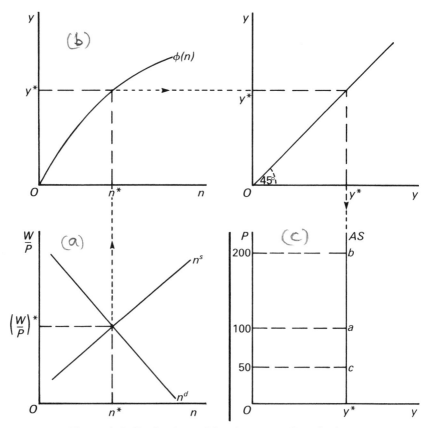

Figure 9.7 *Derivation of the Aggregate Supply Curve*

The aggregate supply curve shows the amount of output which will be supplied as the price level varies when firms are hiring the profit-maximising quantity of labour and households are supplying the utility-maximising quantity of labour. There is a unique level of output y^* that will be produced by the equilibrium level of labour input n^* at the equilibrium real wage $(W/P)^*$. That level of supply will be independent of the price level, so that the aggregate supply curve is vertical.

Now go back to the question, How does equilibrium output vary as the price level varies? Suppose that initially the price level is equal to 100. We can arbitrarily define our units so that is true. This would mean that there is a point on an *aggregate supply curve*, given by the point identified by the letter *a* in Frame (c). Suppose now that the price level was doubled from 100 to 200. What would happen to the amount of output which firms would be willing to supply? The answer is quickly seen — nothing would happen to it. If the price level doubled to 200, then the *money wage* would also have to double to preserve labour market equilibrium (Frame (a)). The quantity of employment would remain unchanged as would the amount of output supplied. The economy would move, therefore, to the point identified by the letter *b* in Frame (c). Next, suppose the price level halved, from 100 to 50. The effects of this on the amount of output that the economy would produce are exactly the same as the effects of the doubling of the price level. In this case the money wage would have to fall to one-half of its previous level in order to maintain the real wage at its market equilibrium value, and employment and output would remain constant at n^* and y^*. The economy would thus move to the point identified with the letter c in Frame (c). These three points (and all the other points above, below, and between them) trace an *aggregate supply curve* for this economy.

The *aggregate supply curve* in the basic model is *perfectly inelastic*. The level of output will be equal to y^* no matter what the price level.

SUMMARY

A. Short-Run Aggregate Production Function

The *short-run aggregate production function* shows how the maximum amount of *output* will vary as the *number* of workers *employed* varies, holding constant the stock of capital, the state of technology, and the skills of labour. Its properties are the same as an ordinary microeconomic short-run production function in that it displays diminishing marginal productivity.

B. Competitive Aggregate Labour Market

A competitive aggregate labour market will determine an equilibrium real wage and level of employment where the downward sloping demand curve (derived from the marginal product curve) cuts an upward sloping supply curve (derived from individual households' utility maximising decisions).

C. Aggregate Supply Curve

The *aggregate supply curve shows how the amount of output varies as the price level varies when firms are maximising profits, households are maximising utility and the labour market is in equilibrium*. In the *basic model* developed in this chapter *aggregate supply* is *perfectly inelastic with respect to the price level*.

Note on Elasticity

Elasticity is a measure of responsiveness. The elasticity of demand measures, in a precise way, the responsiveness of the quantity demanded to a change in the price. The higher is the elasticity the more responsive is the quantity to a price change. Elasticity is a unit-free measure of responsiveness. To be precise, it is the percentage change in the quantity demanded divided by the percentage change in price or, equivalently, the proportionate change of quantity demanded divided by the proportionate change in price. Calling the elasticity η, the change in quantity ΔQ, the change in price ΔP, the quantity Q, and the price P, the elasticity is measured as

$$\eta \equiv \frac{\Delta Q}{Q} \div \frac{\Delta P}{P} \tag{1}$$

This may equivalently be written as

$$\eta = \frac{\Delta Q}{P} \cdot \frac{P}{Q} \tag{2}$$

For future reference it is useful to notice that one over the elasticity (the inverse of the elasticity) is

$$\frac{1}{\eta} = \frac{\Delta P}{\Delta Q} \cdot \frac{Q}{P} \tag{3}$$

To obtain the formula used in the text, notice that total revenue (R) is equal to price (P) multiplied by quantity (Q), that is

$$R = PQ \tag{4}$$

Suppose that there was a change in price that induced a change in quantity and a change in revenue. Then the new revenue which we could call $R + \Delta R$ will be determined as

$$R + \Delta R = (P + \Delta P)(Q + \Delta Q) \tag{5}$$

Multiplying out equation (5) gives

$$R + \Delta R = PQ + P\Delta Q + Q\Delta P + \Delta P\Delta Q \tag{6}$$

If the change in price (ΔP) is very very small, then equation (6) is approximately

$$R + \Delta R \simeq PQ + P\Delta Q + Q\Delta P \tag{7}$$

(you see that we are treating the last term in equation (6) as if it was zero). Now subtract equation (4) from equation (7) to give

$$\Delta R \simeq P\Delta Q + Q\Delta P \tag{8}$$

This can be manipulated by multiplying and dividing the second term on the right-hand side by P to give

$$\Delta R \simeq (\Delta Q + \frac{Q}{P}\Delta P)P \tag{9}$$

Dividing all through this equation by ΔQ gives

$$\frac{\Delta R}{\Delta Q} \simeq (\frac{\Delta Q}{\Delta Q} + \frac{Q}{P}\frac{\Delta P}{\Delta Q})P \tag{10}$$

The left-hand side of equation (10), $\Delta R/\Delta Q$ is what is called marginal revenue — the change in revenue induced by a change in the quantity sold. Obviously, the first term in brackets in equation (10) is equal to one. You can also see, by referring back to equation (3), that the second term in brackets in equation (10) is the inverse of the elasticity of demand. Equation

(10) may, therefore, be written more simply as:

$$\frac{\Delta R}{\Delta Q} \simeq (1 + \frac{1}{\eta})P \qquad (11)$$

This is the relationship used in the text. Expressed in words, it states that marginal revenue equals one plus one over the elasticity of demand multiplied by the price. Clearly, if the elasticity of demand is infinitely big (the case of perfect competition), price and marginal revenue are the same as each other. Another interesting special case is when the elasticity of demand is minus one (the case of a rectangular hyperbola demand curve). In that case you can verify from equation (11) that marginal revenue is equal to zero. Notice that in general, marginal revenue will be positive but less than the price, since η, in general, will be negative and lie between minus infinity (perfect competition) and minus one.

Review Questions

1. A firm produces a good from inputs of labour and capital. Labour is measured by the number of men employed. Use the following data to draw the firm's short-run production function.

No. of men	1	2	3	4	5	6	7	8	9	10
Output	10	21	33	45	56	66	75	83	90	96

    If the money wage is £18 and the firm sells the good it produces for £2, how many men will the firm employ?

2. If the economy consisted of 1000 firms, all identical and all exactly like the firm described in Question 1, draw the *aggregate* short-run production function. Also draw the aggregate demand for labour curve. If the aggregate labour supply curve is

    $$n^s = 2000 \left(\frac{W}{P}\right) - 2000$$

    how many men will be employed and what will be the economy-wide average real wage?

3. What is an aggregate supply curve?

4. Use your answer to Question 2 to derive the aggregate supply curve for the hypothetical economy described in that question.

5. In drawing the aggregate supply curve several assumptions are made. List these assumptions.

6. Labour allocates its time between work and leisure in order to maximise its utility. Along which curve in Question 4 is utility maximised?

7. Firms produce that output which maximises profit. Along which curve in Question 4 are firms maximising profit?

8. Is the aggregate supply curve fixed in position forever or does it shift from time to time? If it does shift, list some of the things that would cause it to do so.

10

Aggregate Demand and the Money Market

You have studied the first ingredient of the basic model — the theory of aggregate supply, and it is now time to move on to the second ingredient — the demand side of the economy. There are two tasks under this topic, which are to:

    A. understand the concept of aggregate demand;
      and
    B. understand the monetary theory of aggregate demand.

The second topic, **B**, is the major part of this chapter and is divided into a series of subsidiary tasks which you should work through very carefully.

A. Aggregate Demand

Aggregate demand is the demand for goods and services in total. It is the *demand* for *aggregate output.*

The *aggregate demand function is defined as the relationship between the aggregate quantity of goods and services which people want to buy in a given period of time and the price level.*

The questions in which we shall be interested concerning the aggregate demand curve, are:

    1. What is the shape of the aggregate demand curve? Does it slope downwards? That is, would the level of aggregate demand rise if the price level fell?
    2. What variables cause the aggregate demand curve to shift? That is, what variables, other than the price level, cause aggregate demand to vary?

These two questions occupy the rest of this chapter.

B. The Monetary Theory of Aggregate Demand

This section introduces a variety of new concepts and is analytically fairly heavy. You are encouraged to work through the material several times, if necessary, in order to be sure that you have a thorough grasp of the monetary theory of aggregate demand. The starting point for understanding what determines aggregate demand is an analysis of the determination of the demand, not for goods, but for money.

(i) The Demand for Money[1]

First, what do we mean by the *demand for money*? You already know what money is: it is the *stock* of currency and demand deposits in existence at a given point in time. Most of us acquire money as a *flow* of income which, typically, is received at either weekly or monthly intervals. On payday, the amount of money that we are holding just before we are paid is at a minimum, and just after we have been paid, is at a maximum. In the period between the moment that we have been paid through to the next payday we typically spend our income gradually, thereby running down our money balances. Figure 10.1 illustrates the pattern of money holdings for an

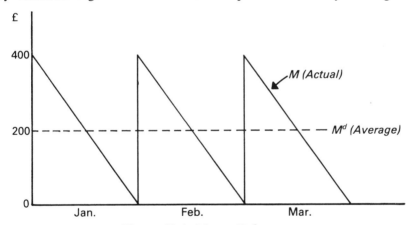

Figure 10.1 *Money Balances*

Actual money balances are at their peak at the beginning of each month and are gradually run down to their minimum as expenditure takes place throughout the month. The demand for money refers to the average money holdings (indicated in the diagram by the dashed line).

individual who receives an income of £400 per month at monthly intervals and who spends that £400 in equal daily amounts through the month. The sawtooth line shows the actual money holdings of that individual. Those money holdings are £400 at the beginning of each month and 0 at the end of each month. The broken line through the middle of the diagram shows the *average money holding* of this individual which, in

1. The analysis of the demand for money presented here is highly simplified. A comprehensive treatment of this topic may be found in David Laidler (1978) *The Demand for Money: Theories and Evidence*, 2nd edn (Harper and Row).

this case, is £200. It is the *average money holding* which we refer to as the individual's *demand for money*. The amount of money demanded is an *average stock*, and the income is a *flow*. Call the quantity of money demanded M^d (the superscript d on the M is to remind you that M^d is the *demand* for money), and call money income Py (the price level, P, multiplied by real income, y). Then let us *define the ratio of money demanded* (M^d) *to money income* (Py) as k. That is,

$$k = \frac{M^d}{Py} \tag{10.1}$$

The individual in the above example has an annual *income* of £4800 (£400 each month) and a *demand for money* of £200. For this individual, therefore, the ratio of average money holdings to money income is

$$k = \frac{£200}{£4800} = \frac{1}{24}$$

An alternative way of writing equation (10.1) would be (by multiplying both sides of the equation by Py) as

$$M^d = kPy \tag{10.2}$$

This says that the *demand for money* is some fraction k of money income. Let us give a name to k: we will call it *the propensity to hold money*.

The next question to be dealt with is, Will the propensity to hold money be constant? Put slightly differently, Would it make sense for individuals mechanically to hold money balances equal, on the average, to one-half of their periodic income? That is, would it make sense for an individual who is paid weekly to hold money balances equal, on the average, to one-half of a week's income, for a person who is paid monthly to hold money balances equal, on the average, to one-half of a month's income, etc.? In fact, for people paid at very frequent intervals, such as a week, it may well be that there is little else to be done than to hold money balances that roughly equal one-half a period's income. For such individuals, the propensity to hold money, k, would be 1/104. For those incomes which are received less frequently, however (and therefore in larger instalments), it would be sensible to attempt to *economise* on money holdings.

Consider the example of a person who receives £4800 a year, paid at quarterly intervals. Specifically, suppose a person receives £1200 on the 1st of January, April, July, and October. Would it make sense for such a person to run down his money balances at an even rate over each quarter? Notice that if such a person did spread his outlays evenly, the propensity to hold money would be 1/8. That is, on the average, one-eighth of a year's income would be held in the form of money. The average money holding of such a person would be £600. What could such a person do to economise on his money holdings? There are two possibilities; he could make a loan by buying and holding some financial asset other than money which, unlike money, pays interest. Alternatively, he could bunch the purchase of goods towards the beginning of the income period, thereby holding less money, on the average, and a higher average inventory of goods.

The higher is the rate of interest the more it will pay to lend unspent income, thereby lowering the propensity to hold money.

Also, the faster prices are rising, or equivalently, the higher is the rate of inflation, the more it will pay to bunch purchases of goods so that most goods are bought soon after payday. Equivalently, the higher is the rate of inflation, the lower will be the propensity to hold money. To see this point more clearly, suppose there is inflation going on at 10 per cent per annum. This will mean that over a three-month period the value of money, in terms of the goods and services that it will buy, will fall by (approximately) $2\frac{1}{2}$ per cent. If, instead of spending income evenly over the three-month period, a stock of goods was bought at the beginning of the period and then consumed during the period, the prices of the goods bought would be the January prices rather than the March prices and would therefore be some $2\frac{1}{2}$ per cent lower than those prevailing in March. It would therefore pay to stock up on all those items which are easily storable, thereby bunching expenditures into the early part of the income period. The effect of this, of course, would be to lower the amount of money balances which on the average are held. You can think of inflation as being a *tax on money holdings*, and the bringing forward of expenditures in time as a way of reducing the amount of the tax that the individual has to pay.

To summarise: there are two ways of economising on money holdings — making loans and buying real goods. Making loans earns interest, and buying goods avoids some of the loss in the value of money resulting from inflation. The higher are interest rates and the higher is the inflation rate, the more people will seek to economise on money holdings and the lower will be the propensity to hold money.

(ii) Interest Rates and Inflation

The next step in developing the monetary theory of aggregate demand is the simplified theory of the rate of interest.

The starting point of the simplified theory is an important definition which states that: *the rate of interest equals the rate of inflation plus the* **real** *rate of interest.*

The rate of interest actually paid and received is sometimes called the *money* (or, equivalently, *nominal) rate of interest*. This is to emphasise its distinction from the *real rate of interest*. The distinction between *real* and *money* (or *nominal*) interest is a vital and natural one. In an economy in which prices are rising by, say, 10 per cent a year, then money that is borrowed and lent will be losing value at the rate of 10 per cent a year. This means that someone who lends money for a year will, at the end of the year, be repaid in pounds that are worth 10 per cent less than the pounds that were lent. Similarly, the borrower will be repaying a loan with cheaper pounds. This lowering in the value of money — inflation — must be subtracted from the rate of interest — the *money* rate of interest — in order to calculate the interest rate *really* paid and received. All this can be summarised in two simple equations. Call the money rate of interest r_m and the real rate of interest r. Then, the money rate of interest is the sum of the real rate of interest and the rate of inflation, i.e.

$$r_m = r + \pi$$

and, equivalently the real rate of interest is the difference between the money rate of interest and the rate of inflation, i.e.

$$r = r_m - \pi$$

The next step in the simplified theory of interest is the proposition that *the real rate of interest is constant*.

This does not say that all borrowers and lenders will pay the same real rate of interest. Rather, it says that whatever real rate of interest prevails between a particular borrower and lender (which will vary across individuals), that *real rate of interest will not vary because of variations in the rate of inflation*.

The reasoning behind this proposition is that lenders will demand compensation for the loss in the value of the money they will receive when their loan is repaid, and borrowers, recognising that they are repaying loans with devalued money, will willingly pay the demanded compensation.

This means that according to this theory, each one per cent rise or fall in the rate of inflation will be associated with an equivalent one per cent rise or fall in rates of interest.

(iii) Inflation and the Demand for Money

Now that we have a theory about the determination of the rate of interest it is possible to return to the demand for money and make a simpler proposition about the determination of the propensity to hold money. The simplified theory of the rate of interest implies that although there are *two* ways of economising on money holdings — making loans and buying goods — there is only *one* factor which induces that economising — inflation.

The entire lengthy discussion may thus be summarised with the proposition: the *propensity to hold money* will vary *inversely* with the *rate of inflation*. We can write this as an equation which says

$$\frac{M^d}{Py} = k\ (\underset{(-)}{\pi})$$ (10.3)

where $k(\pi)$ stands for 'k is a function of — or depends on — π, the rate of inflation'. The minus sign $(-)$ below the equation is there to remind you that as inflation rises, the propensity to hold money *falls*. We can also illustrate the proposition in Figure 10.2. The downward sloping curve $\pi'k'$ shows how k rises as π falls. If inflation was as high as π', people would no longer want to use money, and trade would be undertaken with barter or some commodity means of exchange. If inflation was zero, then k would equal k'. Equivalently, we can write equation (10.3) in the form of (10.2), as

$$M^d = k\ (\underset{(-)}{\pi})\ Py$$ (10.4)

which says that the *demand for money* (M^d) is a function of (depends on) the level of *money income* (Py) and the *rate of inflation* (π). The minus sign $(-)$ below π in equation (10.4) is there to remind you that a *rise* in *inflation* has the effect of *lowering* the *demand for money*.

Notice that there is a crucial difference between the effect of *inflation* and the effect of the *price level* on the demand for money. If the *price level* doubled overnight, and if everything else (including the rate of inflation) remained the same, then the amount of money that people would want to hold would also double. Thus,

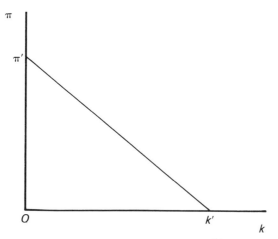

Figure 10.2 *The Propensity to Hold Money*
Inflation is a tax on money holdings. The higher is the tax — the higher is inflation — the more will people economise on their money holdings and the lower, therefore, will be the propensity to hold money.

---

the *demand for money is proportional to the level of prices*. This idea, that the amount of money demanded is proportional to the price level, enables us to make use of a simpler statement about the demand for money, based on a definition of *real money*. Real money is the quantity of money, (M), divided by the price level, (P). That is,

$$Real\ Money = \frac{M}{P}$$

You can express the demand for money as the demand for *real money*. The *demand for real money* depends on the level of *real income* and on the *rate of inflation*. The higher is the level of real income, the more real money will be demanded, and the higher is the rate of inflation, the smaller is the amount of real money demanded.

You can represent this in terms of a simple equation derived directly from equation (10.4), which says:

$$\frac{M^d}{P} = k\underset{(-)}{(\pi)}\, y \qquad\qquad\qquad (10.5)$$

For the rest of the material that we are covering in this chapter it is going to be a convenient simplification to suppose that the rate of inflation is constant. (We shall be dealing with varying inflation rates and the determination of inflation in Chapter 13.) It will also be convenient to set that constant inflation rate equal to zero for the moment so that the propensity to hold money is k' (see Figure 10.2) and the demand for real money is

$$\frac{M^d}{P} = k'y \qquad\qquad\qquad (10.6)$$

This simple theory of the demand for money is a central ingredient in developing the monetary theory of aggregate demand. Each individual decides how much money to demand in real terms, relative to his level of income. For the economy as a whole we may add up all the individual demands to arrive at the economy's aggregate demand for real money balances, which will depend on the economy's aggregate real income.

(iv) The Supply of Money

The stock of money in the economy is called the *supply of money*. That supply is determined by the actions of the central bank and the banking system, and this will be analysed in some detail in Chapter 36. For present purposes we shall treat the supply of money as being determined exogenously. The private individuals who hold the money have no control over what the supply of money will be. The *supply of money* will be called M.

When proper account is taken of the linkages between the domestic economy and the rest of the world, it is not always possible to regard the supply of money as determined exogenously. If the economy has a floating exchange rate, such an assumption may be in order. In the case of an economy with a fixed exchange rate, however, it is inappropriate to regard the money supply as being determined exogenously. For present purposes, therefore, you should regard the exercise that is being conducted as one which applies to an economy that does not have any trading links with the rest of the world, or you should regard it as applying to an economy that has a floating exchange rate. (The world as a whole is the only interesting example of an economy that does not have trading links with the rest of the world!)

Making the assumption that the supply of money, M, is exogenous, enables us to move on to examine how money market equilibrium determines the level of aggregate demand for goods and services.

(v) Money Market Equilibrium

Suppose that the supply of money was bigger than the amount of money which people wanted to hold. How would people react in such a situation? Since we are thinking of a competitive economy, there would be nothing that any individual could do, acting alone, to affect prices. All individuals are price takers. However, every individual has to make a decision about how much to spend. If the amount of money made available by the central bank was to exceed the amount of money that individuals wanted to hold, then the only remedy available *for the individual* would be to increase spending. What one individual spends, however, is the income received by other individuals. Therefore, if the amount of money in the economy exceeded the amount of money demanded, expenditure (and therefore income) would rise.

Conversely, if the amount of money made available by the central bank was less than the amount of money that people wanted to hold, then individuals would cut back their expenditures in order to replenish their money balances. Thus, if

$$M > M^d, \text{ then } Py \text{ will rise,}$$
$$\text{if } M < M^d, \text{ then } Py \text{ will fall,}$$
$$\text{and if } M = M^d, \text{ then } Py \text{ will be constant.}$$

Now although we have just conducted a conceptual experiment to analyse what would happen if the amount of money which people wanted to hold was different from the amount of money supplied, a moment's reflection will reveal that in the ordinary course of events these situations will not be observed. Individuals will not ordinarily be holding an excess or a deficiency of money, on the average. Rather, they will vary their expenditures in order to eliminate either a money balance deficiency or an excessive amount of money holdings. In the ordinary course of events, therefore, what we shall observe is a situation in which the amount of money which people want to hold is equal to the amount of money that the central bank has made available. That is

$$M = M^d \tag{10.7}$$

This is a situation of *money market equilibrium*.

Another analogy may be useful here. Suppose that the North Sea was arbitrarily divided by a straight line running north-south midway along its length. Now ask the question, What would happen if the water level on the left-hand side of this line was 10 feet higher than the water level on the right-hand side? This is a perfectly sensible question to ask. The answer is that the molecular structure of the water is such that the force of gravity would very quickly act upon the higher level to reduce it to equality with that of the lower level. We would never, in the ordinary course of events, observe such an inequality, although the theory that explains why the water surface is flat involves conceptually letting the level be temporarily and hypothetically perturbed. It is the same in the money market. The very forces that would lead to money market equilibrium will, in the ordinary course of events, prevent the money market from ever straying very far away from such an equilibrium.[2]

(vi) Aggregate Demand

We are now almost at the point of being able to derive the monetary theory of aggregate demand. With money market equilibrium we know that

$$M = M^d \tag{10.7}$$

We also know that the demand for money is

$$\frac{M^d}{P} = k'y \tag{10.6}$$

It follows, therefore, that

$$\frac{M}{P} = k'y \tag{10.8}$$

That is, we know that the amount of real money being held is, in equilibrium, going to be proportional to real income (continuing to assume for the present that the inflation rate is constant and zero).

---

2. David Hume first suggested this water level analogy. See his essay, Of the balance of trade, in *Essays: Moral, Political and Literary* (Oxford University Press, 1963), p. 317.

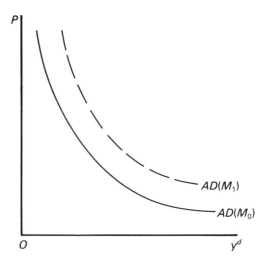

Figure 10.3 *The Aggregate Demand Curve*
The aggregate demand curve traces the relationship between output demanded and the price
level when people have equilibrium money holdings — when the supply of money equals the
demand for money. The aggregate demand curve has an elasticity of -1. The higher is the
stock of money the further to the right is the aggregate demand curve. The dashed curve is
associated with a bigger money stock than the continuous curve.

The *aggregate demand curve* is the relationship between the level of *planned real
expenditure* (= *real income* = *output*) and the *price level*. To find the *aggregate
demand curve* we want conceptually to let the price level vary, holding constant the
level of the money supply, and ask the question, How would the level of planned real
expenditure (= real income = output) vary in order to preserve money market
equilibrium as the price level varies? *Call the level of planned real expenditure* (= *real
income* = *output*), *which maintains money market equilibrium, the level of aggregate
demand* (denoted as y^d). The answer to the question just posed is obtained directly by
'solving' the money market equilibrium equation for the value of y^d as we
conceptually vary the price level P. That is,

$$y^d = \frac{1}{k'}\frac{M}{P} \tag{10.9}$$

You see immediately that *aggregate demand varies* **inversely** *with the price level*. You
also see that the relationship between aggregate demand and the price level is a very
simple one, having an *elasticity of minus one*. The aggregate demand equation (10.9)
is plotted in Figure 10.3 as the curve labelled AD.

You have now answered the first question posed at the beginning of this chapter.
That is, you have discovered that the aggregate demand curve slopes downwards,
indicating that aggregate demand rises as the price level falls. More precisely, you
have discovered that the elasticity of that demand curve is minus one.

The second question, what variables other than the price level cause aggregate
demand to vary, is easily answered. In this simple framework there is only one thing:
the money supply. The higher is the money supply, the higher is aggregate demand

or, equivalently, the further to the right is the aggregate demand curve. The curve labelled ADM_1 in Figure 10.3 illustrates the aggregate demand curve for higher money supply than in the case of the curve $AD(M_0)$.

To summarise: the monetary theory of aggregate demand is based on the idea that strong equilibrating forces ensure that the supply of money equals the amount of money demanded. This implies that for a given money supply, the amount of real goods and services demanded will fall as the price level rises and will, for a given price level, rise as the money supply rises.

SUMMARY

A. Aggregate Demand

Aggregate demand is the *demand for all goods and services* — the demand *for output*. The *aggregate demand curve* is the relationship between the *price level* and the *demand for output*.

B. The Monetary Theory of Aggregate Demand

The monetary theory of aggregate demand states that the level of aggregate demand will fall as the price level rises. It also states that aggregate demand will rise as the money supply rises. These propositions are derived from the assumption that the amount of money which people want to hold is proportional to the price level, rises as real income rises, and falls as the inflation rate rises. Equilibrating forces ensure that, in the normal course of events, the supply of money equals the demand for money and that the amount of goods and services demanded is proportional to the supply of real money balances.

Review Questions

1. What does the term aggregate demand mean?

2. What does the term demand for money mean?

3. Calculate your own average holding of money. What are the units of this quantity? Is it a stock or a flow?

4. Calculate your own demand for money.

5. Calculate your own propensity to hold money. What are the units of this quantity?

6. If the interval between when you are paid is lengthened (i.e., multiplied by 2 or 4) would your demand for money change? Explain why or why not.

7. Some people 'economise' on their money holdings. What does this mean? Explain why they would 'economise'.

8. If the inflation rate dropped to zero tomorrow and remained there, would your demand for money change? Explain why or why not.

9. If the inflation rate doubled tomorrow and remained at that level, would you 'economise' on your money holdings? Explain why or why not.

10. The propensity to hold money is related to the inflation rate. What is this relationship? Draw a diagram to illustrate this relationship.

11. What is the relationship between the demand for money and money income?

12. What is the relationship between the demand for money and the price level?

13. What is the relationship between the demand for money and real income?

14. What is money market equilibrium?

15. If the supply of money exceeded the demand for money, what would happen?

16. Explain the connection between aggregate demand and money market equilibrium.

17. Derive the relationship between aggregate demand and the price level. Draw the aggregate demand curve. Where, on this diagram, is the money market in equilibrium? Where is there excess demand for money and where is there excess supply?

18. What is the effect on the aggregate demand curve of a once-and-for-all rise in the money supply?

11

Equilibrium in the Basic Model

You have now studied the labour market and the determination of the aggregate supply of goods and services in the basic model. You have also studied the money market and the determination of aggregate demand. Your task now is to bring these two aspects of the basic model together and to see how the actual level of output, employment, real wages, and the price level are determined. This chapter builds on the presumption that you have understood the material contained in the two previous chapters. You may find it necessary to refer back from time to time to reinforce that understanding.

Your task in this chapter is to:

understand how the equality of aggregate supply and aggregate demand determines the level of output, employment, the real wage and the price level.

(i) Equilibrium

It is now possible to bring together the theory of aggregate supply and the monetary theory of aggregate demand to determine the price level and the level of output (real income). Figure 11.1 illustrates this. The curve AS is the aggregate supply curve derived from the theory of the competitive labour market (Chapter 9). The downward sloping curve labelled AD is the aggregate demand curve derived in Chapter 10. You will see that these curves cut at the point marked e. At this point, the price level is equal to P^*, and the value of output is equal to y^*. We call these values of the price level and output the *equilibrium values*. This is the point at which the economy will operate. To understand why this is so, consider what would happen if the economy were at some different point. For example, suppose the economy was at the point marked a in Figure 11.1. At the position marked a, the price level is P_1 and output is y_1. At that point, the level of output y_1 is bigger than the aggregate supply output level y^*, and the price level P_1 is higher than the equilibrium price level P^*. In

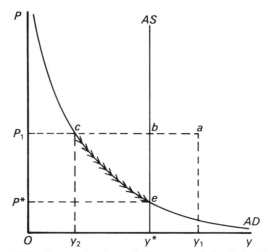

Figure 11.1 *The Determination of Output and the Price Level*
Equilibrium output and the price level are determined where the aggregate demand curve
(money market equilibrium) cuts the aggregate supply curve (labour market equilibrium). At
a point like a, (P_1, y_1), neither market is in equilibrium. At a point like b, the labour market
would be in equilibrium but the money market not. At a point like c, the money market would
be in equilibrium but the labour market not. Only at point e, (P^*, y^*), are both markets in
equilibrium.

a situation such as this, the labour market would not be in equilibrium. To produce
an output of y_1, either firms must employ more labour than the profit-maximising
quantity, or households must supply more labour than the quantity which maximises
utility. For the purpose of tracing a possible sequence of events starting from point a,
assume that the real wage is always at a level that ensures that the required supply of
labour is forthcoming. This would mean that, at point a individual producers would
not be making maximum profits. It would pay firms to cut back on their production.
They would do so until they had returned all the way to the level of output y^*. That is,
if the price level remained at P_1, firms would move back to the point marked b in the
diagram. At b producers would be unable to improve their situation in the sense that
they would be maximising profits and feel no need to take any further action. The
economy would still have forces operating upon it, however, that would move it from
point b. In particular, at point b there would not be enough money to sustain the level
of prices at P_1 and the level of output y^*. That is, the demand for money would still
exceed the supply of money, and individuals would seek to cut back on their
expenditure plans. At the price level P_1, people would only want to spend y_2. This is
shown as point c in the diagram. If, indeed, individuals did cut back their
expenditures all the way to point c, then producers would not be able to sell the
output y^* that maximises their profits.

   Thus, at the price level P_1, there would be an excess supply of goods and services in
the economy. The supply which would maximise producers' profits, y^*, exceeds the
demand that would be forthcoming, y_2. This excess supply would drive down the
price level as firms sought to sell their outputs for a slightly lower price than that
prevailing. This process would go on until the price level had moved down to P^*, at
which point there would be sufficient money balances to sustain the level of prices

and the level of real economic activity. At P^*, producers are maximising their profits so that there is nothing further that they can do to improve their situation. In short, the point e, with income at y^* and the price level at P^*, is the only point at which there are no incentives for individuals to change their behaviour.

It is the essence of the equilibrium theory that the equilibrating process, as described in the above story, that would lead the economy from any hypothetical point such as a or b or c to the equilibrium e is so strong and rapid that we would never observe the economy at points like a or b or c. *Only the equilibrium is observed.*

This is the basic model of the determination of output and the price level. Subsequent chapters in this part will examine what happens when there are changes in the economy which lead to a change in the equilibrium. The theory will be used to analyse the effects of certain policy actions on the levels of output and prices.

Implicit in the above analysis has been the determination of the level of employment. If you go back to Chapter 9 you will see that a given level of output implies a given level of employment and, by combining the aggregate demand and aggregate supply analysis contained in Figure 11.1 above with the analysis contained in Figure 9.7, you can determine all the variables that have so far been introduced into the analysis, namely, output (real income), employment, the real wage, and the price level.

(ii) Summary of the Basic Model of Output, Employment, the Real Wage, and the Price Level

Frame (b) of Figure 11.2 shows the *aggregate production function* — the relationship between output, y, and the level of employment, n. Frame (a) shows the *competitive labour market*. The demand for labour curve, labelled n^d, comes from the profit-maximising decisions of competitive producers. The labour supply curve, labelled n^s, comes from the utility-maximising decisions of households. (Remember that n is the number of workers and not the number of man-hours. As the real wage rises we are assuming that more and more people make an all-or-nothing choice to become workers. As n varies we suppose there is no variation in hours per worker, but a variation in the number of workers, each working a fixed number of hours.) The labour market is assumed to equilibrate. That is, the forces of supply and demand are assumed to be strong enough to bring about a *real wage* that makes the *demand for labour equal to the supply of labour*. The labour market will settle down at the point indicated by n^* (which denotes equilibrium employment) and $(W/P)^*$ which denotes the equilibrium real wage.

From the equilibrium level of employment determined in Frame (a) you can work out the value of the equilibrium level of output (real income) by using the production function shown in Frame (b). By transferring the equilibrium level of output shown on the vertical axis of Frame (b) to the horizontal axis of Frame (c) (follow the dotted line), the *aggregate supply curve* may be derived. This is shown as the vertical line in Frame (c), labelled *AS*. This is the relationship between the *price level* and the level of *output* that profit-maximising producers will want to supply.

The model is completed by the *monetary theory of aggregate demand* (Chapter 10) which predicts the rectangular hyperbola relationship between the price level and output (real income), labelled *AD*. This curve traces out those levels of prices and

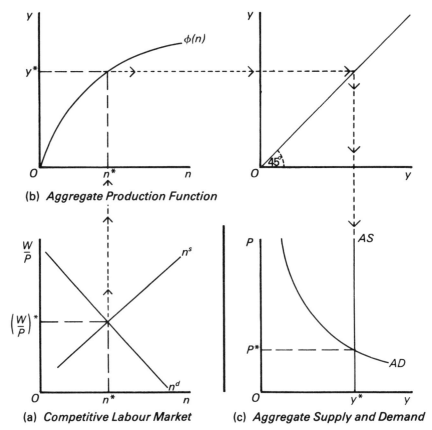

Figure 11.2 *Summary of the Basic Model of Output, Employment, the Real Wage, and the Price Level*

Equilibrium in the labour market (Frame (a)) determines the level of employment and real wage at which both firms are maximising profits and households maximising utility. The equilibrium level of employment generates, through the short-run production function, the equilibrium level of aggregate supply, y^*. This is the equilibrium level of output. The price level is determined by the point at which the aggregate demand curve cuts the aggregate supply curve — the point P^* in Frame (c).

output which ensure an equilibrium in the money market. At the combinations of the price level and output traced out by that curve, the amount of money demanded is equal to the supply of money.

Where the aggregate demand curve (which represents monetary equilibrium) cuts the aggregate supply curve (which represents labour market equilibrium), the price level at which all markets are simultaneously in equilibrium is determined.

SUMMARY

When the amount of money which people wish to hold is equal to the money supply and when producers are unable to increase their profits by changing their output and employment, then the economy is in equilibrium. It is the essence of the basic model that the equilibrating forces are sufficiently strong for the economy normally to be observed only at an equilibrium.

Review Questions

1. When aggregate demand and aggregate supply are equal the economy is in equilibrium. Explain exactly which markets are in equilibrium. Are households maximising their utility? Are firms maximising profits? Explain why or why not.

2. At the equilibrium level of output, but at a price level which exceeds its equilibrium level, is there an excess supply, excess demand, or equilibrium in the markets for goods, money, and labour?

3. At the equilibrium price level, but at a level of output which is less than the equilibrium level, is there an excess demand, excess supply, or equilibrium in the markets for goods, labour, and money? If, for some market or markets, you cannot determine whether there is excess demand or excess supply, state what extra information would be needed to resolve the ambiguity.

4. What is the effect of a once-and-for-all rise in the money supply on the price level, output, employment, unemployment, and the real wage?

5. What is the effect of technological improvement which raises the productivity of labour on the price level, output, employment, unemployment, and the real wage?

6. If the income payment interval for all households was quadrupled, would there be any effect on the price level, output, employment, unemployment, and the real wage? Use a diagram to illustrate your answer.

12

Unemployment

You do not need reminding that unemployment is an important problem in the United Kingdom at the present time. In December 1981, the number of unemployed exceeded three million, higher than at any time since the years of the Great Depression. Further, as you saw in Chapter 2, there has been a tendency for the unemployment rate to trend upwards throughout the entire post-war period.

The objective of this chapter is to help you to understand some of the reasons why unemployment exists, why it persists, and why it has increased over the post-war years.

Chapters 9, 10, and 11 developed the basic model designed to explain the determination of the level of output, employment, the real wage and the price level. That model is now going to be used to analyse the effects of minimum wage laws, trade unions, unemployment benefits, and employment taxes and income taxes on the level of employment and unemployment. In the next chapter the model will be used to analyse the effects of these same things on the level of prices; we shall also, in the next chapter, analyse the effects of changes in the money supply on prices.

The rest of this chapter will help you to understand some of the reasons why unemployment arises and what leads to variations in its rate.

You have four tasks which are to:

A. **understand how minimum wage laws create unemployment;**
B. **understand how trade unions raise wages and create unemployment;**
C. **understand how unemployment benefit schemes create unemployment;**
   and
D. **understand how taxes create unemployment.**

In Chapter 15 you will have an opportunity to review the importance of the last three of these factors in recent United Kingdom history. For the time being you will find it best to concentrate on the mechanics of the theory.

A. Minimum Wage Laws and Unemployment

There are no explicitly legislated minimum wage regulations in the United Kingdom. In many countries, however, such laws have been enacted. Even though such laws do not exist in the United Kingdom, an analysis of how minimum wages create unemployment provides a useful starting point from which to move on to analyse other factors which are present in the United Kingdom and which influence the rate of unemployment.

What are the effects of minimum wages on the level of output, employment, unemployment, and the real wage?

The starting point is to recognise that minimum wages are determined by government regulation at a level higher than that which would prevail in competitive labour markets. The minimum wage is set in terms of so many pounds per hour — that is, it is set as a *money wage*. The money wage is revised from time to time, however, and it is clear that what the legislators have in mind is the establishment of a *minimum real wage* which is above the *competitive equilibrium real wage*.

It is clear that minimum real wages do not *directly* affect a very large fraction of the labour force. They impinge directly only upon those workers who would otherwise have been paid a wage below the minimum. However, *they do affect* the *economy average real wage,* for two reasons. First, since the economy average real wage is simply a weighted average of all the individual real wages, there is automatically a rise in the economy average real wage resulting from chopping off the bottom end of the wage distribution (those wages that would be lower than the minimum wage). In addition, however, there will be a rise in the economy average real wage as a result of competitive pressures. If the lowest income workers are paid a higher wage than the competitive market would pay, there will be pressure to raise other wages as well. On the supply side, there will be a tendency for people to try to substitute away from slightly higher-paid but more demanding jobs and enter those jobs that now attract the minimum wage rate. On the demand side, firms will substitute more expensive (but more productive) grades of labour for those grades of labour whose prices have been increased by the minimum wage regulation. These shifts of supply towards lower productivity jobs and of demand towards higher grades of labour will put upward pressure on real wages all the way up the scale (with the pressure of course diminishing as you move further up the income scale).

For these two reasons, then: (a) chopping off the bottom end of the wage distribution, and (b) the competitive pressures pushing up the real wages in substitute activities, *the imposition of a minimum wage will raise the economy average real wage above the competitive equilibrium level.* The higher is the minimum wage relative to the competitive equilibrium wage, the bigger will be the rise in the economy average real wage relative to its competitive equilibrium.

It is now possible to analyse the effects of minimum wages. We may conduct the analysis in Figure 12.1. The vertical axis of Figure 12.1 measures the economy average real wage (W/P) and the horizontal axis measures the aggregate level of employment, n. The curves labelled n^d and n^s are the labour demand and supply curves, respectively. The competitive equilibrium in this labour market is the real wage $(W/P)^*$ and the employment level n^*.

Now suppose that a minimum wage is established which has the effect of raising the

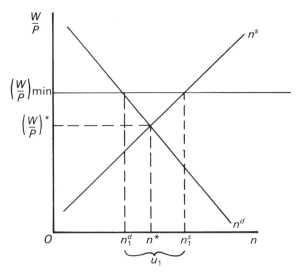

Figure 12.1 *How Minimum Wages Create Unemployment*
A minimum wage set higher than the competitive equilibrium wage creates a regulated
equilibrium at which the quantity of labour employed is equal to the quantity demanded n_1^d,
which is less than the quantity supplied n_1^s. The gap between the quantity supplied and
demanded u_1 measures the quantity of unemployment.

economy average real wage to the level marked in Figure 12.1 as (W/P) min. What is
the effect of this minimum wage law?

In a market economy in which all exchange is voluntary, no one can compel
employers to hire more workers than they choose to hire. At the minimum wage the
demand for labour is less than the supply of labour. It is therefore the demand curve
for labour which will determine how much labour is employed. The level of
employment will be n_1^d. This is the amount read off from the demand curve at the
average real wage induced by the minimum wage legislation. The supply of labour at
that wage rate will be n_1^s.

The gap between the supply of labour n_1^s and the demand for labour n_1^d represents
the number of people who will be unemployed, u_1. If you recall the definition of
unemployment and the way in which unemployment is measured in the United
Kingdom, you will verify that the people in the group u_1 will be recorded as
unemployed. When registered, they will show up as being available for work,
capable of work, but not having work. The higher is the minimum wage relative to
the competitive equilibrium wage, the greater will be the reduction in employment,
the larger will be the supply of labour, and the greater will be the amount of
unemployment created.

The economy will now be in a *regulated equilibrium*. It is important to realise that
an *equilibrium* is nothing more than a *state of rest*, or equivalently, a *state in which all
the forces acting on a variable exactly offset each other*. One of the forces acting on the
economy in this case is the minimum wage regulation, and so the real wage and
employment level come to rest at a point different from the *competitive equilibrium*
which they would reach in the absence of the regulation.

If you recall the water level analogy (Chapter 10), a minimum wage regulation is like a dam which alters the equilibrium levels of water on either side of it.

To summarise: a minimum wage which raises the economy average real wage above its competitive equilibrium level will generate a regulated equilibrium in which there is lower employment, a larger labour supply, and persistent unemployment.

B. Trade Unions and Unemployment

Trade unions are a dominant institution in the labour market. They act as an agent for households in the negotiation of employment and wage contracts. A much larger fraction of the labour force works on contracts negotiated by unions than are members of unions. In analysing the effects of unions on the macroeconomic variables it will be convenient to proceed in two steps. First, we will analyse the effect of an economy-wide union — one that embraces the entire labour force; and secondly, we will analyse the effects of unions in an economy where there is a non-union as well as union sector in the labour market.

(i) An Economy-Wide Union

The economy will be described using Figure 12.2. First, focus your attention on the competitive equilibrium. The curves labelled n^d and n^s are the demand and supply curves (identical to those in Figure 12.1), and the real wage $(W/P)^*$ and the

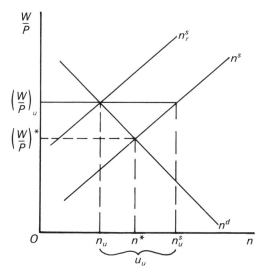

Figure 12.2 *Labour Market Equilibrium with an Economy-Wide Union*

An economy-wide union would either restrict the supply of labour below the competitive supply, n^s_r, or would raise the wage rate above the competitive equilibrium rate, $(W/P)_u$. The effect would be the same in either case. It would lower the quantity of employment from n^* to n_u, but raise the supply from n^* to n^s_u. The gap between the quantity of labour supplied and demanded would be the amount of union-induced unemployment, u_u.

employment level n^* are the competitive equilibrium values for those variables. Now suppose that all the workers in this economy join an economy-wide trade union which seeks to raise real wages.

There are two types of things that the trade union could do in order to raise the real wages of its members. One possibility would be to declare that no one may work for a real wage of less than, say, $(W/P)_u$ and to enforce that either by having some sort of legal power or by using more indirect pressures.

Alternatively, the union could restrict the supply of labour by, for example, defining minimum acceptable qualifications for particular jobs such that the number of people able to meet the minimum qualifications was less than the labour supply in the absence of the union. In that event supply would be artificially restricted, and the supply curve would move to the left of the non-union supply curve.

Either way, the result would be a higher real wage and a lower level of employment. Figure 12.2 illustrates this. In examining Figure 12.2 keep the competitive equilibrium firmly in mind as a reference point. If the union declares a *minimum wage*, below which no one can be employed, of (say) $(W/P)_u$, we can illustrate this by recording that wage on the vertical axis of the figure, above the competitive equilibrium real wage. Then, simply by reading off from the demand for labour curve you can see that at the real wage $(W/P)_u$ the level of employment becomes n_u. This is less than the competitive employment level n^*. At the real wage set by the union, n_u^s people would like to have a job, and the difference between n_u^s and n_u represents the level of unemployment induced by this economy-wide trade union.

If, alternatively, the union enforced *minimum qualifications* which had the effect of shifting the labour supply curve to the left to a position such as that shown as n_r^s, this would have the effect of raising wages and lowering employment. (The diagram is drawn so that the same effect arises from either of these policies. This has been done only to simplify the diagram. There is no presumption that both union strategies would have exactly the same effect.)

In this case the people unemployed are unemployed because they do not meet the minimum qualification standards for the job. This can often be made to look semi-respectable, for example, by dressing up the restriction as 'protecting the consumer', and is therefore a much more commonly employed practice among trade unions than that of simply declaring that no one may work for less than a certain wage. It is especially widely practised by professional unions such as those in the legal and medical industries. It is an easier restriction to enforce.

Either way, whether it sets a minimum real wage or restricts supply, an economy-wide trade union will have the same kind of effect on employment and real wages as would a government-enforced minimum wage law. The economy-wide union will raise the real wage above its competitive equilibrium level, will lower the level of employment, raise the supply of labour, and generate unemployment. The greater the ability of the union to raise the real wage above the competitive equilibrium level, the bigger these effects will be.

(ii) An Economy with a Union and a Non-Union Sector

Analysing the effects of trade unions in an economy where the unions do not control the entire labour force and where there is a non-union sector is not quite as straightforward as the case that we have just dealt with. By working carefully through this section, however, it will be possible for you to get a good understanding of how unions operate in this case and what their macroeconomic effects will be. Figure 12.3 is going to be the vehicle through which you gain your understanding, and it will be described to you in stages.

First of all, imagine that the economy can be divided into two identical sectors, so that we can represent the labour market of the economy with two diagrams that are identical to each other. This is a fiction, of course, but one which makes the understanding of the principles clearer. Frames (a) and (b) represent these two sectors. The aggregate labour market (the sum of the two sectors) is shown in Frame (c). If you ignore the curve n_r^s in Frame (a) and the curve n_s^s in Frame (b) you will see that a competitive equilibrium is shown in the three separate parts of that figure. Each labour market is in equilibrium and each has an identical real wage and employment level.

Now suppose a trade union gets established in one of these markets (that shown in Frame (a)) and establishes some minimum qualifications for employment in that part of the economy. Suppose the effect of that is to shift the effective labour supply curve in the union sector leftwards, so that it is represented by the curve n_r^s. The real wage in the union sector and the level of employment will now move to $(W/P)_u$ and n_u, as indicated in Frame (a). Thus, in the union sector the real wage will rise and the level of employment will fall. That is not, however, the end of the story. The people who do not qualify for work in the union sector now that the qualifications have been increased by the union will *spill over* into the non-union sector. The supply curve in the non-union sector will therefore shift rightwards by an amount equal to the leftward shift of the supply curve in the union sector. This is shown as the supply curve n_s^s in Frame (b). The real wage in the non-union sector will now fall, and the number of people employed in that sector will rise to the amounts shown as $(W/P)_s$ and n_s in Frame (b).

From a macroeconomic point of view, (Frame (c)), *nothing has happened in this economy.* The real wage, on the average, will still be $(W/P)^*$, and the level of employment will still be n^*. The union has simply redistributed income away from non-union workers towards union workers. No employment is created. All that the unions have done is to redistribute incomes.

To summarise: an economy-wide trade union which restricts the supply of labour, or raises the real wage above the competitive equilibrium level by other means, will lower the aggregate level of employment and raise the level of unemployment. A union which does not control the entire economy will have the effect of raising the real wages of unionised workers and lowering the real wages of non-union workers, leaving the macroeconomic magnitudes — the average real wage and the average levels of employment and unemployment — undisturbed.

You will now be able to understand better why minimum wage laws are so popular, especially among trade union leaders. If a trade union behaved in the way described in the above section, raising the wages of its own members at the expense of the wages of non-members, it would become extremely unpopular. Trade unions therefore lobby for minimum wage regulations. These have the effect, of course, as we analysed in Section A above, of creating unemployment. However, it is possible to blame the unemployment on the selfishness of the employer for refusing to pay a decent living wage, or on the incompetence of the government in failing to provide an

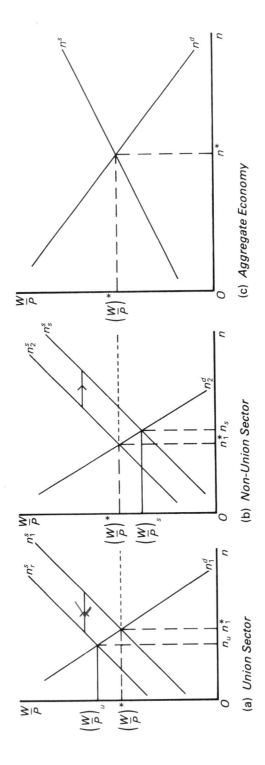

Figure 12.3 *An Economy with a Union and a Non-Union Sector*

The union restricts the supply of labour n_r^s or raises the union wage rate above the competitive rate $(W/P)_u$ (Frame (a)). This results in a drop in employment in the union sector from n_1^* to n_u. Those who cannot find work in the union sector spill over to the non-union sector, shifting the supply curve there from n_2^s to n_s^s. The result is a drop in the real wage below the competitive equilibrium level and a rise in employment. In this example, *aggregate* employment and *average* real wages remain unchanged (Frame (c)).

adequate level of overall demand. This diverts the attention from the unions as the villains that they are and, indeed, because they are pressing for better wages and working conditions for the poorest members of the labour force, makes them look highly virtuous.

C. Unemployment Benefits and Unemployment

(i) Job Search Unemployment

As a prelude to analysing the effects of unemployment benefits, it is necessary to introduce the idea of *job search*. People allocate their time to three major economic activities: *work, leisure,* and *job search.*

Jobs cannot be found without search, and search is costly. It is useful to think of job search as being an *investment*. There is a cost and an expected return. The higher is the expected return or payoff, the bigger will be the amount of job search activity undertaken.

Much job searching is done on a casual basis while a person is employed. Some job searchers, however, specialise in searching; that is, they cease to be workers for a period in which they spend all their non-leisure time in job search activities. These job searchers are interesting from a macroeconomic point of view for they will be *recorded as unemployed.*

For a given cost of job search it seems reasonable to suppose that the larger is the labour force, the greater will be the number of people engaged in full-time job search. Further, the higher is the real wage, the bigger is the labour force. We would suppose, therefore, that the supply of job search is related to the real wage in the manner shown in Figure 12.4.

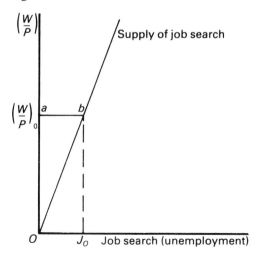

Figure 12.4 *The Supply of Job Search*

Job search is an alternative activity to working and consuming leisure. The higher is the real wage, the more people will join the pool of job searchers. At the real wage $(W/P)_0$, J_0 workers will join the labour force and search for jobs.

If the real wage rate was $(W/P)_0$, there would be J_0 full-time job searchers recorded as unemployed (equivalently shown as the distance ab).

Next, let us distinguish between the *supply of labour* and the *labour force*. Define the *labour force* as the *supply of labour* plus *the supply of job search*. Define the *supply of labour* as the number of people who, at a given real wage, are willing to supply their labour services to full-time employment.

Figure 12.5 shows how these magnitudes will be related to the real wage. The curve n^s is the supply curve which was used in the above analysis. It shows at each real wage the number of people available for work instantaneously, without further search. Adding horizontally to that curve the amount of job search that would be undertaken at each real wage gives the labour force (the curve *lf*). This shows the total number of people available for work right now, plus the total number of people at each real wage who will still be searching for a job. The distance ab in Figure 12.5 is equivalent to the distance ab in Figure 12.4. Thus, the curve *lf* simply adds the supply of job search curve to the supply of labour curve. If the real wage was $(W/P)_0$ the supply of labour would be n_0, and the labour force would be l_0.

The vertical distances ac and bd are interesting economic magnitudes. The marginal person in employment (the last person to become employed at the employment level n_0) who is just willing to work for the wage rate $(W/P)_0$ is on the margin of indifference between accepting a job and continuing to search for a job. If the real wage was marginally below $(W/P)_0$, that person would quit and start to search for a new job. The distance ac measures the value which that marginal worker places upon job search.

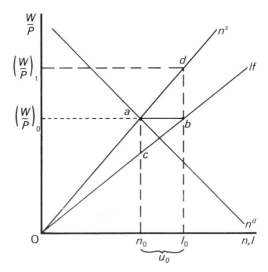

Figure 12.5 *Equilibrium Employment, Unemployment, and Real Wage*
If the supply of job search is added to the supply of labour n^s the labour force supply curve *lf* is derived. (The distance ab in Figure 12.5 is the same as the distance ab in Figure 12.4.) With the demand curve n^d the equilibrium is at $(W/P)_0$ and n_0. The labour force at that equilibrium wage will be l_0 and the unemployed job searchers will be u_0. The length ac measures the value placed on job search by the last person to be employed. The real wage would have to drop by ac to induce that person to leave the labour force. The length db measures the value placed on job search by the last person to join the labour force. The real wage would have to rise by db to $(W/P)_1$ to induce that person to take a job.

There is another margin, that between being in the labour force and not being in the labour force. That individual is at l_0. At a real wage $(W/P)_0$ such an individual feels that it is just worthwhile searching for a job. The value which that individual places upon job search is the distance db. A real wage equal to $(W/P)_1$ would be necessary to induce that marginal worker to actually accept a job instantaneously with no further search.

It is important that you realise that the labour market as depicted in Figure 12.5 is not in a static state, with a certain number of people being permanently employed and another group being permanently unemployed. Rather, there is a continuous turnover, with people quitting jobs to search for new ones, other people entering the labour force to search for jobs, yet others leaving the labour force, and yet others being hired. Thus, the flows of hires and quits will be matched, and the flows of people into and out of the labour force will be balanced, so that the individuals involved are continuously in a state of flux, although the economy, on the average, is in the position shown in Figure 12.5.

Given the demand curve, n^d, the real wage $(W/P)_0$ will be the competitive equilibrium real wage, and the economy will be in an equilibrium characterised by less than complete knowledge about job opportunities, so that there is a need for people to search for jobs. The labour force will be l_0, the employment level n_0, and there will be u_0 unemployed job searchers.

(ii) How Unemployment Benefits Affect the Level of Employment, Unemployment, and the Real Wage

Suppose the government introduces an unemployment benefits scheme which makes it possible for people, while searching for a new job, to receive an income from the government equal to some fraction of the wage which they had previously been earning while employed. What effects would this have?

It is immediately clear that such a policy would lower the cost of job search. It would therefore make job search activity at the margin more attractive. You have already seen that there are two relevant margins of job search. One is the margin between search and employment, the other is the margin between job search and complete leisure (withdrawal from the labour force). Improving unemployment benefits would alter both of these margins. There would be a tendency for people to search longer before accepting employment, thereby lowering the amount of work that people in aggregate would be willing to do at any given real wage. This would have the effect of rotating the labour supply curve n^s upwards. This is shown in Figure 12.6 as the movement from n_0^s to n_1^s. Additionally, people who previously were not in the labour force will now be induced to enter the labour force, take a temporary job to qualify for earnings-related unemployment benefits, and thereafter search for a more acceptable long-term job.

There will therefore be a rotation of the labour force curve in a rightward direction. This again is illustrated in Figure 12.6 as the movement from lf_0 to lf_1. The curves n_0^s and lf_0 and the equilibrium $(W/P)_0$ and n_0 represent the economy with no unemployment benefits scheme and are the same as those illustrated in Figure 12.5. The curves n_1^s and lf_1 represent the new labour supply and labour force curves induced by an unemployment benefits scheme.

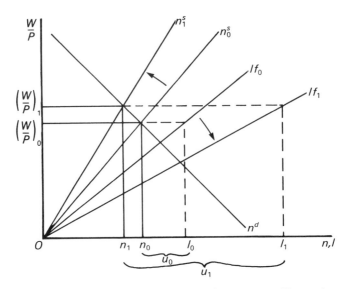

Figure 12.6 *How Unemployment Benefits Increase Unemployment*
Unemployment benefits make job search a more attractive activity relative to either working or consuming leisure. The supply of labour falls from n_0^s to n_1^s and raises the labour force supply curve from lf_0 to lf_1. The real wage rises, the unemployment level falls, the labour force rises, and the number of unemployed rises.

It is now possible to read off the effects of an unemployment benefits scheme on the variables. The labour market will be in equilibrium at the real wage $(W/P)_1$ and the employment level n_1. The labour force will rise to l_1 and unemployment will be $u_1 = l_1 - n_1$. Thus, an unemployment benefits scheme raises the real wage, lowers the level of employment, raises the size of the labour force, and increases the number of unemployed.

The analysis that has just been conducted has ignored the question of who pays the taxes that provide the unemployment benefits. The next section of this chapter will go on to analyse the effects of employment taxes and income taxes on the level of employment, unemployment and real wages. This analysis applies more generally than to taxes used to pay unemployment benefits. It applies to any taxes. The analysis just conducted may be augmented by the analysis of the effects of taxes to which we shall now turn.

D. Taxes and Unemployment

It will be convenient, in analysing the effects of taxes, to abstract from the considerations of job search that were the central feature of the analysis of the previous section. This is not to say that the above analysis is irrelevant when

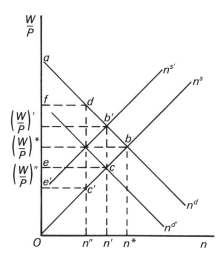

Figure 12.7 *The Effects of Taxes on the Labour Market*

A competitive equilibrium is shown at the real wage $(W/P)^*$ and employment level n^*. That equilibrium is disturbed by the introduction of a tax on labour income or by a tax on consumption which shifts the labour supply curve to $n^{s'}$. The real wage rises to $(W/P)'$ and employment falls to n'. After-tax wages fall. Alternatively, the equilibrium is disturbed by the introduction of an employment tax that shifts the labour demand curve down to $n^{d'}$. Again the level of employment falls to n' and wages become $(W/P)''$ equivalent to the after-tax wage level of e in the previous experiment. Both sets of taxes introduced together lower the level of employment to n''. As taxes on employment are successively increased, labour's share in national income (defined to include the taxes) increases, while the share accruing to the owners of capital decreases.

---

considering the effects of taxes. It is simply a convenient way of considering one thing at a time. Once you have thoroughly mastered the material in this and the preceding sections it will be a straightforward matter for you to consider both effects simultaneously. There is no gain, however, from presenting them as a simultaneous analysis.

The questions that we want to address now are: first, what are the effects of income taxes — taxes on labour income — on real wages, employment and unemployment? Secondly, what are the effects of employment taxes — taxes on firms that vary with the number of workers they employ — on the level of employment, unemployment and real wages? And thirdly, what are the effects of expenditure taxes — taxes on consumption — on the level of employment, unemployment and real wages?

As a starting point let us begin with an economy that has no taxes and then consider what happens as we introduce these alternative taxes first separately and secondly simultaneously. Figure 12.7 will illustrate the analysis. The curves labelled n^s and n^d are the supply and demand curves for labour in a world in which there are no taxes. The competitive equilibrium in that economy is at point b where the real wage is $(W/P)^*$ and the employment level is n^*. This is exactly the position shown as the competitive equilibrium in Figure 12.1 with which we started this analysis of the labour market.

There is one additional thing which you can work out about the economy to which attention has not been drawn previously but which is of some interest for the purpose of the present exercise. That is, the distribution of national income between labour and the owners of capital. Labour income will be equal to the rectangle $O(W/P)^*bn^*$. You can readily verify that this is so by noting that the number of workers is n^* and the wage per worker is $(W/P)^*$, so that labour income, being the product of employment and wages, is given by the area of that rectangle. The income accruing to the owners of capital is the triangle $(W/P)^*ab$. This is a less obvious proposition than the previous one. You may, however, verify that that triangle represents that part of total product not paid to labour. To do this, begin by recalling that the demand for labour curve measures the marginal product of labour. Thus, the first worker taken on would produce a marginal product of a (that is, where the demand curve hits the real wage axis). As more and more workers are taken on so the marginal product declines until the final worker is taken on at the equilibrium level of employment n^* by which time the marginal product has fallen to b. For each extra worker taken on, the extra output produced is equal to the marginal product and so, the total product accruing to the producer is given by the entire area underneath the marginal product curve all the way up to the level of employment n^*. Total product in the economy, then, is the trapezium $Oabn^*$. That which is paid to labour is $O(W/P)^*bn^*$ and that which is paid to the owners of capital is $(W/P)^*ab$. (In the economy shown in Figure 12.7, labour gets $\frac{2}{3}$ and capital $\frac{1}{3}$ of the economy's output.)

Now consider the introduction of an income tax. Instead of keeping all the wages they earn, workers now have to pay some fraction of their labour income to the government in the form of a tax. This means that for any given real wage paid by employers, the wage received by the worker is being reduced. Assuming, as we are, that a higher real wage always brings forth a higher supply of labour, this will imply that for any given real wage paid by the firm there will now be a drop in the supply of labour. This can be represented by shifting the labour supply curve to the left. For simplicity, Figure 12.7 has been drawn on the presumption that the labour supply curve shift is a parallel one, so that the new curve after allowing for taxes is the one labelled $n^{s'}$. The way to read $n^{s'}$ is as follows: for any given level of employment, without taxes, the wage that would have to be paid would be read off from the n^s curve; with the taxes in place however, the wage that would have to be paid to call forth an equivalent level of employment would be read off from the higher curve $n^{s'}$. To determine the equilibrium in this case we have to find the point where the new effective labour supply curve $n^{s'}$ intersects the demand for labour curve n^d. This occurs at the point b' with a real wage equal to $(W/P)'$ and an employment level n'. Thus, the real wage has risen and the employment level has fallen as a result of the introduction of a tax on labour income. The after-tax income of workers will have fallen from a wage rate of $(W/P)^*$ to a wage rate given by the position e on the vertical axis. In fact, total wages will be $Oecn'$. The tax receipts of the government will be $e(W/P)'b'c$ and the income accruing to capital will be the triangle $(W/P)'ab'$. The overall effects, then, of the imposition of a tax on labour income are for there to be a drop in after-tax wages, a rise in pre-tax wages, a fall in labour income, a rise in the government's income and a fall in the income accruing to the owners of capital. There is also a fall in the level of employment.

The drop in employment from n^* to n' cannot, properly speaking, be regarded as unemployment. Although there are fewer people in employment in the situation n' as compared with n^*, the situation that prevails is a competitive equilibrium. It may, nevertheless, be the case that the workers who withdraw from the labour force as the effective wage rate falls from $(W/P)^*$ to e, will be entitled to unemployment benefits and will, therefore, appear to swell the ranks of the unemployed, if not forever, at least for a period equal in length to the duration of unemployment benefits. In this sense the raising of taxes on labour income can be said to 'create unemployment'.

Let us next consider the effects of imposing a tax on the other side of the labour market — on the employers. Imagine that firms have to pay a tax on each worker that they employ. This will mean that the firm no longer regards the marginal product of labour as being equivalent to the value of labour. Rather, firms will regard labour as being worth its marginal product minus the tax that it has to pay on each worker employed. This means that the demand for labour curve will shift downwards. The curve $n^{d'}$ illustrates such a demand curve. What will be the effect of this tax on employment, unemployment and wages? Let us first answer this question in the absence of income taxes. In that case, the new equilibrium will be where the curve $n^{d'}$ cuts the original supply curve n^s. That occurs at the wage rate $(W/P)'' = e$ and at the employment level n'. Notice that this experiment has been set up so as to yield an identical amount of revenue for the government as the income tax did in the previous experiment. In principle, we could analyse cases where different amounts of revenue are raised. It does, however, seem to be more instructive to hold the government revenue constant for the purpose of comparing the effects of alternative taxes. It is now possible to read off all the effects of this employment tax on the level of employment and wages. These effects are, evidently, exactly the same as in the previous case. Employment falls from n^* to n', the share of labour in national income falls to the same level as before, namely, $Oecn'$, the government revenue is exactly the same as before, as also is the share of income accruing to the owners of capital. The only difference between the two cases is that the wages paid by firms fall and firms pay the taxes to the government. In the first experiment conducted the wages paid by firms increased, but after workers had paid their taxes, the effective, net of tax wage decreased. Workers had exactly the same net of tax income in the previous situation as they do in this one.

Next, consider what happens when taxes are imposed on the expenditure on consumer goods by workers. From the perspective of the analysis conducted here, this will have identical effects to the first tax analysed — a tax on labour income. The easiest way to see this is to see the way in which both income taxes and expenditure taxes affect the relative price between labour and consumption. Equivalently, we may ask how income taxes and expenditure taxes affect the rate at which labour may be traded for consumption goods. The wage rate that a worker receives is equal to the gross wage paid, scaled down by the income taxes levied by the government. Suppose that we call the income tax rate t_y. Then, the effective wage rate is $W(1 - t_y)$. When a worker purchases consumer goods the price paid is equal to the price received by the producer, P, plus any taxes levied by the government. Call the rate of tax on expenditure t_c. This means that the price paid by the consumer will be equal to $P(1 + t_c)$. Evidently, the ratio of the price received by the worker to the price paid for goods by the worker is equal to:

$$\frac{W(1 - t_y)}{P(1 + t_c)} \tag{12.1}$$

You may think of the expression $(1 - t_y)/(1 + t_c)$ as the wedge which taxes drive between the price that firms have to pay for their labour, W, and the price that they receive for their output, P. From the household's point of view, for any given real wage, W/P, the bigger is the tax wedge the smaller will be the supply of labour. Thus, you may think of the shift in the labour supply curve analysed in the first experiment conducted above, from n^d to $n^{d'}$ as arising from either the imposition of an income tax or an expenditure tax having an equivalent total yield.

Finally, consider what happens when all of these tax measures are introduced simultaneously. In this case, the relevant supply curve in Figure 12.7 is $n^{s'}$ and the demand curve is $n^{d'}$. In this case, the equilibrium employment level falls still further to n'' but, by the construction of the example, the real wage remains at the no tax equilibrium level of $(W/P)^*$. (To avoid having too many equilibrium positions on the one diagram we have caused these two curves to intersect at the original real wage, $(W/P)^*$.) Workers' incomes will now be $Oe'c'n''$; the government's tax receipts will be $e'fdc'$ and the income accruing to capital owners will be fad. Employment will have fallen from n^* to n''.

It is worth highlighting what is happening to the relative shares of national income in the economy as we move from the initial no tax equilibrium to the after-tax equilibrium. To do this it will be most convenient to use the accounting conventions employed in the National Income Accounts. In those accounts, labour income is defined to include the payments of employment taxes by firms to the government. The fiction is that this is really part of the wages of the workers that is being deducted as a tax at source and handed over to the government in much the same way as the workers' income taxes are also deducted by the employer and paid to the government. Thus, in the no-tax situation, labour income is $O(W/P)^*bn^*$ and in the after-tax situation (after all taxes) labour income is $Ofdn''$. Using this accounting convention, it is evident that, as taxes are increased, so the share of national income accruing to labour increases. You can see this visually in Figure 12.7. In the initial situation labour income was equal to $\frac{2}{3}$ of total income, whilst in the after-tax situation it is equal to $\frac{6}{7}$. What is happening as taxes are increased is that, although the number of workers employed declines, the average wage per worker (defined in the gross sense in which it is being defined here) increases. Total product, of course, declines in the experiment conducted here.

The experiments just reviewed have started with an economy that had zero taxes and then introduced some positive taxes. The same results could have been generated, however, starting out with an economy with a given level of taxes and then raising those taxes. Thus, if taxes on labour (whether paid by workers or employers) are increased, the prediction is that there will be a drop in the level of employment, a rise in labour's share in the national product, and, at least as measured, the creation of additional unemployment.

SUMMARY

A. Minimum Wage Laws and Unemployment

Minimum wage laws raise the economy average real wage above the competitive equilibrium level. With voluntary exchange this means that the number of people employed will be less than the competitive equilibrium quantity and the number of people who would like jobs will be greater than the competitive equilibrium quantity. There will, therefore, be a rise in the real wage, a fall in employment, a rise in the labour force, and a rise in unemployment.

B. Trade Unions and Unemployment

(i)   An economy-wide trade union has exactly the same types of effects as a government-regulated minimum wage.

(ii) A trade union which does not control the whole economy, but which leaves some part of the economy competitive, will have the effect of raising the real wage in the union sector and lowering employment in that sector, while the real wage will fall and employment will rise in the non-union sector. In such a case no unemployment will be created. If, however, the trade union successfully lobbies for minimum wages, then unemployment will arise, but because of the minimum wage, not the activity of the union.

C. Unemployment Benefits and Unemployment

Unemployment benefit schemes lower the cost of job search and make job search more attractive than work and more attractive than leisure at the margin. There will therefore be a rise in the labour force and a fall in the supply of labour; the equilibrium real wage will rise, employment will fall, the labour force will rise, and unemployment will rise.

D. Taxes and Unemployment

If the level of taxes is increased there will be a fall in the level of employment and a rise in labour's share in the domestic product. The fall in employment will manifest itself as measured unemployment if the workers who withdraw from labour avail themselves of unemployment benefits to which they have earned an entitlement.

Review Questions

1. Suppose the labour market in some particular industry is described in the following way. The demand for labour is

    $$n^d = 100 - 5\left(\frac{W}{P}\right)$$

    and the supply of labour is

    $$n^s = 5\left(\frac{W}{P}\right)$$

    (a) Plot the demand curve and state in words what the demand equation means.
    (b) Plot the supply curve and state in words what the supply equation means.
    (c) Calculate (either algebraically or graphically) the equilibrium real wage and level of employment.
    (d) How much unemployment is there in the equilibrium calculated in (c)?
    (e) If the price level is 1.2, what is the equilibrium money wage?
    (f) If a minimum wage of £15 a day is set in this industry, what is the new equilibrium money wage and how much unemployment is created in this industry?
    (g) Suppose that all the workers in this industry become unionised, and the union sets its wage at £18. What is the money wage that is paid and how many workers are now employed and how many cannot find work in this industry?

2. An economy consisting of 1000 firms has a labour demand given by

    $$n^d = 4000 - \frac{1}{2}\left(\frac{W}{P}\right)$$

    and a labour supply given by

    $$n^s = 3000\left(\frac{W}{P}\right) - 2000$$

    (a) What is the equilibrium real wage?
    (b) If the price level is 2, what is the money wage?
    (c) If a minimum wage of £5 is legislated, how many workers are employed and how many unemployed?
    (d) If there is no minimum wage, but half of all the firms become 100 per cent unionised, and the union sets the union wage at £5, what is the average money wage paid in this industry and how many unionised workers are employed and unemployed and how many non-union workers are employed and unemployed?
    (e) Assume that there is no minimum wage and no unionisation of labour, but that the government introduces an unemployment benefits scheme which compensates any unemployed worker 75 per cent of the money wage paid to employed workers. Using a diagram, show the impact of this scheme on: (i) the money wage paid; (ii) the number of workers employed; (iii) the number of workers unemployed; and (iv) the cost to the government of this scheme.

3. An economy with a competitive labour market has a demand curve given by

    $$n^d = 1008 - 4\left(\frac{W}{P}\right)$$

    and a labour supply given by

    $$n^s = 960 + 2\left(\frac{W}{P}\right)$$

(a)   What is the equilibrium real wage?
(b)   Assume the price level to be 1 so that the equilibrium real wage is the equilibrium
       money wage. Now assume that the government imposes an employment tax of £1
       per worker. Calculate the new equilibrium level of employment and the money
       wage.
(c)   Calculate the level of real national income, the share of national income accruing
       to labour, the government, and the owners of capital.
(d)   Now suppose that the government introduces a tax on labour income that shifts
       the labour supply curve to

$$n^s = 954 + 2\left(\frac{W}{P}\right)$$

What is the new equilibrium real wage, employment level and share in national
income accruing to labour, government, and owners of capital?

13

Inflation

At its peak, in 1975, inflation in the United Kingdom was running at more than 20 per cent per annum. In fact, the inflation rate as measured by the GDP Deflator has not fallen below double-digits since 1974. These rates of inflation are historically unusually high. Average inflation in the United Kingdom over the period since 1900 has been just over 4 per cent per annum.

The question of what causes inflation and what can be done to control it is one which is surrounded by a great deal of mythology as well as sheer nonsense. The material presented in this chapter is designed to help you arrive at a clear understanding of what can and cannot cause inflation and also to help you understand and avoid the principal mistakes that are made in the popular press and by non-economist commentators, and even by a few economists! This chapter deals with an economy that is insulated in its inflationary experience from what is occurring in the rest of the world. It could also be viewed as explaining how, on the average, inflation in the world as a whole is determined. The next chapter deals with the complications that arise when international economic linkages are introduced into the analysis.

You have three tasks in this chapter which are to:

A. **review the distinction between a once-and-for-all rise in the price level and inflation;**
B. **know the effects on the price level of labour market shocks: (i) a rise in the legislated minimum wage; (ii) a trade union-induced wage rise; (iii) a rise in unemployment benefits; and (iv) a rise in taxes;**
   and
C. **understand how a continuing growth in the money supply leads to inflation.**

A. Once-and-for-All Price Level Rises and Inflation

Inflation is an ongoing process whereby prices are rising persistently year after year. A once-and-for-all rise in the price level occurs when the economy experiences a price level which is generally stable but which occasionally jumps to a new level. Recall Figure 5.1 in Chapter 5 above. There, two economies are illustrated. One has a price level that increases from 100 to 200 over a period of four years. In the other economy the price level suddenly rises from 100 and 200, and for the rest of the time prices are stable. The first economy is one which is experiencing *inflation*. The second economy has experienced a *once-and-for-all price rise*. This distinction is important in analysing the effects of various shocks on prices.

B. Labour Market Shocks and the Price Level

The analysis which is presented in the previous chapter can now be extended to enable you to work out the effects of labour market shocks on the level of output and prices. Figure 13.1 illustrates. Frame (a) shows the labour market with a competitive equilibrium at n_0^* and $(W/P)_0^*$. That competitive equilibrium level of employment will generate a level of output equal to y_0^*, which is calculated by reading off the level of output from the short-run production function at the equilibrium level of employment (Frame (b)). This competitive equilibrium level of output is then translated to Frame (c) to give the vertical aggregate supply curve AS_0. The equilibrium price level P_0^* is determined where the aggregate demand curve AD cuts the aggregate supply curve AS_0.

Before going further, be sure that you understand the basic model. If necessary, review Chapters 9, 10, and 11.

Each of the four shocks that we are considering — a rise in the legislated minimum wage, a trade union-induced real wage rise, a rise in unemployment benefits or a rise in taxes on labour — have qualitatively the same effect on the real wage and employment. They each raise the real wage above its competitive equilibrium level and they lower the level of employment below its competitive equilibrium level. (They have other effects which differ and which are analysed and discussed in Chapter 12. For the purpose of analysing price level consequences, however, those other effects may be ignored.)

In Figure 13.1, Frame (a) captures these effects by showing a rise in the real wage to $(W/P)_1$ with a drop in the employment level to n_1. This may be thought of as having arisen from any one of the four labour market shocks which we are considering. The lower level of employment n_1 will generate a lower level of output y_1, as read off from the production function in Frame (b). This, in turn (following the dotted line to Frame (c)), implies that the aggregate supply curve will shift to the left to a position AS_1 as shown in Frame (c).

With a *fixed money supply*, and therefore a *fixed aggregate demand curve*, you can now read off the effect on the price level. Unambiguously, the *price level will rise*.

Can anything be said about the amount by which prices will rise? Within the framework of the basic model, *the price level will rise by the same percentage as that by which output falls*. How is this known? It follows directly from the assumption made about the relationship between the level of income and the amount of money which people will choose to hold — the demand for money function. Specifically, it was assumed that:

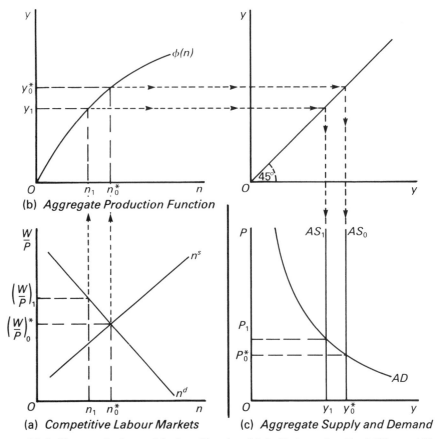

Figure 13.1 *How a Labour Market Shock which Raises the Real Wage Affects Employment, Output, and the Price Level*

A rise in the minimum wage, a rise in union wages, an improvement in unemployment benefits or a rise in taxes on labour will raise the equilibrium real wage and lower the level of employment (Frame (a)). This will lower the level of aggregate supply (Frame (b)). The shift in aggregate supply from y_0^* to y_1 (Frame (c)) will be associated with a rise in the price level. Because the aggregate demand curve is unit elastic, the percentage rise in the price level will equal the percentage drop in output.

$$\frac{M^d}{P} = k'y \qquad (13.1)$$

Further, it was assumed that planned expenditure y^d adjusts so that the demand for money M^d is equal to the supply of money M. This gives us the *aggregate demand curve* described by the equation:

$$y^d = \frac{1}{k'}\frac{M}{P} \qquad (13.2)$$

This aggregate demand curve is *unit elastic with respect to the price level.*

So, since the aggregate demand curve is unit elastic with respect to the price level, if the money supply is held constant, a labour market intervention which lowers real income by 1 per cent will raise the price level by 1 per cent.

With a constant money supply, the price level rise induced by a rise in the legislated minimum wage, a trade union-induced wage rise, a rise in unemployment benefits, or a rise in taxes on labour is clearly a once-and-for-all rise. The only way in which these 'shocks' could cause an ongoing inflation would be if the minimum wage, union wage, scale of unemployment benefits or tax on labour were persistently increased *in the face of rising unemployment, falling employment, falling output,* and *rising real wages.* Thus, if we observed an economy experiencing this combination of events, we might infer that the inflation had its origins in labour market conditions or what are sometimes called 'wage-push' forces.

Although a rise in the legislated minimum wage, a trade union-induced wage rise, a rise in unemployment benefits, or a tax rise has the effect of raising the price level in a once-and-for-all manner, it may be that it will take more than an instant for the price level to rise from its initial equilibrium level to its new equilibrium level. If it did indeed take a sizeable amount of time to move from the initial level to the new level, then it would not be unreasonable to describe the economy as experiencing inflation. However, once the price level has reached its new equilibrium level, there would be no further tendency for it to increase. There is no mechanism arising from these labour market 'shocks' for generating a *permanent* or *ongoing inflation.*

To summarise: legislated rises in the real wage in the form of minimum wage laws or real wage rises induced by trade unions or by a rise in unemployment benefits or a rise in taxes on labour will have the macroeconomic effect of lowering output relative to its competitive equilibrium level and raising the price level. The price level will rise by the same percentage as that by which output falls. However, with a constant money supply, none of these labour market 'shocks' is capable of generating ongoing inflation.

C. Money Supply Growth and Inflation

It will help your understanding of how inflation is generated by money supply growth if the problem is broken up into three parts. First, consider the effects of a once-and-for-all rise in the money supply on the price level. Secondly, determine the behaviour of the price level when the money supply is growing at a constant, steady rate, and thirdly, work out what happens to the rate of inflation when the rate at which the money supply is growing changes — that is, for example, analyse what would happen if the money supply had been growing at (say) 5 per cent per annum and then suddenly increased to a growth rate of (say) 10 per cent per annum.

(i) A Once-and-for-All Rise in the Money Supply

Suppose the economy was at an equilibrium price level and output level as shown in Figure 13.2, where the aggregate demand curve AD_0 cuts the aggregate supply curve at the price level P_0^* and the level of output y^*. Let us call the value of the money supply in that situation M_0. Now imagine that there is a rise in the money supply to a

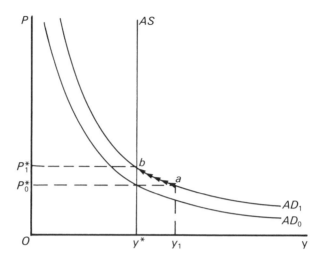

Figure 13.2 *A Once-and-for-All Rise in the Money Supply*
A once-and-for-all rise in the money supply shifts the aggregate demand curve from AD_0 to
AD_1. At the price level P_0^* there would be excess demand $(y_1 > y^*)$. The price level would have
to rise to P_1^* to restore equilibrium.

higher level (call the new level M_1). The aggregate demand curve will shift upwards
as a result of this rise in the money supply. In Figure 13.2 AD_1 represents the new
aggregate demand curve. If the price level remained at P_0^*, the amount of output
(real income) demanded would exceed the amount which firms would supply. The
level of demand would be y_1, while supply would be y^*. Firms could not be induced to
supply the level of output y_1, consistent with expenditure plans being at point a. In a
situation like a firms would be making less than maximum profits and would have
every incentive to contract production from y_1 to y^*. They would, therefore, never
find it profitable to be at point a. The excess demand pressures which would be
operating upon the economy if the level of demand was at point a would raise prices.
There would be severe shortages and prices would quickly be marked up in order to
eliminate the shortages. The price level at which the shortages would be eliminated is
P_1^* at point b. It is the essence of the equilibrium theory that the equilibrating forces
are strong enough for the price level to move from P_0^* to P_1^* (point b) quickly enough
for only the equilibrium observation P_1^*, y^* to be observed following the money
supply increase.

You should think of the rise in the price level that follows a once-and-for-all rise in
the money supply as being a sudden affair which catches people by surprise and
which does not lead them to attempt to economise on their money balance holdings.
(We shall deal with the complications that do arise in that case later in this chapter.)

Can anything be said about the amount by which the price level rises? Just as in the
case analysed in the previous section, the amount by which the price level rises is
known precisely. *The percentage rise in the price level will be the same as the
percentage rise in the money supply.* How is this known? Consider the equation for
the aggregate demand curve which was derived in Chapter 10. That equation is

$$y^d = \frac{1}{k'} \frac{M}{P} \qquad\qquad (13.3)$$

Alternatively, write the aggregate demand equation with the price level on the left-hand side. This is the way in which it is most natural to write the aggregate demand equation as plotted in Figure 13.2. Rewriting the aggregate demand equation with the price level on the left-hand side, it becomes

$$P = \frac{1}{k'} \frac{M}{y^d} \qquad\qquad (13.4)$$

But in equilibrium, aggregate demand y^d is equal to aggregate supply y^*. Replacing y^d in equation (13.4) with y^* gives

$$P = \frac{1}{k'} \frac{M}{y^*} \qquad\qquad (13.5)$$

Simply by inspecting equation (13.5) it is obvious that *the price level is proportional to the money supply* (the proportion is equal to $1/k'y^*$).

Thus, it is evident that a one per cent rise in the money stock will move the aggregate demand curve upwards by one per cent, and since the aggregate supply curve is totally inelastic (vertical), the equilibrium price level will rise by that same one per cent.

(ii) A Constant Rate of Growth of the Money Supply

Now that you understand what happens to the price level in the event of a once-and-for-all rise in the money supply, consider the more complicated case and ask what will happen to the price level if the money supply is increasing at a constant rate of, let us say, 5 per cent per annum. So as to get some important principles clear, suppose that the money supply has been increasing at 5 per cent per annum for as long as anybody can remember, and that everybody fully expects that it is going to continue to increase at 5 per cent per annum into the indefinite future.

The situation to be analysed is called the *steady state*. The steady state value of a variable is the value at which the variable eventually settles after it has been disturbed. If the rate of inflation has settled at some particular value, then it is called the *steady state rate of inflation*. Notice that if the steady state rate of inflation is not equal to zero, then the price level is continuously rising. However, the price level may be an equilibrium level in the sense that, at each moment in time, it is determined by the intersection of the aggregate demand and aggregate supply curves. In that case, the position of the aggregate demand curve will be rising at a constant rate.

Returning to the substance of our analysis, you have already seen that a once-and-for-all rise in the money stock of a certain percentage generates a once-and-for-all rise in the price level of that same percentage, provided the level of aggregate supply remains constant. Does this once-and-for-all result extend to the ongoing money supply growth case? The answer is that it does: with a constant level of real income (with a fixed aggregate supply curve) *the rate of inflation will equal the rate of growth of the money supply*. In the case of our example, if the money supply is growing at 5

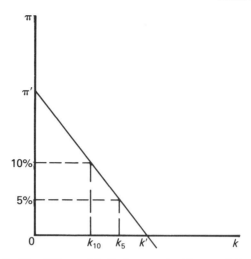

Figure 13.3 *The Effect of Inflation on the Demand for Money*
At an inflation rate of 5 per cent the propensity to hold money would be k_5. At an inflation rate of 10 per cent the propensity to hold money would be the smaller quantity k_{10}. Although the propensity to hold money falls as the inflation rate rises, for a given rate of inflation, the propensity to hold money is a constant. This means that the rate of inflation must be equal to the growth rate of the money supply minus the growth rate of output.

___

per cent per annum and if the aggregate supply curve is fixed, then the price level will be inflating at a rate of 5 per cent per annum.

This proposition about ongoing inflation may seem to follow directly and obviously from the analysis of the effects of a once-and-for-all rise in the money stock. However, we do have to be careful to convince ourselves that the result is correct in the case of an ongoing money supply growth process. You will recall that when analysing the determination of the demand for money, we noticed that at higher rates of inflation there would be an incentive for individuals to economise on their holdings of money balances. Specifically, we postulated that the demand for real money would depend positively on the level of real income (output) and negatively on the rate of inflation. Thus, if the economy experiences a 5 per cent rate of inflation year in and year out, individuals will, on the average, hold a smaller quantity of real money balances than they would if the economy experienced price stability.

You can think of this in the following way: if there is no inflation in the economy, the propensity to hold money, k, will take on a particular constant value. If, however, that same economy has a 5 per cent rate of inflation, then the propensity to hold money will take on a lower value than in the zero inflation economy. Figure 13.3 illustrates this. Recall that the propensity to hold money, k, is simply the ratio of the money supply to the flow of nominal GDP. That is:

$$k = \frac{M}{Py} \tag{13.6}$$

Figure 13.3 shows the value of M/Py plotted against the inflation rate. The relationship is downward sloping, showing that at higher rates of inflation people will economise on their money holdings and hold a smaller quantity of money relative to the flow of money expenditures which they seek to undertake. If the rate of inflation was zero, then the value of k would be k'. If the rate of inflation was 10 per cent, then the value of k would be the smaller number read off on the horizontal axis of Figure 13.3, indicated as k_{10}.

You are now almost able to see that an ongoing rate of growth of the money supply of (say) 5 per cent will indeed lead to an ongoing rate of inflation of 5 per cent. Let us write the equation for the aggregate demand curve, with the price level on the left-hand side and with the value for k that coincides with a 5 per cent rate of inflation on the right-hand side. That is:

$$P = \frac{1}{k_5} \frac{M}{y} \tag{13.7}$$

This equation looks exactly like equation (13.4) which we used to establish the proposition that a rise in the price level will be proportional to the rise in the money supply. If the money supply is growing at 5 per cent per annum and if real income is constant, there is only one rate at which the price level can be increasing to maintain equilibrium. That rate is the same rate at which the money supply is growing — 5 per cent per annum. To see this, consider what would be happening in the economy were it not the case that the price level was inflating at the same rate as the money supply was growing. Suppose the money supply is growing by 5 per cent per annum, real income is fixed, and the price level is only inflating by, say, $2\frac{1}{2}$ per cent per annum. In such a case, the amount of *real money* in the economy would be increasing. We know that if the amount of real money in the economy increases (if the money supply rises relative to the price level), then aggregate demand rises. This would cause an excess demand for goods, thereby forcing the inflation rate upwards.

Consider the opposite extreme. Suppose that with the money supply growing at 5 per cent per annum and real income constant, the inflation rate is 10 per cent per annum. In this case the amount of *real money* in the economy is falling. With the money supply in real terms falling, people will cut back on their demand for goods and services to try to build up their money balances to the desired level, and this will have the effect of lowering the rate at which prices are rising.

Thus, if the inflation rate is lower than the rate of growth of the money supply, excess demand for goods will force the inflation rate up. If the money supply growth rate is lower than the rate at which inflation is proceeding, an excess supply of goods will force the inflation rate down. There is only one inflation rate which is consistent with maintaining equilibrium, and that is the rate at which the money supply is growing.

Thus, *an ongoing steady rate of growth of the money supply of x per cent will, with constant real income (output), lead to an x per cent rate of inflation.*

The above conceptual experiment has been conducted in the context of an economy which is not growing in real terms. That is, the aggregate supply curve has been assumed to be fixed. It is more natural to think of an economy which experiences output growth over time. You can think of capital accumulation and technical progress as shifting the short-run production function upwards and therefore continuously moving the aggregate supply curve out rightwards at a steady trend rate.

From our analysis about the once-and-for-all effects of labour market shocks on the aggregate supply curve and on the price level, you already know that a one per cent drop in aggregate supply leads to a one per cent rise in the price level. It follows immediately, therefore, that a one per cent rise in aggregate supply will lead to a one per cent drop in the price level. If the economy experienced continuing real income growth, with the aggregate supply curve moving rightwards at a constant rate of, say, 3 per cent per annum, and if the money supply was held constant so that the aggregate demand curve did not move, then it is immediately obvious that the price level would be falling by 3 per cent per annum.

It is an easy matter now to allow for output growth in calculating the relationship between the rate of growth of the money supply and the rate of inflation. You have seen that with no output growth, that is, with a fixed aggregate supply curve, a 5 per cent growth rate in the money supply leads to a 5 per cent rate of inflation. You have also seen that a (say) 3 per cent rise in real aggregate supply with a fixed money supply leads to a 3 per cent per annum fall in the price level. These two offsetting effects can be brought together. If the money supply is growing at 5 per cent per annum and at the same time output is growing at 3 per cent per annum, the rate of inflation will be 2 per cent per annum. You have just used the *fundamental steady state inflation equation*. That equation says that: *the rate of inflation equals the rate of growth of the money supply minus the rate of growth of output.*

If we call the rate of inflation π, the rate of growth of the money supply μ, and the rate of growth of output ρ, then we can write this in a more compact form as:

$$\pi = \mu - \rho \qquad\qquad\qquad (13.8)$$

(iii) The Effects of a Rise in the Rate of Growth of the Money Supply

Now that you understand the effects of a once-and-for-all rise in the money supply on the price level and the effects of a constant ongoing rate of money supply growth on the steady state rate of inflation, you are in a position to tackle the most difficult part of the analysis: that is, to analyse the effects of a **change** in the rate of growth of the money supply. You are now going to discover a very important proposition, *the overshooting proposition*, which states that: a rise in the rate of growth of the money supply will lead to a rise in the rate of inflation which will overshoot its steady state value and approach its steady state·value from a *higher* rate of inflation. The proposition can be stated equivalently for a fall in the growth rate of the money supply as: a fall in the rate of growth of the money supply will lead to a fall in the rate of inflation which will overshoot its steady state value and approach its steady state value from a *lower* rate of inflation.

To explain the overshooting proposition, the rest of the chapter concentrates on the first case, a rise in the growth rate of the money supply. To be sure that you thoroughly understand the overshooting proposition, let us state it again in a slightly more long-winded, though simpler, way. If the money supply has been growing at a steady rate of 5 per cent per annum and if the inflation rate has settled down at 5 per cent per annum (its steady state rate with a constant level of real income) and if the money supply *growth rate* is then increased to 10 per cent per annum, the inflation rate will eventually settle down at 10 per cent per annum. However, in the process of reaching the 10 per cent inflation rate, inflation will go higher than 10 per cent, i.e. will overshoot the 10 per cent rate and will approach 10 per cent from that higher

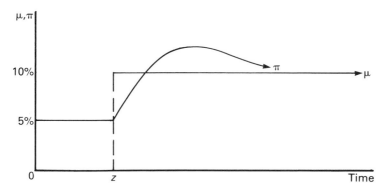

Figure 13.4 *The Overshooting Proposition*
When the money supply growth rate suddenly, and previously unexpectedly, rises, the rate of inflation also rises. On its route to a new steady state level, however, inflation overshoots the growth rate of the money supply. This happens because the higher rate of inflation induces economising on money holdings so that a drop in the demand for money adds to the effects of a rise in the supply of money on the level of aggregate demand and prices.

level. Figure 13.4 illustrates a possible path for the inflation rate. The figure shows the rate of inflation and the rate of growth of the money supply (π and μ) on the vertical axis and measures time on the horizontal axis. Let us suppose that from time 0 to time z the rate of inflation and the rate of money supply growth were both 5 per cent per annum. Then, at time z, the money supply growth rate is suddenly increased to 10 per cent per annum and maintained at that level forever thereafter. The inflation rate will begin to increase and at some stage (perhaps very early in the process) will overshoot the 10 per cent rate and move to yet higher levels. Eventually the inflation rate will approach its steady state value, but from *above* the steady state value, 10 per cent, not from below it.

Why does this happen? The key to the answer is contained in Figure 13.3. You will notice (turning back to that figure) that if we move from a 5 per cent inflation rate to a 10 per cent inflation rate, the propensity to hold money, k, which is the same thing as the ratio of money supply to nominal income, M/Py, falls from k_5 down to k_{10}. Therefore if the economy moved from a 5 per cent inflation rate to a 10 per cent inflation rate, it would be necessary during that process for the ratio of the money supply to nominal income, M/Py, to fall. Remember that we are holding y constant during this experiment (it actually doesn't make any difference to the answer but makes the argument more complicated if we let y change at the same time). With y being held constant, the only way in which the ratio of the money supply to nominal income can fall is for nominal income to increase by a larger percentage amount than the money supply increases. Therefore, in moving from k_5 to k_{10}, the price level must rise by more than the total rise in the money supply. This could not happen if the inflation rate never exceeded the rate of money supply growth. If the inflation rate was always equal to the rate of growth of the money supply and if real income (output) was constant, then M/Py could not change. But M/Py does change: it falls when the inflation rate rises. It follows directly, then, that the inflation rate must overshoot the money supply growth rate in order to achieve this.

Now let us try to give you some simple economic intuition as to what is going on here. The above argument has been a purely abstract logical one. It is a correct argument, but perhaps it will be better appreciated if it is filled out with an economic story.

Imagine the economy with a 5 per cent steady state rate of inflation such as depicted at time z in Figure 13.4. Then suppose that at time z the money supply growth rate is increased to 10 per cent per annum. This will have the immediate effect of increasing the demand for goods, since the money supply is now growing at a faster rate than the rate of inflation. With a fixed level of aggregate supply, this will force up the price level and force up the inflation rate. However, the higher inflation rate will now lead people to start economising on their holdings of money balances. They will seek to hold a smaller quantity of money relative to income. There will therefore be an even bigger excess demand for goods as a result of people economising on their money holdings than there would otherwise have been. This will put yet further upward pressure on prices as people try to lower their money balances by increasing their expenditures. This yet further rise in the rate of inflation will lead to yet further economising on money balances. It sounds as if this could very well be an unstable process. In fact, there are some conditions under which it might be unstable, although they do not appear to occur in the real world. Rather, what happens eventually is that the inflation rate exceeds the money supply growth rate by such a large amount that the amount of real money balances in the economy is falling at a rate even faster than the rate at which people want to reduce their real money balances. When that happens people will cut back on their expenditures and attempt to increase their real money balances. At this stage the rate of inflation will begin to fall. This part of the process will continue until the steady state rate of inflation is reached.

The precise path followed will depend on how quickly people's expectations of inflation adjust to the changed money growth rate. If that expectation adjusts slowly (perhaps because of uncertainty as to whether the new higher money supply growth rate is going to be maintained) then the path illustrated is representative of the path the economy would take. If, at the other extreme, inflation expectations adjust instantly and completely to the new money supply growth path, the price level would 'jump' — the inflation rate would be infinitely large for an instant — to lower real money balances to their new equilibrium level and, therefore, the inflation rate would immediately settle down at its new steady state rate.

SUMMARY

A. Once-and-for-All Price Level Rises and Inflation

Inflation is an ongoing process of persistently rising prices. A once-and-for-all rise in the price level occurs when the price level moves from one steady state level to another steady state level.

B. Labour Market Shocks and the Price Level

A rise in the legislated minimum wage, a trade union-induced wage rise, a rise in unemployment benefits, or a rise in taxes on labour all have the effect of raising the real wage and lowering the level of employment. A lower level of employment will generate a lower level of output, and therefore, aggregate supply will fall. A lower level of aggregate supply will induce a higher price level. The percentage rise in the price level will equal the percentage fall in output. Thus, these shocks will have the effect of generating a once-and-for-all rise in the price level.

C. Money Supply Growth and Inflation

A continuing growth in the money supply leads to inflation. The steady state rate of inflation will equal the rate of growth of the money supply minus the rate of growth of output. A rise in the rate of growth of the money supply will cause the rate of inflation to 'overshoot' its steady state value and to approach the steady state from above.

Appendix: The Algebra of Inflation

This appendix sets out in a slightly more rigorous form some of the ideas developed intuitively in the text of this chapter. You might find this treatment helpful. However, if you find algebraic arguments difficult, you can safely ignore this appendix. The important thing is that you have understood the text.

The starting point for an algebraic analysis of inflation is to recall the theory of the demand for money developed in Chapter 10. You will recall that we worked out that the demand for real money will be higher the higher is the level of real income and will be lower the higher is the rate of inflation. Specifically, we wrote:

$$\frac{M^d}{P} = k(\pi)y$$

We could make this slightly more general by writing

$$\frac{M^d}{P} = g(y,\pi) \atop (+-)$$ (A1)

If we have equilibrium in the money market then we can remove the superscript d and set the demand for money M^d equal to the supply of money M so that

$$\frac{M}{P} = g(y,\pi)$$ (A2)

Take the logarithms of both sides of this equation to give

$$\log M - \log P = \log [g(y, \pi)]$$ (A3)

Now suppose that the demand for money function takes on a very specific form and, in particular, is given by

$$\log [g(y, \pi)] = \alpha \log y - \beta \pi$$ (A4)

This is simply making the demand for money function take on the special functional form that the logarithm of real money balances demanded be equal to a constant, α, times the logarithm of real income minus another constant, β, times the rate of inflation. Substitute the right-hand side of (A4) into the right-hand side of (A3) to give:

$$\log M - \log P = \alpha \log y - \beta \pi$$ (A5)

Now consider how equation (A5) changes over time. Use the operator Δ to denote a change so that

$$\Delta \log M - \Delta \log P = \alpha \Delta \log y - \beta \Delta \pi$$ (A6)

Now the change in a logarithm of a variable is nothing other than its growth rate. Therefore we will define

$$\Delta \log M \equiv \mu$$
$$\Delta \log P \equiv \pi$$ (A7)
$$\Delta \log y \equiv \rho$$

We are defining μ as the growth rate of the money supply and ρ as the growth rate of output and π as the inflation rate. We then obtain

$$\mu - \pi = \alpha \rho - \beta \Delta \pi$$ (A8)

If the inflation rate is constant, then $\Delta \pi$ is equal to zero, and we obtain the steady state rate of inflation as

$$\pi = \mu - \alpha \rho$$ (A9)

This is the fundamental steady state inflation equation developed more intuitively in the text. This equation differs slightly from that in the text in that the growth rate of output is multiplied by a constant α, which is nothing other than the elasticity of demand for money with respect to income. We assumed that to be equal to unity — not a bad approximation as it turns out — in the text and in Chapter 10 above.

Review Questions

1. From the following, label those that are a once-and-for-all rise in the price level and those that are inflation:
    (a) The price of beef this week rose by 10 per cent.
    (b) The General Index of Retail Prices, after having been steady for one year, jumped 10 per cent at the beginning of last winter but has been steady ever since.
    (c) Over the past decade the General Index of Retail Prices has gradually and consistently increased so that today it is double what it was a decade ago.
    (d) Over the last decade the General Index of Retail Prices doubled, but this is the result of two big jumps, one in 1974, and one in 1979.

2. What happens to the price level when a strong trade union successfully raises the money wage rate? Does inflation ensue? What happens to employment, unemployment, real wages, and the level of output?

3. Imagine an economy which has been experiencing stable prices for as long as anyone can remember. Suddenly there is a doubling in the quantity of money. The money supply then remains constant at its new level. What happens in that economy to output, employment, real wages, and the price level? Why? Trace out all the effects and fully set out your reasoning.

4. Does the price level 'overshoot' the money supply in the situation described in Question 3? If so, why? If not, why not?

5. Imagine an economy that has experienced 10 per cent inflation for as long as anyone can remember. Output has been constant and the money supply has grown at the same 10 per cent rate as inflation. Suddenly there is a doubling in the growth rate of the money supply, after which the new higher (20 per cent) growth rate is maintained. What happens in this economy to output, employment, real wages, and inflation?

6. Does the inflation rate 'overshoot' the money supply growth rate in the economy described in Question 5? If so, why? If not, why not?

7. Describe what would happen to interest rates in the event of monetary shocks such as those set out in Questions 3 and 5 above.

14

Inflation, the Balance of Payments and the Exchange Rate

The balance of payments and the exchange rate are frequently in the news. There is a constant cry, especially from politicians, for Britain to 'pay her way in the world'. Also, manufacturing interests are constantly pleading for protection from the competition arising from cheap foreign imports. Even the scientific community joins in this cry, with suggestions that the government should subsidise British scientific research to enable us to compete with US and continental European technology.

The exchange rate also attracts a great deal of attention. In the period since the pound started floating in the early 1970s, it has depreciated in value against the major currencies. During 1979 and 1980, however, the pound appreciated very strongly, especially against the American dollar. During 1981, the pound again began to depreciate and this time very strongly.

This chapter deals with the forces that determine the balance of payments and the exchange rate.[1] You are going to discover that there is a great deal of mythology about these matters and that the factors which actually determine the balance of payments and the value of the pound have very little to do with those factors which the popular mythology supposes to be relevant. In addition, the chapter continues the analysis of inflation begun in Chapter 13. In particular, it extends the analysis of

---

1. The origins of this theory, which has not changed much in more than two hundred years, is David Hume, Of the balance of trade, in *Essays: Moral, Political and Literary*, Oxford University Press, 1963, pp. 316–33 (first published in 1741). An excellent modern restatement of Hume's theory in slightly more general terms than that given in this chapter, is Harry G. Johnson (1972) *Further Essays in Monetary Economics*, Allen & Unwin, pp. 229–49.

inflation to an open economy with international trading and investment links with the rest of the world. You will discover how the analysis of the previous chapter needs modification in order to understand the inflationary process of a fixed exchange rate economy. Further, you will discover that the analysis of the previous chapter emerges with little need for modification in the case of an economy operating on a flexible exchange rate.

You have five tasks in this chapter which are to:

A. **understand the connection between the money supply and foreign exchange reserves;**

B. **understand the 'law of one price':**
   (i) purchasing power parity (PPP)
   (ii) interest rate parity (IRP);

C. **understand how inflation and the balance of payments are determined when the exchange rate is fixed;**

D. **understand how inflation and the exchange rate are determined when the exchange rate is flexible;**
   and

E. **understand how the balance of payments and the exchange rate are linked in a managed floating regime.**

A. Money Supply and Foreign Exchange Reserves

(i) The Banking Sector Balance Sheets

As a preliminary to understanding the factors which determine the balance of payments and the exchange rate, it is necessary to understand the connection between the money supply and the country's stock of foreign exchange reserves. This connection is most readily seen by considering the items in the balance sheets of the central bank and the commercial banks (columns 3 and 4 of Table 4.2, Chapter 4) and by examining the balance sheet of what is called the *consolidated banking sector*. The consolidated banking sector is the central bank and the commercial banks viewed as a whole. Table 14.1 sets out the relevant balance sheets. (You might like to refer back to Chapter 4 on aggregate balance sheet accounting to see how these balance sheets fit in with those in the other sectors of the economy.)

First consider the balance sheet of the central bank. The assets of the central bank are aggregated into two items: *gold and foreign exchange reserves,* and *domestic credit*.

The gold represents actual gold in the vaults of the central bank. The foreign exchange reserves are either bank accounts which the central bank maintains with other central banks (i.e., central banks of other countries) or highly liquid foreign currency denominated securities. From the point of view of the country as a whole, the stock of gold and foreign exchange reserves serves the same purpose as currency and a current account do for you as an individual. Denote the stock of: *gold and foreign exchange reserves* as *F*.

Table 14.1 Banking Sector Balance Sheets

(i)   Central Bank

Assets		*Liabilities*	
Gold and Foreign Exchange Reserves	F	Monetary Base	MB
Domestic Credit	DC_c		

(ii)   Commercial Banks

Assets		*Liabilities*	
Currency plus Deposits at Central Bank	MB_b	Deposits	D
Domestic Credit	DC_b		

(iii)   Consolidated Banking Sector

Assets		*Liabilities*	
Gold and Foreign Exchange Reserves	F	Currency in Circulation with Public $(MB - MB_b)$	MB_p
Domestic Credit $(DC_c + DC_b)$	DC	Deposits	D
Money Supply	M	Money Supply	M

The second item in the central bank's balance sheet is government securities which the central bank has purchased. You will recall that the central bank creates *monetary base* by buying government securities, either from the government directly or from the general public, and making the purchase with newly created money. The whole collection of securities held by the central bank is called the *domestic credit of the central bank*. Denote *domestic credit of the central bank* as DC_c.

Apart from miscellaneous items such as real estate, which may be ignored, these constitute the entire stock of assets of the central bank.

The liability of the central bank is the *monetary base*. That is the stock of currency that has been issued and is held either by the general public or in the tills of commercial banks, together with the stock of bank deposits maintained by the commercial banks at the central bank. Denote the *monetary base* as MB.

The central bank's balance sheet balances so that

$$MB = F + DC_c$$

Next consider the commercial banks. As in the case of the central bank, it is useful to distinguish between two sets of assets. First, the commercial banks hold reserves in the form of notes and coins as well as deposits with the central bank. Denote *commercial bank reserve assets* as MB_b.

Notice that the same letters are being used to denote commercial banks' reserves as those used to denote monetary base because they are in fact the same thing. Part of the monetary base, MB, which is a liability to the central bank, is held as an asset by the commercial banks.

The other assets of the commercial banks have all been grouped into a single item, *domestic credit of the commercial banks*. This item consists of all the securities held by commercial banks, including any loan obligations which private individuals and firms have with the banks. Denote *domestic credit of the commercial banks* as DC_b.

Apart from some real estate, which may be neglected, these two items constitute the entire assets of the commercial banks.

The liabilities of the commercial banks consist of the deposits which have been placed with them by households and firms. Denote *bank deposits* as D.

The balance sheet of the commercial banks balances so total deposits are equal to the stock of reserves plus the domestic credit. That is,

$$D = MB_b + DC_b$$

Next consider the consolidation of these two balance sheets. A consolidated balance sheet is simply the balance sheet that arises from adding together the individual balance sheets and netting out any items which appear as an asset in one balance sheet and as a liability in another. To consolidate the two balance sheets of the central bank and commercial banks, first notice that *gold and foreign exchange reserves* appear only once in the central bank's balance sheet and therefore will appear in the consolidated balance sheet. *Domestic credit* appears twice, DC_c and DC_b. If those two items are added together, the domestic credit of the economy as a whole is obtained. Denote *domestic credit* as DC.

On the liability side of the consolidated balance sheet, notice that the *monetary base*, MB, is partly held as the reserve asset of the commercial banks MB_b. In the consolidated balance sheet the difference between these two items is recorded. This difference is *currency in circulation with the public* (denoted MB_p).

Bank deposits appear just once, in the commercial banks' balance sheet, and therefore, appear again in the consolidated balance sheet.

The total liabilities of the consolidated banking system now have a familiar look. The total liabilities of the consolidated banking system consist of *currency in circulation plus bank deposits*. That total, of course, is precisely the definition of *money*.

Since the two underlying balance sheets balanced, so also the consolidated balance sheet will balance. From this fact it will be clear that the *money supply* can be defined either as: *currency in circulation plus bank deposits*, a definition with which you are already familiar, or as *gold and foreign exchange reserves plus domestic credit*, that is,

$$M = MB_p + D$$

or

$$M = F + DC$$

These, of course, are simply definitions. The second definition, however, is a very useful one in helping us to organise our thinking about the determination of the balance of payments and the exchange rate.

(ii) Changes in Reserves, the Money Supply, and Domestic Credit

The next step is to recognise that the relationship between the *money supply* and the stock of *foreign exchange reserves and domestic credit* is going to hold each and every year, and therefore, the *change in the money supply* from one year to the next will be equal to the *change in foreign exchange reserves* plus the *change in domestic credit*. That is (using Δ to denote change),

$$\Delta M = \Delta F + \Delta DC$$

This is a very important equation because ΔF is the *balance of payments*. That is, the change in the stock of foreign exchange reserves is what we mean by the balance on the official settlements account. Thus, the official settlements balance is related to the change in the money supply and the change in domestic credit. The *change in domestic credit*, ΔDC, is usually called *domestic credit expansion*.

It will be convenient for the next step of the story to look at the equation that describes the change in reserves, money supply, and domestic credit in terms of growth rates, or the proportionate rates of change, rather than in terms of absolute changes. To convert the equation into growth rates, first divide both sides of the equation by M. That will give

$$\frac{\Delta M}{M} = \frac{\Delta F}{M} + \frac{\Delta DC}{M}$$

Terms like $\Delta F/M$ and $\Delta DC/M$ do not have intuitive meanings. They become more intuitive if the first term is multiplied and divided by F and if the second term is multiplied and divided by DC. This will give

$$\frac{\Delta M}{M} = (\frac{F}{M})\frac{\Delta F}{F} + (\frac{DC}{M})\frac{\Delta DC}{DC}$$

(*Stop*: be sure that you understand how the above equation was obtained.)

The equation will look simpler if you recall that the first term, $\Delta M/M$, is the growth rate of the money supply, which we have been calling μ.

Further, define $F/M \equiv \psi$ so that $DC/M \equiv (1 - \psi)$.

The symbol ψ (the Greek letter psi) is the fraction of the money supply which is held by the banking system in foreign exchange reserves, and $1-\psi$ is the fraction of the money supply held by the banking system in domestic assets. (*Stop*: check that $F/M + DC/M = 1$, since $F + DC = M$.)

Also define $\Delta F/F \equiv f$ and $\Delta DC/DC \equiv dc$.

The letter f is the rate of change of foreign exchange reserves, and dc is the rate of change of domestic credit.

The somewhat cumbersome equation above may, with the new definition, be written as the simpler equation

$$\mu = \psi f + (1 - \psi) \, dc \tag{14.1}$$

This is a fundamental relationship between the rate of growth of the money supply, the rate of change of foreign exchange reserves, and the rate of growth of domestic credit. It says that the growth rate of the money supply, μ, is a weighted average of the growth rate of the stock of foreign exchange reserves and domestic credit. The weights, which add up to one, are the fraction of the total money supply backed by holdings of foreign exchange reserves, ψ, and the fraction of the total money supply backed by domestic credit $(1 - \psi)$.

This relationship may be used in order to understand how, in a fixed exchange rate setting, the balance of payments is determined, and how, in a flexible exchange rate regime, the exchange rate itself is determined. Before we can take those next steps, however, we need to pursue one further preliminary task.

B. The 'Law of One Price'

A fundamental law of economics which is of great use in understanding the forces which determine the balance of payments and the exchange rate is the *law of one price*.

The law of one price is a proposition concerning the effects of *arbitrage*. Arbitrage is the buying of a commodity at a low price and simultaneously contracting to sell it for a higher price, thereby making a profit in the process. If it is possible to buy a particular good for some price, say, p_b, and sell the good for a price p_s, then it is possible to make a profit at a rate

$$\frac{p_s - p_b}{p_b}\%$$

If such a situation exists, individuals who see the profit opportunity available will increase their demand for the good whose price is p_b. They will also increase their supply of the good at the price p_s. This arbitrage activity of increasing demand at the price p_b and increasing supply at the price p_s will put upward pressure on the buying price — that is, p_b will rise — and downward pressure on the selling price — that is, p_s will fall. Arbitrage will continue to the point at which one price prevails, that is, $p_s = p_b$, and there are no arbitrage profits to be made.

This is the *law of one price*, namely, that arbitrage will compete away all price differences between identical commodities. Of course, where there are transport costs between two locations, or where there are tariffs and impediments to trade imposed by government, or where there are costs of acquiring information about the prices of alternative sources of supply, arbitrage will not compete price differential all the way to zero. However, it will compete differentials down to the level such that the only remaining price differential reflects underlying real technological or government-induced barriers to further reductions in the price gap.

The law of one price has two important implications which are useful for understanding the determination of inflation, the balance of payments and exchange rates, namely, the *purchasing power parity* and *interest rate parity* theorems.

(i) Purchasing Power Parity (PPP)

The *purchasing power parity* theorem states that the *price of a good in one country will be equal to the price of that same good in another country where the prices are expressed in units of local currency and converted at the current exchange rate.* (Of course, this has to be modified to allow for tariffs and transportation costs.)

As an example, if a computer in the United States costs $500,000 US, that identical computer (trade barriers and transport costs absent) would, at an exchange rate of $2 US per £1, cost £250,000 in the United Kingdom. Even allowing for transport costs and tariffs, if these factors are *constant*, then although the *level* of prices in the United Kingdom might be different from the level of prices in the United States, the *rate of change of prices* in the United Kingdom and the rate of change of prices in the United States will be linked to each other by the relation:

<blockquote>

percentage change in £ price

equals   percentage change in $US price

plus   the percentage rate of depreciation of the
£ against the $US.

</blockquote>

To go back to the computer example, suppose that computer prices in the US are falling by 5 per cent a year. This will mean that a computer that would sell for $500,000 this year will sell for $475,000 next year. Further, suppose that the £ depreciates from $2 US per £1 to $1.90 US per £1 — a five per cent depreciation — then the purchasing power parity theorem states that the price of a computer in the United Kingdom next year will stay constant at £250,000. That is, computer prices in the United Kingdom will change by the percentage change of computer prices in the US, adjusted for the percentage change in the value of the £.

(ii) Interest Rate Parity (IRP)

The interest rate parity theorem is a very close cousin of the purchasing power parity theorem. It arises from arbitrage activities in asset markets. The interest rate parity theorem states that (abstracting from political risk differences) the rate of interest available in one country will be equal to the rate of interest available in another country adjusted for the expected rate of change of the exchange rate between the currencies of the two countries.

Thus, suppose for example, the rate of interest in the United Kingdom is 10 per cent, and the rate of interest in the United States is 8 per cent. Then, if it is expected that the £ is going to depreciate by 2 per cent, the rate of interest that would be obtained by an American investing in a British security will be the 10 per cent interest on British bonds minus the expected depreciation of the £ of 2 per cent, which would equal 8 per cent, the same as he could obtain in the United States. Conversely, a United Kingdom resident investing in the United States would obtain 8 per cent interest on the US security, plus a 2 per cent gain from the appreciation of the $US *vis-à-vis* the £ totalling 10 per cent. This would, of course, be equivalent to what could be obtained in the United Kingdom. If the rate of interest in the United Kingdom was greater than 10 per cent, and the rate of interest in the US, 8 per cent, and the expected rate of depreciation of the £, 2 per cent, there would be gains to be made from investing in the United Kingdom. As investors sought to exploit these gains they would increase the demand for British securities and lower the demand for US securities. This would raise the price of, and lower the rate of interest on, British securities and lower the price of, and raise the rate of interest on, US securities. If there were flexible exchange rates, the flow of funds into the United Kingdom would also lead to a fall in the value of the pound relative to its expected future value. This would mean that the expected rate of future depreciation of the pound would rise. The combination of a higher US interest rate, a lower British interest rate, and a rise in the expected rate of depreciation of the pound would restore the interest rate parity relation. That is, the interest rate in the United Kingdom would equal the interest rate in the United States plus the expected rate of depreciation of the pound.

These two propositions will be used to enable you to understand the basic forces which determine inflation, the balance of payments and the exchange rate.

C. Determination of Inflation and the Balance of Payments under Fixed Exchange Rates

The rate of change of foreign exchange reserves, f, is the balance on the official settlements account (expressed as a proportion of the existing stock of reserves). The things which determine f are therefore exactly the same as the things that determine the official settlements balance. It is tempting to rearrange equation (14.1), derived in Section A above, so that the variable in which we are interested, f, appears on the left-hand side. If you divide the above equation by ψ and then subtract $[(1-\psi)/\psi]dc$ from both sides of the equation, you obtain

$$f = \frac{1}{\psi}\mu - (\frac{1-\psi}{\psi}) dc \qquad (14.2)$$

This equation says that the percentage change in the stock of foreign exchange reserves — *the official settlements balance* expressed in percentage terms — *depends on the rate of growth of the money supply and the rate of growth of domestic credit.* If it is possible to work out what determines these two factors, then we shall have a theory that explains the balance of payments.

(i) Domestic Credit Expansion

Let us deal first with domestic credit expansion, dc. In an open economy with a fixed exchange rate, domestic credit growth is the variable which the monetary authorities can control by their monetary policy actions. If the central bank wants to see the growth of domestic credit increased, then all it has to do is to buy bonds from individuals, thereby increasing its own stock of domestic securities. This also makes more reserves available to the commercial banks and encourages them to acquire more domestic securities. Conversely, if the central bank wants to contract the amount of domestic credit, it can do so by selling government securities, thereby reducing its own holdings of those items. This will also encourage the commercial banks to sell securities, since the availability of reserves to the commercial banks will have been tightened.

Thus, the central bank controls the growth rate of domestic credit. This is an exogenous variable. Under fixed exchange rates, however, the central bank cannot control the money supply. The very act of pegging the foreign exchange rate means that the central bank must always be willing to buy and sell foreign exchange. That is, the central bank must always be willing to raise or lower its own stock of foreign exchange in order to preserve the fixed value of its currency in terms of foreign currencies. Thus, although the central bank can decide how many domestic assets to buy and hold, it has no control over the gold and foreign exchange reserves that it holds. It follows, therefore, that it cannot control the money supply, since the money supply is the sum of domestic credit (which the central bank can control) and foreign exchange reserves (which it cannot control).

Now recall that the official settlements balance equation (14.2 above) tells us that the official settlements balance depends both on the growth rate of the money supply and the growth rate of domestic credit. Although the growth rate of domestic credit may be treated as being under the control of the central bank, the money supply growth rate may not be regarded as being controlled by the central bank, so it is necessary to enquire what does determine its value.

(ii) Growth Rate of Money Supply

When the central bank is pegging the foreign exchange rate and is, as a result, unable to determine the supply of money, the quantity of money in existence will be determined by the amount of money demanded. We have already discovered, in Chapter 10, what determines the demand for money — it depends upon the price level, the level of real income, and the rate of inflation. The demand for money will change therefore as the price level changes, as real income changes, and as the inflation rate changes. In a steady state, when the rate of inflation is constant, the growth rate of the money supply will be equal to the rate of inflation plus the rate of growth of output. That is,

$$\mu = \pi + \rho \tag{14.3}$$

Now recall that the rate of output growth depends on such things as demographic trends, capital accumulation, and technical progress, all of which are being treated as exogenous to, and independent of, the processes that have been analysed here. The rate of output growth, then, may be taken as given. However, that still leaves two variables — the rate of inflation and the rate of money supply growth — which have to be determined.

The theory of inflation developed in Chapter 13 (which dealt only with a closed economy) used the above equation to determine the rate of inflation. In the closed economy, the central bank was viewed as determining the growth rate of the money supply (μ) and, with a given output growth rate, that determines the rate of inflation. In a fixed exchange rate open economy, however, it is not possible for the central bank to decide what the money supply growth rate will be, since it has no control over one of the components of the money supply, namely, the change in the foreign exchange reserves. The above equation, therefore, cannot be regarded as one that determines the rate of inflation. Indeed, given the inflation rate and the growth rate of output, that equation will determine the growth rate of the money supply under fixed exchange rates. The growth rate of the money supply is determined by the growth rate of the demand for money.

What determines the rate of inflation in a fixed exchange rate economy? The answer is the law of one price.

(iii) The Law of One Price

The next step in the story is to recall the law of one price and its implication, the purchasing power parity proposition. Recall (Section B above) that the law of one price says that the rate of change of prices in one country (where the prices are expressed in the currency of that country) will be equal to the rate of change of prices in another country (expressed in units of currency of that other country), plus the rate of depreciation of the first country's currency against that of the second country. In other words, calling the rate of inflation in the rest of the world π_f and the rate of depreciation of the currency, $\Delta\epsilon$,

$$\pi = \pi_f + \Delta\epsilon \tag{14.4}$$

This equation may be better understood with an example. Suppose that inflation in the rest of the world was running at 8 per cent and that the currency was depreciating at 2 per cent per annum. This would imply that the rate of inflation in the domestic economy would be 10 per cent. Thus, there is a relationship between inflation rates in different countries and the exchange rate arising from arbitrage operations in the markets for goods and services.

Now recall that the analysis being conducted here refers to an economy with a fixed exchange rate. If the exchange rate is fixed, then the rate of change of the exchange rate will be zero. From this it follows that in a fixed exchange rate economy the domestic rate of inflation, π, will equal the inflation rate in the rest of the world, π_f. That is,

$$\pi = \pi_f \tag{14.5}$$

This is a fundamental proposition concerning the behaviour of the rate of inflation in an open economy operating under a fixed exchange rate. It does not hold exactly because there are other real things going on to change *relative* prices in the world. How useful an approximation to reality it is, we shall see in the next chapter.

You can think of the rate of inflation in the rest of the world as being given to the small economy which is being analysed. It is probably true that a change in the inflation rate in the United Kingdom will have some slight effect on the inflation rate in the United States and other countries. It is a useful first approximation, however, to assume that effect to be zero. What happens in the United States, the EEC and Japan in aggregate will not, of course, have a negligible effect on what happens in the United Kingdom by virtue of the sheer size of the aggregate of those economies.

You may think of the world inflation rate as being determined by world aggregate money supply growth in exactly the same way as was analysed in Chapter 13. It is as if the world has one money, since all monies can be converted into any money at a known fixed exchange rate. The relevant money supply, therefore, is not the national money supply, but the sum of all the national money supplies (converted into a common unit). Its growth rate is the growth rate that determines world average inflation.

With domestic inflation being determined by world inflation, it is now clear that in a fixed exchange rate economy, the fundamental inflation equation becomes an equation that tells us about the rate of growth of the money supply rather than about the rate of inflation itself. That is, the equation

$$\mu = \pi_f + \rho \tag{14.6}$$

determines μ. The rate of inflation π_f is determined in the rest of the world, and the rate of output growth ρ is determined by long-run forces that are exogenous. What this says is that in a fixed exchange rate open economy the rate of growth of the money supply will be equal to the rate of growth of the demand for money. More money is demanded if prices become higher, and more money is demanded if output increases. The growth in the demand for money is equal to $\pi_f + \rho$. Money is supplied to meet this demand automatically as a result of the central bank's operations in the foreign exchange market, designed to peg the value of the exchange rate. If, when there was a rise in the demand for money the central bank did not supply the extra money needed, the currency would tend to rise in value. To prevent this from happening the central bank would have to take in additional foreign exchange reserves and supply additional domestic money in exchange for the foreign money taken into its reserves.

(iv) The Official Settlements Balance

It is now possible to see what determines the official settlements balance. The official settlements balance (expressed as a proportion of the stock of reserves) is equal to

$$f = \frac{1}{\psi}\mu - (\frac{1-\psi}{\psi})dc \tag{14.2}$$

Also, the money supply growth rate is given by

$$\mu = \pi_f + \rho \tag{14.6}$$

By combining these two propositions, it is apparent that

$$f = \frac{1}{\psi}\pi_f + \frac{1}{\psi}\rho - (\frac{1-\psi}{\psi})dc \tag{14.7}$$

This is a fundamental proposition concerning the determination of the official settlements balance under fixed exchange rates. It says that if a country has a fixed exchange rate, it may have either a balance of payments surplus or a deficit or an equilibrium, and it is a simple matter to achieve whichever of these outcomes is desired. The one policy variable which determines the overall balance on official settlements is the rate of growth of domestic credit. By selling government securities from its portfolio, tightening reserves and forcing commercial banks to sell securities from their portfolios, the central bank can achieve a surplus on the official settlements balance. By doing the contrary, buying domestic securities from the general public and giving the commercial banks enough reserves to increase their holdings of domestic securities, the central bank can generate a deficit on the official settlements balance.

    The official settlements balance is fundamentally a monetary phenomenon caused by the monetary policies of the central bank. As a first approximation, the official settlements balance is independent of the trade flows and capital flows that underlie it.

(v) Aggregate Demand and Supply

Since the money supply is endogenous and not subject to control, you may be wondering what has become of the theory of aggregate supply and aggregate demand in an open economy with a fixed exchange rate. Figure 14.1 illustrates what is going on. This is a standard aggregate supply, aggregate demand diagram. If the rate of growth of output is zero, then y^*, full-employment output, is constant. Also, if the level of foreign prices is held constant, the inflation rate will be zero. Suppose the foreign price level is P_f so that the domestic price level implied by that foreign price level is P_f converted into domestic currency at the exchange rate E i.e. EP_f as marked on the vertical axis. The aggregate supply curve is shown as AS. These two curves intersect at the point a. That is the equilibrium point for the economy. You now ask the question, but what if the aggregate demand curve does not pass through the point a? The answer is that the aggregate demand curve cannot avoid passing through the point a because the money supply, which determines the position of the aggregate demand curve, is determined by the *demand* for money, and not by an exogenous money supply. The demand for money at point a is an amount such that the aggregate demand curve evaluated for that money supply passes exactly through a. If you

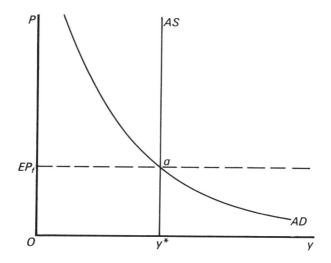

Figure 14.1 *Output, The Price Level, and Aggregate Demand in a Fixed Exchange Rate Open Economy*

The aggregate supply curve AS determines full-employment output, y^*. The foreign price level P_f, when converted to domestic prices by the exchange rate E, determines the domestic price level as EP_f. The position a denotes the equilibrium. Aggregate demand AD will automatically pass through this point because the supply of money, which influences the position of the aggregate demand curve, is determined by the demand for money and therefore by the price level and output level at the point a (rather than being determined exogenously, as in the case of the closed economy).

conduct a thought experiment you can see that the economy can only be at point *a*. Such a thought experiment was conducted in 1741 by David Hume and is still relevant today.

> Suppose four-fifths of all the money in Great Britain to be annihilated in one night, and the nation reduced to the same condition, with regard to specie[2] as in the reigns of the Harrys and Edwards, what would be the consequence? Must not the price of all labour and commodities sink in proportion, and every thing be sold as cheap as they were in those ages? What nation could then dispute with us in any foreign market, or pretend to navigate or to sell manufactures at the same price, which to us would afford sufficient profit? In how little time, therefore, must this bring back the money which we had lost, and raise us to the level of all the neighbouring nations? Where, after we have arrived, we immediately lose the advantage of the cheapness of labour and commodities: and the farther flowing in of money is stopped by our fulness and repletion.
>
> Again, suppose that all the money of Great Britain were multiplied fivefold in a night, must not the contrary effect follow? Must not all labour and commodities rise to such an exorbitant height, that no neighbouring nations could afford to buy from us — while their commodities, on the other hand, became comparatively so cheap, that, in spite of all the laws which could be formed, they would be run in upon us, and our money flow out — till we fall to a level with foreigners, and lose that great superiority of riches, which had laid us under such disadvantages?
>
> Now it is evident, that the same causes, which would correct these exorbitant inequalities, were they to happen miraculously must prevent their happening in the common course of nature, and must for ever, in all neighbouring nations, preserve money nearly proportionable to the art and industry of each nation. All water, wherever it communicates, remains always at a level. Ask naturalists the reason: they tell you, that, were it to be raised in any one place, the superior gravity of that part not being balanced, must depress it, till it meet a counterpoise: and that the same cause, which redresses the inequality when it happens, must for ever prevent, without some violent external operation.[3]

This completes the basic theory of inflation and the balance of payments in a fixed exchange rate economy. Let us now go on to see how inflation is determined in a flexible exchange rate regime, and how the exchange rate itself is determined.

D. Determination of Inflation and the Exchange Rate under a Flexible Exchange Rate Regime

(i) Fundamental Inflation Equation Again

The starting point for understanding what determines inflation and the exchange rate in a flexible exchange rate regime is to recall the inflation theory of Chapter 13. You will recall that, provided the rate of money supply growth is steady, the rate of inflation will settle down at a rate equal to the difference between the growth rate of

---

2. Specie means gold, but in modern parlance is the money stock.

3. David Hume, Of the balance of trade, in *Essays: Moral, Political and Literary*, Oxford University Press, 1963, pp. 318–9 (first published in 1741).

the money supply and the growth rate of full-employment output. That is, the *fundamental inflation equation* is

$$\pi = \mu - \rho \tag{14.8}$$

Recall why this relationship holds. If the rate of money supply growth (less the growth rate of output) is higher than the rate of inflation, then real money balances will be increasing faster than the demand for money is increasing, and the aggregate demand of goods curve will shift outwards, thereby raising the rate at which prices rise. If the rate of money supply growth (less the growth rate of output) is slower than the rate of inflation, then real money balances will be declining faster than the demand for real money balances is declining, and as people attempt to restore their money balances to the desired level, the level of demand for goods will be cut, and this in turn will slow the rate at which prices rise. These forces will always operate when the rate of inflation is different from the rate of growth of the money supply less the rate of output growth.

Although the above theory was developed in the context of a closed economy, a moment's reflection makes it evident that the proposition is equally applicable to an open economy provided the exchange rate is flexible. In a flexible exchange rate economy the central bank has no commitment to use its stock of foreign exchange reserves to maintain the price of its currency in terms of other currencies. The central bank may choose its holdings of foreign exchange reserves in exactly the same way as it chooses how much domestic credit to hold. The implication of this is, of course, that the central bank may, under flexible exchange rates, control the quantity of money as an exogenous policy variable. This being so, equation (14.1) determines the rate of inflation. The growth rate of the money supply, μ, is determined by the central bank and the growth rate of output, ρ, is determined by the real forces that are exogenous to the processes being analysed here. Thus, the predictions about inflation made by the basic model are identical in both the closed economy of Chapter 13 and the flexible exchange rate open economy whose behaviour we are now analysing.

(ii) What is True for One Country is True for Another

The fundamental inflation equation

$$\pi = \mu - \rho \tag{14.8}$$

is not a proposition that is true for only one country. It is true for all countries. Consider some other country, called f, for foreign. The fundamental inflation equation must also be true for the foreign country. That is,

$$\pi_f = \mu_f - \rho_f \tag{14.9}$$

This simply says that in the foreign country the rate of inflation will be equal to its rate of money supply growth minus its rate of full-employment output growth.

(iii) Purchasing Power Parity Again

Next recall the proposition that arbitrage in goods generates purchasing power parity. You will recall that although tariffs, transport costs, and other impediments to trade may drive a wedge between the level of prices in one country and the level in another, arbitrage will ensure that, for given levels of trade distortions, the rate of change of prices in one country will be brought to equality with the rate of change of prices in the other when adjusted for any change in the exchange rate. That is,

$$\pi = \pi_f + \Delta\epsilon \tag{14.4}$$

This says that the rate of inflation in the domestic economy (π) will be equal to the rate of inflation in the foreign economy (π_f) plus the rate at which the currency of the domestic economy is depreciating against the currency of the foreign economy ($\Delta\epsilon$).

(iv) Movements in the Exchange Rate

The above propositions may now be brought together to work out what determines the *foreign exchange rate*. Combining the *domestic forces* which make for *domestic inflation* with the *international arbitrage forces* which ensure that *purchasing power parity* is, on the average, maintained, produces a theory of the exchange rate. To see this, first of all notice that the purchasing power parity relationship, equation (14.4), may be rewritten using the two fundamental inflation equations (14.8) and (14.9). Since the domestic inflation rate π is equal to the domestic money supply growth rate μ minus the rate of output growth ρ, the left-hand side of the purchasing power parity equation π may be replaced with $\mu - \rho$. The same is true of π_f. Notice that π_f is equal to the rate at which money supply is growing in the foreign country μ_f minus the rate of output growth in that country ρ_f. Let us therefore replace π_f on the right-hand side of the purchasing power parity equation by $\mu_f - \rho_f$. This simply says that

$$\mu - \rho = \mu_f - \rho_f + \Delta\epsilon$$

This is nothing other than the purchasing power parity proposition combined with the fundamental inflation equation for each country. This equation may now be rearranged so that it provides an explicit statement as to what is happening to the exchange rate ($\Delta\epsilon$). That is,

$$\Delta\epsilon = (\mu - \mu_f) - (\rho - \rho_f) \tag{14.10}$$

This is the *fundamental exchange rate equation*. It says that:

> the rate of change of the foreign exchange rate between the currencies of two countries

equals the difference between the money supply growth rates in the two countries

minus the difference between the output growth rates in the two countries.

This equation also says that:
  (i)   the faster is the money supply growth rate in the domestic economy, the faster will the currency depreciate (the bigger will be $\Delta\epsilon$);
  (ii) the faster is the money supply growth rate in the foreign country, the faster will the domestic currency appreciate in terms of the foreign currency;
  (iii) the faster is the growth rate of output in the domestic economy, the stronger will be the domestic currency ($\Delta\epsilon$ will be smaller); and

(iv)   the faster is the rate of growth of output in the foreign economy, the weaker will be the domestic currency.

(v) Supply and Demand Yet Again

The factors which determine the exchange rate in the above analysis are nothing other than the forces of *supply* and *demand*. The exchange rate is a price like any other price. It is the relative price of two national monies. *The exchange rate is determined by the supply of and the demand for domestic money relative to the supply of and demand for foreign money.* (Remember that money is a stock, not a flow.)

   Look again at the fundamental exchange rate equation. The first part of that equation tells us about the growth rate of the relative supplies of two monies $(\mu - \mu_f)$. If $\mu - \mu_f$ is positive, the domestic money supply is growing at a faster rate than the foreign money supply, as the domestic money supply is rising relative to the foreign money supply. The second part of the equation $(\rho - \rho_f)$ tells us about the growth rate in the relative demands for the two monies. If the growth rate in output is greater in the domestic economy than that in the foreign economy, then the demand for domestic money will grow at a faster rate than the demand for foreign money.

   Now, if the growth in the relative supplies of money $(\mu - \mu_f)$ is just equal to the growth in the relative demands for money $(\rho - \rho_f)$, the exchange rate will not change, i.e., $\Delta\epsilon$ will be zero. This means that there is a critical growth rate for the domestic money supply (let us call it μ^c) at which the exchange rate will be steady. To find the growth rate μ^c, simply solve the fundamental exchange rate equation for that value of μ which is associated with $\Delta\epsilon = 0$, i.e.,

$$\Delta\epsilon = (\mu - \mu_f) - (\rho - \rho_f) = 0$$

so

$$\mu^c = \mu_f + (\rho - \rho_f)$$

If the money supply grows at a faster rate than μ^c, the currency will depreciate ($\Delta\epsilon$ will be positive) and if the money supply grows at a slower rate than μ^c, the currency will appreciate ($\Delta\epsilon$ will be negative).

   So, *the key thing which a country can control to influence its exchange rate is its money supply growth rate*. Other things being equal, the faster the money supply grows, the faster will the currency depreciate (or the slower will it appreciate). The exchange rate will only be steady if the money supply grows at that critical rate which equals the foreign money supply growth rate plus the difference between the domestic and foreign output growth rates.

(vi) Does a Depreciating Currency Cause Inflation?

There is a popular view which says that inflation is caused by a depreciating currency and that a country can be trapped in a vicious circle of inflation and depreciation about which nothing can be done. You now know enough to know that that is not true. *A depreciating exchange rate is a* **symptom** *of inflation and is caused by the same thing that causes inflation.* You know from the fundamental inflation equation that, other things being equal, inflation will be higher the higher is the money supply growth rate. You also know from the fundamental exchange rate equation that the exchange rate will depreciate faster ($\Delta\epsilon$ is positive and increasing) the bigger is the growth rate of money supply (μ). Thus *both inflation and a weak currency are caused by too high a growth rate of the money supply.*

If a country wants to maintain a steady exchange rate, it is necessary for that country to achieve a money supply growth rate relative to the growth rate of money supply in the rest of the world which exactly offsets the difference in the growth in demands for domestic and foreign money arising from any differences in output growth rates. That being the case, however, with a steady exchange rate the country must accept the inflation rate that is generated in the rest of the world. If, on the other hand, a country wants to achieve a zero rate of inflation, it becomes necessary for the country to make its own money supply grow at the same rate as its own output growth. That is, set μ equal to ρ. This will not ensure a constant value for the exchange rate, however, since the exchange rate will depend on both domestic monetary policy and the monetary policy of the rest of the world. If the rest of the world is undergoing inflation, whereas the domestic economy is maintaining stable prices, then the exchange rate will appreciate ($\Delta\epsilon$ will be negative). If, however, the foreign economy is experiencing deflation, that is, has falling prices, while the domestic economy is maintaining steady prices, then the exchange rate will depreciate ($\Delta\epsilon$ will be positive).

(vii) *Stable Exchange Rates versus Stable Prices*

The above remarks serve to emphasise that *a country cannot choose both its inflation rate and the behaviour of its exchange rate simultaneously.* A country must make a choice as to whether it wants to achieve stable prices, thereby allowing its exchange rate to adjust from time to time to reflect the difference between domestic and foreign inflation, or whether it wants to achieve a fixed exchange rate with the rest of the world, in which case it will have to allow the foreign inflation rate to be fully reflected in the domestic inflation rate.

You now have an understanding of the factors which determine the long-term movements in exchange rates. You see that there are no effects on the exchange rate in the long run arising from such things as import and export demands and the flow of goods and services across national boundaries. In the long run, the exchange rate is determined by monetary equilibrium. With a fixed exchange rate the country abdicates control over its money supply. The automatic changes in the stock of foreign exchange reserves ensure that the growth rate of the money supply is exactly equal to the growth rate of the demand for money, the latter being equal to the world rate of inflation plus the domestic output growth rate. In the case of a flexible exchange rate, the domestic monetary authority controls the stock of foreign exchange reserves and the domestic money supply, thereby forcing the adjustment onto the exchange rate itself. It is movements in the exchange rate that ensure that the stock of money which has been determined by the central bank is willingly held by private economic agents.

E. Determination of the Balance of Payments and the Exchange Rate in a Managed Floating Regime

The basic theory of the determination of the exchange rate under a floating regime and of the balance of payments under a fixed exchange rate regime may be combined in a fairly natural and perhaps even obvious way to set out the fundamental constraints upon the actions of a central bank seeking to pursue a managed (or dirty) floating exchange rate policy. To see these constraints, we simply need to combine three bits of information that have already been examined in the previous sections of this chapter. The first is the relationship between the growth of the money supply, the growth of foreign exchange reserves, and the growth of domestic credit, that is, equation (14.1) which says that

$$\mu = \psi f + (1-\psi)dc \qquad (14.1)$$

The second ingredient is the steady-state relation between money growth, inflation, and output growth, equation (14.3), that is,

$$\mu = \pi + \rho \qquad (14.3)$$

The final ingredient is the purchasing power parity proposition, equation (14.4), that is,

$$\pi = \pi_f + \Delta\epsilon \qquad (14.4)$$

Combining these three propositions — substituting the inflation rate out of equation (14.3), using (14.4), and substituting the money supply growth rate out of (14.1) using (14.3) — gives

$$\pi_f + \Delta\epsilon + \rho = \psi f + (1 - \psi)dc$$

If you subtract the foreign inflation rate from both sides of this equation and also subtract $\psi f + \rho$ from both sides, you obtain

$$\Delta\epsilon - \psi f = [(1 - \psi)dc - \pi_f - \rho] \qquad (14.11)$$

The left-hand side of this equation contains the rate of change of the exchange rate ($\Delta\epsilon$) minus the rate of change of foreign exchange reserves (weighted by the fraction of the money stock backed by those reserves, ψ) ψf. Let us give a name to the left-hand side of this equation: *exchange market pressure*. The right-hand side is simply the growth rate of domestic credit (weighted by the fraction of the money supply backed by domestic credit, $1 - \psi$) i.e. $(1 - \psi)dc$, minus the foreign rate of inflation π_f and minus output growth ρ. All equation (14.11) says is that for a given foreign rate of inflation, a given π_f, the greater is the rate of domestic credit expansion, and the lower is output growth, the stronger will be the exchange market pressure. Exchange market pressure will have to be reflected in either the exchange rate or the stock of reserves. Either the exchange rate will have to rise (the currency will have to depreciate) or reserves will have to fall. Some combination of these two things cannot be avoided. If the central bank wants to manage the exchange rate and keep the exchange rate from falling, then it will have no alternative but to accept a drop in its foreign exchange reserves. The converse of all this is that the lower is domestic credit growth and the higher is output growth relative to the foreign rate of inflation the less will be the exchange market pressure. This would imply that, the lower is the growth rate of domestic credit, the more would the foreign exchange reserves rise and/or the stronger would be the rate of appreciation of the currency ($\Delta\epsilon$ negative). A central bank wishing to pursue tight domestic credit policies (low dc) but at the same time prevent the exchange rate from appreciating (prevent a high negative value of $\Delta\epsilon$) would have to be willing to allow the foreign exchange reserves to rise. Equation (14.11) states the fundamental constraint on the freedom of the central bank to pursue a managed floating policy. A fixed exchange rate is the special case of equation (14.11) where the central bank manages the value of $\Delta\epsilon$ equal to zero, permitting all of the exchange market pressures to come out in the stock of foreign exchange reserves — in the balance of payments. A flexible exchange rate regime is the other opposite extreme, where f is set equal to zero (reserve changes do not occur) and all exchange market pressures are felt by the exchange rate itself. A managed or dirty float is simply a combination of these two extremes determined by the political and other pressures that operate upon the conduct of monetary policy.

SUMMARY

A. Money Supply and Foreign Exchange Reserves

The money supply is, by definition, equal to the sum of foreign exchange reserves and domestic credit.

B. The 'Law of One Price'

The *law of one price* asserts that arbitrage will reduce price differentials to the minimum consistent with transport costs, tariffs, and other physical barriers and impediments to trade.

(i) The *purchasing power parity* theorem states that the price of a particular good in one country will be the same as the price in another country (when the prices are converted at the current exchange rate). This proposition does not strictly apply to price *levels*, since tariffs and transportation costs drive a wedge between price *levels*. However, it does apply to price *changes* expressed in percentage terms. That is, the percentage change in the price of some commodity in the United Kingdom (say) will be equal to the percentage change of the price of the same commodity in the United States plus the percentage rate of depreciation of the pound.

(ii) The *interest rate parity* theorem is an application of the law of one price to asset markets. It states that the rate of interest in the United Kingdom will be equal to the rate of interest in the United States plus the expected rate of depreciation of the pound.

C. Determination of Inflation and the Balance of Payments under Fixed Exchange Rates

In an economy with a fixed exchange rate, inflation is determined by the world rate of inflation. The balance of payments is determined by the domestic credit policies of the central bank. If the central bank creates too much domestic credit, there will be a balance of payments deficit. If the central bank creates too little domestic credit, there will be a balance of payments surplus. The central bank can always achieve a zero balance by permitting exactly the right amount of domestic credit to be created.

D. Determination of Inflation and the Exchange Rate under a Flexible Exchange Rate Regime

When the exchange rate is flexible, the money supply and its growth rate are controllable by the central bank. Inflation is determined in such a case in exactly the same way as it is in the closed economy, by the growth rate of the money supply. The exchange rate is determined by differences in money supply growth rates and output growth rates between countries. Specifically, the exchange rate, being a price like any other price, is determined by supply and demand. Since the exchange rate is the relative price of two monies, it is determined by the relative supplies (stocks) of the two monies and the relative demands for them. There is a sense in which the exchange rate is unlike any other price in that its value depends directly upon the relative monetary policies of the two countries.

E. Determination of the Balance of Payments and the Exchange Rate in a Managed Floating Regime

For a given foreign rate of inflation, the faster is the growth rate of domestic credit, the greater will be the amount of exchange market pressure. Exchange market pressure must come out either in a depreciation of the currency or a loss of foreign exchange reserves. The central bank can select a policy that favours smoothing exchange rate adjustments, by permitting reserves to take the strain, or may select a policy which favours steady reserve behaviour by permitting the foreign exchange rate to take the strain. The central bank cannot choose both the exchange rate and the stock of foreign exchange reserves.

15

Post-War United Kingdom Macroeconomic History: How Well is it Explained by the Basic Model?

The last seven chapters have taken you through the basic model and have generated a variety of predictions about the determination of output, unemployment, inflation, interest rates, the exchange rate and the balance of payments. This chapter provides an opportunity to go back to the facts and to examine the extent to which the basic model is in conformity with those facts and, perhaps more importantly, the extent to which it is not. The chapter will take you through six tasks which are to:

A. **review the movements in the macroeconomic variables which the model seeks to explain;**

B. **summarise the predictions of the basic model;**

C. **review the main labour market shocks;**

D. **examine the growth rate of the money supply;**

E. **examine the course of world inflation;**
   and

F. **understand what the basic model does and does not explain.**

Let us begin with the first of these tasks.

A. Review of Facts

In reviewing the facts — the movements in the main macroeconomic variables which the basic model seeks to explain — all that is necessary is to recall the material presented in Chapters 2 and 7. In this chapter we shall concentrate just on the post-war (post-1946) period and, for some purposes deal only with experience since the middle 1950s. Let us review the main patterns in the data that were presented in those earlier chapters.

First recall the main trends. Three variables — unemployment, inflation, and interest rates — all display clear upward trends through the post-war years. There is no strongly discernable trend in output growth (the *level* of output has grown at a constant trend rate of 2.6 per cent a year). Nor is there any clear trend in the balance of payments. A strong downward trend is evident in the behaviour of the foreign exchange value of the pound. That variable has not, however, fallen in a steady way. Rather, there was a step devaluation in 1949 and again in 1967, after which there was a more gradual depreciation.

Next, let us review the main cyclical features of the data. As we saw in Chapter 7, real income deviates from its trend in a systematic way. In particular, there is a tendency for the deviation in any one year to be related to the deviation in the previous year — output is autocorrelated. The cycles in unemployment closely follow those in output (but of course unemployment moves countercyclically). There is a tendency for inflation and interest rates to move procyclically. The procyclical movements in inflation, whilst clearly present in certain sub-periods, are not the only movements in that variable. From time to time there have been sizeable jumps in the inflation rate which have not been accompanied by a fall in unemployment and often, on the contrary, have been accompanied by a rise in unemployment.

A further feature of Britain's post-war macroeconomic history which is worth highlighting concerns the balance of payments. Although there is no discernable trend in that variable, it is evident that it became much more volatile in the 1970s than it had been in the 50s and 60s.

These, then, are the broad facts concerning Britain's post-war macroeconomic history which we would like to be able to explain: trend increases in unemployment, inflation and interest rates; systematic autocorrelation in deviations of output from trend; countercyclical co-movements in unemployment and procyclical co-movements in interest rates and inflation; and an increasingly volatile balance of payments. Let us now return to the basic model and summarise its key predictions concerning the behaviour of these variables.

B. Predictions of the Basic Model

(i) Output and Unemployment

According to the basic model, fluctuations in output and unemployment are generated by shocks which affect the supply side of the economy — in particular, the labour market. A rise in wages or restriction in employment induced by an economy-wide trade union, a drop in the supply of labour induced by improved unemployment benefit arrangements, or a drop in the supply of labour or the demand for labour induced by a tax wedge, will lower employment, lower output and raise unemployment. Such labour market shocks will also have the effect of raising the price level. Thus, in the face of such shocks there will be negative co-movements in output and prices. The price level will rise (and for a period the inflation rate may appear to have risen) while output falls and unemployment rises.

(ii) Inflation and Interest Rates

The basic model predicts that inflation and interest rates will be closely related to each other. A rise in the inflation rate will induce an equivalent rise in the nominal rate of interest. The basic model further predicts however, that the way in which inflation and interest rates are determined depends in an important way on the foreign exchange rate regime. Under a fixed exchange rate regime the rate of inflation will be determined by international arbitrage and will vary one-for-one with variations in the world rate of inflation. Under a flexible exchange rate regime international arbitrage does not cease to operate. It does, however, cease to be the single most important factor influencing the domestic price level and inflation rate. Instead, both the domestic inflation rate and the foreign exchange rate are determined by the growth rate of the domestic money supply relative to the growth rate of money (and therefore of inflation) in the rest of the world.

(iii) The Balance of Payments

Under a fixed exchange rate regime the balance of payments is determined by the difference between the growth rate of the demand for money and the rate of domestic credit expansion. Under a flexible exchange rate regime the balance of payments is determined purely by the policy decisions of the central monetary authority. Under a managed floating exchange rate regime the balance of payments is determined in a manner analogous to that of a fixed exchange rate setting. In that case however, the monetary authorities do reserve the option of allowing pressures to come out in terms of a change in the exchange rate rather than a rise or fall in foreign exchange reserves.

(iv) Summary

The key predictions of the basic model which we shall check out in the rest of this chapter are as follows: labour market shocks which cut the supply of or demand for labour lower output, raise unemployment and raise prices; under fixed exchange rates, a rise in the world inflation rate leads to a rise in the domestic inflation rate and a rise in domestic interest rates; under a flexible exchange rate regime, a rise in the rate of growth of the money supply leads to a rise in the inflation rate; under a fixed exchange rate or managed floating exchange rate regime, fluctuations in domestic credit expansion lead to fluctuations in the balance of payments.

None of the shocks is predicted to lead to a systematic cycle in real output and employment. Further, none of the shocks makes the prediction that inflation and interest rates will be procyclical. For the basic model to generate cycles in output and unemployment and procyclical movements in prices and interest rates, it will be necessary for the labour market shocks themselves to be cyclical and, furthermore, for monetary shocks (domestic or world) to be positively related to domestic labour market shocks. In the absence of such a coincidence of shocks the basic model is inconsistent with the facts.

Let us now turn to an examination of the shocks starting with those in the labour market.

C. Labour Market Shocks

(i) Union Strength

The labour market shocks that we analysed in Chapter 12 were a trade union-induced rise in real wages, a rise in unemployment benefits, and an increase in the tax wedge that lowers both the supply of and demand for labour. Let us review the broad facts about these three shocks in Britain in the post-war years.

First consider the trade unions. Since there have been many influences on real wages in post-war Britain, it would not be helpful simply to examine the movements in wages. No matter what we found we would not be able to attribute movements to any one particular source. What we can do, however, is to examine the strength of trade unions as measured by some other independent characteristic. A commonly employed measure of trade union strength is the percentage of the labour force that belongs to trade unions. It might be thought that the larger is that percentage the stronger are trade unions, and the more able are they to press *real* wage demands. Of course, as we saw in Chapter 12, if part of the labour force is unionised and part not, a rise in wages in the union sector merely leads to a fall in wages in the non-union sector and has, as a first approximation, no *macro*economic consequences. In the United Kingdom setting, it is probably not unreasonable to proceed on the assumption that the economy is entirely unionised. Whilst many workers do not belong to trade unions, very few of them are able to negotiate their employment terms independently of the terms negotiated by the unions. In other words, the fraction of workers whose wages and other employment conditions are not determined by the outcome of a union-employer negotiation is very small. That being so, changes in the percentage of the labour force belonging to unions may well be regarded as a good indicator of the ability of what is in effect an economy-wide union to press for higher real wages.

What are the facts about union strength on this criterion? Figure 15.1 provides the broad picture in the period from 1950 to 1977. Evidently union strength declined from the early 1950s through to about 1963. For the next 5 years (1963–1968) union strength was virtually constant at just under 40 per cent of the labour force. Since 1968 there has been a dramatic rise in union strength. In 1969 and 1970 there was a jump of more than 4 per cent. Through the decade of the 70s union strength has continued to rise until, by 1977, it had reached 48 per cent of the labour force.

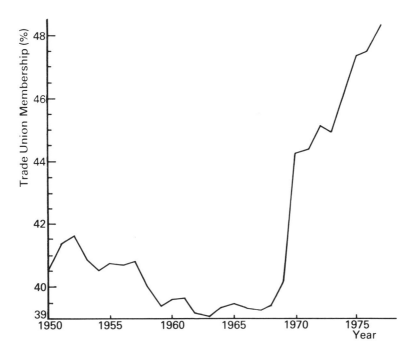

Figure 15.1 *Trade Union Membership 1950–1977*

The fraction of the labour force in trade unions declined steadily through the 1950s, remained constant in the middle 1960s and then grew rapidly in 1969–70 and again in the second half of the 70s. *Source: British Labour Statistics Historical Abstract 1886–1968*, HMSO, 1971, Tables 118, 119. *British Labour Statistics Yearbook 1969*, HMSO, 1971, Tables 45, 156. *Annual Abstract of Statistics*, HMSO, 1980, pp. 146, 182.

Whilst these facts by themselves prove nothing, they do indicate an increasingly strong trade union movement during the decade of the 1970s. That increased strength would bring with it increased bargaining power and increased union funds with which to subsidise strikes thereby yet further strengthening the bargaining position of union negotiators. We shall examine the relationship between these movements in union strength and other variables later in this section. Next let us turn to an examination of unemployment benefits.

(ii) Unemployment Benefits

There have been many minor and one major change in the arrangements concerning unemployment benefits in post-war Britain. The major change was the introduction, in 1966, of the Earnings Related Supplement. Prior to that date unemployment benefits were paid at rates which were independent of the prior earnings of the unemployed person. Further, the benefits were fixed in money terms and increased from time to time by statute. In 1966 unemployment benefits consisted of two parts: one, unrelated to the person's previous earnings and the other, directly tied to the earnings of the person experiencing unemployment. This provided an automatic

Table 15.1 Unemployment Benefits

	Unemployment Benefits as a Percentage of Net Average Earnings
1951	33.1
1961	42.1
1966	66.7
1971	69.6
1976	66.0
1977	65.8
1978	55.5

Source: *Social Trends* 10, 1980, p. 139 (London, HMSO). Figures after 1966 are with the Earnings Related Supplement. Figures before 1971 refer to manual workers only and after 1971 to manual and non-manual workers.

adjustment for unemployment benefits as earnings and prices increased at increasing rates throughout the 1970s. The effects of the changes in the rules governing unemployment benefits can most usefully be summarised by calculating the amount of unemployment benefit that would be paid to an unemployed person, on the average expressed as a percentage of net-of-tax average earnings. Unemployment benefits themselves are not subject to tax, but earnings of course are, so the relevant comparison becomes that of total unemployment benefits expressed as a percentage of after-tax earnings. Table 15.1 provides an outline of the main trends in this variable since 1951. What you see from inspecting the figures in that table is that unemployment benefits rose from being about $\frac{1}{3}$ of net average earnings in 1951 to almost 70 per cent by 1971. Since then, they have slipped back to $\frac{2}{3}$ in 1976–77 and down to 55 per cent by 1978. The slippage since 1971 has occurred as a result of the incomplete linking of benefits to the cost-of-living. The earnings related component of benefits has kept pace with the growth of earnings but the fixed component has not. The pattern presented in Table 15.1 then is one of a strong rise in unemployment benefits up to 1971, but a gradual decline since then.

Let us now turn to the third labour market shock that we analysed in Chapter 12, namely, the tax wedge.

(iii) The Tax Wedge

There have been literally hundreds of changes in tax regulations that may be expected to have effects on the supply of and demand for labour in post-war Britain. We have tried to condense and summarise those changes into a single number. In so doing we have necessarily had to make some simplifying assumptions. What we have done is to calculate the effects of taxes on employment by considering separately three types of taxes and then aggregating them in an appropriate way. The three

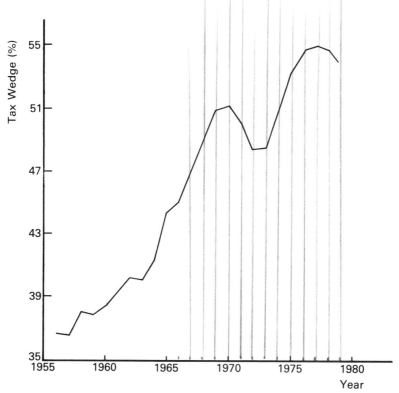

Figure 15.2 *The Tax Wedge 1956–1980*

The tax wedge, the difference between what firms pay for labour and what households receive expressed as a percentage of the total wage bill, has increased steadily from less than 40% in the middle 50s to almost 55% at the end of the 70s. There were distinct cycles around the rising trend. *Source:* Note to this chapter.

taxes are: taxes on employment (employer's National Insurance contributions), income taxes, and expenditure taxes. The taxes on employment and income were expressed as percentages of total income from employment. The taxes on expenditure were expressed as an equivalent tax on income, the idea behind this being simply that, from the point of view of workers and firms, it makes no difference whether the wedge between the real wage paid and the real wage received arises from taxes levied directly in the labour market or in the market for output. (This is a simplification, but one which should not do violence for the purpose at hand.)

The tax wedge, calculated in this way, is set out in Figure 15.2.[1] Evidently the tax wedge has increased dramatically in the period since 1956. The rise was especially strong from 1963 to 1970. There was a dip in the early 70s followed by a further strong rise to 1976–77 and then a subsequent dip. Nevertheless, the positive trend in the tax wedge is very clear.

---

1. The precise sources of data and method of calculation of the tax wedge are set out in a note at the end of this chapter (page 221).

(iv) Explaining Unemployment

How well do these developments in the labour market explain the movements in unemployment? Figure 15.3 provides a summary basis for answering this question. The movements in unemployment since 1950 are shown as the thick line displaying a clear systematic cycle superimposed around a trend that is gently rising through the middle 1960s and rising strongly from the end of the 1960s through the 70s. The various labour market shocks are also shown in that figure. Union strength is seen gradually declining through the 1950s, virtually constant for the middle years of the 60s, and then rising sharply in 1970 and for the rest of that decade. Evidently, the relationship between these two variables is not that close. The falling fraction of the labour force unionised in the 1950s was not matched by a fall in the average rate of unemployment. The constant union strength measure through the 60s was accompanied by a trend rise in unemployment. The sharp rise in union strength at the end of the 1970s is followed by a sharp rise in unemployment during the 1970s. There is no close alignment, however, between those movements. The strong rise in unemployment comes between 1974 and 1977, while the strong rise in union strength occurs in 1969/70. Whilst it may well have been an important influence on unemployment, the direction and timing of changes in union strength do not seem to be closely related to the general movements in unemployment.

Consider next the unemployment benefits. These are shown as the 7 points representing the 7 years for which data are recorded in Table 15.1. Comparing those movements with unemployment, we again see at best a loose connection and, especially in the 1970s, a relationship that is contrary to that which is predicted by the basic model. The rise in unemployment benefits between 1951 and 1971 relates quite well to the trend rise in unemployment over that 20 year period. The fall in the benefits ratio in the 1970s accompanied by the strong rise in unemployment through that decade does not relate well to the theory.

Finally, consider the tax wedge. It is evident than in this case there is a much closer correspondence with unemployment than in the case of the two preceding shocks. The tax wedge rises in line with the rising unemployment rate all the way through the 60s and 70s. There is a tendency for the wedge to rise faster than unemployment in the late 60s and slightly less quickly in the 70s. What this implies is that the relationship between the wedge and unemployment is non-linear. Figure 15.4 illustrates this more clearly. In that figure the unemployment rate is plotted on the vertical axis and the tax wedge on the horizontal axis. Evidently, as the tax wedge rises from around 40 per cent in the late 1950s and early 1960s to the 50 per cent mark around 1970, so the average unemployment rate rises from around 2 per cent to 3 per cent. As the tax wedge rises a further 5 percentage points (from 50 to 55 per cent) through the second half of the 1970s, the average unemployment rate climbs to around $5\frac{1}{2}$ per cent. Thus, the elasticity of unemployment with respect to the tax wedge is increasing as the tax wedge increases from the high 30 per cent range to the mid-50 per cent range.

None of the analysis of the labour market shocks that we have just conducted can be regarded as definitively settling the issue of which labour market shocks have been important and which not. It may well be that all three shocks can be shown to have played some independent role. However, in broad terms, it seems that movements in trade union strength and in unemployment benefits do not, at least by themselves,

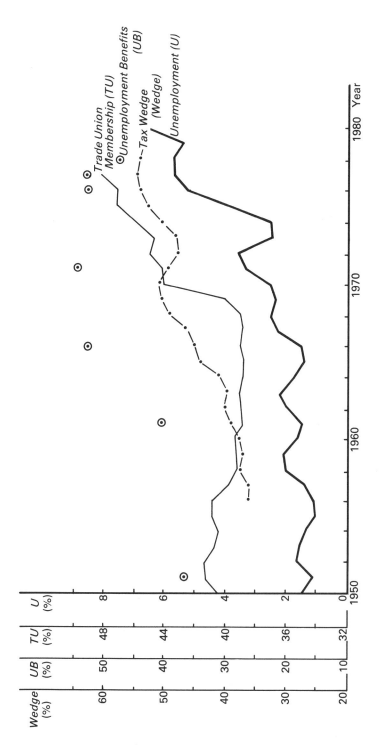

Figure 15.3 *Labour Market Shocks and Unemployment*

Unemployment (the thick line) is not closely related with unemployment benefits or trade union membership, but does correspond closely to movements in the tax wedge. *Source:* Unemployment rate, Appendix to Chapter 2; Tax wedge, see Figure 15.1; Unemployment benefits, Table 15.1; Trade union membership, see Figure 15.2.

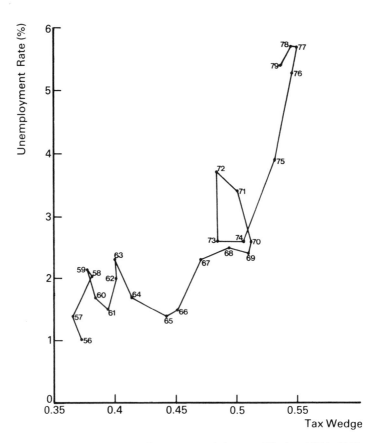

Figure 15.4 *Unemployment and the Tax Wedge 1956–1979*
The relationship between unemployment and the tax wedge is non-linear. The effect of a rise
in the tax wedge on unemployment becomes larger as the tax wedge itself rises. There are
other independent cyclical movements in each of the two variables which are not closely
related. *Source:* Unemployment rate, Appendix to Chapter 2; Tax wedge, see Figure 15.2.

adequately account for movements in unemployment. In contrast, there does appear
to be a strong relationship between the tax wedge and the unemployment rate. Even
this positive finding cannot, of course, be taken as indisputable evidence for the
effect of the tax wedge on unemployment. It is, however, a striking relationship and
one that would have to be explained away if it was to be shown that the tax wedge and
unemployment were not related to each other.

   Although the tax wedge seems well capable of explaining the broad trend in
unemployment in the post-war period, it rather evidently is not capable of
accounting for the cycle. This can be seen both in Figure 15.3 and perhaps more
clearly in Figure 15.4. Clearly, the movements in unemployment are more volatile
than movements in the wedge and there are systematic cycles in the former which are
not present in the latter variable.

   Let us now turn to an examination of the shocks emanating from the rest of the
world and from the monetary sector.

D. Money Supply and World Inflation

In examining the monetary shocks that have hit the United Kingdom economy in the post-war years we need to distinguish between the fixed exchange rate period (up to 1972) and the flexible exchange rate period (after 1972). Under fixed exchange rates, the prediction is that inflation in the United Kingdom will be closely related to inflation in the rest of the world. Under floating exchange rates there is no such prediction. Rather, in that case, United Kingdom inflation will be influenced by United Kingdom money growth.

Let us look first at the relationship between world inflation and United Kingdom inflation. Figure 15.5 provides a description of that relationship. The continuous line sloping upwards in that figure shows the line of equality between United Kingdom inflation and world inflation. The two broken lines show a range of 2 per cent around the equality between the inflation rates. In other words, any observations lying inside those two broken lines show that world inflation and United Kingdom inflation did not deviate by more than 2 percentage points. The inflation rates used in constructing Figure 15.5 are those of consumer price indexes. This has been dictated by the availability of a world inflation measure put together by the International Monetary Fund. Evidently, there is a tendency for United Kingdom inflation to lie within a 2 per cent band of the world inflation rate. There have been exceptional years when United Kingdom inflation has been above that rate and just one year (1959) when the United Kingdom experienced inflation of more than 2 per cent below the world rate. It is striking that in the 1970s, after exchange rates became flexible, there were three years (1975–7) when United Kingdom inflation substantially exceeded the world average rate. In 1971 United Kingdom inflation was also substantially ahead of the world average. It is noteworthy that in the years immediately following devaluations of the pound (1949 and 1967) there was no tendency for United Kingdom inflation to be unusually higher than world inflation. There has, however, been a tendency for United Kingdom inflation to exceed world inflation on the average. Only nine of the years between 1950 and 1979 were ones in which United Kingdom inflation fell short of that of the world average. This would seem to imply that when devaluations occurred they had, to some extent, already been anticipated by United Kingdom inflation running slightly ahead of the world average rate.

In broad terms the predictions of the basic theory concerning the relationship between United Kingdom and world inflation are borne out by Figure 15.5. They are not, however, borne out in any precise detail. There is quite a lot of independent movement in United Kingdom inflation not accounted for by variations in the world inflation rate.

Let us now turn to an examination of the money supply growth rate in the United Kingdom. Figure 15.6 charts the course of the growth rate of three monetary aggregates, the monetary base (*MB*), narrow money (*M1*), and a broad money (*sterling M3*). Perhaps the most noteworthy feature of the money supply growth figures shown in Figure 15.6 are their erratic nature and the lack of a tendency for the different aggregates to move in unison with each other. A more careful examination of the figure does reveal, however, that the money supply growth rate, however measured, was higher in the 1970s than it had been in the 1960s. This observation is entirely consistent with the tendency for inflation in the 1970s to exceed what it had

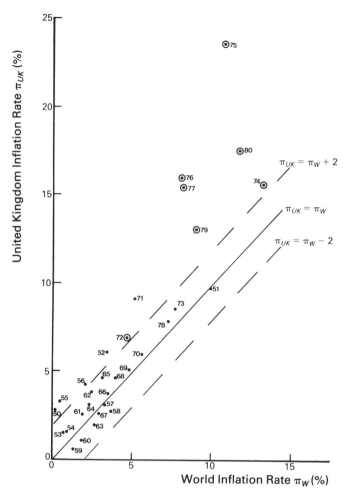

Figure 15.5 *United Kingdom and World Inflation*
Usually, United Kingdom inflation has been within 2% of world inflation. Only during the floating exchange rate years of the 1970s did United Kingdom inflation break away strongly from world inflation and then only in 1975. ~~Source: Unemployment rate, Appendix to Chapter 2; Tax wedge, see Figure 15.2.~~ *Source:* UK inflation rate, Appendix to Chapter 2; World inflation rate, *IFS Yearbook*, 1980, pp. 58–9, *IFS*, p. 45, line 10.)

been in the 1960s. The relationship between the rise in money supply growth and inflation, however, is far from being a precise one. Furthermore, the different monetary aggregates behave in different ways and, therefore, there is considerable ambiguity as to which of the aggregates is the one that we ought to look at in order to explain movements of inflation.

Although not resolving the issue, it is of some interest to examine the relationship between money growth on the average (the average of the growth rate of the money base, *M1* and *sterling M3*) and also averaged over time to remove some of the erratic fluctuations. We have constructed an average of the three growth rates (*MB, M1* and *sterling M3*) and then constructed a three-year moving average of that averaged growth rate. This takes out the more volatile reversals in money growth and enables

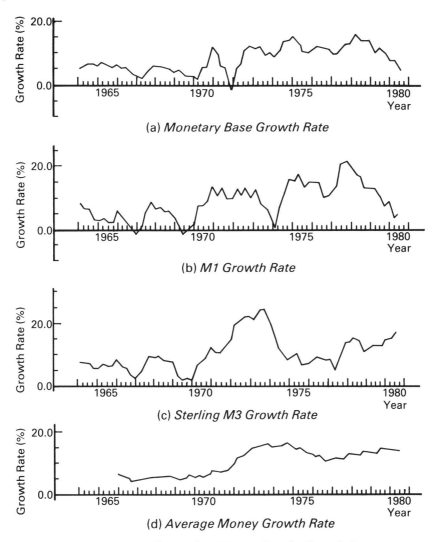

Figure 15.6 *United Kingdom Money Supply Growth Rates*
Monetary base (Frame (a)), *M1* (Frame (b)) and *sterling M3* (Frame (c)) growth rates are
shown from 1963 to 1980. They are extremely volatile and each seems to have a life of its own.
The one striking feature they have in common, however, is that money growth in the 1970s was
higher than in the 1960s on all three definitions. Frame (d) shows the average of the three
growth rates further averaged over three preceding years. This displays very strongly the rise
in money growth at the beginning of the 1970s. *Source:* Monetary base, *Bank of England
Quarterly Bulletin*, Vol. 21, No. 1, March 1981, pp.63–4; *M1* and sterling *M3*, *Quarterly
Money Stock* Series 1963I–1979III, Bank of England, December 1979 & *Bank of England
Quarterly Bulletin*, Vol. 21, No. 2, 1981, Table 11.1.

us to focus on its broad trend. That average money growth rate is also shown in
Figure 15.6. Its relationship with inflation is shown in Figure 15.7. It now becomes
evident that there is a strong positive relationship between inflation and money
growth. According to the basic model, that relationship implies that inflation
generates money growth during the fixed exchange rate period and, conversely, the

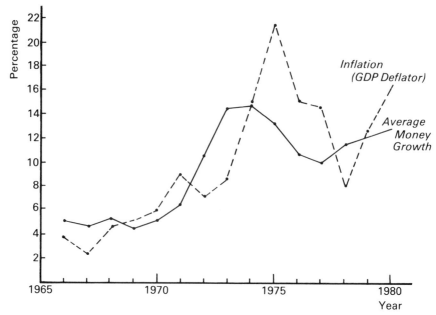

Figure 15.7 *United Kingdom Money Growth and Inflation 1966–1980*
The three-year moving average growth rate of the average of the three monetary aggregates is
well related with movements in inflation. As predicted by the theory inflation overshoots
money growth very strongly during the upturn in 1973–75 and 1978–80 as well as during the
downturn in 1975–78. *Source:* Inflation rate, Appendix to Chapter 2; Money growth, see
Figure 15.6.

money growth itself generates the inflation during the flexible exchange rate period.
Of course, the relationship cannot tell us in which direction causation runs. What it
does tell us, however, is that the predictions of the basic model are not inconsistent
with the facts, provided we are prepared to average out the more volatile aspects of
money growth.

A further prediction of the basic model is that, when there is a change in the growth
rate of the money supply, the inflation rate will change in the same direction but by a
larger amount. That is, inflation will overshoot money growth changes. This
prediction is strongly borne out by the data shown in Figure 15.7, in both major
upturns of 1974–75 and 1978–80 as well as in the downturn of 1975–78.

A yet further prediction concerning the effects of the growth rate of money is that,
when domestic money growth runs ahead of world money growth, the foreign
exchange value of domestic currency will fall. Recalling the behaviour of the
exchange rate, charted in Figure 2.8 (Chapter 2), it is evident that the foreign
exchange value of the pound fell all the way through the 1970s up to 1978. From 1978
to 1980 the pound appreciated but, in 1981 depreciated again. The trend
depreciation of the pound is reasonably well accounted for by the tendency for
United Kingdom money growth to generate inflation in the United Kingdom which,
in the years 1975, 1976 and 1977 strongly exceeded the inflation rates being
experienced in the rest of the world. The tendency for the pound to appreciate

between 1978 and 1980 is not accounted for, however, by these events. United Kingdom inflation did move back into alignment with world inflation in 1979. That, however, would lead to the prediction that the pound's value would stabilise on the foreign exchange markets rather than appreciate. Thus, the broad trend decline in the foreign exchange value of the pound up to 1978 is well accounted for by the basic model, but the rebound after 1978 is not explained by this model.

The basic model predicts that the balance of payments depends upon the difference between the growth rate of the money supply and domestic credit expansion. Now under a fixed exchange rate, the growth rate of the money supply (*nominal* money) is determined entirely by the demand for money and therefore fluctuates with fluctuations in the inflation rate. The increased volatility in inflation (both world and domestic) in the 1970s would be predicted to have increased the volatility in the United Kingdom's demand for money. This in turn would be predicted to lead to increased volatility in the balance of payments unless it was exactly matched by an increasingly volatile domestic credit expansion. In fact, domestic credit expansion has fluctuated more in the 1970s than it did in the 1950s and 60s. It has not, however, behaved in such a way as to offset the increased volatility in the demand for money and so some of the effects of increased volatility in demand for money have come out as an increasingly volatile balance of payments. Here then is a further set of stylised facts well accounted for by the basic model.

E. What the Basic Model Fails to Explain

We have now reviewed the main facts about labour market and monetary shocks in the United Kingdom in the post-war period and have seen that some of these shocks appear to be capable of accounting for some of the patterns in unemployment and inflation as well as in the exchange rate and balance of payments. In particular, the trend rise in unemployment through the 1960s and 70s is not inconsistent with the basic model and, according to that model, could have arisen as a result of a rise in the scale of the tax wedge in the labour market. Fluctuations in inflation in the United Kingdom are reasonably well accounted for by fluctuations in world inflation during the fixed exchange rate period, and in the 1970s with flexible exchange rates, are reasonably well accounted for by a rise in the growth rate of United Kingdom money. The volatility of the balance of payments in the 1970s is not inconsistent with the basic model and, according to that model would have arisen from the increasingly volatile movements in the demand for money. The depreciating pound from 1971 to 1978 is consistent with the basic model and arises from the tendency for United Kingdom inflation (money growth) to run ahead of that in the rest of the world.

There are, however, some important patterns in the data that are not well explained by the basic model. In particular, the autocorrelation (systematic fluctuations) in output and unemployment cannot be viewed as having been generated by well-defined cycles in the labour market shocks that we have analysed. Thus, these regular cycles in activity are inconsistent with the predictions of the basic model. Further, although the broad trends in inflation are predicted by the basic model, the tendency for there to be, from time to time, procyclical movements in inflation and real economic activity do not line up with the predictions of the model. Also the rebound in the foreign exchange value of sterling at the end of the 1970s and into 1980 is not consistent with the predictions of the model.

SUMMARY

A. Review of Facts

The dominant features of post-war United Kingdom macroeconomic history are as follows:
  (1) unemployment, inflation, and interest rates have trended upwards;
  (2) there has been no trend to output growth or the balance of payments;
  (3) the exchange rate has trended downwards and the balance of payments has become more volatile; and
  (4) there have been systematic cycles in output and unemployment with procyclical movements in prices and interest rates.

B. Predictions of the Basic Model

The basic model predicts that movements in output and unemployment will be caused by labour market shocks induced either by trade unions or by government policy actions. Inflation and interest rates will be determined by world inflation and world interest rates under a fixed exchange rate regime, but by the growth rate of the domestic money supply when exchange rates are flexible. The balance of payments will be determined by the growth of the demand for money minus domestic credit expansion.

C. Labour Market Shocks

Trade unions declined in strength in the late 1950s, held a constant strength through the middle 1960s and then grew strongly to encompass almost 50 per cent of the labour force by the late 1970s. Unemployment benefits were improved from roughly $\frac{1}{3}$ of net wages to more than $\frac{2}{3}$ of net wages between 1950 and the middle 1970s. Toward the end of the 70s the benefit to wage ratio declined slightly. The tax wedge in the labour market increased strongly through the post-war years. The trends in unemployment seem to be reasonably well related to the trends in the labour market tax wedge, though not to unemployment benefits and the strength of trade unions. Whilst there are some cyclical movements in the tax wedge, they do not line up well with the cycles in unemployment and output.

D. Money Supply and World Inflation

Fluctuations in world inflation have been closely related with fluctuations in United Kingdom inflation with the notable exception of 1975–7. During that period of the 70s the pound was floating and United Kingdom money growth was very strong. There is a strong relationship between United Kingdom inflation and money growth when the latter is averaged over a number of years and over a number of alternative definitions of money. That relationship is consistent with the predictions of the basic model — that world inflation generates United Kingdom inflation which in turn generates United Kingdom money growth under fixed exchange rates and conversely, that United Kingdom money growth generates United Kingdom inflation under flexible exchange rates.

E. What the Basic Model Fails to Explain

Although the basic model is capable of explaining some of the broad trends in unemployment, inflation and other variables, it is not capable of accounting for the tendency for output and unemployment to display a systematic cycle. Further, it cannot explain the procyclical co-movements in inflation which are observed from time to time. Neither can it explain the tendency for the foreign exchange value of the pound to rise between 1978 and 1980.

Note on the Tax Wedge

The tax wedge was calculated in the following way: From the point of view of the household, the real wage received is equal to the gross money wage minus all income taxes all divided by the average price level of goods bought by households. The latter is the price received by firms plus expenditure taxes. The difference between this net-of-tax real wage and the gross-of-tax real wage, W/P, may be called the 'household tax wedge' and is given by the following equation

$$Household\ Tax\ Wedge = Gross\text{-}of\text{-}Tax\ Real\ Wage\ (W/P)$$

$$\textbf{less}\ Net\text{-}of\text{-}Tax\ Real\ Wage\left(\frac{W(1-t_y)}{P(1+t_c)}\right) \tag{1}$$

W stands for the money wage rate, P for the price level, t_y for the average rate of income tax, and t_c for the average rate of expenditure tax. Equation (1) can be rearranged to give

$$Household\ Tax\ Wedge = \frac{W}{P}\left(\frac{t_c+t_y}{1+t_c}\right) \tag{2}$$

From the point of view of the firm, the cost of labour is equal to the gross wage paid to households plus employment taxes. The tax wedge for firms is the difference between the total cost of labour and W/P; that is

$$Firm's\ Tax\ Wedge = Total\ Cost\ of\ Labour\left(\frac{W}{P}(1+t_e)\right)$$

less Gross-of-Tax Real Wage (W/P)   (3)

where t_e is the average rate of taxes on employment paid by firms. Equation (3) may be rearranged to give

$$Firm's\ Tax\ Wedge = \frac{W}{P}\,t_e \tag{4}$$

The tax wedge shown in Figure 15.2 (p.211) is the sum of the household's and firm's tax wedges and is

$$Tax\ Wedge = \left(\frac{t_c + t_y}{1 + t_c} + t_e\right)\frac{W}{P} \tag{5}$$

The tax rates were calculated according to the following formulae:

$$t_y = DT \div YW \tag{6}$$

$$t_c = ET \div (C - ET) \tag{7}$$

$$t_e = EC \div (YW - EC) \tag{8}$$

where DT is total direct taxes paid by persons, ET is total expenditure taxes, YW is total income from employment, C is consumers' expenditure, and EC is employers' National Insurance contributions.

The sources for these variables are as follows:

Total Income from Employment (YW), Consumers' Expenditure (C) and Direct Taxes on Income (DT):

         1956–1960 *National Income and Expenditure* 1967, p. 4
         1961–1968 *National Income and Expenditure* 1972, p. 5
         1969–1979 *National Income and Expenditure* 1980, p. 28

Expenditure Tax (ET):

         1956–1960 *National Income and Expenditure* 1966, p. 58
         1961–1965 *National Income and Expenditure* 1972, p. 56
         1966–1968 *National Income and Expenditure* 1978, p. 60
         1969–1979 *National Income and Expenditure* 1980, p. 58

Employers' Contributions (EC):

         1956–1960 *National Income and Expenditure* 1967, p. 53
         1961–1968 *National Income and Expenditure* 1972, p. 47
         1969–1979 *National Income and Expenditure* 1980, p. 53

Review Questions

1. What are the main trends in the United Kingdom's macroeconomic variables which the basic model seeks to explain?

2. What predictions does the basic model make concerning the effects of:
   (i)   a union-induced rise in wages
   (ii) a rise in unemployment benefits and
   (iii) a rise in the size of the tax wedge?
   Distinguish between the effects on real variables and the price level and also highlight the predicted co-movements between prices and the real variables.

3.   How have the labour market variables — union strength, unemployment benefits, and the tax wedge — behaved in the United Kingdom in the post-war years?

4.   Which, if any, of these labour market shocks seems capable of accounting for the trend in unemployment? How would you go about criticising and possibly overturning the conclusions reached in this chapter concerning those effects?

5.   What have been the main patterns of money growth in the United Kingdom since 1963? Have all the different definitions of money behaved in the same way? In what respects have they differed and in what respects have they shared a common pattern? What are the main predictions of the basic model concerning the relationship between money and inflation

     (i)   under fixed exchange rates

     (ii) under flexible exchange rates?

6.   Does the observed relationship between money growth and inflation in the United Kingdom contradict the predictions of the basic model?

7.   What are the main failings of the basic model? Which of its predictions are not seen in the data?

Part IV

The Keynesian Model of Income, Employment, and the Price Level

16

Introduction to the Keynesian Model

You have now studied the *basic model* of output, employment, and the price level and have discovered that there is a good deal of our recent macroeconomic history which that model is capable of explaining. You also know however, that it has some serious shortcomings. It cannot explain several features of the business cycle. Nor can it account for the long and deep depression that the United Kingdom and the rest of the world suffered throughout the entire decade of the 1930s.

You are now going to embark upon a study of an important modification to the basic model. When you see the major feature of that modification in the next chapter, you will think it very trivial. In a sense, it *is* a trivial modification. It does, however, have radical implications, both for our understanding of macroeconomic phenomena and for the design and conduct of macroeconomic policy. The modification to the basic model which you are about to study is one suggested by *John Maynard Keynes* in the middle 1930s.

The implications of Keynes's modification of the basic model are so radical, in fact, that it is worthwhile giving the resulting model a name of its own. We shall call it the *Keynesian model*.

You have just two tasks in this short chapter, which are to:

A. **know why you are studying the Keynesian model;**
   and
B. **know the main strengths and weaknesses of the Keynesian model.**

A. Why Study the Keynesian Model?

There are three main reasons why you are studying the Keynesian model. First, it is the model which has, more than any other, shaped the thinking and understanding about macroeconomic phenomena of several generations of economists and policy

226

makers and, more importantly, it is the model which shapes the views of many of those who are in positions of authority and power today. Keynes's revolutionary ideas were published in 1936 in his book *The General Theory of Employment, Interest and Money*. In the closing paragraph of that book (pp. 383–84) Keynes wrote:

> The ideas of economists and political philosophers, both when they are right and when they are wrong, are more powerful than is commonly understood. Indeed the world is ruled by little else. Practical men, who believe themselves to be quite exempt from any intellectual influences, are usually the slaves of some defunct economist. Mad men in authority, who hear voices in the air, are distilling their frenzy from some academic scribbler of a few years back. I am sure that the power of vested interests is vastly exaggerated compared with the gradual encroachment of ideas. Not, indeed, immediately, but after a certain interval; for in the field of economic and political philosophy there are not many who are influenced by new theories after they are 25 or 30 years of age, so that the ideas which civil servants and politicians and even agitators apply to current events are not likely to be the newest. But, sooner or later, it is ideas not vested interests, which are dangerous for good or evil.

As you see from this passage, Keynes was not just a brilliant economist, but also an incredibly perceptive observer of the human condition in a broader sense. Keynes was writing in 1936 of the ideas held by politicians and civil servants at that time. He would have been the last to be surprised to discover that his own ideas, radical and revolutionary though they were in 1936, are regarded by the leading economists of today in the same way as he regarded the ideas of his precursors. Nevertheless, the very fact that the ideas of Keynes are so pervasively believed in today and so widely used as the justification for much current economic policy making requires that you, as a student of modern macroeconomics, understand that body of knowledge and understand its major strengths and weaknesses. This, then, is the first and perhaps most important reason why you are embarking upon a study of what is, in many ways, an outdated way of looking at macroeconomics.

The second reason for studying the Keynesian model is that it remains the only, even rudimentary, explanation that we have for the event known as the *Great Depression*. The persistence, for more than a decade, of unemployment rates in excess of 10 per cent with no tendency for prices to fall, remains a challenge to those who seek a rational explanation for economic phenomena. Keynes did not offer a rational explanation of that phenomenon. That remains a task for a future generation of students of economics. Nevertheless, Keynes did provide us with an explanation which, rudimentary and unsatisfactory though it may be, is the only one available. Even though Keynes's explanation for the Great Depression is not a satisfactory one, by understanding that explanation you will be better able to understand the current research challenge that remains ahead of us.

The third reason for studying the Keynesian model is that, in the process of attempting to explain the phenomenon of the Great Depression, Keynes made some innovations in macroeconomics which have stood the test of time and remain a useful part of modern macroeconomics. This is the area of generalising the theory of aggregate demand. In this area Keynes made innovations which are today almost universally accepted by economists of all schools of thought and shades of opinion. Part of the Keynesian model is therefore a central ingredient in mainstream modern macroeconomics.

B. Strengths and Weaknesses of the Keynesian Model

The main strength of the Keynesian model is that it provides an explanation (though unsatisfactory) of the phenomenon of the Great Depression. This phenomenon of high and persistent unemployment with rather stable prices is hard to explain with the basic model. The main strength of the Keynesian model is that it does provide an internally consistent rationalisation for the Great Depression.

The major weakness of the Keynesian model is that the explanation of the Great Depression which it provides seems to involve irrational behaviour. That is, it seems to involve behaviour that is inconsistent with profit maximisation and utility maximisation on the part of firms and individuals. Modern Keynesians (new Keynesians) seek to show that although the Keynesian model in fact *appears* to involve irrational behaviour, it actually does not. You will be given a brief account of some of this work in Part V of the book, when the new macroeconomics is developed.

SUMMARY

A. Why Study the Keynesian Model?

You are studying the *Keynesian model* for three reasons:
  (i)   it is the model which governs the thinking of those in positions of authority and power today and is the basis of most current macroeconomic policy making;
  (ii)   it provides the only available rudimentary explanation of the phenomenon of the Great Depression; and
  (iii) it contains some modifications to the basic theory of aggregate demand which have been absorbed into the mainstream body of macroeconomics.

B. Strengths and Weaknesses of the Keynesian Model

The main strength of the Keynesian model is that it provides a rudimentary explanation for the Great Depression.

The main weakness of the Keynesian model is that the explanation of the Great Depression which it provides seems to be inconsistent with the notion that individuals and firms seek to maximise utility and profits.

Review Questions

1. What are the three main reasons for studying the Keynesian model?

2. Examine the facts about unemployment, output, and inflation in the years of the Great Depression (1930–1933) set out in the Appendix to Chapter 2 and contrast those facts with the predictions of the basic model.

3. One of the difficult tasks still outstanding for economists is to find an explanation of the Great Depression that does *not* involve assuming that people behave irrationally — that they do not maximise profits and utility. Why do we regard explanations which involve assuming irrational behaviour as unsatisfactory?

17

The Keynesian Theory of Aggregate Supply

The objective of this chapter is to enable you to understand the Keynesian theory of aggregate supply. You have four detailed tasks. They are to:

- **A.** know Keynes's modification to the basic model's theory of aggregate supply;
- **B.** understand the nature of the Keynesian aggregate supply curve;
- **C.** know how to derive the Keynesian aggregate supply curve; and
- **D.** understand the approximate Keynesian aggregate supply curve — the inverse 'L'.

A. Keynes's Modification to the Basic Model

If your memory of the analysis in Chapter 9 on aggregate supply and the labour market is not fresh, you will perhaps find it helpful before going any further to review the material in that chapter. It is possible to illustrate Keynes's major modification to the basic model by recalling the labour market equilibrium of the basic model. Figure 9.6 illustrated that equilibrium, and it is reproduced in Figure 17.1. You will recall that the real wage is measured on the vertical axis of the diagram and the number of people employed is measured on the horizontal axis. The curve labelled n^d represents the demand for labour that will be forthcoming from profit-maximising firms. In order to achieve a maximum profit, firms hire labour up to the point at which the real wage is equal to the marginal product of labour. The upward sloping curve, labelled

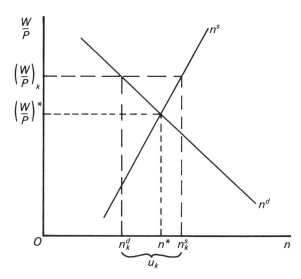

Figure 17.1 *The Labour Market in the Keynesian Model*
The money wage rate will rise quickly to achieve an equilibrium in the labour market if the quantity of labour demanded exceeds the quantity supplied. When, however, the quantity of labour demanded is less than the quantity of labour supplied, the money wage rate will not fall quickly. More strongly, the money wage is rigid in a downward direction. This means that the real wage can become stuck at a level like $(W/P)_k$ so that there is an excess supply of labour and unemployment u_k.

---

n^s, represents the supply of labour that will be forthcoming from utility-maximising households. To induce more people to work (that is, to induce more people to consume less leisure) a higher real wage has to be offered. The labour market of the basic model achieves an equilibrium at the real wage $(W/P)^*$ and at the employment level n^*. At that real wage, the demands for labour by firms and the supplies of labour by households are exactly balanced, and no forces are at work making either households or firms want to change the situation.

Keynes's modification of the basic model is to deny that the labour market always achieves an equilibrium at the point at which the demand for labour equals the supply of labour. For Keynes, that position, represented in Figure 17.1 as the real wage $(W/P)^*$ and the level of employment n^*, is just a *special case*.

Keynes dropped the assumption of the basic model that the real wage adjusts quickly to achieve a labour market equilibrium in which the quantity of labour supplied equals the quantity demanded. In place of that assumption Keynes introduced a far-reaching modification. Keynes's modification is that *the money wage rate will **rise** quickly to achieve an equilibrium in the labour market if the quantity of labour demanded exceeds the quantity of labour supplied. When, however, the quantity of labour demanded is less than the quantity of labour supplied, the money wage rate will not fall quickly.* Indeed, Keynes made the stronger assumption that *the money wage rate is rigid in a downward direction.*

You can think of this as meaning that the money wage rate behaves a bit like a ratchet. It will move in one direction but not in the other. Excess demands for labour will never be observed because the money wage rate will always rise quickly enough to achieve equality between the quantity of labour supplied and demanded. Excess supplies of labour, however, will be observed and they will arise in situations in which the real wage is higher than the labour market clearing real wage. They will persist so long as the real wage stays too high. Since, by Keynes's assumption, the money wage rate will not fall, a situation of excess supply of labour can only be cured by a fall in the real wage being brought about by a rise in the price level.[1]

The remarks made above can be illustrated with the help of Figure 17.1. The basic model solution is shown in Figure 17.1 as n^* and $(W/P)^*$. Now imagine that because the money wage rate is downwardly rigid, the real wage is stuck at $(W/P)_k$, as shown in the figure. At this real wage rate, n_k^d workers will be demanded by firms. The quantity of labour that households want to supply at that real wage is shown as n_k^s. Evidently, the quantity of labour supplied exceeds the quantity demanded. Since trade is voluntary, firms cannot be forced to hire more workers than they wish to hire, and the quantity of labour actually employed will equal the quantity of labour demanded. The difference between the quantity of labour supplied and the quantity demanded will be the quantity of labour that is involuntarily unemployed. This is shown in the diagram as u_k. This is *Keynesian unemployment*. Keynesian unemployment is different from the type of unemployment that you met in Chapter 12. It is a consequence of the assumption that the money wage rate will not move downwards in order to clear the labour market. In contrast to this, in the basic model, the money wage rate was assumed to have unlimited flexibility in both directions so as always to achieve a cleared labour market. Unemployment arose in that model as a result of utility-maximising withdrawals from work in order to undertake job search or as the result of government- or union-imposed real wage rigidities.

The situation depicted in Figure 17.1 as $(W/P)_k$ and n_k^d is just one of the possible Keynesian unemployment positions. The higher is the real wage, the lower will be the demand for labour and the higher the supply of labour. The lower, therefore, would be the level of employment and the higher the level of unemployment.

According to Keynes's theory the real wage can never be lower than $(W/P)^*$. If momentarily it was below $(W/P)^*$, the money wage would rise quickly to restore the real wage to $(W/P)^*$, thereby choking off any excess demand for labour.

B. The Keynesian Aggregate Supply Curve

Recall the definition of the aggregate supply curve given in Chapter 9. *The aggregate supply curve shows the amount of output which the economy will supply at each different price level.* In the basic model, the aggregate supply curve embodies the profit-maximising decisions of producers and the utility-maximising decisions of households. When drawn in a diagram with the price level on the vertical axis and output on the horizontal axis, the basic model's aggregate supply curve is simply a

---

1. A thorough working out of the implications of the assumption of wage rigidity has been provided by Robert W. Clower, The Keynesian counter-revolution: a theoretical appraisal, in F. Hahn and F. Brechling (eds), *The Theory of Interest Rates*, Macmillan, 1965, and by Herschel I. Grossman and Robert J. Barro, in *Money, Employment and Inflation*, Cambridge University Press, 1976.

vertical line at that output level which is associated with the quantity of labour employed being equal to the quantity of labour demanded *and* supplied.

The Keynesian aggregate supply curve, like the basic model aggregate supply curve, is *the amount of output which the economy will supply at each different price level*. It is, however, importantly different from that in the basic model. The Keynesian aggregate supply curve, like that of the basic model, recognises that output will not be supplied in excess of that capable of being produced by profit-maximising firms. Because, however, the labour market does not necessarily achieve an equilibrium between the quantity of labour supplied and demanded, the utility-maximising decisions of households do not, except in the special case of full employment, affect the amount of output that will be supplied. The only thing that matters for the Keynesian aggregate supply curve is the profit-maximising decisions of firms.

C. How to Derive the Keynesian Aggregate Supply Curve

The Keynesian aggregate supply curve may be derived in a manner quite similar to that used to derive the aggregate supply curve of the basic model. The four-quadrant diagram illustrated in Figure 17.2 provides the basis for the derivation.

First, focus on Frame (a), in which the Keynesian labour market is illustrated. The demand for labour is shown by the curve n^d. The supply of labour is shown with the broken line n^s. This curve has been drawn with breaks to remind you that the supply curve of labour does not, except at the special point of full employment, determine the real wage in the Keynesian analysis. As a reference point, however, let us first focus on the full-employment equilibrium case. If the labour market is cleared (as it is in the basic model), then the quantity of employment will be n^* and the real wage will be $(W/P)^*$. (For the moment, ignore the subscripted numbers on W and P. They come into the story below.) Now, focus on Frame (b). It displays the short-run production function that tells us how much output will be supplied at each level of employment. By transferring the equilibrium quantity of employment n^* from the horizontal axis of Frame (a) to the same axis on Frame (b), you may read off from the aggregate production function the quantity of output that will be supplied at full employment. That quantity is shown on the vertical axis of Frame (b) as y^*. So far, you have used Figure 17.2 simply to do an exercise that is identical to that which you did with Figure 9.7 in Chapter 9. That is, you have discovered that at full-employment equilibrium, the level of employment is n^* and the level of output that will be produced is y^*. It is now possible to obtain a single point on the Keynesian aggregate supply curve. To do this, focus on Frame (c). Define the price level to be equal to 1. Then, with the price level equal to 1 and with the quantity of labour employed n^* and output y^*, the point a is obtained as a point on the aggregate supply curve. That is, with a price level of 1 and with an equilibrium real wage, the quantity of output supplied is equal to y^*. Define the money wage rate in the economy also as 1. The equilibrium real wage, therefore, is equal to (W_1/P_1). This is equal to $(W/P)^*$, the equilibrium real wage.

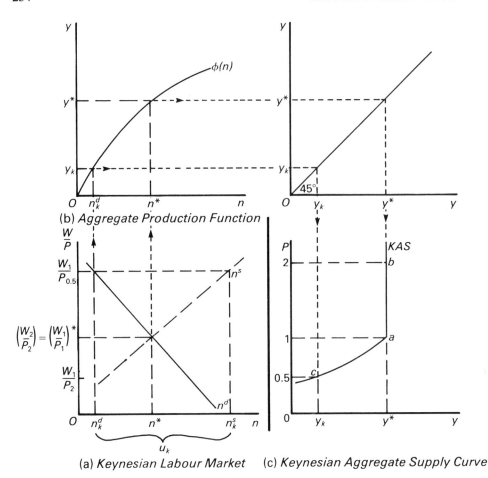

(b) Aggregate Production Function

(a) Keynesian Labour Market   (c) Keynesian Aggregate Supply Curve

Figure 17.2 *The Derivation of the Keynesian Aggregate Supply Curve*
This figure is similar to Figure 9.7 (Chapter 9). If the real wage is $(W/P)^*$, then the employment level will be n^* and output y^*. The money wage rate is downwardly rigid but flexible upwards. By setting things up so that when the price level is 1 the real wage is at its full-employment equilibrium level, the Keynesian aggregate supply curve may be derived. At price levels higher than 1, the money wage rate is dragged up with the price level. This maintains full-employment equilibrium so that output remains at y^*. At price levels below 1, the real wage rises and the level of employment declines (following the demand for labour curve). For example, at a price level of 0.5, the real wage is $W_1/P_{0.5}$ and the level of employment n_k^d. The output level is y_k. The curve cab traces the Keynesian aggregate supply curve (KAS).

Now imagine that the price level doubles to 2. This is shown on the vertical axis of Frame (c). Also imagine, for the moment, that the money wage rate is held rigid at 1. This means that the real wage will halve to (W_1/P_2) as shown in Frame (a). At that low real wage there will be an excess demand for labour. You can read that off the diagram in Frame (a) by noting that at the real wage (W_1/P_2) the quantity of labour demanded exceeds the quantity of labour supplied. By the assumptions discussed in the first section of this chapter, a situation in which there is a bigger demand for labour than supply will quickly lead to a rise in the money wage rate. The situation in which the real wage is equal to (W_1/P_2) could only be temporary and would quickly disappear. It would disappear because the money wage rate would rise and continue rising until the excess demand for labour had been eliminated. You can easily work out the required rise in the money wage rate. You know from the initial assumption that the price level has doubled from 1 to 2. The only way the economy can get back to a situation in which there is no excess demand for labour is for the money wage rate also to double. The Keynesian theory predicts that this will happen and that the real wage will be restored to $(W/P)^*$, with the money wage rate rising to 2, so that the equilibrium real wage is given by (W_2/P_2), which, of course, equals (W_1/P_1) and which in turn equals $(W/P)^*$.

As a result of the analysis just performed, it is now possible to find another point on the Keynesian aggregate supply curve. You have just discovered that if the price level doubles, the money wage rate also doubles, and the real wage remains constant. Not only does the real wage remain constant, so also do the levels of employment and output. They remain at n^* and y^*, respectively. The point b in Frame (c) is therefore another point on the Keynesian aggregate supply curve. Further, all the points between a and b joined together by the vertical continuous line are points on the Keynesian aggregate supply curve. Indeed, over the range a,b (and at price levels above 2 — i.e., at points above b) the Keynesian aggregate supply curve is identical to the aggregate supply curve of the basic model.

Next, consider the opposite experiment. Imagine that instead of rising to twice its initial value, the price level fell to one-half that initial value. (This is a fairly unlikely thing to actually happen, but by imagining an extreme shock we see more clearly the implications of a smaller, more likely one.) What would then happen in the Keynesian model? The first step towards the answer is contained in Frame (a). If the price level halves, with the wage rate stuck at 1, the real wage would rise to $W_1/P_{0.5}$ as shown on the vertical axis of Frame (a). The quantity of labour demanded at this higher real wage would be n_k^d, which, of course, is less than n^*. The amount of output that would be produced at the level of employment n_k^d is obtained by travelling up to Frame (b) and reading off on the vertical axis of that figure the quantity of output that n_k^d can produce. That quantity is shown as y_k. The quantity y_k may now be transferred (through the 45° line in the top right) to Frame (c) so that the point c is arrived at. Point c is that at which the price level is 0.5 and the level of output is y_k. You might find it helpful to your understanding to trace out another point or two and satisfy yourself that you can follow the analysis that led up to point c. For example, put in a price level of 0.25 and then work out the quantity of output that would be supplied at that price level. Also, put in a price level of 0.75 and work out what the level of output is in that case. You will discover that the output levels achieved trace out a line similar to the continuous upward sloping line shown in Frame (c).

The continuous line which slopes upwards through point c to point a and then becomes vertical above a, labelled KAS, is the *Keynesian aggregate supply curve*. It says that because the money wage rate is stuck at a point below which it will not move, at very low price levels, the real wage is so high that firms are unwilling to hire as many workers as are available for work. The output which firms are willing to produce is therefore less than the full employment quantity of output. As the price level rises, so the real wage falls, and the quantity of labour demanded rises. As the quantity of labour demanded rises, so the quantity of output produced rises. This process can go on until the quantity of labour demanded is equal to the quantity supplied. That happens when the real wage has fallen to $(W/P)^*$ and the level of

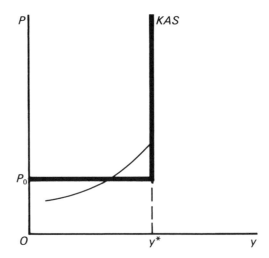

Figure 17.3 *The Inverse 'L' Aggregate Supply Curve*
An approximation to the Keynesian aggregate supply curve is the inverse 'L'. This implies that
the price level itself is downwardly rigid (at P_0), but that at full-employment output (y^*), any
higher price level is possible.

---

output has risen to y^*. If the price level rises above that level, the money wage rate
will rise in sympathy with it, maintaining the equilibrium real wage $(W/P)^*$ and
therefore leading the economy to produce the full-employment quantity of output y^*,
regardless of how high the price level goes.

At all output levels below y^* there is unemployment. That is illustrated for the
price level of 0.5 and the output level y_k in Frame (a). At a price level of 0.5 with the
real wage $(W_1/P_{0.5})$, the quantity of labour supplied is n_k^s, which exceeds the quantity
demanded by the amount shown as u_k.

D. The Approximate Keynesian Aggregate Supply Curve — The Inverse 'L'

There is a useful approximation to the Keynesian aggregate supply curve. It is an
approximation which simplifies considerably the analysis of the determination of
output and employment in the Keynesian model. It is also an approximation which is
not violently at odds with the Keynesian story. That approximation is shown in
Figure 17.3. It is an aggregate supply curve which is horizontal at the price level P_0 for
all levels of output below y^* and which, at y^*, becomes the vertical aggregate supply
curve of the basic model. This is the inverse 'L' approximation to the Keynesian
aggregate supply curve. It says that, as an approximation, we may think of the price
level as being downwardly rigid, so that it will not fall below P_0.

It is an important implication of the Keynesian theory of aggregate supply, that at
full employment aggregate demand determines the price level, but that at less than

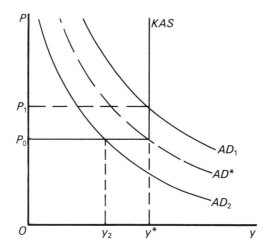

Figure 17.4 *Output Determined by Aggregate Demand in the Keynesian Model*
At full employment, the Keynesian model behaves exactly like the basic model. Aggregate demand AD_1 cuts the vertical part of the aggregate supply curve to determine the price level, P_1. If aggregate demand is below the critical curve AD^*, for example, at AD_2, then it is the position of the aggregate demand curve alone that determines the level of output and employment, such as the level y_2, where the aggregate demand curve AD_2 cuts the inverse 'L' aggregate supply curve.

---

full employment aggregate demand determines the level of output and employment. You can see this very clearly with the inverse 'L' supply curve. It is approximately true with the general Keynesian aggregate supply curve as depicted in Frame (c) of Figure 17.2. If you were to draw in an aggregate demand curve (as derived in Chapter 10) in Figure 17.3 you would be able to determine the price level and the level of output as the point at which that aggregate demand curve cuts the Keynesian aggregate supply curve. Figure 17.4 illustrates. The curve AS is the inverse 'L' approximation to the Keynesian aggregate supply curve. The curves AD_1 and AD_2 are aggregate demand curves of the type derived in Chapter 10. AD_1 is drawn for a larger money supply than AD_2. If the money supply was such that the aggregate demand curve was indeed AD_1, then the economy would be at a point depicted by the price level P_1 and the output level y^*. If, however, the money supply was the lower amount such that the aggregate demand curve was AD_2, then the economy would be stuck at the price level P_0 and with an output level equal to y_2. Fluctuations in the level of aggregate demand that did not take the aggregate demand curve as high as the dashed curve AD^* would lead to fluctuations in the level of output and leave the price level unaffected. Rises in the aggregate demand curve above AD^* would lead to rises in the price level and would leave output unchanged at y^*.

You can now see that on the horizontal part of the Keynesian aggregate supply curve the level of aggregate demand is the all-important matter determining the level of output and employment in the economy. For this reason, the theory of aggregate demand becomes very important for understanding the forces making for fluctuations in output and employment. Much of what Keynes went on to do in modifying the basic model had to do with the theory of aggregate demand, and these matters will be taken up in the next two chapters.

SUMMARY

A. Keynes's Modification to the Basic Model

The major modification to the basic model suggested by Keynes was that
of replacing the assumption that at all times the labour market achieves an
equilibrium where the demand for, and supply of, labour are equal, with
the assumption that the money wage rate is downwardly rigid. The money
wage rate will rise to achieve a balance between the demand and supply of
labour if there is an excess demand for labour. *The money wage rate will
not fall* if there is an excess supply of labour. Instead, the economy gets
stuck with a real wage that is too high and with a level of employment
below the quantity of labour supplied. There is *unemployment* in such a
situation.

B. The Keynesian Aggregate Supply Curve

The Keynesian aggregate supply curve, like that in the basic model,
shows the maximum amount of output which the economy will supply at
each different price level. If the price level is high enough to ensure that
the real wage is not above the full-employment real wage, the Keynesian
aggregate supply curve is identical to that in the basic model. At price
levels below that, however, when the real wage is too high, the Keynesian
aggregate supply curve is derived entirely from the demand for labour by
profit-maximising firms and is not influenced by the supply of labour by
households.

C. How to Derive the Keynesian Aggregate Supply Curve

The Keynesian aggregate supply curve is derived in a four part analysis
which links the demand for labour by profit-maximising firms through the
production function to the quantity of output that will be supplied at each
price level. Figure 17.2 illustrates the derivation and should be fully
understood.

D. The Approximate Keynesian Aggregate Supply Curve — The Inverse 'L'

The inverse 'L' approximation to the Keynesian aggregate supply curve
presumes that it is the price level rather than the money wage that is
downwardly rigid. This gives a horizontal segment to the aggregate

supply curve at the fixed price level up to full-employment output, and then gives a vertical segment at the full-employment level of output.

The important implication of the Keynesian aggregate supply curve (made most clear in the inverse 'L' approximate case) is that below full employment, the quantity of output and employment are determined by aggregate demand alone and do not in any way depend upon the aggregate supply conditions, since the aggregate supply curve itself is horizontal (or nearly so).

Review Questions

1. What is the modification which Keynes made to the basic model's theory of aggregate supply?

2. Suppose that an economy was at full employment and that suddenly the price level fell to one-half of its previous level. Trace out what would happen in the labour market according to the basic model and the Keynesian model.

3. In 1922 and 1923, prices in the United Kingdom (measured by the GDP Deflator) fell by 27 per cent. Using your answer to Question 2 above and any other relevant facts in the Appendix to Chapter 2, compare the predicted effects of such a price fall in the basic and Keynesian models with the actual performance of the United Kingdom labour market.

4. Define the Keynesian aggregate supply curve. What happens as the economy moves along that curve? Which markets are in equilibrium? Are firms maximising profits and households maximising utility?

5. Why is there no difference between the Keynesian and basic theory of aggregate supply at full employment?

6. Why is the inverse 'L' aggregate supply curve only an approximation to the Keynesian theory of aggregate supply?

7. Why does the Keynesian aggregate supply curve slope upwards at output levels below full employment?

8. What will cause the Keynesian aggregate supply curve to shift?

9. What is the main *implication* of the Keynesian theory of aggregate supply that distinguishes it from the basic theory?

18

Aggregate Demand in the Keynesian Model: Consumption and the 45° Cross Model

The subject matter of this and the next four chapters was, for the twenty years from the late 1950s through to the late 1970s, the heart of macroeconomics. Several generations of intermediate textbooks on the subject, many important research monographs, and literally thousands of important articles in learned journals deal with various aspects of the material presented here. It is the *Keynesian theory of aggregate demand*. You should be aware that the material presented in this book covers only the essential features of that theory. As a result of the developments in macroeconomics in the past ten to fifteen years, developments which will be explained in some detail in Part V of this book, we now have a much better perspective than ever before on the Keynesian theory of aggregate demand. It no longer stands as the whole of macroeconomics. It does not even provide the centrepiece of the explanation for macroeconomic fluctuations. That is not, however, to say that the Keynesian theory of aggregate demand is wrong. Like the basic model, there is nothing wrong with an analysis which is but one part of the complete story. The basic model, with which you are now familiar, contains some of the complete story. The Keynesian theory of aggregate demand contains more of the story. The part of the story that the Keynesian analysis contains deals with the determination of aggregate demand at a given price level.

To embark upon your study of the Keynesian theory of aggregate demand you have five tasks, which are to:

A. **know the components of aggregate demand;**
B. **know the theories of the consumption function proposed by Keynes, Friedman, and Modigliani;**
C. **understand the connection between wealth and income and why current income is a major determinant of consumption;**
D. **know how to represent the consumption and savings functions in simple equations and diagrams;**
    and
E. **understand the 45° cross model.**

First, it will be useful to examine the components into which aggregate demand is divided.

A. Components of Aggregate Demand

Just as a matter of arithmetic, aggregate demand could be divided up in an infinite number of different ways. It would be possible to distinguish between the demand for beer, the demand for food, the demand for hydro-electric power stations, the demand for nuclear submarines, etc., etc. For some purposes no doubt such a detailed disaggregation of the total volume of demand in the economy is useful. For the purpose of the questions addressed in macroeconomics, however, such a detailed classification of the components of aggregate demand appears to be unnecessary. It has turned out to be useful, nevertheless, to divide aggregate demand into a small number of key components, the determination of each of which involves different theoretical considerations. Specifically, for the purpose of doing macroeconomic analysis, aggregate demand is divided into four components. They are:

(i) consumption demand
(ii) investment demand
(iii) government demand
(iv) net foreign demand.

Each of these will now be briefly described.

(i) Consumption Demand

Consumption demand is the aggregate expenditure by households on goods and services to be used up for current consumption purposes. Examples of consumption demand would be the demand for beer and food. Other examples would be expenditures on holidays, travel, films and entertainment, rent of houses and flats, the purchase of electricity, gas or oil, the purchase of haircuts, driving lessons — indeed, any of the many thousands and thousands of activities on which we spend our income.

(ii) Investment Demand

Investment demand is distinguished from consumption demand by the fact that an investment *is the purchase of* a capital good — that is, a piece of equipment which is durable and which provides services over a number of years. Sometimes the services will be in the form of consumption services and sometimes they will be production services. Both households and firms make investment expenditures. Examples of investment expenditures made by households are the purchase of a new house, a new car, a new refrigerator, or any of the other many thousands of new consumer durable goods. Examples of investment expenditures by firms are the purchase of a new steel mill, a hydro-electric generating plant, a car assembly line, a computer, or again, any of the many thousands of different types of new capital goods used in the production process.

It is important that you clearly understand the distinction between consumption and investment. Consumption is the purchase of goods and services for current use. Examples of consumption goods are haircuts, food and drinks, and holidays. Investment is the purchase of goods and services for current and future use. Examples are cars, car assembly plants, and computers. When you buy a consumption good you buy a flow of services. When you invest, you buy a capital good which is a stock of equipment that gives rise to a flow of either production or consumption services.

It is also important to distinguish sharply between the term investment in the sense in which economists use it when doing macroeconomic analysis and the way in which the term is used in everyday speech. In everyday usage, investment often means the purchase of a stock or a share or a bond. That is not investment in macroeconomic analysis. Such an activity is a portfolio reallocation and has very different causes and consequences from the purchase of newly produced capital equipment.

(iii) Government Demand

The third component of aggregate demand is *government expenditure on goods and services.* Much of government expenditure represents the demands by the government for goods and services produced by the private sector of the economy. Examples of the demand by the government for goods and services produced by the private sector are the demand for a nuclear submarine, for a motorway, for a new administrative building, or for paper clips and paper. Notice that the examples just given include both capital and consumption goods. No distinction is made between what might be termed government investment demand (nuclear submarines, motorways and buildings) and what might be government consumption demand (paper clips and paper). For the purpose of macroeconomic analysis, there is no advantage to be gained from dividing government expenditure into its investment and consumption components. Indeed, such a division is, to a large extent, arbitrary. For example, two of the big items of expenditure by the government — health and education expenditure — could be regarded as either consumption or investment. They are consumption in the sense that they provide an immediate flow of services — of good health and knowledge. They may also be interpreted as investment expenditures, for a healthy and an educated person has an asset — has more human capital — which is capable of generating an income stream not just at the present but in the future as well. For some purposes it is crucial to be able correctly to distinguish the investment from the consumption components of government expenditure. For present purposes, however, there is no gain from pursuing that distinction.

In addition to buying goods and services produced by the private sector, the government also demands goods and services which it supplies itself. Examples are administrative services, police and law enforcement services, and military services. You can think of the government as being like a firm. It hires labour from households (soldiers, sailors, airmen, bureaucrats, policemen, judges, etc.) and produces goods and services which are then directly demanded by the government.

Government expenditure on goods and services is treated as being *exogenous*. That is, its quantity is treated as something which it is not our task to explain and which can be determined by the government at whatever level the government so chooses, independently of the values of any of the other variables in our macroeconomic model.[1]

Much of government expenditure in the modern world is excluded from the above definition of government demand. Government expenditures on pensions, welfare programmes, subsidies to various industries, and interest payments on the national debt, although vast in volume, do not represent government expenditures on goods and services. Rather, they are transfers of money — of purchasing power — from the government to private individuals and firms. Those expenditures are called *transfer payments*. Their effects on aggregate demand are analysed by examining their effects on private consumption and investment demand. They are not ignored, therefore, but they are not treated as direct demands for goods and services by the government.

(iv) Net Foreign Demand

Net foreign demand for goods and services is the difference between *exports and imports*. Foreigners place demands on the domestic economy by demanding those goods and services which are exported from the domestic economy. Residents of the domestic economy place demands on the rest of the world, and those are measured by the quantity of imports of goods and services. The difference between these two magnitudes represents net foreign demand. For the purpose of what follows in this and the subsequent four chapters, it will be assumed that net foreign demand is always exactly zero. This, of course, does not correspond well with the facts. By making the assumption, however, it turns out to be possible to simplify considerably the task of understanding the main elements of the Keynesian theory of aggregate demand. In Chapter 23, attention will be paid specifically to the determination of international trade as well as international investment flows. The implications of these international transactions for the Keynesian theory will be fully explored in that chapter.

---

1. As a matter of fact, in some very elaborate statistical models of the economy, government expenditures on goods and services are divided into two parts, those which are exogenous and those parts which respond to the state of the economy. Such a dichotomisation of government expenditure is important for some purposes, but not essential to the task upon which you are currently embarked.

Aggregate demand has been divided into four components: consumption, investment, government, and net foreign demand for goods and services. The last item is being ignored for the present, and government demand is being treated as exogenous and therefore does not have to be explained. The other two items, however, do need explanation. The rest of this chapter deals with the determinants of consumption demand, and the next chapter, with investment.

B. Theories of the Consumption Function Proposed by Keynes, Friedman and Modigliani

In his analysis of the determination of aggregate demand, the so-called *theory of the consumption function* was regarded by Keynes as the centrepiece of his new theory of income and employment. We now suspect that Keynes had an exaggerated opinion of the importance of this innovation. It is, nevertheless, an important ingredient in the theory of aggregate demand.

Keynes's theory[2] of the determinants of consumption was that, of the many possible factors that influence the level of consumption demand, the most important is the level of real disposable income. The way in which consumption demand is influenced by real disposable income is, for Keynes, based upon what he called 'the fundamental psychological law upon which we are entitled to depend with great confidence' (*General Theory*, p. 96). That law, Keynes went on to outline, is the proposition 'that men are disposed, as a rule and on the average, to increase their consumption as their income increases, but not by as much as the increase in their income' (*General Theory*, p. 96). What Keynes is saying is that consumption depends on income such that, for a given rise in income, consumption will rise by some fraction of the rise in income.

Following the first statement of Keynes's consumption function hypothesis, a great deal of statistical work was undertaken which sought to test Keynes's theory with the newly available national income accounting data. Several puzzles and problems revealed by the data lead to a more refined formulation of the theory of the consumption function. The two leading architects of the refining were Milton Friedman, who developed the *permanent income hypothesis*[3] and Franco Modigliani, who developed the *life-cycle hypothesis*.[4] These two contributions have more similarities than differences and hark back to the work of one of the greatest pre-Keynesian economists, Irving Fisher. They can be conveniently summarised by treating them as if they were a single theory.

---

2. Keynes set out his theory of the consumption function in Chapters 8 and 9 of the *General Theory of Employment, Interest and Money*, Macmillan, 1936.

3. Milton Friedman, *A Theory of the Consumption Function*, Princeton University Press, 1957.

4. Franco Modigliani gave a useful and comprehensive appraisal of his work in his paper 'The life cycle hypothesis of saving twenty-five years later', in Michael Parkin and A.R. Nobay (eds), *Contemporary Issues in Economics*, Manchester University Press, 1975, pp. 2–36. That paper also contains a fairly comprehensive bibliography on the consumption function.

Friedman and Modigliani reasoned as follows. If people can borrow and lend freely through financial institutions, then their consumption in any one particular period should not be too closely linked to their income in that particular period. If for some reason income is *temporarily* high, there would be an incentive to save a larger than normal fraction of that temporarily high income, so that consumption would be a low fraction of income. If, in some other year, income was temporarily low, there would be a tendency to consume the whole of income and perhaps also to consume some previous savings (or, if previous savings were inadequate, to borrow against future income). Recognising the possibility of breaking the direct link between income and consumption through borrowing and lending, Modigliani and Friedman suggested that the ultimate constraint upon how much consumption an individual will undertake is the amount of that individual's wealth. On the average, the wealthier an individual is, the more will that individual consume. In the life-cycle analysis of Modigliani, the individual would attempt to smooth out the path of consumption over the life span, even though income received would vary.

It turned out that upon careful investigation of the statistics, the permanent income and life-cycle hypotheses that say that consumption depends on wealth are ones which fit the facts better than the Keynesian hypothesis that consumption depends primarily on disposable income.

C. Connection between Wealth and Income and Why Current Income is a Major Determinant of Consumption

Wealth and income are related to each other in a simple way. As you already know, *wealth is a stock* and *income is a flow*. The relationship between income and wealth can be put in terms of stocks and flows. Income is the flow that is generated by the stock of wealth.

Perhaps a physical analogy which relates to that used in Chapter 3 will be helpful. Suppose that a bathtub contains 500 gallons of water. Suppose that the water is permitted to run from the bathtub at a rate of 50 gallons an hour. After 10 hours the bathtub will be empty, the stock of water in it at that point being zero. You may think of the stock of water initially in the bathtub, 500 gallons, as being analogous to wealth. You may think of the flow of water at the rate of 50 gallons per hour as being analogous to income. The rate of flow of water (50 gallons per hour) multiplied by the number of hours for which the flow occurred (10 hours) gives a number equal to the initial stock of water (wealth) in the bathtub. Notice that this story starts off with a certain amount of water in the bathtub which is used up as the water is allowed to run out of the plug-hole. You can now turn the analogy around and ask the question, how much water would have to be in the bathtub initially in order to have the *equivalent* of a rate of flow of 50 gallons an hour for 10 hours? Now ask the identical questions, but in place of the phrase 'water in the bathtub' use the word 'wealth'; instead of the phrase 'the flow of water' use the word 'income'; instead of 'gallons' talk about 'pounds'; and instead of an experiment which just runs for a few hours think of an hour as being a year and think of the number of years as being an average human life span. The question would then become, how much wealth would an individual need in order to have the equivalent of an income flow of £50 per year over a period of (say) 70 years?

This analogy should help you to see the connection between income and wealth. Wealth is the stock equivalent of the income flow measured at a certain rate over a certain period of time. There is one important additional thing to note that makes the calculation of wealth slightly different from the calculation performed using the water in the bathtub analogy. How much wealth today £1 of income in the future is worth depends on how far in the future that income is earned. One pound earned in the next 5 minutes is worth much more than £1 earned in the last 5 minutes of your life. The reason for this is easy to see. One pound earned in the next 5 minutes could be used to buy an interest-bearing security which would lead to the accumulation of more pounds in the future from interest receipts. One pound earned 50 years in the future would be worth less than £1 earned in the next 5 minutes, because it would be incapable of earning interest for you over the next 50 years. To calculate the wealth equivalent of future income, the future income stream has to be converted to a common valuation basis.

The most useful common valuation basis is known as the *present value*. The present value of a future sum of money is simply that sum of money which, if you were to receive it today, would, when invested at the average rate of interest, accumulate to the pre-stated future value. For example, if the rate of interest is 10 per cent, £100 invested today would accumulate in one year to £110. It would be said, therefore, that the present value of £110 received one year in the future at a 10 per cent rate of interest is equal to £100.

Now that you understand the connection between income and wealth, you will be aware that the permanent income and life-cycle hypotheses of consumption are, in effect, generalisations of the Keynesian theory of consumption. They say that consumption will depend upon today's disposable income and upon all future disposable income. Other things being equal, the larger is today's disposable income, the larger is wealth, and the greater will be the level of consumption. The bigger is future disposable income, other things being equal, the bigger is wealth, and the greater will be today's consumption.

There are two lines of reasoning which lead to the proposition that the most important factor determining current consumption is current disposable income. The first follows directly from the discussion above concerning the relationship between wealth and income. Although it is true that if borrowing and lending in free capital markets are possible, then it is wealth rather than income which is the ultimate constraint on consumption, there is nevertheless good reason for elevating the level of current disposable income to a more important status than wealth. As you saw above, wealth can be equivalently thought of as current disposable income plus all future disposable income converted to a present value. There is an important distinction between the present and future that arises from the information that we have about those two states. The present is known and certain. The future is unknown and only probabilistic. It is very likely, therefore, that what is happening in the present to an individual's disposable income is going to be treated as a signal concerning what is likely to happen in the future. It therefore seems sensible to hypothesise that wealth, as perceived by an individual, is positively related to current disposable income. If that is so, it becomes current disposable income rather than wealth that is, from an operational or observational point of view, the major determinant of current consumption. Another way of putting this would be to say that to a large extent wealth is not a directly observable and measurable variable. It contains, in part, future expected income flows that are not yet known. Those future expected income flows must be forecasted on the basis of things that are known, one important ingredient of which is current disposable income.

There is a second reason why current disposable income will be an important determinant of consumption. The permanent income and life-cycle hypotheses reach the conclusion that consumption will depend on wealth by assuming that individuals may borrow and lend unlimited amounts in order to smooth out consumption over their lifetime. There are very good reasons why this will not, in general, be possible. It is difficult to borrow unlimited funds against future labour income. It may be possible, therefore, that an individual is constrained in the amount of consumption that can be undertaken by the amount of current disposable income, since that amount will be used as an indication to a potential lender concerning the individual's ability to repay the loan and pay the interest on it.

For two reasons, then, because current income provides good information to an individual about future income and therefore about wealth, and because current disposable income provides good information to potential lenders, it seems reasonable to suppose that it is current disposable income that is the most important single factor determining current consumption demand.[5]

---

5. The account of the theory of the consumption function given in this chapter has been highly condensed and selective. The best, lengthy textbook treatment of the subject that will fill in a lot of the detail for you is David F. Heathfield (ed.), *Topics in Applied Macroeconomics*, Macmillan, 1976. An up-to-date survey of the empirical issues (from a US perspective, though) is Walter Dolde, Issues and models in empirical research on aggregate consumer expenditure, in Karl Brunner and Allan H. Meltzer, (eds), *On the State of Macro-Economics*, Carnegie-Rochester Conference Series on Public Policy, Vol. 12, Spring 1980, pp. 161–206. There is an enormous body of published literature on the United Kingdom consumption function. All of this literature is technically much more demanding than the level of material presented in this book. Some examples are: R.P. Byron, Initial attempts in econometric model building at NIESR, in K. Hilton and D.F. Heathfield (eds), *The Econometric Study of the United Kingdom*, Macmillan, 1970, Chapter 1; Angus S. Deaton, Wealth effects on consumption in a modified life-cycle model, *The Review of Economic Studies*, Vol. 39, 1972, pp. 443–54; David F. Hendry, Stochastic specification in an aggregate demand model of the United Kingdom, *Econometrica*, Vol. 42, 1974, pp. 559–78; R.J. Ball *et al.*, The London Business School quarterly econometric model of the UK economy, in G.A. Renton (ed.), *Modelling the Economy*, Heinemann Educational Books, 1975, Chapter 1 (the Renton book also includes papers by John Bispham and James Shepherd and others which explain the National Institute's and Treasury's consumption functions). The most comprehensive and up-to-date treatment of the UK consumption function is that by James Davidson, David Hendry, Frank Srba, and Stephen Yeo, Econometric modelling of the aggregate time series relationship between consumers' expenditure and income in the United Kingdom, *Economic Journal*, Vol. 88, December 1978, pp. 661–92.

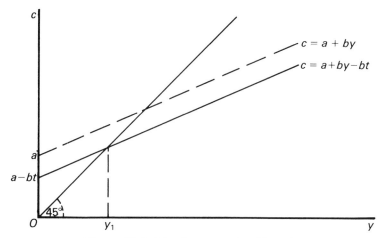

Figure 18.1 *The Consumption Function*
Consumption is a function of disposable income. When graphed against real GDP, the consumption function slopes upwards at the rate of the marginal propensity to consume (the parameter b). Its intercept on the vertical axis is equal to a (the intercept of the consumption function minus the marginal propensity to consume times the level of taxes).

D. Consumption and Savings Functions in Simple Equations and Diagrams

The discussion and analysis that has been conducted above may now be summarised in a very compact form by writing a simple equation to describe the determination of consumption demand. Such an equation would be

$$c = a + b(y-t) \qquad a > 0, 1 > b > 0 \tag{18.1}$$

The value of aggregate real consumption demand is represented by c, y represents real income (real gross domestic product), t represents the total collection of taxes by the government net of transfer payments, and a and b are *constants* or *parameters*. According to Keynes's 'fundamental psychological law', the parameter b will be a positive fraction. An example would be, say, $\frac{3}{4}$. The parameter a (which captures the effects of everything else on consumption and which might itself reasonably be regarded as changing over time as a result of such long-term things as changing demographic patterns and tastes) will presumably be positive, indicating that if people had very low current incomes, they would seek to consume more than their income, thereby using up part of their past accumulated savings.

The consumption function written as an equation above may be shown in a simple diagram. Figure 18.1 illustrates. The vertical axis measures real consumption demand and the horizontal axis measures real income. In order to show the relationship between consumption demand and income on a diagram, it is necessary to be precise about how taxes vary as income varies. For present purposes, it will be assumed that taxes are set by the government to yield a certain total amount of revenue, t, independently of what the level of income is. In other words, taxes will be treated as a constant. This is not the only assumption that could have been made, nor is it necessarily the most natural one. Permitting taxes to vary with income does not, however, modify the result that we shall get in any qualitative way, but does make the presentation of the analysis slightly more cumbersome. Proceeding then with the assumption that taxes are constant we can now illustrate the relationship between real consumption demand and real income in Figure 18.1. The dashed line labelled $c = a + by$ represents the consumption function in an economy in which taxes and transfer payments sum to zero. The continuous line labelled $c = a + by - bt$ represents the consumption function in an economy that has net taxes at the level t. The other line in the diagram is a 45° line and can be read as telling you that at each point on that line consumption would be exactly equal to income. You may use that as a reference line, therefore, to figure out whether or not consumption demand will exceed, equal, or fall short of current income. You see, for example, that at the income level y_1 consumption demand exactly equals income. At income levels above y_1 consumption is less than income, and at income levels below y_1, consumption exceeds income.

This equation and diagram summarise the theory of the determinants of consumption demand. The slope of this line (represented by the parameter b) is given a name, and that name is *the marginal propensity to consume*. If the marginal propensity to consume is high (close to 1) the consumption function will be steep (almost as steep as the 45° line). The lower is the marginal propensity to consume, the flatter is the consumption function.

Notice that the consumption function as drawn in Figure 18.1 will shift each time there is a different level of taxes. You can see this directly in Figure 18.1 by comparing the dashed line drawn for zero taxes with the continuous line drawn for a tax level of t. This tells you that the higher is the level of taxes, the further downwards does the consumption function shift. What this says is that the higher is the tax level, the lower is the level of disposable income, and therefore, the lower is the level of consumption associated with each level of gross domestic product. The amount by which the consumption function shifts down for a £1 rise in taxes is the fraction b. The reason why the consumption function shifts down by the fraction b and not by the whole amount of the taxes is that part of the taxes paid comes from a reduction in savings, and only fraction b of the taxes comes from a reduction in consumption. You will be able to see this more clearly by considering the relationship between consumption, savings, and taxes, which is our next task.

Households can do only three different types of things with their income: they can consume, save, or pay taxes. You can think of this, in effect, as a definition of *savings*. Savings are what are left over after meeting consumption expenditures and paying taxes. This can be written as an equation, namely

$$y = c + s + t \tag{18.2}$$

Clearly, in planning their consumption, households are also implicitly planning how much saving to undertake. If consumption is determined by equation (18.1) above, that is, if

$$c = a + b(y - t) \tag{18.1}$$

it must be the case that households are planning to save an amount given by another equation, namely

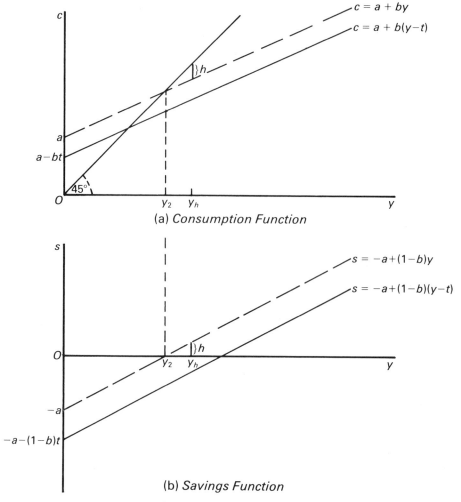

Figure 18.2 *The Consumption and Savings Functions*

Since income must be disposed of either by consuming, saving, or paying taxes, the consumption function implies a savings function. When savings and consumption plans are added together they exactly exhaust disposable income.

$$s = -a + (1 - b)\,(y - t) \tag{18.3}$$

How do we know that equation (18.3) tells us about the households' savings plan? The answer is simply that if we add together the households' consumption plan (18.1) and their savings plan (18.3) we get the proposition that

$$c + s = y - t \tag{18.4}$$

namely, that consumption plus savings is equal to disposable income. You will recognise this as simply a re-arrangement of equation (18.2) above. Equation (18.3) is usually referred to as the *savings function* and the slope of the savings function $(1 - b)$ as the *marginal propensity to save*. The marginal propensity to save plus the marginal propensity to consume always adds up to unity.

You may find it helpful to represent the consumption function and the savings function in a simple diagram that shows how the two are related. Figure 18.2 does this. Frame (a) shows consumption plotted against income, and Frame (b) shows savings plotted against income. Indeed, Frame (a) of Figure 18.2 is nothing other than Figure 18.1. The two frames of Figure 18.2 are related to each other in the following way. Look first at the dashed lines that represent an economy with no taxes, so that disposable income and aggregate income are the same number. In that case, the vertical distance between the consumption function and the 45° line in Frame (a) is equal to the vertical distance between the horizontal axis and the savings function in Frame (b). As an example, at the income level y_2 consumption exactly equals income and savings exactly equals zero. At an income level above y_2 for example, y_h, savings can be represented on Frame (a) by the vertical line marked h and equivalently in Frame (b) by the vertical distance h. Next, consider the economy in which taxes are not zero. In that case the consumption function has shifted downwards by an amount equal to b times taxes. The savings function has also shifted down, but this time by an amount equal to $1-b$ times taxes. What does this mean? It means simply that for a £1 rise in taxes, consumption drops by fraction b of a pound and savings drop by fraction $1-b$ of a pound, the drop in savings and consumption taken together being enough to make up the £1 of taxes. The after-tax consumption and savings functions are parallel to the pre-tax functions. Adding the consumption function and the savings function together gives a number equal to disposable income, that is, a number equal to income minus taxes.

You have now covered the major aspects of the theory of consumption demand and the related theory of saving. It is now possible to explore the simplest flow theory of income determination, the 45° cross model.

E. The 45° Cross Model

The essence of the Keynesian theory of aggregate demand — what has come to be called the 45° cross model — may now be understood. We already know that in the simplest Keynesian framework, output is determined by aggregate demand. That is, except in the special case of full employment, and using the inverse 'L' approximation to the aggregate supply curve, the price level is fixed, and variations in actual output are determined entirely by movements in the aggregate demand curve. In Figure 18.2 you have already become familiar with a diagram in which output is measured on the horizontal axis (recalling that output and income are equal to each other) and in which one of the major components of aggregate demand (consumption demand) is measured on the vertical axis. We don't have to move very far from the content of Figure 18.2 to determine aggregate demand and aggregate output and income in the simplest Keynesian framework. We can do this by broadening our view slightly, as we do in Figure 18.3, and measuring on the vertical axis of the diagram, not just consumption demand, but all the components of aggregate demand added together, that is, y^d. We continue to measure actual output, y, on the horizontal axis.

The first thing to understand about the diagram in this slightly modified form is the

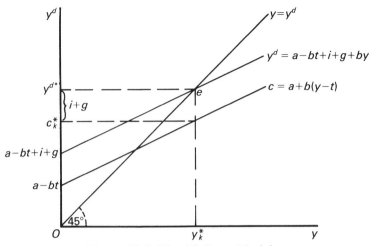

Figure 18.3 *The 45° Cross Model*

The 45° cross model is the essence of the Keynesian theory of output determination. Actual output is equal to aggregate demand (the 45° line). Aggregate demand is the sum of consumption demand and autonomous expenditure. Where the aggregate demand line cuts the 45° line determines the equilibrium level of real income.

---

meaning of the 45° line. That line has been labelled $y = y^d$. You may interpret the 45° line as saying that actual output, y, will be determined as the quantity of output that is actually demanded, y^d. There is a sense in which this might be thought of as the aggregate supply curve, although you must be careful not to confuse it with the aggregate supply curve derived in Chapter 17. Since, in terms of Figures 17.3 or 17.4 of the previous chapter, the price level is fixed and we are operating on the horizontal section of the inverse 'L' aggregate supply curve, we may plot variations in the actual quantity of output supplied (the horizontal axis of Figure 18.3) against the quantity of output demanded (the vertical axis of Figure 18.3). So much for the 45° line, which tells us that the actual quantity of output will be equal to the quantity demanded. Let us now turn to the demand side of the economy.

The consumption function, the line labelled

$$c = a + b\,(y - t)$$

already introduced in Figure 18.2, is reproduced in Figure 18.3. Now consumption demand is only part of total demand. The other elements of aggregate demand (ignoring net foreign demand) are investment and government expenditures on goods and services. We have already agreed to treat government expenditures as exogenous. Let us for the moment treat investment in the same way. That is, let us suppose that investment expenditures are given. (The next chapter actually goes on to discuss the factors that determine investment.) Aggregate demand, then, can be written

$$y^d = c + i + g \tag{18.5}$$

where i and g are real investment expenditures and real government expenditures on goods and services, respectively. In order to graph aggregate demand, y^d in Figure

18.3, all that we have to do is to add the fixed amount of investment expenditure and government expenditure to the consumption function. That is, we need to displace the consumption function upwards by an amount equal to investment plus government expenditures. This is done in the diagram and represented by the line labelled

$$y^d = a - bt + i + g + by$$

This curve tells us what the total level of demand will be at each level of income. Total demand will rise as income rises. It will not, however, rise as quickly as income, since the consumption function itself has a slope of less than one. At low income levels total demand would exceed income, and at high incomes total demand would fall short of income. There is only one income level, y_k^*, that generates a level of aggregate demand equal to itself. That is the equilibrium level of aggregate demand in the 45° cross model. Income, rather than prices, is the variable that adjusts to achieve the equilibrium. To see this, consider hypothetically what would happen if income were greater than y_k^*. This is a purely hypothetical experiment which could not actually happen in the world described in Figure 18.3. In that event, the level of demand would be less than the level of income. You can see that because the curve labelled y^d is lower than the 45° line at all points to the right of y_k^*. This would mean that total spending (gross domestic product) was less than income. You know that to be impossible. Hence, the conjectured income level greater than y_k^* could not occur. The same applies to income levels below y_k^*. There is one, and only one, income level that is compatible with the relationships hypothesised here, and that is the income level y_k^*, or the point e at which the aggregate demand curve cuts the 45° line.

The analysis that you have just gone through is the essence of Keynes's general theory. (Keynes himself was explicit about this on page 29 of *The General Theory of Employment, Interest and Money*.[6])

An important and interesting implication of this analysis is the simple so-called autonomous expenditure *multiplier*. Investment and government expenditure (and taxes) are all variables which change their values autonomously with respect to (independently of) real income. Only consumption changes as income changes. If there is a change in the value of taxes, investment, or government expenditures, there will be an induced change in consumption and in income, and the change in income will be larger than the initial change in autonomous expenditure. To see this, consider, by way of an example, the effects of a rise in investment. Suppose that taxes and government spending are held constant, but investment rises. We know that any change in income that occurs will be equal to the change in investment plus any induced change in consumption. That is, using the symbol 'Δ' to denote 'change in',

$$\Delta y = \Delta c + \Delta i \tag{18.6}$$

But we know from the theory of the consumption function that the change in consumption will be equal to the change in income multiplied by b, the marginal propensity to consume, that is,

---

6. The presentation of this model on pages 28 and 29 of the *General Theory* is slightly disguised by the fact that Keynes uses the level of employment rather than the level of output (income) as the variable determined by the analysis, but if you work carefully through these two pages of Keynes's book, you will find the above model there.

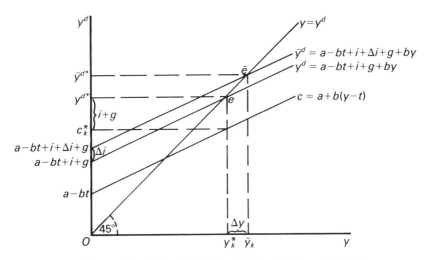

Figure 18.4 *The Multiplier in the 45° Cross Model*
A rise in autonomous expenditure (for example, a rise in investment by Δi) raises aggregate demand and raises equilibrium income (output) by Δy, an amount equal to Δi multiplied by $1/(1 - b)$.

$$\Delta c = b\Delta y \tag{18.7}$$

Substituting this equation into the previous one tells us that the change in income will be equal to b times the change in income plus the change in investment. That is,

$$\Delta y = b\Delta y + \Delta i \tag{18.8}$$

Rearranging this equation by taking the term $b\Delta y$ to the left-hand side and then dividing through by $(1-b)$ gives

$$\Delta y = \frac{1}{1 - b}\Delta i \tag{18.9}$$

You have just worked out the famous Keynesian multiplier. The change in income that is induced by a change in autonomous expenditures (investment in this case) is equal to 1 divided by 1 minus the marginal propensity to consume times the initial change in autonomous expenditure. If the propensity to consume is a number like 0.8, then the multiplier would be a number like 5. Figure 18.4 illustrates this. It is possible to mark the rise in investment (Δi) on the vertical axis of the figure, thereby generating a new aggregate demand curve, the curve labelled

$$\bar{y}^d = a - bt + i + \Delta i + g + by$$

The new equilibrium level of income is at point $\bar{e}$ at an income level $\bar{y}_k$. The rise in income is marked in the figure as Δy, and the initial rise in investment is Δi.

You have now discovered that in the simplest version of the Keynesian theory of aggregate demand, the level of demand (which equals the level of actual income and output) is determined by the level of autonomous expenditure. Change taxes, government spending, or investment and there will be a change in income that is bigger than the initial change in autonomous expenditure. You may be wondering what became of the monetary theory of aggregate demand in the basic model. How is it that the level of aggregate demand can be determined entirely by the relationship between consumption and income and the level of autonomous expenditure? What is going on in the money market? What became of money market equilibrium — the fundamental condition giving rise to the aggregate demand curve in the basic model? These questions will be answered shortly. It will be best, however, if the answer is approached in stages and left until we get to Chapter 22.

SUMMARY

A. Components of Aggregate Demand

The components of aggregate demand are consumption, investment, government purchases of goods and services, and net exports.

B. Theories of the Consumption Function Proposed by Keynes, Friedman, and Modigliani

Keynes hypothesised that the major determinant of consumption was current disposable income. Keynes supposed that the level of consumption would rise as income rose, but the fraction of income consumed would decline. Friedman and Modigliani developed the permanent income and life-cycle hypotheses, which emphasised the role of wealth as the ultimate constraint upon consumption.

C. Connection between Wealth and Income and Why Current Income is a Major Determinant of Consumption

Wealth is the present value of current and future income. By borrowing and lending it is possible to break the direct connection between current income and current consumption. Nevertheless, current income is an important indicator of potential future income and therefore will influence the extent to which an individual can borrow against future labour income and will influence the individual's own assessment of what represents a desirable, sustainable consumption and savings plan. Therefore, current income is a major determinant of consumption.

D. Consumption and Savings Functions in Simple Equations and Diagrams

The consumption function may be written as

$$c = a + b(y - t)$$

Since savings plus consumption must equal disposable income, it follows that the savings function must be

$$s = -a + (1 - b)(y - t)$$

If savings and consumption are added together, they always add up to disposable income $(y - t)$.

E. The 45° Cross Model

The essence of the simple Keynesian theory of aggregate demand can be summarised in the 45° cross diagram. Aggregate demand is measured on the vertical axis and actual output on the horizontal axis. The 45° line says that the level of actual output will equal the quantity demanded. The aggregate demand curve plotted in that diagram shows the consumption function plus the assumed fixed level of investment and government expenditures. Where the aggregate demand line cuts the 45° line determines the equilibrium level of income. It is an equilibrium in the sense that it is the only income level that generates a level of consumption which, when added to investment and government spending, equals that same level of income.

A rise in investment or government spending (or a cut in taxes) will shift the aggregate demand curve upwards and produce a higher equilibrium income level. The rise in income will be equal to the rise in autonomous expenditure multiplied by $1/(1-b)$, where b is the marginal propensity to consume.

Review Questions

1. What are the components into which aggregate demand is separated in order to study the determination of aggregate demand?

2. Classify the following according to whether they are consumption (C), investment (I), government expenditure (G), none of these and not part of aggregate demand (N), or not enough information to say (?):
   (i)   your purchase of lunch today
   (ii)   the purchase of a new car
   (iii)   the purchase of a used car
   (iv)   the purchase of a new office block by the British Government
   (v)   the payment of unemployment benefits by the British Government
   (vi)   the purchase by British Airways of a Boeing 747 aeroplane
   (vii)   the purchase by British Airways of food for in-flight service (Hint: be careful — look at Chapter 3 on the distinction between final and intermediate expenditure)
   (viii) your purchase of a ticket on a British Airways flight
   (ix)   the purchase of a computer by BP
   (x)   your income tax payments to the Inland Revenue.

3. What is Keynes's theory of the consumption function?

4. What, according to the permanent income and life-cycle hypotheses, is the fundamental constraint on consumption?

5. What is the connection between income and wealth?

6. If a person's income was to rise in 1982 by £1000, but thereafter to return to its original path, and if the rate of interest was 10 per cent, by how much would that person's wealth rise in 1981?

7. Why is it that, despite the fact that wealth is the fundamental constraint on consumption, disposable income is regarded as the major determinant of consumption?

8. What is the meaning of the term 'marginal propensity to consume' (MPC)? Why is the MPC less than one?

9. What is the savings function? What is the relationship between the savings function and the consumption function?

10. You are given the following information about a hypothetical economy:
    1) $c = 100 + 0.8(y - t)$
    2) $i = 500$
    3) $g = 400$
    4) $t = 400$
    5) there is unemployment and the price level is fixed
       (c = consumption, i = investment, g = government expenditure on goods and services, y = real income, t = taxes).
    (a) Calculate the equilibrium level of output and consumption.
    (b) If government expenditure is cut to 300, what is the *change* in income and the *change* in consumption?
    (c) What is the size of the multiplier effect of government expenditure on output?

19

Investment Demand

You already know from the definitions given at the beginning of the last chapter that investment demand is the purchase of durable goods by both households and firms. You also know from your examination of the characteristics of the United Kingdom's business cycle in Chapter 7 that the fluctuations in durables are much more volatile than those in non-durables. Understanding what determines investment is therefore of crucial importance in understanding some of the major sources of fluctuations in aggregate demand. What determines investment and why does it fluctuate so much? These are the principal questions for this chapter.[1] Answering these questions is a fairly big task and one which is going to be more easily approached by breaking it up into a series of specific tasks, which are to:

  A. **understand the distinction between investment and the capital stock;**
  B. **understand what determines the demand for capital;**
  C. **understand what is meant by the rental rate of capital;**
  D. **understand how investment demand is related to the demand for capital;** and
  E. **know how to represent the investment demand function in a simple equation and diagram.**

A. Distinction Between Investment and the Capital Stock

Investment demand is the demand for capital goods for use in production or consumption-yielding activities. Investment may be undertaken for two purposes: (1) to add to the existing stock of capital, or (2) to replace capital equipment that has depreciated (that has worn out). You will have noticed that investment is a flow. It is

---

1. The development of the theory of investment presented in this chapter is based very closely on Dale W. Jorgensen, Capital theory and investment behaviour, *American Economic Review Papers and Proceedings*, 53, 1963, pp. 247–59.

the flow of additions to the capital stock, or replacements for worn out capital. In any one year, the amount of investment is likely to be very small relative to the size of the capital stock. For example, in the United Kingdom in 1979, 20 per cent of the gross domestic product was devoted to investment demand. In that same year, it was estimated that the capital stock in the United Kingdom was 5.1 times the level of gross domestic product. This means that the amount of investment undertaken was 4 per cent of the capital stock. So, the capital stock is the total value of the capital equipment located in the economy at a particular point in time. The level of investment is the rate of flow of additions to that capital stock, plus the rate of flow of expenditure on capital goods to replace worn-out capital equipment.

What determines the rate of investment demand? This question is best answered in a slightly roundabout manner. Rather than answering it directly, we are going to approach it by asking first of all, what determines the amount of capital stock which in the aggregate the agents in the economy want to hold? Let us then examine that question.

B. The Demand for Capital

In any productive or consumption-yielding activity there is a range of choice of techniques available. It will be possible to undertake almost any imaginable task by using only labour as the resource and using no capital at all. At the other extreme it would be possible to undertake almost any imaginable task by using a very capital-intensive technology, that is, a technology that involves very little labour and large amounts of capital. (It is, of course, true that there are some tasks which one could not imagine doing in any way other than using large amounts of capital — for example, putting a satellite into earth orbit.) Nevertheless, over a very large range of economic activities it is possible to visualise differing degrees of intensity of use of capital. A classical example would be the building of a dam, which could be undertaken with massive earth-moving equipment or individuals with small wooden shovels, themselves made by hand.

What determines the extent to which a capital-intensive technology will be used rather than a labour-intensive technology? A moment's reflection suggests that the answer depends upon the relative costs of the two factors of production. If capital is very cheap relative to labour, then it would seem efficient to use a capital-intensive technology. If, on the other hand, labour is very cheap relative to capital, then a labour-intensive technology would seem to be indicated. All that seems obvious enough until one reflects a little further and begins to wonder how one would calculate whether or not capital was cheap relative to labour. After all, buying a piece of equipment is buying something which is durable and which is going to be usable over a long period of time, whereas hiring labour is something which is more in the nature of a consumption activity. How can we compare the price of capital and the price of labour in order to know whether capital is cheap or not? The answer lies in a concept called the *rental rate of capital*. By comparing the rental rate of capital with the wage rate of labour we can establish the relative price of capital and labour. It is true that most capital equipment is not rented at all. People buy the capital that they are going to use and then use it without any explicit payment of a rent. It is possible, however, to think of capital which is owned and used as being *implicitly* rented. Often, of course, capital is in fact explicitly rented. Examples of private individuals renting capital abound. Renting a car at an airport, or more commonly, renting a flat or house. Firms often rent equipment, for example, large-scale civil engineering contractors often rent heavy earth-moving and other specialised equipment. Whether capital equipment is explicitly rented or owned by the user and, as it were, implicitly rented by him from himself makes no difference to the general concept of the rental rate of capital. Let us now turn to the task of understanding what is meant by the rental rate of capital.

C. Rental Rate of Capital

The best way of understanding what is meant by the rental rate of capital is to proceed by example. How much would you be willing to pay each year to rent a house which could alternatively buy for £50,000? To answer that question you need to know a little bit more information than you have just been given. Let's supply some more pieces of information. The house will last for 50 years, so that if you bought the house it would wear out at the rate of 2 per cent a year.[2] The interest rate that you would face is 15 per cent per annum. That means that you would have to pay 15 per cent per annum for any money that you borrowed (any mortgage money) to buy the house. Equivalently, if you sold some existing securities to buy the house, you would have to forgo a 15 per cent rate of interest on those securities. Either way, the opportunity cost of the funds that you used to buy the house is going to be 15 per cent. House prices are rising and are expected to rise indefinitely through the future at a rate of 10 per cent per annum. You now have enough information with which to answer the question, how much would you pay each year to rent a house that you could otherwise buy for £50,000? The answer is you wouldn't pay any more rent than the amount which you would implicitly have to pay to yourself if you were to buy the house and live in it for as long as you needed it and thereafter sell the house. How much is that? To figure that out, consider the following three costs of owning the house and renting it to yourself. First, there is a cost in the form of the physical depreciation on the house. Secondly, there is a cost in the form of the interest that you would have to pay in order to acquire the £50,000 needed to buy the house, and thirdly, there is the negative cost, the gain, that arises from the fact that the value of the house on the housing market will rise at the rate at which house prices are projected to rise (in the example, 10 per cent per annum). If you are going to buy a

---

2. Actually, to say that a house will last for 50 years and to say that it will wear out at the rate of 2 per cent a year is slightly contradictory. The two statements are approximately equivalent, however. If a house wore out in 50 years at exactly a rate of 1/50 of the initial house each year, then the depreciation expressed as a percentage of the remaining value of the house would rise. If we express the depreciation rate as a constant per cent each year, what we are really saying is that the asset will never finally wear out. This is known as radioactive depreciation. It makes the arithmetic easier and is approximately the same as a constant absolute amount of depreciation.

£50,000 house, the depreciation of 2 per cent per annum would be £1000 a year. The interest payment at 15 per cent would cost a further £7,500 a year, so your total cost so far is £8,500. However, offset against this is the fact that the house value will appreciate by 10 per cent a year, which will give you a capital gain of £5,000 each year. This has to be offset against the £8,500 to give a net annual cost of £3,500. Ignoring tax considerations and ignoring the costs of searching for a house and of transacting to buy and sell a house, abstracting from all those things, £3,500 per annum is the implicit rental rate that you would have to pay to yourself if you were to buy the house. If houses actually rented for less than £3,500 a year, it would pay you to rent rather than buy. If houses of this type rented for more than £3,500 a year, it would pay you to buy rather than rent. Since everyone is capable of doing the kinds of calculations that you have just performed, it might be expected that there would be some equilibrating forces at work in the marketplace ensuring that the actual rental rates on houses did not stray too far away from the implicit rental rate that we have just calculated. Thus, the actual rent of capital goods (a house in this example) and the implicit rent may be regarded as the same. You have now calculated a formula which can be stated in general terms, namely, the rental rate of a piece of capital equipment is equal to the price of the equipment multiplied by the rate of depreciation plus the market rate of interest minus the expected rate of change of the price of the piece of equipment. Let us write that as an equation, defining P_k as the price of capital, δ as the depreciation rate, r_m as the market rate of interest, $-\Delta P_k/P_k$ as the rate of change of the price of capital equipment, and R as the rental rate. The formula for the rental rate becomes

$$R = P_k \left(\delta + r_m - \frac{\Delta P_k}{P_k} \right) \tag{19.1}$$

Let us check that this formula gives us the right answer for the annual rental rate of a house. Using the numbers introduced above, P_k equals £50,000. δ is 2 per cent per annum which will be expressed in proportionate terms as 0.02. The interest rate, r_m (again expressed as a proportion) is 0.15 and the rate of inflation of house prices, $\Delta P_k/P_k$ (also expressed as a proportion) is 0.1. Putting these numbers into the formula gives:

Rent   = £50,000 (0.02 + 0.15 − 0.10)
          = £50,000 × 0.07
          = £3,500 per annum

Evidently the formula works.

Now that you have got the basic idea of how to calculate the rental rate on a piece of capital equipment, let us return to the task of figuring out how a producer will choose how much capital and labour to employ in the production process. You already know that, in order to maximise profits, a producer will set the marginal product of a factor of production equal to its real price. In the case of labour, this involves setting the marginal product of labour equal to the real wage. For capital, the producer has to set the marginal product of capital equal to the real rental rate. What we have just calculated above is the nominal rental rate. The real rental rate, RR, is obtained by dividing the nominal rental rate by the price level to give:

$$RR = \frac{P_k}{P} \left(\delta + r_m - \frac{\Delta P_k}{P_k} \right) \tag{19.2}$$

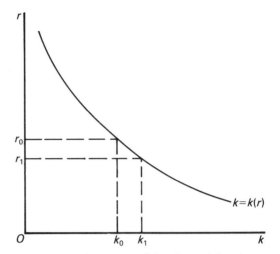

Figure 19.1 *The Demand for Capital Stock*

The demand for capital stock depends inversely upon the rental rate of capital. The rental rate equals the technologically given rate of depreciation plus the difference between the money rate of interest and the rate of inflation of asset prices. The difference between the money rate of interest and the rate of inflation of asset prices is the real rate of interest. The demand for capital therefore depends inversely upon the real rate of interest.

Since we are interested in aggregate economic phenomena we are interested in the economy average real rental rate. In terms of the above equation, that means that we want to interpret P_k/P as the relative price of capital goods to goods and services in general. It is a reasonable approximation to regard that ratio as constant. (In the period between 1960 and 1979 in the United Kingdom capital goods prices decreased by 0.03 of a per cent per annum relative to consumer goods prices.) By calculating a price index for capital goods (P_k) and for goods in general (P) with the same base, we can regard the relative price as being equal to one. Further, since capital goods prices inflate at approximately the same rate as prices in general, we can replace the term $\Delta P_k/P_k$ with the rate of inflation, π. This enables us to write the formula for the real rental rate in a simpler way as:

$$RR = (\delta + r_m - \pi) \qquad\qquad (19.3)$$

Notice that the change in the price of capital now becomes π, the rate of inflation.

You have met before the term $r_m - \pi$. This is nothing other than the real rate of interest which we have previously denoted as r. We can therefore simplify the formula for the real capital rental rate as

$$RR = \delta + r \qquad\qquad (19.4)$$

If the rate of depreciation is a technologically given constant, it is clear that the only *variable* that affects the real capital rental rate is the real rate of interest. Thus, the higher is the real rate of interest, the higher is the real capital rental rate.

If producers utilise capital and labour resources in an efficient way, they will seek to use a more capital-intensive technology the lower is the real rate of interest. Figure 19.1 illustrates the relationship between the capital stock and the real rate of interest. If the real rate of interest was the level r_0, then the capital stock that producers would wish to have is shown as k_0. If the interest rate was lower, at r_1, then the higher capital stock k_1 would be desired.

Now that you understand the relationship between the real rate of interest and the rental rate of capital and also the relationship between the real rate of interest and the demand for capital stock, it is possible to take the next step and see how the rate of investment is determined.

D. Investment and the Demand for Capital

As already stated earlier in this chapter, investment demand is the demand for capital goods for use in productive (or consumption-yielding) activities. Investment is a flow which represents either additions to the existing stock of capital, or replacements of worn-out (depreciated) pieces of capital equipment. Capital equipment that is wearing out will be proportional to the stock of capital in existence, and from the discussion that we had above concerning the rental rate of capital, that depreciation rate, denoted there as δ, implies that the rate at which capital stock is being worn out is equal to δK. The rate at which the capital stock is changing is equal to ΔK. Investment, i, is the sum of these two things, that is,

$$i = \delta K + \Delta K \tag{19.5}$$

There are some very elaborate theories that explain the speed with which firms will seek to add to their capital stock. For our purposes, it seems sufficient to remark that if firms added to their capital stock too quickly, they would incur a variety of high costs in the form of organisational problems and planning bottlenecks. If, on the other hand, they add to their capital stock too slowly, then they will have to put up with having too little equipment for too long. There would seem to be some optimum rate at which to add to the capital stock, which might be thought of as depending on the extent to which the capital stock currently in place falls short of (or exceeds) the desired capital stock. We know what the preferred capital stock is. It is shown in Figure 19.1 and depends upon the real rate of interest. If the change in the capital stock proceeds at some rate that depends on the gap between this preferred capital stock and the actual capital stock, then the rate of investment will depend on two things. First, the rate of interest, since that determines the desired capital stock, and secondly, the existing capital stock, since that affects how much capital shortage or surplus there is. How do these two variables, the real rate of interest and the stock of capital, affect the investment rate? A moment's reflection will reveal that they both have a negative effect on investment. We have already seen that the higher is the real rate of interest, the smaller is the desired capital stock. The bigger is the actual capital stock, the smaller, other things being equal, will be the gap between the desired and the actual capital stock that firms seek to close. Both of these forces, then, would work to reduce the rate of investment.

To summarise then, the rate of investment will depend on the real rate of interest and the capital stock. The higher is either of those two variables, the lower will be the rate of investment.

There is one final simplification which it will be useful to introduce into the analysis, and that concerns the approximation arising from the fact that investment is a small number relative to the capital stock, so that even though positive investment is being undertaken at all times, the capital stock is a very slowly changing variable and may be regarded as approximately constant. That being so, it is possible to simplify the theory of investment still further by ignoring, at least for short-run purposes, the effect of the capital stock on the rate of investment. Thus, the theory of investment used in short-run macroeconomic models is one that supposes that investment depends only on the real rate of interest.

In developing the proposition that investment depends only on the real rate of interest, a great deal has been set aside. Indeed, it would not be an exaggeration to say that the major sources of fluctuation in investment are ignored by focusing exclusively on the real rate of interest as a determinant of investment. There are obviously many things other than the real rate of interest that will influence the pace of investment. Such things as taxes; changes in technology which make some types of equipment outmoded and stimulate massive demand for new, previously unknown types of capital; changes in population (both in terms of its size, age, and sex distributions); changes in entrepreneurs' perceptions of profit opportunities; as well, of course, as the slowly changing capital stock itself are all examples of things that undoubtedly exert a major influence upon investment. Further, because investment is the *flow* which is the means whereby the *stock* of capital is changed, anything which changes the desired stock of capital will have a *magnified* effect on the flow of investment. When the demand for capital (a stock demand) rises, the flow of investment will jump. When the stock of capital reaches its new desired level, the pace of investment will slacken off to a rate consistent with replacing worn out capital.

The bathtub analogy which we have used before illustrates this phenomenon well. The desire to soak in a tub leads to a rise in the demand for a *stock* of water. That results in opening the tap to maximum pressure — a *flow* — for as long as necessary to achieve the desired water level. Then the tap is closed and the flow stops — though the stock remains. Thus, a flow rises from zero to its maximum rate and back to zero very quickly. The flow displays large fluctuations. It is exactly the same with the variables that lead to changes in the desired capital stock. They result in large fluctuations in investment.

The key to understanding the theory of investment as used in macroeconomic analysis is the realisation that all the other factors that influence investment may, as a reasonable approximation, be taken to be independent of all the other variables that a macroeconomic model determines. This means that when such factors change and shift the investment demand curve, they set up repercussions for income, prices, interest rates, and other macroeconomic variables, but there are no significant feedbacks onto the rate of investment itself other than those which go through the real rate of interest.

E. Investment Demand Function

The entire discussion in this chapter can now be summarised very compactly. The investment demand function implied by the previous discussion may be written as a simple equation, which is

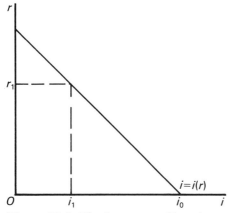

Figure 19.2 *The Investment Function*

Investment will be undertaken to replace existing capital and to close the gap between the desired and actual capital stock. Since the desired capital stock depends inversely on the real rate of interest and since the actual capital stock changes only slowly over time, investment itself will be a function of the real rate of interest. Many other factors, summarised in the intercept i_0, will influence investment. None of the variables that influence the position of the investment demand function, i_0, is determined in the macroeconomic model. Rather, shifts in the investment demand function may be important exogenous sources of fluctuation in aggregate demand.

$$i = i_0 - hr \qquad i_0, h, > 0 \tag{19.6}$$

This equation says that the level of investment will be equal to some amount that is independent of all the other variables in our macroeconomic model, i_0, and over and above that, will vary inversely with the real rate of interest. The way that the equation is specified makes the relationship linear. A one percentage point rise in the real rate of interest would produce an h-million pound drop in the rate of investment. The same relationship as appears in equation (19.6) is shown in Figure 19.2.

You should think of the volatility of investment as being reflected in shifts in the investment function as shown in Figure 19.2, or equivalently, of exogenous changes in the intercept of the investment function, i_0. These changes would arise from the many factors, examples of which are listed at the end of Section D above.[3]

---

3. As in the case of the consumption function, the theory of investment presented here is highly condensed and selective. A superb treatment of the subject at a more advanced level, however, may be found in Frank Brechling, *Investment and Employment Decisions*, Manchester University Press, 1975. Another even more up-to-date but technically yet more demanding study is that by Stephen J. Nickell, *The Investment Decisions of Firms*, James Nisbet and Co. and the Cambridge University Press, 1978. A good, up-to-date, though again fairly demanding survey is Andrew B. Abel, Empirical investment equations: an integrative framework, in Karl Brunner and Alan H. Meltzer (eds), *On the State of Macro-Economics*, Carnegie-Rochester Conference Series, Vol. 12, Spring 1980, pp. 39–92. Empirical studies of investment behaviour in the United Kingdom can be found in the reports of the content of the large-scale econometric models of the National Institute of Economic and Social Research, the London Business School, the Treasury, and the University of Southampton, in G.A. Renton (ed.), *Modelling the Economy*, Heinemann Educational Books, 1975, Part I. A more straightforward though somewhat dated study is that by A. R. Nobay, Forecasting manufacturing investment — some preliminary results, *National Institute Economic Review*, No. 52, 1970, pp. 58–66.

SUMMARY

A. Distinction Between Investment and the Capital Stock

Investment demand is the demand for capital goods for use in production or consumption-yielding activities. It represents additions to the stock of capital or replacement of depreciated capital. Thus, investment is the *flow* which augments or maintains the *stock* of capital.

B. The Demand for Capital

The demand for capital is determined by cost-minimising or profit-maximising considerations. Capital will be demanded up to the point at which its marginal product equals its rental rate.

C. Rental Rate of Capital

Where capital equipment is explicitly rented, as is often the case with houses, and occasionally with carts, TV sets, and industrial equipment, the rental rate of capital is simply the rate per hour that has to be paid for the use of a particular type of equipment. Most capital is not rented explicitly, but is owned by the individual or firm that uses it. In such a case, the rental rate on capital is *implicit*. The individual implicitly rents the equipment from him/herself. That implicit rental rate will be equal to the rate of depreciation plus the market rate of interest (nominal rate of interest), minus the rate of appreciation of the asset in question.

D. Investment and the Demand for Capital

The rate of investment will be determined by the size of the capital stock relative to the profit-maximising capital stock. The bigger is the stock of capital relative to the desired stock, the faster will the rate of investment be. Since the capital stock is a slowly changing variable, as an approximation the rate of investment may be presumed to depend only upon the rental rate of capital. The rental rate will in turn depend primarily upon the real rate of interest. Thus, the simple macroeconomic theory of investment is that it depends upon the real rate of interest. A higher real rate of interest will induce a lower rate of investment. This theory leaves out more than it includes. What is left out, however, may be presumed to be independent of (exogenous with respect to) the other variables that macroeconomics seeks to understand. It is fluctuations in those other variables, however, which are responsible for some of the major swings in investment activity.

E. Investment Demand Function

The investment demand function can be written in a simple equation as $i = i_0 - hr$. This equation states that as the real rate of interest, r, rises, the level of investment falls. The constant, h, is the degree of responsiveness of investment to interest rate changes. Volatility of investment is reflected in changes in i_0 which shift the investment demand function.

Review Questions

1. What is the difference between investment and the capital stock?

2. What is the difference between a *change* in investment and a *change* in the capital stock?

3. How do firms decide on the size of the desired capital stock?

4. What is the rental rate of capital? How does it relate to the price of capital goods?

5. A car which you are thinking of buying costs £6,000 and will, after one year, have a resale value of £5,000. The rate of interest on the bank loan which you would take if you did buy the car is 15 per cent. A friend who already owns an identical car offers to lease you that car for one year for £1,800 (you buy the petrol and pay for maintenance). Should you accept the offer from your friend or should you buy the car? What is the rental rate that your friend is asking? What is the implicit rental rate if you buy the car?

6. What determines the rate of investment?

7. What is the investment demand function? What is being held constant and what is varying as we move along the investment demand function?

8. What causes shifts in the investment demand function?

9. Use *National Income and Expenditure* (the Blue Book), HMSO, London, for a recent year and obtain data on investment expenditure over the last ten years. (Refer back to Chapter 3 if you are not sure how to do this.) Draw a time series graph of investment. Describe the main movements. What relationship, if any, can you find between investment and the *real* rate of interest? (Use the Appendix to Chapter 2 for data on interest rates and inflation rates.)

20

The IS Curve

There are various stages in the process of learning economics that involve mastering some steps of analysis which seem, at the time, completely pointless. It is as if analysis is being mastered for its own sake, rather than to achieve some objective in terms of having greater insights or better understanding of how the economy works. It is not until a later stage in the learning process that the point of a particular piece of analysis becomes fully apparent. You are about to embark on such a piece of analysis in this chapter. The objective towards which you are working is having an understanding of what determines aggregate demand and how aggregate demand is affected by such things as government expenditures, taxes, foreign demand, and the money supply. Achieving a level of expertise and understanding that is worthwhile involves mastering a body of analysis which, in its entirety, is hard to grasp the first time through (and even the second or third time for some of us). It is easier to grasp and understand if it is broken down into a series of individually easy-to-manage steps. That makes the process of comprehension and understanding easier. At the same time, it does give rise to the problem that we describe above; namely, that while a series of small intermediate steps are being taken, the final objective, the point to where it is all leading, may be lost from sight.

Try to keep in mind where you are going. You are going to end up after another two chapters with a clear understanding of the Keynesian theory of aggregate demand. You are going to see how the various bits and pieces, one of which is now going to be developed in this chapter, will fit together.

The part of the aggregate demand story that you are going to master in this chapter involves a relationship called the *IS* curve. *I* stands for investment and *S* for savings. You are going to undertake four tasks which are to:

A. **know the definition of the *IS* curve;**
B. **know how to derive the *IS* curve;**
C. **understand what determines the slope of the *IS* curve;**
   and
D. **understand what makes the *IS* curve shift and by how much.**

A. Definition of the *IS* Curve

The *IS* curve is a relationship between the level of output and the real rate of interest. It is that relationship that links the level of income and the real rate of interest such that investment demand plus government demand equals savings plus taxes.[1] Equivalently, it is that relationship between the level of real income and the real rate of interest which ensures that aggregate demand (consumption demand plus investment demand plus government demand) is equal to the level of real income. It might be helpful to put this slightly differently and more long windedly. Since consumption depends on income, different levels of income will bring forth different levels of consumption. When consumption is added to investment and government spending, the result is a particular level of the total demand for output (real income). The *IS* curve traces the relationship between the level of output (real income) and the real rate of interest when the level of aggregate demand is equal to the level of real income that generates that level of aggregate demand.

The *IS* curve is not a description of the desires or decisions of any single agent or group of agents. Rather, it is the same kind of animal as the aggregate demand curve which you have already met. It is an *equilibrium locus*. It traces the locus of points that give an equality between the aggregated demand for goods and services and the level of output of goods and services. Indeed, you can think of the *IS* curve as a kind of aggregate demand curve. Of course, the aggregate demand curve as we defined it is a relationship between the total demand for goods and services and the price level. That meaning of the term aggregate demand curve is a useful one, and we shall reserve it, even in the Keynesian context, for something other than the *IS* curve. Nevertheless, the *IS* curve tells us the total demand for goods and services as we vary, not the price level, but the real rate of interest. It is important not to interpret the *IS* curve as implying anything about causality. The *IS* curve emphatically does not say that different levels of aggregate demand are caused by different levels of the real rate of interest. All that it is telling us is that the real rate of interest and the level of real income cannot be any values they like. They must be restricted to lie on the *IS* curve. The two variables will be determined simultaneously (by a procedure that we shall get to in Chapter 22).

What you are going to be looking at next, then, is the way the *IS* curve is derived.

B. Derivation of the *IS* Curve

The easiest way to learn how to derive the *IS* curve is to begin by refreshing your memory about the components of aggregate demand for goods and services and the ways in which aggregate income may be allocated by households. Recall that

---

1. You may think that the *IS* curve is peculiarly named since it is a curve that describes the equality of investment (*I*) plus government spending (*G*) and savings (*S*) plus taxes (*T*). Aside from *IGST* being a clumsy name, when the analysis presented here was first invented by Sir John Hicks in 1936 he illustrated the analysis for an economy in which government spending and taxes were zero, hence the name *IS*.

aggregate income may be allocated in three ways. It may be spent on consumption, saved, or paid in taxes; that is,

$$y = c + s + t \tag{20.1}$$

(Recall that c is consumption demand, s is savings, t is taxes, and y is real income [output].) Also recall that aggregate demand is decomposed into three components: consumption demand, investment demand, and government demand for goods and services. That is,

$$y^d = c + i + g \tag{20.2}$$

Subtracting c from both sides of equation (20.1) gives

$$y - c = s + t \tag{20.3}$$

This simply says that income minus consumption demand must be equal to savings-plus-taxes. This does not say anything about behaviour, of course. It is simply a statement about the necessary relationship between income and expenditure. It is nothing other than the household sector's budget constraint. Next, subtract c from both sides of equation (20.2) to obtain

$$y^d - c = i + g \tag{20.4}$$

What this says is that the difference between aggregate demand and consumption demand is equal to investment-plus-government spending. Equation (20.1) says exactly the same thing as equation (20.3), and equation (20.2) says the same as equation (20.4). They are simply different ways of looking at the same thing.

The *IS* curve, the derivation of which you are now embarking upon, traces the relationship between the level of aggregate demand and the real rate of interest when the level of aggregate demand is equal to the level of real income. In other words, the *IS* curve has to be derived satisfying the condition

$$y = y^d \tag{20.5}$$

This says that points on the *IS* curve are points such that aggregate demand is equal to aggregate real income (output). You will notice, if you replace y with y^d in equation (20.3), that the left-hand side of equation (20.3) is exactly the same as the left-hand side of equation (20.4). It follows, therefore, that the right-hand side of equation (20.3) must be equal to the right-hand side of equation (20.4) when we are on the *IS* curve. That is,

$$s + t = i + g \tag{20.6}$$

Equation (20.6) says that planned savings-plus-taxes must equal investment-plus-government spending at all points on the *IS* curve. It is equation (20.6) that gives the name to the *IS* curve. If there were no government, so that t and g were equal to zero, it would simply say that to be on the *IS* curve, savings plans must equal investment demand. With government spending and taxes not being zero, these have to be added to private savings and investment to obtain the equivalent *flow equilibrium condition in the goods market* that underlies the *IS curve*.

With this background it is now possible to proceed to derive the *IS* curve. It will be helpful to proceed in easy stages, however, and first to examine the right-hand side of equation (20.6), investment-plus-government spending. Figure 20.1 illustrates this

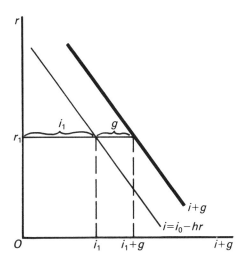

Figure 20.1 *Investment-Plus-Government Spending*
Investment (the thin line) varies inversely with the real rate of interest. Government spending
is fixed independently of the rate of interest. Investment-plus-government spending (the thick
line) has the same slope as the investment line, but is shifted to the right by the amount of
government spending (g). For example, at the real interest rate r_1 investment is i_1 and
investment-plus-government spending is $i_1 + g$.

aspect of the demand for goods. The real interest rate is measured on the vertical axis
and investment-plus-government spending on the horizontal axis. The thin curve
labelled $i = i_0 - hr$ is the investment demand schedule, the derivation of which is
discussed in Chapter 19. It shows that the level of investment demand increases as the
real rate of interest falls. For example, at the interest rate r_1 the level of investment
demand will be i_1. At higher interest rates the level of investment demand will be less
than i_1. The thicker line in the figure, which is drawn parallel to the investment
demand curve, is the level of investment demand plus the level of government
demand for goods and services. You will recall that the level of government demand
is assumed to be exogenous. It is determined independently of the level of the
interest rate or of any other of the variables in the model. The horizontal distance
between the investment demand curve and the curve labelled $i + g$ is the fixed level of
government expenditure. It is illustrated by the horizontal line g at the interest rate
r_1. You can see, however, that the distance between i and $i + g$ is the same at all rates
of interest. The thick line $i + g$ represents the total amount of investment demand
and the total demand for goods and services by the government added together —
investment-plus-government spending. This diagram will be returned to below.
Next, consider the other side of equation (20.6), savings-plus-taxes.
   This is slightly trickier than the previous analysis. The reason why it is trickier is
that savings depend on *disposable* income. Disposable income, in turn, depends in
part on taxes, so taxes have a double influence on the volume of savings-plus-taxes;
higher taxes mean lower savings, but higher taxes mean bigger savings-*plus*-taxes all
taken together. You need to be slightly careful, therefore, in sorting out the
relationships involved here. Figure 20.2 illustrates what goes on. Looking at Figure
20.2, first focus on the middle line in that figure. That line shows the level of savings

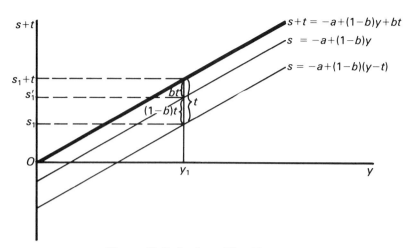

Figure 20.2 *Savings-Plus-Taxes*

In the absence of taxes, the savings function would be the centre thin line. With taxes at level t, the savings function is the lower thin line. It is displaced downwards by the propensity to save $(1 - b)$ times taxes. Taxes are treated as constant. The savings-plus-taxes function is therefore displaced upwards above the savings function by the amount of taxes, and shown as the thick line. If taxes rise, the savings-plus-taxes line rises by the marginal propensity to consume (b) times the rise in taxes.

---

that would be forthcoming at each level of income if taxes were equal to zero. It is simply describing the equation $s = -a + (1-b)y$. That is the savings relation implied by the consumption function that was discussed in Chapter 18. Now, focus on the income level y_1 and notice that if taxes were indeed zero, savings would be equal to s_1' at the income level y_1. Now, drop the assumption that taxes are zero and allow taxes to be some positive number, t. You will recall, from the discussion in Chapter 18, that with taxes at level t, the savings function will shift downwards by an amount equal to $(1 - b)$ times the level of taxes. This is because when taxes go up, consumption and savings must fall by an amount equal to the tax rise. Fraction b of the taxes is paid for by reducing consumption, and fraction $1 - b$ is paid by reducing savings. The bottom line in Figure 20.2 illustrates the savings function, allowing for taxes at level t. With taxes at level t and income at y_1, savings will be equal to s_1. The vertical distance between the line $s=-a+(1 - b)y$ and the line $s = -a +(1 - b)(y - t)$ is equal to $(1 - b)t$. Now, according to equation (20.6), it is savings-plus-taxes that must be equal to investment-plus-government spending and it is therefore the total of savings-plus-taxes we are interested in. The top line of Figure 20.2 is a graph of savings-plus-taxes. It is nothing other than the level of taxes, t, added (vertically) to the lowest of the three lines in the diagram. That is illustrated at the income level y_1 by the distance indicated by t.

You are now in a position to understand the nature of the relationship between savings-plus-taxes and income. That relationship is similar to the relationship between savings and income. If you start from the curve describing the relationship between savings and income when taxes are zero, the savings-plus-taxes curve is equal to that original savings curve plus taxes times the marginal propensity to consume. What this says is that a rise in taxes does not raise savings-plus-taxes one-

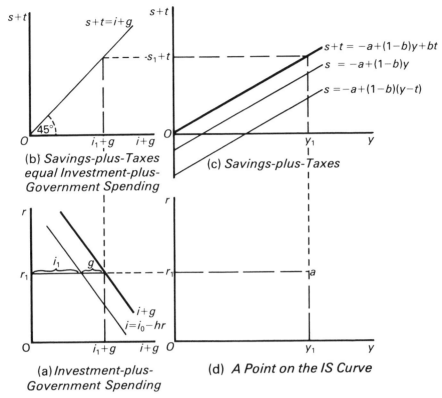

Figure 20.3 *The Derivations of a Point on the IS Curve*

The *IS* curve traces the relationship between the real rate of interest and the level of real income at which investment-plus-government spending equals savings-plus-taxes. Point *a* is a point on the *IS* curve. At point *a*, real income is y_1 (horizontal axis of Frames (d) and (c)) so that savings-plus-taxes are $s_1 + t$. At *a* the interest rate is r_1 (vertical axis of Frames (d) and (a)) so that investment-plus-government spending is $i_1 + g$. Looking at Frame (b) you see that $s_1 + t = i_1 + g$, so that the point *a* satisfies the definition of the *IS* curve.

for-one. A rise in taxes raises savings-plus-taxes by less than the rise in taxes, because there is going to be a drop in savings in order to meet part of the tax payments.

You are now in a position to derive the *IS* curve graphically. Figure 20.3 is the source of the derivation. It looks much more formidable than it is, so try not to be put off by your first glance at that figure. Just follow the text carefully and slowly as it leads you through what, as you will soon see, is a straightforward derivation. Frame (a) is nothing other than Figure 20.1 — investment-plus-government spending. The interest rate r_1 and the investment level i_1, and the government spending level g shown in that frame are the same as the values shown in Figure 20.1. Frame (c) is exactly the same as Figure 20.2 — savings-plus-taxes. Again, the income level y_1, the savings level s_1, and the tax level t are the same in Frame (c) as those shown and already discussed in Figure 20.2. The new frames of Figure 20.3 are Frames (b) and (d). Frame (b) of the figure is just a graphical representation of the equilibrium condition that defines the *IS* curve. It is a 45° line. You will readily verify that measuring investment-plus-government spending on the horizontal axis in the same units as savings-plus-taxes are measured on the vertical axis implies that at each point on that 45° line, savings-plus-taxes are equal to investment-plus-government spending. You can think of the IS curve now as being a relationship between the level of real income and the real rate of interest such that the economy is located on each of the three curves depicted in Frames (a), (b) and (c). Such a point on the IS curve is the point a depicted in Frame (d). Notice that the axes in Frame (d) measure the real rate of interest and real income. Opposite the real interest rate axis, in Frame (a) the real interest rate is measured in the investment-plus-government spending diagram. Transferring the real interest rate r_1 across from Frame (a) to Frame (d) takes us horizontally across to point a. You will also notice that the level of real income on the horizontal axis of Frame (d) is the same as the horizontal axis of Frame (c) immediately above it. Transferring the income level y_1 down from Frame (c) to Frame (d), we shall reach the same point a. Notice that the level of savings-plus-taxes generated by income level y_1 is exactly the same as the level of investment-plus-government spending generated by the interest rate r_1. You can verify this by tracking up vertically from Frame (a) to Frame (b) and across horizontally from Frame (c) to Frame (b). Point a, then, is a point on the IS curve.

Let us complete the derivation of the IS curve in a slightly less cluttered-up diagram, but one which in every respect is identical to Figure 20.3 except that it has some of the lines removed for clarity. Figure 20.4 simply reproduces the curves $i + g$ and $s + t$ from Figure 20.3. First of all familiarise yourself with Figure 20.4 and satisfy yourself it is identical to Figure 20.3 except that some lines have been left off to give the diagram a fresher and clearer appearance. Now choose a higher interest rate than r_1, such as r_2. Notice that at r_2, the level of investment-plus-government spending, is $i_2 + g$, which is less than $i_1 + g$. Now track up from Frame (a) to Frame (b) and record the level of investment-plus-government spending $i_2 + g$ on the horizontal axis of Frame (b). Notice that if $i + g$ is equal to $s + t$ (if we are going to be at a point on the IS curve), the level of savings-plus-taxes must equal $s_2 + t$ as shown on the vertical axis of Frame (b). Now transfer that amount of savings-plus-taxes horizontally across to Frame (c). You may now read off from Frame (c) the level of real income that is necessary to ensure that the volume of savings-plus-taxes equals $s_2 + t$. That level of income is given by y_2. Now transfer the income level y_2 down to the horizontal axis of Frame (d) and transfer the interest rate level r_2 horizontally across from Frame (a) to Frame (d). Where these two lines join, labelled b, is another point on the IS curve. Joining together points a and b with other intermediate points traces out the IS curve.

You will find it helpful to derive an IS curve for yourself by setting up the diagrams shown as Frames (a), (b) and (c), and then deriving points on the IS curve for a series of interest rates such as r_1, r_2, and other intermediate rates. Be sure that you are thoroughly conversant with the way in which the IS curve is derived before moving on to the next two sections of this chapter.

C. Determination of the *IS* Curve Slope

You already know that the IS curve slopes downwards. You can see that simply from Frame (d) of Figure 20.4 in which you have derived an IS curve. You can also see

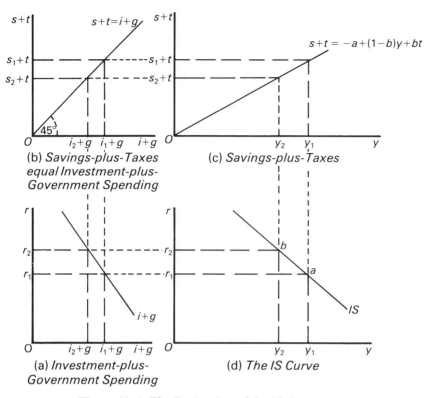

Figure 20.4 *The Derivation of the IS Curve*

This figure is exactly like 20.3 except that in Frames (a) and (c) only the $i + g$ and $s + t$ curves are plotted. Point *a* in this figure is the same as point *a* in Figure 20.3. The point *b* (in Frame (d) of the diagram) is equivalent to point *a*, but relates to the income level y_2 and the interest rate r_2. At point *b*, the income level is y_2 and savings-plus-taxes are $s_2 + t$. The interest rate at point *b* is r_2, so that investment-plus-government spending is $i_2 + g$. By looking at Frame (b), you can see that $i_2 + g = s_2 + t$, so that *b* is also a point on an *IS* curve. Joining up *a* and *b* and extending the line beyond those points traces out the *IS* curve.

from inspecting Figure 20.4 and comparing Frame (d) with Frame (a) that the *IS* curve is flatter than the slope of the investment demand curve. What does this mean? It means that as the interest rate falls from, say, r_2 to r_1, the investment rise from i_2 to i_1 is less than the amount by which income rises from y_2 to y_1. Call the *change in investment* Δi and call the *change in income* Δy. What is the relationship between the change in income and the change in investment when the interest rate is (hypothetically) allowed to drop from r_2 to r_1? You can figure this out by using a small amount of secondary school geometry. Figure 20.5 illustrates. A thickened right-angled triangle is shown in Frame (c). What are the properties of that triangle? Its base clearly has length Δy. Its height has length Δi. You also know that the hypotenuse of that triangle has a slope equal to $1 - b$, the marginal propensity to save or, equivalently, 1 minus the marginal propensity to consume. Now recall your secondary school geometry. The proposition that you need is the one that goes 'slope

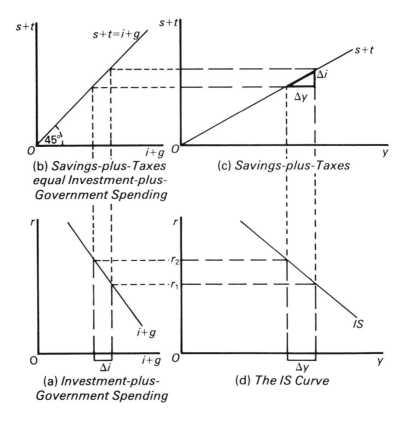

Figure 20.5 *The Slope of the IS Curve*

The *IS* curve slopes downwards. The lower the real rate of interest, the higher the level of investment, and since investment-plus-government spending must equal savings-plus-taxes, the higher too must be the level of savings. Since savings depend on income, higher savings will require higher income levels. Hence, to be on the *IS* curve, the lower rate of interest will have to be associated with a higher level of income. For a given drop in the rate of interest, the rise in income will be equal to the rise in investment divided by the marginal propensity to save, or $\Delta i/(1 - b)$.

---

equals rise over run'. The 'slope' in this case is $1 - b$, the 'rise' is Δi, and the 'run' is Δy. Translating 'slope equals rise over run' into the numbers that represent the 'slope', 'rise' and 'run' of the triangle in Frame (c), we have

'slope' $= 1 - b$
'rise' $= \Delta i$
'run' $= \Delta y$

so that

$1 - b = \Delta i/\Delta y$

Now multiply both sides of that equation by the change in income (Δy) to give

$\Delta y(1 - b) = \Delta i$

Now divide both sides of the equation by the marginal propensity to save $(1 - b)$ to give

$$\Delta y = \frac{1}{1 - b} \cdot \Delta i$$

This is the famous Keynesian *multiplier* which you have already met in Chapter 18. It says that the change in income will be related to the change in investment by the amount $1/(1 - b)$. Clearly, since b is a fraction, $1 - b$ is also a fraction, and $1/(1 - b)$ is a number bigger than 1, a multiple giving rise to the name multiplier.

You have now discovered that the slope of the *IS* curve is negative and that it is flatter than the slope of the investment demand curve and related to the slope of the investment demand curve by 1 divided by the marginal propensity to save, or 1 divided by 1 minus the marginal propensity to consume.

D. Shifts in the *IS* Curve

The *IS* curve will shift if government spending changes, if taxes change, if autonomous expenditure, i_0 or a changes. We shall focus only on changes in government spending and taxes. Changes in i_0 and a have identical effects on the *IS* curve to changes in government spending, as you will be readily able to verify for yourself once you are familiar with the analysis.

First, let us look at the effects of a change in government spending. Figure 20.6 will illustrate the analysis. The thickened curves simply reproduce the curves already introduced and used in Figures 20.4 and 20.5. Now suppose that there is a rise in government spending by an amount that will be called Δg. What does that do to this diagram? The answer is shown in Frame (a). The curve labelled $i+g$ which shows investment-plus-government spending shifts to the right by an amount equal to the rise in government spending. This is illustrated by the thinner line in Frame (a) that is displaced horizontally to the right from the original $i+g$ line by an amount indicated as Δg.

Holding taxes constant for the moment, there are no changes to be recorded in Frame (c). All that remains is to work out the implications of the shift in the curve $i+g$ for the *IS* curve. You can do that by deriving a new *IS* curve, using the new $i+g+\Delta g$ line in Frame (a). Applying the method which you have learned in Section B of this chapter, you will discover that the new *IS* curve is the one labelled IS_2 in Frame (d). (If you are not sure how to derive that *IS* curve you should go back to Section B of this chapter and reinforce your understanding of how to derive the *IS* curve.)

What is the effect on the *IS* curve of the rise in g? Suppose that g rises by an amount that will be called Δg. You can see by inspecting Figure 20.6 what happens to the *IS* curve. It shifts to the right. Further, it shifts to the right by more than the rise in government spending (Δg). You can see that by visual inspection of Frames (a) and (d). By how much more to the right has the *IS* curve shifted than the rise in government spending? The answer to that question turns out to be identical to the answer that you have already derived concerning the relationship between the slope of the $i+g$ curve and the slope of the *IS* curve. You can see this directly because of a

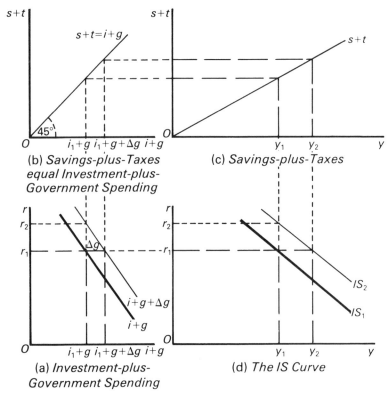

Figure 20.6 *A Change in Government Spending Shifts the IS Curve*

A rise in government spending of Δg shifts the investment-plus-government spending function to the right by the amount Δg. The *IS* curve is shifted to the right as a result of this by an amount equal to $\Delta g/(1 - b)$.

visual trick that we have used in selecting the amount by which to raise government spending, Δg. Notice that we chose the rise in government spending, Δg, to be an amount such that when the interest rate is r_2 with the new higher level of government spending, the total level of investment-plus-spending is identical to what it had been previously at the interest rate r_1. If, therefore, you conduct the analysis at the interest rate r_2, you will see that at the interest rate r_2 the rise in investment-plus-government spending indicated as Δg is the same as the rise in investment in the experiment conducted above when discussing the slope of the *IS* curve. You will also see that the rise in income that we have derived from this rise in government spending is exactly the same as the rise in income discussed and analysed in Figure 20.5 above. By applying exactly the same logic and exactly the same reasoning you can therefore see that the *shift in the IS curve is equal to the rise in government spending multiplied by* $1/(1 - b)$.

Now let us turn to an analysis of the effects of a rise in taxes on the *IS* curve. This is slightly more complicated, and the extra complexity arises from the fact that the savings-plus-taxes schedule is a slightly more tricky animal than the investment-plus-government spending schedule. Figure 20.7 will illustrate the analysis. Let us again

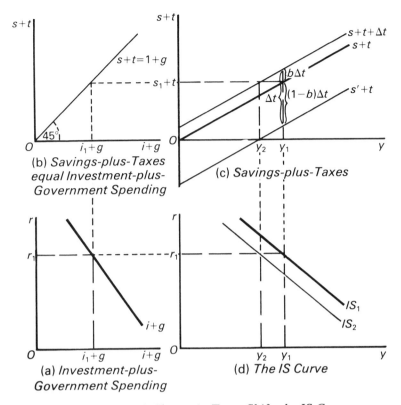

Figure 20.7 *A Change in Taxes Shifts the IS Curve*
A rise in taxes of Δt will raise the savings-plus-taxes curve by $b\Delta t$. This will result in a *backward* shift in the *IS* curve.

familiarise ourselves with the set-up by noting that the thick curves in Figure 20.7 are identical to those used in Figure 20.4. The *IS* curve labelled IS_1 is the *IS* curve that would be derived under the conditions prevailing in Figure 20.4.

We now want to ask what happens to the *IS* curve if taxes rise by an amount that will be called Δt. The impact effect of the rise in taxes is to be seen in Frame (c). You know from the material that you have already mastered in Section B of this chapter that if taxes rise, this will raise the savings-plus-taxes schedule, but not by the full amount of the tax rise. This is because savings themselves will fall somewhat. If taxes rise by Δt, the savings-plus-taxes schedule will move to the schedule labelled $s+t+\Delta t$. You should satisfy yourself that this new schedule is higher than the original schedule by an amount equal to $b\Delta t$. Savings will have dropped to s', which is $(1-b)\Delta t$ lower than originally. The total rise in taxes is the distance between the top line and the bottom line in Frame (c).

Now let us figure out what this change in taxes has done to the *IS* curve. Derive a new *IS* curve, using exactly the same technique as before, but using the curve labelled $s+t+\Delta t$, the new savings-plus-taxes curve in Frame (c). That *IS* curve, you will discover, is the one labelled IS_2 in Frame (d). How does this *IS* curve compare with the curve IS_1? First, you will notice that a rise in taxes leads to a shift in the *IS* curve, but in the opposite direction to the shift occurring when government spending

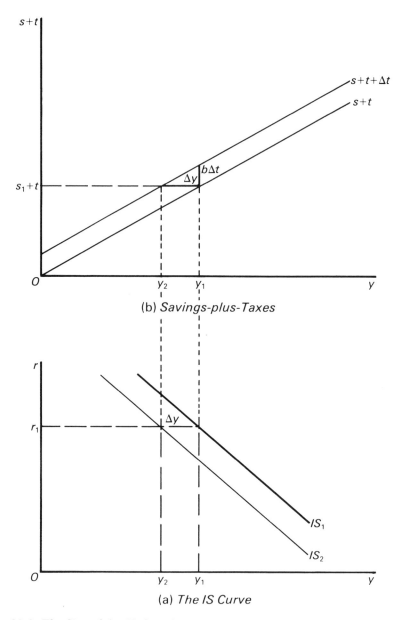

Figure 20.8 *The Size of the Shift in the IS Curve Resulting from a Change in Taxes*
A tax rise of Δt will raise the savings-plus-taxes curve by $b\Delta t$. The backward shift in the *IS* curve that results from this will be equal to $b\Delta t/(1 - b)$. The effect on a tax change on the *IS* curve is less than the (opposite) effect of an equivalent change in government spending. Government spending affects aggregate demand directly, whereas taxes affect aggregate demand indirectly through their effect on consumption. A £1 change in taxes produces a £b change in spending. Thus, the tax multiplier is $-b/(1 - b)$, whereas the government spending multiplier is $1/(1 - b)$.

increases. By how much does the *IS* curve shift leftwards when the level of taxes is increased? You can answer this question with another piece of secondary school geometry illustrated in Figure 20.8. Figure 20.8 reproduces Frames (c) and (d) of Figure 20.7. Focus on the interest rate at r_1 with the income level at y_1. Notice that at the interest rate r_1 the tax rise shifts the *IS* curve such that, if the interest rate was to remain constant at r_1, income would fall to y_2. Call the change in income from y_1 to y_2, Δy. That income change is labelled Δy in Frame (a). Transferring that income level up to Frame (b), you see that it forms the base of a triangle whose height is given by b times the change in taxes. Again, use the formula 'slope = rise/run' to figure out what the change in income is in this case. You know that the 'slope' of the hypotenuse of that triangle is $1-b$; the 'rise' is $b\Delta t$ and the 'run' is $(-\Delta y)$, so you may establish that 'slope = rise/run' becomes $1-b=b\Delta t/(-\Delta y)$. (Why have we put a minus sign in front of Δy? *Because income* **falls** *as taxes* **rise**, so they move in opposite directions.) Now multiply both sides of this equation by the change in income (Δy) to give

$$\Delta y(1-b) = -b\Delta t$$

Now divide both sides of this equation by $(1-b)$, the marginal propensity to save, and obtain

$$\Delta y = \frac{-b}{1-b}\Delta t$$

What does this say? It says that a change in taxes changes income in the opposite direction and by an amount that is equal to the marginal propensity to consume divided by the marginal propensity to save, times the change in taxes.

SUMMARY

A. Definition of the *IS* Curve

The *IS* curve is the relationship between the aggregate demand for goods
and services and the real rate of interest when flow equilibrium prevails in
the goods market; that is, when investment-plus-government spending is
equal to planned savings-plus-taxes.

B. Derivation of the *IS* Curve

The *IS* curve is derived from the investment-plus-government spending
curve, the planned savings-plus-taxes curve, and the equality of
investment-plus-government spending and savings-plus-taxes. Figures
20.1 – 20.4 illustrate this and should be thoroughly understood.

C. Determination of the *IS* Curve Slope

The *IS* curve slopes downwards. That is, at lower real interest rates higher
levels of real income are required to maintain flow equilibrium in the
goods market. This arises because at lower interest rates there is more
investment spending, and with higher investment there need to be higher
savings to maintain equilibrium. Higher savings require a higher level of
income, so that lower interest rates require higher income levels. More
precisely, the slope of the *IS* curve is equal to the slope of the investment
demand curve multiplied by $1/(1 - b)$, where b is the marginal propensity
to consume.

D. Shifts in the *IS* Curve

The *IS* curve shifts when government spending and taxes change. A rise in
government spending will lead to a rightward shift in the *IS* curve by an
amount equal to $1/(1 - b)$ times the change in government spending. A
rise in taxes will cause the *IS* curve to shift leftwards. The amount of the
shift will be equal to the rise in taxes times $b/(1 - b)$.

Appendix: The Algebra of the *IS* Curve

This appendix sets out the algebra of the *IS* curve. The material presented in this appendix is simply another way of looking at the derivation given in the body of the chapter. For those who prefer an algebraic treatment, this may be found to be more compact and straightforward. It does not, however, contain anything of substance that is not stated in words and diagrams in the chapter.

Aggregate demand for goods and services is

$$y^d = c + i + g \tag{A1}$$

Consumption demand is determined by

$$c = a + b(y - t), \qquad a > 0, 0 < b < 1 \tag{A2}$$

and investment demand is determined by

$$i = i_0 - hr \qquad i_0, h > 0 \tag{A3}$$

Substituting c and i in (A2) and (A3) into (A1) gives

$$y^d = a + b(y - t) + i_0 - hr + g \tag{A4}$$

To be on the *IS* curve,

$$y = y^d \tag{A5}$$

so replacing y^d with y in (A4),

$$y = a + b(y - t) + i_0 - hr + g \tag{A6}$$

which may be rearranged as

$$(1 - b)y = a + i_0 + g - bt - hr \tag{A7}$$

and, dividing both sides by $1 - b$,

$$y = \frac{1}{1 - b} (a + i_0 + g - bt - hr) \tag{A8}$$

or, equivalently,

$$y = \left(\frac{a + i_0}{1 - b}\right) + \left(\frac{1}{1 - b}\right)g - \left(\frac{b}{1 - b}\right)t - \left(\frac{h}{1 - b}\right)r \tag{A9}$$

Equation (A8) or the equivalent (A9) are alternative ways of writing the equation for the *IS* curve. The second way of writing the equation for the *IS* curve is perhaps the clearest and the one that makes interpretation of it most straightforward. The variables that enter the *IS* curve are government spending, g, taxes, t, and the rate of interest, r. The parameters that affect the *IS* curve are the constant in the consumption function, a, the constant in the investment demand function, i_0, the slope of the investment function, h, and the marginal propensity to consume, b. The way in which these various parameters enter the *IS* curve is made very precise in equation (A9). First, the constant in the *IS* curve (the level of output that would occur even if government spending, taxes, and the rates of interest were all zero) is the first term in equation (A9), that is

$$\frac{(a + i_0)}{1 - b}$$

The slope of the *IS* curve (the change in income that occurs when the rate of interest changes by one percentage point) is given by the coefficient in front of the rate of interest, namely

$$\frac{-h}{1-b}$$

Since $-h$ is the slope of the investment curve, you can immediately verify the proposition derived in the text that the slope of the *IS* curve is equal to the slope of the investment curve multiplied by $1/(1-b)$.

A change in government spending will shift the *IS* curve by an amount indicated by the coefficient that multiplies g in equation (A9). That coefficient is $1/(1-b)$ and agrees with the derivation in the text.

A rise in taxes will lower the level of income (will shift the *IS* curve leftwards), since the coefficient in front of taxes has a minus sign attached to it. The size of the change in income that results from a rise in taxes will be equal to $b/(1-b)$ times the change in taxes. This also agrees with the derivation in the text.

Review Questions

1. What is the *IS* curve?

2. Which markets are in equilibrium along the *IS* curve?

3. Why does the *IS* curve slope downwards?

4. Why is the *IS* curve flatter than the investment demand curve?

5. What happens to the position of the *IS* curve if there is a £1 million rise in government expenditure on goods and services?

6. What happens to the position of the *IS* curve if there is a £1 million rise in government transfers to individuals in the form of increased pensions and unemployment benefits?

7. What happens to the position of the *IS* curve if the government cuts pensions and raises defence spending by £1 million?

8. You are given the following information about a hypothetical economy:

   $$c = 100 + 0.8(y-t)$$

   $$i = 500 - 50r$$

   $$g = 400$$

   $$t = 400$$

   (c = consumption; i = investment; g = government expenditure on goods and services; t = taxes; y = real income; r = real rate of interest).
   (a) Find the equation for the *IS* curve.
   (b) Show that the slope of the *IS* curve is the same as the slope of the investment demand curve divided by one minus the marginal propensity to consume.
   (c) Show that a rise in g shifts the *IS* curve to the right by 5 times the rise in g.
   (d) Show that a rise in t shifts the *IS* curve to the left by 4 times the rise in t.

21

The Demand for Money, the Supply of Money and the LM Curve

The subject matter of this chapter is very closely related to that of Chapter 10. If it is a little while since you studied Chapter 10 you will probably find it helpful to review the material in that chapter again before proceeding any further. In the basic model, the analysis of the demand for money, the supply of money, and monetary equilibrium gave rise to the basic model's aggregate demand curve. The aggregate demand curve of the Keynesian model is a bit more complicated than that. Fundamentally, the additional complication arises because, in the Keynesian model, unlike the basic model, the real rate of interest is not regarded as fixed, but rather is a variable to be determined in the analysis. The rate of interest is determined simultaneously with the level of output in the Keynesian model. The determination of consumption and investment summarised in the *IS* curve is one of the ingredients in that Keynesian theory of interest and income. An analysis of the demand for money and money market equilibrium summarised in the *LM* curve is the other ingredient in the Keynesian theory. This chapter deals with this second ingredient. You have four tasks ahead of you in this chapter, which are to:

A. know the definition of the *LM* curve;
B. know how to derive the *LM* curve;
C. understand what determines the slope of the *LM* curve; and
D. understand what makes the *LM* curve shift and by how much.

A. Definition of the *LM* Curve

Like the *IS* curve which you have already studied, the *LM* curve is also a relationship between the rate of interest and the level of real income. Specifically, *the LM curve is that relationship between the rate of interest and the level of real income that makes the demand for money equal to the supply of money.* Thus, like the *IS* curve, the *LM* curve is an equilibrium locus. It is worth emphasising again that the *LM* curve does not imply any causal relationship from the rate of interest to the level of income or in the reverse direction. Like the *IS* curve, it places further restrictions on the values that these two variables may take on. Let us now proceed to see how the *LM* curve is derived.

B. Derivation of the *LM* Curve

The starting point for the derivation of the *LM* curve is the theory of the demand for money.[1] That theory, set out in Chapter 10, says that the amount of real money balances that people will want to hold in the aggregate will vary directly with the level of real income and vary inversely with the level of the market or *money* rate of interest and the rate of inflation. In Chapter 10 we went on to hypothesise that the market rate of interest would be equal to a *constant real* rate of interest plus a potentially variable rate of inflation. This led us to focus on the rate of inflation as the sole determinant of the propensity to hold money. In the Keynesian model, the price level is fixed, so that inflation is constant and zero, while the real rate of interest is a variable to be determined in the analysis. This difference of focus between the Keynesian model and the basic model does not mean that the Keynesian theory has to have a different theory of the demand for money. It does, however, lead us to write the demand for money function in the Keynesian model in a way that focuses attention on the variables which that model seeks to determine and explain.

Purely for the convenience of manipulating the Keynesian model, the demand for money function will be treated as *linear* in real income and the rate of interest.[2]

---

1. There are several excellent discussions of the theory of, and empirical evidence on, the demand for money function. In our view you can do no better than study David Laidler's *The Demand for Money: Theories and Evidence,* 2nd edn, Harper and Row, 1978 and M.J. Artis and M.K. Lewis's *Monetary Control in the United Kingdom,* Philip Allan, 1981. A very good survey of studies of the demand for money in the United Kingdom may be found in C.A.E. Goodhart and A.D. Crockett, The importance of money, *Bank of England Quarterly Bulletin,* Vol. 10, No. 2, June 1970, pp. 159–98. A more up to date survey of the evidence is presented by Graham Hacche in The demand for money in the United Kingdom: experience since 1971, *Bank of England Quarterly Bulletin,* Vol. 14, No. 3, September 1977, pp. 284–305.

2. The precise functional form of the demand for money that best fits the facts is a logarithmic function which says that the logarithm of real money demanded is a linear function of the logarithm of real income and the level (not logarithm) of the rate of interest. The different forms of the function used in Chapter 10 and here are selected for analytical convenience and may be regarded as holding approximately for small enough movements in the variables.

Specifically, we shall suppose that the demand for money is determined by the equation

$$\frac{M^d}{P} = ky + m_0 - lr_m \qquad \text{(21.1)}$$

Exactly the same as in Chapter 10, M^d stands for the quantity of nominal money balances demanded, P is the price level, y is real income, r_m is the market rate of interest, and k, m_0, and l are constants. This equation says that for each extra pound of real income in the economy, k real pounds of extra money balances will be demanded. For every 1 per cent point rise in the market rate of interest on bonds, the demand for bonds would rise and the demand for money balances would drop by l pounds. Even at a zero level of income and a zero rate of interest there would be some rock-bottom level of money balances demanded equal to m_0.

As reviewed and explained in Chapter 10, the market rate of interest will be equal to the real rate of interest plus the inflation rate. That is,

$$r_m = r + \pi \qquad \text{(21.2)}$$

In this Keynesian model that you are now studying, the price level is assumed to be fixed at some number P_0 so that the inflation rate, π, is equal to zero. Taking account of that and calling the fixed price level P_0 enables us to write the demand for money function as follows:

$$\frac{M^d}{P_0} = ky + m_0 - lr \qquad \text{(21.3)}$$

This equation incorporates the fact that the amount of nominal money demanded is deflated by a particular fixed price level, the price level called P_0, and the market rate of interest, r_m, is exactly the same as r, the real rate of interest, since, with a fixed price level, the inflation rate, π, is equal to zero.

In equilibrium in the money market, the demand for money must be equal to the supply of money. Calling the supply of money which is determined by the actions of the monetary authorities, M, the equilibrium condition in the money market may be written as:

$$M^d = M \qquad \text{(21.4)}$$

Just as in the previous chapter government spending and taxes were regarded as exogenous, so in this chapter M is treated as being exogenous. That is, the money supply, M, does not respond directly to the values of any of the variables in the model, but rather is determined externally to the model and influences the values of those variables.

If M^d is replaced in equation (21.3) with M, we obtain

$$\frac{M}{P_0} = ky + m_0 - lr \qquad \text{(21.5)}$$

which is the equation for the *LM* curve. Notice that there are two variables in this equation, y and r. All the other terms in the equation are constants. M is a constant determined by the monetary authorities, P_0 is a constant determined by the Keynesian assumption about the money wage rate (using the approximation of the 'inverse L' aggregate supply curve), and m_0, l and k are constants, being parameters of the demand for money function.

By dividing through equation (21.5) by k, the equation for the LM curve can be written with real income, y, on the left-hand side as

$$y = \frac{1}{k}\frac{M}{P_0} - \frac{m_0}{k} + \frac{l}{k}r \qquad (21.6)$$

Alternatively, by dividing (21.5) through by l and rearranging things slightly, the equation for the LM curve can be written as

$$r = -\frac{1}{l}\frac{M}{P_0} + \frac{m_0}{l} + \frac{k}{l}y \qquad (21.7)$$

which is an equation relating y to r. Equations (21.6) and (21.7) are identical and, indeed, are identical to (21.5). Let us see if we can illuminate a bit more fully the properties of the LM equation by looking at the LM curve and its graphical derivation.

Figure 21.1 illustrates the derivation of the LM curve. To draw Figure 21.1, first of all decompose the amount of money demanded into two parts. Define

$$ky \equiv m_A^d$$

and

$$m_0 - lr \equiv m_B^d$$

so that

$$\frac{M^d}{P_0} = ky + m_0 - lr$$

is the same as

$$\frac{M^d}{P_0} \equiv m_A^d + m_B^d$$

The first part, m_A^d, is equal to ky, and the second part is equal to $m_0 - lr$.

Now turn to Figure 21.1. The figure has four parts. Frame (c) contains a graph of that part of the demand for money m_A^d. Frame (a) contains the other part of the demand for money m_B^d. Notice that Frame (a) is very similar to Figure 10.2 which you studied in Chapter 10. Frame (b) measures m_B on the horizontal axis and m_A on the vertical axis. The line drawn in Frame (b) slopes at 'minus one' and is located in the following way. Measure on the horizontal axis the total exogenously given amount of money divided by the price level P_0; measure the same distance on the vertical axis; then join together the two points. What that line tells us is the amount of money that is in existence and that must be held and 'allocated' to m_A^d and m_B^d. In effect, it is the supply of money. The LM curve, derived in Frame (d), is a relationship such that the supply of money depicted in Frame (b) is held and is demanded in accordance with the two-part demand function plotted in Frames (a) and (c). To derive the LM curve proceed as follows.

First, pick an interest rate — say, r_1. Focus on Frame (a) and notice that at the

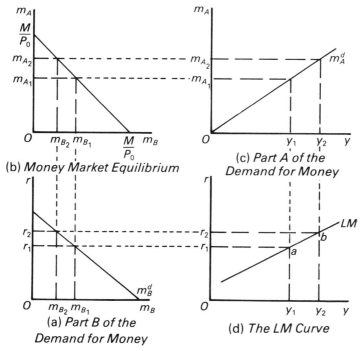

Figure 21.1 *The Derivation of the LM Curve*

The *LM* curve traces the relationship between the rate of interest and level of income which ensures that the demand for money equals the supply of money. The *LM* curve slopes upwards. For a given amount of money, a higher income level (which gives rise to a higher demand for money) can only be sustained if there is more economising on money balances. A higher rate of interest is needed to induce such economising.

interest rate r_1 the amount of money demanded under the B part of the demand for money is m_{B_1}. Transfer that amount of money demanded up to Frame (b) and notice that if m_{B_1} is demanded under part B, then under part A, m_{A_1} money must be demanded ($m_{B_1} + m_{A_1}$ exactly equals the supply of money available). Transfer m_{A_1} across to the vertical axis of Frame (c) and then, using the curve drawn in that frame, work out the level of income that is necessary to ensure that m_{A_1} is demanded. That level of income is y_1. Now transfer the initially selected interest rate, r_1, rightwards across to Frame (d) and transfer the income level y_1 vertically downwards from Frame (c) to Frame (d). These two lines meet at point a, indicating that with the interest rate r_1 the income level y_1 will generate a sufficient demand for money to ensure that the quantity of money in existence is willingly held.

Now repeat the above experiment with the interest rate r_2. At interest rate r_2, m_{B_2} balances are demanded in part B. That leaves m_{A_2} balances to be demanded in part A of the demand for money. According to Frame (c), in order that m_{A_2} balances be demanded, the income level would have to be y_2. Thus, the interest rate r_2 and the income level y_2, taken together, would lead to a demand for money equal to the supply of money. This gives point b in Frame (d). The points a and b are both points on the *LM* curve as defined above. Joining those points together and extending the curve beyond those points plots the *LM* curve.

C. Determination of the *LM* Curve Slope

You can see from inspecting Frame (d) of Figure 21.1 that the *LM curve slopes upwards*. What determines how steep or flat the *LM* curve will be? There are only two things that underlie the slope of the *LM* curve — the parameters l and k that determine the sensitivity of the demand for money with respect to changes in the level of real income and the rate of interest. Figure 21.2 illustrates the effects on the *LM* curve of varying the sensitivity of the demand for money function to changes in the rate of interest, changing the parameter l. The curve LM_2 is derived from the steeper demand for money function plotted in Frame (a). Notice that the steeper demand for money function makes the *LM* curve steeper. That is, the less sensitive the demand for money is to changes in the interest rate, the steeper the *LM* curve. In the limit, if the demand for money became perfectly elastic with respect to the rate of interest, the *LM* curve would become horizontal, and if the demand for money became completely inelastic with respect to the rate of interest, the *LM* curve would become vertical. Check that you can derive those two extreme cases.

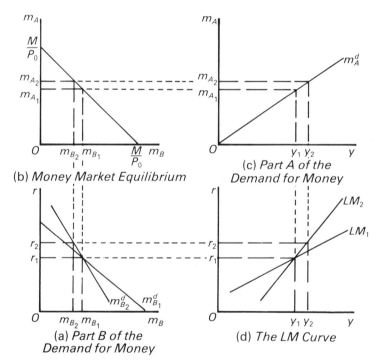

Figure 21.2 *How Different Interest Elasticities of the Demand for Money Affect the Slope of the LM Curve*

The less sensitive is the demand for money to interest rate changes, the steeper will be the slope of the *LM* curve. As the demand for money becomes steeper (Frame (a)) so the *LM* curve rotates to become steeper (Frame (d)). In the extreme, if the demand for money were completely elastic (horizontal demand in Frame (a)), the *LM* curve would be horizontal: if the demand for money were totally inelastic (vertical in Frame (a)) then the *LM* curve would become vertical.

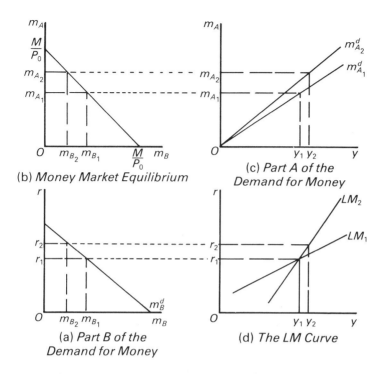

Figure 21.3 *How Different Income Elasticities of the Demand for Money Affect the Slope of the LM Curve*

The bigger the effect of a change in income on the demand for money, the steeper the slope of the *LM* curve. As the demand for money becomes more sensitive to the level of income (Frame (c)), so the *LM* curve becomes steeper (Frame (d)).

Figure 21.3 illustrates the effects of varying the sensitivity of the demand for money to changes in income, varying the parameter k. Again, LM_1 is identical to the *LM* curve in Figure 21.1. LM_2 is derived for the steeper m_A demand curve in Frame (c). Notice that the more sensitive is demand for money to changes in income (the bigger is the value of k), the steeper is the *LM* curve.

You can see the results just derived directly in equation (21.7). Notice that there the *LM* curve equation says that the rate of interest will equal some constants that just involve the money supply, the price level, and the parameters l and m_0 plus a term equal to $(k/l)y$. Clearly, the ratio (k/l) measures the slope of the *LM* curve. The bigger is k, the steeper is that slope, the bigger is l, the flatter is that slope.

What this all means is very simple. If money is a poor substitute for bonds so that the demand for money is inelastic with respect to the rate of interest (l is very small), then the *LM* curve will be very steep. Small changes in income would require big changes in the rate of interest in order to preserve money market equilibrium. Conversely, if money and bonds are very close substitutes for each other so that the demand for money is elastic with respect to the rate of interest, big variations in income will be possible with only small variations in the rate of interest, while maintaining money market equilibrium.

D. Shifts in the *LM* Curve

There are two things that can make the *LM* curve shift. One is the money supply, and the other is the price level. Notice that in the equation that defines the *LM* curve, the money supply is divided by the price level. In other words, *the position of the LM curve depends upon the real money supply*. It follows immediately from this that *a one per cent rise in the money supply will have exactly the same effect on the position of the LM curve as a one per cent cut in the price level*. It is possible, therefore, to discuss both the factors that shift the *LM* curve by considering what would happen to the *LM* curve if the money supply changed. Once you know how the *LM* curve shifts when the money supply changes, you also know, by implication, how the *LM* curve shifts in response to price level changes.

Figure 21.4 illustrates the effects on the *LM* curve of a rise in the money supply. The thick curves in Figure 21.4 are identical to those in Figure 21.1. Now suppose that there is a rise in the money stock of an amount ΔM. This is shown in the diagram in Frame (b) by the parallel shift of the money supply relation. Notice that it is shifted by an amount $\Delta M/P_0$, indicating that at all interest rates and income levels there is an extra $\Delta M/P_0$ of real money balances to be held. You can derive the new *LM* curve for this new higher quantity of money in exactly the same manner as the original *LM* curve, LM_1, was derived. You will notice that this new *LM* curve, LM_2, is to the right of LM_1. Thus, *a rise in the quantity of money shifts the LM curve to the right*. The amount by which the *LM* curve shifts to the right is evidently equal to $1/k$ times the rise in the quantity of real money balances. How do we know that? We know it by exactly the same line of reasoning that led us to work out the size of the shift in the *IS* curve in the previous chapter. Notice that the thickened triangle in Frame (c) provides the detailed calculation of the amount of shift in the *LM* curve. The rise in the money stock $\Delta M/P_0$ measures the height of that triangle. We know that its slope is equal to k and we know that its base is the change in income that would occur at a given interest rate. Using the formula 'slope equals rise over run' we can see that

$$k = \frac{\Delta M}{P_0} \bigg/ \Delta y$$

Dividing both sides of that equation by k and multiplying both sides by Δy gives 'run equals rise over slope', or

$$\Delta y = \frac{1}{k} \frac{\Delta M}{P_0}$$

That is, the size of the shift of the *LM* curve to the right, Δy, equals $1/k$ times the rise in real money supply, $\Delta M/P_0$.

A percentage fall in the price level equal to the rise in the money stock just considered would shift the *LM* curve in exactly the same way.

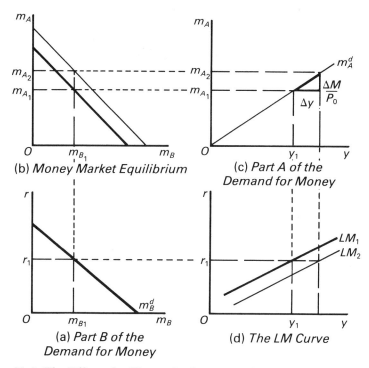

Figure 21.4 *The Effect of a Change in the Money Supply on the LM Curve*

A rise in the supply of money shifts the *LM* curve to the right. The rise in the money supply ($\Delta M/P_0$) is illustrated with a horizontal shift in the money supply curve (Frame (b)). The resulting shift in the *LM* curve is equal to $(1/k)$ times the rise in the money supply.

SUMMARY

A. Definition of the *LM* Curve

The *LM* curve is defined as an equilibrium locus that traces out the relationship between the rate of interest and the level of real income when the money supply is equal to the amount of money demanded.

B. Derivation of the *LM* Curve

The *LM* curve is derived graphically in Figure 21.1. That derivation should be thoroughly understood.

C. Determination of the *LM* Curve Slope

The *LM* curve slopes upwards. That arises from the fact that as the interest rate rises, so people economise on their holdings of money. With a given quantity of money in existence, the only way that monetary equilibrium can be maintained at higher interest rates is for there to be a higher level of real income to induce a rise in the demand for money to offset the economising on money holdings. The less elastic is the demand for money with respect to the rate of interest, the steeper will be the *LM* curve. Also, the more responsive is the demand for money to income changes, the steeper will be the *LM* curve.

D. Shifts in the *LM* Curve

The *LM* curve will shift if the money supply changes or if the price level changes. A rise in the quantity of money will make the *LM* curve shift to the right by an amount equal to $1/k$ times the rise in the real money supply. A rise in the price level will have an equivalent but opposite effect on the *LM* curve to that of a rise in the money supply.

Review Questions

1. What is the *LM* curve?

2. Which markets are in equilibrium along the *LM* curve?

3. Why does the *LM* curve slope upwards?

4. If money was a perfect substitute for bonds, what would be the slope of the *LM* curve?

5. If money and bonds were completely non-substitutable, what would be the slope of the *LM* curve?

6. What happens to the position of the *LM* curve when the money supply rises?

7. What happens to the position of the *LM* curve when the price level rises?

8. What happens to the position of the *LM* curve if the money supply grows at a constant rate?

9. Why does the demand for money depend on the money rate of interest rather than the real rate of interest?

22

Equilibrium in the Keynesian Model

It is now possible to see the light at the end of the Keynesian tunnel. You may feel that you have been groping in the darkness of that tunnel for the last two chapters. Very soon you should be able to see the light! You are going to do five things in this chapter.[1] They are as follows:

A. **understand why the intersection of the *IS* and *LM* curves determines the equilibrium levels of output and the interest rate in the Keynesian model;**

B. **know the properties of the *IS–LM* equilibrium;**

C. **understand the effects of changes in government expenditure and taxes in the Keynesian model;**

D. **understand the effects of a change in the money supply in the Keynesian model; and**

E. **understand how to interpret the Keynesian model as a more general theory of aggregate demand than that of the basic model.**

A. Equilibrium at *IS–LM* Intersection

From the discussion in Chapter 17 concerning the Keynesian theory of aggregate supply, you will recall that, at least as an approximation, the Keynesian aggregate supply curve is perfectly elastic at the price level P_0 for all income levels, up to the full-employment income level, y^*. At y^* the aggregate supply curve becomes the

---

1. This chapter presents the analysis developed by J.R. (now Sir John) Hicks in, Mr. Keynes and the 'Classics': a suggested interpretation, *Econometrica*, Vol. 5, April 1937, pp. 147–59. The sheer brilliance of John Hicks is displayed in this paper which managed to cut through the complexities of *The General Theory* so soon after the work appeared.

same as that of the basic model and is perfectly inelastic with respect to the price level. The Keynesian theory refers to the determination of economic magnitudes in that region of output between zero and full employment. As was explained in the final part of Chapter 17, the fact that the Keynesian aggregate supply curve is perfectly elastic over the relevant range means that the level of output is determined purely on the demand side of the economy. In the last two chapters we have, in fact, developed a theory of aggregate demand that is capable of telling us what the level of real income will be. The first part of that theory is the *IS* curve analysis, which tells us what the level of aggregate demand will be at each level of the rate of interest. The second ingredient is the *LM* curve analysis, which tells us the relationship between the level of real income and the level of the interest rate at which the amount of money supplied will equal the amount demanded. In effect, the *IS* curve and the *LM* curve give us two equations in two unknown variables, the level of real income and the rate of interest. When we are on both the *IS* curve and the *LM* curve, there is determined a unique level of real income and rate of interest.

According to the Keynesian analysis, we shall never observe the economy 'off' either of these two curves. If we were, in an imaginary sense, 'off' the *IS* curve, investment-plus-government spending would not be equal to savings-plus-taxes. Equilibrating forces (which will be described below) would be set up which would quickly produce an equality between these two variables. If we were 'off' the *LM* curve, the demand for money would not be equal to the supply of money. Again, strong equilibrating forces would be set up to bring about this equality. Only when the demand for money and the supply of money are equal, and savings-plus-taxes are equal to investment-plus-government spending, will individuals' plans all be compatible with each other, and only in such a situation will the economy be observed. These remarks are very similar to the remarks made in Chapter 11, which discussed the general equilibrium in the basic model.

Notice that the concept of equilibrium is of a position of rest. It is a position in which, given the assumptions made, the plans of all economic agents are compatible with each other, and no one has any incentive to behave in a different manner. In the Keynesian model, this equilibrium may involve non-market clearing in the labour market as a result of the assumption that the money wage rate is incapable of downward adjustment to achieve a balance between supply and demand in that market. The very forces which, by assumption, hold the money wage rate fixed are, of course, part of the forces describing the overall equilibrium. Thus, you must distinguish sharply between equilibrium in the economy and market clearing. The two terms are not synonymous.

Let us now go on to characterise the equilibrium level of output and interest rate in the Keynesian model.

B. Properties of the *IS–LM* Equilibrium

The *IS* curve derived in Figure 20.4 and the *LM* curve derived in Figure 21.1 are brought together and shown in the same diagram in Figure 22.1. Since the *IS* curve slopes downwards and the *LM* curve slopes upwards, these two curves cut in just one

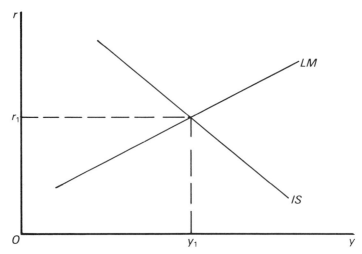

Figure 22.1 *Equilibrium in the Keynesian Model*
When investment-plus-government spending equals savings-plus-taxes (on the *IS* curve) and
when the demand for money equals the supply of money (on the *LM* curve), then the economy
is in equilibrium. Such an equilibrium is shown as r_1, y_1 in the diagram.

---

place. Label this point y_1, r_1. It is a property of the interest rate r_1 and the income level
y_1 that two sets of equilibrium conditions are simultaneously satisfied. First, planned
savings-plus-taxes are equal to investment-plus-government expenditures. Second,
the stock of money in existence is equal to the stock of money demanded. The
interest rate r_1 and income level y_1 represent the only point at which those two
equilibrium conditions are simultaneously satisfied. That position is the equilibrium
level of real income and the interest rate in the Keynesian model.

To determine the values of the other variables in the economy, the level of
investment and savings, all that is necessary is to use a diagram like Figure 20.4 and
work backwards from the frame that displays the *IS* and *LM* curves. Figure 22.2
illustrates. In Frame (d), the *IS* and *LM* curves from Figure 22.1 are reproduced. The
IS curve itself is derived from the underlying savings and investment decisions that
are shown in Frames (a) and (c). By working backwards from Frame (d) we can work
out the equilibrium levels of savings and investment. Transfer the equilibrium
income level y_1 from Frame (d) to Frame (c) and you can read off immediately the
equilibrium level of savings in the economy. Tracking leftwards across to Frame (a),
you can read off the equilibrium level of investment that is generated by the
equilibrium interest rate r_1. By tracking that level of investment-plus-government
spending vertically upwards to Frame (b) and by tracking the level of savings-plus-
taxes horizontally leftwards across from Frame (c) to (b), you can see that the
position depicted is indeed in equilibrium for the two lines meet on the 45° line that
describes the equality of $i+g$ with $s+t$.

Just what are the forces that bring about the equilibrium between investment and
savings on the one hand and the supply of and demand for money on the other? To
answer this question it is necessary to perform a purely conceptual experiment.
Suppose, in a hypothetical sense, that the economy is 'off' the *IS* curve. Frame (a) of
Figure 22.3 can be used to illustrate the discussion. If the economy was 'off' the *IS*

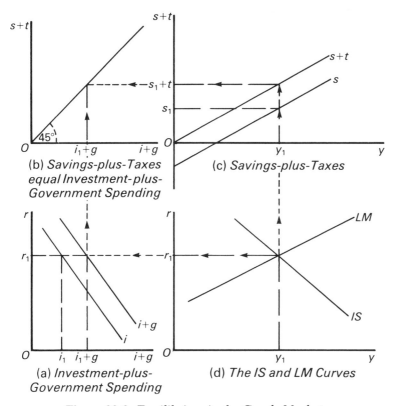

Figure 22.2 *Equilibrium in the Goods Market*
Once the equilibrium level of income and the rate of interest are determined by the intersection of *IS* and *LM* (Frame (d)), it is possible to trace backwards to establish the levels of savings (Frame (c)) and investment (Frame (a)). When taxes are added to savings, and government spending to investment, as Frame (b) shows, investment-plus-government spending is equal to savings-plus-taxes.

---

curve and to its right, investment-plus-government spending would be less than savings-plus-taxes. That is, you could view the interest rate as being too high depressing investment to too low a level, or income too high raising savings to too high a level. Either way, savings-plus-taxes would exceed investment-plus-government spending. On the left side of the *IS* curve, the reverse inequality will hold. The interest rate is too low, stimulating too much investment, or conversely, income is too low and is generating too little saving. Either way, investment-plus-government spending exceeds savings-plus-taxes.

Suppose we are in this second situation of too much investment-plus-government spending relative to the amount of savings-plus-taxes. What would happen? According to the Keynesian story, this would be a situation in which income would not be stationary, but would be rising. The reason why income would be rising is that the total amount of spending that individuals are attempting to undertake exceeds the level of income out of which they are attempting to undertake that spending. To see this, recall that consumption is simply income minus savings minus taxes; this means that if savings-plus-taxes are less than investment-plus-government spending, consumption plus investment plus government spending must add up to a bigger number than income. Such a situation clearly cannot be, because we know that, as a matter of fact, income is equal to consumption plus investment plus government spending. Still, we can tell a story (analogous to the story told earlier in the book about different levels of water in the North Sea). The story would go like this. As people *try* to spend more than current income, so income rises and keeps on rising until it has reached a high enough level to be equal to the total level of planned spending that individuals are undertaking. We know where that point is. For any given interest rate it is the point at which income is read off from the *IS* curve.

To reinforce your understanding, consider the reverse situation. Suppose we are to the right of the *IS* curve, with savings-plus-taxes bigger than investment-plus-government spending. In that case, total spending plans add up to a number less than income. In such a case, income would be falling and would continue to fall until it had reached a low enough level for spending plans to have reached equality with income. Again, that is a point on the *IS* curve.

Thus, part of the Keynesian equilibrating story is one that says that if investment-plus-government spending is different from savings-plus-taxes, income will adjust and achieve an equality between those two variables, putting us on the *IS* curve. *Income, not prices, is the equilibrating variable in the goods market.*

Next, consider a conceptual experiment in the money market. Suppose that we are 'off' the *LM* curve. Frame (b) of Figure 22.3 illustrates. If we are below the *LM* curve, then the demand for money exceeds the supply of money. That is, the interest rate is too low or income too high, generating more demand for money than money available. If we are above the *LM* curve, the demand for money is less than the supply of money. That is, the interest rate is too high and/or the income level too low, making the amount of money demanded fall short of the amount available to be held. What would happen if we were in one of these situations? Imagine that we are in a situation in which the demand for money is less than the supply of money. Obviously, since the supply of money is physically present in the economy, even though the amount demanded is less than the amount supplied, the amount supplied is the amount that is being held. In other words, individuals have in their pockets and purses and bank accounts more money than they want to be holding on current conditions. What do they do in such a situation? The answer is they try to get rid of the money. The Keynesian story is that they get rid of that money by buying securities. That is, they try to buy bonds and other kinds of financial assets. The effect of buying bonds is to raise the demand for bonds and bid up the price of bonds. Bidding up the price of a bond has the effect of bidding down the rate of interest on the bond. (You might find it helpful to have that spelled out. Suppose a bond pays £5 a year in interest in perpetuity, and suppose that the bond has a current market price of £50. Clearly, the rate of interest then is 10 per cent — £5 divided by £50. Now suppose that instead of being £50, the bond price is £25. The interest payment is still £5 a year, but now the interest rate has increased to 20 per cent (£5 divided by £25). Yet again, suppose that instead of being £50, the bond price moved to £100. In that case, with the interest payment of £5 a year, the interest rate would become 5 per cent (£5 divided by £100). You see, then, that the rate of interest on a bond (the market rate of interest in the economy) is inversely related to the price of a bond.

Continuing now with the story; as people try to get rid of their unwanted money balances by buying bonds and, as a result, bidding up the price of bonds and bidding

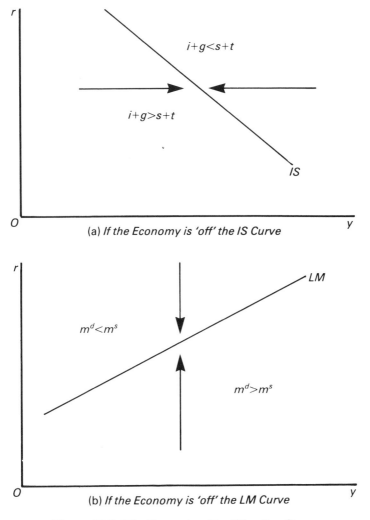

(a) *If the Economy is 'off' the IS Curve*

(b) *If the Economy is 'off' the LM Curve*

Figure 22.3 *The Keynesian Equilibrating Story*

If the economy is 'off' the *IS* curve, planned expenditures will differ from income. In such a case income would have to rise $(i + g > s + t)$ or fall $(i + g < s + t)$. The movement in income would be rapid and the economy quickly brought to a point on the *IS* curve.

If the demand for money was not equal to the supply of money, the economy would be 'off' the *LM* curve. This would lead to the buying or selling of securities, which would produce a rise or fall in the interest rate, so that money market equilibrium was achieved. These equilibrating forces are assumed to operate quickly so that the economy is not, in the normal course of events, observed to be 'off' either the *IS* or *LM* curve.

down the interest rate, so the situation in which there is an excess supply of money is eliminated. The interest rate will fall far enough to eliminate the excess supply of money because people will continue to buy bonds, bidding up their price and bidding down the interest rate, until they are satisfied that the money they are holding is equal to the amount of money they want to hold.

The same mechanism will work in the opposite direction. If the demand for money exceeds the amount of money in existence, individuals will seek to add to their money balances. They will do this by selling bonds. As they sell bonds, so the price of bonds will fall, and the interest rate on them will rise. This process will continue until the interest rate has risen sufficiently to make the amount of money that is in existence enough to satisfy people's demand for money. Either way, then, an excess demand or excess supply in the money market will lead to a movement in the rate of interest by an amount sufficient to place the economy on the *LM* curve.

Now bring these two stories together. If we are 'off' the *IS* curve, income adjusts to bring about an equality between savings-plus-taxes and investment-plus-government spending. If we are 'off' the *LM* curve, the interest rate adjusts to bring about an equality between the demand for money and the supply of money. These two forces, operating simultaneously, ensure that both the stock equilibrium in the money market and the flow equilibrium between investment-plus-government spending and savings-plus-taxes is simultaneously achieved. It is an assumption of the Keynesian analysis that these forces operate with sufficient speed for the economy to be observed only at points of intersection of the *IS* and *LM* curves.

Now that you understand the nature of the equilibrium in the Keynesian model it is possible to go on to analyse the effects of changes in government spending, taxes, and the money supply on real income and the interest rate.

C. Changes in Government Expenditure and Taxes

You have now studied all the key ingredients of the Keynesian model and are in a position to analyse in a fairly straightforward manner the effects of changes in government spending and taxes on the level of real income and the rate of interest.

(i) Changes in Government Expenditure

First, let us analyse the effects of a change in government spending. You already know that a change in government spending leads to a shift in the *IS* curve. Specifically, you know that a rise in government spending leads to a rightward shift of the *IS* curve by an amount equal to the change in government spending multiplied by one over one minus the marginal propensity to consume. What, though, is the effect of the change in government spending, not on the shift in the *IS* curve, but on the equilibrium level of income and the rate of interest? Figure 22.4 provides the basis for answering this question. Assume that initially, the level of government spending is such that the *IS* curve is represented by IS_1. This intersects the *LM* curve at the interest rate r_1 and the income level y_1. Now imagine that there is a rise in government spending by an amount sufficient to shift the *IS* curve from IS_1 to IS_2. Recall that the horizontal distance of the shift in the *IS* curve, arrowed, is equal to the change in government spending multiplied by one over one minus the marginal propensity to consume. You can discover, by inspecting Figure 22.4, that the effect on the

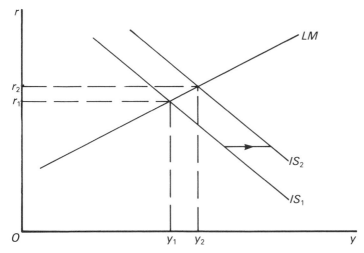

Figure 22.4 *The Effect of Fiscal Policy on the Interest Rate and Real Income*
A rise in government spending or a tax cut will shift the *IS* curve from IS_1 to IS_2. The result will be a higher income level (y_1 to y_2) and a higher interest rate (r_1 to r_2).

equilibrium levels of income and the rate of interest of this shift in the *IS* curve is to raise the interest rate from r_1 to r_2 and to raise income from y_1 to y_2. This result, depicted in Figure 22.4, is a general result. *A rise in government spending raises both real income and the rate of interest.*

The amounts by which income and the interest rate rise depend on both the slope of the *LM* curve and the slope of the *IS* curve. To see how the slope of the *LM* curve affects the outcome, consider Figure 22.5. In this figure are shown two extreme slopes for the *LM* curve. The curve labelled LM_A is horizontal. This would be one limiting case of the slope of the *LM* curve, if money and non-money assets were such perfect substitutes for each other that people really didn't care how much money they were holding, relative to other assets. If the interest rate was slightly above r_1, they would want to hold entirely non-money assets. If the interest rate was slightly below r_1, they would want to hold nothing but money. So r_1 represents the interest rate at which people are entirely indifferent between holding money and other assets. This is a pretty unlikely situation, but one which serves to illustrate one of the extreme values of the effects of a change in government spending. In this particular case you can see that the effect of a change in government spending would be to raise income and leave the interest rate unchanged. The rise in income would be equal to the full amount of the horizontal shift of the *IS* curve. That is, it would be equal to the rise in government spending multiplied by one over one minus the marginal propensity to consume. The other extreme case illustrated is that of the *LM* curve labelled LM_B. The *LM* curve would be vertical if the demand for money did not depend on the interest rate at all. This would be the case if people regarded non-money assets as completely useless as substitutes for money, so that regardless of the cost of holding money, there would be a certain amount of money that they felt they absolutely must hold. In that not so unlikely, but nevertheless slightly exaggerated case, the rise in government spending which shifts the *IS* curve to IS_2 would raise the interest rate to

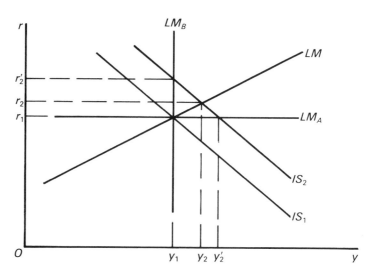

Figure 22.5 *Fiscal Policy and the Steepness of the LM Curve*
The flatter is the *LM* curve, the bigger is the effect of a fiscal policy change on income, and the smaller its effect on the interest rate. In the extremes, with a horizontal *LM* curve (LM_A), income will rise from y_1 to y_2' and the interest rate stays constant, and with a vertical *LM* curve (LM_B), the interest rate will rise from r_1 to r_2' and real income will remain unchanged at y_1.

r_2', but leave the real income level unaffected. What is going on here is that the amount of money which people want to hold is, in effect, a rigid fraction of the level of income. Since the amount of money in the economy has not been changed, then neither can the level of income change. Any change in government spending is fully *crowded out* by a rise in the interest rate, choking off an equal amount of private investment demand.

The analysis in Figure 22.5 serves to illustrate the propositions that *the effect of a change in government spending on real income is smaller, the smaller is the interest elasticity of the demand for money* and that *the effect of a rise in government spending on the rate of interest is larger, the smaller is the interest elasticity of the demand for money*.

The size of the government spending multiplier is also affected by the slope of the *IS* curve. Figure 22.6 illustrates this. Consider first the *IS* curve labelled IS_1, and the equilibrium r_1, y_1. Now imagine that government spending is increased, shifting the *IS* curve to IS_2. That produces a change in income to y_2 and a change in the interest rate to r_2. Now imagine that the *IS* curve is flatter than that depicted as IS_1 and IS_2. In particular, let the initial *IS* curve be IS_1'. Now conduct the same experiment of raising government spending. Raise it by exactly the same amount as before. We know that the new *IS* curve will be parallel to the original one and will shift to the right by the same absolute amount, so that at the interest rate r_1 the *IS* curve IS_2' intersects the *IS* curve IS_2. Now the new equilibrium income level is y_2' and the interest rate level is r_2'. Notice that y_2' is lower than y_2 and r_2' is lower than r_2.

The analysis in Figure 22.6 shows that *the flatter is the IS curve, the smaller is the effect of a change in government spending on income and the smaller is the effect of a change in government spending on the rate of interest*.

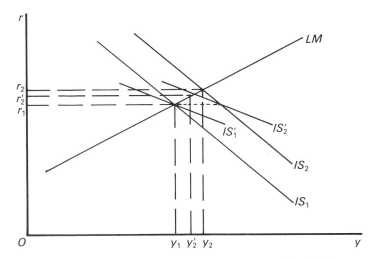

Figure 22.6 *Fiscal Policy and the Steepness of the IS Curve*
The flatter is the *IS* curve, the smaller is the effect of fiscal policy on both interest rates and income. If the *IS* curve is *IS'*, the rise in income and interest rate will be y'_2 and r'_2, compared with the unprimed *IS* curve and unprimed income and interest rate solutions.

The effects of the steepness of the *LM* and *IS* curves may now be summarised succinctly. The effect of a change in government spending on the level of real income will be smaller, the smaller is the interest elasticity of the demand for money and the greater is the interest elasticity of investment demand. The effect of a change in government spending on the interest rate will be larger, the smaller is the interest elasticity of demand for money and the smaller is the interest elasticity of investment demand.

(ii) Changes in Taxes

Considering the effects of tax changes is straightforward. You already know from Chapter 20 that a rise in taxes shifts the *IS* curve in the *opposite* direction to that of a rise in government spending. That is, a rise in taxes will shift the *IS* curve to the left, while a rise in government spending will shift the *IS* curve to the right. You also know that the distance of the shift is fraction *b* (the marginal propensity to consume) of the shift for an equivalent change in government spending. There the differences between the effects of changes in government spending and taxes end. Aside from that, the effects of each of the two changes are identical in this Keynesian set-up. All the remarks made above concerning the effects of the slopes of the *LM* and *IS* curves on the size of the government expenditure multipliers apply identically to the tax multipliers. *The effects on income and the rate of interest of a tax rise are opposite in direction and are fraction b in magnitude of the effects of changes in government spending.*

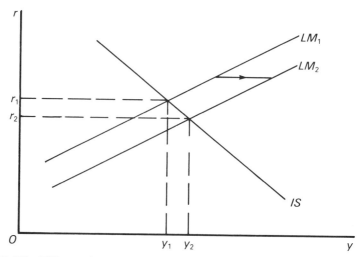

Figure 22.7 *The Effects of Monetary Policy on Real Income and the Rate of Interest*
A rise in the money stock shifts the *LM* curve to the right, lowering the rate of interest and
raising the level of income.

D. Change in the Money Supply

You already know that a change in the money supply will shift the *LM* curve. The
effects of an *LM* curve shift on the equilibrium level of real income and the interest
rate will, like the effects of the *IS* curve shift just analysed, depend upon the slopes of
both the *IS* and *LM* curves. Let us consider first the general case. Figure 22.7
illustrates the effects of a change in the money supply on the equilibrium level of real
income and the rate of interest. The economy is initially in equilibrium, with the *IS*
curve intersecting LM_1 at the interest rate r_1 and the output level y_1. Now imagine the
money supply is increased, so that the *LM* curve moves to LM_2. The new intersection
of the *IS* and *LM* curves is at the income level y_2 and the interest rate r_2. You can see
by inspection of Figure 22.7 that the *rise in the money supply leads to a rise in real
income and a fall in the rate of interest.* This is the general prediction of the Keynesian
model.

Now consider what happens to these effects as the slope of the *IS* curve is allowed
to vary. Figure 22.8 illustrates this. Just as in the previous case, we have drawn in two
extreme slopes for the *IS* curve. If the *IS* curve is the horizontal curve IS_A, the effect
of a change in the money stock is to raise real income by the full amount of the
horizontal shift of the *LM* curve. The interest rate remains unchanged. This result
would arise if the marginal productivity of capital was completely constant,
independent of the size of the capital stock. The opposite case, depicted as the
vertical *IS* curve IS_B, leads to the prediction that the interest rate would drop to r_2',
while income would remain unchanged at y_1. This would arise if, no matter how
much the rate of interest changed, firms saw no reason to change their capital stock.
What is going on in these two cases is straightforward to interpret. With a horizontal

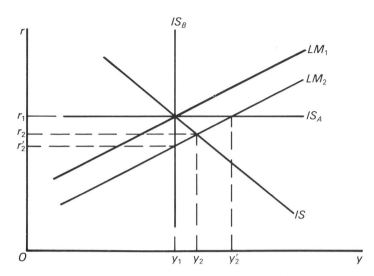

Figure 22.8 *Monetary Policy and the Steepness of the IS Curve*
The flatter is the *IS* curve, the bigger the effect of a change in the money stock on the level of income, and the smaller its effect on the rate of interest. If the *IS* curve was horizontal (IS_A), the shift in *LM* from LM_1 to LM_2 raises income from y_1 to y_2' and leaves the interest rate unchanged. If the *IS* curve was vertical (IS_B), a rise in the money stock that shifts the *LM* curve from LM_1 to LM_2 lowers the interest rate from r_1 to r_2' and leaves income unchanged.

IS curve (with a fixed rate of interest) we are, in effect, in the world of the basic model. The level of aggregate demand moves one-for-one with the level of the money stock. (We are not, of course, in the world of the basic model in all respects, since, in this Keynesian world, the price level is fixed at P_0, and it is real income rather than the price level which does the adjusting as a consequence of the shift in aggregate demand. Nevertheless, as regards the specification of aggregate demand, this case is identical to that of the basic model.) In the case of a vertical *IS* curve, the change in the money supply merely changes the rate of interest leaving the level of aggregate demand unaffected. This arises because, with investment being completely insensitive to interest rates, no matter what the interest rate is, the level of investment will remain unchanged. Since the level of government spending is also constant (by assumption) and since consumption demand depends only on income, there is nothing being altered on the expenditure side of the economy to produce any change in the quantity of output demanded. All the adjustment, therefore, has to come out in a lower interest rate.

What Figure 22.8 illustrates is the general proposition that *the more elastic is the demand for investment with respect to the rate of interest, the bigger is the effect of a change in the money stock on income, and the smaller is the effect of a change in the money stock on the rate of interest.*

Next, consider the effect of the slope of the *LM* curve on the size of the effect of a change in the money stock on income and the rate of interest. Again, let the economy initially be in an equilibrium where the *IS* curve intersects the curve LM_1 at the interest rate r_1 and the income level y_1. Figure 22.9 illustrates this. Now let the money stock be increased, so that the *LM* curve shifts to LM_2. As in the case of Figure 22.7,

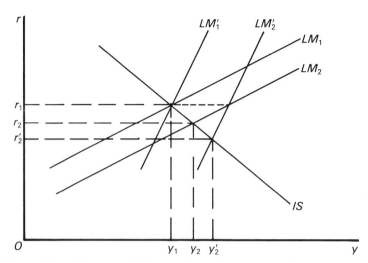

Figure 22.9 *Monetary Policy and the Steepness of the LM Curve*
The steeper is the *LM* curve, the bigger the effects of a change in the money supply on both the level of income and the rate of interest. If the *LM* curve is *LM* primed, then the change in income and the rate of interest is from y_1 to y_2' and r_1 to r_2'. These are larger than the shifts arising in the case of the flatter, unprimed *LM* curves.

this produces a rise in income to y_2 and a drop in the interest rate to r_2. Now imagine that instead of the *LM* curve being LM_1 (LM_2), it is steeper than that, indicating that the demand for money is less elastic with respect to the rate of interest. Specifically, suppose the *LM* curve initially is LM_1'. When the money stock rises, the *LM* curve will shift to LM_2'. (Remember that the horizontal shift at a given interest rate [in this case r_1] is independent of the steepness of the *LM* curve.) What is the effect of an equivalent change in the money stock in this case? It is to raise income to y_2' and lower the interest rate to r_2'. Notice that the change in both income and the interest rate is bigger in this case than it was in the previous case. This serves to illustrate the general proposition *that the smaller the interest elasticity of the demand for money, the bigger the effect of a change in the money supply on both the rate of interest and the level of income.*

You have now completed your investigation of the properties of the Keynesian model. The final section of this chapter is designed to help you see the connection between the Keynesian model and the basic model with which you are already familiar and also to prepare the way for helping you to understand how the useful and valid parts of the Keynesian model carry over and form an integral part of the new macroeconomics that you will be studying in the next part of this book.

E. The Keynesian Model as a General Theory of Aggregate Demand

Begin by recalling the concept of the aggregate demand curve. As set out in Chapter 10, the aggregate demand curve is defined as the relationship between the aggregate quantity of goods and services which people want to buy in a given period of time and the general price level. That definition and concept is sufficiently general to embrace all conceivable theoretical frameworks, and certainly that of the Keynesian model. We have not bothered to derive the aggregate demand curve of the Keynesian model primarily because, although it does exist, it is not very useful in the framework of analysis employed by Keynes. You will see this more clearly, perhaps, if we do in fact derive the Keynesian aggregate demand curve.

It is easy to derive the Keynesian aggregate demand curve and this is set out in Figure 22.10. Frame (a) shows the rate of interest on the vertical axis and real income on the horizontal axis. Frame (b) shows the price level on the vertical axis and real income on the horizontal axis. In Frame (a) are shown an IS curve and an LM curve, labelled $LM(P_0)$. These two curves intersect at the income level y_1 and r_1. This is exactly the solution that we have been working with throughout this chapter. That solution point can also be characterised in Frame (b) of the figure. It is the point a. We know that it is the point a because we know that the Keynesian aggregate supply curve is horizontal at the predetermined price level P_0 and we know that the model has determined for us, on the demand side, an output level of y_1. It is possible, as a hypothetical matter, to ask what the level of aggregate demand would be in the Keynesian framework if the price level was different from P_0. Suppose the price level was higher than P_0, say, P_1. What then would be the quantity of goods and services demanded? From the analysis of the IS curve you can quickly verify that the position of the IS curve is independent of the price level. It is entirely a real curve that relates real income to the rate of interest and depends only on other real variables, namely, real taxes and real government spending. The LM curve, in contrast, is not independent of the price level. You can quickly verify from its definition and derivation that a change in the price level has a similar (but opposite in direction) effect on the LM curve to a change in the money supply. If we raise the price level to P_1 we know, therefore, that the LM curve will shift to the left. Let us suppose that it shifts to become the curve $LM(P_1)$ in Frame (a). This new LM curve intersects the IS curve at the interest rate r_0 and the output level y_0. Since we know the price level that gave rise to that LM curve is P_1, we can read off from Frame (b) the point at which the income level y_0 is associated with the price level P_1. That point is b. Point b is, like point a, another point in the Keynesian aggregate demand curve. Unlike point a, the point b is not a point at which we shall observe the economy. Point a is the economy equilibrium. Nevertheless, simply tracing out the locus of points that link the price level and the level of output that simultaneously satisfies equilibrium in the money market and in investment and savings plans yields the point b. Next, imagine that the price level is at some lower level than P_0, say, P_2, as shown on the vertical axis of Frame (b). With a lower price level we know that the LM curve would shift to the right (equivalent to a rise in the money stock). Suppose, in fact, that the LM curve shifts to that labelled $LM(P_2)$, which generates the income level y_2 and the interest rate r_2. Dropping that income level y_2 down to Frame (b) shows that the point c is also a point on the Keynesian aggregate demand curve. Joining up points b, a, c and extrapolating to points beyond b and c traces out the Keynesian aggregate demand curve.

In conducting the Keynesian analysis of the determination of output, it was possible, of course, to focus only upon point a. By looking at what happens to the IS and LM curve intersections, we are simply examining how the point a travels horizontally along the aggregate supply curve. There is no need in the Keynesian

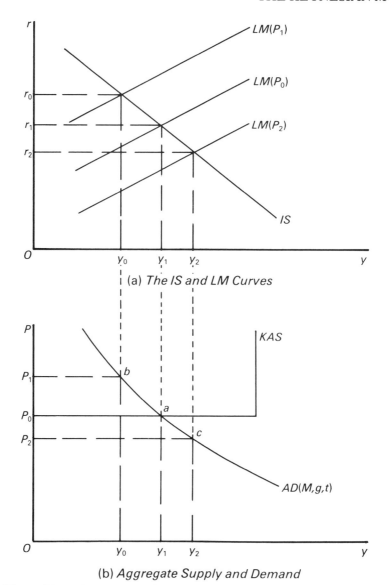

(b) *Aggregate Supply and Demand*

Figure 22.10 *Derivation of the Keynesian Aggregate Demand Curve*

By hypothetically allowing the price level to vary, the *LM* curve will shift (Frame (a)) generating different equilibrium interest rate and income levels. These income solutions and price levels may be mapped into a standard aggregate supply and aggregate demand diagram (Frame (b)) to trace out the Keynesian aggregate demand curve. In general, aggregate demand will depend on the money supply, government spending, and taxes.

---

framework to derive the aggregate demand curve at all. Nevertheless, the curve is there, and it is useful to help us understand the relationship between Keynesian theory and the basic model of output and employment determination. It is also going to be useful in the work that follows in the next part of the book.

The key thing to understand about the analysis of aggregate demand that we have conducted in the Keynesian framework is that the entire analysis may be interpreted as telling us about the factors which cause horizontal shifts in the aggregate demand curve. Anything that shifts the point *a* will also shift the point *b* and the point *c* in the same horizontal direction. Thus, a rise in government spending or a cut in taxes or a rise in the money stock will all produce a rightward shift of the aggregate demand curve. The *AD* curve in Frame (b) is labelled *AD*(*M, g, t*) to remind us of this. The size of that shift will depend on the slopes of the *IS* and *LM* curves. Those slopes will in turn depend upon the slopes of the demand for money function and the investment demand function. In general, the steeper is the demand for money function with respect to the interest rate and/or the flatter is the investment demand function with respect to the interest rate, the bigger will be the effect of a change in the money supply on the horizontal shift of the aggregate demand curve, and the smaller will be the effect of a change in government spending or taxes. In the limiting case where the *IS* curve is horizontal (the interest rate is fixed) or where the *LM* curve is vertical (money is completely non-substitutable for other assets), then only changes in the money supply will lead to changes in the aggregate demand curve, and changes in government spending and taxes will leave the aggregate demand curve unaffected. At the other extreme, if money is a perfect substitute for other assets so that the *LM* curve is horizontal, or if investment demand is completely unresponsive to interest rate changes so that the *IS* curve is vertical, then only changes in government spending and taxes will lead to shifts in the aggregate demand curve, and changes in the money stock will leave the aggregate demand curve unaffected.

You can now see that the monetary theory of aggregate demand developed in Chapter 10 is, in effect, a special case of this more general Keynesian theory of aggregate demand. In general, the aggregate demand curve will shift both because of changes in the money stock and because of changes in the levels of government spending and taxes.

SUMMARY

A. Equilibrium at *IS–LM* Intersection

Because the price level is fixed in the Keynesian analysis, the level of output is determined purely by the level of aggregate demand. The *IS* curve shows the level of income at each level of the interest rate, which equates savings-plus-taxes with investment-plus-government spending. The *LM* curve gives another relationship between income and the interest rate, which equates the supply of and the demand for money. There is just one level of the interest rate and of income at which both of these relationships are simultaneously satisfied. That output and interest rate is the equilibrium of the Keynesian model.

B. Properties of the *IS–LM* Equilibrium

The *IS–LM* equilibrium occurs when both the demand for money equals the supply of money and savings-plus-taxes equal investment-plus-government spending. It is assumed that the forces making for equality of both these sets of magnitudes are strong enough to ensure that the economy is never observed away from equilibrium. If savings-plus-taxes were to exceed investment-plus-government spending, real income would fall quickly enough and far enough to restore the equality. If the supply of money exceeded the demand for money, the act of attempting to reduce money balances and acquire bonds would put downward pressure on interest rates to the point at which the amount of money in existence was willingly held. Both sets of forces will occur sufficiently quickly for the economy never to be observed 'off' either the *IS* or *LM* curves. Thus, the intersection point of the *IS* and *LM* curves is the point that describes the state of the economy.

C. Changes in Government Expenditure and Taxes

In general, a rise in government spending or a cut in taxes will raise the level of real income and raise the rate of interest. The rise in both variables will be greater, the steeper is the *IS* curve. The rise in income will be greater and the rise in the interest rate smaller, the flatter is the *LM* curve.

D. Change in the Money Supply

In general, a rise in the money supply will lead to a rise in real income and a fall in the rate of interest. The change in both variables will be larger, the steeper is the *LM* curve. The change in income will be greater and the change in interest rate smaller, the flatter is the *IS* curve.

E. The Keynesian Model as a General Theory of Aggregate Demand

Although there is no need to derive a Keynesian aggregate demand curve for the purpose of conducting Keynesian analysis, such an aggregate demand curve is implied by the Keynesian theory. By hypothetically varying the price level, a Keynesian aggregate demand curve may be traced out. Like that of the basic model, that curve will be downward sloping. In general, the aggregate demand curve will shift when the money stock changes, when government spending changes, or when taxes change. There are special extreme cases (the basic model case being one such) in which some of the variables under government control have no effect on the aggregate demand curve. If the *IS* curve is vertical or the *LM* curve is horizontal, only government spending and taxes shift the aggregate demand curve, changes in the money supply leaving the curve unaffected. At the other extreme (the basic model case) if the *IS* curve is horizontal or if the *LM* curve is vertical, then changes in the money supply will shift the aggregate demand curve, but changes in government spending and taxes will leave it unaffected.

Appendix: The Algebra of the Keynesian Model

This appendix takes you through the algebra of the determination of the equilibrium levels of output and the rate of interest in the Keynesian model. Like the Appendix to Chapter 20, it contains nothing of substance that is not explained in words and diagrams in the body of the chapter. It may, nevertheless, provided that you feel comfortable with algebraic formulations, give you a clearer picture of how the Keynesian model works. The case analysed in this Appendix is that in which the price level is fixed at P_0 so that output is varying only in ranges up to, but not including, full-employment output.

Aggregate demand is determined by the sum of consumption, investment, and government demand. That is

$$y^d = c + i + g \tag{A1}$$

Consumption demand is determined by the consumption function, which is

$$c = a + b(y - t), \qquad a > 0, 0 < b < 1 \tag{A2}$$

Investment demand is determined by

$$i = i_0 - hr, \qquad i_0, h > 0 \tag{A3}$$

Flow equilibrium prevails in the goods market when aggregate demand equals actual income. That is

$$y^d = y \tag{A4}$$

The above four equations taken together constitute the equation for the IS curve. That equation may be derived by using equations (A2), (A3), and (A4) together with equation (A1) to give

$$y = a + b(y - t) + i_0 - hr + g \tag{A5}$$

This may be arranged or 'solved' for real income as

$$y = \frac{1}{1 - b}(a + i_0 + g - bt - hr) \tag{A6}$$

Equation (A6) is the equation for the IS curve.

The demand for money function is given by

$$\frac{M^d}{P_0} = m_0 + ky - lr, \qquad k > 0, l > 0 \tag{A7}$$

Monetary equilibrium requires that the demand for money be equal to the supply of money, that is

$$M^d = M \tag{A8}$$

Substituting equation (A7) into equation (A8) yields an equation for the LM curve which may be 'solved' for income as

$$y = \frac{1}{k}\left(\frac{M}{P_0} - m_0 + lr\right) \tag{A9}$$

Equation (A9) is the equation for the LM curve.

Equations (A6) and (A9), the equations for the IS and LM curves, are two equations in two unknowns, real income and the rate of interest. By setting the income level in (A6) equal to the income level in (A9) and solving for the rate of interest, you readily obtain

$$r = \frac{(k/l)(a + i_0 + g - bt) - [(1 - b)/l][(M/P_0) - m_0]}{(1 - b) + (kh/l)} \tag{A10}$$

Equation (A10) is an algebraic expression for the equilibrium value of the rate of interest in the Keynesian model. By substituting equation (A10) back into equation (A9) to eliminate the rate of interest, you may obtain an expression for the level of real income. It is possible to 'tidy up' the expression to give

$$y = \frac{a + i_0 + g - bt + [(h/l)(M/P_0 - m_0)]}{1 - b + (kh/l)} \tag{A11}$$

Equation (A11) is the solution of the Keynesian model for the equilibrium level of real income.

In order to obtain a better understanding of what those equations are saying, let us examine equations (A10) and (A11) to see how the interest rate and the level of income vary as we vary the three policy instruments — government spending, taxes, and the money supply. Imagine that each of those three policy variables took on a different value from g, t, and M. Specifically, suppose that g was to increase to a number g' and t to increase to t' and M was to increase to M'. In that case, we know that the solutions for the interest rate and the level of income could be expressed as

$$r' = \frac{(k/l)(a + i_0 + g' - bt') - [(1-b)/l][(M'/P_0) - m_0]}{1 - b + (kh/l)} \tag{A12}$$

$$y' = \frac{a + i_0 + g' - bt' + (h/l)[(M'/P_0) - m_0]}{1 - b + (kh/l)} \tag{A13}$$

Equations (A12) and (A13) are, of course, identical to equations (A10) and (A11) except that the value of the variables (r and y on the left-hand side, and g, t, and M on the right-hand side) have all changed from their original values to their new (primed) values. Now subtract equation (A10) from equation (A12) to obtain equation (A14). Also subtract equation (A11) from equation (A13) to obtain equation (A15). Notice that in equations (A14) and (A15) the terms c_0, i_0, and m_0 have disappeared, since they are common to both the original solutions and the new solutions for y and r.

$$r' - r = \frac{1}{1 - b + (kh/l)} [\frac{k}{l}(g' - g) - \frac{bk}{l}(t' - t) - (\frac{1-b}{l})(\frac{M'}{P_0} - \frac{M}{P_0})] \tag{A14}$$

$$y' - y = \frac{1}{1 - b + (kh/l)} [g' - g - b(t' - t) + \frac{h}{l}(\frac{M'}{P_0} - \frac{M}{P_0})] \tag{A15}$$

Now call the gap between y' and y the change in y, and label it Δy. Similarly, call the gap between r' and r, Δr, and likewise for the policy variables. That is, $g' - g$ is Δg, $t' - t$ is Δt, and $M' - M$ is ΔM. Using that convention, you can write equations (A14) and (A15) slightly more compactly as equations (A16) and (A17), that is

$$\Delta r = \frac{1}{1 - b + (kh/l)} [\frac{k}{l}\Delta g - \frac{bk}{l}\Delta t - \frac{(1-b)}{lP_0}\Delta M] \tag{A16}$$

$$\Delta y = \frac{1}{1 - b + (kh/l)} [\Delta g - b\Delta t + \frac{h}{lP_0}\Delta M] \tag{A17}$$

You can now interpret equations (A16) and (A17) very directly. Notice that the expression $1/[1 - b + (kh/l)]$ will be a positive coefficient relating the changes in the policy variables to the changes in the rate of interest and the level of real income. (You know that it will be positive since b is a positive fraction so that $1 - b$ is also a positive fraction, and k, h and l are all positive parameters.) You can immediately see that equation (A16) says that, in general, a rise in g will raise the interest rate, and a rise in t and a rise in M will cut the interest rate. From equation (A17) you can see that, in general, a rise in g or a rise in M will raise income, but a rise in t will cut income. Equations (A16) and (A17) are nothing other than algebraic expressions for the equivalent propositions obtained in Chapter 22 by direct inspection of the diagrammatic solution for equilibrium output and the interest rate.

In the chapter some extreme cases were examined, and the way in which the policy instrument multipliers are affected by the slopes of the IS and LM curves examined. This can now be done fairly precisely with the algebraic solutions in equations (A16) and (A17). Let us now look at this.

Some Special Cases

First, suppose that the parameter h became infinitely big. An infinitely big h means that the investment demand curve and, hence, the IS curve, is horizontal and means that the rate of interest remains constant. This, in effect, is the special case that we have called the basic model. What do the multipliers become when h is infinitely big? By inspecting equations (A16) and (A17) you can establish that the multipliers are as follows:

$$\Delta r = 0 \tag{A18}$$

$$\Delta y = \frac{1}{k} \frac{\Delta M}{P_0} \tag{A19}$$

What this says is that the aggregate demand curve will shift (y will change by Δy) as a result only of a change in the money stock. The shift will be equal to $1/k$ (divided by the price level). Changes in government spending and taxes will have no effect on aggregate demand in this special case.

Consider as the next special case that in which $l = 0$. This would be where the demand for money is completely insensitive to interest rates. You can think of this as arising when money is such a unique asset that it is completely non-substitutable for any other assets. In that case, by inspection of equations (A16) and (A17), you will discover that the multipliers become

$$\Delta r = \frac{1}{h}(\Delta g - b\Delta t - \frac{(1-b)}{kP_0}\Delta M) \tag{A20}$$

$$\Delta y = \frac{1}{k} \frac{\Delta M}{P_0} \tag{A21}$$

In this case, the interest rate will change when government spending, taxes, and the money stock change. It will rise with a rise in government spending and fall with a rise in taxes or the money supply. The change in y will be exactly the same as in the previous special case.

Now consider the opposite special case to the first one, where instead of h being infinitely big, it becomes infinitely small, specifically, 0. This would be the case where firms' investment plans were completely unresponsive to interest rates. In that case, the changes in the rate of interest and income level will be given by

$$\Delta r = \frac{1}{1-b} \left[\frac{k}{l}\Delta g - \frac{kb}{l}\Delta t - \frac{(1-b)}{lP_0}\Delta M \right] \tag{A22}$$

$$\Delta y = \frac{1}{1-b}[\Delta g - b\Delta t] \tag{A23}$$

This tells you that in this case, a rise in government spending will raise the interest rate, and a rise in taxes or the money supply will cut the interest rate. Unlike the two previous special cases, a rise in government spending or a cut in taxes will raise real income, but a change in the money stock will leave real income unaffected. Equation (A23) says that in the special case $h = 0$, the aggregate demand will change only as a result of changes in fiscal policy variables and will remain unchanged when the money stock changes.

Now consider the opposite special case to the second one, in which we let the parameter l become infinitely big. This would be the case where money is regarded as a perfect substitute for other non-money assets. Substituting an infinite value for l in equations (A16) and (A17) gives the solutions for the change in interest rate and the change in income as

$$\Delta r = 0 \tag{A24}$$

$$\Delta y = \frac{1}{1-b}(\Delta g - b\Delta t) \tag{A25}$$

This time the interest rate is entirely unaffected by changes in any of the variables. Real income changes, however, as a result of changing government spending or taxes (rises when government spending rises and falls when taxes rise), but is unaffected by a change in the money stock.

Notice that equations (A23) and (A25) are identical, just as equations (A19) and (A21) are identical. Equations (A19) and (A21) say that only money affects aggregate demand, while equations (A23) and (A25) say that only fiscal policy variables affect aggregate demand.

These two sets of results are the two extreme cases that arise as the parameter values l and h are allowed to vary. The result of a change in government spending, taxes, and the money supply on real income actually only depends upon the ratio of h to l. As that ratio goes from 0 to infinity, so the value of the fiscal policy mutiplier falls from $1/(1-b)$ to 0 and that of the money multiplier rises from 0 to $1/k$.

Review Questions

1.   Which markets are in equilibrium at the point of intersection of the IS and LM curves?

2.   What would be happening if the economy was 'off' its IS curve?

3.   What would be happening if the economy was 'off' its LM curve?

4.   Show the effects in the IS–LM model of a rise in government expenditure on the level of real income and the rate of interest. What conditions would lead to only the rate of interest changing? What conditions would lead to only real income changing?

5.   Suppose there was a rise in the government's budget deficit (g rises relative to t). What does the IS–LM model predict will happen to the rate of interest?

6.   Could your answer to Question 5 be part of the reason for high interest rates in the United Kingdom in the 1970s? (Be careful to distinguish between real and money rates of interest in your answer to this question.)

7.   Show the effect in the IS–LM model of a rise in the money supply on the rate of interest and the level of real income. What conditions would lead to only the interest rate changing? What conditions would lead to only the level of real income changing?

8.   What is the Keynesian aggregate demand curve? Which markets are in equilibrium along that aggregate demand curve? What is being held constant along the aggregate demand curve? Why does the curve slope downwards? Are there any conditions that would make the aggregate demand curve vertical?

9.   You are given the following information about a hypothetical economy:
    1) $c = 100 + 0.8(y - t)$
    2) $i = 500 - 50r$
    3) $g = 400$
    4) $t = 400$
    5) $M/P = 0.2y + 500 - 25r$
    6) there is unemployment
    7) the price level is fixed at 1
    8) the money supply is 520
    (c = consumption; i = investment; g = government expenditure; t = taxes; r = rate of interest; M = money supply; P = price level; y = real income).
    (a) Find the equilibrium values of real income, consumption, investment, and the rate of interest.
    (b) Find the effect on those equilibrium values of a unit rise in (i) M, (ii) g and (iii) t.

23

The Keynesian Model of the Open Economy

In the last chapter we analysed how, in the Keynesian model, the equilibrium levels of output and the rate of interest are determined in a closed economy. This chapter extends that analysis[1] and examines the determination of output and the rate of interest along with the balance of payments and the exchange rate in an economy which is operating on the horizontal section of the Keynesian inverse 'L' aggregate supply curve. We shall extend the analysis of the previous chapter to examine the effects of domestic monetary policy and fiscal policy actions on aggregate demand and also analyse the effects of foreign shocks on the domestic economy. We shall do this in the context of both a fixed exchange rate economy where the shocks affect the balance of payments and of a flexible exchange rate economy where the exchange rate itself is also going to be influenced by the various shocks that we shall consider.

The chapter pursues its objectives by taking you through six tasks, which are to:

A. **know how to derive the *IS* curve for an open economy;**
B. **know the definition of the *BP* curve;**
C. **know how to derive the *BP* curve;**
D. **understand what makes the *IS, LM,* and *BP* curves shift;**
E. **know how to determine the levels of output, interest rate, and the balance of payments in a fixed exchange rate regime;**
     and
F. **know how to determine the levels of output, interest rate, and the exchange rate in a flexible exchange rate regime.**

---

1. The material presented in this chapter was developed primarily by Robert Mundell and J. Marcus Fleming. The most important papers by these two outstanding scholars are: Robert A. Mundell, The appropriate use of monetary and fiscal policy under fixed exchange rates, *IMF Staff Papers*, Vol. 9, March 1962, pp. 70–77; and J. Marcus Fleming, Domestic financial policies under fixed and floating exchange rates, *IMF Staff Papers,* Vol.9, March 1962, pp. 369–77. Although Keynesian, the material in the chapter is often called the Mundell–Fleming analysis.

A. Derivation of the *IS* Curve for an Open Economy

You already know the meaning of the *IS* curve for an economy which has balanced trade or, equivalently, a 'closed economy'. It is the relationship between the rate of interest and level of income at which savings-plus-taxes are equal to investment-plus-government expenditures. In the 'open economy' there are two additional expenditure flows to be taken into account in defining and deriving the *IS* curve. They are exports and imports of goods and services. In a closed economy, aggregate demand is the sum of consumption plus investment plus government spending, while in an open economy aggregate demand is equal to the sum of those three items plus net foreign demand or, equivalently, exports minus imports. That is, defining exports as *ex* and imports as *im*, aggregate demand in an open economy is

$$y = c + i + g + ex - im \tag{23.1}$$

Subtracting consumption from both sides of equation (23.1) gives

$$y - c = i + g + ex - im \tag{23.2}$$

The left-hand side of the above equation $(y - c)$ is, of course, simply the sum of savings and taxes. We could equivalently, therefore, write that equation as

$$s + t = i + g + ex - im \tag{23.3}$$

Adding imports to both sides of the above equation gives

$$s + t + im = i + g + ex \tag{23.4}$$

This is the condition which, for the open economy, must be satisfied at all points on the *IS* curve. That is, savings-plus-taxes-plus-imports must equal investment-plus-government spending-plus-exports.

To derive the open economy *IS* curve, we need some propositions about how imports and exports are determined. Let us now proceed to do that.

First, consider exports. Two key variables determine a country's exports. The first of these is the total level of income of the people who are demanding those exports. That income level is, of course, the aggregate income of the rest of the world. It is the sum of the gross national products of all the countries in the world other than the country whose economy we are analysing. The second variable that influences exports is the price of the goods produced in the domestic economy relative to the prices ruling in the rest of the world. That relative price, expressed as an economy-wide average, could be stated precisely as

$$\theta = \frac{EP_f}{P} \tag{23.5}$$

Here, θ (the Greek letter theta) is the price of foreign goods, P_f, converted into domestic currency at the exchange rate E, relative to the domestic price level, P. The bigger is the value of θ, the bigger will be the volume of exports. That is, the higher is the foreign price level relative to the domestic price level, the bigger will be the rest of the world's demand for domestically produced goods.

We can summarise these propositions about exports as follows: *exports will be higher the higher is world income and the higher are world prices relative to prices in the domestic economy.*

Next, consider the factors that determine imports. Again there are two key variables which may be isolated as having important effects on imports. The first is the level of domestic income (real GDP). The higher is that, the higher will be imports. The other influence is the same relative price variable that influences exports. Its effect will, however, be opposite in sign to its effect on exports. That is, a rise in world prices relative to domestic prices will lead to a reduction in imports. To summarise: *imports will be higher the higher is real income and will be lower the higher are world prices relative to domestic prices.*

We may now proceed to derive the *IS* curve for an open economy. Figure 23.1 illustrates this. It is set up with an *IS* curve labelled *IS(C)* — C standing for closed economy — which is identical to the *IS* curve derived in Figure 20.4. To see the differences between that *IS* curve and that of the open economy, begin by considering Frame (c) of Figure 23.1. There, on the horizontal axis, we are measuring investment-plus-government spending-plus-exports. For given values of world income and prices, the domestic price level and the exchange rate, exports will be constant. We may therefore add exports to investment-plus-government spending by drawing a line parallel to the $i + g$ curve, the new curve representing $i + g + ex$. The horizontally shaded area in Frame (c) represents the volume of exports.

The second change occurs in Frame (a) of Figure 23.1. There we are measuring savings-plus-taxes-plus-imports on the vertical axis, and investment-plus-government spending-plus-exports on the horizontal axis. The 45° line defines the open economy equilibrium condition for the *IS* curve.

The third change comes in Frame (b). In this frame we measure savings-plus-taxes-plus-imports on the vertical axis. It is necessary, therefore, to add imports to the previously derived savings-plus-taxes schedule. To do this, recall that imports are presumed to depend on the level of domestic income, the exchange rate, and on the domestic and world price levels. As in the case of exports, hold the last three variables at some fixed value. That done, the level of imports will depend solely on the level of domestic income. We can show this in Frame (b) by drawing a line above the savings-plus-taxes line which is steeper than that line. The vertical distance between the two lines will then measure the volume of imports (the shaded area in Frame (b)). To derive the *IS* curve for the open economy, we proceed in the same way as for the closed economy, but we use the $i + g + ex$ and the $s + t + im$ lines. Following exactly the same procedure as in Chapter 20 you can readily verify that the curve *IS (O)* — *O* for open — is the open economy *IS* curve. Notice that it is steeper than that for the closed economy. It cuts the closed economy *IS* curve at that level of income which generates a volume of imports exactly equal to the fixed volume of exports.

Since, in deriving the *IS* curve, we hold the exchange rate fixed, it follows that at each different exchange rate there will be a different *IS* curve. Precisely how the *IS* curve shifts as the exchange rate (and other variables) change will be explored in Section D below. Before that, let us go on to define and derive a new curve — the *BP* curve.

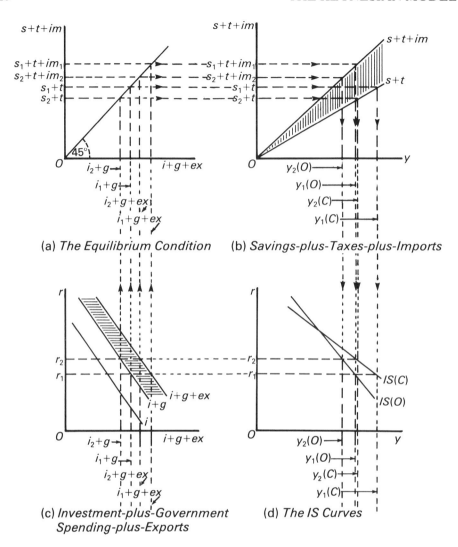

Figure 23.1 *The Derivation of the IS Curve for an Open Economy*

Frame (a) shows the equilibrium condition that defines the *IS* curve in an open economy — the equality of savings-plus-taxes-plus imports with investment-plus-government spending-plus-exports. In Frame (c), exports are added to investment-plus-government spending (the shaded area). In Frame (b), imports are added to savings-plus-taxes (the shaded area). In Frame (d), the *IS* curve, *IS* (C), is that for a closed economy (ignoring exports and imports) and that labelled *IS(O)* is for the open economy. The two curves intersect at the income level that generates a volume of imports equal to the fixed volume of exports. A rise in exports shifts the $i + g + ex$ line and shifts the *IS* curve. The relationship between the two shifts depends on the slope of the $s + t + im$ curve. The steeper is the slope of $s + t + im$, the smaller the shift in the *IS* curve for a given shift in $i + g + ex$.

B. Definition of the *BP* Curve

The BP curve is a relationship between the rate of interest and level of income such that at all points on the BP curve there is a balance of payments equilibrium. Put differently, at all points on the *BP* curve, the balance on the official settlements account is zero. Equivalently, there is a capital account surplus that exactly matches the current account deficit (or capital account deficit that exactly matches the current account surplus).

C. Derivation of the *BP* Curve

The starting point for deriving the *BP* curve is the balance of payments equilibrium condition which states that the sum of the current account balance and the capital account balance is zero. The prices at which a country exports and imports goods and services is determined by the world price level P_f, converted into domestic money units at the exchange rate E, so that the current account balance is $EP_f ex - EP_f im$. Dividing this by the domestic price level P, and remembering that EP_f equals θ, gives the *real* current account balance as $\theta(ex - im)$. Adding the real capital account surplus, denoted by *kas*, gives the condition for the *BP* curve as

$$\theta(ex - im) + kas = 0 \tag{23.6}$$

We have already discussed the determinants of the *volume* of exports and imports and the international relative price, θ, and need now only concern ourselves with the things that determine the capital account surplus.

The capital account of the balance of payments depends primarily upon rates of return on investments that are available in the domestic economy compared with rates of return available in the rest of the world. As a general proposition, the higher are the rates of return available in the domestic economy relative to those available in the rest of the world, the greater will be the tendency for domestic capital to stay at home and for foreign capital to be sucked into the domestic economy. Conversely, the lower are domestic rates of return relative to foreign rates of return, the greater will be the tendency for domestic capital to seek the higher returns available in other countries, and the greater will be the tendency for foreign capital to stay at home. In order to compare rates of return between two countries, it is necessary to look at the rates of interest that are available in the two countries and also to make an allowance for any change in the value of one money in terms of another (change in the exchange rate). As was discussed in Chapter 14, if there were two securities, identical in all respects except for the currency of denomination, then the rates of interest on those two securities would be related by the interest rate parity condition; that is,

$$r = r_f + \Delta\epsilon^e \tag{23.7}$$

Recall that r is the domestic rate of interest, r_f the foreign rate of interest, and $\Delta\epsilon^e$ the expected rate of depreciation of the domestic currency. Although the interest rate

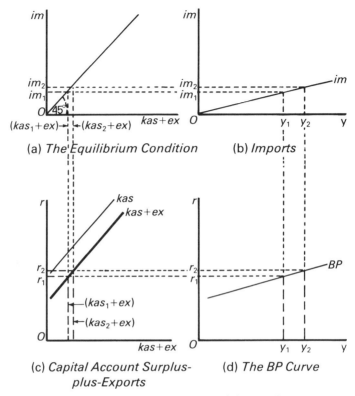

Figure 23.2 *The Derivation of the BP Curve*

Frame (a) contains the condition that defines the *BP* curve — the equality of imports with exports-plus-the capital account surplus. Frame (c) shows the capital account surplus rising with the rate of interest. Exports are added to the capital account surplus in Frame (c). Frame (b) shows imports rising with income. Frame (d) shows the *BP* curve as the relationship that satisfies the three lines in the other frames. The *BP* curve will shift if there is a rise in exports. The distance of the horizontal shift of the *BP* curve relative to the shift in *kas* + *ex* depends solely on the slope of the import function. The flatter is the *im* curve, the greater will be the shift in the *BP* curve for any given change in the *kas* + *ex* curve.

parity condition may be expected to hold exactly under the precise conditions that are used to define it — identical assets — it will not hold when applied to average interest rates across the entire collection of assets issued in one economy and the rest of the world. In general, domestic interest rates will have some room to move higher or lower, on the average, than what is predicted by the interest rate parity condition. The more domestic interest rates rise above the interest rate parity level, the more will be the tendency for foreign capital to enter the economy; the lower are domestic interest rates relative to their interest parity value, the less will foreign capital flow into the economy.

We are now in a position to derive the *BP* curve. Figure 23.2 illustrates the derivation. First, it will be useful to familiarise yourself with what we are measuring on the axes of the different frames: Frame (d) is going to show the *BP* curve and measures the rate of interest against the level of income; Frame (c) measures the rate of interest against total receipts from the rest of the world — exports-plus-capital account surplus; Frame (b) measures imports against the level of income; and Frame (a) measures imports on the vertical axis and exports-plus-capital account surplus on the horizontal axis. The line in Frame (a) defines the balance of payments equilibrium condition. It is a 45° line indicating that when imports equal exports-plus-capital account surplus, there is a zero balance on the official settlements account. In Frame (c), the upward-sloping line, *kas*, denotes the capital account surplus. It slopes upwards, indicating that the higher is the domestic rate of interest, other things being equal, the larger will be the capital account surplus. In drawing that line, the foreign rate of interest and the expected rate of depreciation of the domestic currency are being held constant. The second, thicker line in Frame (c) results from adding the fixed volume of exports to the capital account surplus to denote the total inflow of money from the rest of the world. In deriving the *BP* curve it will be convenient to assume that purchasing power parity (*PPP*) holds, so that $\theta = 1$.

Frame (b) shows the import function — the relationship between imports and income. In drawing the line in Frame (b), as in Frame (c), the exchange rate is being held constant. To derive the *BP* curve, select a rate of interest r_1 and notice that in Frame (c), at the interest rate r_1, there is a capital account surplus of kas_1 and a total inflow of money from the rest of the world of $kas_1 + ex$. Tracing up from Frame (c) to Frame (a), we know that if there is to be a balance of payments equilibrium, the level of imports must equal im_1. Taking that import level across to Frame (b), we discover that in order for the import level to equal im_1, it will be necessary for domestic income to be y_1. Transferring that income level into Frame (d), and transferring the initially assumed rate of interest r_1 across to Frame (d) gives a point on the *BP* curve. The income level y_1 combined with the interest rate r_1 generates a level of imports and capital account surplus such that there is a zero balance on the official settlements account. By selecting other interest rates, it is possible to derive other income levels, and by experimenting you will discover that you can generate the entire line labelled *BP*.

The *BP* curve will slope upwards in general, but could, in a special and important circumstance, be horizontal. That special circumstance would be one of *perfect capital mobility*. Perfect capital mobility means that any interest differential between the domestic economy and the rest of the world would automatically and instantly bring in, or drive out, funds, so that the domestic interest rate always equals the rate given by the interest rate parity relation. In that case, the domestic interest rate would always be equal to the foreign rate of interest plus the expected rate of depreciation of the domestic currency, and would never deviate from that level. The *BP* curve would be a horizontal line at that rate of interest. Although as a general matter, the *BP* curve will slope upwards, as shown in the figure. It may be presumed, however, that it will not be a very steep relationship, since modest interest differentials seem to be sufficient to induce large international movements of capital. (The perfect capital mobility case will feature prominently in Chapter 32.)

Let us now go on to consider the things that make the open economy *IS*, *LM*, and *BP* curves shift.

D. Shifts in the *IS, LM,* and *BP* Curves

Recall that when we derived the *IS* curve we held constant the level of world income, which influences exports, and international relative prices, which influence both exports and imports. What happens to the *IS* curve if either of those variables changes? If world income rises, exports rise. This has the effect of shifting the *IS* curve to the right. If the world price level rises relative to the domestic price level, that also raises exports and lowers imports. That, too, shifts the *IS* curve to the right. The international relative price level might rise either because of a rise in the exchange rate (depreciation), a rise in the foreign price level, or a fall in the domestic price level.

The *LM* curve in the open economy is exactly the same (at least in the presentation given here) as that of the closed economy. As in the case of the closed economy, the only thing that shifts the *LM* curve is a change in the stock of money. There is an important difference between the open and closed economies, however, concerning the sources of variation in the quantity of money. You know from the analysis in Chapter 14 that a change in the quantity of money may be decomposed into two parts: a change in foreign exchange reserves and a change in domestic credit. The first of these items is the balance on the official settlements account. If domestic credit is held constant, which would be the natural way of interpreting a neutral domestic monetary policy, then unless the economy is on the *BP* curve, the quantity of money will be changing. Specifically, at all points above the *BP* curve the quantity of money will be rising, and at all points below it the quantity of money will be falling. This means that if the economy is above the *BP* curve, it is experiencing a balance of payments surplus, and the *LM* curve will be shifting to the right. Conversely, if the economy is below the *BP* curve, it is experiencing a balance of payments deficit, and the *LM* curve will be shifting to the left.

An alternative domestic monetary policy would be to stabilise the quantity of money regardless of the state of the balance of payments. This would involve changing domestic credit by an equal but opposite amount to the change in foreign exchange reserves resulting from the balance of payments deficit or surplus. Such an action is known as *sterilising the balance of payments*. Such a policy can be undertaken, but only for limited periods of time, since, in general, sterilisation actions accentuate the balance of payments problem. Pursuing tighter and tighter domestic monetary policies in the face of the balance of payments surplus tends to make that surplus bigger, and pursuing slacker and slacker monetary policies in the face of the balance of payments deficit tends to make the deficit worse. A situation in which the quantity of money changes by the same amount as the change in foreign exchange reserves is, therefore, an interesting one to analyse, since it represents the only policy action that can be sustained over an indefinite period. Sterilisation cannot.

Next, consider the factors that shift the *BP* curve. In drawing the capital account surplus line in Figure 23.2, we held constant the world rate of interest and the expected rate of change of the exchange rate. A rise in either the rest of the world rate of interest, or in the expected rate of depreciation of the domestic currency will shift the *kas* line to the left (or upwards). The factors that determine exports and imports have already been discussed in the above discussion of the factors which shift the IS curve. Changes in world income or international relative prices which shift the IS curve will also, necessarily, shift the BP curve. Anything that raises exports or lowers imports will shift the BP curve to the right. Thus, a devaluation of the currency (a higher value of E), a rise in foreign prices, a rise in world income, or a fall in domestic price level will all have the effect of shifting the BP curve to the right.

You have now seen that some factors shift the IS curve and the BP curve simultaneously. It is of some importance to establish which of these two curves shifts more, in the event of a change that shifts them both. There is no ambiguity about this when the factor leading to a shift in both curves is a change in world income. In that case, both curves will shift in the same direction as each other, but the BP curve will shift by more than the IS curve. To see this, all that you need do is examine Figures 23.1 and 23.2 again. Consider the effect of a rise in world income, which raises exports. In Figure 23.1, that would shift the investment-plus-government spending-plus-exports line to the right, and shift the IS curve to the right. The amount by which the IS curve shifts depends solely on the initial change in $i + g + ex$ and on the slope of the savings-plus-taxes-plus-imports line in Frame (b). The steeper is that line, the smaller will be the shift in the IS curve.

Now consider what happens to the BP line. In Frame (c) of Figure 23.2, the $kas + ex$ line would shift to the right. Further, the BP curve in Frame (d) would shift to the right. The amount by which the BP curve shifts depends solely on the initial shift in $kas + ex$ and on the slope of the import line in Frame (b). The flatter is that line, the bigger will be the shift in the BP curve. The initial change in exports recorded in Frame (b) of both figures is identical, of course. Since we know that the slope of the savings-plus-taxes-plus-imports line is steeper than the slope of the imports line (convince yourself of this by simply noting that savings also rise as income rises), we also know that the BP curve must shift to the right by more than the IS curve shifts.

A change in world income is not the only factor that leads to shifts in both the IS and BP curves. A change in international relative prices (a change in the exchange rate or the domestic or world price level) will also shift both curves. In this case there is a potential ambiguity as to which of the two curves shifts more. The ambiguity arises from the fact (apparent by comparing equations (23.4) and (23.6) above) that the definition of real expenditure underlying the IS curve is one based on constant (base period) relative prices (refer back to Chapter 3, Section D and to equation (3.6)), while the definition of the balance of payments underlying the BP curve is one based on current relative prices. Thus, when analysing a change in international prices, it is necessary to work out its effects on the *volume* of exports and imports to calculate an IS curve shift and its effect on the real *value* of exports and imports to calculate its effect on the BP curve. To avoid a lengthy treatment of all possible cases, we shall *assume* that a change in international relative prices has the same type of effect on the IS and BP curves as that of a change in world income which we have just analysed. That is, we shall assume that a rise in international relative prices (a rise in $\theta = EP_f/P$) will raise both the volume and value of (net) exports and shift both the IS and BP curves to the right. The BP curve will be assumed to shift further to the right than the IS curve.

It will be useful for the subsequent analysis to introduce a further curve that summarises the IS and BP shifts. Let us call that curve the IS–BP curve. Figure 23.3 illustrates its derivation. Imagine the economy starts out on IS and BP at the interest rate r_1 and income level y_1. There is then some shock that shifts both the IS and BP

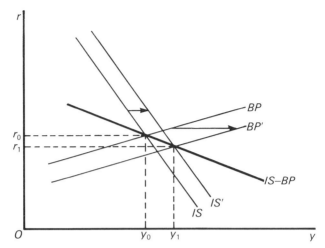

Figure 23.3 *The IS–BP Locus*

Because a shock that influences both the *IS* and *BP* curves shifts the *BP* curve by more than the *IS* curve, the intersection points of successive *BP* and *IS* curves fall on a downward sloping line *IS–BP*.

---

curves to *IS'*, *BP'*. The new income level is y_2 and the interest rate r_2. The line traced by the intersection points of the *IS* and *BP* curves will be called the *IS–BP* curve. It slopes downwards because we are assuming that the *BP* curve shifts by more than the *IS* curve following any shock that shifts both of these curves. The *IS–BP* curve will be useful for analysing the effects of changes in world variables and in the exchange rate, all of which shift both the *IS* and *BP* curves in the manner illustrated in Figure 23.3.

You now have all the tools that are needed to analyse the determination of output, interest rates, the balance of payments, and the exchange rate and how these variables respond to various policy and other shocks when the price level is constant and output is below its full-employment level.

E. Determination of Output, Interest Rate, and the Balance of Payments in a Fixed Exchange Rate Regime

Let us now determine the equilibrium values of output, the interest rate, and the balance of payments when the exchange rate is fixed. We shall do this for given levels of world income, interest rate, and the price level; for the given fixed exchange rate; for fixed levels of government spending and taxes; and for a fixed domestic price level (remembering that throughout we are dealing with the Keynesian situation in which full-employment output exceeds any output level that we are considering). The equilibrium levels of output, the rate of interest, and the balance of payments will be determined at the triple intersection point of the *IS, LM, BP* curves as shown

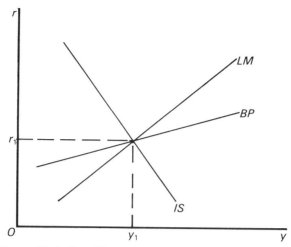

Figure 23.4 *Equilibrium with Fixed Exchange Rates*

Equilibrium output and the interest rate are determined at the point of intersection of the *IS* and *BP* curves. The *LM* curve will also pass through that intersection point because the money supply adjusts to ensure that.

---

in Figure 23.4. The *IS* and *BP* curves are exactly the same as those derived in Figures 23.1 and 23.2. The *LM* curve is exactly the same as the curve derived in Section B of Chapter 21.

(i) Equilibrium

The way the model works to determine the equilibrium is slightly more complicated than the standard closed economy variant of the *IS–LM* analysis. The idea is that income and the rate of interest are determined at each instant by the intersection of the *IS* and *LM* curves, as they were before in the closed economy analysis. That is not, however, the end of the story. If the intersection of *IS* and *LM* is above the *BP* curve, then there is a balance of payments surplus, and the money supply will be rising. A rising money supply means that the *LM* curve will be shifting to the right so that income will be rising and the rate of interest falling (the economy will be sliding down the *IS* curve). Such a process would continue until the *LM* curve comes to rest where the *IS* curve intersects the *BP* curve. At such a point, the balance of payments will be zero and the money supply constant so that the *LM* curve will no longer be shifting. Conversely, if initially the *IS* and *LM* curves cut each other below the *BP* curve, then there will be a balance of payments deficit. The money supply will be falling, and the *LM* curve will be moving to the left. In the process, the level of income will fall and the interest rate will rise (the economy will slide up the *IS* curve). This process will continue until the *LM* curve intersects the intersection point of the *IS* and *BP* curves. At that point the balance of payments deficit will have disappeared and the money stock will be constant. You will probably get a better feeling for what is going on here by working through a series of experiments which result from the economy being shocked by a variety of domestic and foreign disturbances. We shall now turn to such an exercise.

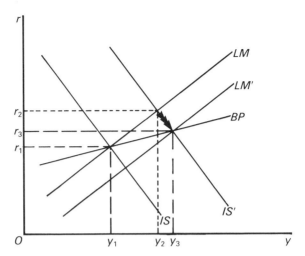

Figure 23.5 *The Effects of an Expansionary Fiscal Policy Under Fixed Exchange Rates*

An initial equilibrium y_1, r_1 is disturbed by a rise in government spending or tax cut that shifts *IS* to *IS'*. The impact effect of this is to raise interest rates and income to r_2 and y_2. In that situation a balance of payments surplus raises the money supply, thereby shifting the *LM* curve to the right. The final equilibrium is the interest rate r_3 and income y_3 where *IS'* intersects *BP*. The *LM* curve will by then have become *LM'*. The adjustment process will take the economy down the *IS* curve.

(ii) Fiscal Policy

First, consider the effects of an expansionary fiscal policy. Figure 23.5 illustrates. The economy is at an initial equilibrium exactly like that depicted in Figure 23.4, with the interest rate at r_1 and income at y_1. There is then a rise in government spending or a cut in taxes which shifts the *IS* curve to *IS'*. The impact effect of that fiscal policy action is to raise the rate of interest and the level of income to r_2 and y_2 respectively. The economy would now, however, be experiencing a balance of payments surplus, since it is operating at a point above the *BP* curve. With a balance of payments surplus, the money supply will be rising, so the *LM* curve will shift to the right. As this happens, so a succession of *LM* curves intersect *IS'* at lower and lower interest rates, but at higher and higher income levels (along the arrowed path). The economy will finally settle down at the interest rate r_3 and income level y_3. The effect, then, of an expansionary fiscal policy in a fixed exchange rate, fixed price level, underemployed economy will be to produce higher interest rates and higher income levels. A balance of payments surplus will bring an inflow of money that will subsequently lower interest rates, but not to their initial level,[2] and raise income still further.[3]

---

2. In the special case of perfect capital mobility, the interest rate will return to its initial level.

3. There is a possible, though most uninteresting, case which would arise if the *BP* curve was steeper than the *LM* curve. In that case, the impact effect of the expansionary fiscal policy would be to produce a balance of payments deficit. Money would flow out of the economy, thereby shifting the *LM* curve leftwards, raising the rate of interest, and lowering the level of income. The new equilibrium would be one in which both interest rates and income had increased above their initial levels.

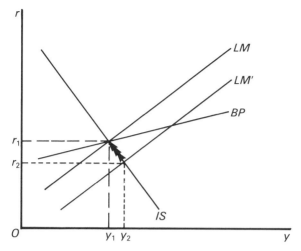

Figure 23.6 *The Effects of a Rise in the Money Supply Under Fixed Exchange Rates*
An initial equilibrium at y_1, r_1 is disturbed by a once-and-for-all rise in domestic credit that shifts the *LM* curve to *LM'*. The impact effect of this is to lower the interest rate to r_2 and raise income to y_2. A balance of payments deficit results, and this leads to an outflow of money. As the money supply falls, the *LM* curve shifts back to the left and settles eventually at the initial equilibrium y_1, r_1.

(iii) Monetary Policy

Next, consider the effects of an expansionary monetary policy. Again, let the economy start out at the initial equilibrium level r_1, y_1 depicted in Figure 23.4. Figure 23.6 shows the effect of a monetary disturbance. Imagine raising the quantity of money (by raising domestic credit) in a once-and-for-all manner, so that the *LM* curve shifts to *LM'*. Initially, the interest rate drops to r_2 and income rises to y_2. Clearly, with a higher income level bringing in more imports and a lower interest rate lowering the capital account surplus, there will be a balance of payments deficit. In that situation the money stock will fall and the *LM* curve will move to the left. As it does so, it will intersect the *IS* curve at higher and higher interest rates and lower income levels (the arrowed path). Eventually, the quantity of money will have returned to its initial level, and the economy will have returned to its initial interest rate and income position. All that will have happened is that the quantity of money will be backed by a higher amount of domestic credit and a smaller amount of foreign exchange reserves in the final situation than initially. This will be the only change between the initial and final situation. Thus, in a fixed exchange rate economy, monetary policy has no permanent effects on aggregate demand.

(vi) Devaluation and Foreign Shocks

Thirdly, consider the effect of a devaluation of the currency. A devaluation is a once-and-for-all rise in the value of the exchange rate, E. Again, suppose the economy starts out at the income and interest level y_1, r_1, as depicted in Figure 23.7. Then imagine that there is a once-and-for-all rise in the value of the exchange rate (devaluation). This raises exports and lowers imports, thereby shifting both the *IS*

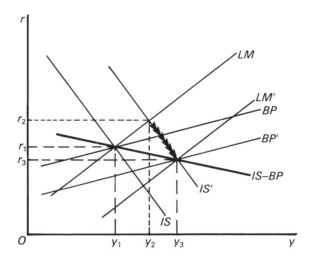

Figure 23.7 *The Effect of a Devaluation*

The initial equilibrium y_1, r_1 is disturbed by a devaluation of the currency. This raises exports and lowers imports, shifting the *IS* and *BP* curves to the right. The impact effect of this is to raise the level of income to y_2 and interest rate to r_2. There will be a balance of payments surplus in this situation which will lead to a rising money supply. The *LM* curve will shift to the right, producing a falling rate of interest and continuing increase in income. The resting point will be where *IS'* intersects *BP'*, at which stage the *LM* curve will have become *LM'*. The devaluation then raises income and initially raises the rate of interest, but eventually lowers the rate of interest.

curve and *BP* curve to the right. The new curves are shown as *IS'* and *BP'* and are drawn to reflect the assumption that the *BP* curve shifts rightwards by more than does the *IS* curve. The initial impact of the devaluation will be to take the economy to the equilibrium y_2, r_2 where the original *LM* curve intersects the new *IS* curve. In that situation there is a balance of payments surplus, since the economy is above the new *BP* curve (*BP'*). The balance of payments surplus causes the quantity of money to rise and the *LM* curve to start shifting to the right. As it does so, it intersects the *IS* curve at lower and lower interest rates and higher and higher income levels (along the arrowed adjustment path). Eventually income rises to y_3 and the interest rate falls to r_3. The final effect of a devaluation, therefore, is to raise income and lower interest rates. The balance of payments moves into surplus during the adjustment process, but is in equilibrium at the end of the process.

It should be emphasised that this set of responses to a devaluation is all conditional on the price level remaining constant. If the price level was to rise by the same percentage amount as the devaluation, then international relative prices would not be affected, and the economy would remain at its initial equilibrium level. Alternatively, if the price level *initially* remained constant, the path described in Figure 23.7 would be set up, and the economy would move from r_1, y_1, to r_2, y_2, and then start to proceed towards r_3, y_3. If, during that process the price level began to rise and eventually rose all the way to full proportionality with the devaluation, then instead of continuing to travel down the curve *IS'*, both the *IS'* and *BP'* curves would shift leftwards, and the economy would gradually move back to r_1, y_1.

Shocks emanating from the rest of the world would have similar effects to a devaluation. A rise in world income or a rise in the world price level would have exactly the same effects as a devaluation. A fall in the world rate of interest, which would shift the *BP* line but not the *IS* curve, would have no impact effect on income and the interest rate. It would, however, set up a process in which the balance of payments was in surplus, and so would start the *LM* curve moving to the right. Income would rise, and the interest rate would fall until the point of intersection of the original *IS* curve with the new *BP* curve was reached.

This completes our analysis of the effects of domestic policy and foreign shocks on output, interest rates, and the balance of payments in a fixed exchange rate regime. Let us now turn to examine a flexible exchange rate economy.

F. Determination of Output, Interest Rate, and the Exchange Rate in a Flexible Exchange Rate Regime

Analysing a flexible exchange rate economy is slightly harder than the fixed exchange rate case. The problem arises because the *IS* and *BP* curves have three variables in them — income, the rate of interest, and the exchange rate — all of which we want to determine, and it is therefore hard to construct diagrams in two dimensions that have the simplicity of those in the fixed exchange rate case. In order to make the analysis of the flexible exchange rate economy as comparable as possible with that of the fixed exchange rate economy, we shall use a series of diagrams drawn in interest rate real income space, as we did before. This means that the exchange rate will not appear explicitly on one of the axes of the picture. It will be possible, nevertheless, to work out directions of change of the exchange rate when various shocks are administered to the economy. This is analogous to the way in which the balance of payments was determined in the previous section.

(i) Equilibrium

It will be useful, as a starting point, to re-interpret Figure 23.1 as a flexible exchange rate equilibrium rather than as a fixed exchange rate equilibrium. Under flexible exchange rates, the quantity of money (both the foreign exchange reserve and domestic credit) are determined by the central bank. The position of the *LM* curve is therefore bolted down, so to speak, by monetary policy. If the point of intersection of the *IS* and *BP* curves is not on the *LM* curve, something has to adjust. The adjustment that occurs is in the exchange rate. Different values of the exchange rate generate different values of exports and imports and therefore produce different *IS* and *BP* curves. Since the *IS* curve slopes downwards and the *BP* curve slopes upwards, there is one, and only one, point at which they intersect and at the same time lie on the *LM* curve. The value of the exchange rate that underlies the *IS* and *BP* curves when they cut the *LM* curve is the equilibrium exchange rate. Thus, you may interpret Figure 23.1 as a flexible exchange rate equilibrium, in the sense that the

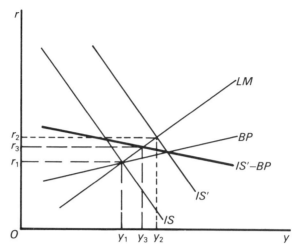

Figure 23.8 *The Effects of an Expansionary Fiscal
Policy Under Flexible Exchange Rates*

An initial equilibrium y_1, r_1 is disturbed by a rise in government spending or a tax cut that shifts
the *IS* curve to *IS'*. If there was no change in the exchange rate, income would move to y_2 and
the interest rate to r_2, thereby producing a balance of payments surplus. With a flexible
exchange rate that does not happen. Instead, the exchange rate falls (the currency
appreciates) thereby lowering exports and raising imports. The *IS* curve and *BP* curve shift to
the left. The equilibrium will be at the point at which the *IS'–BP* locus intersects the *LM* curve,
at the interest rate r_3 and income y_3. Thus, the effect of an expansionary fiscal policy is to raise
income, raise the rate of interest, and appreciate the currency.

---

exchange rate has to be that particular value that causes the *IS* and *BP* curves to
intersect each other at a point on the *LM* curve. This contrasts with the fixed
exchange rate interpretation of Figure 23.1, which is that the *IS* and *BP* curves are
fixed in position, while the *LM* curve takes up the slack — the money supply varying
to ensure that the *LM* curve is located at the point of intersection of the fixed *IS* and
BP curves.

To repeat for emphasis, in a fixed exchange rate world the *IS* and *BP* curves are
fixed in position and determine the steady-state equilibrium while the quantity of
money and, therefore, the *LM* curve are dragged along to that fixed intersection
point. In the case of the flexible exchange rate economy, the *LM* curve is fixed in
position, while the exchange rate is free to move, thereby shifting the *IS* and *BP*
curves to an intersection point on the *LM* curve.

(ii) Fiscal Policy

Let us now proceed to analyse the effects of the same set of policy and foreign shocks
that were analysed in the preceding section, in the flexible exchange rate case. First,
consider the effect of an expansionary fiscal policy. The economy is initially in an
equilibrium, such as that shown in Figure 23.8, at y_1, r_1. There is then expansion of
government spending or a tax cut that shifts the *IS* curve from *IS* to *IS'*. The impact
effect of that is to raise the income level to y_2 and the interest rate to r_2. In that
situation, if the exchange rate was fixed, there would be a balance of payments

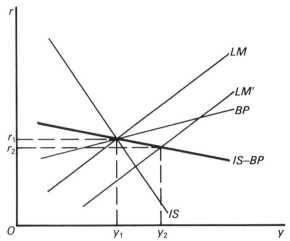

Figure 23.9 *The Effects of an Expansionary Monetary Policy Under Flexible Exchange Rates*

An initial equilibrium at y_1, r_1 is disturbed by a rise in the money stock which shifts the *LM* curve to *LM'*. This leads to a higher exchange rate (devaluation) which shifts the *IS* and *BP* curves along the *IS–BP* locus until they intersect the new *LM* curve at y_2, r_2. Thus, the effect of an expansionary monetary policy under flexible exchange rates is to lower the interest rate, raise income, and depreciate the currency.

---

surplus. With a flexible exchange rate, however, the balance of payments surplus is not allowed to occur. The central bank simply does not stand ready to take in foreign exchange at a pegged exchange rate. Instead, the exchange rate adjusts. If there is an excess supply of foreign currency, its price falls or, alternatively, the domestic currency appreciates. This lowers world prices relative to domestic prices, raising imports and lowering exports. In this process, the *IS* and *BP* curves shift to the left. Since we are assuming that the *BP* curve shifts by more than the *IS* curve, as they move, they intersect along the line marked *IS' – BP*. They will eventually come to rest, intersecting the *LM* curve at the interest rate r_3 and income level y_3. The exchange rate at that point is lower than the initial exchange rate (the currency has appreciated). Thus, the effects of an expansionary fiscal policy in a flexible exchange rate economy are to raise income and the rate of interest and to appreciate the currency. Domestic manufacturing interests may be hostile towards such an outcome and complain about the difficulty of doing profitable business in foreign markets. In effect, what is happening is that because the government is spending more, real resources have to be diverted from the rest of the economy to the government, and that is done by making total world demand for domestic goods decline and domestic demands for rest of world goods increase. The appreciation of the currency is the mechanism whereby this happens. It is not the *cause* of the problem perceived by domestic manufacturers.

(iii) Monetary Policy

Next, consider the effects of an expansionary monetary policy. Again, start out with the economy at the equilibrium (y_1, r_1) shown in Figure 23.9. This is at the triple

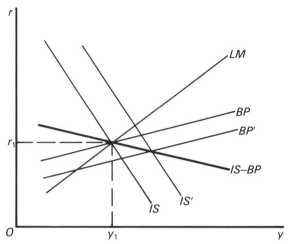

Figure 23.10 *The Effects of a Rise in World Income Under Flexible Exchange Rates*
An initial equilibrium y_1, r_1 is disturbed by a rise in world income which shifts the *IS* and *BP*
curves to *IS'* and *BP'*. The currency appreciates to produce an equivalent shift back of those
curves to their initial positions so that the income level and interest rate are undisturbed. Thus,
the effect of a world income rise under flexible exchange rates comes out entirely as a change in
the exchange rate.

intersection of *LM, BP,* and *IS.* Then let there be a rise in the quantity of money to
shift the *LM* curve to *LM'* . The new equilibrium clearly has to be somewhere on
LM'. At the initial exchange rate, the *IS* and *BP* curves intersect on the old *LM*
curve. There must be another exchange rate (a higher value of the exchange rate)
that would have the curves intersecting on the new *LM* curve, *LM'*. The *IS–BP* curve
traces out the intersection points of the *IS* and *BP* curves as the exchange rate
changes. The intersection of the *IS–BP* curve and the *LM'* curve determines the new
equilibrium level of income y_2 and the interest rate r_2. We know that the exchange
rate is higher than the initial one because we know that it is associated with a higher
level of exports and lower level of imports than prevailed initially. Recall that a
higher value of the exchange rate implies a depreciation of the currency. The effects
of an expansionary monetary policy in a fixed price level, flexible exchange rate
economy may be summarised as follows: a rise in the money supply leads to a lower
rate of interest, a higher level of income, and a depreciation of the currency.

(iv) Foreign Shocks

Finally, consider the effects of a change in world income. Imagine that the economy
is at (y_1, r_1) in Figure 23.10 and that then the rise in world income shifts the *IS* and *BP*
curves to *IS'* and *BP'*. They necessarily intersect along the line *IS–BP*. Varying the
exchange rate changes exports and imports, thereby shifting the *IS* and *BP* curves.
Varying foreign income (the shock that we are considering here) also changes
exports and shifts the *IS* and *BP* curves. Since the *LM* curve has not changed (the
domestic money supply being held constant), we know that the final equilibrium
must be at a point on the *LM* curve. We further know that it has to involve the

intersection of *IS* and *BP*. We can see that there is only one such point and that is the initial equilibrium income and interest rate level (y_1, r_1). What happens is that the exchange rate has to change (appreciate in this case) so as to return the *IS* and *BP* curves from their shocked positions *IS'*, *BP'* to their initial positions. The initial *IS* and *BP* curves then describe the initial exchange rate and the initial level of world income and also the new higher level of world income and lower value of the exchange rate (appreciated currency).

(v) Comparison of Fixed and Flexible Exchange Rates

It is of some interest to compare the responses of the economy in the fixed and flexible exchange rate cases. You can do this by comparing Figure 23.5 with 23.8 (fiscal policy), 23.6 with 23.9 (monetary policy), and 23.7 (interpreted as a foreign shock) with 23.10 (for a rise in world income). An expansionary fiscal policy has a bigger output effect, but smaller interest rate effect under fixed exchange rates than under flexible exchange rates. An expansionary monetary policy raises income and lowers the interest rate under flexible exchange rates, but has no effect, in the steady state, under fixed exchange rates. An expansion of world income raises domestic income and lowers domestic interest rates under fixed exchange rates, but it has no effect on interest rates and income, in the steady state, in a flexible exchange rate economy.

SUMMARY

A. Derivation of the *IS* Curve for an Open Economy

The *IS* curve for an open economy shows the relationship between the rate of interest and level of income at which savings-plus-taxes-plus-imports equals investment-plus-government spending-plus-exports. It is steeper than the *IS* curve for a closed economy and intersects the latter at the income level and interest rate at which imports equal exports.

B. Definition of the *BP* Curve

The *BP* curve shows the relationship between the rate of interest and level of income at which the balance of the official settlements account is zero.

C. Derivation of the *BP* Curve

For a given level of domestic and foreign prices and exchange rate and a given level of world income, exports will be fixed. The capital account surplus depends upon the domestic rate of interest, and imports depend on domestic income. By finding the level of income that generates an import volume equal to the exports-plus-capital account surplus generated by a given interest rate, it is possible to trace out the *BP* curve. The curve slopes upwards, except in the case of perfect capital mobility, in which case it is horizontal.

D. Shifts in the *IS*, *LM*, and *BP* Curves

In addition to the factors that shift the *IS* curve in a closed economy, a change in world income, the exchange rate, or the foreign price level shifts the *IS* curve in an open economy. A rise in world income, a rise in the world price level, or a depreciation of the domestic currency all shift the *IS* curve to the right. The *LM* curve shifts because of changes in the money supply. In an open economy when the exchange rate is fixed, this occurs if the balance of payments is other than zero. The balance of payments surplus is associated with a rising money supply, the balance of payments deficit with a falling money supply. Thus, if the economy is off the *BP* curve, the *LM* curve is shifting if the exchange rate is fixed. The *BP* curve shifts as a result of changes in world income, the exchange rate, the world price level, or the world rate of interest. A rise in world income, a rise in the world price level, a fall in the world rate of interest, or depreciation of the currency all shift the *BP* curve to the right. A change in world income which shifts both the *IS* and the *BP* curves shifts both curves in the same direction but shifts the *BP* curve by more than it shifts the *IS* curve. A change in international relative prices also shifts both the *IS* and *BP* curves and we have assumed that the *BP* curve shifts by more than the *IS* curve.

E. Determination of Output, Interest Rate, and the Balance of Payments in a Fixed Exchange Rate Regime

At each instant, the income level and interest rate are determined at the point of intersection of the *IS* and *LM* curves. If that intersection point is off the *BP* curve, the *LM* curve is shifting. The steady state occurs where the *IS* and *BP* curves intersect. The *LM* curve intersects that point as a result of the money supply adjusting while the balance of payments is out of equilibrium.

Expansionary fiscal policy raises output and interest rates and leads to a temporary balance of payments surplus. Expansionary monetary policy leads to a temporary balance of payments deficit and no steady-state change in income or the rate of interest. A devaluation initially raises the rate of interest and income level, but eventually lowers the rate of interest below its initial level and raises income still further. In the process, the balance of payments will have been in surplus. A rise in world income has a similar effect to that of a devaluation.

F. Determination of Output, Interest Rate, and the Exchange Rate in a Flexible Exchange Rate Regime

Under flexible exchange rates the *LM* curve is fixed in position. The portions of the *BP* and *IS* curves depend on the value of the exchange rate. As the exchange rate varies these curves shift to intersect each other along a downward sloping *IS–BP* locus. The equilibrium exchange rate is that exchange rate which locates the *BP* and *IS* curves at an intersection point along the *LM* curve. In a flexible exchange rate economy an expansionary fiscal policy raises income and the rate of interest and appreciates the currency. An expansionary monetary policy lowers the rate of interest, raises the level of income, and depreciates the currency. An expansion in world income leads to an appreciation of the currency, but no change in income or the rate of interest.

Review Questions

1. What is the equilibrium condition that an open economy satisfies as it moves along its *IS* curve?

2. How does the *IS* curve of an open economy differ from that of a closed economy?

3. What determines the *slope* of the open economy *IS* curve?

4. What makes the open economy *IS* curve shift, and in what directions?

5. What is the equilibrium condition that is satisfied as the economy moves along its *BP* curve?

6. What determines the slope of the *BP* curve?

7. What makes the *BP* curve shift, and in what directions?

8. Explain how a rise in world income shifts the *IS* and *BP* curves. Which shifts by most? Why?

9. What happens to the *LM* curve if the economy is (a) above, (b) below, and (c) on, its *BP* curve?

10. Work out the effects on all the relevant variables, under fixed exchange rates, of the following shocks:
    (a) a rise in government spending
    (b) a rise in domestic credit
    (c) a rise in the exchange rate
    (d) a rise in world income
    (e) a rise in world prices
    (f) a rise in the world rate of interest.
    How do the effects depend on the degree of capital mobility?

11. Work out the effects on all the relevant variables, in a flexible exchange rate regime, of the six shocks listed in Question 10. How do the effects depend on the degree of capital mobility?

12. On the basis of your answers to Questions 10 and 11, how would you choose between the two alternative exchange rate regimes?

24

The Neoclassical Synthesis

The Keynesian model, with its fixed money wage rate (and in the approximate version developed in the above chapters, with its fixed price level), is obviously of limited usefulness in a world that experiences continuously rising prices. All the major economies of the Western world, as they came out of the Great Depression of the inter-war years and into World War II, began to experience rising prices. With trivial exceptions, prices have risen each and every year since then. The Keynesian model was developed to cope with the facts of the inter-war years, a period in which prices were steady and even falling at times. Clearly, the model needed modification to cope with the facts of the post-war world. It was under the pressure of the facts of stubborn, persistent inflation that the Keynesian model came to be modified as a result of contributions by a series of scholars. The resulting system became known as the *neoclassical synthesis*. That is what you are going to learn about in this chapter. In effect, the content of this chapter is a summary of the mainstream way of looking at macroeconomic problems that developed sometime in the 1950s and 1960s. This mainstream analysis gave rise to countless important and lasting contributions to our subject. It is, however, gradually being replaced by a new revolution in macroeconomic thinking. That revolution is described in the next part of this book. For now, however, the task immediately ahead is one of understanding the nature of the neoclassical synthesis. To that end, you have six tasks in this chapter. They are to:
   A. **know what is meant by the term 'neoclassical synthesis';**
   B. **understand how the Keynesian theory of aggregate demand works at full employment when the price level is rising;**
   C. **understand the neoclassical theory of price adjustment;**
   D. **understand the role of price level expectations in the neoclassical theory of price adjustment and understand the 'natural rate' hypothesis;**
   E. **understand the explanation of the business cycle given by the neoclassical synthesis;**
       and
   F. **understand the policy implications of the neoclassical synthesis.**

In order to keep the analysis manageable, we shall revert to the special case of dealing only with a closed economy. In abstracting from international trading and investment activities we do lose some of the richness of the neoclassical synthesis. To deal with the matters raised in this chapter and at the same time to keep all the complexities of the open economy introduced in the last chapter would, however, make your task unmanageable and would result in a less clear understanding of the issues involved.

With this qualification in mind let us now move on to the first of our tasks.

A. Definition of the 'Neoclassical Synthesis'

The term 'neoclassical synthesis' describes a body of analysis in macroeconomics that deals with the determination of the level of output, the rate of interest, and the price level (including its rate of change — the inflation rate) which incorporates three elements:
  (1) the Keynesian theory of aggregate demand;
  (2) the basic model's theory of aggregate supply; and
  (3) a theory of the adjustment of prices in a situation in which aggregate demand does not equal aggregate supply.
The equality of aggregate demand and aggregate supply is the state of rest (or equilibrium) of the neoclassical system. It is not, however, the only state in which the economy will be observed. Starting from any given rate of inflation, if aggregate demand exceeds aggregate supply, inflation will accelerate. If aggregate demand is less than aggregate supply, inflation will slow down. The actual level of output and the actual rate of change of prices will be determined by a rather complicated dynamic adjustment process.

Before it is possible to explain in full detail the characteristics of the neoclassical synthesis, it is necessary to become familiar with the way in which the Keynesian theory of aggregate demand behaves at full employment when the price level is changing. Let us now turn to that task.

B. Keynesian Theory at Full Employment[1]

(i) How the Keynesian Theory of Aggregate Demand Determines the Price Level at Full Employment When the Price Level is Constant

Figure 24.1 is going to illustrate the analysis of this process of price level determination. Notice that Frame (a) contains an *IS–LM* analysis and Frame (b) an

---

1. A seminal treatment of this material is Franco Modigliani, Liquidity preference and the theory of interest and money, *Econometrica*, Vol. 12, January 1944, pp. 45–88. The definitive presentation, however, with attention being paid to many issues ignored here, is Don Patinkin, *Money, Interest and Prices*, 2nd edn, Harper & Row, 1965, Chapters IX, X and XI.

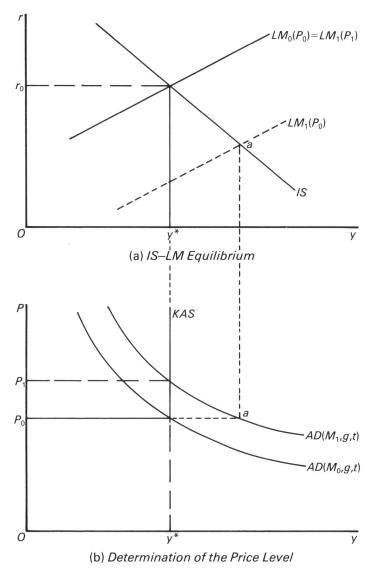

Figure 24.1 *The Effect of a Once-And-For-All Rise in the Money Supply on Output and the Price Level*

At full employment in the Keynesian model, as in the basic model, a rise in the money supply produces a proportionate rise in the price level. An initial equilibrium (y^*, r_0, P_0) is the intersection of the *IS* and *LM* curves in Frame (a) and the intersection of *AD* and *KAS* in Frame (b). This equilibrium is disturbed by a rise in the money stock. If the price level stayed constant, the *LM* curve and *AD* curve would shift, and the economy would move to the position *a*. Point *a* cannot be an equilibrium because output cannot exceed y^*. The price level has to rise to P_1 (Frame (b)) and the *LM* curve shifts back to its original position (Frame (a)).

---

aggregate supply–aggregate demand analysis. The level of real income is measured on the horizontal axis of each diagram and refers to the same magnitude in each case.

Begin by focusing on an initial equilibrium which, by a happy accident, is exactly at full employment and at the price level P_0. Such an equilibrium is depicted in the *IS–*

LM diagram as the intersection point of the curve $LM_0(P_0)$ and the IS curve, that is, the income level y^* and the interest rate r_0. The same equilibrium is depicted in Frame (b) as the point at which the aggregate demand curve, labelled $AD(M_0, g, t)$ intersects the corner of the 'inverse L' aggregate supply curve KAS. The price level is P_0 and the output level is y^*.

Now imagine that the money supply rises from M_0 to some higher level, say, M_1. If the price level remained at P_0, the LM curve representing a money stock of M_1 and the price level of P_0 would be to the right of the original LM curve. Such an LM curve is shown in Frame (a) as that labelled $LM_1(P_0)$. It intersects the IS curve at the point a. This higher money stock (M_1) can be represented in Frame (b) by showing an aggregate demand curve that is wholly to the right of the original aggregate demand curve. Such an aggregate demand curve is shown as that labelled $AD(M_1, g, t)$. Notice that the point on that aggregate demand curve marked a in Frame (b) corresponds to the point a in Frame (a) and is at the price level P_0, but displaced horizontally to a higher level of real income. That level of real income corresponds to the intersection of the IS and $LM_1(P_0)$ curves. Now recall that according to the Keynesian model, wages and prices are completely flexible in an upward direction. They are only rigid downwards. It is evident that a position like a cannot be sustained, given the Keynesian assumptions. At a there is an excess demand for goods and therefore an excess demand for labour. Such a situation would produce higher wages and prices. How much higher? The answer to that is read off immediately by looking at the point at which the new aggregate demand curve (that drawn for a money stock of M_1, $AD(M_1, g, t)$ cuts the full-employment vertical section of the aggregate supply curve. That point is at the price level indicated in Frame (b) as P_1. It is a price level that is higher than P_0 by the same percentage amount that the money stock M_1 exceeds the money stock M_0. At that higher price level, the LM curve would not be the curve shown as $LM_1(P_0)$, but rather would be the curve $LM_1(P_1)$. That LM curve is, of course, identical to the curve $LM_0(P_0)$. (If you are not sure about that, check back to Chapter 21, where the LM curve was derived and where the factors that cause the LM curve to shift were analysed.)

You have now analysed the effects of a once-and-for-all rise in the money stock at full employment in the Keynesian analysis. Those effects are so simple and yet, so important, that they are worth emphasising and highlighting. The initial equilibrium is r_0 and y^* on the IS curve and on the LM curve labelled $LM_0(P_0)$. Now there is a one shot rise in the money stock, from M_0 to M_1. If the price level remained constant, the LM curve would move to the broken LM curve, $LM_1(P_0)$. The price level will not, however, remain constant at full employment. It will have to rise, and by an amount such that the LM curve shifts back to the original position, so that it becomes the same curve as before, relabelled $LM_1(P_1)$.

What are the effects of this one shot rise in the money stock at full employment in the Keynesian model? The answer is very clear from the diagram. There is *no effect on the rate of interest, no effect on real output: the price level rises proportionately to the one shot rise in the money stock*.

Where have you seen that result before? In the analysis of the effects of a one shot rise in the money stock in the basic model. At full employment the Keynesian model predicts precisely the same things as the basic model does. This is what Keynes meant when he called his theory a *general theory*. He meant that the basic model was simply a special case of his more general theory.

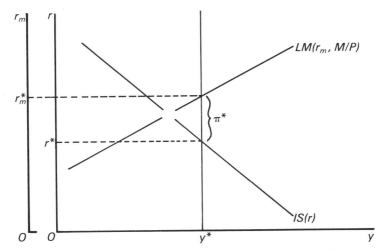

Figure 24.2 *The Effect of a Continuously Rising Money Supply*

A continuously rising money supply drives a wedge of inflation between the real and money rate of interest. The *IS* curve is drawn against the real rate of interest r, and the *LM* curve is drawn against the money rate of interest r_m. The real interest rate r^* is determined where *IS* cuts the full-employment line, and the money rate of interest r_m^* is determined where the *LM* curve cuts the full-employment line. The vertical distance between *IS* and *LM* at full employment is the rate of inflation, π^*.

Let us now analyse what happens at full employment when money and prices are continuously rising and more difficult and important, when the growth rate of the money supply (and the inflation rate) changes.

(ii) How a Continuously Rising Money Supply Generates Inflation and a Gap Between the Market Rate of Interest and Real Rate of Interest

The starting point for this analysis is to recall that the demand for money depends upon the rate of interest that is available on other financial assets. That is, the demand for money will vary inversely with the market rate of interest. The market rate of interest will equal the real rate of interest when there is no inflation. In an inflationary world, however, as you have already discovered, the market rate of interest will be higher than the real rate of interest by precisely the same amount as the inflation rate. That is,

$$r_m = r + \pi \tag{24.1}$$

Since the demand for money depends on r_m and not on r, it is necessary to be rather careful in figuring out how to determine equilibrium at full employment when the inflation rate is not zero. Figure 24.2 is going to help you to understand how to determine a full-employment equilibrium with inflation that is not zero.

First of all, notice that the vertical axis of Figure 24.2 measures two rates of interest, the real rate, r, and the market rate, r_m. The diagram also shows the full-employment output level y^*. We shall conduct the analysis entirely in terms of the economy being at that output level. Since the demand for money depends on the market or nominal rate of interest, it is necessary to plot the *LM* curve against that market rate of interest. You should be careful to remember that the *LM* curve is indeed plotted against the market rate of interest.

The position of the *LM* curve depends, as you know, on the real money supply, M/P. If we are going to analyse a situation in which both M and P are rising, it is evident that the *LM* curve will be continuously shifting, unless M and P are growing at the same rate. When M and P are growing at the same rate, M/P will be constant and so the *LM* curve will be stationary. To remind you that the *LM* curve is plotted against the market rate of interest r_m and that it depends on the real money supply M/P, the *LM* curve has been labelled $LM(r_m, M/P)$.

The *IS* curve, depending as it does on the equality of investment-plus-government spending with savings-plus-taxes, depends upon the real rate of interest. To remind you of that, we have labelled the *IS* curve $IS(r)$. Notice that the *IS* and *LM* curves have been drawn with a break in them. The break coincides with the point at which those two curves would have intersected if they had been drawn continuously. That has been done for a very important purpose. It is to remind you that the point at which those two curves cut in this diagram is a completely uninteresting point. (Strictly speaking, there is no point at which these two curves cut because one of them is plotted against the market rate of interest and the other against the real rate of interest. So, in effect, the two curves are not really drawn in the same space at all.) You may perhaps find it helpful to think of there being two diagrams, one with an *IS* curve plotted against the real interest rate and another one with an *LM* curve plotted against the market rate of interest. Nevertheless, it is useful to draw the two curves in the same picture because we do know that there is an interesting and simple link between the two interest rates. That link, of course, is the rate of inflation. It is possible, therefore, to depict the rate of inflation as the vertical gap between the *LM* curve and the *IS* curve. That is shown as the distance π^* in the diagram, when income is at y^*. Figure 24.2 now can be interpreted as characterising a full-employment equilibrium with an inflation rate of π^*. The real interest rate is r^*, and with an income level y^*, that puts the economy on the *IS* curve, so that there is an equality between the expenditure and income flows in the goods market. The market interest rate is the real interest rate plus π^*, which equals r_m^*. That, with an income level of y^*, puts the economy on its *LM* curve, so that there is an equality between the supply of and demand for money.

There is just one further thing that you need to be aware of and that concerns the money supply and price level that lies behind the *LM* curve. If the price level is rising at a rate π^*, other things being equal, that would be moving the *LM* curve leftwards. If the *LM* curve is not moving, it must be that something else is happening which is just offsetting that pressure to move the *LM* curve as a result of rising prices. It is rather clear what that is; it is a continuously rising money supply. Underlying the *LM* curve when inflation is proceeding at the rate π^* is a rising money stock and a rising price level, each rising by precisely the same percentage amount, leaving the real money supply unchanged. That is, a *continuously rising money supply generates inflation and a gap between the market rate of interest and the real rate of interest*.

You have seen that result before in the basic model. Recall that the fundamental inflation equation says that the rate of inflation is equal to the growth rate of the money supply minus the growth rate of real income. In the analysis depicted in Figure 24.2, the growth rate of real income is zero (y^* is a constant) so that the rate of inflation equals the growth rate of the money supply.

(iii) What Happens When the Growth Rate of the Money Supply is Increased from its Initial Level to Some New Higher Level

What would happen to the equilibrium depicted in Figure 24.2 if there were a rise in the growth rate of the money supply? This is illustrated in Figure 24.3. It is evident that the increasing rate of money supply growth, other things being equal, would tend to make the *LM* curve move to the right. If the inflation rate stayed constant at π_0, that would lower the market rate of interest and the real rate of interest and generate an excess demand for goods. The excess demand for goods would put pressure on the inflation rate, and the rising inflation rate would offset the rightward movement of the *LM* curve and start the *LM* curve moving in the opposite direction. The only new equilibrium that is possible is the one that arises when the *LM* curve has shifted, not to the right at all, but to the left and by enough to have raised the market rate of interest above the real rate of interest by the amount of the new, higher rate of money growth and rate of inflation. By the time the economy settles down on the *LM* curve labelled LM_1 $(r_{m_1}, (M/P)_1)$, such a situation will have arisen. In that situation the *real interest rate is unaffected*, the output level is unaffected, but the market rate of interest is higher, the inflation rate is higher, and the money supply growth rate is *higher all by the same amount as each other*.

How does the economy get from the curve LM_0 to LM_1? The answer must be that the real money supply has fallen between those two situations. How could that have happened? The answer to that lies in the proposition that you have also met before in the basic model, namely, the *overshooting proposition*. As the economy moves from a low inflation rate to a high inflation rate, the price level must overshoot the rate of inflation in the process. It necessarily has to do this in the Keynesian model for exactly the same reasons as discussed in the basic model. You may find it useful to

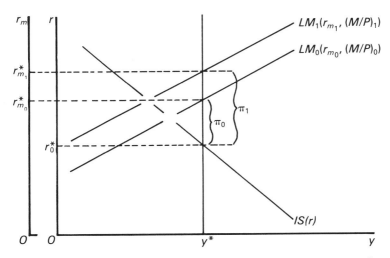

Figure 24.3 *The Effect of a Rise in the Growth Rate of the Money Supply*

The initial equilibrium (subscripted 0) is disturbed by making the money supply grow at a faster rate. This produces a faster rate of inflation which initially overshoots the growth rate of the money supply to lower real balances (shifting the *LM* curve to the left). The new equilibrium is subscripted 1. The result is exactly the same as that in the basic model.

refresh your memory and understanding of why that occurred in the earlier discussion and then satisfy yourself that it applies in this case.

You now have a much richer understanding of the Keynesian theory of aggregate demand. That theory simplifies when the price level is fixed and output is less than full-employment output and becomes a theory of the determination of output and employment. At full employment the Keynesian theory of aggregate demand becomes a theory of the price level. The analysis is slightly more complicated because a distinction has to be made between the market rate of interest, upon which the demand for money depends, and the real rate of interest, upon which the demand for investment depends. Therefore, the equilibrium at full employment is not determined by the intersection of *IS* and *LM* curves, but determined at a point at which there is a vertical gap between the *IS* and *LM* curves that measures the rate of inflation.

You are now in a position to go on to see how the neoclassical theory of price adjustment operates and how it smooths the transition between the two states of the Keynesian model, of which you have now developed a thorough understanding.

C. The Neoclassical Theory of Price Adjustment

The neoclassical theory of price adjustment consists of two propositions.[2] The first proposition is that *when demand is greater than supply, prices rise*. (The equivalent proposition is that when supply is greater than demand, prices fall.) The second proposition of the neoclassical theory of *price adjustment* is that the adjustment process is *asymmetrical*. A given percentage amount of excess demand will produce a bigger price rise than the price fall that would be generated by the same percentage of excess supply. As an example, suppose that a one per cent excess demand produced a five per cent rise in prices. Then a one per cent excess supply would produce something less than a five per cent fall in prices, perhaps, say, a 2 per cent fall in prices.

These two propositions can be summarised in a simple diagram such as Figure 24.4. The vertical axis measures the rate of inflation (the percentage change in prices), π, and the horizontal axis measures excess demand, $y^d - y^s$. The curve which slopes upwards, and increasingly so, illustrates the two propositions. The first proposition is about the slope of the curve — the curve slopes upwards; the second proposition is about its curvature — it slopes upwards at an increasing rate.

Often, the neoclassical theory of price adjustment is applied specifically to the labour market and to wage adjustment. Excess demand is thought of as being related to the unemployment rate, so that the neoclassical theory of wage adjustment —

---

2. The neoclassical theory of price adjustment, as a macroeconomic proposition, was introduced by A.W. Phillips in, The relation between unemployment and the rate of change of money wages in the United Kingdom, 1861–1957, *Economica*, New Series, Vol. 25, November 1958, pp. 283–99. The price adjustment function is often referred to simply as the Phillips curve.

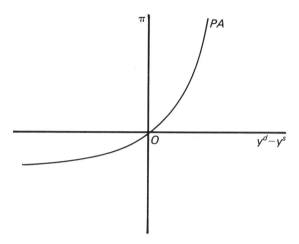

Figure 24.4 *The Neoclassical Theory of Price Adjustment*
Two propositions are embodied in the neoclassical theory of price adjustment: prices rise
when there is excess demand ($y^d > y^s$) and fall when there is excess supply ($y^d < y^s$); prices rise
faster for a given percentage of excess demand than they fall for an equivalent percentage of
excess supply.

---

usually called the Phillips curve — says that the rate of change of money wages will
vary inversely with the unemployment rate. Figure 24.5 illustrates how the Phillips
curve might be derived. Frame (a) shows the same thing as Figure 24.4, but looked at
through a mirror, that is simply the mirror projection of Figure 24.4. The horizontal
axis measures excess supply rather than excess demand. Frame (b) plots the rate of
inflation on the vertical axis and the unemployment rate on the horizontal axis. It
seems reasonable to suppose that there is some unemployment rate (often called the
natural rate of unemployment) which would be associated with a zero excess demand
for goods and services. If there is an excess demand for goods and services, then
unemployment will fall below the natural level u^*, and if there is an excess supply of
goods and services, unemployment will rise above u^*. The Phillips curve can be
viewed as being of a similar shape to the price adjustment curve and passing through,
for its origin, the point u^*. When unemployment is u^*, there is no excess demand for
labour and no pressure for wages and prices to rise. If unemployment is below that
level, there is a positive excess demand for labour, and wages and prices rise. If
unemployment exceeds u^*, there is an excess supply of labour, and wages and prices
fall.

You should be clear that these neoclassical propositions about price and wage
adjustment are different from Keynes's theory. Keynes assumed that wages and
prices would not move downwards at all and that they would move upwards
instantaneously to clear any excess demand. What the neoclassical theory of price
adjustment does is to weaken that proposition. It says that *wages and prices will fall,
but only slowly, and they will rise faster than they will fall, but not at an infinitely fast
rate.*

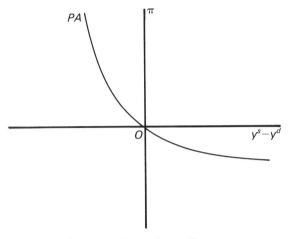

(a) *Neoclassical Price Adjustment*

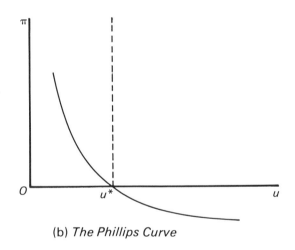

(b) *The Phillips Curve*

Figure 24.5 *The Phillips Curve Version of the Neoclassical Theory of Price Adjustment*

Frame (a) is the same as Figure 24.4, but in mirror image. The horizontal axis of Frame (a) measures the excess supply of goods. If unemployment and excess supply move together, the neoclassical theory of price adjustment in Frame (a) implies the Phillips curve, Frame (b).

D. Price Level Expectations and the 'Natural Rate' Hypothesis

The neoclassical theory of wage and price adjustment set out in the previous section became widely accepted as a useful description of the processes at work in the real world in the late 1950s and early 1960s.

In the middle of that decade, however, two independent, but closely related contributions, one by Milton Friedman of the University of Chicago and the other by Edmund Phelps of Columbia University, pointed out that there was a logical flaw in the proposed price adjustment theory.[3] The flaw arose from a failure on the part of the theory to capture the possibility that prices could change, provided that everyone correctly anticipated that they should change because of changing demand conditions, without the necessity of there being an interim period of excess demand or excess supply. The role of expectations is perhaps most easily understood by telling the story in the way that Edmund Phelps told it. Phelps began with the notion that firms and workers determining prices and wages would want to have their prices (or wages) set at a level that was compatible with an equilibrium in the market in which they were trading. Neoclassical economic theory tells us that the relevant prices for achieving equilibria are relative prices, not absolute prices. (Recall from Chapter 9 that it is the real wage that determines the demand for and supply of labour. The real wage is, of course, a relative price — the price of labour relative to goods — and not an absolute price. Similarly, the standard microeconomic analysis of the consumer and producer predict that demands and supplies will depend upon the price of the good in question relative to the prices of all other goods.) It follows from this that the amount by which an individual firm or union would want to change the price of its output or the price of its labour would, in general, be equal to the rate at which it was expecting prices and wages, on the average, to be changing. It would not always be the case, however, that a desired price change would equal the expected rate at which prices were changing elsewhere. If an individual sector of the economy viewed itself as being in a boom state and likely to experience some excess demand, then that sector would seek to raise its price (or wage) by more than it was expecting prices and wages, on the average, to rise. If an individual sector of the economy thought it was going into a depression phase, with a shortage of demand for its output or labour, then it would rationally seek to raise its price (or wages) by less than it was expecting wages and prices to rise, on the average. What this amounts to, at the individual sector or firm level, is a proposition that *the change in prices* (or *wages*) *will equal the expected average change in prices* (or *wages*) *adjusted for an amount that is positive if there is excess demand,* and *negative if there is excess supply.*

If now we consider the *aggregate* movements in prices (or wages) that would result from these individual wage and price adjustment decisions, the average change in prices (or wages) — inflation — would equal the expected change in prices (or wages) — the expected rate of inflation — plus an amount representing the contribution of excess aggregate demand.

Viewed in this way, the original Phillips curve version of the neoclassical theory of price adjustment can be regarded as having confused relative and absolute price adjustments. What the Phelps and Friedman propositions amount to is a statement that the rate of change of the relative price in question will be a function of excess demand. This means that the *rate of change of the nominal price will change one-for-one with the expected rate of inflation.* This can be illustrated in a diagram such as

---

3. Milton Friedman, The role of monetary policy, *American Economic Review*, Vol. 58, March 1968, pp. 1–17; and Edmund S. Phelps, Money wage dynamics and labor market equilibrium, *Journal of Political Economy*, Vol. 76, July/August 1968, pp. 687–711. These two papers represent the watershed between the neoclassical and new macroeconomics.

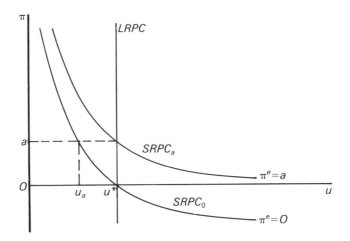

Figure 24.6 *The Expectations-Augmented Phillips Curve*

The neoclassical theory of price adjustment is a theory of *relative* price change. When translated into a theory of movements of the *absolute* price level, it has to be augmented. There is a short-run Phillips curve *SRPC* for every expected rate of inflation. $SRPC_0$ refers to a zero expected rate of inflation and $SRPC_a$ refers to an expected rate of inflation of a. The long-run Phillips curve is vertical.

Figure 24.6. The lower curve in Figure 24.6 is exactly the same as the curve shown in Figure 24.5. It is a Phillips curve. However, it is a Phillips curve drawn for an expected rate of inflation equal to zero. If, on the average, no inflation is expected, then when there is an unemployment rate of u^* (and therefore zero excess demand for labour), there will actually be no inflation. If, however, the unemployment rate was as low as u_a so that there was a large amount of excess demand, but if no inflation is expected, then inflation will in fact occur and at the rate of a.

The Phelps–Friedman story now asks us to suppose that this rate of inflation a continues for a long period of time and becomes fully anticipated. What will happen to the price adjustment process? The answer is that the more people come to expect the rate of inflation to be a, the more will they build that expectation into their own price adjustments. If it became fully expected that prices would rise at the rate a, then the Phillips curve would shift upwards by the whole amount a so that the new Phillips curve, drawn for an expected rate of inflation equal to a, is directly above the point u^* at the inflation rate a. The two Phillips curves shown in Figure 24.6 are known as short-run Phillips curves and are labelled *SRPC* to remind you of that. The vertical line at u^* is sometimes called the long-run Phillips curve (*LRPC*). It embodies the so-called 'Natural rate' hypothesis. The 'natural rate' hypothesis is nothing other than the proposition that *if inflation is fully anticipated, unemployment is equal to its 'natural rate'*. Only when the rate of inflation is different from the expected rate will the unemployment rate be different from its natural rate.

In the neoclassical synthesis, the expected rate of inflation is assumed to be a slowly evolving variable and one which imparts a great deal of inertia to the actual rate of inflation. Although it is a slight exaggeration, it is not a serious distortion to assert that *the expected rate of inflation is exogenous in the neoclassical synthesis.*[4] It plays a very similar role to the exogenous money wage assumption of the narrower Keynesian model. This is not to say that the expected rate of inflation does not change. Rather, it is viewed as a variable which changes as a result of forces which are determined independently of the variables determined within the neoclassical synthesis.

You are now in a position to understand how the neoclassical synthesis explains the business cycle.

E. The Neoclassical Explanation of the Business Cycle

The business cycle, the autocorrelation of output, and the procyclical co-movements of employment, inflation, and interest rates are all explained, in qualitative terms at least, by the neoclassical synthesis. To see this, we will take you through two exercises that disturb an economy which is initially at rest at full employment with no inflation. In one case a slump will be generated, and in the other case, a boom. These exercises are designed to show you the mechanisms that are at work in the process. The actual cycle is generated by swings to and fro in either the *IS* curve or the *LM* curve or both. The illustration that we shall give here visualises the stimulus coming from a shifting *IS* curve.

(i) From Full-Employment Equilibrium to Slump and Back

Figure 24.7 is used to illustrate the mechanisms at work as the economy is disturbed from a full-employment equilibrium, put into a recession, and then allowed to adjust gradually back to a new full-employment equilibrium. Frame (a) contains the *IS–LM* analysis. Frame (b) contains the aggregate demand and supply analysis and Frame (c) contains the neoclassical price adjustment process (with a zero expected rate of inflation throughout the analysis).

The curves IS^*, LM^* and AD^* represent the initial equilibrium curves for the economy. The interest rate is therefore initially r^* and the income level y^* and the price level P^*. Now let the economy be disturbed by a shock in the form of a drop in either government spending or investment demand that shifts the *IS* curve from IS^* to IS_0. The impact effect of that is to lower the rate of interest from r^* to r_0 and to lower income from y^* to y_0. That is the new *IS–LM* equilibrium. Equivalently, the impact effect can be shown in Frame (b) as the shift in the aggregate demand curve from AD^* to AD_0 with the income level being y_0, read off as the point on the new aggregate demand curve AD_0 at the momentarily constant price level P^*. The economy is now in a slump condition.

---

4. Often the so-called 'adaptive expectations' hypothesis is employed in neoclassical models. That hypothesis says that expectations of inflation change by some fraction of the most recent error in forecasting inflation. For a rather thorough, though already dated, discussion of expectations, see David Laidler and Michael Parkin, Inflation: a survey, *Economic Journal*, Vol. 85, No. 340, December 1975, pp. 741–809.

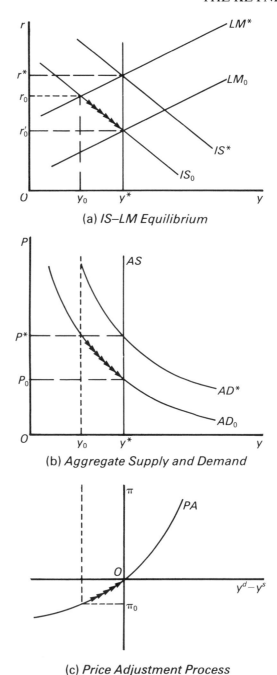

(a) *IS–LM Equilibrium*

(b) *Aggregate Supply and Demand*

(c) *Price Adjustment Process*

Figure 24.7 *From Neutral to Slump and Back in the Neoclassical Model*

An initial equilibrium, (r^*, y^*, P^*) is disturbed by a leftward shift in the IS curve from IS^* to IS_0. Equivalently, the aggregate demand curve shifts from AD^* to AD_0. The impact is for there to be a fall in income and the interest rate (r_0, y_0) and for prices to start to fall at the rate π_0. As prices fall, the LM curve shifts to the right, and the economy follows the arrowed track down the IS curve, down the AD curve, and up the price adjustment curve back to full-employment output, but with a lower price level and interest rate (P_0, r_0).

If we were analysing the simple Keynesian model of the previous chapters, that would be the end of the story. The economy would stay there until something else happened to aggregate demand. In the neoclassical synthesis, however, that is not the end of the story. Frame (c) shows why. With output less than y^*, there is excess supply, and prices will begin to fall. They will not fall by much, but they will begin to fall — π_0 in the figure. As prices fall, so the quantity of real money balances in the economy begins to rise, and the LM curve begins to shift rightwards. As that happens, it intersects the IS curve at lower and lower rates of interest and at higher and higher levels of real income. The arrows on the IS curve indicate the adjustment path the economy takes with a falling interest rate and a rising income level. The same path is illustrated in Frame (b) of the diagram. As the price level falls, in effect, the economy is travelling down its new aggregate demand curve. Again, the arrows show that adjustment process. As the output level rises and approaches full employment, the rate at which prices are falling slackens off. That is illustrated in Frame (c), showing that the economy travels up the price adjustment curve. A new equilibrium will eventually be reached at full employment with a real interest rate of r_0', with a price level of P_0, and with prices constant again.

What you have just analysed is one-half of a business cycle, the half that takes the economy from a neutral position into a slump and back again to a neutral position. Now consider the other half of the cycle.

(ii) From Full-Employment Equilibrium to Boom and Back

Figure 24.8 will illustrate the analysis. The initial set-up is exactly the same as that in Figure 24.7. The interest rate is r^*, income is y^*, the price level is P^*, and the inflation rate is zero.

Now let there be a shock to the IS curve as a result of a rise in government spending or a boom in investment demand that shifts the IS curve to IS_1. The impact of this shift in the IS curve is for it to intersect the LM curve at the higher interest rate r_1 and the income level y_1. The same effects can be illustrated in Frame (b). There, the aggregate demand curve is shown to have shifted from AD^* to AD_1, and the economy is at a point a on that aggregate demand curve. Frame (c) illustrates what is happening to the inflation rate at this moment of shock. With an excess demand equivalent to $y_1 - y^*$, prices are rising at a rate π_1. The economy is in a boom.

In the Keynesian analysis, the economy could never be observed in this position. What would happen is that prices would rise immediately and instantly choke off the excess demand. That is, the price level P_1 and the interest rate r_1' would be the instantaneous end of the story.

In the neoclassical synthesis, that is the end of the story, but not an end that is arrived at instantaneously. The neoclassical view is that it takes time for the economy to arrive at that new full-employment equilibrium with a higher price level. What happens is that the economy gradually adjusts. The inflation rate gradually slows, but the price level rises from P^* to P_1, the output level gradually falls from y_1 back to y^*, and the interest rate gradually rises from r_1 to r_1'. The economy has gone from a neutral position into a boom and back again to a neutral position, half a business cycle.

Now, a *complete cycle would involve a swing in investment or government spending* so that the IS curve would swing from IS_0 to IS^* (Figure 24.7) and IS^* to IS_1 (Figure

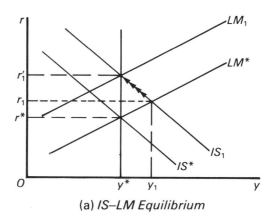

(a) *IS–LM Equilibrium*

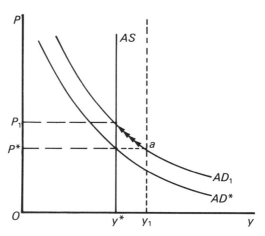

(b) *Aggregate Supply and Demand*

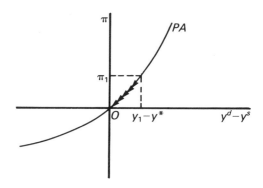

(c) *Price Adjustment Process*

Figure 24.8 *From Neutral to Boom and Back in the Neoclassical Model*

An initial equilibrium (r^*, y^*, P^*) is disturbed by a rightward shift in the IS curve, from IS^* to IS_1. Equivalently, the aggregate demand curve shifts from AD^* to AD_1. The impact is for there to be a rise in income and the interest rate (r_1, y_1) and for prices to start to rise at the rate π_1. As prices rise, the LM curve shifts leftwards, the economy moves up the IS curve and up the AD curve and back down the price adjustment curve to a stable price full-employment equilibrium in which the price level has increased to P_1 and the interest rate to r'_1.

24.8) and back again. If you visualise the *IS* curve systematically swinging to and fro between the limits IS_1 and IS_0, you can easily visualise the generation of an ongoing cycle in output and inflation and the rate of interest.

If, superimposed upon such a cycle, the money supply is growing at a positive constant rate, then superimposed upon the process described here will be an ongoing, positive average rate of inflation. All the diagrams would need modification to incorporate the considerations discussed in Section B of this chapter. There is nothing new, in principle, however, to understand in that case.

F. Policy Implications of the Neoclassical Synthesis

The policy implications of the neoclassical synthesis are clear. *If inflation and unemployment are to be avoided, swings in aggregate demand are to be avoided.* Such swings can, in principle, be avoided by making government spending, taxes, and the money supply move in such a way that whatever is happening to investment demand and perhaps to consumption demand is offset by equivalent changes in the government policy instruments so that aggregate demand remains steady. By preventing aggregate demand from moving, the cyclical forces described in the previous section can themselves be prevented. There is much more to the modern policy debate than is contained in this brief paragraph, but that must await the development of the new macroeconomics developed in Part V of this book.

SUMMARY

A. Definition of the Neoclassical Synthesis

The term neoclassical synthesis describes a body of macroeconomic analysis designed to explain the determination of output, prices, employment, and interest rates and to account for the cyclical fluctuations in those variables. It is an amalgamation of the basic model, the Keynesian model, and a gradual price and wage adjustment hypothesis.

B. Keynesian Theory at Full Employment

The Keynesian theory of aggregate demand, which determines output at less than full employment, becomes a theory of the price level at full employment. It yields all the same predictions as those generated by the basic model. A once-and-for-all rise in the money stock raises the price level proportionately. A continuing rise in the money stock generates an inflation rate that is equal to the growth rate of the money stock (minus the growth rate of output). A rise in the growth rate of the money supply produces a rise in the inflation rate, but the inflation rate overshoots the money supply growth rate en route to the new equilibrium.

C. The Neoclassical Theory of Price Adjustment

The neoclassical theory of price adjustment asserts that prices rise when there is excess demand and fall when there is excess supply. The adjustment process is asymmetrical. A one per cent excess demand would produce a faster price rise than the price fall that would be generated by a one per cent excess supply.

D. Price Level Expectations and the 'Natural Rate' Hypothesis

Properly understood, the neoclassical theory of price adjustment is a theory of relative price adjustment. Nominal price adjustment will therefore be greater at each and every level of excess demand, one-for-one as the expected inflation rate rises. The expected rate of inflation is a slowly evolving variable, which may be treated as exogenous in the neoclassical analysis.

E. The Neoclassical Explanation of the Business Cycle

The neoclassical synthesis explains the business cycle as the working out of the effects of swings in the aggregate demand curve generated either by shifts in the *IS* curve or shifts in the *LM* curve. These shifts themselves arise from changing investment demand, changes in government spending and taxes, and changes in the money supply.

F. Policy Implications of the Neoclassical Synthesis

The neoclassical synthesis implies that by moving government spending, taxes, and the money supply in a manner that offsets the changes in aggregate demand arising from private behaviour, the aggregate demand curve can be stabilised, and as a result, so too can the level of output, prices, and interest rates.

Review Questions

1. What is the neoclassical synthesis?

2. What distinguishes the neoclassical synthesis from the Keynesian model?

3. What happens, according to the Keynesian model, if at full employment there is:
    (i) a rise in government expenditure
    (ii) a once-and-for-all rise in the money supply
    (iii) a rise in the growth rate of the money supply
    (iv) a rise in both the excess of government spending over taxes and in the growth rate of the money supply?

4. What is the neoclassical theory of price adjustment?

5. Why do actual price adjustments depend, one-for-one, on expected price adjustments?

6. Trace the effects in the neoclassical model of the following shocks (assume the economy to be at full employment initially):
    (i) a once-and-for-all rise in investment demand
    (ii) a once-and-for-all rise in the money supply
    (iii) a cycle in investment demand
    (iv) a cycle in the money supply.

25

The United Kingdom's Recent Economic History: How Well is it Explained by the Neoclassical Synthesis?

The neoclassical synthesis is the post-Keynesian orthodoxy which has reigned supreme in macroeconomics for more than twenty-five years. It has defined the rules that have governed the research program over that period. Questions have been posed and answered in terms of the concepts of the *IS–LM* framework for analysing aggregate demand and of the expectations-augmented Phillips curve (or neoclassical price adjustment hypothesis) for analysing aggregate supply. Examples of such questions are: How steep are the *IS* and *LM* curves? Is the long-run Phillips curve vertical? How much inflation reduction can be obtained for a given per cent of excess supply (or unemployment?) What is the magnitude of the marginal propensity to consume? These are but examples of a long list of similar questions which have been posed and answered within the framework of analysis set out in Chapters 17 to 24.

More than this, the system has formed the basis for complete *econometric models*. These were pioneered in the inter-war years by the Dutch economist Jan Tinbergen. Developments in macroeconometric modelling in the post-war years have been highly innovative and have employed some of the best minds in the subject. Lawrence Klein, of the University of Pennsylvania, has been one of the leading architects of this movement. In the United Kingdom, the most comprehensive of such exercises have been the development of the London Business School Quarterly econometric model directed by R.J. Ball and Terry Burns (now Chief Economic Advisor to Her Majesty's Government); the Southampton econometric model of the United Kingdom initiated by Professor Ivor Pearce and others; the National Institute of Economic and Social Research model directed by David Worswick and models developed in the Treasury and the Bank of England.[1]

There are literally thousands of learned papers written and published on the topic of this chapter — the correspondence between the predictions of the neoclassical synthesis and the facts, and there is no way in which it is going to be possible to do justice to this large, and in many respects exemplary, scientific literature. It would not be sufficient arbitrarily to pull out examples from the literature, nor would it be possible to attempt a faithful and comprehensive summary of it.

What this chapter is going to do is to try to give you a general feel for what parts of the neoclassical synthesis are a success and, in the current state of knowledge, must stand as the best model available; and what parts are in some sense failing us. In pursuit of this objective, we shall seek to:

A. **know the main predictions of the neoclassical model;**
B. **know the facts which are explained by the neoclassical model;**
C. **know the facts which are not well explained by the neoclassical model;** and
D. **understand the main strengths and shortcomings of the neoclassical model.**

A. Main Predictions of the Neoclassical Model

Chapter 24 has already taken you through an analysis of how the neoclassical synthesis works by setting out the model and examining what happens when that model is subjected to various types of shocks. We are now going to expand that analysis somewhat in order to track out the time series predictions of the neoclassical model when subjected to three types of shocks. Those shocks are (i) a shift in the *IS* curve generated either by fiscal policy or by a shift in investment demand; (ii) a shift in the *LM* curve generated by a rise in the growth rate of the money supply; and (iii) a shift in the neoclassical price adjustment function generated by a temporary or permanent drop in the trend value of aggregate supply.

First, consider an *IS* curve shock. The analysis is going to be illustrated in Figure

---

1. G.A. Renton (ed.), *Modelling the Economy*, Heinemann Educational Books, 1975 and P. Ormerod (ed.), *Economic Modelling*, Heinemann Educational Books, 1979, are useful summary sources of these models and related work.

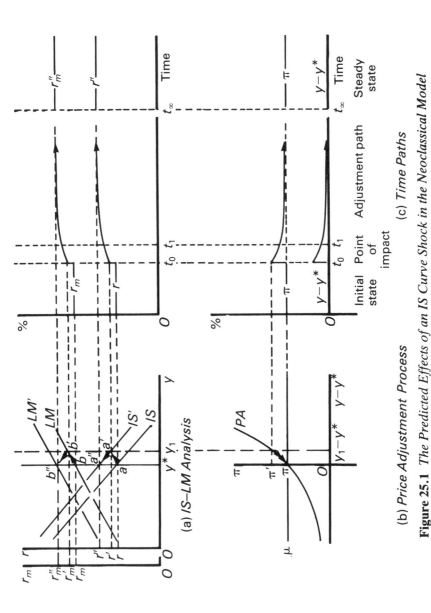

(a) *IS–LM Analysis*

(b) *Price Adjustment Process*

(c) *Time Paths*

Figure 25.1 *The Predicted Effects of an IS Curve Shock in the Neoclassical Model*

The economy starts out with an interest rate r, money interest rate r_m, and inflation rate π at full employment. At time t_0 it is disturbed with an IS curve shift to the right (to IS'). This immediately raises interest rates and the inflation rate and creates excess demand for goods. With inflation higher than the growth rate of the money supply, the LM curve starts to drift to the left, raising interest rates still further but choking off the excess demand and lowering the inflation rate. Eventually, the economy reaches a steady state with higher interest rates, the initial inflation rate, and full-employment output.

25.1, and it will be best to begin by familiarising yourself with how that figure works. First, notice that Frames (a) and (b) on the left-hand side are exactly the same diagram as Figure 24.7, with which you are already familiar. Frame (c), on the right, is going to track the evolution over time of the variables determined by the neoclassical model. Look at the labelling below those time graphs. We are going to be dealing with four distinct periods of time. The first, referred to as the *initial state,* is the period prior to the shock that we are going to administer to the economy. The second is a single point in time, labelled t_0 on the graph. That is the *point of impact* of the shock that we shall administer. The third block of time is the *adjustment path* of the economy. In general that will be an infinitely long path, and the time axis is broken to indicate that. Finally, beyond the point labelled t_∞, we shall be concerned with the *steady state* of the economy following the shock that we shall administer. Before we begin any analysis, you should be clear that these time intervals are constructions of the theory and do not refer to any specific units of calendar time. How long it would take to get from the point of impact to a position like t_1 on the adjustment path is an empirical matter on which the neoclassical theory is silent. Likewise, how long it would take in calendar time to reach the steady state is a matter on which the theory does not place restrictions. Nevertheless, it is important that you recall that the steady state predictions of the neoclassical model are identical to the steady state predictions of the basic model. If the neoclassical theory is to be of any interest, therefore, it must be that it is asserting that the steady state does not occur until a long period of time has elapsed. This is the view that will be taken of the neoclassical synthesis in this chapter. The neoclassical synthesis is concerned primarily with impact effects and early adjustment paths. In terms of the Figure 25.1 and the subsequent figures, that part of the adjustment path on which the neoclassical synthesis focuses will be taken to be the interval between t_0, the point of impact, and the point marked as t_1 along the adjustment path.

With these general introductory remarks, let us now consider the effects of an *IS* curve shock. Imagine that the economy is in an inflationary equilibrium on the *IS* and *LM* curves shown in Figure 25.1. The real rate of interest is r, the money rate of interest is r_m, the inflation rate is π, and output is equal to its full-employment level y^*. Imagine that the economy runs along on this path with a constant real and money rate of interest and with prices constantly rising at rate π. A constantly rising money supply at rate μ keeps the *LM* curve in a fixed position. Now imagine that at t_0 there is a rise in government spending or a cut in taxes or a rise in investment spending that shifts the *IS* curve from *IS* to *IS'*. What happens in this economy as a result of the impact of this shock? In answering this question we are going to suppose that the expected rate of inflation remains constant at the initial rate of inflation π and that the gap between the money rate of interest and the expected real rate of interest also remains constant at that same expected rate of inflation π. With that assumption we can work out the effects of the shift in the *IS* curve. The impact of the shift in the *IS* curve to *IS'* will be to raise interest rates, income, and inflation. To see this, first note that the gap between the *IS* and *LM* curves at the full-employment line (the distance ab) is the initial actual and expected rate of inflation, π. Hold that gap constant when the *IS* curve shifts. To do this, focus on the points $a'b'$ on the *IS* and *LM* curves. The line aa' is parallel to bb', so that $a'b'$ is equal to ab. At the position a' on *IS'* you can read off the impact expected real rate of interest as r', and at the position b' on the *LM* curve you can read off the impact money rate of interest as r'_m. The vertical gap between b' and a' represents the expected rate of inflation. Only at the level of income y_1 is the vertical gap between the LM and IS curves equal to that initial anticipated inflation rate. Point y_1 then, is the amount of demand at the point of impact. Excess demand becomes $y_1 - y^*$, read of on the horizontal axis of Frame (b), and π' is the impact inflation rate. At the point of impact, then, the two interest rates rise by the same amount, and the rate of inflation and the level of output both rise. *By assumption,* the expected rate of inflation remains constant.

This is not the end of the story. Since the price level is now rising at a faster rate than π and since, by assumption, we have not changed the growth rate of the money supply, it must be that the real money stock is falling. This must further mean that the LM curve is shifting to the left. As that happens, interest rates will rise still further, and the economy will slide back up the IS' curve and down the price adjustment curve. As this process moves on, consider first Frame (a). The money rate of interest will rise along the line from a' to a'' and the expected real rate of interest will rise from b' to b''. Secondly, look at Frame (b) and notice that inflation and excess demand will gradually fall along the price adjustment curve to the initial inflation rate and full-employment output level. This adjustment path is sketched in Frame (c), showing a gradual convergence to the steady state.

If the neoclassical model (as opposed to the basic model) is to be regarded as the relevant model for dealing with what happens in actual economies, it must be that the steady state effects are regarded as occurring only in the very distant future and the impact and early adjustment effects are the ones that are dominant and relevant. That being so, the main prediction of the neoclassical model is that the effect of a rightward shift in the IS curve is to raise interest rates, output, and inflation and to set up a process in which interest rates continue rising, while inflation and output embark on a path which will eventually, but gradually, return them to their initial equilibrium levels.

You can easily work out the effects of the reverse shock (a leftward shift of the IS curve) for yourself.

Next, consider the effects of a change in the growth rate of the money supply. This is a harder experiment to analyse because more steady state changes occur. Figure 25.2 will take you through this analysis. As before, there is an initial full-employment equilibrium, with the inflation rate π, real interest rate r, and money interest rate r_m, higher than r by the amount of the actual and expected rate of inflation π. The money supply is growing at the same rate as the inflation rate, holding the LM curve steady in the position marked LM.

Suppose that at time t_0, the point of impact, the money supply growth rate is increased from μ to μ'. This is marked on the time series graph (Frame (c)) as a step increase from μ to μ' and also shown as a horizontal line in the price adjustment diagram (Frame (b)).

Before we begin to try to work out what happens to the economy when it is administered this shock, let us do something that we are fairly familiar with; that is, let us look at the steady state. It is always a good idea to try to find out where you are going to wind up in an analysis of this kind before you embark upon the adjustment path. That will help to keep directions clear en route. You already know from your analysis in the previous chapter and, indeed, from the analysis of the basic model (for they are both the same in terms of their steady state effects) that a rise in the growth rate of the money supply will lead to a higher inflation rate and a higher money rate of

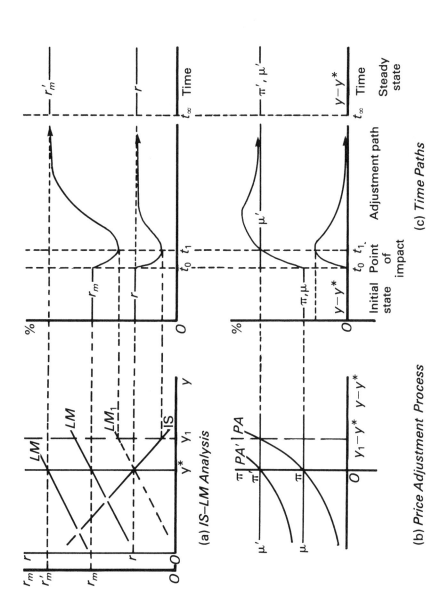

(a) *IS–LM Analysis*

(b) *Price Adjustment Process*

(c) *Time Paths*

Figure 25.2 *The Predicted Effects of a Rise in the Money Supply Growth Rate in the Neoclassical Model*

An initial equilibrium exactly the same as that of Figure 25.1 is disturbed by doubling the growth rate of the money supply from μ to μ'. There is no impact effect of this. All the variables gradually adjust from their initial values, interest rates initially falling and inflation rates and output initially rising. Eventually, interest rates turn upwards, and, the inflation rate, having overshot the money supply growth rate, approach their new steady state values. Output returns to a steady state full-employment level.

interest, but to an unchanged real rate of interest. The economy will also be at full
employment again when it reaches the steady state. The final part of the time series
(Frame (c)) shows the economy in its new steady state. The LM curve, LM' in Frame
(a) is also the new steady state LM curve. Recall that it gets to the left of the initial
LM curve because the inflation rate overshoots the money supply growth rate in the
adjustment process, thereby lowering real money balances. Also, the price
adjustment curve PA' is the position in which that curve will be in the new steady
state when the expected rate of inflation is π' (which equals μ').

Now let us come to the harder task of working out the sort of path that will take us
from the initial equilibrium to the new one. What is the path that the neoclassical
model predicts for the adjustment? The answer, perhaps fairly surprisingly, is that
there is no specific prediction contained in the neoclassical model. Why is that? The
key to understanding why the neoclassical model does not predict any specific time
path in the adjustment process is that it does not have a specific theory about how the
expected rate of inflation changes, and therefore, how the PA curve shifts. If the
expected rate of inflation was to remain constant at π' forever, regardless of the
actual growth rate of the money supply and actual rate of inflation, then the economy
would forever experience a state of excess demand, and expectations would be
forever wrong. Although it does not say how expectations change, the neoclassical
model does insist that, on the average, in the long run, expectations are correct. It
therefore predicts that the expected inflation rate will rise from π to π' *at some stage
or other*. What it is silent on is precisely how that change will occur.

To see why this is important, consider what would happen if the expected rate of
inflation increased from π to π' at the moment of t_0, the point of impact of the change
in the growth rate of the money supply. In that event, the PA curve would
immediately shift up to PA' and there would be a once-and-for-all jump in the price
level. The real money balances would fall and the LM curve would shift to LM', the
money interest rate would rise instantly to its steady state value, and the inflation rate
would immediately thereafter be on the steady state path. There would, in effect, be
a spike in the inflation rate at the moment of impact, and thereafter the inflation rate
would be at its steady state level. There would be no excess demand at any stage in
this process. The economy would stay at full employment all the time. This is nothing
other than the prediction of the basic model analysed in Chapter 13.

At the alternative extreme, suppose that the expected rate of inflation did not
change from π for a very long period of time. While the expected inflation rate
remainded constant, the path of adjustment of the economy would look like the path
from t_0 to t_1 in Frame (c). That is, at the moment of impact, when the money supply
growth rate increased, the LM curve would start to move to the right. It would do this
because the money supply growth rate at that moment would be higher than the
inflation rate. So long as the LM curve is moving to the right, the inflation rate is
rising and real income is also rising. There will come a point at which the LM curve
will have shifted so far to the right, having generated so much excess demand, that
the inflation rate will be equal to the growth rate of the money supply. This happens
in the picture when the LM curve gets to the dashed curve, LM_1, with an income
level, y_1. By construction, that happens on the time diagram (Frame (c)) at time t_1. If
the expected rate of inflation never changed, the situation in which the economy
finds itself at time t_1 would never change. It is a point of rest, given a false expected
rate of inflation.

To work out the adjustment path of the economy it is necessary to specify a path of adjustment for inflation expectations. Since the neoclassical theory is silent on that matter, there is nothing that we can do to provide a detailed picture of the adjustment path. All we know is that the theory predicts that eventually the expected inflation rate will equal the actual rate. That being so, the theory does predict that the steady state, with which you are already familiar, will indeed be arrived at by some means or other. The adjustment path sketched out in Frame (c) is the simplest conceivable path which the economy could follow to its steady state. Many other types of paths are possible, including some which cycle around before settling down at the steady state. The path shown is one which would arise if the expected rate of inflation gradually increased from π to π', so that the PA curve gradually drifted upwards to PA'.

Again, recall that the neoclassical model claims to be more useful than the basic model in understanding what is going on in the actual world. It must be, therefore, that the impact and early adjustment path phase is to be regarded as the relevant set of predictions of this model. To summarise those, a rise in the growth rate of the money supply will at first have the effect of gradually lowering interest rates, raising output, and raising the inflation rate. All of these effects will occur gradually rather than suddenly. Eventually, the money rate of interest will rise above its initial level, but this will not happen in the early phase of the adjustment process.

Finally, let us analyse a shock which many proponents of the neoclassical theory believe to have been an important shock in the early 1970s, that of a temporary (or permanent) drop in aggregate supply. Figure 25.3 will illustrate the analysis in this case. As before, the economy is in full-employment equilibrium with an inflation rate π up to time t_0. The IS and LM curves illustrate this equilibrium, as does the price adjustment relation in Frames (a) and (b) of Figure 25.3. At time t_0, the shock which the economy receives is a drop in aggregate supply. Analytically, we can represent this by a leftward shift of the price adjustment curve. In effect, shifting the price adjustment curve to the left implies that at each level of demand there will now be more excess demand and, therefore, given the price adjustment proposition of the neoclassical model, more inflation.

What are the impacts of this shift in the price adjustment relation? By hypothesis the IS or LM curves do not shift. The impact effect must therefore simply be to raise inflation to the point at which the price adjustment curve cuts the zero excess demand line. This is shown as the jump in the inflation rate from π to π' in Frame (b) and Frame (c). Is this the end of the story? The answer is clearly no. If the initial state was an equilibrium, then the money supply growth rate must have been compatible with the inflation rate π. At an inflation rate π', the money supply growth rate is less than the inflation rate, so real money balances are falling and the LM curve is shifting to the left. As the LM curve shifts to the left, so real and money interest rates rise (shown in Frame (c)) and the economy moves into an excess supply situation. That is, the economy starts to travel down the price adjustment curve PA' with falling inflation and falling output. If the supply shock is a permanent one, so that the price adjustment curve is going to be at PA' forever, then by the time the economy reaches the position t_1 it is back at a full equilibrium. Output is y_1, the inflation rate is back at π, and interest rates are higher than initially, but necessarily so, because the full-employment aggregate supply is lower. If, on the other hand, the supply shock is temporary so that the price adjustment curve gradually moves back to PA, then the

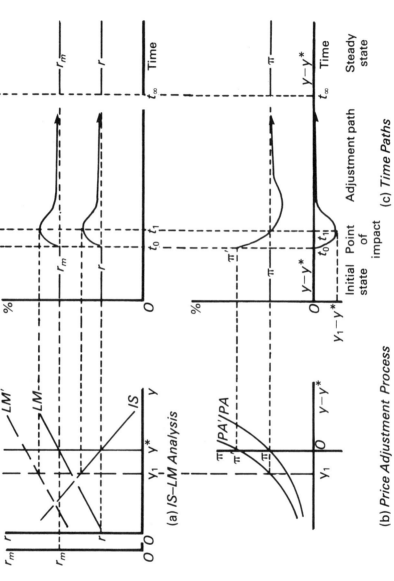

(a) *IS–LM Analysis*

(b) *Price Adjustment Process*

(c) *Time Paths*

Figure 25.3 *The Predicted Effects of a Temporary Fall in Aggregate Supply in the Neoclassical Model*

The same initial equilibrium is disturbed by a temporary drop in aggregate supply. This is depicted as a leftward shift of the price adjustment curve. The impact effect of this is to raise the inflation rate from π to π'. With inflation bigger than money supply growth, real balances fall and the LM curve drifts to the left. This lowers the level of demand (output falls below trend), the inflation rate falls, and interest rates begin to rise. If the shock is temporary so that the price adjustment curve drifts back from PA' to PA, then the inflation rate will fall and undershoot its initial value, eventually returning to its original steady state. All the other variables also will return to their economy will follow an adjustment path similar to that traced out in Frame (c), eventually returning to the initial equilibrium.

Again, since the emphasis in the neoclassical model is on impact effects and early phases of the adjustment path, the presumed relevant predictions of the model concerning the effects of a supply shock are that, if aggregate supply is reduced, there will be an impact rise in the inflation rate, a gradual rise in interest rates, and a gradual depression of output below trend. In the early phases of the adjustment process, interest rates will continue to drift upwards, the inflation rate will moderate, but output performance will deteriorate.

Let us now turn to the task of examining some recent British facts and the extent to which they conform with the predictions of the neoclassical model set out above.

B. The Facts Explained by the Neoclassical Model

The facts about the evolution of the three directly observable variables whose paths we have just analysed, covering the period from 1970 to 1980 in the United Kingdom, are set out in Frame (c) of Figure 25.4. This figure has been arranged to be the actually observed counterpart of the analytical exercises that we have just been conducting. As in the previous three figures, Frame (a) of Figure 25.4 shows the interest rate and output points in *IS–LM* space. It contains the facts about nominal interest rates and deviations of output from full employment. According to the neoclassical theory, all the points in Frame (a) are points on the *LM* curve. We cannot see the points on the *IS* curve because, although we can calculate the actual, *ex post* real rate of interest, we cannot calculate the *expected* real rate of interest that will have determined people's expenditure plans. Frame (b) of Figure 25.4 shows the facts about inflation plotted against excess demand. According to the neoclassical theory, these are all points on the price adjustment curve.

This section is going to focus on those aspects of the facts which the neoclassical model seems to be well capable of explaining. Those facts are the ones contained in Frame (a) of Figure 25.4 — the relationship between the rate of interest and real income. This could be put more directly as saying that the neoclassical model is fairly good at explaining income and interest rates, *given* the behaviour of *the price level* (and the inflation rate). Further, and even more simply, it turns out that we can make reasonable sense of the pattern of interest rate and income movements simply by examining shifts in the *LM* curve. Recall that all the points in Frame (a) are points on the *LM* curve. Of course, they are not on the *same LM* curve. The presumption must be that the *LM* curve shifted each year over the eleven years under review. In order to assess how the curve moved, it is necessary to look at movements in the real money supply. Table 25.1 sets out the relevant calculations. It itemises the monetary base growth, the growth rate of the GDP Deflator and the difference between these two variables.

The way to read this table is as follows. The final column tells us the *direction* of shift of the *LM* curve. A (+) means it moved to the right (real balances were increasing), and a (−) means it moved to the left (real balances were decreasing).

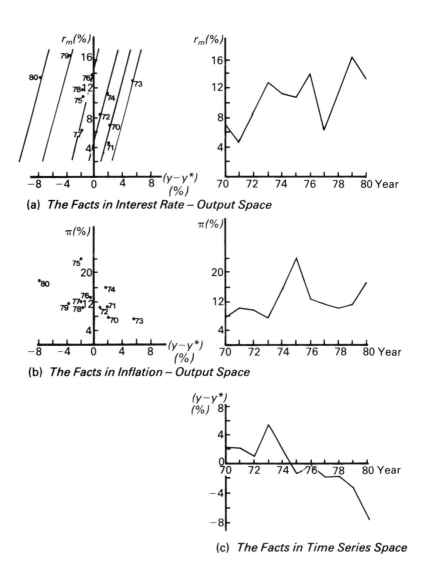

(a) *The Facts in Interest Rate – Output Space*

(b) *The Facts in Inflation – Output Space*

(c) *The Facts in Time Series Space*

Figure 25.4 *The Facts 1970–1980*

The relationship between the interest rate and real income (Frame (a)) is well described by the notion that the *LM* curve shifted left in 1971–72, shifted strongly to the right in 1973 and then shifted massively to the left through to 1980. The relationship between inflation and excess demand (Frame (b)) is not well explained by the neoclassical theory of price adjustment.

Table 25.1 *LM* Curve Shifts (per cent per annum)

Year	Money Growth	Inflation of GDP Deflator	Indicator of Direction and Size of LM Curve Shift
1971	8.3	10.2	− 1.9
1972	5.6	9.9	−4.3
1973	11.9	7.7	4.2
1974	11.4	15.8	−4.4
1975	14.2	23.9	−9.7
1976	12.2	13.1	−0.9
1977	10.9	11.5	−0.6
1978	15.0	10.6	0.8
1979	13.3	11.7	1.6
1980	7.9	17.4	−9.5

Sources and Methods:
> Money growth is the growth in monetary base calculated as the percentage change in the annual average monetary base, *Bank of England Quarterly Bulletin,* Vol. 21, No. 1, March 1980, p. 62. Inflation is from the Appendix to Chapter 2.

The magnitude of the number entered in the third column of the table indicates the magnitude of the shift in the *LM* curve. It does not, however, tell us in any useful units the size of the shift. (To know that you would have to know the slope of the demand for money function with respect to both income and the rate of interest.) According to these figures the *LM* curve shifted to the left between 1970 and 1972 , moved to the right again in 1973 but then in 1974 returned to more or less its 1972 position. In 1975 it moved substantially to the left, but then stayed more or less stationary until 1980, when it moved further to the left again. These shifts are illustrated in Frame (a) of Figure 25.4. The only anomalies occur in 1979 when, according to the figures in Table 25.1, the *LM* curve does not move much but, according to the interest rate and income movements in Frame (a), the *LM* curve must have shifted somewhat to the left and second, the small leftward shift in 1971 which is not apparent in the diagram though indicated by the relative magnitudes of money growth and inflation in the table.

The *LM* curve shown in Frame (a) is intended to be illustrative only and, whilst based on reasonable estimates of its likely slope, is not derived from any rigorous statistical estimation process. Its movements nevertheless do give a feel for what has been happening in the monetary sector of the United Kingdom over the decade of the 1970s. In the early part of the decade, money growth began to increase and initially, at a faster pace than the inflation. As a result, the *LM* curve started to move to the right. Eventually, the inflation initiated by the faster money growth began to overshoot the money growth rate itself (as predicted by the neoclassical theory) and, as a consequence, the *LM* curve started shifting back to the left.

Of course, a precise, complete, and detailed tracking of the points in Frame (a) would require that we identify the *IS* curve as well as the *LM* curve and that we be sure that we can reconcile the movements in output and the interest rate with what was happening to the *IS* curve. To do that in any detail would take us well beyond what can be done in this chapter. It is worth noting, however, that a substantial loosening of fiscal policy occurred in 1972–73 which would have been associated with a rightward shift of the *IS* curve at that time. In the later part of the 1970s, there have been repeated attempts at fiscal restraint which would have tended to pull the *IS* curve back to the left. Additionally, a great increase in uncertainty and lack of confidence in the medium-to-long-term future has produced a slowdown of investment demand, shifting the investment demand schedule to the left. This would act in a manner that reinforced the fiscal restraint of the later part of the 1970s.

To summarise the above, it is evident that taking the movements in the price level as given, the movements of real money balances have generated shifts in the *LM* curve, the directions of which are entirely compatible with the pattern of evolution of output and the rate of interest as predicted by the neoclassical model. Let us now turn to a set of facts with which the neoclassical model has difficulty.

C. The Facts Not Explained by the Neoclassical Model

The key facts which are not well explained by the neoclassical model concern the relationship between inflation and excess demand. According to the neoclassical theory of price adjustment, the greater is excess demand, the faster will prices rise. It is recognised that the expected rate of inflation also plays a role. Nevertheless, the neoclassical theory regards inflationary expectations as evolving only slowly in response to actual inflationary experience and the major changes in those expectations to be exogenous. This hardly constitutes an explanation.

To see the failure of the neoclassical model in this regard, examine Frame (b) of Figure 25.4. You see there that the relationship between the rate of inflation and excess demand is an exceedingly loose one. We could, of course, pass a neoclassical price adjustment (*PA*) through each of the points in that figure. In order to do so, however, we would have to make the curve shift every year. You may be thinking, 'but that is what we had to do to get the *LM* curve to fit the facts.' That is true, but we also have independent means of working out the major influence upon the position of the *LM* curve — real money balances. In the case of the *PA* curve, we have no independent predictions on how it would have shifted. In effect, we would have to be willing to change the expected rate of inflation every year. Since there is no theory as to how that expectation evolves, this would simply amount to an *ex post* rationalisation of the phenomenon that we have observed and would be completely devoid of predictive content.

Of course, it is possible that our calculation of the trend value of real national income and therefore our calculation of excess demand (measured as deviations from trend) is inappropriate. Even if that turned out to be so, the pattern of data relating inflation to deviations of output from trend has none of the properties it would require to be compatible with the neoclassical theory of price adjustment. If there is any slope to the relationship between those two variables (and it's only a very loose one) it appears to have the wrong sign! That is, the higher is the state of excess demand, the lower is the rate of inflation according to the data plotted in Frame (b).

One of the shocks that we examined in Section A of this chapter, a supply-side shock, is widely believed to have been an important actual event in 1973–74. In the final part of 1973 the world economy was administered an enormous shock in the form of a quadrupling of the price of oil. There was at that time an oil embargo. This cut back the productive potential of all the nations of the Western world. You will recall, from the analysis of Section A of this chapter, that the effects of such a shock as predicted by the neoclassical theory are to raise the inflation rate and start output falling. This certainly seems to have been a feature of that period. Between 1973 and 1974, excess demand fell from more than 5 per cent to less than 2 per cent and at the same time, the inflation rate climbed to almost double its 1973 rate. Thus, the evolution of inflation and output in that immediate post-oil shock period seems to be compatible with the predictions of neoclassical theory.

What is not well explained by the neoclassical model, is the fact that inflation continued to accelerate through 1975, even though the economy moved into a state of excess supply at that time. Further, the acceleration of inflation from 1978 to 1980 while the economy was in a state of unusually slack demand, defies explanation in the framework of this model. According to the neoclassical model, inflation should accelerate normally when there is an excess demand and should decelerate when there is excess supply. If the biggest movements in inflation, even though not the most common ones, occur independently of the state of excess demand, then there is a serious deficiency in the neoclassical theory.

D. Strengths and Shortcomings of the Neoclassical Model

We have seen that the major strength of the neoclassical synthesis is its capacity to predict interest rates and income, given the behaviour of the price level. We have also seen that its major weakness is its failure to predict the inflation rate, given the state of excess demand. Movements in inflation which are independent of excess demand are more important historically than those associated with excess demand. Implicit in this shortcoming is the failure of the neoclassical model to supply an adequate theory of inflation expectations. In effect, the model takes one step behind the Keynesian assumption of a downwardly rigid money wage and assumes slowly evolving and largely exogenous inflationary expectations. Not only does this make the theory weak as a predictor of inflation, it also builds into the analysis the presumption of irrational behaviour on the part of individuals. People see inflation around them, have some knowledge and understanding of what causes it, and yet for some reason they don't use that information to figure out what to expect the inflation rate to be in the current or immediate future. They behave like 'clockwork mice'. You wind them up and they run their course, repeatedly bumping into the wall and never learning from their experience. This, as much as its failure in predictive terms, is a deep shortcoming of the Keynesian and neoclassical models.

SUMMARY

A. Main Predictions of the Neoclassical Model

The neoclassical model predicts that a shock which shifts the *IS* curve (expansionary fiscal policy or rise in investment spending) will raise interest rates, inflation, and output. After the impact, interest rates will continue to rise, but inflation and output will drift downwards towards their previous values. A rise in the growth rate of the money supply will have no impact effects. It will set up a process, however, of initially falling interest rates, rising inflation, and rising output. Eventually interest rates will also rise to reflect fully the higher inflation. The impact effect of a negative supply-side shock will be to raise inflation. The adjustment process will set up rising interest rates, falling inflation, and falling output.

B. The Facts Explained by the Neoclassical Model

The neoclassical model explains well the determination of output and interest rates for a given price level and inflation rate. It is a good theory of aggregate demand.

C. The Facts Not Explained by the Neoclassical Model

The neoclassical model does not explain well the behaviour of the inflation rate, given the state of excess demand. There are sizeable movements in the inflation rate which are independent of excess demand and for which the neoclassical model cannot account.

D. Strengths and Shortcomings of the Neoclassical Model

The main strength of the neoclassical model is its demand side. It is the best theory of aggregate demand that is available. Its major shortcomings are on the supply side. It does not give a good explanation of inflation. Further, it lacks a satisfactory theory of inflationary expectations.

Review Questions

1. Using an analysis and diagrams similar to those set out in Figures 25.1, 25.2, and 25.3, analyse the effects of the following shocks (be careful to distinguish between impact effects, adjustment paths, and steady states):
    (a) a 10 per cent cut in real government purchases of goods and services;
    (b) a once-and-for-all rise in the money supply of 10 per cent (not a continuing ongoing rate of growth of the money supply of 10 per cent);
    (c) a postal strike which leads to a large rise in the demand for money that is not matched by a rise in the supply of money; and
    (d) a sudden rise in inflationary expectations.

2. Using the predictions of the neoclassical model concerning impact effects and early adjustment path effects, try to figure out a combination of shocks capable of completely explaining the movement shown in Frame (c) of Figure 25.4 in interest rates, inflation, and output. Is it always necessary to 'fiddle' by letting exogenous changes in inflationary expectations adjust to validate the theory *ex post*?

3. What is wrong with letting inflationary expectations adjust in whatever way is necessary to make the neoclassical theory fit the facts?

Part V

Rational Expectations Theory of Income, Employment and the Price Level

26

Introduction to the Rational Expectations Theories of Income, Employment and the Price Level

You have now reviewed the basic and Keynesian models and have discovered that while there is much in Britain's economic history that these models can explain, there is also an important set of facts of which neither of them gives an entirely satisfactory account. These facts are the co-movements between real economic activity (output, employment, and unemployment) and inflation. The basic model predicts that movements in prices (and in inflation) will be independent of movements in real variables. That model *does* explain the main trends in inflation, but it is incapable of accounting for the procyclical co-movements in prices and inflation that often occur. The Keynesian model, on the other hand, as extended in the form of the neoclassical synthesis, can, in a crude way, account for the procyclical co-movements of prices. It cannot, however, account for some of the strong bursts of inflation that have occurred in the 1970s at times when unemployment was high or real output close to or below trend.

This and the following six chapters are going to introduce you to some of the recent innovations in macroeconomic theory which seek to overcome these shortcomings of the earlier models. You just have one task in this chapter, which is to:

know the main components of the rational expectations theories of income, employment, and the price level.[1]

The innovations in macroeconomic analysis begun by Keynes were a response to the need for a theory of how the economy operated when there was a substantial amount of excess capacity and unemployment. Keynes characterised the economy as operating on a horizontal section of the aggregate supply curve so that output and employment were determined by the position of the aggregate demand curve alone. This made it necessary to be rather careful to develop an adequate theory of aggregate demand. That is precisely what Keynes and his followers did, and the theory embodied in the *IS–LM* analysis stands as a component part of the rational expectations theories of the determination of output, employment and prices.

As we have seen, the major shortcoming of the Keynesian and neoclassical analyses is their inability to explain the facts about inflation and output. It is as if the Keynesian theory, being a careful theory of aggregate demand, has been too cavalier in its treatment of the aggregate supply-side of the economy. Just as it became necessary to be very careful about the theory of demand when the economy was operating in a region of considerable excess capacity, so it becomes equally important to be careful about the theory of aggregate supply when the economy is operating at or in the neighbourhood of its full employment output point.

It is on the aggregate supply side that the new theories of macroeconomics make their major contribution. The starting point of the innovations in the theory of aggregate supply has, in effect, already been accepted and incorporated into the body of analysis presented earlier as the neoclassical synthesis. The theoretical innovations of Milton Friedman and Edmund Phelps have already been briefly introduced. In order that you have a thorough understanding of the nature of their innovations, one of the major tasks in this part of the book is to examine the theory of aggregate supply implied by the analyses of these two scholars. Harkening back to the ideas of Irving Fisher, they emphasise the role of *expectations* in the labour market and modify the theory of aggregate supply of the basic model. They develop what we shall call the *expectations-augmented aggregate supply curve*.

Once expectations become a key part of any model, it becomes crucial to develop a theory of how expectations are formed and changed. The innovation in this area was first introduced into economics by John Muth in 1961. Its implications for macroeconomics and the understanding of economic fluctuations was not seen until the seminal contributions of Robert E. Lucas Jr. in the early 1970s. Lucas showed us

---

1. An excellent review of the rational expectations hypothesis and its implications for macroeconomics is contained in David G. Mayes, The controversy over rational expectations, *National Institute Economic Review*, No. 96, May 1981, pp. 53–61. David Mayes' conclusions are different from those reached by us. The paper contains a fairly comprehensive bibliography of the recent literature in this area. Of the several excellent survey articles on the modern theories of macroeconomics, the one which is most readable is that by William Poole, Rational expectations in the macro model, *Brookings Papers on Economic Activity,* 2, 1976, pp. 463–505. A useful critical appraisal of the modern theories is Robert J. Gordon, Recent developments in the theory of inflation and unemployment, *Journal of Monetary Economics,* 2, April 1976, pp. 185–220.

how we could develop a theory which was capable of explaining both the procyclical co-movements in inflation and at the same time explain why, from time to time, inflation would surge ahead independently of the state of excess demand. This theory is based on the idea that individuals supply and demand labour and supply and demand goods, acting upon expectations which are formed rationally and based on all the information that is available to them. This *rational expectations* approach, while still controversial, has a great deal of economic appeal because it assumes that people are indeed rational, do not waste information, and behave in the most efficient and economical manner that they can. It would be too costly for them to acquire full or perfect information and to renegotiate contracts every instant in the light of new information; hence, people commit themselves to actions based on incomplete information and sometimes make mistakes. It is the consequence of these mistakes that leads to the observed procyclical co-movements in prices.

Making sense of this and understanding the full implications of the previous paragraphs will be the subject of the next six chapters. As a preview of those chapters the following 'story' may be helpful. The notion of a story, by the way, is a useful one in this context. Just as a fairy story vividly illustrates particular phobias, fears, or moral attitudes, so it is possible to tell a story about the economy that emphasises particular features of the world. The abstractions used in the story are intended to be useful in making predictions about the world.

A Story About the Economy

Our story about the economy begins with rational, maximising individuals. Households maximise their utility and firms their profits. This means that the lower the real wage, the more labour will be demanded, and the higher the real wage, the more labour will be supplied. It also means that for a given level of the variables that determine aggregate demand (the money supply, government spending, and taxes), the lower the price level, the more goods will be demanded. Individuals do not have full information. They have to do the best they can in the face of limited information. In particular, people have to form expectations about the general price level at which they will be able to buy consumer goods.

There are two variants of the story concerning the way in which people do business with each other: one called *new classical* and the other *new Keynesian*. In the new classical version of the story, individuals do business with each other in markets which are sufficiently efficient to achieve equilibrium quickly. It is as if there is an effective auctioneer finding the prices at which people can trade with each other and in so doing exploit all the potential gains from trading activities. From a scientific point of view, building a theory on the notion that markets equilibrate quickly is not very different from primitive ideas about gravity. Without really knowing why, man observed that apples tended to fall to the ground rather than to fly around the orchard. A physical theory could be constructed to explain many observations by assuming the existence of gravity. It is much the same with market equilibrium.

In the new Keynesian version of the story, markets do not achieve equilibrium at each and every instant. They do, however, achieve equilibrium *on the average*. Labour is traded not on a market that behaves like an auction but on contracts. A money wage is fixed to achieve an expected equilibrium between supply and demand

and, in exchange for a fixed money wage, households agree to supply whatever labour firms demand over the duration of the contract.

Standing alongside the incompletely informed, rational, maximising individuals, trading with each other in markets that are in equilibrium (either always or on the average) there is a government and central bank that undertakes a certain volume of spending, raises a certain volume of taxes and creates a certain quantity of money. If the level of aggregate demand so generated is such that it determines a price level which is the same as the expected price level, then the economy settles down at a full-employment equilibrium. If aggregate demand exceeds that quantity, the economy moves to a higher level of prices, employment, and output. If aggregate demand is less than that quantity, the economy moves to a lower level of output, employment, and prices. These movements occur as the rational profit-maximising and utility-maximising responses of individuals. Everybody does the best he can for himself and positions of employment above or below the full-employment level have many of the characteristics of an equilibrium at full employment. They are all positions at which, given the state of information, no one finds it worthwhile to make any adjustment in his output or employment. The next six chapters will fill out the details of this story.

Throughout this and the next part of the book, which deal with the predictions and policy implications of rational expectations models, the analysis will be conducted for an economy whose trend inflation rate is zero. This is a convenient simplification which makes it possible to conduct all the analysis in diagrammatic terms. It is not a limitation of the analysis. The theories that are to be reviewed are equally applicable at *any* trend rate of inflation. You may, therefore, conveniently regard the analysis presented as representing deviations from the trend rate of inflation. Thus, when we talk about a rise in the price level or a fall in the price level you may, provided you are careful to remember what is going on, interpret that as a temporary rise in the inflation rate above its trend or a temporary fall in inflation below its trend. In making that interpretation you need to be constantly on guard to maintain the sharp analytical distinction introduced earlier concerning the difference between inflation and a once-and-for-all change in prices.

The new models of macroeconomics make predictions about trend inflation which are in most respects identical to those of the basic model with which you are already familiar.

As in the development of the basic and Keynesian models, the new theories will first be developed ignoring the linkages between the domestic economy and the rest of the world. Subsequently, in Chapter 32, the complications arising from international economic transactions will be explored.

SUMMARY

The rational expectations theories of income, employment, and the price level seek to explain the procyclical co-movements of prices and, at the same time, account for the important independent movements which occasionally occur between output and prices. They achieve this by radically modifying the neoclassical theory of aggregate supply, though accepting the *neoclassical theory of aggregate demand*. The new theories of aggregate supply generalise that of the basic model by introducing the *expectations-augmented aggregate supply curve*. They also incorporate the notion of *rational expectations* which assumes that people form their expectations on the basis of all the information available to them. That is, they assume that people are rational, do not waste information, and behave in the most efficient and economical manner that they can.

27

Information, Expectations, and the New Classical Theory of Aggregate Supply

This chapter develops what we shall call the 'new classical' theory of aggregate supply[1] and the expectations-augmented supply curve. There are a variety of alternative particular 'stories' that lead to the same conclusions as those reached in this chapter. The 'story' used here is, in our view, the simplest one. It will not be until Chapters 30 and 31, however, that the full story will emerge. This chapter then deals with the first building block of the new theories. Subsequent chapters will show how this theory of aggregate supply, when combined with the rational expectations hypothesis and the Keynesian theory of aggregate demand, is capable of providing an explanation of the facts about output and prices. In order to get you moving towards that objective, this chapter has four tasks, which are to:

A. **understand how incomplete information affects the supply of and demand for labour;**
B. **understand how the money wage and level of employment (and unemployment) are affected by wrong expectations;**
C. **know the definition of the expectations-augmented aggregate supply curve;** and
D. **how to derive the expectations-augmented aggregate supply curve.**

---

1. The theory of aggregate supply presented in this chapter had its origins in Milton Friedman, The role of monetary policy, *The American Economic Review*, 58, March 1968, pp. 1–17. It is also similar to that developed by Robert E. Lucas Jr. in, Some international evidence on output-inflation tradeoffs, *The American Economic Review*, Vol. LXIII, No. 3, 1973, pp. 326–34.

A. Incomplete Information and the Labour Market

In the basic model of the labour market, the demand for labour, the supply of labour, and the market equilibrating process paid no attention to any special characteristics of labour. We could have been talking about stocks and shares, wheat, futures contracts in gold, or just about any competitive market for any commodity at all.

There are some features of labour which make it unlike many other commodities. One important feature concerns the scale of the transactions costs which individuals (both suppliers and demanders of labour) have to incur in order to find someone with whom to do business. From the household side, there is a heavy transactions cost in finding a job that is attractive enough, well paid enough, and satisfactory in other dimensions. From the point of view of the firm demanding labour, there is a transactions cost in finding potential employees with the required skills and personal attributes.

The fact that there are heavy transactions costs implies that the labour market will typically not be organised as a *continuous auction* as, for example, are the stock market and the various commodity markets. Instead, the labour market will be characterised by *contracts*. Individuals will enter into arrangements with each other for a finite period of time (often, in the case of labour markets, a year or even more ahead). The worker and the employer will agree to trade labour services for a certain *money wage* for a certain period of time into the future. The employer will typically *not* undertake to guarantee employment at that wage and will be free to vary the number of workers hired. Individuals will also be free to quit their jobs if they can find better jobs with other firms. Usually, however, when entering into a transaction in the labour market, both suppliers and demanders of labour will be expecting to enter into an arrangement which has some durability.

Labour market contracts could, in principle, be very complex documents which incorporate hundreds (perhaps thousands) of contingency clauses specifying wages and other employment conditions. In practice, presumably because the costs of negotiating, writing, monitoring, and enforcing contracts are high, labour market contracts are relatively simple. They specify a *money wage* (and other non-wage terms) that will be paid for a certain type of labour over a specified future period. If the contract is to run for more than one year, it will also typically specify an adjustment in the *money wage*, either in *money terms*, or as some fraction of the rise in the cost of living as measured by the Retail Price Index — an *indexed* contract. Since individuals enter into medium-to-long-term contractual arrangements in the labour market and since those contracts are not typically 100 per cent *indexed*, but specify an agreed *money wage*, it becomes necessary for the contracting parties to form an *expectation* of the *price level* so that they may translate a *known money wage* into an *expected real wage*.

When a firm is figuring out how much labour to demand for a particular money wage, it has to calculate the real wage based on the price of the goods that it is selling. Recall that the firm needs to do this calculation because, if it is to maximise its profits, it will want to hire labour up to the point at which the *marginal product of labour equals the real wage*. From the household's point of view, the amount of labour that will be supplied for any particular *money wage* will depend upon the *household's expectation of the price level* of the basket of consumer goods which it anticipates buying with its money wage.

There is an interesting and important potential asymmetry here which may be used to generate the new theories of aggregate supply. As we noted above, the price which is relevant on the demand side of the labour market is the price of the firm's *own* output. The price which is relevant on the supply side of the labour market is the price of the basket of goods that consumers will be buying — which can be thought of as including the prices of the output of *all* firms, the Retail Price Index. It seems reasonable to suppose that both the individual firm and its workers are able continuously to observe the price of the individual good (or prices of the range of goods) which the firm produces. On the other hand, it seems very unlikely that anyone will be sufficiently well-informed to be able to make a correct estimate of average consumer prices when deciding how much labour to supply. People will, of course, do their best; they will use all information that is available to them and, on the average, will probably estimate the price level accurately. They will not, however, be right each and every time; sometimes they will over-estimate and sometimes they will under-estimate the actual level of prices. It is important to note that this is not an asymmetry between households and firms. It is that both firms and households know the prices in their own sector, but are incompletely informed about other sectors of the economy.

Now individual prices will vary partly as a result of shocks that affect *all* prices and partly as a result of factors affecting supply and demand in an individual industry. In other words, *relative prices* will be in a continuous state of change. This being so, it will not be possible for people (either for workers or their employers) to figure out what the general price level is simply from their knowledge of the levels of prices in their own industry.

The starting point for developing the new classical theory is an analysis of the labour market which builds on the above remarks.

B. Wrong Expectations and the Labour Market

(i) The Labour Market and Money Wages

Recall the basic model of the labour market as shown below in Frame (a) of Figure 27.1. That figure shows a competitive labour market in equilibrium at a real wage of $(W/P_0)^*$ and employment level n^*. The demand for labour increases as the real wage falls because of profit-maximising labour demand decisions by firms (marginal product = real wage); the supply of labour increases as real wages rise, since more households enter the labour force the higher is the real bundle of goods which they can buy in exchange for their work.

Suppose for a moment that the price level is equal to one, i.e. $P_0 = 1$. With the price level equal to one we may simply rename the vertical axis of Figure 27.1 to measure the money wage. If the price level is fixed at one and we plot the demand and supply curves against the money wage, this is exactly the same as plotting them

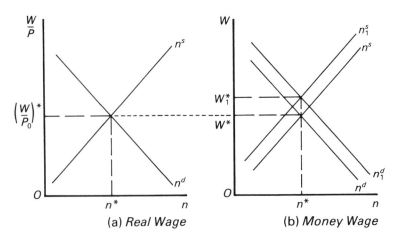

Figure 27.1 *The Labour Market and the Money Wage*

The supply and demand curves in the labour market which are drawn against the real wage (Frame (a)) may equivalently be drawn against the money wage (Frame (b)). In that case, there is a separate supply and demand curve for each price level. Both curves move vertically one-for-one as the price level varies.

against the real wage. Frame (b) reproduces the demand and supply curves, n^d and n^s, and shows the same employment equilibrium n^* and the equilibrium *money wage*, W^*.

Next, notice that the equilibrium real wage $(W/P_0)^*$ (shown in Frame (a)) could be attained at *any money wage*. All that is necessary is that the money wage and price level stand in the appropriate relationship to each other; if the price level doubled, the money wage would have to double; if the price level rose by x per cent, the money wage would have to rise by x per cent. Now in Frame (a), where we draw the demand and supply curves against the real wage, changes in the price level are not visible. The equilibrium determined in Frame (a) is a *real equilibrium* and is independent of the price level.

Is the same true of the equilibrium in Frame (b)? Is the equilibrium depicted in that frame independent of the price level? The answer is that the *real* equilibrium — real wage and employment level — is independent of the price level, but the money wage, measured on the vertical axis of Frame (b), is not. Since in Frame (b) the *money wage* is measured on the vertical axis, it is necessary to be aware that the demand and supply curves can only be drawn for a *given* level of prices. The supply and demand curves, illustrated as n^d and n^s, are drawn for a price level equal to one. Suppose the price level were to increase to P_1, which is higher than P_0 by x per cent, i.e., suppose $P_1 = (1 + x)P_0$. (You may find some numbers helpful: If $x = 5$ per cent, i.e., $5/100$, then $P_1 = (1 + x)P_0$ is the same as $P_1 = (1 + 5/100)P_0$ or $P_1 = (1.05)1 = 1.05$.) If the price level rose by x per cent, how would the demand and supply curves in Frame (b) move? It is clear that the *money wages* that firms would now be willing to pay for each quantity of labour would be higher by the same x per cent as the price level has increased. Since the firm is only interested in the real wage, an x per cent rise in the price level means that at a money wage x per cent higher, the firm would be willing to hire the same number of workers as it would be at the lower price level and lower money wage. Thus, the demand for labour curve will shift upwards by the same x per cent as the price level has risen. This is shown as the curve n_1^d.

What happens on the supply side? Precisely the same as on the demand side: the quantity of labour which households are willing to supply depends on the real wage. Therefore, if the price level rises by x per cent, the money wage will have to rise by x per cent if the quantity of labour supplied is to remain unchanged. Thus, the curve n_1^s shows the supply of labour at the price level P_1. That is, the supply curve moves upwards by x per cent in exactly the same way as the demand curve does.

It is now a simple matter to see that since the two curves have both moved upwards by the same percentage amounts, they must cut at the same employment level as before and at a money wage that is x per cent higher than before. This new equilibrium *money* wage is shown in the diagram as W_1^* and is equal to $(1 + x)W^*$. The equilibrium level of employment remains unchanged at n^*.

So far, nothing new has been introduced other than the idea that the labour market can be analysed so as to determine the equilibrium wage and employment in the basic model, with the *money wage* on the vertical axis of the supply–demand diagram instead of the *real wage*. With the money wage on the vertical axis, the demand and supply curves shift when the price level changes. With the real wage on the vertical axis, the curves are fixed independently of the price level. How the labour market works with incomplete information will now be analysed.

(ii) Incomplete Information and Expectations

First, although a simplification, it will be assumed that firms and households know only the price at which the firm will be able to sell its output. Neither firms nor households know any other prices — prices in other sectors — that make up the general price level. Labour supply decisions will be made on the basis of the best available estimates of the price level. Call the price level which consumers expect to have to pay to buy their basket of consumer goods the *expected price level*, and denote it as P^e.

Next, assume that although firms and households do business with each other by agreeing on a money wage, contractual arrangements are sufficiently flexible, and job turnover — people switching between jobs with different rates of pay — sufficiently rapid, to ensure that the average money wage rate continuously adjusts to maintain labour market equilibrium. This is a crucial assumption of the 'new classical' analysis which distinguishes it from the 'new Keynesian' analysis that you will look at in the next chapter.

Let us now see what these assumptions imply. Figure 27.2 will be the main vehicle for following the analysis. The vertical axis measures the money wage and the horizontal axis the level of employment. The curve $n^d(P_0)$ is the demand curve for labour when the price level is fixed at P_0. The supply curve of labour is plotted for a given *expected* level of prices. The supply curve, marked $n^s(P^e = P_0)$, is for a level of expected prices which equals the actual price level P_0. Thus, the supply curve $n^s(P^e = P_0)$ and the demand curve $n^d(P_0)$ can be thought of as representing the original curves, n^d and n^s, in Frame (b) of Figure 27.1. They determine an equilibrium money wage W^* and employment level n^*, which will now be called the *full-employment* values. *The full-employment values of employment and the real wage are identical to those determined in the basic model.*

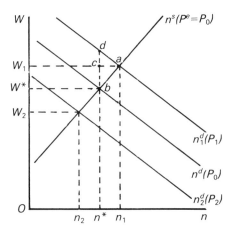

Figure 27.2 *Expectations Equilibria in the Labour Market*
The demand for labour by each firm depends upon the firm's own output price. This means
that the aggregate demand for labour depends on the actual price level. The supply of labour
depends on the expected price level. The equilibrium wage rate and employment level will be
different at each different price level. At the price level P_0 there is full-employment
equilibrium. At the price level P_1 there is over-full employment (wages W_1, employment n_1),
and at the price level P_2 there is unemployment (wage rate W_2, employment level n_2).

You may think it strange that the demand for labour is shown as depending on the
actual price level when we are assuming that no one knows the actual price level. A
moment's reflection will convince you that there is no paradox or inconsistency here.
Each firm's demand for labour depends on its own output price so that, when we
aggregate overall firms to obtain the aggregate demand for labour, the relevant price
which determines that aggregate demand is the average of the prices actually faced
by each firm — the actual price level.

Now consider what would happen if the price level was higher than P_0, while the
expected price level remained at $P^e = P_0$. In particular, consider what would happen
if the actual price level increased by x per cent to $P_1 = (1+x)P_0$. Each firm, knowing
that its own selling price had risen by x per cent would now be willing to pay a higher
money wage for its labour. That is, the demand for labour curve would shift upwards.
The new demand curve that would result is shown as $n_1^d(P_1)$. Recall that we are
conducting a conceptual experiment in which the general price level *expected* by
consumers and labour suppliers does not change. Since the *expected* price level has
not changed, the supply curve is not affected by the change in the actual price level
and remains in its original position.[2] The labour market will now attain an

---

2. Strictly speaking, there is an inconsistency in the treatment here. Everybody knows the
   price in the market for the commodity whose production they are concerned with, and yet
   they do not seem to take that information into account in forming an expectation of the
   general price level. This is wasteful of information. A more complete, but more difficult,
   treatment would extract information from the known price of a particular commodity to
   obtain a better inference about the general price level. The essence of the new classical
   theory of aggregate supply is not affected, however, by ignoring this piece of information.
   For the reader able to follow the statistical analysis, Robert E. Lucas Jr., Some
   international evidence on output-inflation tradeoffs, *The American Economic Review*,
   Vol. LXIII, No. 3, 1973, pp. 326–34, deals with this problem. That paper, in fact, is the
   most important, accessible and original presentation of the new classical theory of
   aggregate supply.

equilibrium at the money wage W_1 and the employment level n_1. That is, with the actual price level higher than the expected price level, the money wage will be higher than its full-employment value, and the level of employment will be higher than its full-employment value. The real wage, however, will be lower than its full-employment value. This can be seen in the diagram. The price level increase is measured by the full vertical shift of the labour demand curve, for example, the distance ab in the diagram. The money wage, however, rises by a smaller distance cb. You see, therefore, that the price level rise is greater than the money wage rise and, therefore, the real wage has fallen. This fall in the real wage has induced firms to hire more labour and has generated the increase in employment from n^* to n_1. Households expect the price level to be P_0 and, therefore, as the money wage rises households expect the real wage to be (W_1/P_0). This encourages households to supply the extra amount of labour n^* to n_1. While they are doing business with each other, households and firms are in equilibrium. Both households and firms are happy, and there is nothing that either could do to improve their situation. However, after the event households will realise that they have made a mistake. They will realise that they did too much work and at too low a real wage. Of course, bygones are bygones and there will be nothing that can be done about that. All that households can do the next time around is again to use all the information that is available to them and make the best deal they can. The situation just analysed is called one of *over-full employment*.

Next, consider the opposite experiment, of a fall in the price level below P_0 while the expected price level remains constant at $P^e = P_0$. In particular, let us suppose that the price level falls by x per cent, from P_0 to P_2, but that the expected price level remains at P_0. The demand for labour curve will now shift downwards and is illustrated by the new demand curve $n_2^d(P_2)$. The supply curve does not shift because the expected price level has not changed. What happens in this event? Again, the answer is clear and is contained in the diagram. This time the labour market will come to what is called an *unemployment* equilibrium. The equilibrium wage rate will be W_2, and the employment level n_2. Thus, with a lower price level than that expected, employment and the money wage will fall below their full-employment levels. The real wage, in this case, will rise above its full-employment level. The real wage rises because the price level falls by more than the fall in the money wage. By a similar argument to that given above, the demand curve falls by the full percentage amount of the fall in the price level, but as you can see, the money wage falls by only a fraction of that. It is the higher real wage that creates the fall in employment, inducing firms to hire fewer workers. The expected real wage falls, however, because households do not expect the fall in the price level, and when they see a fall in the money wage, they read this as being a fall in the real wage. There is, therefore, full agreement between the households and the firms concerning the drop in employment and the change in the money wage. Households willingly reduce their employment to n_2 in the face of an expected fall in the real wage, while firms willingly cut their hiring to n_2, since they are facing a higher real wage. While the households and firms are trading labour, everyone is happy; both firms and households are doing the best they can for themselves. The workers $n^* - n_2$ will choose not to be employed, and their decision to be unemployed is correct in the light of their expectation of a low real wage. They expect a low real wage because their expectation is that the price level will remain constant, while they have observed that the money wage has fallen. Each firm, on the other hand, knowing its own output price, regards the drop in the money wage as insufficient to compensate for the drop in its own price, and so the resulting higher actual real wage induces them to hire less labour.

You see, then, that if the price level that is expected actually comes about, the economy will settle down at an equilibrium that is the same as the equilibrium in the basic model. That equilibrium is called *full employment*. If the price level is higher than expected, the labour market will equilibrate at a higher level of employment and a lower level of the real wage than the full-employment levels. In this case there will be *over-full employment*. If the price level turns out to be lower than that expected, then there will be a cut in the employment level and a higher real wage — there will be *unemployment*. In the institutional setting of the United Kingdom, such unemployment will usually be recorded as unemployment, since the individuals involved will be 'capable of', 'available for work' and registered as unemployed. They are not willing to work at the wage which is available, but in registering as unemployed no mention is made of wages. Further, such people will usually be receiving unemployment benefits.

There is no single unique equilibrium in the labour market once expectations are introduced. The equilibrium level of employment and the real wage will be influenced by the actual price level relative to its expected level. The higher the actual price level relative to its expected level, the higher will be the level of employment and the money wage, and the lower will be the level of unemployment and the real wage.

C. Definition of the Expectations-Augmented Aggregate Supply Curve

The expectations-augmented aggregate supply curve shows the maximum amount of output which the economy will supply at each different price level but **with a fixed expected price level**.

This is an extension of the concept of the aggregate supply curve which was introduced earlier in the basic model. The aggregate supply curve of the basic model can be thought of as showing the maximum amount of output which the economy will supply when there is no difference between the actual and the expected price levels. That is, the aggregate supply curve of the basic model is the same as the expectations-augmented aggregate supply curve when everyone has full information and everyone knows the actual price level.

D. Derivation of the Expectations-Augmented Aggregate Supply Curve

It is a straightforward matter to derive the expectations-augmented aggregate supply curve from the analysis that you have already conducted. Figure 27.3 illustrates how

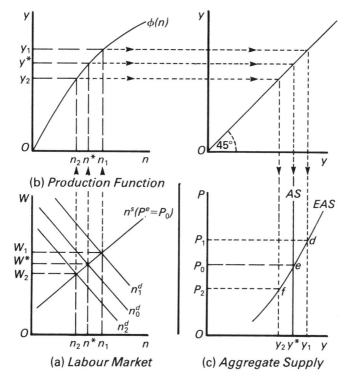

Figure 27.3 *Derivation of the Expectations Augmented Aggregate Supply Curve*
Frame (a) is the same as Figure 27.2. At each different price level there is a different labour
market equilibrium. The employment levels associated with those different equilibria
translate into different output levels (Frame (b)). By associating the initially assumed different
price levels with the output levels generated (Frame (c)) the expectations-augmented
aggregate supply curve is derived. Position *e* is the same as full-employment equilibrium in the
basic model. The expectations-augmented aggregate supply curve cuts the basic model
aggregate supply curve at the expected price level.

---

this is done. Frame (a) simply reproduces Figure 27.2. If you have understood Figure
27.2, you also understand Frame (a), for it contains nothing new. The demand for
labour curve n_1^d is drawn for the price level P_1, the curve n_0^d for the price level P_0, and
the curve n_2^d for the price level P_2. The supply curve is drawn for a fixed expected
price level P^e equal to P_0.

First, Figure 27.3 is used to do something with which you are already familiar. It is
used to derive the aggregate supply curve of the basic model. This is done by reading
off the equilibrium level of output for which the expected price level equals the actual
price level. In this case, everyone has full information — no one is fooled. The
equilibrium in the labour market is where the demand curve n_0^d cuts the supply curve
$n^s(P^e = P_0)$. At this point, employment is n^* and the money wage is W^*. Transferring
this employment level up to Frame (b), you can read off from the production
function the equilibrium level of output that will be supplied at full-employment
equilibrium. That is y^*. Translate that level of output (following the dotted line)
round to Frame (c) and plot the level of output which will be produced in full-
employment equilibrium against the price level P_0, point *e*. Now as the price level is

varied *and* provided we also vary the expected price level so that actual and expected prices are always equal to each other (recall Frame (b) of Figure 27.1), nothing would happen to the equilibrium level of employment or real wage. The money wage would change proportionately with the price level, and the real equilibrium in the labour market would be undisturbed. That is essentially the exercise we performed when deriving the aggregate supply curve in the basic model: as the price level is varied and the expected price level is varied so as to always equal the actual price level, the equilibrium level of employment remains constant, and from Frame (b) the equilibrium level of output also remains constant. This traces out the aggregate supply curve of the basic model, AS, in Frame (c).

Next, consider what happens when the expected price level is held constant but the actual price level changes. First, suppose the actual price level rises from P_0 to P_1, while the expected price level stays at P_0. This higher price level is shown on the vertical axis of Frame (c) as P_1 which is equal to $P_0(1 + x)$. What is the level of output which profit-maximising producers would want to supply at that price level? The answer is obtained by starting in the labour market. You know that the demand for labour curve will shift upwards to n_1^d. You know that the supply curve of labour will not move because its position depends on the expected price level, and this has not changed. The labour market will clear at a higher money wage W_1 and a higher level of employment n_1. At this higher level of employment firms will produce a higher level of output y_1, which is read off from the production function in Frame (b). If we translate this level of output (by following the dotted line) to Frame (c), we generate the new point d in Frame (c). Point d shows the output level y_1 which profit-maximising firms are willing to supply if the price level is P_1 and the expected price level is P_0.

Next, consider what would happen if the price level fell to x per cent below P_0. Such a price level is shown on the vertical axis of Frame (c) as P_2 (which equals $P_0(1 - x)$). What is the profit-maximising supply of output in this case? The answer is again obtained by starting in the labour market. You know that the demand for labour curve falls to n_2^d, so that the equilibrium level of employment and money wage will now move to n_2 and W_2 respectively. At this lower level of employment firms will produce the lower level of output y_2 (read off from Frame (b)). Now transferring this output level y_2 (following the dotted line) to Frame (c) shows that profit-maximising firms will supply the level of output y_2 at the price level P_2. That is, the economy would operate at point f. Point f says that if the price level is P_2, but the expected price level is P_0, firms will choose to supply y_2 as their profit-maximising output.

If we join together the points d, e, and f and all other points in between and beyond these, we will generate the *expectations-augmented aggregate supply curve* labelled *EAS*.

The expectations-augmented aggregate supply curve shows how the profit-maximising and utility-maximising quantity of supply varies as the price level varies, but when the expected price level is fixed. Notice that the expectations-augmented aggregate supply curve (EAS) cuts the aggregate supply curve (AS) at the point at which the actual price level is equal to the expected price level. In the example in Frame (c), this is at the price level P_0. This is not a coincidence. It happens because only when expectations turn out to be correct do we get the same aggregate supply as we would if everyone always had complete information.

This new aggregate supply analysis will be combined with the theory of aggregate demand in Chapter 29 to re-examine the effects of a change in the money supply on the level of output and prices.

SUMMARY

A. Incomplete Information and the Labour Market

Because it is costly for workers to find suitable jobs and because it is costly for firms to find suitable employees, individuals typically do not change their jobs frequently, and labour is not traded as if in a continuous auction market. Rather, contracts are entered into which run for a year or more. Because contracts last for a sizeable length of time and because it is expensive to write complicated contracts with detailed contingency clauses, it is typically the case that firms and households fix the price at which they will buy and sell labour in money units — i.e., they fix a money wage. However, because their decisions to buy and sell labour are influenced by the real wage, it is necessary for both households and firms to form an expectation about the price level that will prevail over a wage contract period.

Firms and households can do a better job of forming a reliable expectation about the prices in their own sector of the economy than they can about prices in general. Firms typically sell a small number of commodities and have a large amount of information about the markets in which they operate. Households buy a very large range of commodities and are not typically well-informed about prices in those markets. As an approximation, it is assumed that everyone knows the prices at which he will be selling his output over the wage contract period; no one knows *all* the prices which he will be facing when buying, so it is necessary to form an expectation of those prices, based on incomplete information.

B. Wrong Expectations and the Labour Market

For a given expectation of prices, a rise in the money wage will be read by households as a rise in the real wage, and they will increase their supply of labour. A cut in the money wage will be read as a cut in the real wage, and they will decrease their supply of labour. In contrast, on the demand side, firms having full information about the prices of their limited range of commodities will not be misled. The higher is the actual price level relative to the expected price level, the lower will be the real wage, and the greater will be the amount of labour which firms hire, the higher will be the expected real wage, and the greater will be the amount of labour which households supply. There are many equilibrium levels of the real wage and level of employment. The only equilibrium that corresponds to

that in the basic model is the one in which the expected price level is equal
to the actual price level. This occurs when everyone's expectation is
correct.

C. Definition of the Expectations-Augmented Aggregate Supply Curve

The expectations-augmented aggregate supply curve traces out the
quantities of aggregate output which firms will be willing to supply as the
price level varies at a given expected price level.

D. Derivation of the Expectations-Augmented Aggregate Supply Curve

This is done in Figure 27.3. You should review Figure 27.3 as many times
as necessary until you are thoroughly familiar with the derivation of the
expectations-augmented aggregate supply curve.

Review Questions

1. What are the key assumptions of the new classical theory of the labour market?

2. What is the asymmetry in the labour market on which the new classical theory of
    aggregate supply is based? Does it imply that workers are more ignorant than their
    employers about prices?

3. What are the ways in which firms can vary the wage rate, independently of negotiating a
    new contract?

4. Why does the aggregate demand for labour in the new classical model depend upon the
    actual real wage? How can it do so, when, by the assumptions of the model, no one
    knows the actual real wage?

5. Why, despite the fact that there is never any involuntary unemployment in the new
    classical model, might there be concern about unemployment even in the context of that
    model?

6. What markets are in equilibrium along the new classical *EAS* curve? Is there any
    involuntary unemployment?

7. What determines the slope of the new classical expectations-augmented aggregate
    supply curve? Show how the slope of the *EAS* curve changes as the supply of labour
    curve becomes more elastic.

28

The New Keynesian Theory of Aggregate Supply

There has recently emerged a new Keynesian theory of aggregate supply[1] which differs in subtle but important ways from the new classical theory. The principal architects of the New Keynesian theory are Stanley Fischer of the Massachusetts Institute of Technology, Edmund Phelps of Columbia University, and John Taylor of Princeton University.

The point of departure of the new Keynesian theory, as contrasted with the new classical theory, is that there are important institutional aspects of the labour market from which the new classical theory abstracts, but which are emphasised by the new Keynesian theory. These features were discussed and described at the beginning of the previous chapter. It was also made clear in that chapter, however, that the descriptive institutional detail was downplayed by the new classical theory. The key assumption of that theory is that money wages continuously adjust to ensure a continuous clearing of the labour market.

The new Keynesian theory regards the contractual fixing of money wages as being such a crucial feature of the labour market that it must figure prominently in any

---

1. The main contributions to what we are calling the new Keynesian theory of aggregate supply are Stanley Fischer, Long-term contracts, rational expectations and the optimal money supply rule, *Journal of Political Economy*, 85, February 1977, pp. 191–206; Edmund S. Phelps and John B. Taylor, Stabilizing powers of monetary policy under rational expectations, *Journal of Political Economy*, 85, February 1977, pp. 163–90; and John B. Taylor, Staggered wage setting in a macro model, *The American Economic Review, Papers and Proceedings*, May 1979, pp. 108–13. The paper by Taylor is the most straightforward and focused of these. The first two cited deal with a broader range of issues than this chapter and extend to the policy questions dealt with in Chapters 37 and 38.

theory of how the labour market works. According to the new Keynesian theory, labour markets do not look like markets that are in a state of continuous auction, with prices (wages) being frequently adjusted to achieve an ongoing equality between supply and demand. On the average, supply equals demand, but at any particular moment in time, demand may exceed or fall short of supply. Taking explicit account of the institutional fact of contractually fixed money wages has important implications for the specification of the aggregate supply curve. This chapter explores those implications. Four specific tasks will help you in that objective. They are to:

A. know the key assumptions of the new Keynesian analysis;
B. understand how money wages are determined in the new Keynesian theory of aggregate supply;
C. understand the implications of the new Keynesian theory of wage determination for the expectations-augmented aggregate supply curve; and
D. understand the implications of overlapping labour market contracts.

A. Assumptions of the New Keynesian Analysis

There are three key assumptions in the new Keynesian theory of aggregate supply. The first of these is that *wages are set in money terms for a fixed contractual period before the quantity of labour supplied and demanded is known*. Wages are *not* set so as to equate the *actual* supply of labour with the actual demand for labour, but to *equate* the *expected* supply with the *expected* demand. No explicit theory of maximising behaviour on the part of labour suppliers and demanders is set out which rationalises this. It is asserted that, for whatever reason, the real world is so obviously characterised by such arrangements in labour markets that it is inappropriate to develop an analysis of the labour market that ignores the contractual fixity of money wages.

The second key assumption of the new Keynesian analysis is that the *actual quantity of labour traded is equal to the quantity demanded*. After wages are set so as to equate expected demand with expected supply, the actual supply and demand conditions become known. Once those conditions are known, both suppliers and demanders in the labour market are already tied into a wage contract. There has to be some rule for determining the quantity that will be traded. That rule could be that the short side of the market dominates. What this means is that if demand is less than supply, the quantity traded is the quantity demanded, but if demand exceeds supply, the quantity traded is the quantity supplied. This is not the assumption employed in the new Keynesian analysis. Instead, it is assumed that the demand side dominates. The suppliers of labour are assumed to stand ready to supply whatever labour is demanded in exchange for the certainty of a fixed money wage over the duration of the existing contract.

The third key assumption of the new Keynesian theory of aggregate supply is that not all labour market contracts are signed on the same day to run for the same duration. Contracts are signed on different dates for different durations (although the differences in durations are not as important as the differences in the dates on which the contracts are signed). The fact that *contracts overlap* or are 'staggered' rather than bunched to the same date and time interval has important implications which will be discussed in Section D of this chapter. The next two sections will not take account of the overlapping nature of labour market contracts but, for simplicity, will proceed as if all contracts are signed on the same day and run for the same duration.

B. Determination of Money Wages

The process whereby the money wage rate is determined in the new Keynesian theory is most straightforwardly illustrated in a simple diagram analogous to that contained in Figure 27.2. Figure 28.1 illustrates. The level of employment is measured on the horizontal axis, and the money wage rate on the vertical axis. The supply curve of labour $n^s(P^e = P_0)$ is drawn for a fixed expected price level equal to P_0. It is supposed that the labour market convenes and negotiations take place, and the money wage contract is signed prior to the commencement of the period for which the labour will be supplied and demanded. The price level at which the demanders of labour will sell their output is therefore unknown at the time that the labour market contract is signed. The demand for labour which is relevant for the determination of the wage contract is that based on the expected price level. Such a demand function is drawn in Figure 28.1 as the curve labelled $n^d(P^e = P_0)$. This is the expected demand for labour curve, given the expected price level equal to P_0. Where the expected demand curve cuts the expected supply curve determines the expected

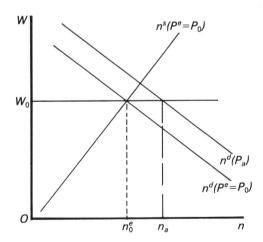

Figure 28.1 *The Labour Market in the New Keynesian Model*
The labour market meets and a money wage is set before the actual price level is known. That wage rate, W_0, is set to achieve an equilibrium in the labour market based on the expected price level (P_0). When the actual price level (P_a) is revealed, the quantity of labour traded will equal the quantity demanded (n_a).

labour market equilibrium. The level of employment n_0^e is the expected equilibrium level of employment, and the wage rate W_0 is the expected market clearing money wage rate. The *contractually determined money wage rate will be set equal to this expected market clearing money wage*. Once that money wage is determined, nothing is allowed to change it until the next bargaining date at some time in the future. In the meantime, the actual level of employment will be determined at the contracted money wage by the *actual* demand for labour curve. Suppose that the actual price level turns out to be P_a and that the actual demand for labour curve turns out to be $n^d(P_a)$. In that case, the quantity of labour employed will be n_a, and the wage rate, of course, will remain at W_0. The real wage will fall because the price level P_a is higher than the expected price level P_0, on which the fixed money wage rate W_0 is based.

C. The New Keynesian Expectations-Augmented Aggregate Supply Curve

The new Keynesian theory of aggregate supply implied by the theory of wage determination just presented is very similar, in qualitative terms, to the new classical theory. The derivation of the new Keynesian expectations-augmented aggregate supply curve is presented in Figure 28.2. It will be recognised that this figure is almost identical to Figure 27.3, which was used to derive the new classical expectations-augmented aggregate supply curve. The labour market analysis presented above in Figure 28.1 is repeated in Frame (a). The production function appears in Frame (b), and the aggregate supply curve is generated in Frame (c). As described above, the money wage is determined at W_0, which is that money wage which achieves an expected equilibrium in the labour market. That is, it achieves an equality between the expected supply of labour and the expected demand for labour with the expected price level P_0. If the actual price level turned out to be P_1 so that the demand for labour curve was, in fact, $n^d(P_1)$, then the quantity of labour demanded would be n_1. The quantity of labour n_1 would, through the production function, generate a level of output equal to y_1. That output level y_1 could be traced around through the 45° quadrant to the aggregate supply diagram in Frame (c), being the output level y_1 on the horizontal axis of Frame (c). That output level y_1 is, of course, associated with the price level P_1, so that the point d' is a point on the expectations-augmented aggregate supply curve of the new Keynesian analysis.

If, conversely, the price level was lower than P_0 at, say, P_2 so that the demand for labour curve dropped to the curve $n^d(P_2)$, then the quantity of labour demanded would become the quantity n_2 on the horizontal axis of Frame (a). That level of employment would generate an output level y_2 read off from the vertical axis of Frame (b). Transferring the output level y_2 through the 45° quadrant to Frame (c) shows that the output level y_2 is associated with the price level P_2 at the point f'. If the price level turned out to be that which was expected, namely P_0, then the quantity of labour employed would, of course, be n^* and the output level would be y^*, generating a point on the aggregate supply curve of e. Joining together f', e, and d' and extrapolating beyond those points traces out the new Keynesian expectations-augmented aggregate supply curve, labelled $EAS(K)$ in Frame (c).

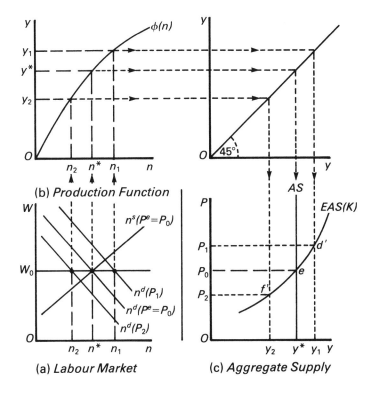

Figure 28.2 *Derivation of the Expectations-Augmented Aggregate Supply Curve in the New Keynesian Model*

The development in this diagram parallels that of Figure 27.3. In Frame (a), the labour market sets a money wage at W_0, based on the expected price level P_0. Full employment equilibrium would be at n^*. Different actual price levels (P_0, P_1, P_2) generate different demand curves. The quantity traded is read off from the demand curve (n_1 at price level P_1, and n_2 at price level P_2). The output produced by these different labour inputs are read off from the production function (Frame (b)). The resulting new Keynesian expectations-augmented aggregate supply curve is traced out as $f'ed'$. The aggregate supply curve based on correct information is that of the basic model, labelled AS.

So that you can see clearly the relationship between the new Keynesian expectations-augmented aggregate supply curve and the new classical expectations-augmented aggregate supply curve, Figure 28.3 superimposes the two analyses on top of each other. You can easily verify that Figure 28.3 contains everything that is in Figure 28.2 that generates the curve $EAS(K)$ (the new Keynesian aggregate supply curve) and also everything that is in Figure 27.3 that generates the new classical aggregate supply curve, the curve $EAS(C)$. Notice that the *new Keynesian aggregate supply curve is flatter than the new classical curve*. This says that the new Keynesian analysis gives rise to more pessimistic predictions than the new classical analysis about the effects on prices of a cut in aggregate demand, but to more optimistic predictions concerning the inflationary consequences of stimulating aggregate demand.

Aside, however, from the slopes of the two curves, the two theories as presented

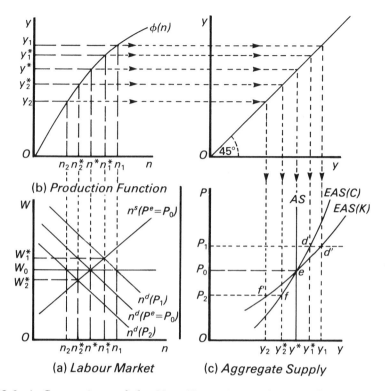

Figure 28.3 *A Comparison of the New Keynesian and New Classical Aggregate Supply Curves*

This diagram superimposes Figure 28.2 upon Figure 27.2. The key differences between the new Keynesian and new classical models are seen in Frames (a) and (c). In the new Keynesian model the money wage is fixed at W_0 so that as the price level varies between P_1 and P_2, the quantity of labour traded varies between n_1 and n_2, and output between y_1 and y_2. In the new classical analysis, as the price level varies between P_1 and P_2 shifting the demand curve between $n^d(P_1)$ and $n^d(P_2)$, so the money wage rate fluctuates between W_1^* and W_2^*. These fluctuations in the wage rate damp off fluctuations in the quantity of labour demanded so that employment and output fluctuate between n_1^* and n_2^* and output between y_1^* and y_2^*. The two expectations-augmented aggregate supply curves cut the basic aggregate supply curve at the expected price level, point e. The new classical curve is steeper than the new Keynesian curve.

---

so far look very similar. There is, however, a crucial difference between the two that has not yet been revealed as fully as it needs to be, and that arises from the fact that the contractually determined wages are not all set on the same date but, rather, overlap each other. Let us now turn to an examination of the implications of this.

D. Overlapping Wage Contracts

The new Keynesian theory of aggregate supply developed above is based on the idea that at the beginning of each period of time workers and employers sit down together, form an expectation of what the price level will be over the coming period (say a year), agree on a money wage rate that will achieve an expected equilibrium in the labour market, and then agree to trade at that wage for the coming year. The amount of labour that they trade will be determined by the actual demand for labour once the general price level is revealed. Suppose, however, that that is not a good characterisation of the situation. Specifically, suppose that half of the labour force sits down at the beginning of January each year and negotiates a wage that is to prevail, not for one year, but for two years. The other half of the labour force will negotiate a wage on the alternate January, again for a period of two years. The analysis contained in Figures 28.1 and 28.2 still applies, but now only to half of the labour force. The other half of the labour force has already performed that same exercise one year earlier and will be performing it one year later. The actual wage rate that is observed at any one point in time in the economy will be an average of the wages that have been set at various dates in the past on contracts that are still current. In the example, if half of the labour force sets its wages in January of one year and the other half in January of the alternate year, then the wage that prevails in any one year will be equal to a half of the wage determined at the beginning of January of the year in question, plus half of the wage determined at the beginning of the preceding January. This wage will be based on expectations of the general price level that were formed at two different dates in the past. This being so, the aggregate expectations-augmented aggregate supply curve will depend not only upon current expectations of the current price level, but on older (and perhaps by now known to be wrong) expectations of the current price level. Once agents are locked into a money wage decision based on an old, and perhaps falsified, expectation of the price level, there is, by the hypothesis embodied in the new Keynesian analysis, nothing they can do about it until the next wage review date comes along. This has very important implications for the analysis of economic policy, as you will see in subsequent chapters of this book.

This new Keynesian analysis is a way of rationalising 'sticky money wages'. *Money wages are sticky*, not because of some mysterious downward rigidity as in Keynes's analysis, but *because contractual commitments prevent people from adjusting money wages in the light of new information*. In effect, workers and firms have said to each other, 'These are the terms on which we are willing to do business *come what may* until the next time we sit down two years from now'. There is a lively debate in the current literature concerning the efficiency of the labour market contracts which the new Keynesian economists use in their theory of aggregate supply. New classical economists such as Robert Barro insist that such contracts are inefficient and cannot be rationalised as the kinds of contracts which rational profit-maximising and utility-maximising agents would enter into. The new Keynesians agree that it is hard to think of convincing reasons why people would enter into contracts such as these. They insist, however, that we do observe such contracts as commonplace, and in the absence of a really firm understanding as to why, they argue that we have no alternative but to incorporate them into our macroeconomic models.

The new Keynesian analysis can be viewed as having replaced the traditional Keynesian assumption of a fixed money wage with the assumption of a fixed timing structure to the changes in money wages that arise in a rather rigid contractual setting.

SUMMARY

A. Assumptions of the New Keynesian Analysis

There are three key assumptions of the new Keynesian analysis:
(1) that money wages are determined to achieve an expected equilibrium in the labour market;
(2) that the actual quantity of labour traded is determined by the quantity demanded; and
(3) that wage contracts overlap in time.

B. Determination of Money Wages

Money wages are determined in the new Keynesian theory of aggregate supply by equating the supply of labour which is expected on the basis of the expected price level with the demand for labour which is expected on the basis of the expected price level. Figure 28.1 illustrates this and should be thoroughly understood.

C. The New Keynesian Expectations-Augmented Aggregate Supply Curve

The new Keynesian theory of wage determination implies that the expectations-augmented aggregate supply curve will have the same basic shape as the new classical expectations-augmented aggregate supply curve. The new Keynesian aggregate supply curve will, however, be flatter than the new classical curve. This arises because, when the demand for labour function shifts because of changes in the actual price level, there are no partially compensating adjustments in the money wage rate to dampen off some of the effects of the shift in demand function on the quantity demanded. The quantity of labour demanded adjusts fully to reflect shifts in the demand function at the fixed money wage rate, and the level of output therefore fluctuates by a larger amount than otherwise would be the case.

D. Overlapping Wage Contracts

The fact that not all labour market contracts are signed on the same date, but overlap each other, has fundamental implications for the aggregate supply curve. Instead of the position of the aggregate supply curve depending only upon *current* expectations of the price level, it will also depend upon previous expectations of the current period's price level. Expectations formed all the way back to the date on which the oldest existing contract was signed will be embodied in the position of the Keynesian expectations-augmented aggregate supply curve.

Review Questions

1. What are the three key assumptions of the new Keynesian theory of the labour market?

2. Why is the new Keynesian expectations-augmented aggregate supply curve flatter than the new classical curve?

3. Why do the new Keynesian, new classical, and basic model aggregate supply curves all intersect at full-employment output and the expected price level?

4. The new Keynesian theory of the labour market assumes that households can be 'off' their supply curves. How might firms induce households to behave in such a way? Could households be induced to be permanently off their supply curves?

5. What are the implications of overlapping labour market contracts?

6. Compare the new Keynesian with the old Keynesian theory of the labour market. What are the main differences? Why do you think the new Keynesian theory is so called?

7.(a) An economy is described by the following equations: the marginal product of labour curve is described by the equation

$$MPL = 5,000,001 - 5n$$

The supply of labour is given by

$$n^s = 999,990 + 10(W/P)$$

What is the equilibrium level of employment and real wage given complete information? That is, what would the equilibrium of the basic model be?

(b) If the production function is $y = 5,000,001n - 2.5n^2$, calculate and plot an equation for the new classical expectations-augmented aggregate supply curve assuming that the expected price level remains constant at unity.

(c) Calculate and plot an equation for the new Keynesian expectations-augmented aggregate supply curve, assuming that the expected price level is fixed at unity. (Hint: try actual price levels of 1/2, 1, and 2 for the purpose of this exercise.)

29

Equilibrium Income, Employment and the Price Level with Fixed Expectations

You have now begun to modify the basic model of aggregate supply to allow for incomplete information on the part of market participants. In particular, in Chapters 27 and 28 you were introduced to two theories leading to the expectations-augmented aggregate supply curve. This chapter employs the expectations-augmented aggregate supply curve and analyses what happens when aggregate demand changes, but when the expected price level is fixed. However, before embarking on that analysis, there are two preliminary tasks that need attention. Overall, then, you have three tasks in this chapter, which are to:

A. **know the definition of full-employment equilibrium;**
B. **know how to characterise full-employment equilibrium in a simple diagram;** and
C. **know how output, employment, the real wage, the price level, and the money wage are affected by a rise or fall in aggregate demand when the expected price level is fixed.**

A. Full-Employment Equilibrium

Full-employment equilibrium is a situation in which the actual price level is equal to the expected price level. The full-employment equilibrium levels of output, employment, and the real wage are the levels of those variables which occur when the actual price level is equal to the expected price level.

Although the name full-employment equilibrium is used to describe a situation in which the price level is equal to the expected price level, that does not mean that there is no unemployment in full-employment equilibrium. This may seem like a contradiction of terms, but it is really nothing more than a convenient use of language. You will remember from your analysis of the basic model of aggregate output and employment determination, that you were able to generate unemployment even in that model. Recall that there are no wrong expectations in that model. Minimum wages which raised the economy-average real wage above the equilibrium real wage, an economy-wide labour union which raised the real wage above the equilibrium wage, a rise in unemployment benefits, or a rise in employment or income taxes were all seen as factors which could produce a level of employment of labour below the labour supply. That amount of unemployment is sometimes named *natural unemployment. At full-employment equilibrium, the unemployment rate is equal to the natural unemployment rate.* This will be obvious to you if you recall that in developing the basic model no distinction was made between the expected and the actual price level. Workers were presumed to supply their labour in accordance with full knowledge of the actual price level. So, the basic model always depicts a full-employment equilibrium. As a matter of definition, then, when the unemployment rate is equal to the natural unemployment rate, the term full employment is used to describe the condition of the labour market.

In what follows in the rest of this chapter and in subsequent chapters, the analysis abstracts from the natural rate of unemployment. That does not mean that it is ignored or assumed not to exist. Rather, the analysis will be thought of as determining the level of unemployment relative to the natural rate of unemployment. In the formal analysis, the natural rate of unemployment will be treated as if it were zero. That is only an analytical convenience. The reason for making this abstraction is that the natural unemployment rate itself is not affected by the factors which are being considered. Further, the natural unemployment rate does not affect the factors that will be considered. It is possible, therefore, to analyse fluctuations of unemployment around the natural rate independently of what the natural rate of unemployment is.

To summarise: full-employment equilibrium values of real income, employment, and the real wage occur when the price level is equal to its expected level. There will be some unemployment in that situation, determined by the real factors (discussed in Chapters 12 and 15) that determine the natural rate of unemployment.

B. Simple Diagram to Characterise Full-Employment Equilibrium

It is important to characterise full-employment equilibrium before moving on to analysing the effects of a change in aggregate demand on the levels of output, employment, and prices. Figure 29.1 illustrates a full-employment equilibrium, and the text in this section guides you through that figure.

Notice that the diagram is similar to Figures 11.2 and 27.3. Frame (a) shows the labour market with the money wage on the vertical axis and employment on the horizontal axis. Frame (b) shows the production function — the relationship between the maximum amount of output that can be supplied and the level of employment. Frame (c) shows the aggregate goods market with aggregate demand and aggregate supply for goods plotted against the price level.

First, pretend that there are no curves in Frame (a) at all. Instead of using Frame (a), recall the diagram for the labour market which was employed in the basic model

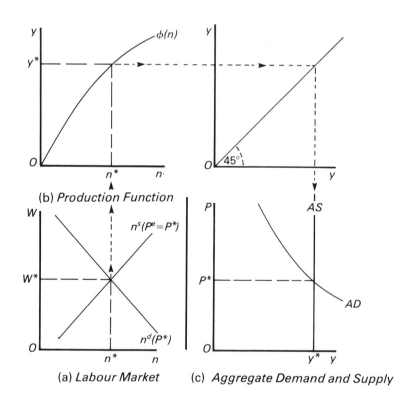

(b) *Production Function*

(a) *Labour Market*   (c) *Aggregate Demand and Supply*

Figure 29.1 *Full-Employment Equilibrium*

Where the aggregate demand curve cuts the basic model aggregate supply curve (Frame (c)) is determined the full-employment equilibrium price level. When the supply of labour and demand for labour curves are plotted in Frame (a) against the money wage rate, but given the price level fixed at P^*, they intersect at n^* and determine the money wage rate W^*.

of real income and employment (Figure 11.1(a)). You will recall that in that Frame, we plotted the level of employment against the *real* wage. Where the supply of labour curve cuts the demand for labour curve, the equilibrium real wage and the level of employment are determined. Let us suppose that the level of employment determined in Figure 11.1(a) is the value n^* plotted on the horizontal axis of Frame (a) in Figure 29.1. That is, we have determined n^* from the basic model of Chapter 11.

You can now determine the level of output which will be produced with the level of employment n^*. Following the dotted line from Frame (a) to Frame (b), you see that the level of output associated with n^* is equal to y^*. Transferring that level of output (following the dotted line) to the aggregate supply and demand diagram (Frame (c)) generates the aggregate supply curve shown as the vertical line labelled AS.

From either the simple monetary theory of aggregate demand or, more satisfactorily, from the Keynesian *IS–LM* theory of aggregate demand (recall Chapter 22, Section D), we may obtain the aggregate demand curve. This is shown in Frame (c) as the curve labelled AD. Where the aggregate demand and aggregate supply curves intersect determines the equilibrium price level P^*.

Now that the equilibrium price level P^* has been determined, it is possible to work backwards and determine the money wage. This could not have been done before determining the equilibrium price level because you would not have known where in Frame (a) to plot the labour supply and demand curves. Recall that although these curves are fixed when graphed against the real wage, they shift with the price level when plotted against the money wage. The demand for labour curve, recall, depends upon the actual price level, and we can draw that as the curve labelled $n^d(P^*)$. This is the demand for labour curve plotted against the money wage rate when the price level is equal to the equilibrium price level P^*. The supply of labour curve is plotted against the expected price level. Since the diagram is characterising full-employment equilibrium, the supply of labour curve is drawn for an expected price level equal to the actual price level, which in turn is equal to P^*. The supply curve is shown as the curve labelled $n^s(P^e = P^*)$. This supply curve cuts the demand curve at the level of employment n^*. This follows directly from the fact that the demand and supply curves are fixed when plotted against the real wage and shift proportionately to each other as the price level varies when plotted against the money wage. It follows, then, that if both the supply and demand curves are plotted against the money wage, but for the same given price level for both curves, then these curves must cut at the full-employment level of employment n^*.

You can now read off, finally, the money wage that is associated with an equilibrium in the labour market at the given actual and expected price level P^*. This money wage is denoted in Frame (a) as W^*.

This completes the characterisation of full-employment equilibrium. It is worth emphasising that there is no difficulty in representing, in this diagram, a positive value for the natural rate of unemployment. You could, for example, supplement Frame (a) with a minimum wage rate, thereby shifting the regulated equilibrium level of employment and the aggregate supply curve, or you could, for example, modify Frame (a) along the lines suggested in the earlier analysis of the effects of unemployment benefits, again generating an equilibrium level of unemployment. All that these things do is to raise the equilibrium money wage and lower the level of employment relative to that shown in Frame (a).

C. Effects of a Change in Aggregate Demand with a Fixed Expected Price Level

Suppose that the expected price level P^e is equal to P^* and is fixed at that value. Later (in the next chapter) we shall inquire what determines the expected price level and how it might change. It will be clearer, however, if we proceed in steps, and the first step is to examine what happens to the levels of output, employment and unemployment, the real wage, and the price level when the economy experiences a change in aggregate demand, but when the expected price level does not change.

(i) The Expectations-Augmented Aggregate Supply Curve

The starting point for the analysis is the *expectations-augmented aggregate supply curve* discussed at length in the previous two chapters. Either the new Keynesian or new classical version of the *EAS* curve could be employed. The treatment here uses the new classical version. You may find it a useful exercise to carry out a parallel exercise using the new Keynesian version. Figure 29.2 summarises the derivation of the new classical aggregate supply curve. You will recall that the supply of labour curve shown in Frame (a) depends on the expected price level. Since the expected price level is being held constant, so the supply of labour curve is also held constant. You will also recall that the demand for labour curve depends upon the *actual* value of the price level. The demand curve labelled $n^d(P^*)$ is drawn for a level of prices equal to P^*. Where that curve intersects the supply of labour curve determines the full-employment equilibrium money wage W^* and employment level n^*. The production function in Frame (b) shows that the employment level n^* will produce a level of output supplied equal to y^*. Following the dotted line from Frame (b) to Frame (c), you arrive at the point a, which represents the full-employment equilibrium point where P^*, the actual price level, is equal to the expected price level.

If the price level being considered is at a higher value than P^*, say P_1, as shown on the vertical axis of Frame (c), then you have to replot the demand for labour curve, showing it to have shifted upwards. This is shown as $n^d(P_1)$ in Frame (a). This determines a new higher money wage and employment level (W_1 and n_1) and, through Frame (b), a higher level of output y_1. If this output level is transferred (following the dotted line) to Frame (c), we see that at the price level P_1 the output level will be y_1 and the economy will operate at the point marked b.

Now consider the price level as being less than P^*, say at P_2, as marked on the vertical axis of Frame (c). In this case the labour demand curve has to be shifted downwards. This is shown as $n^d(P_2)$ in Frame (a). This labour demand curve intersects the fixed labour supply curve to determine the lower money wage and employment levels W_2 and n_2. At the employment level n_2 the economy will produce an output level of y_2. Transferring the output level y_2 (following the dotted line) to Frame (c) shows us that the economy will produce at the point marked c where the price level is P_2 and the output level is y_2. Joining up all the points c, a, b, generates the *expectations-augmented aggregate supply curve* marked *EAS*.

Now that your knowledge of the expectations-augmented aggregate supply curve

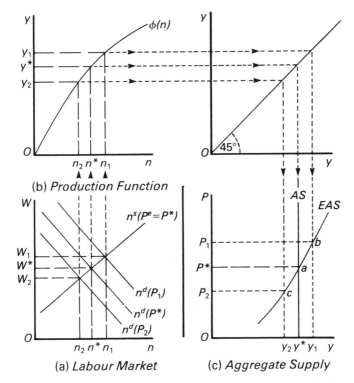

Figure 29.2 *The Expectations-Augmented Aggregate Supply Curve*
As the actual price level varies between P_1 and P_2 (Frame (c)), so the demand for labour curve shifts between $n^d(P_1)$ and $n^d(P_2)$ (Frame (a)). With the expected price level fixed at P^*, the supply of labour curve does not shift. Labour market equilibrium employment and wages vary between n_1 and n_2 and W_1 and W_2, generating output fluctuations between y_1 and y_2. Thus, as the price level moves from P_1 to P_2, output moves from y_1 to y_2 along the curve *EAS*.

has been reviewed, it is a very simple matter to see how changes in aggregate demand affect output, employment, the real wage, and the price level. First of all, the effects on prices and output will be considered and then subsequently the effects on the labour market.

(ii) The Effects of a Change in Aggregate Demand on the Levels of Output and Prices

Figure 29.3 summarises the effects of a change in aggregate demand on prices and output. The starting point, *a*, is a full-employment equilibrium. Here the price level, P^*, and output level, y^*, are determined by the intersection of the aggregate demand curve, AD^*, and the aggregate supply curve, *AS*, as well as the expectations-augmented aggregate supply curve, *EAS*. The point *a* is the full-employment equilibrium as defined above in the sense that the actual price level P^* is equal to the expected price level that underlies the *EAS* curve.

Hold the expected price level constant at P^* and ask what happens if the level of

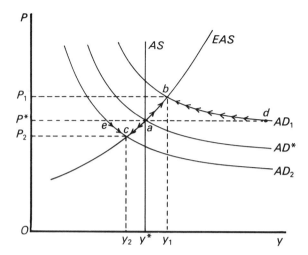

Figure 29.3 *The Effects of a Rise or Fall in Aggregate Demand with Fixed Price Level Expectations*

If the expected price level is fixed at P^*, the EAS curve does not move. When aggregate demand is AD^*, the actual price level is P^* and the economy is at full employment. If aggregate demand was AD_1, the equilibrium would be at point b with a higher price level and output level (P_1, y_1). If aggregate demand fell to AD_2, then the price level and output would fall to P_2 and y_2 at point c.

---

aggregate demand changes. You can think of aggregate demand changing either because the money supply rises, government spending rises, taxes are cut, or there is a shift in the demand for investment goods. (Depending on which of these shocks occur, the rate of interest that is simultaneously determined with the variables being considered here will either rise or fall. It is a fairly straightforward matter to work out the implications for the rate of interest by going back to the $IS-LM$ analysis of Chapter 22. In the development here and in the rest of the book, with the exception of a brief section of Chapter 33, movements in interest rates, while occurring, will not be emphasised.) Suppose that, for whatever of the above reasons, the aggregate demand curve shifts from AD^* to AD_1. It is clear that with this new higher level of aggregate demand, there is only one point where the economy can come to an equilibrium, and that point is marked b. At the point b, output is y_1 and the price level is P_1.

How does this new equilibrium point b come about? Suppose the economy started out in the full-employment equilibrium at point a. Suppose then that aggregate demand suddenly increased from AD^* to AD_1. At the new higher level of aggregate demand, but with the price level remaining at P^*, there would be an excess demand for goods equivalent to the distance ad in the diagram. That excess demand would generate rising prices, as people who sought to raise their expenditure would find it necessary to offer higher prices in order to acquire the goods that they were demanding. As the price level was forced upwards, the level of aggregate demand would decline. This is shown in the diagram by the arrows moving up the aggregate demand curve.

There would also be a response on the supply side of the economy. As the prices of some goods began to increase, firms, being well-informed about the markets in which they operate and observing the rising price of their output, would start to increase their demand for labour. Their demand for labour curves would begin to shift upwards (as in Figure 29.2(a)). This would produce a rise in the money wage but a fall in the real wage and, therefore, a rise in employment and a rise in the aggregate supply of goods. There would therefore be, on the supply side, a tendency for firms to slide up the aggregate supply curve from a to b, as shown by the arrows in the diagram. As the price level increased, the excess of demand over supply would be choked off, and the economy would come to rest at point b, with firms satisfied that they were supplying the profit-maximising quantity and households satisfied that they were buying the right quantity of goods in total.

Next, consider what would happen if aggregate demand was to fall. Specifically, suppose aggregate demand fell from AD^* to AD_2. This aggregate demand curve cuts the expectations-augmented aggregate supply curve at c. This is the new equilibrium point, with the price level P_2 and y_2. To see how this equilibrium comes about, perform a similar conceptual experiment to that which you have just performed in the case of a rise in aggregate demand. Suppose that the price level is initially at P^* and that aggregate demand has just fallen to AD_2. In such a case there will be a cutback in demand and there will be an excess of supply over demand equal to the distance ae in the diagram. This excess of supply over demand will cause prices to fall. As prices begin to fall, firms' demand for labour curves (in Figure 29.2(a)) will be shifting downwards. This will lower the amount of labour employed and the amount of output supplied. Firms will travel downwards along their supply curves, resulting in movement along the expectations-augmented aggregate supply curve from a to c, as shown by the arrows. Households will move along their demand curves, resulting in a movement along the aggregate demand curve from e to c. At point c there is a balance between supply and demand and there is no further tendency for the price level or the level of output to change.

Although the analysis that has just been performed has been done explicitly within the framework of the new classical theory of aggregate supply, the same broad predictions would have been generated if the new Keynesian theory had been used. In that case, however, the output movements would have been greater and the price movements less than in the new classical case. You can easily verify that this is so by checking back to the comparison of the new Keynesian and new classical expectations-augmented aggregate supply curves. Since the new Keynesian curve is flatter than the new classical curve, swings in aggregate demand have bigger output and smaller price effects in the new Keynesian than in the new classical case.

(iii) Key Assumption of Equilibrium Analysis

We assume that the equilibrating processes just described, which move the economy from position a to position b when aggregate demand rises and from position a to position c when aggregate demand falls, occur quickly enough for points a, b, and c to be the only points observed.

(iv) Summary of Effects of Change in Aggregate Demand on Output and Price Level

We can now summarise the effects of a rise or fall in aggregate demand on the level of output and prices.
   (a) If the expected price level is constant and aggregate demand rises, then output and the price level will both rise.
   (b) If the expected price level is constant and aggregate demand falls, then output and the price level will both fall.

(v) Effects of a Change in Aggregate Demand on Employment and Wages

The effects on the level of employment, money wages, and the real wage will now be analysed. Because of the way in which the aggregate demand experiment has been set up, these effects can immediately be read off by referring back to Figure 29.2.

First, consider the case of a rise in aggregate demand. This moves the economy, as you saw in Figure 29.3, to position b. Position b is also shown in Figure 29.2, so that you can easily see the effects on the labour market. At the price level P_1, which is the consequence of a rise in aggregate demand to AD_1, the demand for labour curve will shift to the right and be in the position shown as $n^d(P_1)$. This produces a higher money wage, W_1 and a higher employment level, n_1. It also produces a lower real wage. The real wage has fallen because the money wage increased by less than the price level has increased. (Refer back to Chapter 27, Figure 27.2 and the associated discussion if you cannot see that this is true.) Indeed, it is the fall in the real wage that induces a higher level of employment. Firms, seeing that the real wage has fallen, find it profitable to hire additional workers. Households, on the other hand, having a fixed expectation of the price level, think that the real wage has increased and therefore are willing to supply more labour.

Next, consider the case of a cut in aggregate demand. If aggregate demand is cut to the curve AD_2, it will intersect the expectations-augmented aggregate supply curve at point c in Figure 29.3. Point c is also shown in Figure 29.2(c). You see that at that price level the demand for labour curve is shown as $n^d(P_2)$ and determines an equilibrium level of wages and employment of W_2 and n_2. So a cut in aggregate demand leads to a cut in the money wage and in the level of employment. In this situation *real wages* will have increased. This occurs because the price level will have fallen by more than the money wage has fallen. Firms, knowing this, will cut back on their demand for labour. Households will not resist this cutback in the demand for labour because, as far as they are concerned, the real wage that they have been offered has fallen. This arises because the money wage has fallen while the expected price level has remained constant.

Although the above effects have been stated in terms of the new classical theory, similar effects would occur in the new Keynesian case. The key difference between the two would be that in the new Keynesian case, households would be knocked off the supply of labour curve. When aggregate demand increased to AD_1, the money wage rate would remain constant, the price level would rise, and the real wage would fall. This would induce an increase in the demand for labour which would not be matched by an increase in the supply of labour. Nevertheless, because of the assumed nature of the contract that workers have with their employers, they would be required to supply the extra labour even though this was in excess of their labour supply. In the reverse case, when aggregate demand falls to AD_2, workers are knocked off their supply curve in the opposite direction. In this case, the price level falls, so that with a fixed money wage rate, the real wage rises, thereby lowering the demand for labour. Firms now hire less labour than would like to work. In this case, there will be unemployment over and above any natural unemployment in the economy, and it will have the appearance of being involuntary, in the sense that if they could have signed different contracts, workers would have done so.

(vi) Summary of the Effects of a Change in Aggregate Demand with a Constant Expected Price Level

To summarise, the effects of a rise in aggregate demand with a fixed expected price level on all five variables in our model are as follows:
- (a) With a fixed expected price level, a rise in aggregate demand will raise output, raise the price level, raise the level of employment, and lower the real wage. Unemployment will fall below the natural rate of unemployment.
- (b) With a fixed expected price level, a cut in aggregate demand will lower the level of output, lower the price level, lower the level of employment, and raise real wages. It will also create unemployment in excess of the natural rate of unemployment.

This completes the formal analysis of the effects of a change in aggregate demand on the levels of output, employment, the real wage, and the price level when price expectations are fixed.

You may find it useful, to ensure that you have understood the analysis that lies behind the movement of the economy from position a to position b in the face of a rise in aggregate demand and from position a to position c in the face of a fall in aggregate demand, to check that these movements are consistent with people's rational maximising choices as described in the story set out at the end of Chapter 26.

Although positions b and c in this economy are equilibrium positions in the sense that a is an equilibrium position, they differ from equilibrium a in a fundamental respect. They cannot be sustained forever, whereas position a can. To see why they cannot be sustained forever takes us into an analysis of how expectations are formed and changed, and that will be the subject of the next chapter.

SUMMARY

A. Full-Employment Equilibrium

Full-employment equilibrium values of output, employment, unemployment, and the real wage occur when the price level is equal to the expected price level. The unemployment present at full-employment equilibrium is called the *natural rate of unemployment*.

B. Simple Diagram to Characterise Full-Employment Equilibrium

This is done in Figure 29.1, and you should be thoroughly familiar with that figure. You should also understand that it is identical to the equilibrium in the basic model which we examined in Chapter 11.

C. Effects of a Change in Aggregate Demand with a Fixed Expected Price Level

If the expected price level is fixed, a rise in aggregate demand will raise the level of output, employment, and the price level. It will lower the real wage and will make unemployment fall below its natural rate.

When the expected price level is fixed and aggregate demand falls, there will be a fall in output, employment, and in the price level. The real wage will rise, and unemployment will rise above its natural rate.

Review Questions

1.   Define full-employment equilibrium.

2.   Explain why there will be some unemployment at full-employment equilibrium.

3.   Define the natural unemployment rate. Is the natural unemployment rate affected by the price level? Why or why not? Explain.

4.(a) Characterise full-employment equilibrium in a set of diagrams like those shown in Figure 29.1.
  (b) Now introduce a minimum-wage law which fixes the *money wage* above the equilibrium and work out the new equilibrium level of output, employment, and prices. (This is a tricky question.)

5.   Consider Figure 29.2. Suppose the expected price level was to rise to P_1. What would happen to the *EAS* curve? Draw a new curve to illustrate your answer.

6.   Why does the *EAS* curve slope upwards?

7.   What happens to the levels of: (a) output, (b) employment, (c) unemployment, (d) the money wage rate, (e) the real wage, (f) the price level, if the money supply rises but the expected price level remains constant?

8.   What happens to all the variables listed as (a) to (f) in Question 7 if the expected price level falls while the money supply remains constant?

9.   What happens to all the variables listed as (a) to (f) in Question 7 if both the expected price level and aggregate demand rise by the *same* percentage amount?

10.   Review the following terms or concepts:
      (i) rational maximising behaviour
      (ii) equilibrium.

30

Price Level Expectations

We saw, when we dealt with the neoclassical synthesis, that a major shortcoming of that body of analysis was the lack of a theory of how price level expectations were formed and how they changed. So far, in the development of the new theories of aggregate supply, the expected price level has been taken as fixed; no attempt has been made to explain where it comes from or what might cause it to change. It is certain that the expected price level *does* change, especially in an inflationary environment. There is much imprecise popular talk about an 'inflation psychology' being one of the causes of inflation. You are going to discover that if by an 'inflation psychology' people mean inflation (or price level) expectations, then there is no rational basis for the view that inflation can be *caused* by an 'inflation psychology'. Rather, the very things which generate inflation also generate inflation expectations. The questions dealt with in this chapter are:

  (i) what determines the expected price level?
  (ii) what factors lead to changes in the expected price level?

You have four tasks, which are to:

  A. **understand the distinction between a subjective expectation and a conditional mathematical expectation;**
  B. **understand the concept of a rational expectation;**
  C. **understand the concept of the rational expectation of the price level; and**
  D. **know how to work out the rational expectation of the price level.**

A. Subjective Expectation and Conditional Mathematical Expectation

(i) Subjective Expectation

The term *expectation* has two distinct meanings. In ordinary speech it is used to describe a more or less vague feeling about some future event. This is a *subjective expectation*. For example, we might be travelling by car along a congested motorway and *expect* that it will take an hour to reach our destination; or we might be standing at a bus stop and *expect* the bus to come along in five minutes. Another example concerns the expectations of a skilled snooker player. Such a person might have an expectation as to what will happen when the cue is aligned in a particular direction and applied to the cue ball with a particular direction of spin and force. That expectation may be, for example, that the cue ball will collide with a second ball at a specific angle, force, and spin such that the second ball is dispatched to a pocket and the cue ball is aligned optimally for the next shot.

Typically, we do not explicitly analyse the reasons why we hold the expectations that we do. We have ways of arriving at subjective feelings which, *on the average*, seem to work out all right, and we don't consciously examine the sources of these expectations. The snooker player, for example, does not ask himself where his expectation comes from. He simply knows how to play the game and uses a well-developed instinct and skill to achieve the appropriate movements of the balls.

A subjective expectation, then, is simply a feeling that an individual has about the likely consequences of some particular action or as to the likely outcome of some particular event.

(ii) Conditional Mathematical Expectation

There is a more precise usage of the term expectation — a *conditional mathematical expectation*. A mathematical expectation is nothing other than an average. An example will make it easy to understand this. Suppose we have 3000 cards: 1000 of them are printed with the number 4 on one side, another 1000 with the number 5, and another 1000 with the number 6. These cards are put into a bag and are shaken up so that they are thoroughly mixed. Then, 300 cards are drawn from the bag at random. You are asked to predict what the average of the numbers drawn will be. You know that there are three kinds of cards in the bag; that one-third of them has the number 4, one-third has the number 5, and one-third the number 6. Since the cards have been shuffled very thoroughly and they have been drawn at random, you will predict that, on the average, out of 300 cards drawn, 100 will have the number 4, 100 the number 5, and 100 the number 6. You calculate the average of that and you arrive at a prediction that the average of all the cards drawn will be 5. You have just calculated a mathematical expectation.

A *conditional mathematical expectation* is a mathematical expectation calculated when some *information* is already *given*. For example, suppose in the numbered card game described above, you were told that of the 300 cards drawn, 200 were numbered 6. (This would be an improbable, though possible, outcome.) You are now asked to predict the average value of all 300 cards drawn. You know that there are as many 4's as 5's in the bag, so you will expect that, of the remaining cards, 50 will be 4's, and 50 will be 5's. The average which you will calculate from 200 6's, 50 4's, and 50 5's is $(200/300)6 + (50/300)4 + (50/300)5 = 5.5$. You have now calculated a conditional mathematical expectation, or more simply, a *conditional expectation*. You have calculated the expected average value of the cards, *given* that two-thirds of them are 6's.

Let us go back to those earlier examples of subjective expectations and see whether we can think of a mathematical expectation interpretation of them.

Consider first of all your car journey along a congested motorway. Many factors will determine the number of minutes that it will take you to arrive at your destination. It will depend on the number of cars on the road ahead of you, whether there are any road works that have closed one or more of the lanes, whether or not there are any accidents blocking the road and perhaps a thousand other things which are difficult to enumerate. Suppose, however, that you have travelled this particular road over this particular distance many times in the past. You have a stock of experience from those previous journeys concerning the length of time that it takes. If you had actually kept a written record of the number of minutes it took each time you went on this particular road from a given starting point to a given destination then you could calculate the average journey time. That is, you could calculate the mathematical expectation. You may, however, be able to do better than that. It may be that you know that in certain circumstances the journey is quicker than others. Perhaps you know that if you travel between 8.00 a.m. and 9.00 a.m., or between 5.00 p.m. and 6.00 p.m., it takes longer than if you travel at other times of the day. You might also know that the journey typically takes less time on Tuesdays, Wednesdays and Thursdays than it does on Mondays and Fridays. You might also know that it takes longer in rain or icy weather than on a sunny day. Given all this extra information you could calculate the average number of minutes it takes you to complete this particular journey at different times of the day, different days of the week, in different weather conditions and allowing for any other factors that you have noticed affect the outcome. These averages would be conditional expectations. They would be conditional on the information concerning the time of day, day of the week, state of the weather, etc.

We could tell an identical story concerning the number of minutes that you expect to have to wait for a bus.

In the case of the snooker player example, if the snooker player could solve complicated geometrical problems in a very short span of time in his head and program himself to carry out the instructions implied by those solutions, he could make the cue ball follow exactly the trajectory and with exactly the force required to achieve his objective. This would be a rather complicated mathematical expectation calculation; it would be the calculation of a mathematical expectation of the paths of (at least) two balls.

Of course, just as in the case of the numbered cards in the bag, there will be no certainty as to the outcome in any of these examples. Unless we were to pull all three thousand cards from the bag we would not be able to predict for sure the average value of the cards drawn. Likewise, going back to the car journey example, unless we knew absolutely everything about the conditions on the road ahead of us we would not be able to make an exact prediction concerning the time at which we would arrive at our destination. We would nevertheless be able to calculate a mathematical expectation. That is, we would be able to calculate the expected value of the relevant variable, conditional on all the information available.

Let us now apply these ideas of a subjective expectation — a vague feeling about some likely event — and a mathematical expectation — a precise calculation of the expectation of some outcome based on all the information that is relevant and available — to the concept of a rational expectation.

B. Rational Expectation[1]

(i) Definition

The definition of a rational expectation is as follows. *An expectation is* said to be *rational when the subjective expectation coincides with the conditional mathematical expectation based on all available information.* Notice that the definition says that when a mathematical and a subjective expectation *coincide*, then the expectation is rational. It does not say that a rational expectation is arrived at by performing all the complicated calculations which it would be necessary to perform in order to arrive at the appropriate conditional mathematical expectation. As in the example given above, an expectation about the length of time it would take to complete a particular journey would be rational if the expectation arrived at by instinct, intuition, or judgment, based on past experience, turned out to coincide with the expectation based on a careful recording of previous experience and the calculation of a conditional expectation from those data.

(ii) Some Further Intuition on the Meaning of Rational Expectations

In order to get a better feel for what a rational expectation is, it might be helpful to consider expectations of a particular variable in which man has always been interested, namely, the future state of the weather. There are many ways in which we can arrive at an expectation of the future state of the weather. One would be to turn on the TV or radio station and hear the latest forecasts being put out by the meteorological office. Another would be to watch the squirrels and observe how many nuts they are stockpiling. Yet a further method would be to recall the various traditional sayings, such as the proposition about the number of days it will rain or not rain following a rainy or a fine St. Swithin's Day, or the proposition about March beginning like a lion and ending like a lamb, or *vice versa*. All of these would be methods of forming a view about some future state of the weather.

At the present time and in the present state of knowledge, it is clear that the rational expectation of the future state of the weather is obtained by employing the first of these devices. Expectations based on the other procedures, unless they are

---

1. The concept of rational expectations presented here is that of John F. Muth, Rational expectations and the theory of price movements, *Econometrica*, 29, July 1961, pp. 315–35 and introduced into macroeconomics by Robert E. Lucas Jr. (see footnote 2, Chapter 27).

based on well-established empirical regularities would not be rational. It may be, of course, that the squirrel actually does have some antennae which enable it to know what the likely future winter length, for example, is going to be and to react accordingly by stockpiling the appropriate quantity of nuts. In that event, it would be rational to base an expectation of the likely future winter length on the basis of that observed behaviour. This simply says that a rational expectation can be based on any information, provided that information can be demonstrated to be relevant to the forecasting of the future value of the variable of interest.

Although, in the current state of knowledge, forming a rational expectation of the weather involves the taking of meteorological observations followed by the use of meteorological theory to generate inferences concerning the implications of those observations for the future course of the weather, such predictions are not exact. This inexactness arises from the fact that meteorological information collection is far from total. It would cost an infinite or close to an infinite amount of resources to collect enough information to make predictions about the state and movement of every last molecule of air. Rather than do that, we invest a smaller amount of resources in sampling the atmosphere at various levels and in various places and make inferences concerning the behaviour between those points. Further, we do not evaluate intricate, complicated meteorological models involving millions and millions of equations. Rather, the meteorologists rely upon simpler theories which, on the average, work out all right, but which do not work out in every last instant. So, in the area of the weather, a rational expectation is an expectation that is based on all the information that is available, even though that information is far from the total set of information which one could imagine making available. This means that a rational expectation will not always be right. It will only be right on the average.

Notice, that in this meteorological example, we do not require that each and every individual be an expert meteorologist and be able to work out the weather forecast for himself. All that is necessary is that there be a body of science, and a systematic observation process to inform that body of science, to enable the scientific community to make the relevant predictions. The rest of us can then consume the fruits of that scientific activity.

C. Rational Expectation of the Price Level

(i) The Concept of Rational Expectation Applied to the Price Level

A rational expectation of the price level follows very directly from the examples that have been introduced so far. The rational expectation of the price level is that price level which is predicted on the basis of *all* the available information at the time at which the expectation is formed. Such information might include all the past history of the key economic variables, such as the price level itself, output, the real wage, the money wage, the money supply, and many other economic variables.

Expectations (forecasts) concerning economic variables are typically made available to the general public by the economics profession in much the same way as weather forecasts are made available by the meteorological profession. Such newspapers and journals as *The Financial Times*, *The Economist* and *The National Institute Economic Review* bring together and appraise forecasts of diverse groups of economic analysts. Of course, economic science is less settled than is meteorology. There are, as you were made aware of in Chapter 1, a variety of schools of thought concerning the way the economy works. In the present state of economic knowledge it is necessary, therefore, for each individual, in forming a rational expectation, to weigh the 'economic weather forecasts' which are put out by the economics profession against that individual's own personal knowledge, information and experience. Each individual's expectation will be arrived at using a large variety of inputs. That expectation will, however, be a rational expectation if it coincides with the conditional expectation based on all the information that is available.

(ii) A More Precise Definition of the Rational Expectation of the Price Level

We can make the definition of the rational expectation of the price level (or the inflation rate) more precise in a way that utilises the brilliant insights of John F. Muth. The ideas advanced by Muth are fairly deep and apparently difficult to grasp. Let us proceed then with some care. First, let us remind ourselves (and keep on reminding ourselves) that a rational expectation is just an average. Secondly, consider the question (which seems at first thought totally irrelevant to what we have just been discussing), 'what is theory?' Theory is, of course, a set of propositions designed to make predictions about the behaviour of some variable or variables. A theory of the price level (or the inflation rate) for example, is designed to make predictions about prices. Now no theory, of course, is exact. The best that we can expect of any theory is that it will be right on the average. This can be put more directly: all theories are designed to make predictions about the average behaviour of the phenomena that they address. Realising that theories are designed to make predictions about averages and also realising that a rational expectation is nothing other than an average led John Muth to a neat and powerful operational definition of a rational expectation. That definition states that a rational expectation is the same thing as the prediction of the relevant theory. Thus, the rational expectation of the price level is the same thing as the prediction of the relevant theory for determining the price level.

This is not, of course, to say that the rational expectation of the price level is the prediction of *any* theory of the price level. Theories that are clearly wrong would not yield predictions that coincided with the rational expectation. Only a theory that is not wrong would do so.

Now of course, in the current state of knowledge, we do not know, at least not with any certainty, what the relevant theory for predicting prices is. We are still in that stage of scientific inquiry of advancing alternative hypotheses and determining which if any of these alternatives are compatible with the facts. Although we do not know for sure that any particular theory is the correct theory, each time we advance a theory we do so in the hope that it will turn out to be the right one. Where that theory contains as part of its structure people's expectations of magnitudes predicted by the theory, the only internally consistent assumption that we can make concerning the way in which those expectations are formed, is to postulate that they are formed in the same way as that particular theory says the variable is determined. In so doing, we have a very powerful technique for developing, testing, and usually, though hopefully not always, rejecting a succession of alternative hypotheses concerning the determination of the macroeconomic variables.

You may be suspecting that to assume that people form their expectations in the same way that a particular theory says the variables in question are determined somehow stacks the cards in favour of the theory by making the predictions self-fulfilling. Nothing could in fact be further from the truth. It is harder to get theories to pass the test of prediction when they incorporate rational expectations than when they adopt some more mechanical *ad hoc* expectations hypotheses such as that embodied in the neoclassical model. A moment's reflection will convince you of the reason for this. We saw, when examining the co-movements of inflation and deviations of output from trend over the last decade (in Chapter 25) that, provided we were willing to make *ad hoc* assumptions about how the expected inflation rate changed each year, we would be able to account for the facts using the neoclassical model. Clearly, if we restricted ourselves by insisting that the expectations of inflation were not allowed to change conveniently so as to 'fit the facts', but insisted that inflationary expectations evolve only to coincide with the predictions of the theory, then we would be giving ourselves no additional 'degrees of freedom' with which to explain the facts. Thus, insisting that expectations be formed in such a way that they coincide with the predictions of the model places greater demands on the model and forces us to work harder to find the right one.

In the next section we shall go on to employ these ideas to calculate the rational expectation of the price level. Specifically, we shall use macroeconomic theory to make predictions about the price level and we shall assume that people's expectations of the price level coincide with the prediction of the theory.

D. How to Work Out the Rational Expectation of the Price Level

(i) The Boot-Laces Problem!

There is a preliminary problem which needs some discussion, arising from a key difference between the rational expectation of the price level and the rational expectation of something like the length of the winter or the amount of rain that is going to fall tomorrow. Tomorrow's weather is not going to be affected, at least as far as we know on the basis of existing information, by our expectations of what it will be.

From the work already done in Chapter 29 however, you know that this is *not* true of the price level. The price level next year, according to our theory, will depend on our expectation of the price level next year. To see this more clearly, consider Figure 30.1.

It shows the goods market as described by the theory developed in Chapter 29. The vertical axis measures the price level, and the horizontal axis measures the level of output. The curve *AD* is the aggregate demand curve, and *AS* is the aggregate supply curve derived from the labour market equilibrium conditions and the production

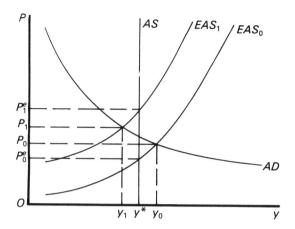

Figure 30.1 *The Effect of the Expected Price Level on the Actual Price Level*
Aggregate demand is held constant at the curve AD. If the expected price level is P_0^e then the expectations-augmented aggregate supply curve is EAS_0 and the actual price level is P_0 (and income y_0). If the expected price level was P_1^e, the EAS curve would be EAS_1 and the actual price level would be P_1 (and income y_1). Thus, holding everything else constant, the higher is the expected price level, the higher will be the actual price level.

function. The curve EAS_0 is the expectations-augmented aggregate supply curve drawn for an expected price level equal to P_0^e. Notice that the curve EAS_0 cuts the aggregate supply curve AS at the price level P_0^e. If the expected price level is P_0^e so that we are on EAS_0, and if aggregate demand is AD, then the intersection of EAS_0 and AD will determine the actual price level as P_0 and the level of output as y_0. If, however, the expected price level was higher than P_0^e at, say, P_1^e, then the expectations-augmented aggregate supply curve would become the curve shown as EAS_1, which cuts the aggregate supply curve AS at P_1^e. In this case, with the money supply constant so that the aggregate demand curve is held constant, the actual price level will be determined as P_1 and the level of output as y_1.

From this exercise you see that the actual price level is not independent of the expected price level. All that has been done in Figure 30.1 is to consider two alternative expectations for the price level, with everything else the same. Reading off the equilibrium solutions shows that there is a direct relationship between the expected and actual price levels. The higher the expected price level, the higher will be the actual price level, given a constant money supply.

How, then, can economic theory be used to determine the expected price level when the actual price level depends on the expected price level? It is rather like asking the question, how can we lift ourselves off the ground by pulling at our own boot-laces? We can pull as hard as we like, but no matter how hard we pull we shall stay put on the ground and make no progress. It looks a little bit as if the same is true concerning the use of economic theory to generate a prediction about the expected price level. If the expectation of the price level is necessary for forcasting the actual price level, how can the predictions of economic theory be used to form an expectation about the price level? How can we get off the ground?.

(ii) Working Out the Rational Expectation of the Price Level

It turns out that we can solve this problem. The way in which it is solved is illustrated in Figure 30.2. Remember that what we want to do is form an expectation of the price level that will prevail in a *future* period, and we want that expectation to be the prediction of the theory about the actual price level that will prevail in that future period.

The starting point has to be to form an expectation of the position of the aggregate demand curve. Suppose that we have done this and that the aggregate demand curve which we expect in the following period is shown as AD^e. What *this means*, of course, is *that we have formed an expectation of the value of the money supply, government expenditure, and taxes in the next period and figured out what they imply for the position of the aggregate demand curve in the next period.* Let us also put in the diagram the aggregate supply curve, the vertical line labelled AS, with the full-employment output level y^*. Now let us perform a purely conceptual experiment. Let us suppose that we start out with an entirely arbitrary expectation of the price level for the next period equal to P_0^e, as shown on the vertical axis of Figure 30.2. This means that we can now locate an expectations-augmented aggregate supply curve based on that expected price level. This is shown as $EAS(P_0^e)$. If P_0^e is the expected price level, then we see, given our expectation of the position of the aggregate

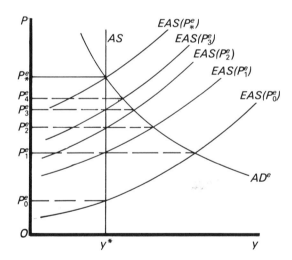

Figure 30.2 *Calculating the Rational Expectation of the Price Level*
The starting point for the calculation of the rational expectation of the price level is the formation of an expectation of aggregate demand. This requires that an expectation be formed of the values of the variables that determine aggregate demand as well as their influence upon demand. The curve AD^e denotes the expected aggregate demand curve. The rational expectation of the price level can be calculated by performing a conceptual experiment. Try P_0^e as the expected price level. That cannot be the rational expectation because the predicted price level is different from that initial trial value. It is P_1^e. P_1^e in turn predicts P_2^e as the actual price level. P_2^e in turns predicts P_3^e, and so on. Only the price level P_*^e predicts an actual price *level equal to P_*^e.* That is the rational expectation of the price level. It is the price level at which the expected aggregate demand curve (AD^e) cuts the full-employment aggregate supply curve (AS).

demand curve for the next period, that we would be forecasting a price level higher than the expected price level P_0^e. In fact, we would be forecasting a price level equal to P_1^e. It is clear that we have a conflict. We started with a purely arbitrary expectation of P_0^e and we see that if P_0^e is our expectation, our theory does not lead to a prediction that the price level will in fact be the value that we are expecting. Therefore, the expectation P_0^e is not a rational expectation. It is not the conditional expectation of the price level that is generated by our theory.

Suppose, continuing to perform the conceptual experiment, we now try a different expected price level. In particular, let us try P_1^e as the expected price level. This is the price level predicted by the first experiment conducted. With this higher expected price level we now have a different expectations-augmented aggregate supply curve, namely, $EAS(P_1^e)$. (Recall that EAS cuts AS at the price level equal to the expected price level.) This higher expected price level, P_1^e, generates, as we see, a forecast for the price level next period of P_2^e. That is the price level at which the expectation of the aggregate demand curve cuts the expectations-augmented aggregate supply curve $EAS(P_1^e)$. Again, we have a conflict. The forecast of our theory is different from the expectation P_1^e, which we arbitrarily assumed. Again, the prediction of the theory is higher than the assumed expectation. Still continuing with the conceptual experiment, let us now try a yet higher expected price level, namely, P_2^e. With this expected price level, the expectations-augmented aggregate supply curve becomes $EAS(P_2^e)$. This curve cuts the expected aggregate demand curve at the price level P_3^e. Yet again there is a conflict.

You can now see what is happening. Each time we use a trial value for the expected price level we are generating a prediction for the actual price level which is higher than the expected price level. However, you will notice that the gap between the initially assumed expected price level and the conditional prediction of the price level is becoming smaller. Can we bring this process to an end? The answer is that we can, and we do this by predicting that the price level will be equal to that value generated by the point at which the expected aggregate demand curve cuts the aggregate supply curve AS at P_*^e. Suppose we started out with that expectation for the price level. The expectations-augmented aggregate supply curve that passes through the AS curve at that point is $EAS(P_*^e)$. That is the expectations-augmented aggregate supply curve based on an expected price level of P_*^e. The theory now predicts that the price level in the next period will also be P_*^e. Notice that we are not saying that the price level next period *will actually turn out to be* P_*^e. Rather, we are saying that the prediction of our theory concerning the price level is that it will be P_*^e, given that our expectation is that the aggregate demand will be AD^e.

This leads to a very important proposition. *The rational expectation is that the price level will be equal to its expected full-employment value.* This is the only expectation of the price level which is consistent with the prediction of our theory concerning what the price level will be. You should not confuse this with the statement that 'everyone expects full employment always to prevail'. People know that random shocks will be hitting the economy and that we may *never* have full employment. They do the best they can, however, before the event, to form an expectation about the price level which, *should that expectation turn out to be correct*, will ensure full employment.

You now know how to determine the rational expectation of the price level in the context of the new theories of aggregate supply and the Keynesian *IS–LM* theory of aggregate demand.

(iii) Individual Thought Experiments

The hypothesis about individual economic agents is that they will behave on the basis of a subjective expectation of the price level which coincides with a conditional mathematical expectation of the price level, given the available information. That is, they behave on the basis of a rational expectation. That is not to say that everybody knows the same piece of economic theory that you know and that they are capable of calculating the rational expectation from this model or any other particular model. Rather, it is to say that people form their expectations of the price level in much the same way as the snooker player forms his expectation of the trajectories of the balls. Just as the snooker player follows instinctive and subjective calculations of the appropriate angles and forces and degrees of spin, so economic agents form their price expectations on the basis of ill-articulated thought processes. Of course, not everyone is a good snooker player and not everyone is good at forming expectations of future levels of prices. Those who are good snooker players, however, typically play a lot and are paid for their skills. Likewise, those who are good at making price level expectations (and who approximate to making rational expectations) typically make the expectations upon which the rest of us base our behaviour. They also get paid for their special skills.

SUMMARY

A. Subjective Expectation and Conditional Mathematical Expectation

A subjective expectation is a vague intuitive feeling about the likely value or outcome of some future event. A conditional mathematical expectation is the true average value of the outcome of a future event conditional on (i.e., given) whatever are the known actual values of all the relevant variables.

B. Rational Expectation

A rational expectation of a variable is a subjective expectation which *coincides* with the conditional mathematical expectation of that variable, given the available information.

C. Rational Expectation of the Price Level

The rational expectation of the price level is the prediction of the price level that is based on all the available information at the time at which the expectation is formed. It will coincide with the prediction of the relevant economic theory for predicting the price level.

D. How to Work Out the Rational Expectation of the Price Level

In the context of the new theories of macroeconomics, the rational expectation of the price level is the price level at which the expected aggregate demand curve cuts the aggregate supply curve. (The conceptual experiment whereby this expectation is worked out is discussed in Section D and illustrated in Figure 30.2 and should be thoroughly understood.)

Review Questions

1. Define a subjective expectation.

2. Define a conditional mathematical expectation.

3. Give the definition of a rational expectation and explain the relationship between a rational, a conditional mathematical, and a subjective expectation.

4. What are the key distinguishing features of a rational expectation?

5. What basic postulate concerning economic behaviour suggests that individuals would form expectations rationally?

6. Give some examples of economic agents (firms, individuals, etc.) who are 'in the business' of providing forecasts and selling other informational services. How do individuals benefit from these services?

7. What factors govern the degree to which the expectation of the price level affects aggregate supply? Under what circumstances will an increase in the expected price level have the greatest effect on aggregate supply?

8. What factors determine the expected price level?

9. Illustrate diagrammatically the derivation of the expected price level.

10. What relationship does the rational expectation of the price level bear to the full-employment price level?

31

Equilibrium Income, Employment and the Price Level with Rational Expectations

This chapter takes the next step in completing the rational expectations theory of the determination of the price level and real economic activity. From what you have learnt so far concerning the rational expectations theory, you will almost be able to guess what this chapter has to deal with. You now know that the expected price level is determined by expected aggregate demand. You also know from your analysis of the determination of output and prices with a fixed price level expectation that the actual price and output levels are determined where the actual demand curve cuts the expectations-augmented aggregate supply curve. All that now needs to be done, therefore, to complete our analysis is to explore the full implications of the distinction between expected (or anticipated) and unexpected (or unanticipated) changes in aggregate demand. Three tasks in this chapter will achieve that. They are to:

   A. **understand the distinction between an anticipated and unanticipated change in aggregate demand;**
   B. **know how output, employment, unemployment, the real wage, money wage, and price level are affected by an *anticipated* change in aggregate demand;** and
   C. **know how output, employment, unemployment, the real wage, money wage, and price level are affected by an *unanticipated* change in aggregate demand.**

A. Anticipated and Unanticipated Changes in Aggregate Demand

(i) Definition of Anticipated and Unanticipated Changes in Aggregate Demand

The level of aggregate demand in any particular year (say year t) may be thought of as being equal to aggregate demand in the previous year (year $t-1$) plus the change in demand over the year (Δy^d). That is

$$y^d_t = y_{t-1} + \Delta y^d_t \tag{31.1}$$

Notice that since actual output is always equilibrium output, y_{t-1} (actual output at time $t-1$) is equal to y^d_{t-1} (aggregate demand at time $t-1$). As soon as time $t-1$ is past, the value of output at that date becomes known (actually it's a little bit strong to say that this becomes known *as soon as* the time is past. It takes a short while for the data to be accumulated). The level of aggregate demand for time t, however, will not be known. Since rational economic agents need to form an expectation of the price level, and since the price level will depend upon the level of aggregate demand, it is necessary, in order to form a rational expectation of prices, to form a rational expectation of the level of aggregate demand. It is necessary, therefore, to forecast the change in aggregate demand so that its future value may be predicted.

The predicted component of the change in aggregate demand is referred to as the *anticipated change in aggregate demand*, and the unpredicted component is known as the *unanticipated change in aggregate demand*.

The actual change in aggregate demand is made up of these two components. That is

$$\Delta y^d_t = \Delta y^{de}_t + \Delta y^{du}_t \tag{31.2}$$

The superscript e denotes the expected or anticipated part of the change in aggregate demand, and the superscript u, the unanticipated or unexpected part. There is not, in general, any reason why the expected and unexpected components of the change in aggregate demand should be of the same sign. They may be, in which case they will each be a fraction of the actual change. It is possible, nevertheless, for the anticipated change to be greater than the actual change so that the unexpected change is negative. Five examples give the range of possibilities. They are set out in Table 31.1. The first example is of a correctly anticipated change in demand. The actual change is 100 and the expected change is 100. The second example is one in which the change in demand is entirely unanticipated. The expected change is 0, but the actual change is 100. The third example is one (which may be thought of as the most likely case) in which the actual change in demand is divided between an anticipated and unanticipated component. In the particular example, the division is 50/50, though in general, of course, it would not be so evenly split. The fourth example is one in which the actual change is less than the anticipated change, so that there is a negative unexpected component. The fifth and final example is one in which the expected change in aggregate demand is negative and, therefore, the unexpected change exceeds the actual change.

Table 31.1   Examples of Divisions of the Actual Change in Aggregate Demand
Between Anticipated and Unanticipated Changes

Example	Δy_t^d	=	Δy_t^{de}	+	Δy_t^{du}
1	100	=	100	+	0
2	100	=	0	+	100
3	100	=	50	+	50
4	100	=	200	−	100
5	100	=	−100	+	200

(ii) Measurement of the Anticipated and Unanticipated Changes in Aggregate Demand

In order actually to measure the anticipated and unanticipated changes in aggregate demand, it is necessary to divide the changes in the variables that determine aggregate demand into their anticipated and unanticipated components. One such variable is the change in the money supply.

What determines the division of the actual change in the money supply between its anticipated and unanticipated components? This is not a settled matter. Robert Barro[1] of the University of Rochester and Cliff Attfield, D. Demery, and Nigel Duck[2] of the University of Bristol have conducted the pioneering studies on this question, using United States and United Kingdom money supply growth respectively. They have attempted to decompose the actual money supply growth into its anticipated and unanticipated components. However, their work is by no means uncontroversial, and matters are not yet settled.

The way in which they proceeded was to search for statistical regularities in the past history of money supply growth and then to suppose that rational agents would exploit those statistical regularities in forming a rational expectation of money supply growth. Specifically, Attfield, Demery and Duck discovered that the money supply growth rate tends to be faster:

(i) the faster the money supply growth has been in the preceding year; and

(ii) the bigger is the real value of the central government borrowing requirement.

These findings are more than statistical patterns. They also make good intuitive sense. The proposition that money supply growth will be faster, the faster has been the previous year's money supply growth, simply reflects the fact that the central bank exhibits some inertia in its decision making. It does not change course suddenly

---

1. The most comprehensive account of Barro's work is Robert J. Barro and Mark Rush, Unanticipated money and economic activity, Chapter 2 in Stanley Fischer, (ed.), *Rational Expectations and Economic Policy*, National Bureau of Economic Research Conference Report, University of Chicago Press, 1980.

2. An account of the work on the United Kingdom may be found in C.L.F. Attfield, D. Demery and N.W. Duck, A quarterly model of unanticipated monetary growth, output and the price level in the UK: 1963–1978, *Journal of Monetary Economics* Vol. 8, No. 3, November 1981, pp. 331–50.

and rapidly in a zigzag fashion; rather, it changes course gradually. This means that the behaviour of the central bank can, on the average, be described by a version of the formula that says that tomorrow will be very much like today. This, after all, is not a bad way of forecasting the weather. It misses the turning points, but it gets more days right than would the prediction that tomorrow will be the opposite of today.

The proposition that money supply growth increases when the central government borrowing requirement increases and decreases when the central government borrowing requirement decreases is a natural consequence of the fact that money creation is a form of taxation. When there is a burst of government expenditure or a sharp drop in government expenditure it is much easier to vary the rate at which money is printed than it is to vary such things as (for example) the sales tax, income tax, or capital gains tax. Hence, the efficient financing of government expenditures will entail varying the growth rate of the money supply to cover unusually large changes in expenditure.

Attfield, Demery and Duck were unable to find any systematic responsiveness of the money supply to other variables such as, for example, the previous year's unemployment, output growth, or inflation. This suggests that despite the widespread belief that governments can manipulate the economy by activist monetary policies, they have not, in the United Kingdom at least, done so. The Keynesian idea that stimulating demand in times of depression and holding demand back in times of boom will moderate the business cycle does not seem to have affected United Kingdom monetary policy action.

The propositions just discussed can be given a precise numerical form by the use of statistical techniques that lie outside the scope of this book. From those statistical exercises it is possible to make a forecast of what the money supply will be in the subsequent year (or in the distant future years for that matter) conditional on information about the previous year's money supply growth and the behaviour of the central government borrowing requirement. Such a forecast becomes the anticipated change in the money supply. A movement in the actual money supply which is different from the calculated anticipated change becomes the calculated value of the unanticipated change in the money supply.

The above discussion concerning the decomposition of changes in the money supply into anticipated and unanticipated components applies in principle to changes in government expenditures, taxes, or any other variables of change which influence aggregate demand.

Now that the distinction between anticipated and unanticipated changes in aggregate demand is understood and we have seen how in practice it is possible to distinguish between them, it will be useful to go on to analyse the way in which these two components of the change in aggregate demand influence the key macroeconomic variables.

B. Effects of an Anticipated Change in Aggregate Demand

The effects of a fully anticipated change in aggregate demand are analysed first. This is an extreme case, but it is the clearest and simplest case with which to begin.

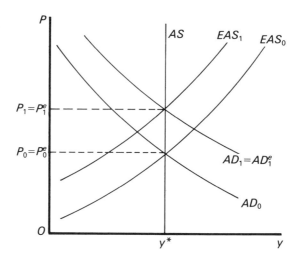

Figure 31.1 *The Effect of an Anticipated Change in Aggregate Demand on the Price Level and the Level of Output*

The economy is initially at full-employment equilibrium where AD_0 intersects EAS_0 at output y^* and price level P_0. Aggregate demand increases in a fully anticipated way from AD_0 to AD_1 ($= AD_1^e$). The expectations-augmented aggregate supply curve shifts to become EAS_1, with the expected price level P_1^e. The actual price level is determined at P_1 and output at y^*. A fully anticipated rise in aggregate demand raises the price level, but leaves real output unaffected.

The analysis will be illustrated using Figure 31.1. You will recognise this as the diagrammatic summary of the theory of the determination of output (real income) and the price level. Suppose that you are looking at an economy at a particular time, called period 0. The aggregate demand curve is the curve labelled AD_0. Suppose that period 0 is one of *full-employment equilibrium*. This is simply a convenient reference point. With period 0 being one of full-employment equilibrium, you know that the *expectations-augmented aggregate supply curve*, the *aggregate supply curve* and the *aggregate demand curve* all intersect at the same point. (If you do not understand why this is so, review Chapter 27, Section C.) Thus, the actual price level and the expected price level equal each other at P_0 and P_0^e.

To summarise, at the starting point, the economy is described by the curves EAS_0 and AD_0; output is equal to y^*; and the price level and the expected price level are equal to each other and equal to P_0.

Now imagine that you are looking forward one year and are trying to form a view about the price level in that period. Suppose that you expect the aggregate demand to rise so that the aggregate demand curve is expected to be the curve labelled AD_1^e. This is where you expect the aggregate demand curve to be next year. You can now calculate the rational expectation of the price level, which is equal to P_1^e. (If you are not sure as to the reason for that, check back with Chapter 30, Figure 30.2.) The expected price level P_1^e is the only expected price level which is consistent with the prediction of this model, given that expected aggregate demand is AD_1^e. This means that the expectations-augmented aggregate supply curve for next year will be the curve EAS_1.

Next, suppose that aggregate demand actually increases by exactly the amount expected so that *the aggregate demand change is fully anticipated*. This means that the *actual* aggregate demand curve will be the same as the *expected* aggregate demand curve. To remind you of this, we have labelled the aggregate demand curve twice as $AD_1 = AD_1^e$. This is to emphasise that the **actual** *aggregate demand curve* is the same as the **expected** *aggregate demand curve*.

What is the new equilibrium level of output and prices in this economy? Recall that equilibrium occurs at the point at which the aggregate demand curve cuts the expectations-augmented aggregate supply curve. The expectations-augmented aggregate suply curve is EAS_1 — the aggregate supply curve when the expected price level is P_1^e, based on the expected aggregate demand curve AD_1^e.

You can now read off the new equilibrium. The aggregate demand curve AD_1 cuts the expectations-augmented aggregate supply curve EAS_1 at the full-employment output level y^* and at the price level P_1. *So the price level rises and the level of output remains unchanged*.

This is the first proposition concerning the effect of a fully anticipated change in aggregate demand. *A fully anticipated rise in aggregate demand raises the price level and leaves output unchanged*.

What happens to the remaining variables in the economy? Specifically, what happens to employment, unemployment, the real wage, and money wage?

You will recall that the diagram displayed in Figure 31.1 was derived originally (in Chapter 29) from an analysis of the labour market and the production function. It is convenient now to recall Figure 29.2. (Refresh your memory by turning back to it.) Starting from the fact that output has not changed, you can travel back (reversing the arrows in Figure 29.2) through the production function and immediately establish that the level of employment has not changed. If the level of employment has not changed, then firms must be willingly hiring the same quantity of labour as they were hiring before. This immediately implies that the real wage has not changed. Furthermore, if the level of employment has not changed, the level of unemployment is also unchanged — it remains at the natural unemployment rate. Finally, since the real wage has not changed, but the price level has risen, it follows that the money wage rate must also have risen and by the same percentage amount as the price level has risen.

It is now possible to summarise all the consequences of a fully anticipated change in aggregate demand.

A fully anticipated change in aggregate demand changes the price level and the money wage by the same percentage amount as each other. It has no effects on any of the real variables in the economy, i.e. on output, employment, unemployment, and the real wage.

It is not difficult to understand the reason for these results. *A fully anticipated change in aggregate demand has the same effects as a change in aggregate demand had in the basic model*.

Let us now go on to analyse the opposite extreme.

C. Effects of an Unanticipated Change in Aggregate Demand

Figure 31.2 will be used to illustrate the effects on the price level and output of an unanticipated change in aggregate demand. Suppose that the economy is initially in exactly the same situation as that depicted in Figure 31.1 for period 0. That is, the aggregate demand curve is AD_0, the expectations-augmented aggregate supply curve is EAS_0. These curves intersect at a price level of P_0, which is also the expected price level P_0^e. Output is at the full-employment level, y^*.

Unlike the previous example, suppose that everyone expects that next year aggregate demand will remain at AD_0. This aggregate demand curve is marked $AD_0 = AD_1^e$ to remind you that aggregate demand expected in period 1 is the same as actual aggregate demand in period 0. From this, the rational expectation of the price level in period 1, P_1^e, remains at P_0^e. The expectations-augmented aggregate supply curve for period 1 is the same as EAS_0, and this curve is marked EAS_1 to remind you of that.

Now suppose that instead of remaining constant at AD_0, aggregate demand actually rises in period 1 to become AD_1. Now you can read off the equilibrium price and output levels in period 1, given that the expected price level P_1^e is constant, but that actual aggregate demand has increased above the level that was expected. Equilibrium will now be at the point at which the expectations-augmented aggregate

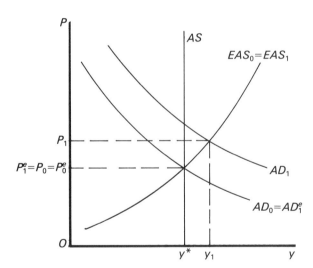

Figure 31.2 *The Effect of an Unanticipated Change in Aggregate Demand on the Price Level and the Level of Output*

An initial equilibrium at P_0 and y^* (exactly as in Figure 31.1) is disturbed by an unanticipated shift in aggregate demand to AD_1. The expectations-augmented aggregate supply curve remains fixed at EAS_0. The new equilibrium price and output is where the new aggregate demand curve cuts the original EAS curve at P_1, y_1. An unanticipated rise in aggregate demand raises output and prices, but raises prices less than proportionately to the rise in aggregate demand.

supply curve EAS_1 cuts the *actual* aggregate demand curve AD_1. The price level and output level determined by this intersection point are P_1 and y_1 respectively.

Notice that in this experiment we have an *unanticipated rise* in aggregate demand. Anticipated aggregate demand remains constant; actual aggregate demand rises, so the unanticipated rise in aggregate demand is exactly equal to the actual rise in aggregate demand.

The effects of this unanticipated rise in aggregate demand are as follows: the price level is above its expected level and output is above full-employment output. The percentage by which the price level is above its expected level is less than the percentage unanticipated rise in aggregate demand. This result arises from the fact that the percentage gap between the expected and actual price level and the gap between full-employment and actual output taken together will equal the percentage unanticipated rise in aggregate demand.

What are the effects on the other variables in the economy? (Again recall Figure 29.2.) Since you know from Figure 31.2 that output has risen, it is immediately obvious that employment must also have risen. The fact that employment has risen also means that unemployment must have fallen below the natural unemployment rate. If there is more than full employment and if firms are still making maximum profits, then they must have slid down their labour demand curves. This means that the real wage must have fallen. As the actual price level is higher than the expected price level, the money wage must also have risen. Since the real wage has fallen while the price level has risen, we know that the money wage must have risen by a smaller percentage than the rise in the price level.

It is now possible to summarise the effects of a completely unanticipated change in aggregate demand. *An unanticipated rise in aggregate demand will raise the price level, but by a smaller percentage amount than the unanticipated rise in aggregate demand. It will also produce a rise in the money wage rate, but by an even smaller percentage than the percentage rise in the price level. It will cause a fall in the real wage and a fall in unemployment below the natural rate. It will also produce a higher level of employment and output than the full-employment levels.* The above can be readily restated for an unanticipated fall in the money supply.

SUMMARY

A. Anticipated and Unanticipated Changes in Aggregate Demand

The change in aggregate demand may be decomposed into its anticipated or expected component and its unanticipated or unexpected component. The anticipated change in aggregate demand may be greater or smaller than the actual change. When it is exactly the same as the actual change we speak of a fully anticipated change in aggregate demand. The unanticipated change in aggregate demand is simply the difference between the actual and anticipated changes. Since the change in actual aggregate demand is determined by changes in the money supply, government spending, and taxes, decomposing the change in aggregate demand into its expected and unexpected components involves decomposing the changes in these determinants of aggregate demand into their anticipated and unanticipated components.

B. Effects of an Anticipated Change in Aggregate Demand

A fully anticipated change in aggregate demand has the effect of changing the price level and the money wage by exactly the same percentage amount as each other and by the same percentage as the rise in aggregate demand. It has no effects on any of the real variables. Specifically, it has no effect on output, employment, unemployment, or the real wage.

C. Effects of an Unanticipated Change in Aggregate Demand

An unanticipated change in aggregate demand has both real and nominal effects. It will raise the price level, but by a smaller percentage amount than the unanticipated rise in aggregate demand, and it will raise the money wage by an even smaller percentage amount than it raises the price level. It thus will lower the real wage, raise the level of employment, raise the level of output, and lower the level of unemployment.

Appendix: The Algebra of Rational Expectations Equilibrium

This appendix sets out the simple algebra of a rational expectations equilibrium model. It presents the simplest example of a rational expectations equilibrium so that you may see the connection between the solution to this model and the solution of the fixed price *IS–LM* model of aggregate demand. There is nothing of substance in this appendix that does not appear in the preceding chapters. As with the other algebraic appendices, if you feel comfortable with this kind of treatment, you will probably find this a convenient, compact summary of the material presented in words and diagrams in the text of the chapter.

The starting point is the *IS–LM* theory of aggregate demand. This may be summarised very compactly in the form of the following aggregate demand equation:

$$y_t^d = \alpha_t + \beta(m_t - p_t), \qquad \beta > 0 \tag{A1}$$

Here, α stands for all the things that cause aggregate demand to vary other than the real money supply. It incorporates, therefore, government expenditure, taxes, and any shifts in the investment function or the demand for money function. The money supply (m) and the price level (p) are expressed as logarithms, so that $m\text{-}p$ is the same as log (M/P). (This formulation, which is linear in the logarithm of real money balances rather than the level of real money balances, makes the explicit calculation of expectations more straightforward.) The parameter β is the multiplier effect of a change in the logarithm of real money balances on aggregate demand. It is very closely related to the money multiplier in the Appendix to Chapter 22. You should think of equation (A1) and equation (A11) in the Appendix to Chapter 22 as approximations to each other.[*]

The expectations-augmented aggregate supply curve may be written in equation form as

$$y_t^s = y^* + \gamma(p_t - p_t^e), \qquad \gamma > 0 \tag{A2}$$

This says what you already know, namely, that if the price level was equal to its expected value ($p = p^e$), then aggregate supply would be equal to full-employment aggregate supply y^*. As the actual price level exceeds the expected price level, so output rises above y^*. The positive parameter γ captures this. The only difference (in this simple treatment) between the new classical and new Keynesian approaches to the aggregate supply curve is that the value of γ would be different in the two theories. For the new Keynesians γ would be bigger than that for the new classicals.

---

[*] The exact connection between (A1) above and the *IS–LM* aggregate demand solution is easy to see. The *IS–LM* aggregate demand solution (Equation (A11) in the Appendix to Chapter 22) is

$$y = \frac{a + i_0 + g - bt + (h/l)[(M/P_0) - m_0]}{1 - b + (kh/l)}$$

Although in the fixed price model this equation determines y, in the rational expectations theory it determines y^d as P varies. Writing it as the y^d equation and changing the order of the items slightly, we may write:

$$y^d = \left[\frac{a + i_0 + g - bt - (h/l)m_0}{1 - b + kh/l} \right] + \frac{h/l}{1 - b + kh/l} \left(\frac{M}{P} \right)$$

The first term is defined as α in (A1) above. The second term becomes $\beta(m-p)$, though (A1) is by assumption, linear in the logarithms, while (A11) in Chapter 22 is linear in the level of real balances.

Next, equilibrium prevails, in the sense that aggregate supply equals aggregate demand, and actual output y is also equal to demand and supply. We can write this as two equations. That is

$$y_t = y_t^d = y_t^s \tag{A3}$$

The first step in finding the rational expectations equilibrium of this model is to calculate the expected values of output and prices, *given* the expected values of α and m. (A full treatment would also have an explicit theory for the determination of α and m. We shall not make that extension here.) Calculating the expected values of y and p, given the expected values of α and m, simply involves taking the expectations of equations (A1) and (A2) using the fact that actual output is the same as aggregate demand and supply. Letting the superscript e stand for the expected value of a variable, you can immediately see that this implies

$$y_t^e = \alpha_t^e + \beta(m_t^e - p_t^e) \tag{A4}$$

$$y_t^e = y^* \tag{A5}$$

Equation (A4) follows directly from equation (A1). If (A1) describes what determines the actual level of aggregate output demanded and if demand equals actual output, then expected output must be equal to the expected value of α plus β times the expected value of real balances. That's all that equation (A4) says. Equation (A5) follows directly from equation (A2). It says what you already know, namely, that expected output will be equal to full-employment output, since the expected price level is the rational expectation. That is, p_t^e is the same thing as the expectation of p_t, and so the second term in equation (A2) is expected to be zero.

You can now solve equation (A5) for the price level. Just by re-arranging equation (A4) you obtain

$$p_t^e = m_t^e - \frac{1}{\beta}(y^* - \alpha_t^e) \tag{A6}$$

Recall that p and m are logarithms, so that this says that the expected price level is proportional to the expected money supply.

To calculate the actual levels of output and prices, first of all subtract equation (A4) from (A1) and equations (A5) from (A2). The results are

$$y_t - y^* = (\alpha_t - \alpha_t^e) + \beta(m_t - m_t^e) - \beta(p_t - p_t^e) \tag{A7}$$

$$y_t - y^* = \gamma(p_t - p_t^e) \tag{A8}$$

Equation (A7) says that output will deviate from full employment by the amount that α deviates from its expected level, plus the amount that the money stock deviates from its expected level, multiplied by the parameter β minus the amount by which the price level deviates from its expected level, multiplied by the same parameter β. The right-hand side of equation (A7) is the deviations of the aggregate demand curve from its expected level. It is, in terms of the concepts discussed in the chapter, the unexpected component of aggregate demand. Equation (A8), in effect, is simply a re-arrangement of equation (A2). It says that deviations of output from full employment on the supply side will be proportional to deviations of the price level from its expectation.

We may now solve these two equations (A7) and (A8) for the actual levels of output and prices. Those solutions are

$$y_t = y^* + \frac{\gamma}{\gamma + \beta}[\alpha_t - \alpha_t^e + \beta(m_t - m_t^e)] \tag{A9}$$

$$p_t = m_t^e - \frac{1}{\beta}(y^* - \alpha_t^e) + \frac{1}{\gamma + \beta}[\alpha_t - \alpha_t^e + \beta(m_t - m_t^e)] \tag{A10}$$

The output equation says that output will equal its full-employment level plus terms involving the unexpected components of α and the money supply. The price level will equal its expected level (the first two terms in equation (A10)) plus some terms involving deviations of α and the money supply from their expected levels.

Thus, you can see it is only unanticipated shifts in aggregate demand that affect output, and it is both fully anticipated and unanticipated shifts in aggregate demand that affect prices. The multipliers of the *IS–LM* analysis tell us about the distance of the horizontal shift of the aggregate demand curve. Equations (A9) and (A10) tell us that, to the extent that the horizontal shift is fully anticipated, it will raise both output and prices and will distribute its effects between output and prices in accordance with the slope parameter γ, the slope of the *EAS* curve. You can see, as a matter of interest, that if γ was infinitely big, the effect of an unanticipated shift in aggregate demand would be exactly the same as the *IS–LM* model says, and it would have no effect on prices. You can see this immediately for the price level (A10). For output, divide the top and bottom of $\gamma/(\gamma + \beta)$ by γ to give $1/[1 + (\beta/\gamma)]$. You now see that as γ approaches ∞, so $1/[1 + (\beta/\gamma)]$ approaches 1, so that (A9) becomes the *IS–LM* solution for income.

Review Questions

1. What is the distinction between anticipated and unanticipated changes in aggregate demand?

2. What factors determine anticipated changes in aggregate demand?

3. What factors determine unanticipated changes in aggregate demand?

4. In what ways do the effects of fully anticipated changes in the money supply differ from the effects of unanticipated changes in the money supply?

5. Illustrate diagrammatically the effect of:
   - (i) a fully anticipated increase in the money stock
   - (ii) an unanticipated increase in the money stock
   - (iii) an increase in the money supply — part of which was anticipated and part of which was unanticipated, and
   - (iv) an anticipated rise in the money stock which turns out to be the opposite of the actual change.

6. 'Whereas an unanticipated increase in the money supply lowers the real wage rate paid by firms, it increases the perceived real wage rate received by employees.' Is this statement true or false? Explain.

7. 'Only anticipated increases in the price level have output effects, since in order for producers to increase production during times of high prices, such increases must be anticipated.' Within the context of the model we have developed, explain what is wrong with this statement.

32

Rational Expectations Theory of the Open Economy: a Selective Sketch

This chapter is going to introduce you to some recent developments in the analysis of the macroeconomic problems of the open economy. This material is of a very recent origin, and is still not fully digested in the professional literature. Although you are going to be given only a selective sketch in this chapter, you are going to be introduced to some of the central issues involved in dealing with the development of a rational theory of the open economy. There are four tasks which will enable you to achieve this, and they are to:

A. understand the need for a rational expectations theory of the open economy;
B. understand the implications of the assumption of perfect capital mobility for the determination of aggregate demand;
C. understand how output and the price level are determined with perfect capital mobility, rational expectations, and a fixed exchange rate; and
D. understand how output, the price level, and the exchange rate are determined with perfect capital mobility and rational expectations in a flexible exchange rate regime.

In pursuing these tasks it will be convenient, as in the case of the closed economy analysis of rational expectations models, to abstract from trends in the variables. We shall determine the price level rather than the rate of inflation and the exchange rate rather than the rate of depreciation of the currency. As before, you can think of what we are doing as analysing movements about trends, but not changing the underlying trends in the variables. The basic model (Chapter 14) analysed the trends.

Let us proceed immediately with the first task.

A. Need for a Rational Expectations Theory of the Open Economy

Chapters 14 and 23 took you through the basic and Keynesian models of the open economy. The basic model is a simple extension of the basic model of the closed economy and analyses what happens to output, prices, interest rates, the exchange rate, and the balance of payments when the economy is at a continuous full-employment position. The Keynesian model of the open economy is a natural extension of the Keynesian model of the closed economy. It tells us what happens to output, interest rates, the exchange rate, and the balance of payments when the price level is fixed and there is excess capacity. Both are extremes. We have seen that each is capable of explaining some of the facts, but neither is capable of explaining all the facts. The virtue of the rational expectations analysis is that, in effect, it combines the best of both the basic and Keynesian models. The basic model is seen as generating the consequences of fully anticipated shocks, while the Keynesian model gives predictions that are approximately the same as those that arise when the economy is administered unanticipated shocks. Using the notion that actual policy processes involve varying degrees of anticipation and of error, in principle at least, enables all the facts to be accommodated by the one theory.

It clearly would be an unsatisfactory state of affairs if we were unable to extend these notions to the open economy. It would be intellectually unsatisfying if we had to live with the basic and Keynesian models as the only models available for handling open economy questions, when we know that in the context of the simpler closed economy, they are in some respects unsatisfactory. Hence, the need for an extension of the rational expectations theory of the closed economy to the open economy.

There are some challenging problems in achieving a completely satisfactory rational analysis of the open economy. In the open economy, there are more variables to be determined and more sources of shocks than in the closed economy, and this raises the dimensionality of the problem which we need to solve. It makes it harder to arrive at simple, intuitive, easily grasped models. In this chapter, we are going to try to give you a feel for how the rational expectations theory can be applied to the problems of the open economy by working with a particular model that employs an extreme assumption. That assumption is that capital is perfectly mobile between the economy that we are analysing and the rest of the world. Our own judgment is that this is only a slightly extreme assumption. It is not quite the way the world is, but it is close. The virtue of making this assumption, aside from the fact that it does not strike us as being wildly at odds with the world, is that it simplifies the analysis considerably. It makes it possible to gain insights about issues that otherwise would be hard to understand. There is an alternative extreme assumption that also yields a much simplified analysis, but that yields very different conclusions. That is the opposite extreme to perfect capital mobility — zero capital mobility. That alternative strikes us as being so violently at odds with the world as to be uninteresting and not worthwhile analysing. Both perfect capital mobility and zero capital mobility simplify the task of analysis. One of them does it in a way that only mildly violates the facts, while the other does it in a way that renders the analysis utterly pointless. By way of an analogy, assuming perfect capital mobility seems to us to be quite analogous to assuming there to be no atmosphere (a vacuum) for the purpose of calculating the length of time it would take for a ten-pound rock to fall from the top of the Post Office Tower and hit the ground. The atmospheric resistance may be presumed to be negligible and, hence, the calculations simplified considerably by assuming it to be zero. The answer obtained will be wrong, but not misleadingly wrong. The alternative assumption of zero capital mobility strikes us as being analogous to simplifying the calculation of the power required to put a satellite into earth orbit by assuming zero gravity. The assumption will be so wildly at odds with the facts that the rocket would never leave the launching pad!

Let us proceed then, using the assumption of perfect capital mobility, and see what we can learn about the behaviour of an open economy under rational expectations.

B. Aggregate Demand when Capital is Perfectly Mobile

In order to develop a theory of the open economy comparable to the closed economy theories worked out in the previous chapters, we need to see how expected aggregate demand determines the rational expectation of the price level and how actual aggregate demand, interacting with the expectations-augmented aggregate supply curve, determines the actual levels of output and prices. We further need to work out how, under a fixed exchange rate regime, the balance of payments is determined, and how, under flexible exchange rates, the exchange rate is determined. The key difference between doing this analysis for an open economy and for a closed economy is in the theory of aggregate demand. We need to take on board the open economy extension of the Keynesian theory of aggregate demand that was set out in Chapter 23. The task of this section is to see how, by assuming perfect capital mobility, we may derive a theory of aggregate demand from the Keynesian model of the open economy, which carries over to the rational expectations theory of output and the price level. We shall continue to assume that there are no ongoing trend changes in prices or exchange rates so that we are, in effect, analysing movements about trends rather than changes in trends.

The first thing to notice is that if capital is perfectly mobile, the domestic rate of interest, r, will be equal to the world rate of interest, r_f. The BP curve will be horizontal at that rate of interest. The exogeneity of the rate of interest has powerful simplifying implications for the analysis. In the IS, LM, BP framework of Chapter 23, we had to determine the values of three variables; output, the rate of interest, and either the balance of payments (under fixed exchange rates), or the exchange rate (under flexible exchange rates). By assuming perfect capital mobility and, therefore, the exogeneity of the rate of interest, the problem reduces to that of determining two variables, namely, the level of income, and either the balance of payments (under fixed exchange rates) or the exchange rate (under flexible exchange rates). The Keynesian analysis does, of course, hold the price level constant. That is one of its major drawbacks and one of the things which the rational expectations theory seeks to improve on. Indeed, we want to interpret the Keynesian analysis as determining an aggregate demand function that can interact with the aggregate supply side of the economy. That being so, although we have eliminated from consideration the determination of one variable, the rate of interest, we want to bring into focus the determination of another variable that the Keynesian analysis treats as fixed namely, the price level. This is a lot easier to do in the case where the interest rate is fixed than where we simultaneously seek to determine the interest rate as well as all the other variables of concern.

(i) Aggregate Demand with Fixed Exchange Rate

With these preliminary remarks in mind, we may now use the Keynesian analysis to develop a theory of aggregate demand for the open economy under fixed and flexible exchange rates. The two exchange rate regimes give rise to different propositions about aggregate demand in a rather interesting way. First, recall what the aggregate demand curve is. It is the relationship between the price level and the quantity of output which will be demanded such that the economy is on the IS and LM curves. Let us derive the aggregate demand curve for an open economy under both fixed and flexible exchange rates in the case where there is perfect capital mobility.

First, consider the fixed exchange rate economy. Figure 32.1 will illustrate the analysis. Frame (a) contains the IS, LM and BP curves, and Frame (b) is where the aggregate demand curve is generated. The BP curve is horizontal at the world rate of interest, r_f. Imagine first, that the price level is arbitrarily given as P_0, marked off on the vertical axis of Frame (b). With the price level at P_0, the IS curve would be the curve labelled $IS(EP_f/P_0)$. We know that under fixed exchange rates, the money supply is endogenous and has to be equal to whatever quantity is demanded at the level of income generated by the intersection of the IS and BP curves. Thus, the LM curve will automatically pass through the intersection of IS and BP at the world interest rate r_f and the income level y_0. Call the money stock in that case M_0, so that the LM curve is $LM(M_0/P_0)$. The point a in Frame (b) at (y_0, P_0) is a point on the aggregate demand curve. Next, consider raising the price level to P_1. In that case, the IS curve becomes $IS(EP_f/P_1)$ to the left of the original IS curve. Why does this happen? It happens because world prices have fallen relative to the domestic price level, thereby lowering the net demand for domestic output in the rest of the world and raising domestic demand for world output. This leftward shift of the IS curve intersects the BP curve at income level y_1. Again, the money supply will adjust through the balance of payments to ensure that the LM curve passes through this point. Call the new money supply M_1, so that the LM curve is that labelled $LM(M_1/P_1)$. The point b in Frame (b) at the income level y_1 and price level P_1 is another point on the aggregate demand curve. Consider a yet higher price level, P_2. That shifts the IS curve yet further to the left to $IS(EP_f/P_2)$ which determines the income level y_2. The money stock would fall yet further through a balance of payments deficit, so that the LM curve becomes $LM(M_2/P_2)$. Point c at income level

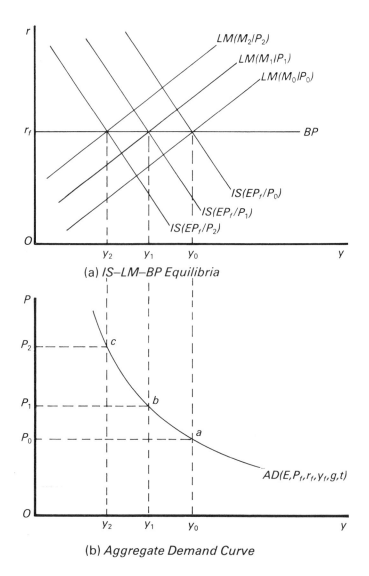

(a) *IS–LM–BP Equilibria*

(b) *Aggregate Demand Curve*

Figure 32.1   *The Aggregate Demand Curve Under Fixed Exchange Rates and Perfect Capital Mobility*

With perfect capital mobility the *BP* curve is horizontal (Frame (a)). Where the *IS* curve cuts the *BP* curve determines the level of aggregate demand. As the price level rises so the *IS* curve shifts to the left with aggregate demand falling. The curve *abc* traces out such an aggregate demand curve. The *LM* curve shifts as a result of a change in the money stock via the balance of payments to ensure money market equilibrium at each point along the aggregate demand curve. Aggregate demand will depend only on the factors that underlie the *BP* and *IS* curves, that is, the exchange rate, the world price level, the world rate of interest, world income, government expenditures, and taxes.

y_2 and price level P_2 is yet another point on the aggregate demand curve. Joining up the points *a, b, c* generates the aggregate demand curve.

You will notice from the way in which the aggregate demand curve has been derived that the things which determine the position of the aggregate demand curve are entirely in the *BP* and *IS* curves. The *LM* curve is a slack relationship which automatically adjusts (via a balance of payments adjustment of the money supply) to ensure an equilibrium money stock to support the interest rate, income, and price level generated by the *IS–BP* intersection. The position of the aggregate demand curve therefore depends only upon those things that influence the position of *IS* and *BP*. Those variables are the world price level, income, and rate of interest; government spending and taxes; and the exchange rate. These are shown in parentheses on the label of the aggregate demand curve to remind you that that curve will shift as a result of changes in those variables. The money supply does not in any way determine the position of the aggregate demand curve in the fixed exchange rate, perfect capital mobility, open economy.

To summarise: *for a fixed exchange rate open economy with perfect capital mobility, the aggregate demand curve is determined by the intersection of the IS and BP curves and in no way depends on the LM curve*. This does not mean that the *LM* curve is irrelevant. Rather, it means that *the LM curve determines the quantity of money, but not the levels of income, prices, or interest rate*.

(ii) Aggregate Demand with Flexible Exchange Rate

Let us now go on to consider the derivation of the aggregate demand curve in a flexible exchange rate, perfect capital mobility economy. Figure 32.2 will illustrate this. For the moment ignore Frame (c) of that figure. Frame (a) contains the *IS, LM*, and *BP* curves, and Frame (b) derives the aggregate demand curve. Again, the *BP* curve is horizontal at the world rate of interest, r_f. Recall that in the flexible exchange rate case, the exchange rate which underlies the position of the *IS* curve is determined in the analysis, while the money supply which underlies the position of the *LM* curve is exogenously determined by the monetary policy actions of the central bank. To derive the aggregate demand curve, again pick a price level (initially P_0) marked on the vertical axis of Frame (b). With a fixed money supply (M_0) and the price level at P_0, the *LM* curve will be $LM(M_0/P_0)$. The level of aggregate demand y_0 is determined where that curve intersects the *BP* curve. The *IS* curve will pass through the point of intersection of $LM(M_0/P_0)$ and *BP* because the exchange rate will adjust until the change in the international relative price generates sufficient domestic demand to ensure that the *IS* curve passes through precisely that point. Indeed, that is how the exchange rate is determined. The output level y_0 determined by the intersection of *LM* and *BP*, along with the price level P_0, marked as point *a* in Frame (b), represents a point on the aggregate demand curve. Next, consider a higher price level P_1, marked on the vertical axis of Frame (b). At this higher price level, while maintaining the money supply at M_0, the *LM* curve will shift to the left to become $LM(M_0/P_1)$. This intersects the *BP* curve at the lower income level y_1. The income level y_1 with the price level P_1 (marked as point *b* in Frame (b)) represents another point on the aggregate demand curve. The *IS* curve will pass through this point because the exchange rate will adjust to E_1, giving the *IS* curve $IS(E_1P_f/P_1)$.

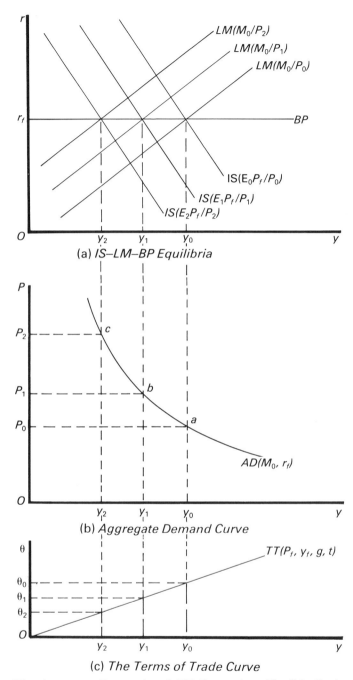

Figure 32.2   *The Aggregate Demand and TT Curves in a Flexible Exchange Rate, Perfect Capital Mobility Economy*

Under flexible exchange rates the intersection of *LM* and *BP* determines aggregate demand. As the price level rises from P_0 through P_2, real money balances fall and aggregate demand falls along the line *abc*. Where the *IS* curve cuts the intersection of *LM* and *BP* determines the real terms of trade. The lower is the level of income, the further to the left must the *IS* curve be, and the lower must be the net demand for domestic goods. The terms of trade must fall, therefore, as income falls.

Finally, suppose the price level was P_2, so that the real money supply was reduced still further, and the LM curve shifted yet further to the left to $LM(M_0/P_2)$. This would generate an income level of y_2, shown as point c in Frame (b). Again, the IS curve would shift to the left with an adjustment in the exchange rate to E_2 to ensure that the international relative price moved by exactly the amount required to put the IS curve at the point of intersection of LM and BP. The points a, b, c, in Frame (b) trace out the aggregate demand curve for the perfect capital mobility economy under flexible exchange rates. Notice that in the derivation of that aggregate demand curve, it was purely the intersection of the LM and BP curves that determined the level of aggregate demand. That curve is therefore labelled as $AD(M_0, r_f)$ to remind you that it is the variables that underlie the LM and BP curve, namely, the money stock and the foreign interest rate, that determine the position of the aggregate demand curve in a flexible exchange rate, perfect capital mobility economy.

To summarise: *under flexible exchange rates with perfect capital mobility, aggregate demand is determined by the intersection of the LM and BP curves, and the position of the aggregate demand curve depends only on the world rate of interest and the domestic money supply. It in no way depends on world income or prices or domestic fiscal policy. The IS curve is not irrelevant in the flexible exchange rate economy, but determines the exchange rate and not output, prices, or the rate of interest.*

(iii) Aggregate Demand: Summary

Both the fixed and flexible exchange rate aggregate demand curves slope downwards, and both depend on the world rate of interest. A higher world rate of interest would shift the fixed exchange rate aggregate demand curve to the left and the flexible exchange rate aggregate demand curve to the right. You can easily see why this is so. Under fixed exchange rates it is the IS–BP intersection that determines aggregate demand, so that a higher world interest rate would mean a lower level of aggregate demand, whereas, under flexible exchange rates it is the LM–BP intersection that determines aggregate demand, so that a higher world interest rate would give a higher domestic velocity of circulation of money and a higher level of aggregate demand for a given money supply. Aside from the world rate of interest, the two aggregate demand curves have no other variables in common. Under fixed exchange rates it is the exchange rate, the world price level, world income, and fiscal policy variables that affect domestic aggregate demand, whereas under flexible exchange rates it is the domestic money stock only that affects aggregate demand.

(iv) The Terms of Trade

Let us now look at Frame (c) of Figure 32.2. It plots on the vertical axis the international relative price, and on the horizontal axis, real income. The international relative price is defined as θ which, as before, is equal to (EP_f/P). The curve shown in Frame (c) will be called the terms of trade curve and is labelled TT. Why does the terms of trade curve slope upwards? The answer to that question is found in the properties of the IS curve. Indeed, the TT curve in effect traces the values of the terms of trade that ensure that the IS curve passes through the intersection points of the LM and BP curves. As the price level was raised from P_0 to

P_1 and P_2, so the exchange rate moved from E_0 to E_1 to E_2 to ensure that the international terms of trade equalled θ_0, θ_1, and θ_2, the values that make the level of income read off from the IS curve equal to the level of aggregate demand determined by the LM–BP intersection.

The variables that make the TT curve shift are the same as those that make the IS curve shift. They are world income, the world price level, and world interest rates, and domestic fiscal policy variables. The TT curve does not shift as a result of any monetary action. It is entirely a real curve. The TT relationship will be important in the subsequent analysis of the behaviour of a flexible exchange rate economy.

We are now in a position to move on to see how we can use the theory of aggregate demand to determine all the aggregate variables of interest to us.

C. Determination of Output and the Price Level with a Fixed Exchange Rate

First, let us consider the fixed exchange rate case. The theory of aggregate demand generated in Figure 32.1 tells us what determines the *actual* demand for goods and services in the economy. That aggregate demand curve may be used in an analogous way to the closed economy aggregate demand analysis to determine the rational expectation of the price level and, therefore, the position of the expectations-augmented aggregate supply curve. Figure 32.3 will illustrate the analysis. In that figure, the basic model aggregate supply curve is shown as AS at the output level y^*. The aggregate demand curve drawn for the expected values of the variables that determine its position, $AD(E^e, P^e_f, y^e_f, r^e_f, g^e, t^e)$, is the aggregate demand curve that is expected on the basis of expectations of the exogenous variables that influence aggregate demand, and given that the economy is operating under fixed exchange rates. The rational expectation of the price level, P^e, is determined where that curve intersects the AS curve. The expectations-augmented aggregate supply curve passes through that point and is the upward sloping curve EAS. If the actual aggregate demand curve is in exactly the same position as the expected aggregate demand curve, then output and prices will be determined at their full-employment and expected levels respectively. The balance of payments will be in equilibrium, with perfect capital mobility ensuring a capital account surplus that exactly matches whatever the current account deficit is (or capital account deficit matching the current account surplus). If, however, the actual values of the variables that determine agregate demand turn out to be different from their expected value, so that the actual aggregate demand curve is in a different position, say, at $AD(EP_f, y_f, r_f, g, t)$, then actual output and prices will be determined where that actual demand curve cuts the expectations-augmented aggregate supply curve at (y_1, P_1). This is exactly the same as in the closed economy, except that the factors that shift the aggregate demand curve in this case are different from those responsible for shifts in the closed economy aggregate demand curve. Random fluctuations in actual demand around its expected value will generate procyclical price and output co-movements.

The balance of payments will be in equilibrium at the higher price and output levels, but the mix between the current account and capital account will be different

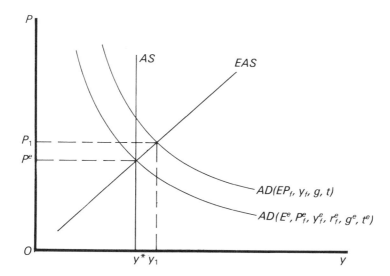

Figure 32.3   *Equilibrium with Fixed Exchange Rates*

With fixed exchange rates the expected price level is determined where the expected aggregate demand curve cuts the aggregate supply curve. That position will depend on the expected values of foreign prices, income and interest rates, of the exchange rate, and of fiscal policy variables. Actual output and prices are determined where the actual aggregate demand curve cuts the expectations-augmented aggregate supply curve. A fully anticipated change in any of the variables that determine aggregate demand will have price level effects only, and an unanticipated change will affect both output and prices.

---

from the full-employment mix. With a fixed exchange rate and fixed world price level, the higher domestic price level will mean that the terms of trade will have fallen, so that imports will rise and exports will fall. The higher income level will also raise imports. Thus, the current account of the balance of payments will move into a smaller surplus or larger deficit. That change in the current account will be matched by an equal, but opposite, change in the capital account.

That is all there is to the determination of output, prices, and the balance of payments in a fixed exchange rate economy with perfect capital mobility under rational expectations. As in the closed economy case, fully anticipated changes in the exogenous variables that determine demand will have price level effects only, and unanticipated changes will have the effects traced out in Figure 32.3. Changes which are partly anticipated and partly not will have effects which combine those shown in Figure 32.3 with the pure price level adjustment that would occur in the fully anticipated case. Notice that the domestic economy is not immune from shocks occurring in the rest of the world. Other things being equal, a fully anticipated change in the foreign price level or a fully anticipated devaluation of the currency will raise the domestic price level by the same percentage amount. Fluctuations in world output, prices, and interest rates will lead to fluctuations in domestic aggregate demand and, if they are not anticipated, will lead to fluctuations in output in the domestic economy are procyclical with fluctuations in the world economy.

Let us now go on to consider the more difficult, but perhaps more interesting, case of flexible exchange rates.

D. Determination of Output, the Price Level, and the Exchange Rate under Flexible Exchange Rates

We shall proceed in a similar way in analysing the flexible exchange rate economy as we did with the fixed exchange rate. The first task is to determine the rational expectation of the price level and, therefore, the position of the expectations-augmented aggregate supply curve. This is not as straightforward in the case of a flexible exchange rate as it was in the case of a fixed exchange rate. The reason for this is that *the exchange rate contains information which it will be rational for people to use in forming their expectation of the price level.* There is a fundamental informational difference between a fixed exchange rate and flexible exchange rate economy. Under fixed exchange rates it is the foreign exchange reserves that adjust on a daily basis to random shocks that hit the economy. These movements in foreign exchange reserves are not continuously reported and are unknown outside the central bank. In a flexible exchange rate economy the exchange rate itself is constantly adjusting to reflect the random forces that influence the economy and is available for all to see at almost zero cost. There is, therefore, more widespread information available in a flexible exchange rate economy than in a fixed exchange rate economy, and that information may be used in order to make inferences about the shocks that are hitting the economy. Making complete sense of this will take a paragraph or two.

(i) Pre-Trading Expectations

Let us begin by imagining that we are at the beginning of a trading period, before any trading has begun. All the markets — labour, money, goods, and foreign exchange — are not yet open for business. We are standing at the beginning of the business 'day' and trying to form expectations about all the variables in the economy. Figure 32.4 will be a useful vehicle for analysing this. Frame (a) shows the aggregate demand and aggregate supply curves and Frame (b) shows the terms of trade curve. (The derivation of the aggregate demand and the terms of trade curves is shown in Figure 32.2.) The top left frame of Figure 32.4 is simply a device for turning the price level through 90° so as to read the same price level on the horizontal axis as we are reading on the vertical axis. Frame (c) is a device for determining the exchange rate. The way to read this is as follows. θ, the international relative price, is defined as the exchange rate times the foreign price level (EP_f) divided by the domestic price level P, that is,

$$\theta = \frac{EP_f}{P}$$

Multiply both sides of this equation by P so that you obtain

$$\theta P = EP_f$$

Now the foreign price level P_f is being treated as fixed and, if we pick an exchange rate, EP_f will be fixed. This says that θP (the terms of trade multiplied by the

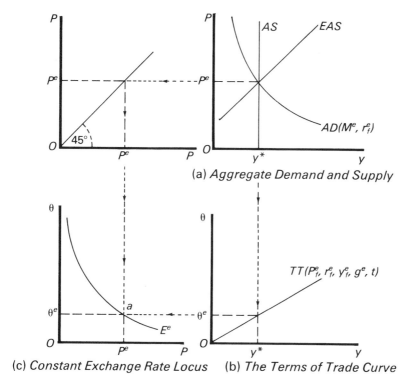

Figure 32.4 *Rational Expectations at the Commencement of Trading*

Before any information is revealed, the rational expectation of the price level, the exchange rate, and the terms of trade can be calculated. Where the expected aggregate demand curve (based on expected money supply and expected foreign interest rates) cuts the *AS* curve, the expected price level P^e is determined. Expected income is y^*, and this determines the expected terms of trade θ^e. There will be one exchange rate only, E^e, that is compatible with the expected price level and the expected terms of trade. This is shown at point a in Frame (c).

---

domestic price level) is equal to a constant, once we have determined the exchange rate. For a particular exchange rate, we could draw a rectangular hyperbola in Frame (c) that shows the relationship between θ and P. Thus, for some particular exchange rate, as shown in the diagram E^e, and for a given world price level P_f, if the domestic price level rises, then the terms of trade θ must fall by an equal percentage amount. That is all that the curve E^e traces out. In principle, there is a whole family of such curves, all rectangular hyperbolae, and all drawn for different values of the exchange rate. We don't need the whole family of those curves for the moment (although we shall need more than one subsequently). Now that you know how to read Frame (c), the only slightly tricky part of the diagram, let us proceed to use the diagram to analyse the determination of the rational expectation of the price level and the exchange rate.

The starting point is in Frame (a). The *AS* curve is determined by the basic model of aggregate supply and is located at y^*. The curve $AD(M^e, r_f^e)$ is the expectation of the aggregate demand curve for a flexible exchange rate economy, based on the derivation in Figure 32.2. Its position depends only upon the expected money stock and expected world rate of interest. The rational expectation of the price level is determined where that curve cuts the AS curve. The rational expectation of output is y^*. Next, calculate the value of the terms of trade that are consistent with this value of output. To do this, simply read off from the TT curve in Frame (b) the value of the terms of trade consistent with the income level y^*. That value is θ^e. That same value may also be read off from the vertical axis of Frame (c). To calculate the rational expectation of the exchange rate, transfer the rational expectation of the price level from Frame (a) through the 45° line to the horizontal axis of Frame (c). Then join θ^e and P^e to give point a in Frame (c). Point a will lie on a rectangular hyperbola, the location of which determines the exchange rate. There will be a unique constant exchange rate locus, labelled E^e, that passes through point a. Any other exchange rate would involve a different combination of the price level and the real terms of trade from that which is implied by the rational expectations of those two variables. Just prior to the commencement of business in this economy, the expectations of output, prices, and the exchange rate are those depicted in Figure 32.4. A higher expected money supply would result in a higher expected price level, no change in the real terms of trade, and a higher expected exchange rate (a depreciated currency). You can easily work that out for yourself by considering what happens in this diagram if we replace the AD curve with an equivalent curve located to the right of the existing curve. There will be no change in expected output or the expected real terms of trade. There will simply be a rise in the expected price level and in the expected exchange rate that would be proportional to each other.

(ii) Extracting Information from the Exchange Rate

Next, imagine that this economy has just started to do business. No one knows what the money supply is that underlies the actual aggregate demand curve, so no one can do any better on the basis of information available about the economic aggregates than continue to expect that the aggregate demand curve is in the position shown in Figure 32.4. There is more information now, however, than there was before trading began. In particular, everyone now knows the actual value of the foreign exchange rate which is being determined on a minute-by-minute basis in the foreign exchange market. In other words, as soon as trading begins, it is known whether or not the exchange rate expectation was correct. If the exchange rate expectation was incorrect, then it will be immediately clear to everyone that the initial expectation of the price level must also have been incorrect. Let us think through the consequences of this, using Figure 32.5.

The starting point is the initial expected values for prices, the exchange rate, and the terms of trade, shown as P^e, E^e, and θ^e. Suppose that the actual aggregate demand curve turned out to be, not $AD(M^e, r_f^e)$, but $AD(M, r_f)$, as shown in Frame (a) of Figure 32.5. According to the theory, the actual levels of income and prices will be determined as y_1, P_1, where the actual aggregate demand curve cuts the expectations-augmented aggregate supply curve. Transferring that solution for income down to Frame (b) shows the actual terms of trade as θ_1. Transferring the price solution, P_1, from the vertical axis of Frame (a) through the 45° line to the horizontal axis of Frame (c), gives the point b in Frame (c) as the terms of trade–price level point. The point b

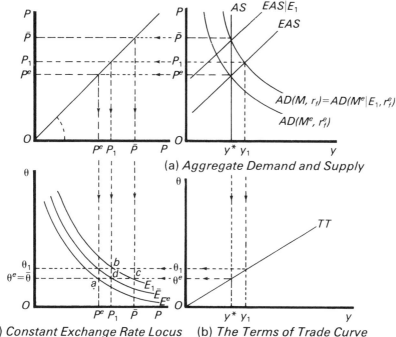

(a) Aggregate Demand and Supply

(c) Constant Exchange Rate Locus   (b) The Terms of Trade Curve

Figure 32.5   *The Information Content of the Exchange Rate Influences the Rational Expectation of the Price Level*

Before trading begins the expected aggregate demand level is $AD(M^e, r^e)$. The expected terms of trade curve is TT. The expected equilibrium for the economy is a price level of P^e, real income of y^*, terms of trade of θ^e and exchange rate of E^e.

The economy is shocked: aggregate demand turns out to be higher than expected at $AD(M, r)$. The terms of trade curve remains at TT. If the expected price level was P^e, it would generate an actual price level of P_1, an actual income level of y_1, actual terms of trade θ_1 and an actual exchange rate of E_1. Since the expected exchange rate, E^e, is different from the actual exchange rate E_1 and since the exchange rate is observed, people will know that their expected price level is wrong. The price level expectation will change. Only if the expected price level is $\bar{P}$ will the expected exchange rate equal the actual exchange rate (at point c). In that case, the actual price level will also be $\bar{P}$, output y^* and the real terms of trade θ^e.

---

lies on the constant exchange rate locus E_1, and so determines the exchange rate at that value. Now, the actual price and income levels, although determined by the analysis, are not known to the people in the economy. They observe only the prices of the small range of goods that they are currently engaged in trading and do not know the general price level or the other aggregates. Everyone, however, knows the exchange rate. It is observed on a continuous basis and is therefore available for all to see. In the situation depicted in Figure 32.5, everyone would know that the exchange rate was E_1 and that it was different from E^e. The economy is not at point a in Frame (c), but at point b. No one would know that, however, for no one would know the real terms of trade. That is not a directly and instantly observed variable. People would, however, know that the exchange rate was different from what they had expected it to be. That being so, everyone would know that a mistake had been made in forming expectations about aggregate demand. Aggregate demand could not be the curve $AD(M^e, r_f^e)$. If it was, the exchange rate would be E^e, and not E_1, which it has turned out to be. The price level P_1 and the income level y_1 cannot therefore be a rational expectations equilibrium. There is some information available, to the effect that a mistake has been made and that information will be utilised in order to rectify the mistake.

If the exchange rate is higher than it was expected to be, then the aggregate demand curve must be higher than it was previously expected to be, and the expected price level needs to be revised upwards. By how much does the expected price level need to be revised upwards? To answer this question we need to see how a change in the expected price level affects both the expected exchange rate and the actual exchange rate. Only when the expected price level is such as to generate an expected exchange rate that is the same as the actual exchange rate will that price expectation be rational. That is, only in such a situation will all the information available have been incorporated into price level expectations.

We can examine how the rational expectation of the price level will be formed when information conveyed by the exchange rate is employed if we perform a conceptual experiment. Imagine that the expectation of the price level is increased from P^e to P_1 (Frame (a)). (Be clear that this is not a description of the *process* that would go on in the real world, for P_1 is not observed and could not therefore be used to calculate an expected price level. This is simply an imagined experiment that will help make clear the *amount* by which the expected price level must rise and not the *process* whereby it does so.) What we need to do is to examine the effects of the higher expected price level on both the actual and expected exchange rate. Consider first its effects on the expected exchange rate. With an expected price level of P_1, the *EAS* curve will shift up (not shown in figure) to intersect the *AS* curve at P_1. In other words, the expected level of aggregate demand will remain constant at y^*. In turn, the expected real terms of trade will remain constant to θ^e. To see what this implies for the exchange rate, all we have to do is to trace through as we have done before to Frame (c) of Figure 32.5. Tracing the price level P_1 and the real terms of trade at θ^e into Frame (c) shows that they imply an exchange rate equal to $\bar{E}$ (meeting at point d on the equal exchange rate locus $\bar{E}$). Thus, raising the expected price level raises the expected exchange rate. In fact, although not transparent from the diagram, there will be a one-to-one correspondence between the expected price level and the expected exchange rate. If the expected price level rises by X per cent, the expected exchange rate will rise by the same X per cent.

Next consider the effect of a change in the expected price level on the actual exchange rate. Stick with the expected price level of P_1. It is clear that with an expected price level of P_1 but with the aggregate demand curve remaining in its position, $AD(M, r_f)$, the actual price level will rise above P_1. Further income will be above y^*. It will, however, be below y_1. (These values have not been shown in the figure.) With income between y^* and y_1, the terms of trade will lie between θ^e and θ_1. With the price level above P_1 and the terms of trade below θ_1 it is evident that the actual value of the exchange rate could rise or fall depending on whether the price level or the real terms of trade effect is larger. The rise in the price level would tend to raise the exchange rate, while the fall in the real terms of trade would tend to lower it.

While there is ambiguity as to the direction of movement of the exchange rate, there is no ambiguity about the fact that the actual exchange rate will have moved closer to the expected exchange rate. How do we know this? We know, first, that in the initial experiment the pre-trading expected exchange rate was E^e and the actual exchange E_1. Thus, the actual exchange rate was higher than the pre-trading expected exchange rate. We also know that a rise in the expected price level raises the expected exchange rate by the same pecentage amount as the rise in the price level, but it raises the actual exchange rate by less than that and could even result in a fall in the actual exchange rate. Thus, raising the expected price level to P_1 closes the gap between the actual and the expected exchange rate. We can see, however, that the expected price level P_1 cannot be the rational expectation of the price level for it does not generate an actual value of the exchange rate equal to its implied expected value. You can see this by noting that, with an expected price level of P_1, the real terms of trade will lie between θ_1 and θ^e. The actual price level will be above P_1 but below $\bar{P}$. (Verify that you indeed agree with the propositions just stated). With the real terms of trade between θ_1 and θ^e and the price level between $\bar{P}$ and P_1, it is evident that the actual exchange rate locus must lie between $\bar{E}$ and E_1. Thus, the actual exchange rate implied by an expected price level of P_1 is higher than the expected exchange rate implied by that expected price level. It is evident that we could repeat the experiment just conducted with a higher price level (equal to the actual price level generated by the expected price level P_1). If we did perform such an experiment we would discover that, with one exception, we repeatedly obtained the same type of result that we have just obtained.

There is just one price level, however, that would give a different result and that is $\bar{P}$. The price level $\bar{P}$ occurs where the actual aggregate demand curve cuts the AS curve. Expected aggregate demand remains y^* and the expected real terms of trade of course remain at θ^e. With an expected price level of $\bar{P}$ that implies an expected exchange rate of E_1 (point c in Frame (c) representing the expected equilibrium). With the actual aggregate demand curve intersecting the AS curve at $\bar{P}$, the actual price level is also determined at $\bar{P}$. Thus, the actual exchange rate is also E_1. Point c becomes not only the expected but also the actual equilibrium position of the economy.

In the set-up in Figure 32.5, we have rigged things such that people are able to work out exactly what the actual aggregate demand curve is from the observation of the exchange rate. This has happened because, purely for the purpose of introducing you to the ideas involved, we have imagined that there is just a single source of random disturbance to the economy, namely, a random disturbance to the aggregate demand curve. That being so, from observing the exchange rate it is possible to infer exactly what that random disturbance is and, as a result, to correct for it by adjusting the expectation of the price level conditioned on the knowledge of the exchange rate. The expectations-augmented aggregate supply curve conditional on the actual exchange rate $(EAS|E_1)$ moves to intersect the actual aggregate demand curve, which in turn becomes the expected aggregate demand curve conditional on the exchange rate $AD(M^e|E_1, r_f^e)$. If there were more sources of disturbance than shocks to the aggregate demand curve, then it would *not* be possible to make a direct inference from the exchange rate back to the aggregate demand curve. Even though people might know they had made a mistake, in the sense that the exchange rate turned out to be different from what they had expected it would be, they would not know for sure the source of that mistake. That being so, they would not be able to do a full and complete adjustment to identify correctly the actual underlying values of the exogenous variables that are influencing the economy.

This will be seen better if we consider a case in which there are two sources of shocks — shocks to the aggregate demand curve (coming from the money supply or the world rate of interest) and shocks to the TT curve (coming from world income, world prices, the world rate of interest, or fiscal policy). We shall consider two experiments. Both of them are highly artificial. Despite their artificiality, they are useful experiments for clarifying the concepts and propositions about the behaviour of a flexible exchange rate economy under rational expectations.

(iii) An Unexpected Change in Aggregate Demand

The first experiment imagines that the economy has always had a completely predictable level of aggregate demand, so that expected aggregate demand and actual aggregate demand have always been one and the same. This could be put more directly by saying that there have never been any aggregate demand shocks in the economy. This economy has, however, often been subjected to terms of trade shocks. In fact, the normal state of affairs is for the terms of trade to be constantly bombarded in a random fashion. Imagine that in a particular period in such an economy, an aggregate demand shock in fact occurs, but no terms of trade shock occurs. This will be a very unusual circumstance for this hypothetical economy. It will in fact be something which, by the hypothetical set-up assumed, has never happened before. Naturally, the exchange rate will adjust in response to the shock that has occurred. It will be rational in that situation for people to infer that there has been a terms of trade shock. It will also be rational for them to infer that there has been no aggregate demand shock. They will be wrong, but they will not be irrational. To see what happens in this situation, let us use Figure 32.6.

The set-up in Figure 32.6 is comparable to that of Figure 32.5. Before trading began, people formed expectations about aggregate demand and the terms of trade and, as a result, formed their pre-trading rational expectations of the price level, the terms of trade, income, and the exchange rate. These are shown in figure 32.6 in the following way. First, the curve labelled AD^e in Frame (a) is the expected aggregate demand curve. Where it intersects the AS curve determines the rational expectation of the price level, as P^e. The expectations-augmented aggregate supply curve EAS passes through the point a' at which the expected aggregate demand curve cuts the aggregate supply curve. The terms of trade curve, both actual and expected, is labelled $TT = TT^e$ in Frame (b). At the expected full-employment income level, the expected terms of trade are given as θ^e on the vertical axis of Frame (b). Transferring the expected price level through the 45° line to Frame (c), and transferring the expected terms of trade also across from Frame (b) to Frame (c), we arrive at a point in Frame (c) that lies on a constant exchange rate locus that determines the expected exchange rate (E^e). This is the pre-trading rational expectation for this economy.

The shock described above is an aggregate demand shock, but one that is completely unexpected. The actual aggregate demand curve that incorporates this shock is shown in Frame (a) as the curve AD. Where the actual aggregate demand curve cuts the expectations-augmented supply curve (point a) determines the actual price level P_1 and income level y_1. At the income level y_1, reading from Frame (b), we may determine the terms of trade as θ_1. If the price level is P_1 and the terms of trade

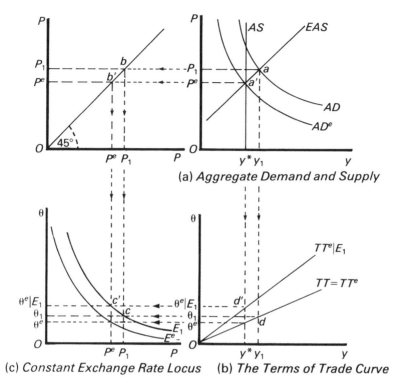

Figure 32.6   *The Effects of an Unanticipated Domestic Monetary Shock*
The economy is initially at y^*, P^e, θ^e, and E^e on the aggregate demand curve AD^e, the expectations-augmented aggregate supply curve EAS, the terms of trade curve $TT = TT^e$, and the constant exchange rate locus E^e. There is then a completely unanticipated rise in aggregate demand to AD. This raises the price level to P_1 and raises income to y_1. It also raises the terms of trade to θ_1. At the price level P_1 and terms of trade θ_1, the exchange rate becomes E_1. The higher exchange rate is incorrectly interpreted as a rise in the real terms of trade to $\theta^e|E_1$. The corners of the square $abcd$ describe the actual situation, and the corners of the square $a'b'c'd'$ describe the situation which agents rationally believe to be occurring. The effect of an unanticipated rise in aggregate demand is to raise the price level, output, the terms of trade, and the exchange rate. The higher terms of trade tell us that the exchange rate rises by more than the price level does.

θ_1, transferring these two magnitudes to Frame (c) takes us to point c on a constant exchange rate locus E_1. Thus, the actual exchange rate in this situation would be E_1, the price level P_1, income y_1, and the real terms of trade θ_1. People will see that the exchange rate is different from what they expected it to be. They will not, however, see any reason to revise their expectations of the price level. As far as they are concerned, there must have been a change in the terms of trade. That is the normal state of affairs. Aggregate demand shocks never occur, so there will be no reason, based on observed regularities in the past, to revise opinions about the level of aggregate demand.

People will be able to reconcile the currently observed exchange rate E_1 with the currently expected level of aggregate demand AD^e and the currently expected price level P^e, by adjusting their expectations of the terms of trade to fall on the line labelled $TT^e|E_1$. To see this, notice that there is a square, the corners of which are a', b', c', d', that just touches the intersection of AD^e and EAS, the 45° line, the constant exchange rate locus E_1, and the expected terms of trade curve $TT^e|E_1$. Thus, the expected price level P^e, the expected terms of trade $\theta^e|E_1$, and the actual exchange rate E_1 are all compatible with each other and with an expectation that the economy is at full-employment output y^*. The other square, $abcd$, represents the actual situation. That is, where the actual aggregate demand curve cuts the expectations-augmented aggregate supply curve, the economy is on the actual TT curve and again on the actual constant exchange rate locus. Both c and c' are on the same constant exchange rate locus. Thus, the actual exchange rate E_1 is compatible with the combined expectation of the price level and the terms of trade.

In effect, people are making two offsetting mistakes. Aggregate demand is actually higher than they believe it to be, and the terms of trade curve is actually lower than they believe it to be. In combination, these two mistakes generate the same expectation of the exchange rate as the actual exchange rate and therefore cannot be corrected simply by observing the exchange rate.

Before leaving this highly artificial economy that has frequently been bombarded with real terms of trade shocks, but never before with an aggregate demand shock, let us consider what would happen if there were no aggregate demand shock, but if the economy did indeed undergo a terms of trade shock. Specifically, imagine that the aggregate demand curve had remained at AD^e, but that the terms of trade had in fact changed, so that the actual terms of trade were denoted by the line $TT^e|E_1$. If that shock had occurred, then the economy would have remained at full-employment y^*, the price level would have remained at P^e, the exchange rate would have moved to E_1, and the real terms of trade to $\theta^e|E_1$. The square $a'b'c'd'$ would describe the actual situation. Thus, by forming expectations on the basis of what usually happens, people would have correctly inferred the real terms of trade shock by using the information given to them by the exchange rate. Thus, in the previous experiment, where there was an unanticipated change in aggregate demand leading to a rise in the price level, output, the real terms of trade, and the exchange rate, it was the unanticipated nature of the aggregate demand change that caused the problems.

(iv) An Unexpected Change in the Terms of Trade

Let us now leave this highly artificial economy and go on to consider another equally highly artificial situation, but at the opposite extreme. Imagine an economy that is always being bombarded by aggregate demand shocks, but which has never before known a change in its real terms of trade. Imagine that in some period that we shall now analyse, the economy suffers a terms of trade shock, but has no aggregate demand shock. Just as before, this is a very unusual event. Something that has perhaps never happened before. The exchange rate responds to the terms of trade shock, but people rationally attribute the exchange rate adjustment to an aggregate demand shock — to something that commonly occurs — and not to the terms of trade shock — something that has never before been known. What happens to output, prices, the exchange rate, and the terms of trade in this case? Figure 32.7 will analyse this.

Let us first use Figure 32.7 to describe the pre-trading rational expectations of the

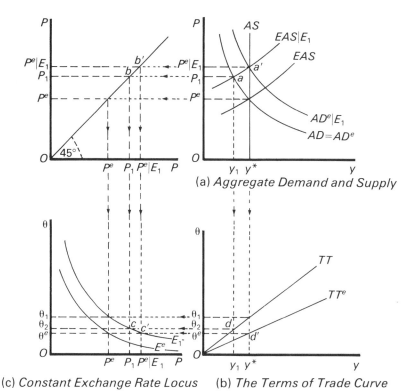

(a) *Aggregate Demand and Supply*

(c) *Constant Exchange Rate Locus*   (b) *The Terms of Trade Curve*

Figure 32.7   *The Effects of an Unanticipated Terms of Trade Shock*
The economy is initially at P^e, y^*, θ^e, and E^e on the aggregate demand curve $AD = AD^e$, the expectations-augmented aggregate supply curve EAS, the terms of trade curve TT^e, and the constant exchange rate locus E^e. There is then an unanticipated rise in the terms of trade to TT. With no change in income and the price level, that would raise the exchange rate to E_1 (the exchange rate compatible with the price level P^e and the terms of trade θ_1). Since the terms of trade shock is unanticipated, the higher exchange rate will be read incorrectly as an aggregate demand shock. The expected price level will be revised upwards to $P^e|E_1$, which will shift the expectations-augmented aggregate supply curve to $EAS|E_1$. Actual output and the price level will be determined at y_1, P_1 and the real terms of trade at θ_2. The price level P_1 and the exchange rate θ_2 are consistent with the exchange rate E_1. The actual situation is described by the corners of the square $abcd$, and the expected situation by the corners of the square $a'b'c'd'$. The unanticipated rise in the terms of trade raises the price level, lowers output, and raises the exchange rate. The exchange rate rises by more than the price level does and so the real terms of trade rises.

variables. The expected aggregate demand curve is AD^e in Frame (a) and, where it intersects the AS curve determines the rational expectation of the price level P^e and the location of the EAS curve. The expectation of the terms of trade in Frame (b) is the curve labelled TT^e, so the rational expectation of the terms of trade is θ^e. Transferring the rational expectation of the price level through the 45° line to Frame (c) and transferring the expected terms of trade to Frame (c) gives a point on the constant exchange rate locus E^e. This, then, is the initial pre-trading rational expectation for the economy. Imagine that there is now a shock to the terms of trade, and the actual terms of trade becomes the line TT. If there were no change in the rational expectation of the price level, and if actual aggregate demand equalled expected aggregate demand, as we shall assume, the level of output and prices would remain constant at P^e and y^*, but the terms of trade would rise to θ_1. At the price level P^e and the terms of trade θ_1, the economy would be on a constant exchange rate locus E_1 shown in Frame (c). Thus, the exchange rate would be higher than expected. Recalling that this is an economy which, by assumption, has never had a terms of trade shock before, but often has aggregate demand shocks, it will be evident that people will read the higher exchange rate as implying that there must have been an aggregate demand shock. As a result, they will revise upwards their expectations of the price level. Since they know the exchange rate to be E_1, and since they firmly expect the terms of trade to remain at θ^e, they will slide down the constant exchange rate locus E_1 to the point c' and read off from that locus the rational expectation of the price level, conditional on knowing that the exchange rate is E_1. This is labelled in Frame (c) as $P_1^e|E_1$. That is, given that people firmly believe that the real terms of trade will remain at θ^e, but that they know the exchange rate to be E_1, it must be that the rational expectation of the price level is compatible with those two facts. Now work backwards from the normal procedure and transfer the rational expectation of the price level $P^e|E_1$ from Frame (c) through the 45° line to Frame (a). This takes us to the point a' in Frame (a). Passing through the point a' is an expectations-augmented aggregate supply curve, given knowledge of the exchange rate as E_1. That is the curve labelled $EAS|E_1$. Where that expectations-augmented aggregate supply curve intersects the actual aggregate demand curve (point a) determines the level of income y_1 and the price level P_1. With the real terms of trade actually being determined by the TT curve, the income level y_1 determines a level of the terms of trade of θ_2. (The terms of trade θ_1 would be associated with full-employment output y^*.) Now transfer the price level P_1 through the 45° line to Frame (c) and transfer the real terms of trade θ_2 across to Frame (c). These meet at point c on the constant exchange rate locus E_1. Thus, the exchange rate E_1 that gives rise to an expectation of the price level of $P^e|E_1$ and an expected real terms of trade of θ^e (point c') also gives rise to an actual price level P_1 and an actual terms of trade θ_2 at point c. The actual equilibrium is described by the corners of the square $abcd$, and the expected equilibrium by the corners of the square $a'b'c'd'$. The effects of this unanticipated rise in the terms of trade curve has been to raise the domestic price level, raise the exchange rate (depreciate the currency), and lower output.[1]

Now consider what would have happened in this economy if it had actually been subjected to the shock to which it is normally subjected, namely, an aggregate demand shock. Imagine that instead of having a terms of trade shock, the terms of trade remained at their normal level TT^e. Imagine further that there was a shock to aggregate demand that took the actual aggregate demand curve to the curve labelled $AD^e|E_1$. Such a shock would have raised the exchange rate, and the higher exchange

1. In order to keep the diagrammatic analysis clean, we have rigged this experiment to yield a rational expectations equilibrium in 'one iteration' by selecting convenient slopes for EAS and TT. In general, although the characterisation of equilibrium shown in Figure 32.7 is correct, a lengthier iterative process would have to be followed in order to establish what the equilibrium is. Its defining characteristics are the two squares: $abcd$, which describes the actual situation, and $a'b'c'd'$, which describes the expected situation. The points c and c' are on the same constant exchange rate locus.

rate would have been interpreted as evidence of a positive aggregate demand shock. People would have adjusted upwards their expectations of prices, thereby building into their current expectations the information being given by the exchange rate. The only equilibrium to which this economy could have come would be the one described by the corners of the square $a'b'c'd'$. That is, the economy would have remained at full-employment output, the price level would actually have risen to $P^e|E_1$, and the exchange rate risen to E_1. The real terms of trade would have remained at θ^e.

This serves to emphasise that the reason why the terms of trade shock in this economy had real effects was because it was unanticipated. This is directly analogous to the reasons why the aggregate demand shock had real effects in the previous extreme example.

(v) Current Account of the Balance of Payments

Let us now briefly turn our attention to what is happening to the current account of the balance of payments during the administration of the shocks that we have just analysed. In the first economy which was subject to an unexpected aggregate demand shock, there is a rise in the price level, the income level, and the terms of trade. The higher terms of trade lead to a rise in world demand for domestic output (exports) and a drop in domestic demand for world output (imports). Other things being equal, this tends to raise the current account surplus (or lower the deficit). Other things are not, however, equal. The higher income level raises imports, thereby contributing to a lowering of the current account surplus (or increasing the deficit). We do not, in general, know which of these two offsetting forces is the stronger and do not therefore know in which direction the current account balance changes. The overall balance of payments (the official settlements balance) would, of course, be maintained at zero as a result of the flexible exchange rate and the perfect capital mobility.

In the case of the economy that is normally subjected to aggregate demand shocks, but is unusually subjected to a terms of trade shock, there is no ambiguity as to what happens to the current account of the balance of payments. In that case, there is a fall in income and a rise in the terms of trade. The combination of these two things is unambiguously to raise the current account surplus (or lower the deficit), since the lower income level lowers imports, while the higher terms of trade reinforce that effect on imports and stimulate exports.

(vi) More General Shocks

The experiments conducted and illustrated in Figures 32.6 and 32.7 are excessively simplified. In practice, *both* the terms of trade and aggregate demand will be shocked simultaneously, and there will be difficulty in disentangling the extent to which each of these two have been shocked. Nevertheless, the conclusions that we have reached using the simplified analyses apply to the more general case. The propositions made above concerning the effects of unexpected changes in money and the terms of trade, taken by themselves, apply to cases where there is a mixture of both shocks. Shocks which reveal themselves through changes in the exchange rate will, in general, be misinterpreted, although as in the two extreme examples used above, not completely but partly. The more common is a particular type of shock, the more inclined people will be to infer the presence of that shock when there is a previously unanticipated change in the exchange rate, the smaller will be the real effects, and the larger will be the price level effects of such a shock. Notice that it is not possible, given that people observe the exchange rate, for there to be unanticipated changes in one variable that are not offset by unanticipated changes in other variables. At least two mistakes must be made.

(vii) Fixed versus Flexible Exchange Rates Again

It is often said that flexible exchange rates give an economy insulation from foreign shocks. What does the above analysis say about this? Certainly we discovered when analysing the fixed exchange rate economy that an unanticipated change in foreign prices, income, or interest rates would produce a change in domestic output and prices. Does the same apply in the flexible exchange rate case? The answer is clearly, yes. Even though these foreign shocks do not in fact affect the position of the aggregate demand curve, they do affect the position of the terms of trade curve, and therefore, they affect the exchange rate. Through their effect on the exchange rate, they lead to inferences about the position of the actual aggregate demand curve which, in general, will be incorrect. Foreign shocks will be partly misperceived as domestic demand shocks. To the extent that they are so misperceived, they will lead to a shift in the expectations-augmented aggregate supply curve and, therefore, to a change in the actual level of output and prices. Interestingly, a foreign shock which raises the expected price level will, other things being equal, produce a stagflation style of result comparable to that which we saw when analysing the effects of labour market shocks in Chapter 12. What the flexible exchange rate does offer is insulation from the effect of fully anticipated foreign shocks. Any such shocks will come out entirely in the exchange rate and leave the domestic price level and output level undisturbed. Of course, it will be pretty hard to imagine such shocks occurring uncontaminated by unexpected components. Nevertheless, and importantly, flexible exchange rates *do* give insulation from ongoing, fully anticipated, trend changes in prices in the rest of the world.

SUMMARY

A. Need for a Rational Expectations Theory of the Open Economy

The need for a rational expectations theory of the open economy arises from the same considerations as in the case of the closed economy. The basic model accounts for some facts, and the Keynesian model for others, but neither accounts for all the facts. The rational expectations theory, which emphasises the importance of the distinction between anticipated and unanticipated shocks, offers, in effect, a method of combining the best of both of those models into a single, unified framework. There is a clear need to extend that framework to handle the determination of output and prices as well as the exchange rate and balance of payments in an open economy.

B. Aggregate Demand when Capital is Perfectly Mobile

If capital is perfectly mobile, the rate of interest is determined exogenously in the rest of the world. In a fixed exchange rate economy, aggregate demand is determined purely by the *IS* curve and the world rate of interest. Shifts in aggregate demand therefore depend on changes in the world price level, world income, world interest rate, and domestic fiscal policy. In a flexible exchange rate world, aggregate demand is determined solely by the domestic demand for money, supply of money, and world interest rate. Changes in aggregate demand in that case therefore depend only on the world rate of interest and the money supply. In the fixed exchange rate setting, the *LM* curve determines the money supply via the balance of payments, and in the flexible exchange rate setting the *IS* curve determines the terms of trade and the exchange rate.

C. Determination of Output and the Price Level with a Fixed Exchange Rate

The expected values of fiscal variables and foreign variables determine the expected aggregate demand curve, which in turn determines the rational expectation of the price level. The actual aggregate demand curve intersecting the expectations-augmented aggregate supply curve determines actual output and the price level. Fully anticipated changes in fiscal policy or foreign variables will have price level effects only; unanticipated changes will affect both output and prices. Fluctuations in the current account of the balance of payments will be countercyclical.

Domestic output will be procyclical with world output. A fully anticipated foreign inflation or depreciation of the currency will raise the price level proportionately.

D. Determination of Output, the Price Level, and the Exchange Rate under Flexible Exchange Rates

With flexible exchange rates, the continuous information given by the exchange rate has to be used to form a rational expectation of the shocks influencing the economy. If there was one, and only one, source of shock, then knowledge of the exchange rate would enable a perfect inference to be made and would ensure that the economy always operated at full-employment equilibrium. The effects of all shocks in that case would be exactly the same as in the basic model. If there is more than one source of shock (for example, a money shock and a terms of trade shock), then observation of the exchange rate alone does not enable a complete inference to be made concerning those shocks. In general, an unexpected rise in the money stock will be associated with an unexpected drop in the terms of trade, and *vice versa*. That is, at least two expectational errors will be made that offset each other and give rise to an expectation of the exchange rate that is the same as the actual exchange rate. An actual rise in the terms of trade, with no change in the money stock will, in general, be partly misinterpreted as a smaller rise in the terms of trade than has actually occurred, and with a rise in the money stock. Its effect will be to lower output, raise the price level, raise the terms of trade, and depreciate the currency. The current account of the balance of payments will move into a smaller surplus or bigger deficit as the fall in income and rise in the terms of trade lower imports and raise exports. A rise in the money stock, which raises the exchange rate, will partly be interpreted as a rise in the terms of trade. Its effect will be to raise output, the price level, the exchange rate, and the terms of trade. Its effect on the current account will be ambiguous, since the higher income level will raise imports, but the higher terms of trade will have an offsetting effect on imports and will stimulate exports.

Review Questions

1. What is wrong with the basic and Keynesian models of the open economy?

2. What determines aggregate demand in an open economy that faces perfectly mobile international capital flows:
    (a) under fixed exchange rates
    (b) under flexible exchange rates?

3. Why does the exchange rate regime make a difference to the determinants of aggregate demand?

4. How is the rational expectation of the price level determined when the exchange rate is fixed and capital is perfectly mobile?

5. Work out the effects on the rational expectation of the price level (with fixed exchange rates and perfect capital mobility) of the following:
    (i) a fully anticipated rise in the world price level of 10 per cent
    (ii) a fully anticipated rise in world income
    (iii) a fully anticipated rise in domestic credit
    (iv) an unanticipated devaluation
    (v) a fully anticipated devaluation of 10 per cent
    (vi) an unanticipated rise in domestic credit
    (vii) an unanticipated tax cut
    (viii) a fully anticipated rise in government spending.

6. Work out the effects on output, the price level, and the current account balance (with fixed exchange rates and perfect capital mobility) of the eight shocks listed in Question 5.

7. What is the fundamental difference between a fixed and a flexible exchange rate regime? Which generates the most information?

8. How is the rational expectation of the price level determined when the exchange rate is flexible and when capital is perfectly mobile
    (a) before the markets begin trading
    (b) when trading is taking place?

9. How is the rational expectation of the price level affected by the eight shocks listed in Question 5, when the exchange rate is flexible and capital is perfectly mobile?

10. How are output, the price level, the exchange rate, and the current account balance affected by the eight shocks listed in Question 5, when the exchange rate is flexible and capital is perfectly mobile?

11. Do flexible exchange rates provide better insulation from foreign shocks than do fixed exchange rates?

33

Explaining the Facts

After we had completed our review of the basic model of income, employment, and the price level, we examined the ability of that model to explain the facts. In Chapter 15 we discovered that the broad trends in inflation and some of the movements in unemployment were reasonably well accounted for by that model. The model was not capable, however, of explaining the procyclical co-movements of prices and output. Also, there were some movements in the unemployment rate (equivalently, deviations of output from trend) that the basic model could not explain. After examining the post-Keynesian neoclassical synthesis, we discovered, in Chapter 25, that that model was capable of explaining one of the main things which was not explained by the basic model, the procyclical co-movements of prices. The major difficulty of the neoclassical model was its inability to account for the surges in the rate of inflation which were not accompanied by low unemployment or, equivalently, positive deviations of output from trend. Now that we have completed our review of the rational expectations theories of income, employment, and prices, it is possible to examine how well these new macroeconomic models cope with the facts.

There is a marked contrast between the rational expectations theories and the mainstream neoclassical theory which arises purely from the length of time that each of them has been around. As was indicated in the introduction to Chapter 25, the post-Keynesian neoclassical synthesis has been the mainstream macroeconomic model for a whole generation, and so a vast amount of work has been done comparing the predictions of that model with the facts. In contrast, the new theories have been around for less than a decade and, in many cases, are still being digested. Not nearly as much work has yet been done on these models[1] as on the mainstream

---

1. The main contributions have been those by Robert Lucas Jr. (referred to in footnote 2, Chapter 27) and Robert Barro (referred to in footnote 1, Chapter 31) and Thomas J. Sargent. Of Sargent's several fine contributions in this area, perhaps the most relevant in the context of this chapter is, A classical macroeconomic model for the United States, *Journal of Political Economy*, 84, June 1976, pp. 631–40. The only empirical work on the UK using rational expectations is that by Attfield, Demery and Duck (see p. 426 above) and by Patrick Minford, A rational expectations model of the United Kingdom under fixed and floating exchange rates, *Carnegie-Rochester Conference Series on Public Policy*, Vol. 12, Spring 1980, pp. 293–355.

neoclassical synthesis. It is not yet clear, therefore, to what extent these new theories are going to be successful in explaining the facts. They look very promising at this stage, and this chapter will indicate to you why that is so.

For at least two reasons, it would be surprising if the rational expectations theories do not do at least as good a job of explaining the facts as the basic model and the neoclassical synthesis do. First, the new theories have been devised with the benefit of hindsight; we know what is wrong with the basic and neoclassical models and can design new theories to take account of the anomalies or failures of prediction of those earlier models. Secondly, as we have seen, there are some areas in which the basic model predicts well and others in which the neoclassical model predicts well. It so happens that the areas where each of those two models predicts badly are exactly the areas where the other does well. We cannot, of course, at least not if we are going to obey some pretty basic rules of logic, simultaneously maintain the neoclassical model and the basic model as explaining the facts. They are mutually inconsistent. Assumptions made by the basic model are denied by the neoclassical model and *vice versa*. What the new theories do, in effect, is to provide us with a trick which enables us to have the best of both models while, as a matter of logic, denying that either of them is correct. The basic model is seen as the special case of the rational expectations theories when shocks are fully anticipated, and the neoclassical model is seen as the special case when the shocks are not fully anticipated. The Keynesian model (in its strict sense) applies when the shocks are entirely unanticipated. Of course, this identification of the basic and Keynesian models as two special cases and the neoclassical synthesis as a set of intermediate cases of the rational expectations theories does not, in and of itself, tell us that the rational expectations theories are going to turn out to be correct. We cannot simply define the shocks that have hit the economy as being anticipated or unanticipated or some combination of the two, so as to ensure that the theory fits the facts. It is necessary to establish *a priori* how changes in policy instruments and other exogenous variables have been perceived — the extent to which they have actually been anticipated and unanticipated — so as to test the rational expectations theories. That task is well beyond anything that can be done in this chapter (or indeed in this book) and is going to be the subject matter of a great deal of research activity in macroeconomics in the coming years. What we can do, nevertheless, is to see how, in principle at least, the new theories are capable of explaining the facts and what is the nature of the research task ahead. In pursuit of that objective, this chapter takes you through six tasks, which are to:

A. **understand how unanticipated changes in aggregate demand generate procyclical co-movements in prices;**

B. **understand how a combination of unanticipated and anticipated changes in aggregate demand generates both surges in inflation which are independent of output and procyclical co-movements in prices;**

C. **know how the rational expectations theories explain the autocorrelation of output and employment;**

D. **understand the implications of rational expectations for interest rate behaviour;**

E. **understand how the rational expectations theories explain the business cycle;** and

F. **understand the nature of the hypothesis testing problem posed by the rational expectations theories.**

A. Procyclical Co-Movements in Prices

You have seen in Chapter 31 how a fully anticipated change in aggregate demand affects only the nominal variables of the economy, and how an unanticipated change in aggregate demand has both nominal and real effects. It is now possible to use this analysis to understand how the swings in economic activity which are characterised by procyclical co-movements in prices occur.

For illustrative purposes it is going to be easiest to suppose that the expected aggregate demand curve does not change. Equivalently, this implies that the expected money supply and expected government expenditures and taxes are constant. (It would be possible to suppose that the expected *growth rate* of the money supply was constant, so that the expected level of the money supply was increasing by a constant percentage amount each period. In that case, the aggregate demand curve would be shifting upwards at a constant percentage rate, and there would be a trend rate of inflation. We would then analyse variations in aggregate demand around its rising trend position. Such an exercise would complicate the analysis without adding any insights and will not be pursued here.)

In order to fix our ideas, let us suppose that the level of aggregate demand that actually occurs differs from that which is expected because the actual money supply is randomly fluctuating around its anticipated level. Figures 33.1 and 33.2 will illustrate what is going on. Figure 33.1 shows a hypothetical random path for the money supply. (These illustrative numbers are random drawings from a normal distribution with a mean of 100 and a standard deviation of 2.) The average value of the money supply is 100; therefore, the rational expectation of the money supply is also 100. The maximum value of the money supply in this example, 104, occurs in the period 5 and is marked a. The minimum value, 95.8, occurs in period 9 and is marked b.

Figure 33.2 shows the aggregate demand and aggregate supply curves. The curve $AD(M^e = 100)$ is the aggregate demand curve drawn for the expected value of the money supply. The expectations-augmented aggregate supply curve, EAS_0, is drawn

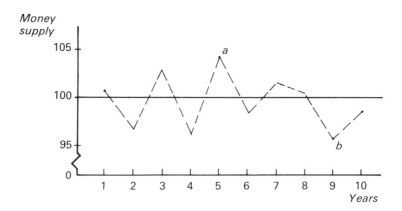

Figure 33.1 *Hypothetical Money Supply Path*

A hypothetical path for the money supply is generated by drawing random numbers from a normal distribution that has an average value of 100 and a standard deviation of 2. The path plotted was generated by taking ten drawings from such a distribution.

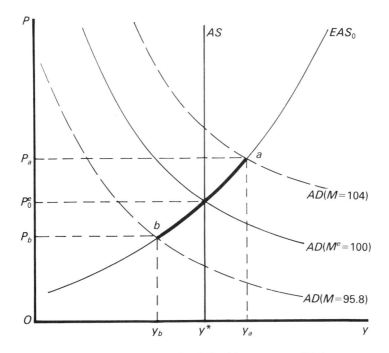

Figure 33.2 *The Procyclical Co-Movements of Prices*
If the money supply was equal to its average value (and rationally expected value) of 100, the aggregate demand curve would be the solid line $AD(M^e = 100)$, output would be y^*, and the price level P_0^e. Actual movements in the money supply will shift the demand function, as shown, between the limits $AD(M = 104)$ and $AD(M = 95.8)$. With a constant expected price level the expectations-augmented aggregate supply curve remains at EAS_0, and the actual levels of output and prices are generated along the thick line ab. This thickened line traces out the generally procyclical price movement.

---

for an expected price level equal to its rational expectation, P_0^e. The vertical curve, AS, is the full-employment aggregate supply curve.

If the money supply behaves as shown in Figure 33.1, then the economy will, on the average, be at the price level P_0^e and, on the average, will have a full-employment output level of y^*. There will, however, be fluctuations around these points. When the money supply is at a, its maximum value in this example, the aggregate demand curve will be the curve shown as $AD(M = 104)$. This determines output as y_a and the price level as P_a. When the money supply is at b, its minimum value in this example, the aggregate demand curve will be at the position shown as $AD(M = 95.8)$. In this case output will be y_b and the price level P_b. For intermediate values of the money supply (periods 1 to 4, 6 to 8, and 10) output and the price level will be determined at points in between these two extremes and along the EAS_0 curve. The thickened portion of that curve traces out the range of values of y and P generated by this hypothetical money supply path.

Although random variations in the money supply about the anticipated level have been stylised as random variations around a *constant* anticipated money supply, as noted above, it would not be difficult to generalise this analysis. If the anticipated money supply were growing, then the expected aggregate demand curve and, therefore, the expectations-augmented aggregate supply curve, would also drift upwards. The actual variations in the money supply, however, would fluctuate around the rising trend, so that the actual aggregate demand curve would fluctuate around the expected curve. We would, therefore, still generate procyclical co-movements of prices, although the amplitude of the price movements would be accentuated and those of the output movements would be smaller than those illustrated.

The predicted procyclical co-movements of prices shown in Figure 33.2 can easily be translated into a predicted negative relationship between inflation and unemployment. When output is above its full-employment level, unemployment will be below its natural rate, and *vice versa*. When the price level is higher than expected, the inflation rate will be higher than expected. Therefore, procyclical co-movements of prices automatically imply a negative relationship between inflation and unemployment — the Phillips curve.

You have now seen how the rational expectations theories generate one aspect of the facts which need to be explained — the sometimes observed, systematic, procyclical movements of prices. This is a phenomenon which the neoclassical synthesis could also cope with, but one which the basic model failed to predict. Let us now move on to consider how the rational expectations theories cope with some other facts.

B. Independent Movements of Output and Prices

There is not much to be said that has not already been said in previous chapters about the effects of a fully anticipated change in aggregate demand. This was explored in Chapter 31, and you saw there that the effects of such a change are identical to the predictions of the basic model. The entire analysis presented in Part III of this book therefore stands as the prediction of the rational expectations theories concerning the effects of a fully anticipated change in aggregate demand. It is particularly worthy of emphasis that the basic model makes the same predictions as do the rational expectations theories concerning the effects of a fully anticipated change in the growth of the money supply. Specifically, the basic model predicts that a change in the growth rate of the money supply will lead to a change in the rate of inflation that will, on the path towards the new steady state, overshoot the growth rate of the money supply. This carries over, without modification, to the rational expectations theories as the predicted effect of a fully anticipated change in the money supply growth rate. Since, in the basic model, changes in the inflation rate occurred *independently of* the level of output, you will recognise as a strength of the rational expectations theories their ability to explain what the Keynesian theory was not able to explain, namely, sudden surges in the rate of inflation that are independent of the level of output.

To see how the rational expectations theories are capable of accounting, in principle, for all the patterns that we observe in the co-movements of output and prices, let us consider separately the effects of anticipated, unanticipated, and combined monetary shocks to the economy.

Suppose first, as described in detail in the previous section, there is a rise in the money supply which raises aggregate demand in an unanticipated fashion. We know that this will raise the price level (and the inflation rate) and raise output. There will thus, from this source of shock, be a procyclical co-movement in prices. Suppose, at the opposite extreme, that there is a rise in the money supply that is entirely anticipated. This will lead to a rise in the price level (inflation rate) with no corresponding movement of output. Now combine these two effects. There are two interesting cases. One is where the money supply increases by an amount that is partly anticipated and partly not. In this case there will be a rise in both output and prices, but the rise in prices will be greater than if the rise in the money supply was unanticipated. Let us translate this into a prediction about inflation and unemployment rather than about prices and output. In the experiment just reviewed, a higher output level will be associated with a lower unemployment rate, and a higher price level with a higher observed rate of inflation. This would mean that a rise in the money supply that was partly anticipated and partly not would generate a rise in inflation and a drop in unemployment. The amount by which prices rise would depend on the anticipated and unanticipated components of the rise in the money supply. The amount by which unemployment falls would depend only on the unanticipated change in the money supply. What this implies is that the slope of the Phillips curve (the pattern of points linking inflation to unemployment) will not be constant and will, in general, depend on the decomposition of the change in the money supply betwween its anticipated and unanticipated components.

We can see this in a more extreme case by considering a second example. Suppose that the money supply *is anticipated* to grow at a high rate. Suppose further that the money supply actually increases at a rate which is lower than anticipated. This is a situation in which there is high anticipated money growth, and negative unanticipated money growth. In such a situation, output will fall and unemployment will rise. The inflation rate may either rise or fall, depending on the strength of the two offsetting effects upon it. The effect of a high anticipated growth of the money supply will be to keep inflation high, while the effect of a negative unanticipated change in the money supply will be to lower inflation. We cannot say, *a priori*, which of these two effects will dominate. It is possible, however, for the first to dominate, thereby producing a higher rate of inflation with a higher unemployment rate and an output rate which is below trend. This would be the case observed on several occasions in the 1970s when there was a tendency for both inflation and unemployment to rise together. The continued rise in United Kingdom unemployment in the late 1970s and 1980–81, with the tendency for output to fall below its trend value, while at the same time the inflation rate, although moderating in 1981, has remained persistently high, may potentially be accounted for by this line of reasoning.

The crucial thing to emphasise and reiterate is that the way in which a change in aggregate demand is divided between a change in output and a change in prices depends upon the extent to which that change in aggregate demand is anticipated. On the average, output and prices will move in the same direction as each other, since swings in actual aggregate demand are likely to have greater amplitude than swings in expected aggregate demand. From time to time, however, there may be large shifts in anticipated aggregate demand, usually less than, but occasionally greater than, the change in actual aggregate demand. These occasional strong changes in expected aggregate demand will produce co-movements that are opposite to those normally observed and, when they occur, will be associated with the appearance of badly deteriorating (or, though it has not happened in the 1970s, of miraculously improving) macroeconomic performance.

The discussion in this section and in Section A has focused on the way in which the price and output co-movements might be understood. There is one further feature of the behaviour of output, however, on which that discussion has not touched and to which we now turn.

C. Autocorrelation of Output and Employment

There are two commonly advanced explanations for autocorrelation of output and employment. The first is based on *costs of adjustment*. The theory of profit-maximising firms' demand for labour and supply of output, as developed in Chapter 9, which underlies all the models — the basic, Keynesian, and rational expectations — implicitly assumes that firms can vary their output and labour inputs instantly and costlessly. That is a reasonable assumption to make for the purpose of getting some theoretical principles straight. It is probably not a good assumption, however, if we want to explain the facts as they appear in actual economies. It is costly to hire and fire labour, and in the event of a change in demand, firms will only gradually adjust their labour inputs and outputs to meet the new demand conditions. Therefore, when the price level rises, instead of the demand for labour curve shifting to reflect the new higher price level *instantly*, it will only *gradually* move. Thus, if the economy experienced an unanticipated (say) rise, in the money supply, then, although the response to that rise will be a higher price level and higher levels of output and employment, it will take firms some time to raise their output and employment levels by the amounts suggested by the theories developed in this book. Instead of the demand for labour function suddenly shifting, it will gradually move to the right, thereby leading to a gradual change in employment and output rather than a sudden change. To make things clearer, suppose that after a period in which there had been an unanticipated rise in the money supply, there was a subsequent unanticipated fall. Firms will already have hired additional labour and be producing additional output, having moved some way towards satisfying the demand associated with the previously unanticipated rise in the money supply. Now that they are confronted with an unexpected fall in the money supply (and therefore an unexpected fall in the price level), they will not suddenly jump to the new lower employment and output position. Rather they will, *starting from where they are*, gradually move towards the new lower output and employment position. This is not to say that firms are irrational and are not maximising profits. On the contrary, it is precisely because they are maximising profits that their adjustments will be gradual. They have to take account, not only of the cost of labour and capital and the price of output in their profit-maximising decisions, but also of the costs of *changing* their output and employment. Thus, the costs of hiring and firing labour make demand for labour curves move slowly, and this imparts gradual adjustment to output and employment.

Gradual adjustment, of course, may be described as autocorrelation. If output and employment adjust gradually, then where they will move to in the current period depends on where they started out from in the previous period, and where they will go to in the next period depends on where they are now. This can be described by saying that the value of output and employment in period t depends in part on the values of those variables in period $t - 1$.

The explanation for autocorrelation just presented is the one that is incorporated in the new classical theory of aggregate supply. A second way in which autocorrelation of output and employment can arise is emphasised in the new Keynesian theory and comes from the fact that *contracts* in the labour market are *long and overlapping*. It is not the case that everyone negotiates a labour contract on the same day of each year for the coming year. Some labour market contracts run for less than a year, some for a year, some for more than a year. Contracts in existence in any particular year were negotiated at different dates in the past, and so *the expectations that are embedded in those contracts are based on information that was available at different dates in the past*. Thus, what was unanticipated when one set of contracts was written, some time in the past, might already have occurred and therefore be part of the information on the basis of which some other, more recent, contracts were written. This means that a monetary (or other aggregate demand) shock which occurs after a contract has been written and which was unanticipated when the contract was written will continue to have effects on output and employment until that particular contract is replaced with a new one. Random shocks will have effects that persist from one period to the next rather than simply dying away instantly.

An Analogy[2]

The idea that costly labour input adjustments and overlapping long-term contracts can generate autocorrelation in output, employment, and prices has a vivid physical analogy which perhaps will make things clearer. Suppose one was to hit a rocking chair at random. The chair is sometimes hit frequently and sometimes infrequently; sometimes with a hard knock and sometimes with a gentle one. Within wide limits the chair will rock in a very systematic and persistent fashion, regardless of how it is hit. It will swing to and fro much more systematically than the shocks which are being imparted to it by the person who is rocking it. It is much the same with the economy. The adjustment costs in labour markets and the negotiation costs in setting up new contracts mean that when unexpected events occur, there is sufficient inertia in the economy to ensure that it does not radically alter its course as a result of the random shock. Rather, its course is much more systematic and smooth than the path of the shocks themselves that are hitting the economy.

---

2. The rocking chair analogy was first suggested as long ago as 1907 by the brilliant Swedish economist, Knut Wicksell, and elaborated upon in 1933 by Ragnar Frisch: 'If you hit a wooden rocking horse with a club, the movement of the horse will be very different to that of the club.' Quoted from Ragnar Frisch, Propogation problems and impulse problems in dynamic economics, *Economic Essays in Honour of Gustave Cassell*, Augustus M. Kelley, New York, 1967, p. 198 (originally published in 1933).

D. Interest Rate Behaviour

Although, in the presentation of the rational expectation theories in Chapters 27 to 31, we have not explicitly analysed the determination of the rate of interest, there are strong implications for interest rate determination in the new theories. To explore those implications fully and completely would require more time and space than is available here and in some respects, would take us into a level of analysis that is substantially more demanding than would be appropriate. Nevertheless, it is possible to obtain a good understanding of the general implications for interest rate determination of the rational expectations theories. This brief section will pursue that task.

You already know that the market rate of interest will, in general, deviate from the real rate of interest because of inflation. When we developed the simple theory of interest in Chapter 10 we were not being careful to distinguish between actual and expected magnitudes. A moment's reflection will tell you, however, that the gap between the real and money rate of interest is going to be the *expected* or anticipated *inflation* rate rather than the *actual* rate. This is obvious, simply from considering the nature of capital markets in which interest rates are determined. People borrow and lend for *future periods* of differing lengths. That being so, the real rate of return that they will obtain at the end of a loan term will be equal to the market rate of interest on the loan minus the actual rate of inflation that emerges over the term of the loan. At the time at which a loan is contracted, that actual rate of inflation is unknown. The only substitute for the actual rate of inflation that both borrowers and lenders can use is their anticipation of the inflation that will occur over the term of the loan. Lenders will demand a premium on the interest rate to compensate for their anticipation of the inflation that is going to occur over the term of the loan, and borrowers will willingly pay a premium equal to their anticipation of inflation. Since both borrowers and lenders occupy the same economic environment and form their expectations in the same rational manner, there should be a consensus as to what the anticipated rate of inflation is. This amounts to saying that the market rate of interest that we should observe will equal the equilibrium real rate of interest, (itself a variable), plus the rational expectation of the rate of inflation *over the term of the loan in question*. For three-month loans this will mean that the anticipated three-month rate of inflation will be added to the real rate of interest and for, say, 15- to 20-year loans, the rate of inflation expected over the long term, on the average, will be added to the real rate of interest.

The anticipated rate of inflation (the rational expectation of the future price level expressed as a percentage change over the current known price level and converted to an annual rate of change) will depend upon the expected growth rate of the money supply and expected output growth. In general, we would expect the actual growth rate of the money supply (and actual growth rate of aggregate demand) to be more volatile than movements in the expected growth rate of the money supply and expected growth of aggregate demand. This is precisely the consideration that led to the prediction of procyclical co-movements in prices in Section A above. Further, in general, we would expect fluctuations in the expected long-term average growth rate of the money supply to be much smaller than fluctuations in expectations of, say, the next three months' growth rate of the money supply or the next twelve months' growth rate. Now, recall that the rate at which prices change depends on *both* the anticipated and unanticipated changes in the money supply. Movements in the interest rate, however, will depend only on the anticipated inflation rate and therefore only on the anticipated movements of the money supply. This implies that fluctuations in prices (inflation) will have greater amplitude than fluctuations in interest rates. Further, because fluctuations in the expected long-term average money supply growth rate will be smaller than fluctuations in the expected money supply growth rate over the short term, fluctuations in short-term interest rates will have greater amplitude than fluctuations in long-term interest rates.

It is an implication of the rational expectations theories that, like prices, interest rates will display procyclical co-movements. Interest rates, however, will have fluctuations of smaller amplitude than prices, and the longer the term of the interest rate, the smaller will be the amplitude of the fluctuation. You will recognise these predictions as being in accord with the facts if you recall the information on British interest rates presented in Chapters 2 and 7 of this book.

E. The Business Cycle[3]

This section does little more than bring together and consolidate what has already been said above. The first feature of the business cycle that was identified in Chapter 7 was the description of the movements of real economic activity (as measured by output) as a low-order stochastically disturbed difference equation. Specifically, we saw that it was possible to describe post-war British real GDP by an equation that said that real GDP in year t would be equal to 0.63 of its value in the previous year, plus a purely random component. You can now see how the rational expectations theories explain that simple description of the evolution of real GDP. The autocorrelation component (the persistence effect) is not the central part of the theory at all. That is rationalised in terms of costly adjustment, either of inputs of labour or of wage and employment contracts. The main part of the theory has to do with rationalising the sources of randomness that hit the economy. The rational expectations theories identify that randomness as the unanticipated components of monetary and fiscal changes as well, of course implicitly, as randomness in decisions concerning private-expenditure and money-holding decisions.

The second feature of the business cycle described in Chapter 7 and identified as being present in the United Kingdom is the procyclical co-movement of prices and interest rates. We have seen in this chapter how the normally observed procyclical co-movements of prices are to be explained as the consequence of fluctuations in actual aggregate demand having greater amplitude than the fluctuations in

---

3. For two brilliant papers dealing with this topic and much more — indeed with the entire subject matter of this book — you will want to read Robert E. Lucas Jr.'s, Understanding business cycles, *Journal of Monetary Economics*, Supplement 1977, Carnegie Rochester Conference Series, Vol. 5 and, Methods and problems in business cycle theory, *Journal of Money, Credit and Banking*, Vol. 12, November 1980, Part 2, pp. 696–715. For a thoughtful critique, you will also want to read James Tobin's discussion paper in the second cited Lucas paper, on pp. 795–99 of the same journal.

anticipated aggregate demand. We have also seen that the procyclical co-movements of interest rates, smaller in amplitude than the fluctuations in prices and of even smaller amplitude in the case of long-term interest rates, are all explicable in these same terms. Basically, fluctuations in expected values of variables are usually less marked than fluctuations in actual values, and the longer the period over which an average expectation is being formed, the smaller the amplitude of the fluctuations in that expectation.

The key ingenuity of the rational expectations theories lies in its ability to account for the autocorrelated movements of output and the procyclical co-movements of prices and interest rates, while at the same time being able to account for the infrequent but, when they occur, important independent movements of inflation and output. You have also seen in this chapter how that explanation is achieved. The final task of this chapter is to set out a few problems that arise in the area of testing the explanation just advanced.

F. The Hypothesis Testing Problem Posed by the Rational Expectations Theories[4]

This chapter has tried to show you how the rational expectations theories of income, employment, and prices are capable, *in principle*, of explaining the facts. That exercise should not be confused with the exercise of actually explaining the facts. That latter task is much more difficult and requires careful, indeed, painstaking measurements and statistical inferences. *Testing* the explanations advanced in this chapter is something which is only in its infancy[5] and is going to occupy a great deal of time and energy in the coming years. This section merely reviews some of the highlights of the problems that arise in that activity.

The first problem that has to be solved is that of finding plausible, *a priori* defendable and, ideally, non-controversial decompositions of changes in money, government spending, taxes (and perhaps other exogenous variables) into their anticipated and unanticipated components. This involves studying the *processes* that describe the evolution of these variables and finding ways of forecasting them that mimic reasonably well the ways in which agents in the real world might go about that task. The example of the money supply, briefly referred to in Chapter 31, describing the money supply as a low-order autocorrelated process which responds to unusually large fluctuations in the government spending level, seems like a promising hypothesis for explaining how people form anticipations of monetary growth. The

---

4. The subject matter of this section is discussed in Stanley Fischer, (ed.), *Rational Expectations and Economic Policy*, National Bureau of Economic Research Conference Report, University of Chicago Press, 1980, especially pp. 49–70.

5. The work of Barro and of Attfield, Demery and Duck referred to in Chapter 32 are good examples. In addition to decomposing money growth into its anticipated and unanticipated components, they go on to show that, as predicted by the rational expectations models, only unanticipated money growth affects output, while both anticipated and unanticipated money growth affect the price level.

work that has been done by Robert Barro and Attfield, Demery and Duck along these lines and is now being extended and applied to government spending and taxes and other related variables makes a useful start.

Even if we were able convincingly and non-controversially to decompose changes in exogenous variables into their anticipated and unanticipated components, our tasks would not be over. A major problem arises in discriminating between the new Keynesian and new classical theories. As you saw, those two theories are very similar. They differ in three respects. First, they imply different slopes for the expectations-augmented aggregate supply curve. Secondly, one theory implies that households will always be 'on' their labour supply curve while the other implies that they may at some stages be 'off' that curve. From an observational point of view it is very difficult to discriminate between these two differences, since we do not know, *a priori*, what the slope of the expectations-augmented aggregate supply curve is, nor would it be very easy, *a priori*, to identify whether or not individuals were 'on' or 'off' their labour supply curves. The third source of difference does provide a potential way of discriminating, but it will not be easy to exploit. It is the difference between the two theories arising from the overlapping nature of labour market contracts emphasised by the new Keynesian theory. The difference in question is the way in which the random shocks combine to affect the current value of output, employment, and prices. According to the new classical theory, the current random shock combined with the previous actual value of output is all that is required to explain what is happening in the current period, whereas for the new Keynesian approach, the shocks from previous periods explicitly have to be combined with the current period shock to generate the current period output, employment, and price level.

There is a third problem known as the 'observational equivalence' problem.[6] Although not quite a precise statement of that problem, you will get an adequate feel for it if you imagine that in the context of the neoclassical synthesis, the hypothesis about how inflation expectations evolve (how they relate to previous values of other observed variables) is specified in such a way that the ultimate relation between the exogenous variables (monetary and fiscal policy and other exogenous variables) and the levels of output, employment, and prices are as close a correspondence (indeed are an identical correspondence) with the facts as the predictions generated by a specific version of the rational expectations theory. It is always possible, as a matter of logic, to construct such an observationally equivalent theory. This says nothing other, however, than that the ultimate test of a theory is its ability to predict the future rather than the past!

6. This problem is explained in Thomas J. Sargent, The observational equivalence of natural and unnatural rate theories of macroeconomics, *Journal of Political Economy*, 84, June, 1976, pp. 631–40.

SUMMARY

A. Procyclical Co-Movements in Prices

Generally, the swings in the actual values of variables which determine aggregate demand (for example, the money supply) are bigger than the swings in the anticipated values of those variables. This means that the aggregate demand curve fluctuates with greater amplitude than the expectations-augmented aggregate supply curve. The consequence of this is procyclical co-movements of prices in general.

B. Independent Movements of Output and Prices

Fully anticipated changes in agregate demand will move the price level but leave real output undisturbed. By combining fully anticipated and unanticipated movements in aggregate demand (generated by fully anticipated and unanticipated movements in monetary and fiscal policy variables) enables us, in principle, to account for the facts about output and prices (or, equivalently, unemployment and inflation). As a general rule, prices are procyclical (inflation and unemployment are negatively related) for the reasons developed in Section A and summarised above. Occasionally there will be a surge in inflation that is independent of, or even sometimes goes in the same direction as, the unemployment rate. This will arise because the anticipated rise in the money supply is high, while the unanticipated change in the money supply is negative.

C. Autocorrelation of Output and Employment

Output is autocorrelated even though the shocks which hit the economy are purely random because the costs of changing labour inputs and the costs of re-negotiating labour contracts impart inertia into firms' adjustments of employment and output.

D. Interest Rate Behaviour

Money rates of interest will exceed real rates of interest by an amount equal to the anticipated rate of inflation. The term over which inflation has to be anticipated is the same as the term over which a loan is made. For short-term loans, the relevant anticipated inflation rate is that over the short term. For longer-term loans, the long-term average anticipation of inflation is required. Anticipated inflation depends only on anticipated money growth, while actual inflation depends on both anticipated and unanticipated money growth. Interest rates will fluctuate in a generally procyclical manner, but with less amplitude than prices because the anticipated money supply growth rate will fluctuate with a smaller amplitude than the actual money supply growth rate. Longer-term interest rates will have an even smaller amplitude of fluctuation because fluctuations in the anticipated long-term average money supply growth rate will have smaller amplitude than those of short-term anticipations.

E. The Business Cycle

The first feature of the business cycle, the autocorrelation of output, is explained by the costs of adjusting labour input and costs of re-negotiating labour market contracts. The procyclical co-movements of prices and interest rates are explained by the tendency for the actual variables that generate aggregate demand (monetary and fiscal policy variables) to fluctuate with bigger amplitude than their expected values. The non-universality of the procyclical movements of prices arises from the occasional jump in the anticipated money supply growth rate (sometimes in excess of that which actually occurs).

F. The Hypothesis Testing Problem Posed by the Rational Expectations Theories

The major problem is that of finding a convincing and non-controversial way of decomposing changes in the actual values of exogenous variables into their anticipated and unanticipated components. Discriminating between the new Keynesian and new classical theories will be difficult because they are almost equivalent from an observational point of view. Further, discriminating the rational expectations theories from traditional theory purely on the basis of the past will be difficult, since it is always possible to patch up the traditional theory with an appropriately general theory of the time lags involved in the adjustment of expectations for the two theories to yield identical predictions. The ultimate test of any theory will lie in its ability to predict the future rather than the past.

Appendix: A Methodological Postscript

We have an aversion to methodological discussions in the abstract — no doubt arising from the fact that we are economists and not philosophers of science. It is possible, however, that extra insights will be obtained into the analysis that has been presented in the last 26 theoretical chapters if we stand back a little from the detail and think about what we have been doing in more general abstract terms. This methodological postscript discusses two interrelated matters. The first has to do with the distinction between *ex post* or realised values of variables and *ex ante* or planned values, as well as the closely related distinction between accounting identities and equilibrium conditions. The second matter discussed is the distinction between equilibrium and disequilibrium methods of modelling economic activity.

Economic Variables and the Relations Between Them

We have, in the last 26 chapters, developed models which purport to make predictions about actual events in the world. These are predictions about the behaviour of such variables as income, output, employment, unemployment, prices, and interest rates. The models seek to make predictions about the *actual* values of variables. These actual values are called *ex post* or realised values. *Ex post* or realised variables are linked together with *accounting identities*. That is, certain realised values of certain variables are defined to be equal to certain sums of other variables. Some of the most obvious such accounting identities are those which say that one variable is identically equal to another. The equality between national income, expenditure and output is an example of this. In general, purchases always equal sales. Certain stocks are related to each other in a similar way, for example the stock of money issued by the central bank is equal to the stocks of money held by the commercial banks and private individuals.

In explaining — in generating predictions about — these actual variables we have developed theories which make statements about the plans of economic agents. We have postulated that rational agents maximise utility or profit and as a result of these maximisation experiments come through with plans for consumption or labour supply or output supply or labour demand. Aggregating these plans over all agents leads to aggregate plans such as aggregate demand, the aggregate demand for money, investment, consumption and the like. These are not actual quantities. They are not even a single quantity. They are conditional quantities: aggregate demand will be so much if the price level is some particular value. If the price level is a lower value then aggregate demand will be a higher value. These planned magnitudes are called *ex ante* or, more directly, planned variables.

It is possible to imagine a situation in which the plans of different individuals are not necessarily compatible with each other. A situation in which plans are compatible is called an *equilibrium*. A situation in which plans are not compatible is called a *disequilibrium*. The statement that one *ex ante* (planned) magnitude is equal to some other relevant *ex ante* (planned) magnitude is known as an equilibrium condition. For example, supply equals demand is such a condition. Equilibrium conditions and accounting identities look very similar to each other. For example, purchases equals sales is an accounting identity and supply equals demand an equilibrium condition. Although they look very similar, the meaning of these two statements is fundamentally different. An accounting identity is always true from the definition of the variables. An equilibrium condition is a statement about the compatibility of plans.

The above discussion of equilibrium and disequilibrium invites us to go further and examine these two concepts as ways of developing economic models.

Equilibrium and Disequilibrium Methods in Economic Modelling

There are two distinct ways in which it is possible to develop an economic model — the equilibrium method and the disequilibrium method. In the equilibrium method 'the concepts of excess demands and supplies play no observational role and are identified with no observed magnitudes.'[7] All observed quantities and prices are at the intersection points of supply and demand curves. That is, they are points in which plans of individual agents are compatible with each other. Movements in prices and quantities are the results of movements in supply and/or demand curves.

Disequilibrium models, in contrast to equilibrium models, are ones in which, to negate the above quotation, excess demands and supplies do play an observational role and are indeed identified with observed quantities. In the context of macroeconomics, unemployment is a phenomenon identified with the concept of the excess supply of labour and inflation is a magnitude identified with the excess demand for goods. In the disequilibrium method, observed quantities are, in general, disequilibrium quantities. Movements in prices and quantities are responses to disequilibrium.

Choosing between these two alternative ways of building an economic model is *not an empirical matter*. It is a matter of axiomatic principle. One may choose to develop a model using equilibrium concepts or using disequilibrium concepts as a matter of taste. There is an ongoing debate in economics (in macroeconomics in particular) as to which of these two methods is going to be the most fruitful.[8]

The following brief diagrammatic analysis will explain to you why it is possible to model the same phenomenon either as a disequilibrium or an equilibrium process. Figure 33.3 illustrates a market for a single quantity q (it could be labour or goods, an aggregate market, or an individual commodity or factor market) the initial quantity traded of which is q^* and the initial price of which is p^*. To keep the picture very simple, imagine that supply is completely inelastic and is illustrated by the vertical line s in both Frame (a) and Frame (b). Initially, demand is given by the curve d which is shown in both Frames (a) and (b). Imagine that at a particular point in time the price began to rise above p^*, but the quantity remained constant at q^*. The economy goes through a process in which the price level gradually rises from p^* to $p^{*\prime}$ but with a constant quantity. How could this process be explained using the two alternative methodologies? First, consider the disequilibrium approach (Frame (a)). According to this theory, the demand function has shifted to d' generating excess demand of $q' - q^*$. With excess demand prices begin to rise (the price adjustment curve in the lower part of Frame (a)). As prices rise, so excess demand falls and eventually, when prices have risen all the way to $p^{*\prime}$, there is no excess demand left and the economy is back at an equilibrium. Throughout the process of moving from p^* to $p^{*\prime}$ the economy has been in disequilibrium. The quantity demanded has exceeded the quantity supplied throughout that process.

The alternative methodology — the equilibrium methodology — would explain the same events in the following way. In the very short run demand does not change, but remains at the level shown by the demand curve labelled d. Something has happened however, to change demand conditions and so demand gradually increases. This will take the form of the demand curve gradually shifting upwards from d to d'. As it does so, it will intersect the supply curve at higher and higher prices and eventually, the demand curve will have moved to d' (the postulated instantaneous shift in the disequilibrium approach.) Throughout the process of adjustment in Frame (b), the economy has been in equilibrium. The quantity demanded has been equal to the quantity supplied. The same facts occur in both situations and are clearly equally amenable to explanation by the two alternative methods.

If two equilibria are compared, the analysis being undertaken is known as *comparative statics*. According to the equilibrium method, comparative statics is an empirically relevant exercise. It involves comparing two situations which, according to the method being employed, are situations that are relevant to the actual economy and not simply relevant to the theoretical construct — the model economy. According to the disequilibrium method,

---

7. Robert E. Lucas Jr., Methods and problems in business cycle theory, *Journal of Money, Credit and Banking*, Vol. 12, No. 4, Part 2, November 1980, p. 709.

8. The entire paper by Lucas cited in the previous footnote is an excellent statement of the case for an equilibrium methodology. Also see, by the same author, Tobin and monetarism: a review article, *The Journal of Economic Literature*, Vol. 19, No. 2, June 1981, pp. 558–85.

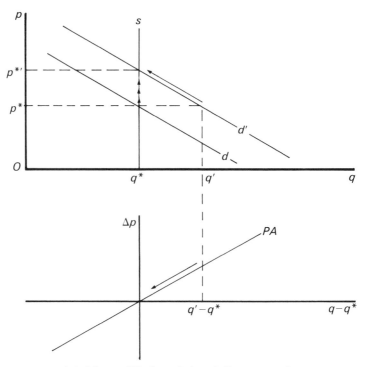

(a) *Disequilibrium Price Adjustment Process*

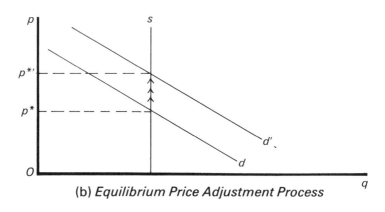

(b) *Equilibrium Price Adjustment Process*

Figure 33.3 *Equilibrium-Disequilibrium Price Adjustment Processes*

The same event, a gradual rise in the price with a constant quantity is explained by two
alternative theoretical methods. Frame (a) describes the event as a disequilibrium process.
The demand curve shifts to d' creating an excess demand. Excess demand leads to rising prices
so that the economy slides up d' and down PA to the new equilibrium price $p^{*\prime}$. Frame (b)
illustrates an equilibrium representation of the same process. Demand conditions change but,
at the moment of impact, the demand curve does not move. The equilibrium price and
quantity remain constant therefore at p^*, q^*. Gradually the demand curve moves upwards
and, as it does so, it intersects the supply curve at higher and higher prices. Eventually, the
demand curve moves all the way to d' (the same curve as that postulated to have arisen
instantaneously in the case of the disequilibrium approach) and the price level has risen to $p^{*\prime}$.

comparative statics is interesting in that it tells us where the economy is headed, but uninteresting as a general description of where the economy was initially and will move to following some exogenous shock.

The process whereby the economy moves from one stationary position (such as p^*, q^*) to another (such as $p^{*'}$, $q^{*'}$) is called a *dynamic* process and the analysis of such a process is called *dynamics*. From what has been said above, it will be clear to you that dynamics is *not* synonymous with disequilibrium. There are equilibrium and disequilibrium theories of dynamic processes.

You may find it helpful, in the light of the methodological discussion presented in this postscript, to review again the material presented in Part II concerning the measurement of economic variables. In that part, all the variables presented as *ex post* or realised and all the relations between them are accounting identities. Additionally, you may find it helpful to review again the alternative theories of macroeconomics. The basic model as well as the new classical model use the equilibrium method. The Keynesian model and the neoclassical synthesis use the disequilibrium method. The new Keynesian model is always in an expected equilibrium, but never in an actual equilibrium (except of course in the event that the random shocks are zero).

Review Questions

1. Explain how, in general, procyclical co-movements in prices and output are explained by the rational expectations theories.

2. Show how the rational expectations theories explain the fact that, on occasion, there is a strong rise in inflation accompanied by low output and high unemployment.

3. Do the new Keynesian and new classical theories differ as regards their explanation for the phenomenon described in Question 2? If so, how?

4. What is the explanation offered by the new classical theory for autocorrelation in output and employment?

5. What is the explanation offered by the new Keynesian theory for autocorrelation in output and employment?

6. What is the explanation of the rational expectations theories for interest rate behaviour? Why do long-term interest rates fluctuate with smaller amplitude than short-term rates and why do short-term rates fluctuate with smaller amplitude than inflation?

7. Review the explanation offered by the rational expectations theories of the business cycle. How do they differ from the neoclassical explanation?

8. Assess the assertion that the modern theories are non-scientific because they can never be falsified.

9. (Similar to 8!) Assess the assertion that since we can decompose the changes in monetary and fiscal variables into anticipated and unanticipated components so as to make the rational expectations theories fit the facts, they will suffer from the ultimate weakness of being capable of explaining everything and predicting nothing.

Part VI

Macroeconomic Policy

34

Introduction to Macroeconomic Policy Problems

You have now completed your study of macroeconomic theory — the problem of explaining macroeconomic phenomena — and are now ready to examine the implications of that theory for the formation and conduct of macroeconomic policy. There has been a good deal of policy discussion implicit in the presentation of the theory itself. It is now time, however, to address the policy issues more directly and systematically. This brief introductory chapter will enable you to start on that process by doing three things. It will enable you to:

A. know what macroeconomic policies seek to achieve;
B. know the highlights in the evolution of the policy debate;
 and
C. understand the idea that policy is a process and not an event.

A. What Macroeconomic Policies Seek to Achieve

There is little disagreement among economists concerning what an ideal macroeconomic performance would look like. There might be some arguments of detail, but they are insignificant compared with the broad agreement on two matters. First, it would be ideal if unemployment, except for that associated with natural job searching and labour turnover, could be entirely eliminated. Equivalently, it would be ideal if output could be maintained at its full-employment equilibrium value on a continuous basis. Secondly, it would be ideal if inflation could be held at a steady, constant, low (perhaps, ideally, zero) rate.[1] Associated with this would be the ideal that the market rate of interest would be equal to the real rate of interest. Recognising that perfection is impossible, the objective could be expressed slightly more generally as that of minimising the deviations of unemployment from its natural rate, of output from its full-employment rate, of inflation from zero, and of market interest rates from real interest rates.

It is worth emphasising that the specification of the unemployment objective is that of keeping unemployment as close to its natural rate as possible, and *not* that of lowering the natural rate to as low a level as possible. It is important to understand that too little unemployment can have serious consequences for the economic welfare of all, even those who are from time to time unemployed. Job search and job changing are productive activities. Further, even if it is judged that the natural rate of unemployment is, in fact, too high, then the only policy measures that can be taken to influence that rate are microeconomic (relative price) policies. It would be necessary to change the arrangements for unemployment benefits, methods of taxing income from employment and job search, or some other similar matter. In other words, the natural rate of unemployment is not itself a variable which can be influenced by aggregate government spending, taxes, or monetary growth.

The objectives of *macroeconomic* policy, then, are to minimise the variability of unemployment and output about their natural rates and to minimise the variability of inflation around some low, stable, possibly zero, value.

B. Highlights in the Evolution of the Policy Debate

In the pre-Keynesian era, the general feeling was that the fluctuations in economic activity which characterised the business cycle were natural phenomena which simply had to be put up with. They were in the same class as storms, floods, and tempests. They buffeted human societies in a serious and sometimes devastating way, but simply had to be accepted as one of the harsh facts of life. The Keynesian revolution, which began in the mid-1930s but didn't achieve its full influence until the 50s and 60s, radically changed that view. The business cycle was then seen as entirely controllable. It was widely believed that monetary and fiscal policy could and should be used to manipulate aggregate demand so as to ensure the close achievement of full employment and stable prices.[2] Some believed that monetary and fiscal policies

1. There is an extensive literature on the optimum rate of inflation as well as on the optimum level of unemployment. The summary of the objectives of macroeconomic policy stated in this chapter is not meant as a substitute for these careful and in some cases deep analyses. For a comprehensive discussion of these issues you should consult Edmund S. Phelps, *Inflation Policy and Unemployment Theory: The Cost Benefit Approach to Monetary Planning*, W. W. Norton, 1972.

2. For a superb account of this view, see Franco Modigliani, The monetarist controversy or, should we forsake stabilisation policies?, *American Economic Review*, 67, March 1977, pp. 1–19.

could achieve high employment and real output, but not price stability. They were nevertheless undaunted in their pursuit of both objectives of macroeconomic policy and regarded the implementation of direct controls on wages and prices or, more euphemistically, 'incomes policies', as the appropriate additional instrument for achieving both sets of objectives.

As we moved into the 1970s, it became increasingly apparent that macroeconomic policy was not delivering the promised stability. Inflation rates accelerated, and this despite the fact that unemployment levels were historically high and output growth sagging. Coinciding with this dismal macroeconomic policy performance, there emerged a radically new view of how economic fluctuations are generated and what might be done to moderate them. The centrepiece of the new view is the hypothesis that expectations are formed rationally.[3] The hypothesis not only leads to a radical transformation in the explanation for the phenomenon of the business cycle, but also to a radically different view of policy. The business cycle is viewed as the outcome of shocks which hit the economy which are either not correctly foreseen or not fully perceived. Policy influences the cycle in that the *unanticipated* variations in policy instruments lead to variations in real output and prices. In this view, policy is a process that has to be decomposed into an anticipated and unanticipated component. By minimising the unanticipated variations in policy, the business cycle will be smoothed as much as is possible. There may be a case for having a pre-announced, countercyclical policy response, but there will never be a case for random, haphazard 'discretionary' policy intervention. The cycle will not go away, and it may sometimes be quite severe. But *ad hoc*, previously unexpected attempts to intervene and boost aggregate demand can only be more destabilising on the average than doing nothing other than pursuing a previously announced policy strategy.

It is this new view of policy to which you will be introduced in the remaining chapters of this part of the book. Before moving on to that, it will be worthwhile spending a moment or two on the final topic of this chapter.

C. Policy — A Process, Not an Event

The old-fashioned way of analysing macroeconomic policy was to ask questions like, what will happen if the level of government spending is raised by 10 per cent? What will happen if the money supply growth rate is cut from 7 per cent to 4 per cent and held there indefinitely? What will happen if taxes and spending are cut by the same amount? Questions of this kind are questions that treat policy as an *event*, in the sense that a certain well-defined policy action occurs. The idea then (several examples of which you have seen in this book) is to trace out the effects of this policy shock on output, prices, interest rates, employment, etc. You now understand that

---

3. A very good presentation of this view, which does not explicitly introduce the rationality of expectations, but which is clearly groping in that direction, is Milton Friedman, The role of monetary policy, *American Economic Review*, 58, March 1968, pp. 1–17. The best discussion in the context of an explicit rational framework is Thomas J. Sargent and Neil Wallace, Rational expectations and the theory of economic policy, *Journal of Monetary Economics*, 2, April 1976, pp. 169–84.

accepting the hypothesis that expectations are formed rationally implies that such exercises are meaningless. It is simply not possible to analyse the effect of a single-event policy change without knowing whether or not that policy was anticipated or unanticipated. Once that is known, it is possible to analyse the effects on output, prices, and the other variables in the economy. It is not possible, however, to know whether or not a particular policy event was anticipated or unanticipated *by considering that event in isolation*. It is unavoidable that the *entire policy process* be analysed in order that a particular policy event may be identified as anticipated, unanticipated, or partly one and partly the other. That is, it is necessary to have a model of the evolution of the policy instruments that enables the policy instruments of any particular time to be decomposed into their anticipated and unanticipated components. It is also necessary to examine the broader institutional and political setting within which policies are being made, for it is the entire policy process which influences the quality of macroeconomic performance. Work of this kind is only in its infancy. It will, however, inevitably become a major part of the next generation of research in understanding and improving macroeconomic policy.

The remaining chapters in this part of the book are first of all going to examine the links between monetary and fiscal policy. This will show you that when viewing the entire monetary and fiscal policy process, these two sets of policies are inextricably linked together. Next, we shall examine the way in which the Bank of England conducts its policies for achieving a particular path for the money supply. After these two preliminary chapters we shall move to the substance of the policy debate and analyse the key reasons for the differences in policy views that were set out in Chapter 1 of this book.

SUMMARY

A. What Macroeconomic Policies Seek to Achieve

Macroeconomic policies seek to minimise fluctuations of unemployment and output about their natural rates and minimise the variability of inflation around some low, stable, possibly zero, value. Other objectives, such as lowering the natural rate of unemployment, are not, strictly speaking, *macroeconomic* policies. They involve *microeconomic* intervention to change relative prices.

B. Highlights in the Evolution of the Policy Debate

The pre-Keynesian view of macroeconomic policy was that none was available. Fluctuations simply had to be lived with in the same way as other natural disorders. The Keynesian revolution led to the optimistic view that by manipulating monetary and fiscal policy, aggregate demand could be controlled in such a way as to achieve full employment and price stability. The new view is that, because expectations are formed rationally, the best that policy can do is to avoid injecting uncertainty into the economy. Fully predictable policy is therefore required. It may be possible to achieve the best outcome with a pre-announced policy feedback rule, but it will not be possible to do better with *ad hoc* discretionary intervention.

C. Policy — A Process, Not an Event

If expectations are formed rationally, analysing the implications of a policy change requires that it be decomposed into an anticipated and unanticipated component. Only by analysing the entire process of policy is it possible to say whether a particular event was usual, and therefore anticipated, or unusual, and therefore unanticipated.

Review Questions

1.   What are the objectives of *macroeconomic* policy?
2.   Review your understanding of the three main stages in the evolution of ideas on the proper role of macroeconomic policy.
3.   What does it mean to say that 'policy is a process and not an event'?

35

The Constraints on Macroeconomic Policy

Although governments are sovereign within the limits of the constitution, even they must obey certain economic laws. The most fundamental of these laws, to which even governments are subject, is the law of opportunity cost or, equivalently, the principle that 'there is no such thing as a free lunch'. Governments cannot command use over real resources without taking those resources from individuals. Like private individuals and firms, the government has a budget which must balance, in the sense that, in the short run, governments must either tax or borrow to cover their spending. In the longer run, their loans have to be repaid so that, in some fundamental sense, the government must raise taxes by an amount sufficient to cover its expenditures. This places some important limitations on the conduct of monetary and fiscal policy and introduces some important linkages between these two areas of policy. Additionally, the government's actions are restricted by the relationship between domestic credit, foreign exchange reserves and the exchange rate — the balance of payments constraint — that we saw in Chapter 14.

Taking account of both the government's budget constraint and the balance of payments constraint implies that there are important linkages between fiscal policy, money supply control, and exchange rate policy. This chapter goes on to explore these linkages and examines in more detail the constraints on government. It takes you through four tasks which are to:

A. **understand the nature of the government budget constraint;**
B. **understand the implications of the government budget constraint for the conduct of monetary and fiscal policy;**
C. **understand the nature of the balance of payments constraint and the implications of the combination of the government budget constraint and the balance of payments constraint for the conduct of fiscal, monetary and exchange rate policy;**
   and
D. **understand the implications of the government budget and balance of payments constraints for the formation of rational expectations.**

A. Government Budget Constraint

Let us begin by examining the main items in the government's budget. Table 35.1 summarises the government's payments and receipts. The first payment listed is government expenditure on goods and services. This is the variable which appears in the National Income Accounts[1] as one of the aggregate expenditure items, and which features prominently in the theory of aggregate demand developed in Part IV of this book. The second item is transfer payments. These are the direct payments by the government to households and firms under various income support programmes. The third item is the interest which the government has to pay on debt outstanding. These three items added together constitute the total payments made by the government. They must be matched by government receipts. The first item listed under receipts is called legislated taxes. The prefix 'legislated' is there to alert you to the idea that there are some receipts by the government which are in the nature of taxes, but which are not explicitly legislated. (More of that in a moment.) The legislated taxes are taxes on incomes, expenditures, wealth, foreign trade, and a variety of specific activities. The second receipt item is net issues of debt. Like any large organisation, the government is constantly borrowing and repaying debt previously contracted. The *net* issue of debt constitutes the excess of newly issued debt over loans repaid. The final receipt is the net issue of currency. In a sense, this is not really a receipt. In effect, the government mints new money simply by stamping the appropriate images on the appropriate bits of metal. Nevertheless, in terms of the

Table 35.1   The Government's Payments and Receipts

Item
(i)   *Payments*
Government expenditure on goods and services
+   Transfer payments
+   Debt interest payments
=   Total payments
(ii)   *Receipts*
Legislated taxes
+   Net issues of debt
+   Net issue of currency
=   Total receipts

---

1. Actually this item does not appear as a single aggregate in the UK National Income Accounts. Government spending on capital goods is aggregated with gross fixed capital formation. The first payment listed in Table 35.1 adds government investment to its current expenditure which appears as a separate item in the National Income Accounts.

Table 35.2   Changes in the Bank of England's Balance Sheet

	Change in commercial bank deposits with the Bank of England
+	Net issue of new bank notes
−	Change in government securities
=	Zero

government's accounts, this has to be reckoned as a receipt, since, from the point of view of the government, it is one of the things that the government can use to cover its expenditures.

The debt issued by the government is not all bought by the general public. Some of it is bought by the Bank of England. Since the Bank of England is owned by the government, in the sense that all its profits are ultimately returned to the government, it is of some importance to consider separately what happens in the Bank of England when new debt issues of the government are purchased by the Bank rather than by the general public. Equally important is to examine what happens inside the Bank of England when the Bank buys existing debt from the public. We can examine these Bank of England transactions very straightforwardly by considering the changes in the Bank of England's balance sheet that occur in any period of time. Table 35.2 summarises this.

This table is very closely related to Table 4.2, which you studied in Chapter 4. In effect, it is the change in any given period in the items in the fourth column (the central bank balance sheet) shown in that table. The first item is the change in commercial bank deposits with the Bank of England; the second is the net issue of new bank notes by the Bank of England; and the third is the change in government security holdings by the Bank of England. The first two items are liabilities of the Bank of England, and the third item is an asset. You already know that the change in assets must equal the change in liabilities so that, if we measure a rise in assets as positive and a rise in liabilities as negative, the sum of all the changes listed in Table 35.2 must always be zero. (This abstracts from any changes in foreign exchange holdings by the Bank of England which, in this treatment, are being assumed to be zero.) The importance of changes in government security holdings by the Bank of England is that they are equivalent to changes in two of the components of the economy's monetary base, commercial bank deposits and bank notes.

We gain important insights if we consolidate the government's receipts and payments with the changes in the Bank of England balance sheet. This is done in Table 35.3. The first two items in the table are exactly the same as in Table 35.1, government expenditures on goods and services and transfer payments. The next two items appeared in Table 35.1 as a single item. Debt interest paid by the government has been divided into two items, that paid to the public and that paid to the Bank of England. Total payments, then, in Table 35.3 are exactly the same as those in Table 35.1, but with debt interest payments separated into those paid to the Bank of England and those paid to the general public. The receipts shown in Table 35.3 are more detailed than those in Table 35.1. The first item, legislated taxes, is

Table 35.3   Consolidation of Government and Bank of England

Item	£
(i) *Payments*	
Government expenditure on goods and services	G
+ Transfer of payments	TR
+ Debt interest paid to public	DI
+ Debt interest paid to Bank of England	
= Total payments	
(ii) *Receipts*	
Legislated taxes	TAX
+ Profits from Bank of England	
+ Net issue of debt to the public	ΔD
+ Change in commercial bank deposits with the Bank of England ⎞	
+ Net issue of bank notes ⎬	ΔMB
+ Net issue of currency ⎠	
= Total receipts	

exactly the same as before. The next receipt shown, however, is the profits from the Bank of England. These profits, of course, will be nothing other than the interest that the Bank of England earns on the government's debt that it holds, minus the operating costs of the Bank. This last item will be very small relative to the amount of debt interest earned. The third item in the government's receipts is the net issue of debt to the public. This is the same as the item in Table 35.1 *less* the net issue of debt to the Bank of England. That is dealt with in the next two items. If we are to count the total issue of debt by the government, we need to count the debt issued to the Bank of England as well as that to the public. This is done by entering as the next two items in the government's receipts the change in the liabilities of the Bank of England, which you already know from Table 35.2 add up to the same number as the change in government debt held by the Bank of England. Thus, the change in commercial bank deposits with the Bank of England plus the net issue of bank notes is equal to the net issue of debt to the central bank. The final item, net issue of currency, is exactly the same as that in Table 35.1.

Now focus on the column on the right-hand side of Table 35.3. It provides a summary of payments and receipts by the consolidated government central bank sector. Government expenditures are called G, transfer payments TR, and debt interest paid to the public DI. Debt interest paid to the central bank is not given a symbolic name; nor are profits received from the Bank of England. Assuming Bank of England operating costs to be small relative to the total interest payments received by the Bank, these two items may be regarded as approximately offsetting each other. There is a receipt and a payment that are of approximately equal magnitude. Legislated taxes are called TAX and the net issue of debt to the public is labelled

ΔD. The final three items, the change in commercial bank deposits with the Bank of England, the net issue of bank notes, and net issue of currency are lumped together as a single item which is, of course, the *change in the monetary base* and labelled ΔMB. Transfer payments, TR, may be thought of as negative taxes and be subtracted from legislated taxes, TAX, to give net taxes which we will call $NET\ TAX$.

The sum of the receipts by government must exactly equal the sum of the payments made by the government. This is the *government budget constraint*. It says that

$$G + DI - NET\ TAX - \Delta D - \Delta MB = 0 \tag{35.1}$$

This says that the government must raise in net taxes or borrow or create money on a scale exactly equal to the volume of its purchases of goods and services and its payments of debt interest. Let us now move on to consider some of the implications of this government budget constraint.

B. Government Budget Constraint and the Conduct of Monetary and Fiscal Policy

The government's budget constraint with which we ended the last section may be rewritten in the following form:

$$\Delta MB + \Delta D = G + DI - NET\ TAX \tag{35.2}$$

This emphasises that the expansion of the stock of money and the stock of government debt will necessarily be equal to the difference between the government's total spending and its tax receipts. This immediately places a link between monetary policy and fiscal policy. You can think of monetary policy as the rate at which the money stock grows. You can think of fiscal policy as the scale of government spending and the scale of taxes. The government budget constraint says that there is a connection between these two. It also says, however, that as long as the government is able or willing to issue debt (ΔD) and pay interest on it (DI), there is no hard-and-fast link between the two branches of macroeconomic policy. Although in any given short-term period (a year or two, or perhaps even five years or so), the government may issue debt to loosen the link between monetary and fiscal policy, on the average over the long run that cannot be so.

To get a feel for the way this is, imagine what would happen if you spent more than your income. For the first year you could perhaps go to the bank and get a loan to cover the deficit. You might even be able to do that for two years, or if you had a very indulgent bank manager, perhaps for a third year. At some stage, however, the day of reckoning would arrive. It would be necessary to pull in your horns, lower consumption, and start to pay off the loans that had accumulated. Although the details differ, exactly the same constraints necessarily apply to the government. To see why this is so, it is necessary to understand that when the government issues debt, it is doing nothing other than deferring taxes.

The government issues all kinds of debt. Some of it is long-term debt, with 25 or more years to run to the date at which the government will redeem it. Some debt is medium-term, with 10 to 15 years to run to the redemption date; some is short-term debt, with up to 5 years to run to the redemption date. In addition, the government issues very short-term debt in the form of three-month Treasury bills. Further, some government debt is non-marketable and takes the form of savings bonds. This type of debt is redeemable on demand, but at a penalty to the holder.

Although the government issues many different kinds of debt, it is sensible to think of government debt as if it was a *perpetuity*. A perpetuity is a bond which will never be redeemed by the issuer. The British government issued such bonds in the eighteenth and nineteenth centuries. They are called consols. Although the British government does not issue such bonds today, it is nevertheless sensible to think of all British government debt as perpetual debt. The reason why this is so is that, although the particular bonds issued by the government today will be redeemed, when they are redeemed they will be replaced by new bonds. Thus, the debt is continuously turned over, with new bonds being issued to replace the old bonds that are retired. One can therefore think of government debt as perpetual debt rather than as debt that will be repaid.

A perpetuity is a bond which promises to pay a certain sum of money every year forever. Call that amount £c. The bond will never be redeemed, so that it has no redemption price. It can be sold to someone else, and that new owner will receive the £c per annum while in possession of the bond. How much would a person be willing to pay for a bond that promised to pay £c per annum in perpetuity? Let us call the price that a person would be willing to pay £p. If you invested £p in the best alternative asset, say a company share or some physical capital or a private business, you would make a rate of return of, let us say, r per cent per annum. Clearly, you would not be interested in buying a government bond that promised to pay £c per annum unless the rate of return that you obtained was at least as great as the r per cent per annum that you could obtain from some other activity. With the price of the bond £p and the payment by the government £c per annum, the rate of return on the bond is, of course,

$$\text{Rate of Return} = \frac{£c}{£p} \times 100$$

If

$$\frac{£c}{£p} \times 100 > r\%$$

then you would be interested in buying government bonds.
If

$$\frac{£c}{£p} \times 100 < r\%$$

you would be wanting to sell government bonds. Buying government bonds would raise their price, and selling government bonds would lower their price. Government bonds will have an equilibrium price when

$$\frac{£c}{£p} \times 100 = r\%$$

From this, it is clear that the price of the government bond will be

$$\pounds p = \frac{\pounds c \times 100}{r\%}$$

For example, if a bond promises to pay £5 per annum and if the rate of interest was 5 per cent per annum, then the price of the bond would be £100. The price of a government bond may be written equivalently as

$$\pounds p = \frac{\pounds c}{r}$$

where r is the rate of interest expressed as a proportion of 1 (i.e., $r\% \div 100$).

Now suppose the government issues a bond and receives $\pounds p$. So that you can see the value of this to the government, let us isolate the bond sale and subsequent interest payments on the bond from the other receipts and expenditures of the government. To do this we must assume that the government is not going to change its expenditures on goods and services or transfers, change the taxes that it legislates, or create any new money. It is simply going to issue its bond and allow the bond to be completely self-financing. You can think of this as meaning that when the government receives the proceeds from its bond sale, $\pounds p$, it has to set aside a fund that will generate sufficient interest income to enable it to meet the interest payments on the bond of $\pounds c$ per annum in perpetuity.

Let us suppose, then, that the government has sold a bond for $\pounds p$ (which is equal to $\pounds c/r$, where $\pounds c$ is the number of pounds per annum the government will pay out on the bond). How much must the government set aside in order for it to be able to meet these interest payments? At the end of the first year the government will need $\pounds c$ from its fund. If it set aside a sum of money $\pounds a_1$ such that $\pounds a_1$ plus the interest received on $\pounds a_1$, $r\pounds a_1$, was equal to $\pounds c_1$, then it would have enough money to pay out $\pounds c$ at the end of the first year. For example, if the rate of interest is 5 per cent and the government is committed to paying £5 on the bond at the end of one year, it will need to set aside approximately £4.76 at the beginning of the year. The £4.76 invested at 5 per cent would yield a 24p interest income which, when added to the £4.76 investment would give the government the £5 that it needs to meet the interest payment on its bond. However, if it set aside only £4.76, the government would not be able to meet the interest payments on its bond in the second and subsequent years. To meet the interest payment in two years' time, it needs to set aside a sum of money such that the interest on the sum plus the interest on the first year's interest would add up to a sufficient sum to pay the bond interest. Call this sum of money $\pounds a_2$. It would be a sum such that $\pounds a_2(1 + r)^2 = \pounds c$. This would enable the government to pay its second-year interest payment, but not the third and subsequent years' payments. In general, then, in order to meet *all* its interest payments into the future, the government would need to set aside sums of money as shown in Table 35.4. Now, if the government is going to have enough funds to meet the interest payments on its bond over the infinite life of the bond, it will need a fund equal to $\pounds a_1 + \pounds a_2 + \pounds a_3 + \dots + \pounds a_i + \dots$. (The dots $+ \dots + \dots$ stand for all the terms not written explicitly.) We can work out the value of each $\pounds a_i$ from Table 35.4. If you divide $\pounds c$ by $(1 + r)$, then you get $\pounds a_1$. If you divide $\pounds c$ by $(1 + r)^2$, then you get $\pounds a_2$; if you divide $\pounds c$ by $(1 + r)^i$, then you get $\pounds a_i$. That is, the amount which the government will have to set aside (S) to meet *all* the future interest payments on its bonds is

Table 35.4   The Funds Needed to Pay Interest on a Perpetuity

---

To pay $£c$ in one year, you need $£a_1$ now such that $£a_1(1+r)$ $\doteq £c$

To pay $£c$ in two years, you need $£a_2$ now such that $£a_2(1+r)^2$ $= £c$

To pay $£c$ in three years, you need $£a_3$ now such that $£a_3(1+r)^3$ $= £c$

To pay $£c$ in i years, you need $£a_i$ now such that $£a_i(1+r)^i$ $= £c$

$$S = \frac{£c}{(1+r)} + \frac{£c}{(1+r)^2} + \dots + \frac{£c}{(1+r)^i} + \dots$$

or, equivalently,

$$S = \left[\frac{1}{(1+r)} + \frac{1}{(1+r)^2} + \dots + \frac{1}{(1+r)^i} + \dots \right] £c \qquad (35.3)$$

To figure out how much this is, we need to add up the infinite sum inside the brackets in equation (35.3) above. To do this, multiply both sides of equation (35.3) by $1/(1+r)$. This will give equation (35.4) below.

$$\frac{1}{(1+r)} S = \left[\frac{1}{(1+r)^2} + \dots + \frac{1}{(1+r)^i} + \dots \right] £c \qquad (35.4)$$

All the missing terms in (35.3) represented by the dots $+ \dots + \dots$ will be identical to the missing terms in (35.4), except for the last term in (35.4). That last term in (35.4) will equal the last term in (35.3), multiplied by $1/(1+r)$. However, as you go further and further into the future, the terms $1/(1+r)^i$ become very very small and can be ignored. So, ignoring that last term in (35.4), subtract equation (35.4) from (35.3) to obtain

$$S - \frac{1}{(1+r)} S = \frac{1}{(1+r)} £c \qquad (35.5)$$

Multiply both sides of (35.5) by $(1+r)$ to give

$$S(1+r) - S = £c \qquad (35.6)$$

or

$$S + rS - S = £c \qquad (35.7)$$

Or, more simply,

$$S = \frac{£c}{r} \qquad (35.8)$$

So, S, the sum which the government would need to set aside in order to meet the interest payments on its bond, is equal to $£c/r$.

But that is exactly the sum the government receives when it sells the bond. *It would be necessary, therefore, if the government was to make its bond self-financing, to set aside all the receipts from the bond to meet future interest payments.* When proper account is made for the future interest payments which a bond will generate, the government gets precisely nothing when it sells a bond. Thus, you can think of selling a bond as simply putting off the evil day of raising taxes. It is possible for the government to increase its revenue in any one year by selling more bonds, but it cannot increase its revenue indefinitely by selling bonds, since it immediately commits itself to an interest stream which exactly offsets the receipts that it obtains from its bond sales.

The implication of this for the government's budget constraint is very important. It means that *the government cannot regard bond financing as anything other than deferred taxes.* Treating bond sales, net of interest payments, as deferred taxes, we can aggregate together not only taxes and transfers, but also bond sales, net of interest, into a single item which we will simply call *taxes*, or T^*. Be careful to notice that this is an unconventional definition of taxes. It includes all *current* taxes minus all *current* tranfers, plus the *future* taxes that are implied by the *current* difference between bond sales and interest payments.

The long-term average government budget constraint may now be condensed into the simpler statement, namely:

$$G - T^* = \Delta MB \tag{35.9}$$

In the next chapter, the connection between the monetary base and the money supply itself will be explored. For the rest of this chapter, let us agree to take on trust the proposition that, on the average over the long run, the growth rate of the monetary base and the growth rate of the money supply will be the same. Equivalently, we could say that the change in the monetary base will be some constant fraction of the change in the money supply. Let us call that fraction q. In that case,

$$\Delta MB = q\Delta M \tag{35.10}$$

We could now use equation (35.10) to replace the change in monetary base with the fraction q times the change in the total money supply in equation (35.9) to obtain

$$G - T^* = q\Delta M \tag{35.11}$$

It is more instructive to view this government budget constraint in *real terms — the real long-term average government budget constraint.* We can do this by dividing through the budget constraint by the price level. Let us divide the above equation by the GDP Deflator P to obtain

$$\frac{G}{P} - \frac{T^*}{P} = q\frac{\Delta M}{P} \tag{35.12}$$

Now define $G/P = g$ and $T^*/P = t^*$. This means that

$$g - t^* = q\frac{\Delta M}{P} \tag{35.13}$$

Now multiply and divide the right-hand side of equation (35.13) by M, i.e.,

$$q\frac{\Delta M}{P} = q\frac{\Delta M}{P} \times \frac{M}{M} \tag{35.14}$$

This, of course, leaves the value of the equation undisturbed. However, you can now see, changing the order of the variables, that

$$q\,\frac{\Delta M}{P} = q\,\frac{M}{P} \times \frac{\Delta M}{M} \tag{35.15}$$

Also, you will recall that $\Delta M/M \equiv \mu$; the growth rate of the money supply. Therefore

$$q\,\frac{\Delta M}{P} = q\,\frac{M}{P} \times \mu \tag{35.16}$$

Using equation (35.16) to replace the right-hand side of equation (35.13) gives

$$g - t^* = q\,\frac{M}{P}\,\mu \tag{35.17}$$

This is the *fundamental government budget constraint equation*. This equation cannot be violated on the average. It tells us that whenever the government changes its expenditures, it must at some time change at least one other variable. It must either change taxes or change the growth rate of the money supply.

Another instructive way of looking at the government's fundamental budget constraint equation is one which emphasises the nature of inflation as a tax. Fundamentally, what is being said is that governments must raise taxes to cover their spending. There are two sources of taxes, legislated taxes, t, and the inflation tax, $\mu q\,(M/P)$. There is no restriction on the government as to the extent to which it uses either of these taxes. The restriction is that it must raise a large enough total from both of them, taken together, to cover its expenditures.

C. Balance of Payments Constraint

The balance of payments constraint was introduced and explained in Chapter 14 when we discussed the constraints upon a managed floating exchange rate. We noticed that if the government fixes the exchange rate, then the balance of payments is determined by the growth rate of domestic credit, the world inflation rate and the growth rate of output. More generally, we were able to show (in equation 14.11) that, if domestic credit expansion was too fast in relation to world inflation and output growth, then either the foreign exchange value of domestic money would have to fall, or the balance of payments would have to go into deficit, or some combination of those two things would have to occur. It will perhaps be helpful to recall equation (14.11) which is reproduced here as:

$$\Delta \epsilon - \psi f = (1 - \psi)\,dc - \pi_f - \rho \tag{35.18}$$

If you have forgotten how to interpret this equation it will be worthwhile returning to Chapter 14 and refreshing your memory before attempting to go further. This equation says that exchange market pressure — the depreciation of the currency (positive values of $\Delta \epsilon$) minus the rate of reserve loss (negative values of f, weighted by the fraction of the money stock represented by foreign exchange reserves ψ) — will be greater the greater is domestic credit expansion (dc) and the lower is world inflation (π_f) and output growth (ρ). This equation, like the government budget constraint, has to be satisfied on the average. Unlike the budget constraint, equation (35.18) incorporates a behavioural proposition and is not a pure budget constraint. The behavioural proposition is that there exists a well-defined, stable, and predictable demand function for real money balances.

For the purposes of what follows it will be most convenient to concentrate, not on the general case of managed floating exchange rates, but on the two purer cases of fixed exchange rates and freely floating exchange rates. If the exchange rate is freely floating, then the authorities may determine the quantity of foreign exchange reserves that they hold and the rate at which those reserves grow, allowing the foreign exchange value of their currency to take on whatever value the market determines. To see what that value is, simply add ψf to both sides of equation (35.18) to give

$$\Delta\epsilon = (1 - \psi)dc + \psi f - \pi_f - \rho \tag{35.19}$$

and notice (refreshing your memory with Chapter 14 if necessary) that, since the first two terms on the right-hand side of (35.19) add up to the growth rate of the money supply (μ), we may express (35.19) equivalently as

$$\Delta\epsilon = \mu - \pi_f - \rho \tag{35.20}$$

This simply says that the rate at which the currency will depreciate (positive values of $\Delta\epsilon$) is equal to the growth rate of the money supply minus the world inflation rate minus the rate of growth of output. In this case, the growth rate of the money supply is the outcome of the policy choice of the government and/or the central bank. In the case where the exchange rate is fixed, $\Delta\epsilon$ is maintained at zero and, in the process of pegging the exchange rate, the monetary authorities must stand ready to allow their stock of foreign exchange reserves to rise or fall according to demand. Thus, in that case, the growth rate of the money supply is determined by the demand for money and evidently will be

$$\mu = \pi_f + \rho \tag{35.21}$$

Putting this equation into words, under fixed exchange rates, the growth rate of the money supply will be equal to the world rate of inflation, plus the rate of growth of output. In this case, the growth rate of the money supply will not be a variable chosen by the government and/or the central bank. It will be determined by market processes and will equal the growth rate of the demand for money.

Let us now explore the implications of the balance of payments constraint when combined with the government's budget constraint. First, consider the case of fixed exchange rates. You have seen in equation (35.21) above that this implies that the growth rate of the money supply is equal to the world inflation rate, plus the rate of growth of output. Let us substitute equation (35.21) into equation (35.17). This gives

$$g - t^* = q\frac{M}{P}(\pi_f + \rho) \tag{35.22}$$

What this says is that the excess of government spending over taxes must, on the average, be financed by the inflation tax. This, of course, is exactly what equation

(35.17) above said. We can see, however, from equation (35.22) that, under fixed exchange rates, the government really has no degrees of freedom left with which to manoeuvre on the average. Its inflation tax rate will be determined entirely by world inflation and by the trend growth rate of output. The inflation tax base which is the quantity of high powered money, $q(M/P)$, is determined by the demand for money and so, once the government has determined the level of spending on goods and services, g, it is also constrained, on the average, to a particular value for taxes. There is, in effect, on the average, no scope for the pursuit of independent monetary and fiscal policy.

In contrast, under flexible exchange rates, the money supply growth rate is directly under the control of the central monetary authority and equation (35.17) becomes the constraint on policy even after allowing for the implications of the balance of payments constraint.

To summarise, under fixed exchange rates there is no scope for independent monetary policy. Once the government's spending level has been selected, that implies a tax level which, on the average, must also be achieved. Under flexible exchange rates the balance of payments does not impose a constraint upon the relationship between monetary and fiscal policy. A constraint on those policy combinations exists as a consequence of the government's budget constraint, but there is no additional constraint arising from balance of payments considerations.

An analogy may be helpful in making the preceding discussion clearer. Let us contrast the constraints upon government spending at the level of local government with those of central government. A local government authority does not have the power to vary the exchange rate of the money used in its jurisdiction against the monies used in other local jurisdictions. In principle, we could imagine there being a Scottish pound, a Welsh pound, a Northern Irish pound, and an English pound and even smaller subdivisions such as the Yorkshire pound and the Cornish pound. Given that we have a unified state with a single unified monetary system, the exchange rates between these imaginable pounds are all fixed and, from a practical point of view, irrevocably so at unity. That being the case, if a given local authority chooses to expand its spending programme it must, of necessity, plan to raise taxes at some date either now or in the future to cover that additional spending. Thus, the fixed exchange rate constraint (35.22) applies to such a level of government. A central government, however, with control over its own central bank and with a monopoly on the issue of money within its area of jurisdiction is free to allow the value of its own money to vary against the value of the monies issued by other governments/central banks. It is therefore constrained by the flexible exchange rate restraint, equation (35.17). Even if such a government decided for a period to maintain a fixed exchange rate, that fixed exchange rate would not be a constraint upon the government's behaviour. If ever the fixed exchange rate became inconvenient it could be abandoned.

Let us now turn to a consideration of the implications of the foregoing discussion for the formation of rational expectations.

D. Government Budget and Balance of Payments Constraints and Rational Expectations

The government budget and balance of payments constraints have dramatic implications for the formation of rational expectations. First, consider the case of a fixed exchange rate economy. We know from the above discussion that, on the average, in such an economy equation (35.22) must be satisfied. That is, the excess of government spending over taxes must equal some number that is determined outside the control of the government. What would happen if the government was running a deficit, spending more than it was collecting in current taxes? In forming expectations about future government spending, taxes and money growth, people will rationally use the knowledge that, on the average, such a deficit cannot persist. They will know that at some stage in the future either government spending must be cut, taxes increased, or the fixed exchange rate system must be abandoned and the growth rate of the money supply increased. The longer government spending exceeds current tax receipts by more than it can do, on the average, in the long run, the stronger will be the expectation that next period some changes in that direction will occur. Conversely, if the government was running too small a deficit and reducing its outstanding debt, it would be rational to expect that at some time in the future, either government spending will rise, taxes fall, or again, the fixed exchange rate system be abandoned and this time the currency allowed to appreciate. In general, it would be rational to expect that the fixed exchange rate regime will not be permanent but will, at some time in the future, be abandoned. The bigger the accumulated change in the stock of government debt, the greater the probability that the fixed exchange rate system will be abandoned. It will always be rational to assign some non-zero probability to such an event. The magnitude of that probability, of course, may be trivial or sizeable. That will depend upon the history of the country in question. A country (or more generally jurisdiction) which has a long history of repeatedly taking serious fiscal policy steps to defend the value of its currency, by raising taxes or cutting spending as appropriate, will be one to which a small probability of future exchange rate changes will be attached. At the other extreme, a country that has a long history of repeatedly abandoning fixed exchange rate regimes and permitting the currency to appreciate or depreciate in order to accommodate a persistent fiscal surplus or deficit, will be one to which a high probability of future exchange rate variability will be attached.

Consider next a country which is not currently pursuing a fixed exchange rate and is therefore not constrained by equation (35.22), but is constrained by equation (35.17). In this case, we know that it is possible for the level of *current* taxes to fall short of or to exceed current spending and for the gap to be made up by *future* taxes, that is by borrowing or reducing outstanding debt. We also know, however, that in the long run, borrowing makes no net contribution to government revenues. It will not be rational to expect a monetary and fiscal policy that violates this fact. To expect such a violation is to expect something which cannot happen. Such an expectation could not be rational. This means that if at some time a government is running a large current deficit and issuing a large quantity of bonds, then the rational expectation will be that at some future date either government expenditures are going to be cut or taxes are going to be increased or the rate of money printing, and therefore of inflation, is going to be increased. Based on an analysis of the constraints operating upon the government, and its likely course in the future, individuals will rationally assign weights to those alternative future changes in government actions. A government, or more generally, a political system, that has a long-run track record of repeatedly inflating its way out of short-run financial problems will rationally be expected to pursue such policies again in the future. A government which has heavily constrained itself from using the inflation tax by, for example, setting up a highly dependent central bank with extensive powers to control the growth rate of the money supply independently of the short-term wishes of the government, will be one that will rationally be expected to correct any short-term deficit, by either raising legislated taxes or cutting spending rather than by increasing the inflation tax. There will be no hard-and-fast, simple to state rule that will enable individuals to make the correct inferences concerning future monetary and fiscal policy. The hard fact of the government budget constraint must, however, be taken into account in forming a rational expectation as to likely future changes in the direction of policy. Only if the government is currently running a deficit that is being financed by its current rate of money printing is it pursuing a policy which can be pursued on the average over the long term. The pursuit of such a policy will simplify the task faced by private individuals in forming rational expectations, but by no means eliminate the problem.

SUMMARY

A. Government Budget Constraint

The government budget constraint states that total government expenditures on goods and services, transfers to individuals, and debt interest must equal receipts from legislated taxes, the sales of new debt, and the creation of new money.

B. Government Budget Constraint and the Conduct of Monetary and Fiscal Policy

Although the government can issue debt, thereby weakening the link between monetary and fiscal policy in the short term, on the average over the long term, debt interest has to be paid which exactly offsets the receipts from debt sales. This means that, in effect, issuing debt is the same thing as deferring taxes. The long-term average government budget constraint does not give the government the option of raising debt. There is, therefore, on the average, a fundamental connection between fiscal policy and monetary policy. Conventionally legislated taxes together with the inflation tax must raise sufficient funds to cover the government's expenditures. Monetary policy and fiscal policy therefore, on the average, are interdependent.

C. Balance of Payments Constraint

If the government permits the exchange rate to be flexible, then it is possible to set the growth of the money supply at any chosen rate. If, however, the exchange rate is pegged, then the growth rate of the money supply will be determined by the growth rate of the demand for money which in turn will depend upon the growth rate of output and world inflation.

The combination of the balance of payments and government budget constraint under fixed exchange rates implies no degrees of freedom, on the average, for the conduct of fiscal and monetary policy. The government can choose the scale of government spending, but it must raise sufficient taxes to cover that spending. Under flexible exchange rates, the balance of payments does not impose any additional constraints upon the government than those implied by the government budget constraint. In such a case, the government must cover its spending either by the inflation tax or other taxes. It may, however, choose the extent to which it uses each of these sources of financing.

D. Government Budget and Balance of Payments Constraints and Rational Expectations

In general, it will not be rational to form an expectation of long-term money growth and inflation that is based on the maintenance in perpetuity of a fixed exchange rate. Under flexible exchange rates, or under fixed exchange rates which are not expected to be permanent, it will not be rational to form an expectation of long-term money growth and inflation that is based on a violation of the government's budget constraint. In a situation in which the government is running a deficit or surplus, issuing or retiring large volumes of debt, individuals will have to form a rational expectation concerning which of the variables in the government's budget constraint will be varied in order to satisfy the long-term average constraint. In situations in which the government has, in the past, satisfied its budget constraint by varying the rate of inflation, it will be rational to expect such action in the future. In other situations, where the government has taken steps to adjust its spending or other taxes in order to maintain a steady (or zero) rate of inflation, then it would be rational to expect a repeat of such actions in the future.

Review Questions

1. Review the items which appear in the government's budget constraint.

2. Sort the following into the three items in the government's budget constraint (i.e., expenditures on goods and services, taxes, and money creation):
   (a) premium savings bond prizes
   (b) welfare payments
   (c) the purchase of a typewriter financed by printing £50
   (d) the purchase of a foreign security (be careful here!)
   (e) social insurance (payments and receipts)
   (f) national defence expenditures.

3. Why are legislated taxes so called?

4. Explain why transfer payments may (as a first approximation) be treated as negative taxes.

5. How does the 'change in the monetary base' get into the government's budget constraint? Review the links between the government and central bank from which it results.

6. What is the relationship between the price which someone will pay for a bond and the stream of interest payments on that bond?

7. Calculate the equilibrium market price of a perpetuity which promises to pay £1 per annum, given that interest rates on alternative available assets are currently 8 per cent.

8. 'The present value of a bond is always zero.' Explain.

9. If the price for which a bond can be sold is exactly the same as the present value of the future stream of interest payments, why would anyone issue bonds?

10. Explain why bond sales are deferred taxes.

11. If the government can issue money on which it does not have to pay interest, why do you suppose we observe governments issuing debt on which they do have to pay interest?

12. Explain why, on the average, the government must finance its expenditures with either legislated taxes or the inflation tax.

13. Review your understanding of why it would be irrational to expect the government to be able to issue debt on an increasing scale indefinitely.

14. Looking at British monetary policy and fiscal policy in the 1970s, what conclusions do you reach concerning a rational expectation about future monetary and fiscal policy changes in the United Kingdom?

36

Control of the Money Supply

The quantity of money in existence — the money supply — features prominently in all macroeconomic models, from the basic model through the Keynesian, and the neo-classical synthesis to the rational expectations theories. The final thing that we need to do before getting on with the substance of analysing macroeconomic policy is to examine how the money supply is determined and controlled. You already know from the analysis that we conducted in Chapters 14 and 35 that, under fixed exchange rates, the money supply is *not* controlled. Rather, it is determined by the demand for money. In effect, monetary policy amounts to the selection of the exchange rate at which to peg the value of the currency. All that remains is for the monetary authorities to conduct their affairs in such a way as to make that selected fixed exchange rate effective. Although there are many interesting technical questions concerning how a central bank may most effectively achieve and maintain a fixed exchange rate, from the perspective of the issues addressed in this book, no further interesting questions arise as to how the monetary authorities control the money supply.

Under flexible exchange rates, things are entirely different. In that case, the central bank may determine the quantity of money and its rate of growth independently of any considerations arising from the balance of payments. There remain, of course, constraints on average money growth behaviour imposed by the government's budget constraint. Nevertheless, the question of how the central bank achieves a particular growth rate of the money supply and how that growth rate may be modified is an important one that needs further discussion.

This chapter and indeed the entire discussion of macroeconomic policy in the subsequent chapters will focus on this more interesting and less heavily constrained flexible exchange rate situation.

In the last chapter we asked you to take on trust the proposition that, on the average, the monetary base and the total money supply stand in some constant

505

relationship to each other. This chapter will explain why that is a reasonable proposition. It will look at the detailed linkages between the money supply and the monetary base. Also, this chapter is going to look at the way in which the Bank of England conducts its monetary policies with a view to achieving its target growth path for the monetary aggregate, sterling *M3*. The chapter will not present a comprehensive description of Bank of England operations, however. In particular, it will sidestep the important foreign exchange market operations of the bank (alluded to above).

This chapter contains two tasks, which are to:

   A. **understand the links between the monetary base and the money supply;** and
   B. **understand how the Bank of England operates to achieve its target growth path for the money supply.**

A. Links Between the Monetary Base and the Money Supply

The starting point for understanding the links between the monetary base and the money supply are two definitions. Both definitions are implied in the structure of the balance sheet of the economy that you studied in Chapter 4. The first is the definition of the money supply. It is convenient when analysing the determinants of the money supply to decompose it into two parts: the monetary base held by the public and the bank deposits held by the public. (Which bank deposits we would count would depend on which monetary aggregate we were dealing with. We are going to deal with £*M3* in this chapter, though we shall use the symbol *M* to denote that aggregate.) Let us write this definition of the money supply as follows

$$M = MB_p + D \tag{36.1}$$

In this definition, *M* stands for the money supply, MB_p for the monetary base held by the general public, and *D* for bank deposits. The monetary base held by the general public is, of course, simply the notes and coins (currency) in circulation.

The next definition concerns the monetary base itself. The monetary base consists of that which is held by the public (MB_p) that is already in the above definition, and the monetary base held inside the commercial banks — we shall call this MB_b. The monetary base, then, is allocated across the two holders, the general public and the banks, so that

$$MB = MB_p + MB_b \tag{36.2}$$

These are just definitions, of course, and they don't tell us anything about what determines either the money supply or the monetary base.

The first behavioural hypothesis that we need is one concerning the general public's allocation of money between base money and deposits. The general idea is that in conducting our everyday transactions, there is a fairly stable fraction of those transactions that we would customarily undertake with currency. This means that we would want to hold a fairly stable fraction of our total money holdings in the form of currency. Let us call that fraction v. This means that we could say that

$$MB_p = vM \qquad 0 < v < 1 \tag{36.3}$$

This simply says that v is some fraction, and the monetary base (currency), which people on the average hold is equal to that fraction v of their total money holdings. Of course, there is an equivalent proposition, which is that bank deposits are equal to one minus the fraction v times total money. That is

$$D = (1 - v)M \tag{36.4}$$

Although this is a pretty mechanical proposition about how people allocate their money between currency and bank deposits, it seems to be a reasonable hypothesis and one that does approximately describe the facts.

The next thing that we need to consider is how the banks decide how much monetary base to hold. That is, what is the demand for monetary base by the banks? This question is a lot like the question, what determines the demand for money by households and firms? Why do the banks hold monetary base, i.e., why do they hold notes and coins and deposits with the Bank of England? The answer, of course, is that they hold notes and coins in order to be able to meet demands for currency on the part of their customers. They hold deposits at the Bank of England so that they can make payments to other banks. They would need to do this if the total value of all the cheques paid by the customers in any one trading period exceeded the value of cheques paid to their customers during that same period. As a general rule, it will be obvious that the bigger is the volume of bank deposits that a bank has accepted, the bigger the size of currency reserves and Bank of England deposits the bank will need to keep on hand. The volume of bank deposits, then, is the first determinant of the demand for monetary base by the commercial banks.

Just as in the case of private individuals, however, holding reserves for a bank involves an opportunity cost. Deposits placed with a bank can be used by the bank for two kinds of purposes. One is to hold monetary base. The other is to buy interest earning assets of various kinds, including making loans to households and firms. Clearly, the bank makes no money on its holdings of monetary base. The profits for a bank are obtained by making loans and buying interest-earning securities. Just as in the case of the analysis of the demand for money for households, it seems likely that the higher is the rate of interest on securities, the more will banks be inclined to try to economise on their holdings of monetary base and make loans.

There are two factors, then, that determine the bank's demand for monetary base. One is the total volume of deposits which the bank has accepted. The more of these, the bigger the amount of base required. The other is the level of interest rates. The higher are interest rates, the more will the bank seek to economise on monetary base, and therefore the lower will be its holdings of monetary base.

We can summarise all this in a very simple equation that looks a lot like the demand for money function of households and firms. That equation says that

$$MB_b = zD + mb_0 - l_b r_m \qquad 0 < z < 1, mb_0, l_b > 0 \tag{36.5}$$

What this equation says is that, other things being equal (for a given market rate of interest), the higher is the level of bank deposits, the more will banks hold in monetary base. For a £1 million rise in deposits, they would hold a fraction z of a million in extra monetary base. The fraction z of total deposits which the banks will want to hold as monetary base represents, in fact, two kinds of influences — one imposed on the bank, and the other part of its voluntary behaviour. Imposed on the bank is a minimum required reserve holding below which the bank is not permitted to let its holdings of monetary base fall. Over and above that, on the average the bank will find it prudent to hold a certain level of reserves in excess of the required reserves. The fraction z represents the sum of both of these influences.

Over and above the effect of deposits on the bank's holdings of monetary base there is the influence of interest rates. Let us suppose that the term $mb_0 - l_b r_m$ is, on the average, equal to zero. That is, if interest rates were at their long-run average level, the demand for monetary base by the banks would be completely described by the fraction z of total deposits. If, however, interest rates go above their average level, then the banks will seek to economise on their holdings of monetary base, and if interest rates go below their average level, then the banks will be less eager to make loans and economise on monetary base. That is what the second two terms in the above equation are saying.

In order to derive the supply of money in the economy, all that is necessary is to examine the equilibrium in the market for monetary base itself. *The supply of money function* is not like an ordinary supply function. Like the aggregate supply function, it is an *equilibrium locus*. The market that is in equilibrium on the money supply function is the *market for monetary base*. By setting the supply of monetary base equal to the demand for base, we can find the quantity of money that will be supplied. To do this, we need the following equation:

$$MB = vM + z(1 - v)M + mb_0 - l_b r_m \qquad (36.6)$$

The left-hand side of this equation is the supply of monetary base. The right-hand side is the demand for monetary base by the public and by the banks. The first term (vM) is the demand for monetary base by the public (fraction v of the total money supply). The remaining terms represent the demand for monetary base by the banks. The first of these is z times bank deposits. Bank deposits are represented as $(1 - v)M$, since we know from the way households allocate their money between currency and deposits that $D = (1 - v)M$. The final two terms represent the interest sensitive component of the demand for monetary base by the banks which, on the average, we are taking to be zero. You can now collect together the first two terms that multiply M and obtain

$$MB = [v + z(1-v)]M + mb_0 - l_b r_m \qquad (36.7)$$

You can now divide both sides of this equation by $[v + z(1 - v)]$ to give

$$M = \frac{1}{v + z(1 - v)}(MB - mb_0 + l_b r_m) \qquad (36.8)$$

What this says is that the money supply will be some multiple of the monetary base (the multiple being $1/[v + z(1 - v)]$ on the average, but will deviate from that in the same direction as variations in the interest rate. The higher is the market rate of interest, other things given, the higher would be the money supply.

You are now in a position to summarise the links between the monetary base and the money supply. When the demand for monetary base equals the supply of monetary base, there is a direct relationship between the supply of money and the supply of monetary base. Other things being equal, a £1 million rise in the monetary base will produce a rise in the money supply of $1/[v + z(1 - v)]$ million pounds. For a given monetary base, the higher is the market rate of interest, the greater will be the money supply. This arises because banks will seek to economise on their holdings of monetary base at higher interest rates.

We can link the above discussion with that in the previous chapter by noting that, *on the average*, the money supply and monetary base will be linked by the simpler relation

$$M = \frac{1}{v + z(1 - v)} MB \qquad (36.9)$$

or, more compactly, defining $v + z(1 - v) = q$,

$$M = \frac{1}{q} MB \qquad (36.10)$$

The fraction q in this equation is exactly the same fraction as q introduced in the previous chapter.

The link that we have established between the monetary base, interest rates, and the money supply is not to be confused for a statement that says the money supply is determined by the monetary base and the rate of interest. It could well be that the monetary base itself responds to interest rates and the money supply in such a way that the actual path of the money supply is determined by some exogenous policy decision, and the monetary base and interest rates are the variables that do the adjusting to make that path possible. This is what we are now going to examine.

B. How the Bank of England Operates to Achieve its Target Growth Path for the Money Supply

If the relationship between the monetary base and the money supply, which we have just examined, was a very precise one, it would be possible for the Bank of England to exploit the relationship in order to achieve the desired path for the money supply. The Bank would simply have to manipulate the monetary base from day to day in whatever way was required in order to make the money supply grow at the desired rate. The Bank of England believes, however, that the relationship between the monetary base and the money supply is not a very precise one and, in fact, is insufficiently precise to give predictable control over the money supply. Whether or not the Bank is correct in that belief is a question of some controversy, and it would not be possible to settle the matter here. There has, in fact, been some movement in the debate in recent years and, in the summer of 1981, the Bank of England modified the procedures whereby it seeks to control the money supply in such a way as to make it easier in the future for it to exploit the relationship between the monetary base and the total money supply.

The changes which the Bank of England has recently made in its technique of monetary control may be described as a 'halfway house' between controlling the aggregate money supply by controlling the monetary base and the bank's traditional techniques of control. It will be helpful therefore if we begin by describing what that traditional technique of control has been.

Instead of using the relationship between the monetary base and the money supply to achieve its monetary target, the Bank of England has operated in an indirect way seeking to manipulate the quantity of money by operating on the demand side of the market for money. You will recall that the demand for money (thought of as the demand for real money) depends on the level of income and the rate of interest — the opportunity cost of holding money. By manipulating interest rates the monetary authorities can cause the economy to slide up and down its demand for money function, thereby resulting in changes in the quantity of money outstanding. This is how the Bank of England has operated. Let us examine in a little more detail exactly what is involved with this technique of monetary control.

The technique starts out with a demand function of the type described in Chapter 21, that is,

$$\frac{M^d}{P} = ky + m_0 - lr_m \tag{36.11}$$

In effect, the way the Bank proceeded was to estimate, using statistical techniques, the values of the parameters of the demand for money function (k, m_0, l). It then selected its target for the money supply — we shall call that monetary target M^*. It then forecasted the price level and the income level that it thought would prevail, on the average, over the coming few months. Let us call the Bank's forecasted values of the price level and real income, respectively, P^f and y^f. The Bank then 'solved' the demand for money function for the market rate of interest that would be required in order to make the amount of money demanded equal the money supply target, given the forecast of prices and income. You can obtain that solution simply by rearranging the demand for money function in the following way. First of all, set the demand for money M^d equal to the target money supply M^* and set the levels of income and prices equal to their forecasted values y^f and P^f. That is,

$$\frac{M^*}{P^f} = ky^f + m_0 - lr_m \tag{36.12}$$

Now rearrange this equation to 'solve' for the market rate of interest. That is,

$$r_m = \frac{1}{l}(ky^f + m_0 - \frac{M^*}{P^f}) \tag{36.13}$$

This equation tells us the market rate of interest which, if the Bank achieved it and if the Bank's forecasts of income and prices were correct, would on the average make the money supply equal to M^*, the target money supply.

This technique of monetary control which was employed by the Bank of England is far from perfect. The Bank could be considerably wrong in its forecasts of prices and income and, to the extent that it is wrong, it will miss its money supply target. You can see this very easily if you perform the following exercise. Use equation (36.13) that we solved above for the Bank's chosen rate of interest and substitute that back into the demand for money function. You will then obtain the following equation:

$$\frac{M^d}{P} = ky + m_0 - \frac{l}{l}(ky^f + m_0 - \frac{M^*}{P^f})$$ (36.14)

Notice that this equation simplifies considerably to the following:

$$\frac{M^d}{P} = \frac{M^*}{P^f} + k(y - y^f)$$ (36.15)

which may be further rearranged by multiplying through by the price level to give

$$M^d = M^* \frac{P}{P^f} + k(y - y^f) P$$ (36.16)

Let us pause and see what this equation is telling us. Given the technique of control of the money supply by the Bank of England, it is the demand for money that will determine how much money is in existence. The left-hand side of the equation therefore tells us what the quantity of money will be. It will be the same as M^d. How will that relate to the Bank's target? The answer is that it will deviate from the target in general. In order to be bang on target, the Bank would have to forecast the price level correctly. That is, the actual price level (P) would have to equal the forecasted price level (P^f). Furthermore, the forecast of income would have to be equal to actual income. If the actual price level turns out to be bigger than the forecasted price level, then, with a correct income forecast, the money supply will exceed the desired money supply by the same percentage as the price level exceeds the forecasted price level. If the level of income turns out to be higher than the forecasted level of income, then the money supply will exceed its target by an amount equal to the excess of actual income over forecasted income multiplied by the price level and by the parameter k.

These imperfections in this technique of monetary control have resulted in spectacular failures on the part of the Bank of England to achieve its money growth targets. It is these failures that are responsible for the tentative steps being taken in the direction of modifying the technique of monetary control. Let us now turn to a brief description of what these steps are.

A central feature of the old technique of monetary control was the Bank of England's manipulation of interest rates so as to influence the opportunity cost of holding money. The interest rates in question which the Bank controlled were, by and large, rates on three-month securities such as Treasury bills and commercial bills of exchange. In order to achieve fine control over rates of interest on three-month securities, the Bank had to stand ready to buy or sell Treasury bills and/or commercial bills in whatever quantities were demanded by the banks and other financial institutions so as to prevent the price of these bills (and therefore their rate of interest) from varying by more than the Bank of England wanted to see. There is an analogy here with a fixed exchange rate. Just as a central bank that is committed to a fixed exchange rate cannot control the quantity of its foreign exchange reserves, so, a central bank that is committed to a particular rate of interest cannot control the monetary base. It must buy and sell securities (raising or lowering the monetary base) on demand, and not at its discretion.

The change introduced in August 1981 was for the Bank of England to redirect its efforts at interest rate control away from three-month interest rates to rates on very short-term securities — bills that have between one and two weeks to run to maturity. In other words, the Bank of England, under the technique of control introduced in 1981, seeks to control very short-term rates of interest permitting interest rates of securities that are still very short-term, but not as short as a week or two, to find their own level in the marketplace. This technique of control remains an interest rate management technique. It is, however, a 'halfway house' between the old policy and a monetary base policy in the sense that, as the bank accumulates experience at controlling very short-term rates, permitting three-month rates and longer rates to be market determined, it puts itself in a position to be able to take a next step, a step of ceasing to control even the seven-day rate of interest and instead controlling the monetary base itself, permitting even those very short-term rates to be market determined.

Although the current policy may be thought of as an intermediate policy between monetary base control and interest rate control, it may in fact have none of the desirable features of either of these policies. The old technique of control at least had the virtue that the Bank was manipulating an interest rate that had reasonably predictable effects upon the monetary aggregate whose growth path the Bank was seeking to influence. The direct control of the monetary base would have the virtue that it was exploiting a remarkably stable relationship between the monetary base and the aggregate money supply.[1] The new technique relies on little-known linkages between the seven-day rate of interest and the three-month rate of interest that seems to be the one that most directly influences the demand for money. Thus, the errors in achieving the money target that are set out and summarised in equation (36.16) above need to be supplemented by an additional error, namely the error on achieving the correct level for the three-month rate of interest. If, in manipulating the seven-day interest rate, the bank allows three-month rates to stay too low or go too high then the discrepancy between the required and actual three-month interest rate, multiplied by the parameter l, would have to be added to the errors set out in that above equation. Thus, the recent change in Bank of England control techniques, whilst a potentially useful step in the direction of changing over to a monetary base control procedure may well turn out to be an unfortunate intermediate resting place.

The implications of the foregoing are that, although the Bank of England has not and still does not exercise precise control over the money supply, we may, nevertheless, regard the money supply as a controllable instrument of macroeconomic policy and go on to analyse the effects of alternative strategies for varying its quantity.

---

1. Between 1972 and 1979, the ratio of the monetary base for £$M3$ was never less than 17.2% and never greater than 21.8% (using end quarter figures). See David Savage, Some issues of monetary policy, *National Institute Economic Review*, No. 91, February 1981, pp. 78–85 and Table 2, p. 82.

SUMMARY

A. Links Between the Monetary Base and the Money Supply

The money supply function is, like the aggregate supply function, an equilibrium locus. The market which is in equilibrium along the money supply function is the market for monetary base. The demand for monetary base by the general public (the demand for currency) may be presumed to be a fairly stable fraction of the demand for money in total. The demand for monetary base by banks will depend partly on the level of deposits and partly on the market rate of interest. The greater the level of deposits, the more monetary base will banks demand; the higher the market rate of interest, the smaller the monetary base demanded by banks.

Other things being equal, the higher the monetary base, the higher the money supply; and the higher the market rate of interest, the higher the money supply. On average the money supply will be a fairly stable multiple of the monetary base, though over shorter periods there will be independent fluctuations in the two variables, associated with movements in market rates of interest.

B. How the Bank of England Operates to Achieve its Target Growth Path for the Money Supply

The Bank of England has recently modified its technique of monetary control. Until 1981, it sought to achieve a target growth path for the money supply (sterling $M3$) by operating on the demand side of the money market. The Bank 'solved' the demand for money function for that level of the short-term interest rate which it was predicted would induce the amount of money demand to equal the target value of the money supply, given the Bank's own forecasts of the price level and the level of real income. That technique of control was far from perfect. Deviation of prices or income from their forecasted value led to serious deviations of the money supply from its target.

In 1981, the Bank abandoned this particular control procedure. Instead of seeking to control those interest rates which influence the demand for sterling $M3$, the Bank now seeks to control only the very short-term one- to two-week interest rates. Three-month interest rates (those which influence the demand for sterling $M3$) are left to be determined by market forces (but of course heavily influenced by the Bank's own operations in the shorter-term, one- to two-week, markets). The Bank views this move as an exploratory move towards possibly controlling the money supply via control of the reserve base of the banking system exploiting the linkages described in Section A of this chapter.

It is quite likely that the current policies of the Bank of England represent an inferior alternative both to the technique that has been abandoned and to the procedure of controlling money by controlling the monetary base.

Review Questions

1. What is the monetary base? Who issues it (whose liability is it) and who holds it (whose asset is it)?

2. What determines the demand for currency by households and firms?

3. What determines the demand for monetary base by the commercial banks?

4. What is the money supply function?

5. What markets are in equilibrium along the money supply function?

6. What would lead to a shift in the money supply function?

7. Does the money supply function imply that the monetary base determines the money supply?

8. How, until 1981, did the Bank of England seek to control the United Kingdom money supply? Did it exploit the money supply function analysed in this chapter?

9. What are the main potential sources of error or looseness in the Bank of England's old and new techniques of monetary control? How would you set about comparing the effectiveness of these two alternative techniques?

10. How does the Bank manipulate the market rate of interest in order to move to its target point on the demand for money function?

11. In light of your answer to Question 10, do you want to reconsider your answer to Question 8?

12. What are the main potential sources of error, or looseness, in the Bank of England's control of sterling $M3$, given the methods used by the Bank to effect that control?

37

Monetary Policy I: Aggregate Demand Shocks

You are now in a position to ask the central macroeconomic policy question, namely, what can and should monetary policy do to offset the business cycle? This is a controversial question. There are two broad views concerning its answer, and this chapter, along with the next, is designed to help you understand the nature of the controversy. The material presented in these two chapters will take you right to the frontiers of the current debate in economics.[1] However, nothing that will be dealt with in these chapters is inherently more difficult than the material that you have handled so far.

This chapter will help you with five tasks. They are to:

A. know the key difference between the monetary policy advice given by Monetarists and that given by Keynesians;

B. know what aggregate demand shocks are and how they affect the aggregate demand curve;

---

1. The leading articles on this topic are much more demanding than the simplified presentation given in this and the next two chapters. On the Monetarist side, the leading pieces are: Thomas J. Sargent and Neil Wallace, Rational expectations and the theory of economic policy, *Journal of Monetary Economics*, 2, April 1976, pp. 169–84; and Robert E. Lucas Jr., Rules, discretion and the role of the economic advisor, in Stanley Fischer, (ed.), *Rational Expectations and Economic Policy*, NBER, University of Chicago Press, 1980, pp. 199–210. On the Keynesian side, the best pieces are Edmund Phelps and John B. Taylor, Stabilizing powers of monetary policy under rational expectations, *Journal of Political Economy*, 85, February 1977, pp. 163–89; and Stanley Fischer, Long-term contracts, rational expectations, and the optimal money supply rule, *Journal of Political Economy*, 85, February 1977, pp. 191–206.

MACROECONOMIC POLICY

C. understand the consequences of following Monetarist monetary policy advice in the face of aggregate demand shocks;
D. understand the consequences of following Keynesian monetary policy advice in the face of aggregate demand shocks;
and
E. understand why Monetarists and Keynesians offer conflicting monetary policy advice.

A. Monetarist and Keynesian Monetary Policy Advice

For present purposes, monetary policy will mean manipulating the money supply. This means that we are going to be dealing only with an economy that operates under flexible exchange rates. As you have seen, an economy which operates with a fixed exchange rate is very severely limited in the monetary policy actions that it can take. The detailed procedures whereby the central bank achieves its money supply objectives, described in the previous chapter, are taken to be capable of delivering whatever supply of money the bank chooses. This chapter will be concerned with the effects of the bank achieving alternative targets for the money supply, rather than with the ways in which those targets are achieved.

The monetary policy advice given by *Keynesians* is:
(i) *raise the money supply* to a higher level than it otherwise would have been *if output* is (or is forecast to be) *below its full-employment level*;
(ii) *lower the money supply* below what it otherwise would have been *if output* is (or is forecast to be) *above its full-employment level*.

The precise value of the money supply and the precise amount by which it should be moved in order to achieve the desired level of output is a technically complex matter, but one which Keynesians believe they can solve with the help of large-scale econometric models of the economy.

The *Monetarist* policy advice contrasts very sharply with the *Keynesian* advice. It is: *keep the money supply growing at a constant known rate each and every year, no matter what the level of output is*.

If output is below its full-employment level so that there is a recession, Monetarists advise holding the money supply on a steady course that is known and predictable, rather than raising the rate of growth of the money supply above that known and predictable path. Conversely, when the economy is in a boom, with output above its full-employment level, the monetarist advice is again to hold the money supply growing at a steady and predictable rate, rather than to reduce its growth rate.

Thus, Keynesian advice is to manipulate the money supply growth rate, raising it in a depression and lowering it in a boom; the Monetarist policy advice is to keep the money supply growth rate steady, regardless of whether the economy is in a boom or a slump.

To see *why* each group of economists gives the advice that it does and to see precisely why there is a disagreement, it is necessary to analyse how the economy reacts to shocks that do not themselves stem from the actions of monetary policy. It is then necessary to ask how monetary policy can (and should) be used to counter the effects of these shocks. There are two broad sources of shocks, one on the aggregate demand side, and the other on the aggregate supply side of the economy. The aggregate demand shocks are considered in this chapter, and the aggregate supply shocks in the next one.

B. Aggregate Demand Shocks and the Aggregate Demand Curve

The *IS–LM* model of aggregate demand, developed in Part IV, did not explicitly contain aggregate demand shocks. It was presented as if the level of output, employment, unemployment, the real wage, money wage, and the price level were determined *exactly* once the value of the money supply and the fiscal policy variables were set. This was an oversimplification, and one which it is now necessary to relax. In this chapter we relax this simplification on the demand side of the economy.

You will recall that the theory of aggregate demand was developed from a theory of consumption, investment, and the demand for money. A moment's reflection will tell you that holding the money supply and fiscal policy variables constant, the position of the aggregate demand curve will be fixed and fully predictable only if the consumption function, investment function, and demand for money function are fixed and fully predictable. If a significant group of individuals decided in one particular year that they would manage with a smaller ratio of money balances to income than normal, then in that particular year there would be a surge of expenditures. This would happen as this group of individuals put into action their decisions to lower their money balances below their normal level in relation to their incomes. Conversely, if a significant group of individuals decided in a particular year that they wanted a higher ratio of money balances to income than normal, they would cut back on their expenditures as they put their decisions into effect.

There are many factors which could lead individuals to vary, over time, their consumption, investment, and demand for money. On the average, such factors would cancel out, and for most of the time, when aggregated over all the individuals in the economy, would not be very important. From time to time, however, such factors could be important and might knock the economy significantly away from its *normal* equilibrium position.

Perhaps some examples will be helpful. Suppose it is widely believed that there is going to be a major drought. This might lead people to invest in a stockpile of food and lower their average money holdings for a period. While this stockpiling was going on there would be an increase in the level of aggregate demand as people attempted to put through their increased expenditure plans. In the opposite direction, suppose that it was widely believed that there was going to be a major technical innovation in, say, cars, such that the current year's model will be quickly superseded by a vastly superior technology. In such a case, the sales of cars in the year in question would be unusually low, and people would hold on to their money or other financial assets in readiness for a subsequent increase in expenditures. In this case there would be a retiming of expenditures, with sales in one year being unusually

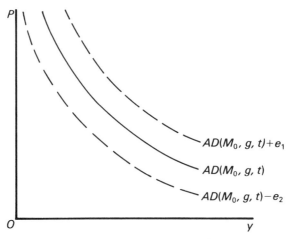

Figure 37.1 *Aggregate Demand Shocks*

Random fluctuations in consumption, investment and the demand for money, summarised as the shock e, shift the aggregate demand curve around its average postition even though monetary and fiscal policy variables are fixed. On the average the shocks will be zero. e_1 is an example of a positive shock, and e_2 of a negative shock.

---

low and sales in some subsequent year, or years, being unusually high.

These are simply examples; you can probably think of many more. Most of the examples which you will think of will turn out to involve *randomness in the timing of people's expenditures in acquiring either durable goods, capital goods, or other goods to store. Random fluctuations in the composition of people's assets — between money and financial assets on the one hand and real asset holdings on the other hand — lead to random fluctuations in aggregate demand.*

You can think of the aggregate demand curve that we have been working with in the earlier parts of this book as being the level of the aggregate demand curve *on the average*. This curve is reproduced in Figure 37.1 as the solid line labelled $AD(M_0, g, t)$. (It is labelled in this way to remind you that the position of the AD curve depends on the money supply M, government spending, g, and taxes, t. The subscript on M is there to denote the initial value of the money supply, M_0. Later we shall analyse what happens when we change M, holding everything else constant.) Now allow also for random shocks arising from the considerations just described to affect the position of the aggregate demand curve. Sometimes aggregate demand will be higher than its average value and sometimes lower than its average value. We can capture such random shocks as an addition to or subtraction from the average position of the aggregate demand curve. Let us call the aggregate of all the random shocks to demand e. On the average e is equal to zero. It will, however, take on large positive or negative values from time to time. If e took on a positive value, say, e_1, then the aggregate demand curve would move to the right, such as the curve shown as the broken line $AD(M_0, g, t) + e_1$. If there was a negative random shock, say, e_2, then the aggregate demand curve would move to the left, such as that shown as the broken line labelled $AD(M_0, g, t) - e_2$. At any particular point in time the aggregate demand curve might lie anywhere inside the range of the two broken line curves. On the average, the aggregate demand curve would be located in the middle of this range at

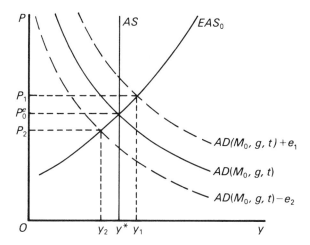

Figure 37.2   *The Consequences of Following Monetarist Policy Advice*
Monetarist policy holds the money stock constant. Expected aggregate demand will be
$AD(M_0, g, t)$ and the rationally expected price level P_0^e. Actual random fluctuations in
aggregate demand will generate fluctuations in output with procyclical co-movements in
prices.

$AD(M_0, g, t)$. Thus, for any given level of the money supply you can think of there
being a whole set of possible aggregate demand curves. The *actual* position of the
aggregate demand curve depends on the size of the random shock e, on the money
supply and on government spending and taxes.

C. Consequences of Monetarist Policy

Let us now analyse what happens when there is an aggregate demand shock and
when the monetary policy pursued is that advocated by Monetarists. Figure 37.2
illustrates this. Let us suppose that the *anticipated money supply* is M_0. Recall that
the Monetarist policy involves making the money supply follow a totally predictable
path under all circumstances. Specifically assume the actual money supply is held
constant at M_0. It will now be obvious that the *actual money supply* will *equal the
anticipated money supply*. In other words, *if the Monetarist policy rule is followed,
there will be no unanticipated changes in the money supply*.

   Since, on the average, the aggregate demand shock e will be zero, it will be rational
to expect a zero aggregate demand shock. So the rational expectation of the price
level (P_0^e) is found where the expected aggregate demand curve $AD(M_0, g, t)$ cuts the
aggregate supply curve AS. This aggregate demand curve is the *expected aggregate
demand curve in the double sense that it is drawn for an expected value of the aggregate
demand shock equal to zero and for the money supply equal to its anticipated level of
M_0. Passing through the point P_0^e and y^* is the relevant expectations-augmented
aggregate supply curve. This is the expectations-augmented aggregate supply curve
drawn for the rational expectation of the price level of P_0^e.

Now suppose that there is a random increase in aggregate demand by an amount e_1 such that the demand curve *actually* moves rightwards to $AD(M_0, g, t) + e_1$. If the monetary policy advice of the Monetarists is followed and the money supply is held at M_0, its anticipated level, the result of this random shock to aggregate demand will be a rise in the price level to P_1 and a rise in output to y_1.

Next consider the opposite case. Suppose there is a negative random shock to aggregate demand — a random fall in aggregate demand — so that the aggregate demand curve shifts leftwards to $AD(M_0, g, t) - e_2$. Again, following the Monetarist policy advice, the actual money supply is held steady at its anticipated level M_0. There is therefore a drop in the price level to P_2 and a drop in output to y_2.

You can now see that the consequences of following the Monetarist policy advice are that the economy will experience random deviations of output from its full-employment level and random deviations of the price level from its expected level as the economy is continuously 'bombarded' by random aggregate demand shocks. These shocks are not offset by changes in the money supply. There will also be fluctuations in employment, unemployment, the real wage, and money wage. You can work out the directions in which these variables will move from Chapter 31. Further, for the reasons discussed in Chapter 33, there will only be a gradual return to full employment following a shock.

Let us now examine the consequences of following Keynesian policy advice.

D. Consequences of Keynesian Policy

Let us begin with exactly the same set-up as before. The anticipated money supply is M_0, and the expected aggregate demand curve drawn for an expected zero aggregate demand shock is the curve $AD(M_0, g, t)$. (For the moment ignore the other labels on that curve in Figure 37.3.) The rational expectation of the price level is P_0^e, and the relevant expectations-augmented aggregate supply curve is EAS_0.

Now suppose that there is a positive random shock to aggregate demand (e_1) taking the aggregate demand curve to the higher curve $AD(M_0, g, t) + e_1$. The Keynesian policy advice in this situation is to cut the money supply. If the money supply is cut by exactly the right amount, it is possible to offset the positive aggregate demand shock, thereby making the actual aggregate demand curve the same as the curve $AD(M_0, g, t)$. Suppose that the money supply which exactly achieves that effect is M_1. Then the aggregate demand curve would be the same as $AD(M_0, g, t)$. We have given that aggregate demand curve a second label, $AD(M_1, g, t) + e_1$. This is to indicate to you that *the same aggregate demand curve can arise from different combinations of the money supply and the random aggregate demand shock*. If the aggregate demand shock was zero and the money supply was M_0, the aggregate demand curve would be the same as in a situation in which the money supply was M_1 (smaller than M_0) and the aggregate demand shock was e_1 (a positive value). Following this Keynesian policy rule of changing the money supply to offset the aggregate demand shock gives the prediction that the level of output will stay constant at y^* and the price level will stay at its rational expectation level P_0^e.

The same conclusion would arise if the consequences of a negative aggregate

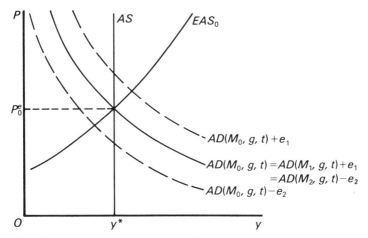

Figure 37.3 *The Consequences of Following Keynesian Monetary Policy Advice*
If a random shock hits the economy, thereby shifting the aggregate demand curve (with the
money stock constant), Keynesian policy would change the money stock so as to offset the
random demand shift. The actual aggregate demand curve would remain constant as the
continuous line in the figure. Output would be stabilised at full employment and the price level
at its expected level.

---

demand shock were examined. If aggregate demand fell by a random amount e_2, with
a fixed money supply M_0, the aggregate demand curve would move to $AD(M_0, g, t) - e_2$. If this random shock was offset by a rise in the money supply, to (say) M_2 — a
value big enough to raise the aggregate demand curve back to its original level —
then the aggregate demand curve would again become the same as $AD(M_0, g, t)$. The
curve $AD(M_0, g, t)$ has been labelled yet a third time as equal to $AD(M_2, g, t) - e_2$ to
remind you that with a higher money supply (M_2) and a negative value of the
aggregate demand shock (e_2) it is possible to place the aggregate demand curve in the
same place as it would have been with a lower value for the money supply (M_0) and a
zero random shock to aggregate demand.

Again, following Keynesian policy advice, the economy stays at the price level P_0^e
and the full-employment output level y^* where the aggregate demand curve $AD(M_2,
g, t) - e_2 (= AD(M_0, g, t))$ cuts the expectations-augmented aggregate supply curve
EAS_0.

You see, then, that the consequences of following Keynesian stabilisation policy
are to remove all the fluctuations from output and to keep the price level at its
rationally expected level.

E. Why Monetarists and Keynesians Offer Conflicting Advice

(i) Comparison: Keynesian Policy Seems to be Better than Monetarist Policy

From the above presentation of the effects of following a Monetarist policy rule and a

Keynesian policy intervention, it is apparent that Monetarist policy leaves the economy contaminated by the effects of random shocks to aggregate demand, while Keynesian policy completely insulates the economy from these shocks by exactly offsetting their effects. It would appear, then, that monetary policy can be used to keep the economy free from random fluctuations in output and the price level, and assuming that to be a desirable end, that monetary policy should so be used. Put more directly, it would appear that Keynesian policy is better than Monetarist policy.

Naturally, since there is a debate about the matter, things are not quite as simple as they have been presented in the above two sections. Let us now try to find out why Keynesians and Monetarists disagree with each other.

(ii) Informational Advantages

In the two monetary policy experiments that we have conducted and compared in the preceding sections, we have not made the same assumptions concerning the information available to the central bank and private economic agents in the two cases.

When conducting the Monetarist policy analysis it was assumed implicitly — and it is now time to be explicit about the matter — *that the central bank and private economic agents all had the same information. No one knew what value e would take in the coming time period.* Everyone, including the central bank, expected that it would be zero.

When conducting the Keynesian policy analysis however, *it was assumed* implicitly — and again it is now time to be explicit — *that no private agent was able to forecast the value of the random shock e, but that the central bank knew the value of e exactly and was able to move the money supply so as precisely to offset its effects on aggregate demand.* In other words, it was assumed that the central bank knew more than the private economic agents concerning the position of the aggregate demand curve.

Instead of assuming that the central bank has such an *informational advantage,* let us analyse what would happen if the central bank had to operate a Keynesian policy with a time lag such that it could only change the money supply when it knew that there *had been an aggregate demand shock* which it had been able to observe. Also, however, let us recognise that *what can be observed by the central bank can also be observed by anybody else.* If the central bank knows that the economy is experiencing a positive (or negative) aggregate demand shock, then it seems reasonable to suppose that everyone else knows that too.

In order to make things as clear as possible, let us look at two periods of time (years). We will analyse what would happen if there was a positive aggregate demand shock (e_1) in the first period and then no aggregate demand shock in the second period. Of course, no one actually sees the shock. All that people see are the changes in output, employment and the price level that are generated by the shock. Suppose that the central bank reacts, in the manner advocated by Keynesians, to an output change, but with a one-period time lag. That is, if there has been a rise in output in the first period, the central bank cuts back on the money supply in the second period in an attempt to offset the observed effects of the first-period aggregate demand shock. Further, let us suppose that everyone knows as much as the central bank knows about the aggregate demand shock. Yet *further, let us suppose that everyone knows that the central bank is pursuing a Keynesian policy and will react with a one-*

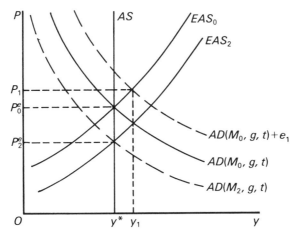

Figure 37.4 *The Consequences of Following Keynesian Monetary Policy Advice with an Information Lag*

An economy initially at full-employment equilibrium (y^*, P_0^e) is disturbed by a random shock to aggregate demand (e_1). Output and prices rise to P_1, y_1, the same as they would if the Monetarist rule was being pursued. The higher output level induces a monetary contraction under the Keynesian rule (lowering the aggregate demand curve to $AD(M_2, g, t)$). Since everyone knows the government is using the Keynesian rule, the aggregate demand curve (in the absence of random shocks) will be the same as the expected curve. The economy will return to full employment, but with a lower price level. Pursuing a Keynesian rule with a one-period lag leaves real output on the same path as in the case of the Monetarist rule, but makes prices more volatile.

---

period lag by changing the money stock. Let us now work out what will happen as a result of this monetary policy response.

Figure 37.4 illustrates the analysis. The economy is initially expected to be on the demand curve $AD(M_0, g, t)$, at a price level P_0^e and an output level y^*. The relevant expectations-augmented aggregate supply curve is EAS_0. Let this be the point at which the economy starts out. Then, in the first period, let there be a positive aggregate demand shock e_1. No one can predict the aggregate demand shock before it happens, and therefore, no one reacts to it until the second period. However, the shock affects the actual behaviour of the economy in the first period, and the price level and output level settle down at P_1 and y_1 respectively. These are the values of the price level and output at which the new aggregate demand curve $AD(M_0, g, t) + e_1$ cuts the expectations-augmented aggregate supply curve EAS_0.

Now, in the next period everyone has observed that there has been a positive aggregate demand shock. Furthermore, everyone can work out the size of the shock from knowing what the actual price and output levels turned out to be. The central bank reacts to this aggregate demand shock by cutting the money supply in the second period to a value of (say) M_2. Assuming that there is no aggregate demand shock in this second period, the new aggregate demand curve will be below the original curve $AD(M_0, g, t)$, since the money supply has been cut below M_0. In particular, the aggregate demand curve will be $AD(M_2, g, t)$. Private agents will expect the aggregate demand curve to be $AD(M_2, g, t)$ because they will expect the monetary authorities to cut the money stock as a reaction to the previous period's aggregate demand shock e_1. They will form a rational expectation of the price level of P_2^e, and the expectations-augmented aggregate supply curve will become EAS_2. If (as we are assuming) there is no aggregate demand shock in the second period, the economy will settle at its full-employment output level of y^* and the price level of P_2^e.

Thus, *following a Keynesian policy rule*, but *with a one-period information lag*, implying that the central bank has no better information than the private sector has, *leads to a movement in output which is exactly the same as that which occurs when the Monetarist policy rule is followed*. However, there is a difference between the two policies in the behaviour of the price level. *The price level fluctuates more when Keynesian policy advice is followed than it does with the Monetarist rule.*

We see, then, that following Keynesian policy advice, which has a one-period lag on information and with no informational advantage for the central bank, is exactly the same as following Monetarist policy advice in its effect on output. However, it leads to bigger fluctuations in the price level than does Monetarist policy.

(iii) The Essence of the Dispute Between Keynesians and Monetarists

The essence of the dispute between Keynesians and Monetarists concerning the effects of monetary policy turns on the question of information *and the use which may be made of new information*. The Monetarist asserts that the central bank has no informational advantage over private agents and that it can do nothing which private agents will not do for themselves. Any attempt by the central bank to *fine tune* or stabilise the economy by making the money supply react to *previous shocks, known to everybody*, will make the level of output behave no better than it otherwise would have done and will make the price level more variable.

Keynesians assert that the central bank possesses an *effective informational advantage*. They agree that individuals will form their expectations rationally, using all the information that is available to them. They go on to assert that individuals get *locked into contracts* based on an expected price level which, after the fact of an aggregate demand shock, turns out to be wrong. *The central bank can act **after** private agents have tied themselves into contractual arrangements based on a false price level expectation* to compensate for and offset the effects of those random shocks. Figure 37.3 can be re-interpreted as showing what happens if the private sector is tied into contracts based on a wrong expected price level. In that case, if both the central bank and private agents *observe* an aggregate demand shock of (say) e_1, *but if* private agents are tied into contracts based on the expected price level P_0^e, *and if* the central bank can change the money supply quickly enough, then the Keynesian policy outcome shown in Figure 37.3 can be achieved.

The essence of the debate, then, concerns the flexibility of private sector responses *vis-à-vis* the flexibility of central bank responses to random shocks that hit the economy. If everyone can act as quickly and as effortlessly as everyone else, there is no advantage from pursuing Keynesian policy and, indeed, there are disadvantages because the price level will be more variable. If, however, the central bank can act more quickly than the private sector, there may be a gain in the form of reduced output and price variability from pursuing Keynesian policy.

(iv) An Unsettled Scientific Question — and a Presumption in Favour of Monetarism

There is no easy way of deciding which of these two views better describes the world, and further scientific research is required before the matter will be settled.

One thing which can be said, however, is that because it is difficult to know exactly what random shocks are hitting the economy, attempts to pursue Keynesian policy will make the money supply more random and less predictable than would Monetarist policy. You have seen (Chapters 31 and 33) that an unpredictable monetary policy gives rise to cycles in economic activity arising from the money supply movements themselves. Thus, Keynesian policy will necessarily impart some cyclical movements into the economy as a consequence of the fact that the money supply itself is less predictable under Keynesian policy than under a Monetarist policy rule. Monetarist policy will (as far as possible) remove any fluctuations from aggregate demand that arise from the money supply itself. The only things that can lead to business cycles under a Monetarist policy rule are the random fluctuations arising from private aggregate demand (or aggregate supply) shocks. The random shocks emanating from the behaviour of the central bank are eliminated. Whether random shocks that arise from the private sector are the dominant shocks is another matter of dispute. Here, however, there seems to be less room for disagreement. It is fairly well established that most of the major fluctuations in economic activity in modern industrial economies arise from instability in monetary policy itself. Unanticipated variations in the money supply seem to account for *most* of the variations that we observe in the level of economic activity. However, they certainly do not account for all the observed fluctuations. The Great Depression of 1929 to 1934 has not yet been satisfactorily explained by *any* theory. We must therefore remain cautious and display a certain amount of humility. This does not, however, bode well for the Keynesian policy recommendation which, in order that it may improve matters, must be based upon the presumption that we know rather a lot about the way in which the economy behaves.

The bottom line defence for the Monetarist policy recommendation is that we are simply too ignorant about the workings of the economy to be able to do better than to remove at least those sources of fluctuation in economic activity that we *can* control, namely, those that stem from instability in the money supply. If those fluctuations were removed, the economy would behave in a much more stable manner than it has in the past. Of course, it would not be ideal. Idealism, however, requires a great deal more information than is currently available to us.

SUMMARY

A. Monetarist and Keynesian Monetary Policy Advice

Monetarists recommend the adoption of a steady and predictable money supply growth rule. The money supply growth rate should be kept constant no matter what the current state of the economy.

Keynesians recommend the use of active variations in the money supply to offset aggregate demand shocks. They recommend raising the money supply when output is below its full-employment level and lowering the money supply when output is above its full-employment level.

B. Aggregate Demand Shocks and the Aggregate Demand Curve

Aggregate demand shocks are random variations in the level of aggregate demand which arise from random movements in the timing of expenditures and from random fluctuations in desired holdings of real assets and financial assets. If people try to hold more real assets and fewer financial assets, there will be a rise in the demand for goods — a rise in aggregate demand.

Aggregate demand shocks shift the aggregate demand curve. For any given price level, the level of aggregate demand will vary around its most likely value, depending on the size of the aggregate demand shock.

C. Consequences of Monetarist Policy

Adopting a Monetarist policy permits fluctuations in output, employment, unemployment, the price level, the money wage, and the real wage. For example, in the case of a positive aggregate demand shock, output, employment, the price level, and the money wage will rise, and the real wage and unemployment will fall.

D. Consequences of Keynesian Policy

Keynesian policy is designed to insulate the economy from a random shock and eliminate fluctuations in output and the price level. In the case of a positive aggregate demand shock, Keynesian monetary policy advice is to lower the money supply so as to leave aggregate demand (and thus the position of the aggregate demand curve) unchanged. This would lead to no adjustment in the rational expectation of the price level so that the level of output, employment, unemployment, the price level, the real and money wage would remain constant.

E. Why Monetarists and Keynesians Offer Conflicting Advice

The dispute between Monetarists and Keynesians rests on whether the central bank has an informational advantage over private agents in the economy. Monetarists argue that the central bank has no more information than do private agents. Any attempt by the central bank to offset *previous* random aggregate demand shocks now known to all agents in the economy by varying the money supply will not reduce the fluctuations in output, while it will increase those in the price level.

Keynesians assert that the central bank has an *effective* informal advantage over private agents. Private agents get locked into contracts which cannot be revised quickly as new information becomes available. When the central bank and private agents observe an aggregate demand shock, private agents are unable to revise their contracts and are thus locked into contracts based on the wrong expected price level. The central bank can respond quickly to the new information (the aggregate demand shock) and change the money supply quickly enough so that output, employment, and the price level remain steady.

The successful application of Keynesian policy would require a vast amount of information on the part of the central bank and government, and there is a strong presumption that, in the present state of knowledge, they do not have sufficient information. Attempts at pursuing Keynesian policies will be likely to generate bigger fluctuations in both output and prices than would the adoption of a Monetarist rule.

Review Questions

1. Summarise and contrast the monetary policy positions of Keynesians and Monetarists.

2. Give some examples of factors which might cause aggregate demand shocks.

3. Work out, using the appropriate diagrams, the consequences of pursuing a Monetarist policy in the face of random fluctuations in aggregate demand.

4. Explain the rationale which Monetarists use for permitting random aggregate demand shocks to influence aggregate output and prices.

5. Work out, using the appropriate diagrams, the Keynesian monetary policy required to stabilise the economy in the face of a positive shock.

6. Work out, using the appropriate diagrams, the effects of pursuing a Keynesian policy, but with the monetary authorities reacting with a one-period lag to aggregate demand shocks.

7. Set out the major differences in the predicted consequences of pursuing Monetarist and Keynesian policies in the face of random aggregate demand shocks.

8. What is the primary source of disagreement between Keynesians and Monetarists which causes each group of economists to give the advice that it does?

38

Monetary Policy II: Aggregate Supply Shocks

In September 1973, the members of the Oil Producing Exporting Countries (OPEC) announced a fourfold increase in the price of crude oil. At the same time they announced an embargo on the shipment of oil to certain countries and a decision to cut back their production levels. In a single afternoon, the OPEC decision delivered a *supply shock* to the Western world which has only been matched by the events of major wars. The consequences of the OPEC oil price rise have been widespread and long drawn out. They also triggered a fierce debate as to what constituted the appropriate macroeconomic policy response.[1]

This chapter is going to help you to understand some of the main macroeconomic effects of the OPEC oil shock and also help you to evaluate alternative policy recommendations for dealing with supply shocks of that kind. You have six tasks, which are to:

- A. **understand how a supply shock affects: (i) the production function, (ii) the labour market, (iii) the aggregate supply curve;**
- B. **understand the distinction between the expectations-augmented aggregate supply curve and the expectation of the aggregate supply curve;**
- C. **understand the consequences of following Monetarist policy advice in the event of an aggregate supply shock;**
- D. **understand the consequences of following Keynesian policy advice in the event of an aggregate supply shock;**

---

1. An excellent presentation of a Keynesian view on this is Robert M. Solow, What to do (macroeconomically) when OPEC comes, in Stanley Fischer, (ed.), *Rational Expectations and Economic Policy,* NBER, University of Chicago Press, 1980, pp. 249–64. Also see Neil Wallace's comment on Solow on pp. 264–67 of the same volume.

E. understand the consequences of following a Keynesian policy with an
   information lag;
   and
F. understand the essence of the dispute and why there is a further presumption in
   favour of Monetarism.

A. Effects of Supply Shocks

(i) The Production Function

You will recall that the theory of aggregate supply developed in Chapter 9 started
from the concept of the *short-run production function*. The *production function* tells
us the maximum output which can be produced using given inputs. The *short-run
production function* tells us how the maximum output level varies as the labour input
alone is varied, holding constant capital, land inputs and the state of technology. An
aggregate supply shock such as the cutback of oil supplies and the quadrupling of the
price of oil can be thought of as shifting the short-run production function. Figure
38.1 illustrates such a shift. The short-run production function $\phi_0(n)$ may be thought
of as that relating to the pre-supply shock situation, and $\phi_1(n)$ to the post-shock
situation. At the employment level n_0, more could be produced before the shock, y_0,
than after the shock, y_1.

There are thousands upon thousands of individual actions which lead to the shift in
the production function. For example, following a supply shock like the oil shock,
many extra resources would be diverted into the search for alternative sources of
lower-cost energy, thereby lowering the volume of output which would result from a
given level of employment. Also, much labour and capital would be diverted to
finding ways of using less fuel, again lowering the available supply of goods produced
at a given level of employment. A concrete example of such a diversion of resources
is in the car industry. As a result of the higher price of oil, there has been a switch to
more fuel-efficient cars. Large quantities of labour (and capital) had to be employed
in designing, testing, and building these cars. The actual output of cars produced by
this labour could have been much higher if the more traditional engines and sizes had
not been discarded in favour of the new types. This example is just one of thousands
in all areas of industrial activity and transportation.

(ii) The Real Wage and Levels of Employment and Unemployment

An aggregate supply shock not only shifts the production function, it has an effect in
the labour market as well. It is possible to imagine situations in which the demand for
labour function shifts in either direction (upwards or downwards). To focus our
attention on a case that seems to have some relevance from the recent past, we shall
consider only the case in which the labour demand function shifts downwards. This is
the case that is consistent with the way in which Figure 38.1 is drawn. Also, it seems
to be in line with the events that occurred following the oil price rise in 1973. Another
way of saying that the demand for labour function will shift is to say that the marginal

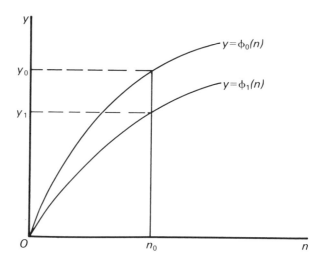

Figure 38.1   *How An Aggregate Supply Shock Shifts the*
Short-Run Production Function

An aggregate supply shock lowers the output rate that can be produced at each level of labour
input. It also lowers the marginal product of labour. For example, a labour input of n_0 would
only be able to produce y_1 after a shock, whereas it could have produced y_0 before the shock.

---

product of labour has changed. If the demand for labour function shifts downwards
as we shall suppose it to have done in the case analysed here, the marginal
productivity of labour has declined. The shift in the production function and the
change in the marginal productivity of labour are one and the same phenomenon.
Following a shock like the oil price rise, much labour gets absorbed in activities
designed to minimise the adverse effects of the price rise, rather than in the direct
production of goods for final consumption and investment. The car industry example
may be used again to illustrate the point. Suppose that, as a result of higher oil prices,
a production line for large cars is scrapped long before it normally would have been
and is replaced by a new line to make smaller cars. Suppose also that the small car is
to be powered with a new engine, completely redesigned for fuel-efficient operation
and with an electronic fuel and pressure monitoring system. The amount of labour
required to produce a given quantity of the new type of car will be substantially larger
than that required for the traditional design and technology. Further, the extra
output (marginal product) which could be produced by raising the labour force by a
given amount will be less than would have been the case with the older technology
car.

The shift in the production function and the associated shift in the demand for
labour function are shown in Figure 38.2. The economy was originally producing y_0^*
with a labour force of n_0, and the real wage was $(W/P)_0$. After the supply shock, the
production function shifts to $\phi_1(n)$, and the demand for labour function shifts to n_1^d.
The labour market equilibrium now is achieved at a *lower* level of employment, n_1,
and a lower real wage, $(W/P)_1$. The difference between n_0 and n_1 will be the drop in
employment resulting from the supply shock. Initially, at least, these workers may
remain in the labour force and be recorded as unemployed as they search for new

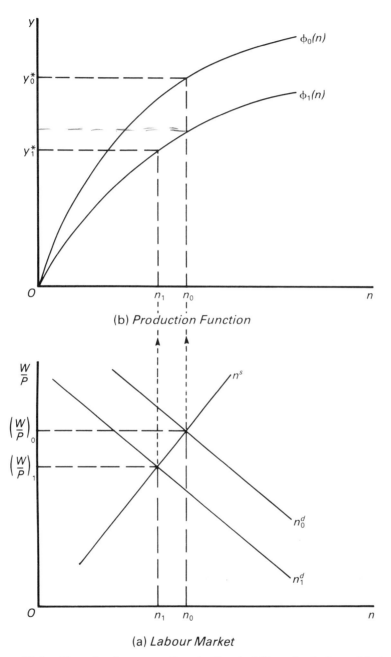

(b) *Production Function*

(a) *Labour Market*

Figure 38.2   *How An Aggregate Supply Shock Affects the Labour Market*

A drop in the production function which lowers the marginal product of labour shifts the demand for labour curve downwards. Employment and the real wage fall from n_0 to n_1 and $(W/P)_0$ to $(W/P)_1$. Output falls from y_0^* to y_1^*.

jobs. Eventually, if the supply shock is permanent, they will leave the labour force as they realise that the real wage has permanently fallen.

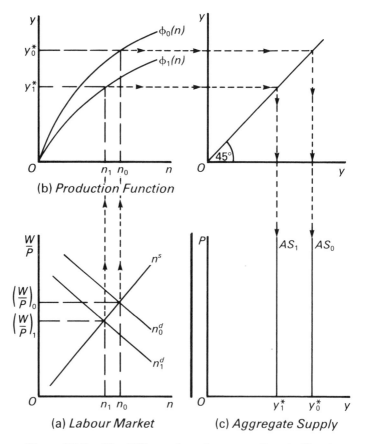

Figure 38.3   *The Effects of an Aggregate Supply Shock
on the Aggregate Supply Curve*

The aggregate supply curve shifts to the left in the face of a negative aggregate supply shock.
The leftward shift is bigger than the drop in output for a given level of employment.
Employment falls because the real wage falls. Thus, aggregate supply falls for two reasons, a
drop in the production function and a drop in the level of employment.

(iii) The Aggregate Supply Curve

The effect of an aggregate supply shock on the aggregate supply curve is shown in
Figure 38.3. Frames (a) and (b) are the same as Figure 38.2. The amount of output
produced initially was y_0^*, and the aggregate supply curve was AS_0. After the supply
shock the level of employment drops to n_1 and the level of output drops to y_1^*, with
the aggregate supply function shifting to AS_1. Notice that the drop in aggregate
supply from y_0^* to y_1^* results from two factors: first, the shift in the production
function from $\phi_0(n)$ to $\phi_1(n)$, and secondly, the cut in employment induced by the
drop in the marginal productivity of labour, which reduces the demand for labour.

B. Expectations-Augmented Aggregate Supply Curve and the Expectation of the Aggregate Supply Curve

Before going further in the analysis of aggregate supply shocks, we want to draw your attention to an important distinction which you need to be clear about. The word 'expectation' is going to be attached to the aggregate supply curve in two very different ways. First, there is the *expectations-augmented aggregate supply curve* (*EAS*). This is what it always has been, namely, a curve showing the level of aggregate supply for a given *expected price level*. Secondly, the concept of the *expectation of the aggregate supply curve* will be used. This is a new concept which has not been used before. The aggregate supply curve is the vertical aggregate supply curve *AS* — which shows the level of aggregate supply when the *expected* and *actual price levels are equal to each other*. If there are no aggregate supply shocks, the position of this curve is determined uniquely by the production function and the condition of equilibrium in the labour market. However, when random shocks affect the production function, they also affect the position of the aggregate supply function. The size and direction of random shocks to the production function cannot be known before they occur, and on the average, those shocks cancel out — are zero. The aggregate supply curve based on a zero aggregate supply shock — the expected or average aggregate supply shock — will be called the *expectation of the aggregate supply curve*.

Keeping this distinction clear, and as a prelude to analysing the effects of alternative policies towards aggregate supply shocks, let us see how each of these aggregate supply curves shifts in response to such a shock.

Figure 38.4 shows the effects of an aggregate supply shock on the aggregate supply and expectations-augmented aggregate supply curves. Suppose that initially the economy was on the curve AS_0, and the aggregate demand curve $AD(M_0, g, t)$, at a full-employment equilibrium y_0^* and P_0^e. The expectations-augmented aggregate supply curve has both a superscript and a subscript. The subscript refers to the value of the money supply, and the superscript refers to the value of the aggregate supply curve. Thus, EAS_0^0 is at the point of intersection of AS_0 and $AD(M_0, g, t)$. Now suppose that there is a random shock to aggregate supply which cuts aggregate supply at each level of employment. This will shift the aggregate supply curve to (say) AS_1. Suppose further that the expected value of the money supply remains at M_0, so that the aggregate demand curve $AD(M_0, g, t)$ is expected to remain unchanged. Also, suppose the aggregate supply shock is *un*anticipated, so that the expectation of the aggregate supply curve is that it remains at AS_0. In this case, the rational expectation of the price level will remain at P_0^e. The aggregate supply curve shift was easy to work out. That curve simply shifts leftwards by the amount of the drop in output that results from the aggregate supply shock. What happens to the expectations-augmented aggregate supply curve? This is not as straightforward to figure out. However, a moment's reflection will tell you that that curve must also shift horizontally by the same amount as the aggregate supply curve has shifted. The expectations-augmented aggregate supply curve always cuts the *actual* aggregate supply curve at the expected price level. Since the aggregate supply shock is (by

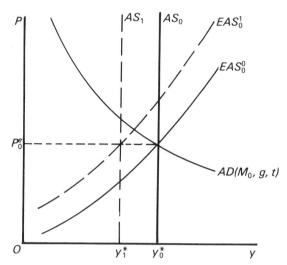

Figure 38.4 *An Aggregate Supply Shock and the Aggregate Supply Curves*
An unexpected aggregate supply shock shifts the aggregate supply, for example, from AS_0 to AS_1. The expectations-augmented aggregate supply curve is dragged along horizontally with the AS curve. EAS_0^0 is the expectations-augmented aggregate supply curve for the expected price level P_0^e (expected money stock M_0) and an expected aggregate supply curve of AS_0. The curve EAS_0^1 refers to the same expected price level and money stock, but to the lower level of aggregate supply.

---

assumption) unanticipated, there is no prior knowledge about it. The aggregate supply curve has shifted, at random, from its expected position AS_0 to an unexpected position AS_1. The expectations-augmented aggregate supply curve will have been dragged along with the aggregate supply curve so as to intersect it at the expected price level P_0^e. Given the aggregate supply shock, there will now be a lower level of output available at all price levels. Nothing has happened to change the expected price level, which remains at P_0^e. That is, nothing has happened to yield new information to economic agents that would lead them to revise their price level expectation. Thus, the effect on the aggregate supply curves of an aggregate supply shock is to shift both the aggregate supply curve and the expectations-augmented aggregate supply curve horizontally by the amount of the shock. The curve EAS_0^1 is the expectations-augmented aggregate supply curve when the expectation of aggregate demand is $AD(M_0, g, t)$ and when aggregate supply has *unexpectedly* dropped to AS_1.

You are now in a position to go on to compare the effects of alternative policies.

C. Consequences of Monetarist Policy

Figure 38.5 illustrates the consequences of following Monetarist policy in the event of an aggregate supply shock. Suppose there is a random drop in aggregate supply from AS_0 to AS_1 and suppose that a Monetarist policy rule of fixing the money stock

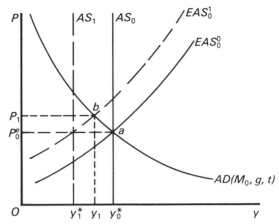

Figure 38.5 *The Consequences of Following Monetarist Policy Advice in the Event of a Supply Shock — Stagflation*

An economy initially at full-employment equilibrium (y_0^*, P_0^e) is disturbed by a negative aggregate supply shock which unexpectedly takes the aggregate supply curve to AS_1 and the EAS curve to EAS_0^1. The impact equilibrium is at P_1, y_1. Prices rise and output falls: the economy experiences stagflation.

---

at M_0 is followed, so that the aggregate demand curve remains as $AD(M_0, g, t)$. The initial equilibrium in the economy is the point a where output is y_0^* and the price level is P_0^e. When the supply shock occurs, the aggregate supply curve shifts to AS_1, and the expectations-augmented aggregate supply curve shifts with it to EAS_0^1. There is no monetary policy reaction, and the economy settles at point b, with a price level of P_1 and an output level of y_1.

If, in the next period, unlike the case of the OPEC oil price shock, the aggregate supply shock disappears, so that the economy reverts to its normal position on the aggregate supply curve AS_0, with the expectations-augmented aggregate supply curve EAS_0^0, the economy will return to the full-employment point a from which it started. Thus, following Monetarist policy in the face of an aggregate supply shock leads to a movement in output and the price level in opposite directions to each other. This is the phenomenon sometimes called *stagflation*. That is, the economy stagnates and inflates at the same time. It is to avoid stagflation in the face of an aggregate supply shock that some economists advocate adjusting the money supply to accommodate the supply shock. Let us now see what will happen if we follow this Keynesian policy.

D. Consequences of Keynesian Policy

Figure 38.6 illustrates the analysis. Again, suppose the economy starts out at point a on the aggregate demand curve $AD(M_0, g, t)$ and the aggregate supply curve AS_0, with the expectations-augmented aggregate supply curve EAS_0^0. As before, let there be a shock to aggregate supply which moves the aggregate supply curve to AS_1, and

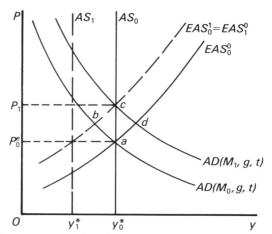

Figure 38.6   *The Consequences of Following Keynesian Monetary Policy Advice in the Event of a Supply Shock — Avoiding Stagflation*

In the same situation as analysed in Fgure 38.5, the Keynesian advice is to raise the money supply, thereby raising aggregate demand from $AD(M_0, g, t)$ to $AD(M_1, g, t)$. This would move the economy to point c (full employment with a price level P_1). What happens in the next period depends on what the government does and what it is expected to do. A fully anticipated return of the money stock to its initial level will return the economy to its initial positition a. A fully anticipated maintenance of the money stock at its new level will keep the economy at point c. If the money stock is expected to fall back to the original position, but actually stays at the new position, the economy will go to d, and if finally the money stock is lowered to its original level, but unexpectedly so, the economy will go to b.

---

the expectations-augmented aggregate supply curve to EAS_0^1. Keynesian policy would counter this drop in aggregate supply by raising the money supply. The Keynesian response would be to raise the money supply to (say) M_1, such that the aggregate demand curve shifts to the curve labelled $AD(M_1, g, t)$. The new equilibrium would then be at point c, with the output level at y_0^* as originally, but with the price level at P_1. If, in the next period, the aggregate supply shock disappeared and the economy reverted to its normal aggregate supply curve AS_0, then one of *four* possibilities arises. First, if the money supply is returned to its original level $AD(M_0, g, t)$ and if everyone expects that to happen, the economy will return to the original position a. Secondly, if the money supply is kept at its higher level M_1 and, again, if everyone anticipates that that will happen, the economy will stay at point c, but the expectations-augmented aggregate supply curve EAS_0^1 will become EAS_1^0, being the expectations-augmented aggregate supply curve drawn for a value of the money stock equal to M_1 with the aggregate supply curve at AS_0. Thirdly, and fourthly, if there is confusion in the minds of economic agents as to whether the monetary authorities will revert to the original money supply or stay with the new money supply, then the expectations-augmented aggregate supply curve will be located somewhere in between positions a and c on the AS_0 curve, and the economy will experience an output boom if the money supply stays at M_1, or an output slump if the money supply is returned to M_0. The price level will be between P_0^e and P_1. At the extremes, if the money supply was expected to revert to M_0, but in fact remained at M_1, the economy would move to point d, and if the money supply was expected to remain at M_1, but in fact reverted to M_0, the economy would move to point b. Thus,

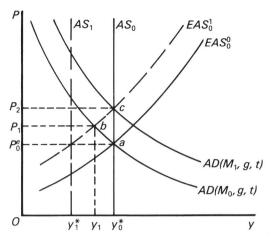

Figure 38.7   *The Consequences of Following Keynesian Monetary Policy Advice in the Event of a Supply Shock with an Information Lag*

The economy is subjected to exactly the same shock as in the previous figures. Since there is a one-period policy response lag, in the first period of the shock the economy behaves in the same way as it would under a Monetarist rule. It moves from *a* to *b*. If the monetary authority now stimulates demand, and if people know that a Keynesian policy is being pursued and therefore expect this policy response, the price level will rise to P_2 and output return to y_0^* in the next period. Thus, the behaviour of real output is identical in the Keynesian case to the Monetarist case, but the price level is more variable under a Keynesian rule.

---

following Keynesian policy advice in the face of an aggregate supply shock leads to inflation initially, with no drop in output and employment. In the next period, whether inflation falls and/or output falls, rises, or stays at its full-employment level turns on what the expected and actual money supplies are. But note that the Keynesian policy of adjusting the money supply so as to accommodate the supply shock avoids the reduction in output generated by following the Monetarist policy, but only at the expense of higher inflation.

E. Consequences of Keynesian Policy with an Information Lag

Next, consider what would happen in the case of following a Keynesian policy with an information lag. Suppose a Keynesian policy is adopted with a one-period reaction lag to the aggregate supply shock. Figure 38.7 illustrates this. Again, let the economy begin at position *a* on the aggregate demand curve $AD(M_0, g, t)$, the expectations-augmented aggregate supply curve EAS_0^0, and the aggregate supply curve AS_0. Then let there be an aggregate supply shock shifting the aggregate supply curve to AS_1 and the expectations-augmented aggregate supply curve to EAS_0^1. Since this is a random shock which no one has been able to predict, the economy will move to position *b*, with an output level of y_1 and a price level of P_1. *This is exactly the response resulting from following the Monetarist policy rule.* Next, suppose that in the following period the central bank reacts to this cut in aggregate output by raising the money supply to M_1. Provided that everyone correctly anticipates this monetary policy reaction, this will put the economy back at the full-employment output level, but at the higher price level P_2, at position c. *Thus, with a one-period information lag, a Keynesian stabilisation policy in the face of an aggregate supply shock leads to exactly the same path for output as occurs under the Monetarist policy, but the price level has a different behaviour. With the Monetarist policy the price level returns to its original level, but with the Keynesian policy the price level rises to P_2.*

F. The Monetarist–Keynesian Dispute: A Presumption in Favour of Monetarism

Exactly the same considerations are relevant in judging the appropriateness of Keynesian and Monetarist policy responses to an aggregate supply shock as were relevant in the case of an aggregate demand shock. There is now, however, an additional reason for suspecting that a Keynesian policy will be difficult to carry out. You have already seen in the previous chapter that a Keynesian policy requires a great deal of information. It requires information about the magnitude of the aggregate demand shocks. You now see that to pursue appropriate aggregate supply corections, it is necessary to have good information about aggregate supply shocks as well. It will be apparent that if *both* of these types of shocks occur simultaneously, it will be necessary for the monetary authorities to have the ability to disentangle the separate shocks that are affecting the economy and to offset both of them in the appropriate way and with greater speed than the private sector can react to them.

Further, if the private sector learns that the public sector is going to react to aggregate supply shocks and if the private sector has as much information as the central bank does concerning those shocks, then the central bank's reaction will always be built into the private sector's expectations, and the central bank's actions themselves will result exclusively in price level variability.

Thus, *the Monetarists' key objection to Keynesian policies is that they do not improve the performance of the economy as regards the behaviour of output and they unambiguously make the price level less stable and predictable than would a Monetarist policy.*

SUMMARY

A. Effects of Supply Shocks

A negative aggregate supply shock lowers the amount of output which can be produced at each level of labour input. It also lowers the marginal productivity of labour and shifts the demand for labour curve downwards. The new equilibrium in the labour market following a negative aggregate supply shock is one with a lower real wage and a lower level of employment. There may be a temporary rise in the measured unemployment rate as people who were previously in employment seek alternative occupations. The aggregate supply curve shifts leftwards, partly as a result of the production function shift, and partly as a result of the reduced equilibrium level of employment.

B. Expectations-Augmented Aggregate Supply Curve and the Expectation of the Aggregate Supply Curve

The expectations-augmented aggregate supply curve traces the amount of aggregate supply as the price level varies for a given expected price level. The expectation of the aggregate supply curve refers to the vertical aggregate supply curve, which traces the quantity which will be supplied at each price level when that price level is fully expected. The expectation of that vertical aggregate supply curve refers to its position in normal or usual periods, when aggregate supply shocks are zero.

C. Consequences of Monetarist Policy

A random negative shock to aggregate supply with a fixed money supply will lower the level of output and raise the price level in the period in which the aggregate supply shock occurs. The level of employment will fall. The economy will experience stagflation.

D. Consequences of Keynesian Policy

Keynesian policy in the face of a negative aggregate supply shock would be to stimulate demand by raising the money supply. Perfectly conducted, this would have the effect of leaving output and employment unchanged, but raising the price level.

E. Consequences of Keynesian Policy with an Information Lag

If a Keynesian policy is followed, but with a one-period lag in the receipt of information concerning the aggregate supply shock, the economy would respond in exactly the same way under a Keynesian policy as it would have done under a Monetarist policy. If, using a Keynesian policy, the monetary authorities stimulate demand with a one-period lag and if everyone correctly anticipates this, there will be a rise in the price level, but no output effect in the second period.

F. The Monetarist–Keynesian Dispute: A Presumption in Favour of Monetarism

The essence of the dispute between Keynesians and Monetarists concerning the appropriate response to aggregate supply shocks is exactly the same as that discussed in the previous chapter concerning aggregate demand shocks. The issue turns on who gets information fastest and who can react fastest to new information. If the central bank has no superior information, then the use of Keynesian policies to correct aggregate supply shocks will leave the behaviour of output unaffected and will produce a greater degree of price level variability than will the pursuit of a Monetarist rule.

Review Questions

1. Explain why an aggregate supply shock shifts the short-run aggregate production function.

2. Trace the effects of an aggregate supply shock on the labour market and on the aggregate supply curve.

3. What is the distinction between the expectations-augmented aggregate supply curve and the expectation of the aggregate supply curve?

4. How does the expectations-augmented aggregate supply curve shift in the event of a negative aggregate supply shock?

5. Work out, using the appropriate diagrams, the effects of pursuing a Monetarist policy in the face of a temporary (one period only), but unpredictable, drop in aggregate supply.

6. For the same shock as in Question 5, work out the effects of pursuing a Keynesian policy.

7. Contrast the output and price level paths in your answers to Questions 5 and 6.

8.   If there was a previously unpredictable but, once occurred, known to be *permanent* shock to aggregate supply, what would happen to output and the price level, if the authorities adopted:
      (a) a Monetarist policy
      (b) a Keynesian policy?

9.   If a negative aggregate supply shock was always responded to with a rise in the money supply, and a positive aggregate demand shock was responded to with an unchanged money supply, what would the path of the inflation rate be like? (This is a tougher question than the others.)

39

Fiscal Policy

This chapter examines how *fiscal policy* affects the level of output, employment, unemployment, the real wage, the money wage, and the price level. You will be aware that there is a great deal of popular discussion concerning the desirability of alternative government spending and tax policy changes. The chapter is designed to help you to understand and evaluate this discussion. Your tasks are to:

A. **understand the key differences between the Monetarist and Keynesian policy recommendations concerning fiscal policy;**

B. **understand the distinction between anticipated and unanticipated fiscal policy;**

C. **know how output, employment, unemployment, the real wage, money wage, and price level are affected by an anticipated change in government expenditures;**
and

D. **know how output, employment, unemployment, the real wage, money wage, and price level are affected by an unanticipated change in government expenditures.**

A. Keynesian and Monetarist Fiscal Policy Advice

The Keynesian and Monetarist disagreement concerning the appropriate use of fiscal policy is much like their disagreement over monetary policy.

(i) Keynesian Fiscal Policy Advice

Keynesians recommend that:
   (a) *when output is* **below** *its full-employment level,* either

542

     (i)   *raise government expenditures*; or

    (ii)   *cut taxes*; or

   (iii)   *raise government expenditures and cut taxes together.*

  (b) when output is **above** *its full-employment level*, either,

     (i)   *cut government expenditures*; or

    (ii)   *raise taxes*; or

   (iii)   *cut government expenditures and raise taxes together.*

Keynesians also tend to favour a political constitution which gives centralised fiscal control so as to facilitate active fiscal policy changes.

(ii) Monetarist Fiscal Policy Advice

Monetarists disagree profoundly with the Keynesian fiscal policy advice. They say that government expenditures should be set at a level that is determined with reference to the requirements of *economic efficiency* rather than with reference to *macroeconomic stability*.

    (a) Government Expenditures: *Monetarists* recommend that *government expenditure should be set at a level such that the marginal utility derived from public expenditures per pound spent is equal to the marginal utility derived from private expenditures per pound spent.* (Recall your microeconomic analysis of the optimum allocation of a consumer's budget. Monetarists assert that the same considerations that apply to an individual's budget allocation are relevant for the allocation of resources between the public and private sector.) If the marginal utility per pound spent on government goods is greater than the marginal utility per pound spent on private goods, then government expenditures are too low and private expenditures are too high, and there is a need to re-allocate resources away from the private sector and towards the government sector — to increase public expenditures. Conversely, if the marginal utility per pound spent on private expenditures is greater than the marginal utility per pound spent by the government, then the government sector is too big, and there is a need to reduce government spending so that private spending may be increased. Monetarists would therefore begin by looking at the marginal utility per pound spent on such items as national defence, law and order, education, health services, and all the other things purchased directly by government and would compare these with the marginal utility per pound of private expenditures. Monetarists assert that government expenditures should be set with reference to this economic efficiency criterion only.

    Monetarists — or at least some of them — go on to point out that there is a problem arising from an imperfection in the political marketplace. They point out that there appears to be a tendency for the interaction of politicians, the bureaucracy, and the electorate to generate a level of government expenditures which exceeds the efficient level. That is, there is a tendency for government expenditures to rise quickly relative to private expenditures, pushing the marginal utility per pound spent on goods bought by the government to levels increasingly below those in the private sector. They therefore advocate a constitutional limitation on the fraction of aggregate output which may be spent by the government. Further, Monetarists tend to favour political constitutions which have decentralised federal and local fiscal authorities, so that those who levy taxes and spend on public consumption are not too distant from the people they represent and also so as to encourage competition between jurisdictions.

To summarise: *Monetarists advocate setting the level of government expenditures on considerations of economic efficiency and independently of the state of the aggregate level of output, employment, unemployment, or prices.* There is a presumption that government expenditures should be held to a steady fraction of aggregate output.

(b) **Taxes:**   *Monetarists recommend that taxes be set at a level which enables the government to buy the utility-maximising volume of public goods and services and maintain a constant money supply growth rate.*

This policy recommendation follows directly from the Monetarist view about the appropriate government spending policy and money supply policy. Recall that the government is constrained by the budget equation:

$$g - t^* = q \, \frac{M}{P} \, \mu$$

Also recall from Chapter 37 that the Monetarists' advice on the money supply growth rate, μ, is that it should be set at a constant and steady value. One possible value would be zero, but usually Monetarists recommend that μ should be set equal to the rate of growth of output so that the level of prices (recalling the fundamental inflation equation) is constant. Since Monetarists recommend that government expenditures be set equal to their utility-maximising level (independently of the state of the macroeconomy) and that the money supply should grow at a steady rate (independently of the state of the macroeconomy), it follows that they want to see the level of legislated taxes set such that these other two objectives may be met. In other words, for Monetarists, taxes and government expenditures go together. Both need to be set at levels such that an efficient allocation of resources between the government and private sector is achieved and, further, so that the money supply growth rate stays at a constant zero inflation rate.

You see, then, that as in the case of monetary policy, Keynesians advocate that fiscal policy be used in an active manner to raise output if it is below its full-employment level and to lower it if it is above its full-employment level, whereas Monetarists recommend that policy be set steady independently of fluctuations in the level of output and the other macroeconomic variables.

B. Anticipated and Unanticipated Fiscal Policy

The distinction between anticipated and unanticipated fiscal policy is directly analogous to the distinction between anticipated and unanticipated changes in the money supply. The level of government expenditures g in any year is equal to the value in the previous year $g_{(-1)}$, plus the change between the previous year and the current year Δg. That is,

$$g = g_{(-1)} + \Delta g$$

The change in government expenditures Δg can be decomposed into the change that was anticipated, Δg^a, and the component that was unanticipated, Δg^u. That is,

$$\Delta g = \Delta g^a + \Delta g^u$$

The same distinction applies to taxes as well.

C. Effects of Anticipated Change in Government Expenditures

(i) The Effects on Output and the Price Level

The effects of a fully anticipated change in government expenditures will be analysed by working out first of all its effects on output and the price level. After that, the implications of those effects for changes in the labour market variables (employment, unemployment, the real and money wages) will be worked out. Figure 39.1 will be used to illustrate the analysis. Suppose that the money supply is fixed at M_0 and the level of government expenditures is initially at g_0 and taxes at t_0. This means that the aggregate demand curve will be the solid curve labelled $AD(M_0, g_0, t_0)$. The rational expectation of the price level, given this aggregate demand level, will be P_0^e. That is the price level where the aggregate demand curve cuts the aggregate supply curve. The expectations-augmented aggregate supply curve EAS_0 cuts the aggregate supply curve at this same point. The economy will initially be at full-employment equilibrium so that the actual price level is equal to the expected price level P_0^e and the actual level of output is y^*.

Now suppose there is a fully anticipated rise in government expenditures. Further, suppose that there is a matching fully anticipated rise in taxes, so that there is a balanced budget multiplier shift in the aggregate demand curve. (If you are not sure about this, check back to Chapter 22.) If government spending was to rise without a rise in taxes, then it would be necessary to raise the rate of money supply growth, and that would generate inflation. It would not be impossible to analyse this case, but the balanced budget fiscal policy is easier to analyse.

Suppose that the balanced budget increase in government expenditures and taxes is such as to shift the aggregate demand curve to the broken line labelled $AD(M_0, g_1, t_1)$. With the money supply being held constant at M_0, but with government expenditures and taxes raised to g_1 and t_1 respectively, the aggregate demand curve has shifted rightwards. Also, recall that the rise in government expenditures to g_1 is assumed to be fully anticipated. This means that all economic agents will be aware that government expenditures have increased to g_1. Everyone will be aware, therefore, that the price level is going to rise because the new aggregate demand curve is to the right of the original one. The new rational expectation of the price level will be calculated as P_1^e. This is the price level where the new aggregate demand curve cuts the aggregate supply curve. A new expectations-augmented aggregate supply curve (the broken line labelled EAS_1) will be located so that it goes through the point where the new aggregate demand curve cuts the aggregate supply curve.

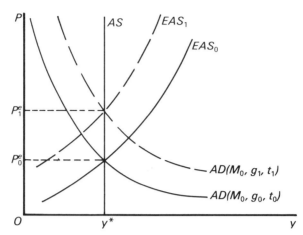

Figure 39.1 *The Effects of an Anticipated Change in Government Expenditures and Taxes on the Level of Output and Prices*

A fully anticipated rise in government spending and taxes with a constant money stock will raise the price level and leave real output undisturbed.

You can now read off directly the effects of a fully anticipated rise in government expenditures on output and the price level. If the levels of government expenditures and taxes *actually* rise to g_1 and t_1, so that the actual aggregate demand curve becomes the same broken curve $AD(M_0, g_1, t_1)$, then the level of prices will be equal to the rational expectation of the price level, namely, P_1^e, and output will remain at its full-employment level y^*.

You can see then at *a fully anticipated rise in government expenditures (matched by a fully anticipated rise in taxes) will raise the price level and leave the level of output unchanged*.

(ii) The Effects on the Labour Market

It is a trivial matter to work out the effects of a fully anticipated rise in government spending (matched by a tax rise) on the labour market variables. Since output has not changed, neither will employment, unemployment, nor the real wage have changed. Since the price level has gone up, so must the money wage rate have risen. The money wage rate will rise by the same percentage amount as the rise in the price level, thereby leaving the real wage unchanged.

That is all there is to the effects of a fully anticipated rise in government expenditures.

There is, however, a *very important caveat*. You should be aware that the analysis which has just been performed is based on the assumption that the extra taxes raised in the experiment are non-distorting. That is, that they are of a form that does not affect the supply of, or demand for, labour. If there were changes in such taxes as income or payroll taxes, there would be further important effects on employment and the real wage to take into account. These in turn would lead to a different response of output to that worked out above. In fact, if higher taxes shifted the labour supply curve to the left, the levels of output and employment would *fall*, and the price level would rise by even more than that shown in Figure 39.1. This is the essence of the *supply-side* analysis of some economists in the US who support the Reagan tax-cut programme. They argue that by *cutting* taxes and government spending, in a predictable, i.e., fully anticipated way, the supply of labour will rise, output and employment will rise, and the inflation rate (the price level in the analysis here) will fall. You can easily see the logic of that view in this model. How important such incentive effects of tax changes are is a controversial and not well-established matter.

(iii) Random Shocks and Policy Responses

If there was a random shock to aggregate demand or to aggregate supply such as discussed in Chapters 37 and 38, it would not be possible to offset those random shocks with a fully anticipated change in government expenditures. Any fully anticipated fiscal policy action would be fully allowed for by private economic agents in forming their own rational expectations and would leave the level of output undisturbed. Therefore, fully anticipated fiscal policy changes cannot be used to stabilise the level of output, employment, and unemployment in the face of random shocks. They only have price level effects.

Let us now go on to analyse the effects of an unanticipated change in government expenditures.

D. Effects of Unanticipated Change in Government Expenditures

(i) The Effects on Output and the Price Level

To analyse the effects of an unanticipated change in government expenditures, let us again begin by working out its effects on the level of output and the price level. Also, let us begin at the same point as before. Figure 39.2 will illustrate the analysis. The economy initially has a money supply M_0 and government spending level g_0 and taxes t_0, so that the aggregate demand curve is the continuous line $AD(M_0, g_0, t_0)$. The aggregate supply curve is AS and equilibrium is at the full-employment output level y^* and the actual and rationally expected price level of P_0^e. Suppose that all economic agents anticipate that government expenditures, taxes, and the money supply will be maintained at their initial levels of g_0, t_0, and M_0 respectively. Suppose, however, that instead of doing the expected, the government unexpectedly increased its expenditures and taxes by equal amounts to g_1 and t_1 respectively. With equal unexpected rises in government expenditures and taxes, the central bank will maintain the money supply constant at the initial level of M_0. The unanticipated rise in government expenditures and the equal unanticipated rise in taxes will shift the aggregate demand curve outwards to the curve $AD(M_0, g_1, t_1)$. Since this shift is unanticipated, the expectations-augmented aggregate supply curve remains the curve EAS_0. The new equilibrium is obtained at the point at which the new aggregate demand curve $AD(M_0, g_1, t_1)$ cuts the expectations-augmented aggregate supply curve EAS_0. You can read off this new solution as the price level P_1 and the output level y_1 in Figure 39.2.

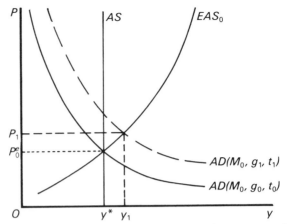

Figure 39.2   *The Effects of an Unanticipated Change in Government Expenditures and Taxes on the Level of Output and Prices*

An unanticipated rise in government spending and taxes with a constant money supply will raise both output and prices.

You can now easily see the effects of an unanticipated rise in government expenditures (matched by an equal tax rise).

An unanticipated rise in government expenditures (matched by an unanticipated tax rise to maintain a balanced budget) will raise the level of output and raise the price level.

We could easily reverse the above experiment and consider an unanticipated cut in government expenditures (matched by a tax cut to maintain a balanced budget), and, of course, this would lead to a fall in both output and the price level.

(ii) The Effects on the Labour Market

It is now possible to work out the effects of these unanticipated changes in government expenditures on the labour market variables. Let us consider for illustrative purposes an unanticipated *rise* in government expenditures. (You can work out the effects of an unanticipated *fall* for yourself.)

Since an unanticipated rise in government spending raises output, it follows immediately that it must also raise the level of employment. You can read this off by considering Figure 29.2 in Chapter 29. Further, since the level of employment rises, the level of unemployment falls below its natural level. In order to induce a rise in employment, firms must willingly hire the additional labour and still be maximising profits. This implies that the real wage must fall. The real wage falls only if the money wage rises by less than the rise in the price level. This therefore is a further implication of the analysis concerning the effects of an unanticipated change in government spending.

To summarise the effects of an unanticipated rise in government spending on the labour market variables: *an unanticipated rise in government expenditures (matched by an unanticipated tax rise) will raise the level of employment, lower the level of unemployment, lower the real wage, and lead to a rise in the money wage, but by a smaller percentage amount than the rise in the price level.*

(iii) Random Shocks and Policy Responses

You see, then, that an unanticipated change in government expenditures is capable of moving the level of aggregate output and employment around. It is possible to stimulate demand and raise output with an unanticipated rise in government spending and to cut back on output with an unanticipated cut in government spending.

It follows, therefore, that an unanticipated change in fiscal policy could be used to offset a random shock to either aggregate demand or aggregate supply. However, exactly the same considerations which were discussed in Chapters 37 and 38 concerning monetary policy apply here. If the government can change its expenditures (and taxes) quickly enough to offset shocks which private agents know have occurred, but which they are contractually unable to respond to, then it would be possible to use fiscal policy along the lines suggested by Keynesians to reduce the amount of variability in economic activity. However, if government expenditure and tax changes can only be engineered slowly and no more quickly than private contracts can be renegotiated, then there is no scope for government expenditure and tax variations to do anything other than lead to price level variability. Because of the legislative and bureaucratic lags in the enactment and implementation of fiscal policy changes, many Keynesians are now coming to the view that fiscal policy is not a useful stabilisation weapon and are placing more emphasis on active variations in the money supply as the appropriate way of stabilising the economy.

There is a further reason for concern over the use of fiscal policy as a stabilising device. This concerns its inflationary consequences. Throughout the exercises conducted in this chapter it has been supposed that the inflation rate was being held at zero, with the money supply growth rate held at the output growth rate (in the case of this model, both zero). If, starting from an initial situation of zero inflation, there was to be a permanent rise in government expenditures, with a permanent commitment not to change taxes, then we know that the money supply would eventually have to start growing at a faster rate. This means that the aggregate demand curve would begin to shift upwards continuously. Also, the expectations-augmented aggregate supply curve would shift upwards continuously as rational agents would continuously revise their price level expectations upwards. Provided the money supply growth was fully anticipated, these two curves would move up at the same pace as each other, with inflation ensuing. With a fully anticipated inflation, the economy would stay at full employment. It is unlikely, however, that the money supply growth rate would be fully anticipated. The money supply growth rate could be either above or below its anticipated level. This being the case, there could either be an output boom or an output slump (stagflation) as the inflation rate increased. Either of these effects is possible, depending on whether the money supply growth accompanying a fiscal policy change is under- or over-anticipated.

There is a final rather subtle argument concerning fiscal policy that arises from our analysis of the rational expectations theory of the open economy operating under fixed exchange rates (Chapter 32). As we noted earlier, the entire discussion of policy in this section has dealt with an economy operating under flexible exchange rates so that there is sufficient room for manoeuvre in the pursuit of an independent monetary and fiscal policy. An interesting asymmetry of information arises, however, in the case of a fixed exchange rate economy. In the fixed exchange rate case, the authorities gather information continuously on the country's stock of foreign exchange reserves. This information, not available to people in general as quickly as it is to the authorities, provides information about the shocks that are hitting the economy. For example, an unexpected drop in foreign exchange reserves would signify that one of the variables on which the demand for money depends has unexpectedly changed. Such information might be exploitable by the authorities simply because they know something that no one else knows. Notice that the case of a flexible exchange rate economy does not produce this informational asymmetry. In the case of a flexible exchange rate economy the value of the foreign exchange rate becomes a random variable that responds to the many shocks that are hitting the economy. Movements in the exchange rate certainly can be exploited (as we saw in Chapter 32) to make inferences about what those shocks might be. The authorities have no advantage over ordinary people, however, in this respect. The question arises: Is it possible under a fixed exchange rate regime for the authorities to use their informational advantage — their knowledge of the stock of foreign exchange reserves — to intervene actively and produce a superior performance for output and prices to that which would be achieved by following fixed rules of the Monetarist type? The answer to this question seems likely to be negative. First, it should be remembered that, under a fixed exchange rate there is little scope for an independent monetary policy. This means that any actions that are to be taken to influence the economy will have to be fiscal actions. In the nature of things, fiscal policy actions take time to agree upon and implement and, by the time they are implemented would be widely anticipated and therefore of negligible value in affecting the course of real variables. Under a regime where policy actions that affect aggregate demand can be taken swiftly — monetary policy actions — the exchange rate is flexible and the informational advantage to the authorities is lost. Thus, although there certainly is an informational advantage to the authorities operating under a fixed exchange rate regime, that informational advantage does not appear to be one that can be exploited to achieve a more desirable performance of output and unemployment.

SUMMARY

A. Keynesian and Monetarist Fiscal Policy

Keynesians recommend the active use of variations in government spending and taxes to raise demand when output is below its full-employment level and to lower demand when output is above its full-employment level.

Monetarists urge the maintaining of a steady fiscal policy that is dictated by resource allocation considerations between the public and private sector, and not by economic stabilisation considerations. They advocate a level of government spending consistent with an optimal division of resources between the government and private sector, and a level of taxes such that the money supply growth target which they advocate may be achieved.

B. Anticipated and Unanticipated Fiscal Policy

Just as in the case of monetary policy, a change in government expenditures or taxes may be decomposed into that part which was anticipated and that part which was unanticipated. The unanticipated change in government spending and taxes is simply the actual change minus the change that was anticipated. When there is no unanticipated change, fiscal policy is fully anticipated.

C. Effects of Anticipated Change in Government Expenditures

A fully anticipated rise in government expenditures matched by an equal fully anticipated tax rise will raise the price level and raise the money wage by the same percentage amount as each other. It will leave the level of output, employment, unemployment, and the real wage unchanged. These predictions assume *neutral* tax changes.

D. Effects of Unanticipated Change in Government Expenditures

An unanticipated rise in government expenditures matched by an equal unanticipated tax rise will raise the level of output and the price level. It will also raise the level of employment and the money wage. However, the money wage will not rise by as much as the price level, and the real wage will fall. There will also be a fall in the unemployment rate.

Exactly the same considerations apply to evaluating the appropriateness of alternative fiscal policies as were discussed in Chapters 37 and 38 concerning monetary policies. That material should be studied carefully and its relevance to the fiscal policy debate understood.

Review Questions

1. Outline the key disagreements between Keynesians and Monetarists regarding fiscal policy.

2. What criterion does the Monetarist use for determining whether or not additional government spending is recommended? What criterion does the typical Keynesian policy adviser use?

3. Why is it that some Monetarists feel there should be a constitutional limitation on the fraction of GNP which may be spent by the government?

4. What are the implications, in terms of the government's budget deficit, of following a Monetarist rule of setting the rate of growth of the money supply equal to the rate of growth of output?

5. Suppose there is a random shock to aggregate demand. Work out, using the appropriate diagrams:
    (i) the consequences for real income, the price level, and the levels of employment, unemployment, and real wages of adopting a Monetarist fiscal policy;
    (ii) the consequences for real income, the price level, and the levels of employment, unemployment, and real wages of adopting a Keynesian fiscal policy; and
    (iii) the consequences for real income, the price level, and the levels of employment, unemployment, and real wages of adopting a Keynesian policy with a one-period lag in changing government spending and/or taxes.

6. Suppose there is a fully anticipated rise in government expenditure not matched by a tax rise. Suppose further that initially the inflation rate was zero. Trace out the future time path of the inflation rate following this policy change.

7. Suppose there is a rise in government expenditure, not matched by a tax rise, which at first is unanticipated, but which is maintained and subsequently becomes anticipated. Trace out the time path which will be followed by the rate of inflation, output, and unemployment.

40

Prices and Incomes Policies

The emergence of rapid inflation combined with high unemployment rates has led, in the post-war years, to a search for new anti-inflation policies.

You already know from your understanding of macroeconomic theory that it is possible to reduce the rate of inflation by reducing the growth rate of the money supply. You also know that, provided the reduction in the growth rate of the money supply is fully anticipated, inflation will fall without causing a recession — without causing a drop in output and a rise in unemployment. However, it is practically impossible for the central bank to engineer a cut in the money supply growth rate that is fully anticipated. Simply to announce a cut is not sufficient. People have to see before they believe. This means that, while the central bank is convincing people of its intentions to lower the money supply growth rate, there will be a tendency for the actual money supply growth rate to be below the anticipated growth rate. In other words, the money supply will be below its anticipated level. As you know, the consequence of this is that the actual price level will be below the expected price level, and the actual level of output below the full-employment level.

Although not necessarily rationalised in this way, it is to avoid the problem of paying the price of higher unemployment in exchange for a lower rate of inflation that new anti-inflation policies have been searched for. The major alternative 'new' policy, which has been widely advocated and used throughout the post-war years, is that of prices and incomes policy — sometimes alternatively and more precisely called wage and price controls.

The United Kingdom and other Western European countries were among the first to embark upon such policies after World War II. In the United Kingdom there have now been eleven distinct episodes of prices and incomes policies. The United States has had three such policies in the post-war years — the Kennedy guideposts, the Nixon controls, and the Carter controls.

Although viewed by their supporters as sophisticated 'new' weapons, wage and price controls are perhaps better described as blunt old instruments.

One of the earliest recorded episodes of wage and price controls was in 301 A.D., when the Roman Emperor Diocletian, in his famous Edict sought to control the prices on 900 commodities, 130 different classes of labour, and a large number of freight rates. Penalties for the violation of Diocletian's controls ran all the way to death. Controls have been used on and off ever since that time (and possibly in earlier times as well).

It is clear, then, that the controls are certainly an old and not a new idea. The view that they are a blunt instrument rather than a sophisticated weapon will take the rest of this chapter to develop. However, as a prelude to that, let us summarise what we think is a reasonable attitude towards controls in the following way:

> [T]he so-called 'new' policies are the oldest and crudest, best likened to medieval medicine based on ignorance and misunderstanding of the fundamental processes at work and more likely to kill the patient than to cure him.
> It was not until relatively recently in the long sweep of human history, in the 17th and 18th centuries, that the principles governing the determination of the general level of prices were made clear. The insights of Bodin and Hume and the refinements which have followed through the work and writings of Irving Fisher, Wicksell, Keynes and modern monetary theorists, such as Milton Friedman, are critical for understanding and influencing the monetary forces which determine the general level of prices [and] the rate of inflation.
> (Michael Parkin, *The Illusion of Wage and Price Controls*, The Fraser Institute, Vancouver, 1976, pp.101–2.)

The new policies for controlling inflation, then, *are monetary policies*. There has been no essential technical advance in this field since the eighteenth century. There have been some refinements, but the fundamental ideas developed by Bodin and Hume remain the theoretical underpinnings of any successful anti-inflationary policy. The rest of this chapter is designed to help you understand and appreciate this.

You have five tasks. They are to:
A. **know the main features of the content of a prices and incomes policy;**
B. **understand the distinction between a posted price and an actual price;**
C. **understand why wage and price controls do not affect the expected price level;**
D. **understand why wage and price controls do not affect the actual price level;** and
E. **understand why wage and price controls can only make matters worse.**

A. Content of a Prices and Incomes Policy

A prices and incomes policy typically has three sets of features:
   (i) a set of rules about wages, prices, and, sometimes, profits;
   (ii) a set of penalties for a violation of the rules; and
   (iii) a monitoring agency.

(i) Rules

The rules concerning wages and prices typically centre on the average allowable rate of increase of wages. There are usually exceptions clauses, typically dealing with the wages of lower paid workers. Sometimes the price rule employed takes the form of a maximum allowed rate of price rise. More often, however, it is couched in terms of a restriction allowing prices to rise only by an amount sufficient to cover the increased costs that arise from labour cost increases allowable under the wage rule.

Profit rules are more complex, both to state and to administer, and are often absent. When explicit profit rules are used, they are typically couched in terms of some maximum percentage of a previous period's average profits.

(ii) Penalties

Penalties for violation of the rules vary enormously. In the case of Diocletian's controls, the penalties ran all the way to death. In modern times they typically involve fines and sometimes 'roll-backs' — a requirement that the wage or price be rolled back to the level that it would have been at had the rules been obeyed.

(iii) Monitoring Agency

Monitoring agencies also vary enormously. Sometimes a special monitoring agency is set up. In other cases, existing government departments are used to provide the policing and monitoring, and the ordinary courts are used to carry out enforcement.

B. Posted Price and Actual Price

There are many dimensions to a transaction. These many dimensions can, however, be conveniently summarised under three headings. Each transaction has a
  (i) price dimension;
  (ii) quantity dimension; and
  (iii) quality dimension.
That is, when you decide to buy something, you are buying a certain quantity of a commodity of a presumed quality for a certain price. This is true, not only for commodities, but also applies to labour services. You might hire a certain quality of (say) plumber for a certain number of hours for a certain price (i.e. wage).

A wage and price control programme seeks to control directly one dimension of a transaction, namely, the price. In principle, of course, what it is trying to control is the price at which a specific quantity and quality of product or labour service is traded. It is extremely difficult, however, to monitor quantity and quality. Some examples will perhaps help to make this clear.

Suppose that the price dimension of a transaction is policed completely effectively. A good example of that would be the policing of the price of a University Professor working for a British University. Suppose the wage of a University Professor is controlled by a wage control programme and effectively controlled to be below the market equilibrium wage. What will the Professor do in that situation? It is clear that he will seek to maximise his utility by changing either the quality or the quantity of the labour that he supplies, so that the marginal disutility of work is equal to the wage rate paid. If the wage rate being offered is below the market equilibrium wage rate, then he will lower the quantity and/or quality of work below the market equilibrium quantity/quality. Specifically, he will either take more leisure or indulge in more non-teaching, non-research, income-earning activities. The effective price of a unit of professorial services will not have been controlled. The *posted price* will have been controlled fully, but the *actual price* — the price for a specific quality and quantity — will be exactly the same as it would have been in the absence of the controls.

As another example, suppose that to perform some industrial job a certain grade of electrician is required (call it a grade three electrician). Suppose that although a grade three electrician is required to do this particular job, the wages of grade three electricians have been controlled below the equilibrium wage, and a particular firm cannot hire enough of this type of labour. Clearly, what the firm will do is to hire the next, more-expensive grade of electrician (call it grade two — and if necessary, upgrade people to that grade) in order to get the job done and maximise profits. Again, the posted price — the price of a grade three electrician — will have been effectively controlled. However, the actual price paid to a particular individual supplier of effort will not have been controlled. People who otherwise would have been grade three electricians now become grade two electricians, and their wages rise in exactly the same way as they would have done in the absence of controls.

Consider a commodity market. The list price of a car is a posted price. However, as you know, the actual price at which a car gets traded is typically different from the list price, and includes a discount. Precisely what discount is offered is very hard to monitor and police. It is true that a discount is a reduction of the actual price below the posted price. However, if the posted price was controlled below its equilibrium level, then by reducing the size of the discount, the actual price could increase to achieve and maintain market equilibrium. Thus, when posted prices are controlled, the gap between posted prices and actual prices — if actual prices are at a discount — will narrow.

The distinction between posted and actual prices should now be clear from the above examples. The posted price is the visible price, but not necessarily the price at which trades actually take place. It is, of course, the actual price and the average of all actual prices that constitute the general price level, and not the fictitious numbers that are stuck on car windscreens or attached to jobs of specific grades.

Let us now move on to examine the effects of wage and price controls on actual prices. As a prelude to this, however, it is necessary to analyse the effects of controls on *expected* prices.

C. Wage and Price Controls and the Expected Price Level

The most sophisticated advocates of wage and price controls base their belief in the potency of these measures on a view that controls can effectively lower inflationary expectations and, as a result, lower the actual rate of inflation without generating a recession. You already know that if inflationary expectations can indeed be lowered,

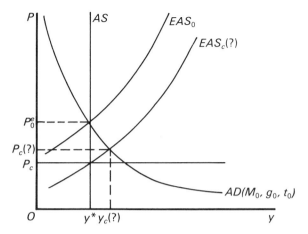

Figure 40.1   *Why Controls do not Lower the Expected Price Level*
If the full-employment equilibrium is y^*, P_0^e, and a price control programme seeks to maintain the price level at no higher than P_c, the expected price level will remain at P_0^e. To see that, notice that if the controlled price level was the expected price level, the *EAS* curve would be $EAS_c(?)$. This would generate a price level of $P_c(?)$. The only expected price level that is rational (that predicts itself) is P_0^e. Thus, controls do not lower the expected price level.

---

then it is possible to lower the inflation rate and even have an output boom while the inflation rate is falling. (Go back to Chapter 29 and study the model shown in Figure 29.3. If the expectations-augmented aggregate supply curve could be lowered while the aggregate demand curve is held constant, then you see that the equilibrium price level falls and equilibrium output rises.)

Let us begin our analysis, then, by working out what the effects of wage and price controls are on the expected price level. *Do wage and price controls lower the expected price level and lower the expectations-augmented aggregate supply curve?*

To analyse this, consider Figure 40.1. The curve $AD(M_0, g_0, t_0)$ is the aggregate demand curve. To focus our attention exclusively on controls, let us hold the level of the money supply and government expenditures and taxes constant at the levels M_0, g_0, and t_0 and, furthermore, suppose that they are fully anticipated. You will recall that this implies that the actual position of the aggregate demand curve and its expected position are one and the same. This assumption enables us to isolate the effects of the controls.

The curve *AS* is the aggregate supply curve generated from equilibrium in the labour market. The expected price level P_0^e is determined by the intersection of the aggregate demand curve and the aggregate supply curve. Through that same point at which the aggregate demand curve cuts the *AS* curve passes the expectations-augmented aggregate supply curve EAS_0. This is the aggregate supply curve drawn for an expected price level of P_0^e which, in turn, is the rational expectation given a money supply of M_0 and a level of government spending of g_0. Let us suppose that the economy is in equilibrium, with the actual price level at P_0^e and the output level at full-employment y^*.

Now suppose the government introduces wage and price controls. Mark on the vertical axis of Figure 40.1 the price level which is implied by the government's control programme. P_c denotes the price level which the government is seeking to achieve with its controls. It is the price level that would emerge if the rules that specify the allowable behaviour of wages and prices in the economy were effectively enforced. So the horizontal line at P_c represents the ceiling which the government would like to enforce on the price level. It is important to recognise that there is a major difference between the government attempting to impose a price ceiling on the general price level and the imposition of a price ceiling on some specific commodity such as, say, flat or house rents. It is imaginable that sufficient resources could be devoted to monitoring and enforcing regulations concerning rent control. However, it is a far cry from being able to control the price level. There are literally trillions of individual prices that make up a modern economy. To monitor, police, and effectively control the actual prices — the actual as opposed to the posted prices — on all the trillions of different kinds of commodities and factor services would almost certainly use up the entire supply of labour and capital in the economy. Private individuals, maximising their utilities and profits, will do the best they can for themselves, subject to the constraints which they face. If, by adjusting the quality dimension of transactions, they can evade without detection the effects of a control on posted prices, then they will find it profitable to do so and, indeed, will do so. There is no presumption, therefore, that the actual price level in the economy will be equal to the price level that would emerge if all the rules that specified the allowable behaviour of wages and prices were followed. Those rules will not be followed, and the price level will be different from the level implied by the exact adherence to those rules. It is possible, of course, that the price level as measured by the economic statisticians will fail to get at the true prices during a period of controls and behave in a way that is not far out of line with the requirements of the controls. That measured price, however, will have no operational significance. It is the actual price level, not the incorrectly measured price level, that is relevant for determining behaviour.

With this in mind, we now want to return to the question, what will be the effects of controls on the expected price level? Specifically, will the price level P_c become the expected price level? Let us conduct a conceptual experiment exactly like the one which we conducted in Chapter 30 when discussing the determination of the rational expectation of the price level. Let us first suppose that the expected price level is indeed the controlled price level P_c. Would this be a rational expectation? If P_c was the expected price level, then the expectations-augmented aggregate supply curve would become the curve $EAS_c(?)$. We have put a $(?)$ after that expectations-augmented aggregate supply curve to remind you that we are conducting a conceptual experiment and we are asking the question, could that be the expectations-augmented aggregate supply curve which is relevant once the controls are imposed? You can see immediately that if the expectations-augmented aggregate supply curve is $EAS_c(?)$ and if the aggregate demand curve remains unchanged (which by assumption it does), then the price level and output level will be determined at $y_c(?)$ and $P_c(?)$. Again, we have put a $(?)$ after these quantities to remind you that they are conceptual experimental values that we are considering and not necessarily actual values that the economy will achieve. Now, recall the concept of a rational expectation. It is the prediction implied by the relevant theory, conditional on all the information available at the time the prediction is made. If the prediction of the theory is that the price level will be $P_c(?)$, it is clear that we cannot have P_c as the rational expectation of the price level. Further, therefore, $EAS_c(?)$ cannot be the relevant expectations-augmented aggregate supply curve. If you follow through the analysis in Section D of Chapter 30 on the determination of the rational expectation of the price level, you will see that there is only one price level which will be rationally expected. That price level is P_0^e. In other words, only the expected price level P_0^e leads to the prediction that the actual price level will be equal to the expected price level; and hence, only the level P_0^e is the rational expectation. It follows, therefore, that the expectations-augmented aggregate supply curve will not move as a consequence of introducing controls and will remain at EAS_0.

Another way of thinking about the above analysis is as follows. Rational economic agents will expect the price level to be determined by the forces that in fact determine the price level, namely, aggregate supply and aggregate demand. Wage and price controls (as a first approximation, to be modified in the final section) will not be expected to have much effect on aggregate supply. Further, again as a first approximation to be modified in the final section, controls will not affect the money supply or the level of government expenditures, so aggregate demand will be unaffected. Holding all these things constant, nothing that the controls have introduced would lead any rational person to expect that the actual price level would change as a result of the imposition of the controls. Hence, the rational person will expect the price level to be exactly the same with controls in place as without them. (The above remarks are to be interpreted as applying only if there is indeed no expectation that either aggregate supply AS, the money supply, or government spending are going to be changed *as a consequence of* the introduction of controls. The possible effects of controls on these variables will be analysed in the final section.)

D. Wage and Price Controls and the Actual Price Level

You have now seen that the rational expectations theory of output and the price level predicts that the introduction of wage and price controls will have no effect on the expected price level and no effect on the position of the expectations-augmented aggregate supply curve. It is now a simple matter to analyse the effects of controls on the *actual* price level.

Figure 40.2 illustrates the analysis. The curves AS, $AD(M_0, g_0, t_0)$ and EAS_0 are the relevant aggregate supply, aggregate demand, and expectations-augmented aggregate supply curves in the immediate pre-control situation. The economy is at full-employment output y^*, with the actual and expected price level at P_0^e. Now suppose that wage and price controls are imposed, which would imply, if they were fully observed, a price level of P_c, as shown on the vertical axis of Figure 40.2. What happens to the actual price level in this situation?

Recall that the actual price level is determined at the point of intersection between the expectations-augmented aggregate supply curve and the aggregate demand curve. By the analysis of the preceding section, the controls will not move the expected price level and will not, therefore, move the expectations-augmented aggregate supply curve. The expectations-augmented aggregate supply curve remains at EAS_0.

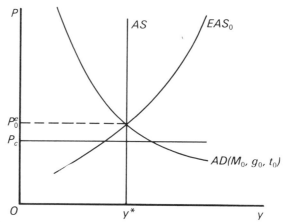

Figure 40.2 *Why Controls do not Lower the Price Level (or the Inflation Rate)*
The imposition of controls does not affect either the *EAS* curve or the *AD* curve. The equilibrium price level is determined at the intersection of those curves and therefore will be independent of the control price level.

Wage and price controls are not monetary policy and are not fiscal policy. As a first approximation, there will be no change in the money supply and no change in government expenditure when the controls are imposed (we will modify this in the next section). Therefore, nothing happens to the aggregate demand curve when we impose controls.

Since nothing happens to the expectations-augmented aggregate supply curve, nor to the aggregate demand curve, it is clear that the point at which these curves intersect remains unchanged. The price level remains at P_0 and the output level remains at y^*. Thus, as a first approximation, *controls have no effect on the actual price level*. They may well control posted prices, and an index of posted prices may not rise by as much as actual prices. Indeed, an index of posted prices may well approximate to P_c for a period. However, the actual price level in the economy will be unaffected, and if the price index is constructed from accurate price sampling, the recorded overall price index will show a price level of P_0^e rather than the controlled price level of P_c.

E. Wage and Price Controls Make Matters Worse

The conclusion of the preceding section is that wage and price controls have no effects. However, there are many reasons for supposing that they will have some effect upon the economy. It is best to regard the conclusion of Section D above as a first approximation rather than as the whole story. Let us now examine some of the possible effects.

First, controls divert real resources from other productive activities. The army of bureaucrats, accountants, lawyers (and even economists!) hired directly and

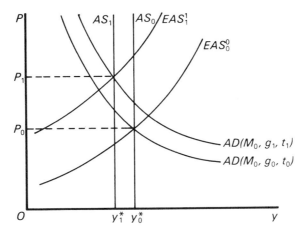

Figure 40.3 *Why Controls Can Only Make Things Worse*

Controls divert resources from productive activity, thereby lowering aggregate supply. They also involve additional government expenditures and taxes to administer the control programme. This raises the aggregate demand curve. The consequence of these two things is to raise the price level and lower output. These effects are probably not large, but they are certainly in the wrong direction.

indirectly by the wage–price monitoring agency could be employed in other productive activities. To the extent that there is a diversion of labour resources from producing goods and services (from producing y), there will be a shift in the aggregate supply available for private and government consumption. You can think of this as a shift in the aggregate supply curve (as illustrated in Figure 40.3) from AS_0 to AS_1. Of course, in asserting that the aggregate supply curve has shifted to the right, we are asserting that the value of the output of the army of bureaucrats, accountants, lawyers, and economists employed in administering the control programme is zero. Just as the price level may very well be incorrectly measured during a period of wage and price controls, so may the value of national income. The national income statisticians would certainly impute a value of output to those employed in administering the wage and price control programme equal to the factor incomes paid to them. In suggesting that income would fall in the event of the diversion of real resources away from productive activities to administering the programme, we are saying that the national income accounts are incorrectly calculated and that the wages of those employed in administering the programme should be regarded as a transfer payment from productive people to those who are unproductive. In this respect, it is no different from other forms of government transfer payments. (Although the remarks made here arise in connection with a discussion of wage and price controls you may reflect on their more general applicability!)

Secondly, a wage and price control programme typically involves additional government expenditures, both on the bureaucratic side and on professional labour hired on a short-term contract basis. Such a rise in government expenditures would lead to a shift in the aggregate demand curve as illustrated, for example, in Figure 40.3, from $AD(M_0, g_0, t_0)$ to $AD(M_0, g_1, t_1)$.

It is clear that the combination of diverting resources from private activities, which lowers the output supplied, and raising government expenditure, which shifts the

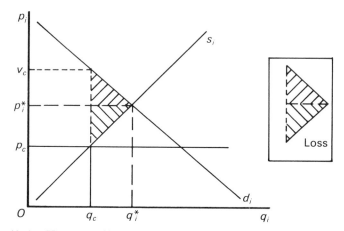

Figure 40.4   *How an Effective Price Control Causes a Loss of Welfare*

If a price control on some particular commodity or group of commodities is effective in holding
the price below the equilibrium level, the value placed upon the commodity at the margin by
the consumer (v_c) exceeds the real cost of production (p_c). A loss of producer and consumer
surplus (the shaded area) results.

aggregate demand curve, exerts separate but reinforcing effects on the price level.
The rightward shift of the aggregate demand curve and the leftward shift of the
aggregate supply curve will both tend to make the price level higher than it would
otherwise have been (and the inflation rate higher than it would otherwise have
been). Also, output will be lower than it would otherwise have been.

It would be wrong to suggest that these effects are likely to be of a large magnitude.
However, they are certainly going to be present in the *directions* indicated in Figure
40.3, and there have been episodes in history when such effects may have been large.

There is a third possible factor to be taken into account. This is the effect of wage
and price controls on monetary policy. With a wage and price control programme in
place to control the inflation rate, it is possible that the central bank and central
government will become less concerned with maintaining anti-inflationary monetary
policy. There may be a temptation to use monetary policy in an attempt to stimulate
aggregate demand while using wage and price controls to keep inflation in check. If
the money supply rises more quickly while the controls are in place, there will be a
tendency for the inflation rate to rise even further than it would have done had there
been no control programme.

A fourth and major consideration concerning the effects of the controls arises from
the fact that some prices are in fact controlled effectively, while others are not. The
overall average effect of controls on the general price level of zero can be seen as
hiding some effective control in some particular areas, with a tendency for demand to
spill over into less controlled areas, where prices will rise to even higher levels than
they would have in the absence of controls. If this happens (and there is good reason
to suppose that it does because of the excessive attention paid by the wage and price
monitoring board to specific sensitive sectors) then there will be some further serious
economic losses inflicted.

Figure 40.4 illustrates the market for some particular good. It could be steel plate
or any other highly visible commodity which the monitoring agency can effectively

and fully control. The price on the vertical axis is the *relative* price of the good in question. This is equal to the money price of the good divided by the price level. That is, $p_i = P_i/P$. The horizontal axis measures the quantity of the good. The curves d_i and s_i are the demand and supply curves (which you develop in your microeconomic theory course). p_i^* and q_i^* are the competitive equilibrium price and quantity respectively. Now suppose that an *effective* price control of p_c is imposed on this particular commodity. Assume that effective policing of quantity and quality ensures that p_c is the actual price, and not just the posted price. It is clear that the quantity supplied will be reduced from q_i^* to q_c as the firms that produce this commodity seek to avoid the heavy losses that would be incurred if they maintained their output at q_i^*. The consumer places a value on the marginal quantity consumed of v_c. That is, the marginal utility of the last unit consumed exceeds the price by the distance $v_c - p_c$. The shaded triangle represents the total loss that results from the imposition of an effective price control of p_c. You can think of the shaded triangle as measuring the total difference between the value placed upon consumption of this commodity and the marginal cost of producing it as we move from the competitive equilibrium position of q_i^* to the controlled position of q_c. There will, in general, be a large number of losses of this kind arising from the unevenness with which wage and price controls are imposed upon the economy.

Overall, then, the effects of wage and price controls which we can detect are all in the direction of either raising prices or lowering output, or lowering economic welfare.

SUMMARY

A. Content of a Prices and Incomes Policy

A prices and incomes policy has three features:
   (i) rules about wages, prices, and profits;
   (ii) sanctions and penalties; and
   (iii) a monitoring agency.

B. Posted Price and Actual Price

A posted price is the published or announced price; an actual price is the price at which a trade actually takes place for a given quantity and quality of product (or factor service).

C. Wage and Price Controls and the Expected Price Level

Since wage and price controls do not (as a first approximation) affect the level of the money supply or the level of government spending, they do not affect the level of aggregate demand. Again, as a first approximation, they do not affect aggregate supply. They do not, therefore, affect anything which determines the actual price level, and it would be irrational to expect the actual price level to be affected by controls.

D. Wage and Price Controls and the Actual Price Level

The actual price level is determined at the intersection of the aggregate demand and expectations-augmented aggregate supply curves. Wage and price controls do not shift either of these curves and do not, therefore, affect the actual price level.

E. Wage and Price Controls Make Matters Worse

To the extent that wage and price controls divert resources from the private sector, they lower output and raise the price level. To the extent that they generate a higher level of government spending to finance the program, they raise the price level. To the extent that they encourage slack monetary policies, they raise the inflation rate. To the extent that wage and price controls are applied unevenly and made to stick in some sectors, they generate relative price distortions and produce losses of economic welfare from a misallocation of resources.

Review Questions

1. What are the three features of a wage and price control programme? Give an example of each of these features.

2. Distinguish between the actual price and the posted price level in terms of the three dimensions of any transaction as outlined in this chapter.

3. Explain why wage and price controls may be used to control posted prices, but not actual prices.

4. List some products and the way in which each product's actual price can be adjusted in response to a posted price control.

5. Explain why wage and price controls cannot influence the rational expectation of the price level.

6. Work out, using the appropriate diagrams, the effects of expansionary monetary policy during a period of price controls.

7. Explain what is meant by the statement that, 'wage and price controls can only make matters worse.'

8. In terms of ordinary demand and supply curves, illustrate the welfare loss associated with a price control.

9. Who benefits from wage and price controls? Why do you think they are so popular?

41

United Kingdom Macroeconomic Policy

We have now completed our examination of the theory of macroeconomic policy. The previous chapters in this final part of the book have taken you through an analysis of what happens to aggregate output and the price level when alternative policy strategies are pursued. This final chapter is going to examine the macroeconomic policies that have been pursued in the United Kingdom in the post-war years. There exist many useful surveys of this topic.[1] None of them, however, with the exception of an excellent recent study of the Thatcher experiment by Willem Buiter and Marcus Miller[2], examines policy from the perspective suggested by the analysis that you have just completed. The analytical viewpoint adopted by most available surveys of United Kingdom macroeconomic policy is that of the

1. The most comprehensive surveys are J.C.R. Dow, *The Management of the British Economy, 1945–1960*, Cambridge University Press, 1964, F.T. Blackaby (ed.) *et al.*, *British Economic Policy, 1960–1974*, Cambridge University Press, 1978, Richard E. Caves *et al.*, *Britain's Economic Prospects*, The Brookings Institution, Washington DC and George Allen & Unwin, 1968 and Richard E. Caves and Lawrence B. Krause (eds), *Britain's Economic Performance*, The Brookings Institution, Washington DC, 1980. A useful study which adopts a narrower focus is Robert Bacon and Walter Eltis, *Britain's Economic Problem: Too Few Producers*, Macmillan, 1976. Two studies which fill in the political background (and which are more journalistic in style than those previously cited) are Michael Stewart, *Politics and Economic Policy in the UK Since 1964*, Pergamon Press, 1978 and William Keegan and Rupert Pennant-Rae, *Who Runs the Economy*, Maurice Temple Smith, 1979.

2. That study is Willem H. Buiter and Marcus H. Miller, The Thatcher experiment: the first two years, *Brookings Papers on Economic Activity*, 2, 1981, pp. 315–80. This book was in production by the time this paper was published and, therefore, this chapter has not been able to benefit from its excellent, balanced (if controversial and tentative) analysis.

neoclassical model. Consequently, policy actions are described, and the likely effects of each policy change are calculated, using the types of policy multipliers that you studied in Part IV of this book. As we have seen, that neoclassical framework for understanding macroeconomic phenomena was, in some important respects, a fairly spectacular failure during the 1970s. The new theories of macroeconomics, which predict that the effects of policies depend on whether those policies are anticipated or not, require that we take a broader view of the policy process in order to evaluate policy and understand the role that it might have played in influencing the economy. Since the new theories are indeed new, it is not possible to give a detailed, definitive, solidly researched account of how policy has influenced the economy. Much more basic research will have to be done before that is possible. What we can do, however, is to take a broader look at the monetary and fiscal policy processes that have been at work in post-war Britain and form some tentative picture as to what the major changes in the direction of policy have been. We may also attempt to reach some tentative judgments as to whether or not the major changes in the thrust of policy were anticipated or not. On the basis of such an assessment we may reach some tentative conclusions concerning the influence of policy on output and unemployment as well as on inflation.

Some specific questions are suggested by the analysis that has been conducted in the previous chapters. For example, has United Kingdom macroeconomic policy been Keynesian or Monetarist in nature? Yet more specifically, did United Kingdom macroeconomic policy become Monetarist in the summer of 1979 following the election of the government headed by Mrs Thatcher?

This final chapter will address these questions, focusing on the period since 1950. It will pursue four tasks which are to:

A. **review the content of fiscal policy;**
B. **review the content of monetary policy;**
C. **understand the main patterns in monetary and fiscal policy and how those policies have influenced inflation and output;**
and
D. **assess whether the policies pursued since 1979 constitute an example of Monetarism.**

A. Fiscal Policy

We may summarise fiscal policy in the United Kingdom in the post-war years by using the accounting relations established in Chapter 35. That is, we may examine the course of government expenditures on goods and services, transfer payments, debt interest payments, tax receipts, receipts from the sale of new debt and the issue of new money. We know that the first three items (the expenditures) must exactly equal the second three (the receipts). The Appendix to this chapter provides a detailed listing of these data covering the period between 1950 and 1979. It is instructive to focus on the values of these variables expressed as a percentage of GDP. So as to remove some of the influence of the cycles in economic activity on those percentages, we have calculated the values of the six items in the government's

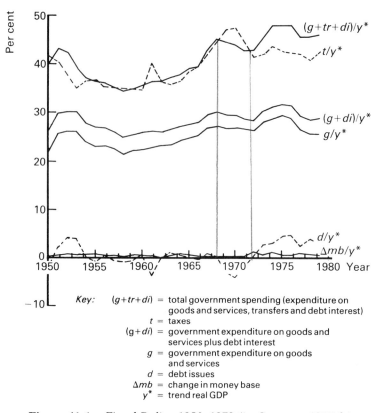

Figure 41.1 *Fiscal Policy 1950–1979 (in Constant 1975 £s)*

Expressed as a fraction of trend real GDP, government spending and taxes fell steadily after 1951 to 1958. Both then began to rise at first gradually but very strongly in the late 1960s. There is a short period (69–72) of renewed tightening of fiscal policy followed by a further burst of growth of spending and taxes in the middle 1970s. In the second-half of the 70s spending and taxes have declined slightly. The balance of expenditures over taxes (the deficit) has fluctuated considerably. Surpluses were recorded in the 1950s and early 60s and again in 1968–71. A large deficit emerged in the middle 1970s which persisted through to the end of the decade and into the early 80s. (*Source*: Appendix to this chapter, Table 1(c).)

---

budget constraint expressed in constant pounds as a percentage of the trend value of GDP.[3] These figures are also shown in the Appendix. More conveniently, they are illustrated in Figure 41.1. Let us study that figure and see what we can learn from it about fiscal policy in the period since 1950.

First, some rather remarkable long-term patterns in the data are very apparent. Focus first of all on government expenditures on goods and services (g/y^*). After an initial expansion of government spending in 1951–52, there was a six year downward trend in this variable that ended in 1958. For the next decade (1958–68) it followed a steady, persistent, upward trend. That trend was halted in 1968 and followed by four years of virtually constant (as a fraction of trend GDP) government spending. The

---

3. This does not remove all cyclical elements from the government's accounts, since both taxes and expenditures, especially transfer expenditures, are sensitive to the state of the economy.

mid-1970s saw a strong bulge in government expenditures which reached a peak in 1975. At the end of the 1970s the share of trend GDP being spent on goods and services by the government had returned to its mid-1960s level.

Transfer expenditures by the government follow a very similar pattern to spending on goods and services. This is visible in the figure as the vertical distance between the total government spending line (g/y^*) and the line that measures spending on goods and services plus debt interest, $(g + di)/y^*$. It is clear that total spending (spending on goods and services and transfers as well as debt interest (i.e. $(g + tr + di)/y^*$) has followed the same general pattern as spending on goods and services, but has been more volatile. The down-trend from 1952 to 1958 is stronger, and the up-trend to 1968 is much stronger — especially so in 1967–8. When spending on goods and services was constant around 1970, transfer spending was declining somewhat. For the most part, however, the two variables have followed very similar paths.

Total tax revenues (t/y^*) have followed a course that has departed from that of total expenditures in some important and interesting ways. At the beginning of the 1950s, taxes fell short of expenditure by a sizeable amount. By 1955, however, the gap had been closed and, for the most part, during the second-half of the 1950s the government accounts showed a modest surplus. A deficit briefly arose in 1956 and again in 1960. In 1961 there was a sudden and very sharp rise in the fraction of trend GDP taken in taxes and that resulted in a substantial budget surplus. In the following year, however, taxes were cut (but not quite as dramatically as they had been increased in the previous year). Taxes continued to be cut in 1963 and a deficit re-emerged in that year. The deficit persisted until 1966 when taxes rose again fairly sharply. Between 1969 and 1971 the government ran a very tight fiscal policy, with taxes increasing in the first of those two years and spending being cut in both of the years. As a result, a sizeable surplus emerged which persisted until 1972. In that year, however, a further tax cut, at the same time as spending was beginning its mid 1970s bulge, turned the government's accounts into a deficit. Taxes rose slightly in 1974 but remained at a rather constant fraction of trend GDP throughout the balance of the 1970s, so that the bulge in spending that we have already examined came through as a bulge in the government's deficit. The deficit persisted through the balance of the decade of the 1970s.

Before attempting to account for these patterns in fiscal policy and also to analyse their likely effects upon the economy, let us turn to a brief description of monetary policy.

B. Monetary Policy

As you know from the analysis of Chapter 35 and from your study of Chapter 14, monetary policy is significantly affected by the exchange rate regime. Under a fixed exchange rate regime there is little scope for the pursuit of an independent monetary policy. In such a case, the money supply is determined by the demand for money rather than by the policy actions of the monetary authorities. Under the flexible exchange rate regime, of course, these constraints no longer operate and the money supply is the outcome of the policy actions of the monetary authority. As you also

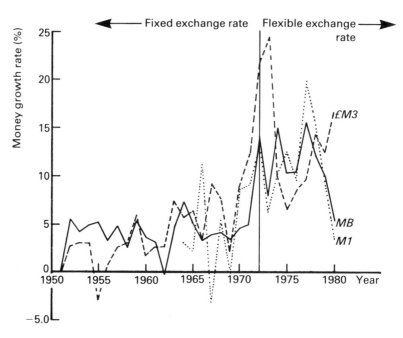

Figure 41.2 *Money Supply Growth 1950–1980*

Up to 1972 the exchange rate of the pound was fixed so that fluctuations in the money supply were determined by fluctuations in the demand for money rather than by monetary policy actions. Since 1972 the pound has been flexible and money supply growth has been determined by the Bank of England's policies. Clearly, after the pound floated, money supply growth became higher than previously and much more volatile. A strong burst of money growth in 1972–73 helped generate the strong inflation in the United Kingdom in the middle 70s. The tightening of monetary policy after 1978 (as measured by *M1* and monetary base) is probably in part responsible for the contraction of economic activity and the slowing of inflation at the beginning of the 80s. (*Source:* Appendix to this chapter, Table 2).

---

already know, the United Kingdom pursued a policy of rigidly adhering to a fixed exchange rate for the pound from 1949, when its value was first pegged at 2.80 US dollars up to 1972 when the exchange rate was allowed to float. There was, of course, a devaluation to 2.40 US dollars in 1967 but, following that devaluation, a renewed commitment to pegging the exchange rate at the new value was made. Further adjustments in the exchange rate followed in the early 1970s and, by the middle of 1972, a fixed exchange rate for the pound was abandoned and flexible exchange rates formally adopted.

Bearing this in mind let us now turn to an examination of Figure 41.2 which summarises monetary policy in the shape of growth rates for three monetary aggregates, the monetary base, *M1* and sterling *M3*. Evidently, the change in exchange rate regime in 1972 brought with it a dramatic shift in the average growth rate of the money supply. Although money growth had been fairly volatile in the fixed exchange rate period, its volatility and average value very clearly became higher in the period after 1972. There was some tendency to increased volatility and increased average money growth in 1970–71, but the really dramatic rise occurred in 1972. Even under fixed exchange rates, it is evident that there was a slight tendency for money growth to be higher in the 1960s than it had been in the 1950s. This, however, is not a reflection on the monetary policy of the United Kingdom authorities. It is a reflection of the fact that world inflation was higher in the 1960s than it had been in the 1950s and, with a fixed exchange rate, the 'law of one price' ensured that United Kingdom inflation and United Kingdom money growth increased to keep pace with the increase in world inflation.

Interpreting monetary policy in the United Kingdom in the flexible exchange rate period is made difficult by virtue of the fact that the different monetary aggregates have grown at very unequal rates. The picture obtained by following the growth rate of sterling *M3* is different from that shown by *M1*. The monetary base falls somewhere in between these two, but is somewhat closer to *M1* in its overall pattern. Judged from the growth rate of sterling *M3*, monetary policy became highly inflationary in the years immediately following the adoption of flexible exchange rates, then tightened substantially in 1974–75 and has been on a rising growth path since then. *M1* became highly expansionary in 1972, but slowed more quickly than did sterling *M3*. The acceleration of sterling *M3* growth after 1976 was matched by *M1* through 1977 but, since then, *M1* growth has been falling. The growth rate of the monetary base did not rise as much as the broad aggregate in 1972–73 but continued to accelerate until 1977. Since that time monetary base growth has fallen very strongly.

Although there is ambiguity, it seems to us that a reasonable judgment of the monetary policy is that it was expansionary in 1972–73. Much of the appearance of tight policy in 1973 in the *M1* growth figure arises from a substitution out of non interest-bearing forms of money and into interest-bearing deposits. To some extent that was reversed in 1974. Policy became tight again in 1974–75. There was a loosening of policy through 1977–78 and, after 1978, policy became tight again. In interpreting monetary policy in this way, we are clearly putting more weight on *M1* and the monetary base than on sterling *M3*. This seems to us to be the correct place to put the weight in view of the fact that the narrower aggregates more nearly correspond to the theoretical concept of money, while sterling *M3* includes term deposits and certificates of deposit which more closely resemble three-month bills of exchange than money.

A feature of the money supply growth rates in the United Kingdom both under fixed and flexible exchange rates, to which it is worth paying some attention, is their exceeding volatility. It is clearly extremely difficult to predict what the growth rate of any of these monetary aggregates is going to be one or more years into the future on the basis of the erratic way in which they have grown in the past. This is of some importance in understanding what has been happening to the United Kingdom economy.

Let us now turn our attention away from describing monetary and fiscal policy towards an attempt to discern patterns in those policies and identify some of their effects.

C. Policy Patterns and Effects

Let us begin by considering briefly the political background to macroeconomic policy.

(a) The Political Background

(i) **Churchill Conservatism:** In 1951 a Conservative government led by Winston Churchill was elected to replace the Labour government of Clement Attlee. The previous Labour government had been active in socialising much of the economy (nationalising the coal, gas, electricity, transport and steel industries) and had been content to keep a good deal of central control over the private sector of the economy by retaining control measures introduced during the war. The newly elected Conservative government was, from a philosophical point of view, very close to the recently elected conservative governments in the United Kingdom (Margaret Thatcher) and the United States (Ronald Reagan). Between 1952 and 1958, pursuing their conservative goals, the Churchill government reduced the fraction of trend GDP spent by the government on goods and services and transfer payments from 43% down to 35%. At the same time, and initially running ahead of the spending cuts, taxes were reduced from 40% to 35% of trend GDP. Thus, the Churchill government cut taxes and cut spending and removed a budget deficit of some 3% of GDP. During this period the exchange rate was pegged and enthusiastically so. Thus, there was no independent monetary policy. World money growth and world inflation were moderate and so were money growth and inflation in the United Kingdom.

(ii) **Macmillan Conservatism:** Following the military activities in Suez, Anthony Eden (Churchill's brief successor) was replaced as Prime Minister and leader of the Conservative government by Harold Macmillan. Unlike Churchill and Eden, Macmillan was what might be described (depending on your preferences) as a progressive or socialistically-inclined Conservative. Macmillan's Chancellor of the Exchequer was R.A. Butler, another progressive left-leaning Conservative. Indeed, at that same time Hugh Gaitskell was the leader of the Labour party and, in view of the difficulty in discerning the difference of political position between the Conservative and Labour parties at that time, the term 'Butskellism' was coined. This more radical form of Conservatism guided the formation of macroeconomic policy from 1958 to 1963. It was during that period that the long, steady trend rise in government spending both on goods and services and transfers began. By 1961, however, the pursuit of steadily rising spending combined with slightly falling taxes gave rise to a deficit on the government's budget. A balance of payments deficit also emerged in that year. Remaining fully committed to a fixed exchange rate, the government had no alternative (as you know from the discussion of the government's budget constraint discussed in Chapter 35) but to make some policy changes. The particular change adopted in 1961 was a massive rise in taxes. The tax rise turned the government's budget position around and restored a surplus in the balance of payments. This gave the Macmillan government the breathing space that it needed to launch a major 'dash for growth' in 1962–63. During those two years, taxes were cut, spending increased and the government budget surplus of 1961 turned into a modest but nevertheless significant deficit by 1963. This renewed expansion of government spending and cut in taxes was not consistent with a balance of payments equilibrium and, accordingly, the balance of payments went into deficit again in 1963–4. This deficit was inherited by a new Labour government in the autumn of 1964.

(iii) ***Wilson's First Labour Government:*** The Labour government headed by Harold Wilson, elected in the autumn of 1964, inherited from the previous Conservative government a growing balance of payments deficit. The new government was as dedicated as ever to both of the objectives that had been pursued by its predecessor — maintaining the exchange rate at 2.80 US dollars and expanding social and other government spending programmes. Further, like its predecessor the new government was reluctant to raise taxes too sharply. Accordingly, from 1964 to 1967 the Wilson government increased public spending and also increased taxes, but the latter not sufficiently to restore a surplus to the balance of payments. Increasing deficits and increasing difficulties in covering those deficits led ultimately, in November 1967, to a devaluation of the pound. In the process of defending the pound, however, and in the process of further defending it from subsequent devaluations, massive foreign borrowing was undertaken both from the International Monetary Fund and other central banks. The result of this was much the same as what happens when an individual finds that debts have been piled up to an uncomfortably high degree. The bank manager steps in and starts ordering the individual to make some economies. That is precisely what happened in the United Kingdom. The International Monetary Fund (IMF) placed severe restrictions on the room of the United Kingdom government for manoeuvre. In the final two years of its term of office the Wilson government, under restraints from the rest of the world monitored by the IMF, cut government spending and raised taxes to open up a large overall surplus on the government account and, in so doing, turned the United Kingdom's balance of payments around to a massive surplus by 1970.

In many ways 1969 was a replay of 1961. During the late 1950s, the Macmillan government had tried to spend more than it raised in taxes and more than was consistent with achieving a balance of payments equilibrium under fixed exchange rates. In 1961 its day of reckoning came. Similarly, the Labour government had to face the fundamental budget constraint when it realised that there was no other way of maintaining external balance at the fixed exchange rate.

(iv) ***Heath Conservatism:*** When the Wilson Labour government took office in 1964 it inherited an economy that was suffering from a government budget deficit and a balance of payments deficit. When the Heath Conservative government succeeded Wilson's Labour administration, exactly the reverse situation prevailed. The last years of the Wilson government had been spent in pursuing very tight policies which had generated a strong balance of payments and government budget surplus. The Conservative government of Heath, like the earlier Macmillan government, shared most of the social objectives of the Labour party. Unlike the Labour party and the previous Conservative governments, Heath and his followers were much more pragmatic on the issue of the fixed exchange rate. Indeed, they saw the fixed exchange rate as an impediment to the pursuit of desirable growth policies. In this, of course, they made a fundamental error. The exchange rate, being a purely monetary phenomenon, is (and some would argue ought to be) an impediment to pursuing *inflationary* policies and not an impediment to pursuing policies of rapid technological progress and real economic growth. Nevertheless, with this philosophical approach to macroeconomic policy, the Heath government embarked upon a programme of massive stimulation to the economy. Taxes were cut dramatically and, though spending was held steady for one year (1971–72), it began

to expand strongly in 1973–74. The large surplus inherited from the Labour government was quickly eroded and a deficit of almost unprecedented peacetime proportions emerged. When the balance of payments began to move into deficit (as it did by 1972) the remedy was simple — abandon the fixed exchange rate and keep the boom going. Money supply growth was accelerated at the same time as taxes were being cut and government spending on goods and services and transfers was being accelerated. By 1974 a strong inflationary situation had clearly developed.

(v) *Labour Under Wilson and Callaghan:*   From 1974 to 1979 a Labour government was back in power, initially led by Harold Wilson but subsequently by James Callaghan. For the second time in post-war history a Labour government inherited a badly overheated economy from its Conservative predecessor. Although dedicated to the same social goals as its predecessor, the Labour government began first to hold the line on spending growth and then subsequently to cut government expenditures from their peak 1974 levels. At the same time, the Labour government permitted tax revenues to decline slightly (as a fraction of GDP) and a deficit of between three and four per cent persisted. Money growth was highly erratic, but, on the average, slowed down, especially during 1978–79.

(vi) *Thatcher Conservatism:*   In May 1979 Margaret Thatcher was elected Prime Minister and inherited an economy that had been experiencing double digit inflation and a large government budget deficit for close on half a decade. The philosophical leaning of Mrs Thatcher represented, in effect, a return to the approach embodied in the government of Churchill in the early 1950s. Smaller government and an enhanced role for personal responsibility and freedom were emphasised. In macroeconomic policy terms this amounted to a desire to cut government spending and taxes. On the monetary policy front the new government adopted, by self-proclamation, a policy described as Monetarism. It even invoked the name of, and was visibly consulting with, such intellectual leaders of the Monetarist school as Milton Friedman and Karl Brunner. During the balance of 1979 and 1980 the Thatcher government continued to pursue a tightening of monetary policy, held the line on government expenditures, and increased taxes. The government deficit was reduced slightly but remained in the neighbourhood of 2% of GDP.

(b) What has Triggered the Major Switches of Policy?

The political narrative of the preceding section serves to account to some extent for the broader trends in macroeconomic policy making over the post-war years. It does not, however, in and of itself explain why there were from time to time sharp movements in the setting of policy instruments. What has triggered the main shifts of direction of policy? For the fixed exchange rate period up to 1972, the answer to this question is undoubtedly found in the commitment to the exchange rate with the need to achieve an external balance (or surplus). The sharp rise in taxes in 1961 and the tax rise and simultaneous spending cut in 1969–70 were clearly triggered by balance of payments problems. Further, the cut in taxes and the attempt to generate a strong output boom in 1962–63 and 1971–72 were triggered by the presence of a healthy payments balance. This strong balance of payments position was judged as allowing the more vigorous pursuit of social objectives, which have been present on a continuous basis between the Macmillan and Callaghan years, to take place.

Of course, the major policy shock in the United Kingdom in the post-war period was the abandonment of the fixed exchange rate in 1972. This policy change can be seen, however, as a natural consequence of the continuous and repeated attempt to run a fiscal policy characterised by high and growing government expenditures on goods and services and transfers, combined with a reluctance to see taxes growing at the required rate to finance those expenditures.

(c) What was Predictable and What was Not?

A careful, historical study which attempted to isolate what was known and not known, anticipated and not anticipated about macroeconomic policy in the United Kingdom over this post-war period would be an undertaking with a very high rate of return. No one has yet provided such a study and, in its absence, all that we can do is to draw some of the more obvious conclusions (tentative though they must be) from the broad patterns in the evolution of policy. First, it seems fairly evident that the commitment to a fixed exchange rate during the 1950s and 60s was a strong one and one that reflected a widely and deeply felt consensus. That being so, policy expectations were almost certainly formed (at least until the mid-1960s) on the presumption that fiscal policy would have to be adjusted to fit in with the requirements of the fixed exchange rate. Further, the balance of payments position was a readily observable and widely known variable so that, as the balance of payments weakened, more and more people would come to anticipate a tightening of fiscal policy. That being so, it may be presumed that most of the fiscal policy actions during the fixed exchange rate period were reasonably well anticipated. Their precise magnitudes and their precise timing may not have been anticipated, but the broad direction and approximate timing almost certainly were.

During the 1960s the consensus on the exchange rate was beginning to break down. Increasingly, professional economists and others including politicians were expressing scepticism about the value of maintaining a fixed exchange rate. The devaluation of 1967 therefore and the subsequent abandonment of fixed exchange rates in 1972 did not come as a bolt from the blue. These things had to some degree been anticipated. What had almost certainly not been anticipated, however, at least not to the extent that it occurred, was the use to which a Conservative government would put the new found freedom from the exchange rate peg. When, in 1973, the government permitted money supply growth to rise to the mid-twenties per cent per annum and permitted the budget deficit to soar, this must, to a large degree, have taken people by surprise. Thus, in 1973 there was almost certainly a large positive random shock to aggregate demand generated by macroeconomic policy. The magnitude of the reversal of that policy (especially the monetary policy) in 1974–75 in the face of severe recession must also have taken people by surprise. Thus, a positive shock was followed by a sizeable negative shock. The rebound of money growth up to 1978 was probably not regarded as surprising, but the firm tightening of money growth after 1978 must, at least at first, have taken people by surprise especially as regards its severity.

There is a further element of confusion being injected into policy in the last years of the 1970s as a result of the continuation of a high government deficit in combination with tight monetary policies. As you know from our discussion in Chapter 35, such a state of affairs cannot continue indefinitely. Either the deficit has to be removed, or money growth will at some stage rebound as the inflation tax is used to replace the transitory and, from the long-run point of view of the government, worthless borrowing. How people will resolve this confusion is not something on which we can make firm propositions. It does, however, seem likely that people will regard a government deficit that has been in place for six years as being a more permanent feature of the scene than a money growth rate that has been low for only two years. Thus, it is likely that from 1978 to 1981 the high government deficit was giving rise to a prediction that money growth will accelerate in the near future. The continuation of low money growth in the face of such an expectation has to be interpreted as being unexpected.

(d) Policy and the Economy

How do these tentative propositions about the decomposition of policy into expected and unexpected components fit the facts? In Chapter 7, where we discussed the business cycle, we described the movements of the deviations of real GDP from trend as being generated by a first-order difference equation disturbed by a random shock. The random shocks themselves were calculated (estimated). It may be worth looking back at Figure 7.6 to refresh your memory about those random shocks. We may interpret those random shocks as arising from a whole variety of sources — foreign prices, foreign income, long-term expectations about profit opportunities influencing investment spending, as well as from unanticipated monetary and fiscal policy. We have suggested that, prior to the floating of the pound, there probably wasn't very much unanticipated policy movement in the United Kingdom. Since then, however, we suspect that there have been some major, unexpected policy shifts. According to our estimates of the shocks hitting the economy in the 1970s, there was a large positive (5.1%) shock in 1973. This seems to coincide well with our supposition that both fiscal and monetary policy became unexpectedly expansionary during 1972–73. Further, according to our estimated shocks, a sizeable negative shock occurred in 1974–75. This too would be consistent with the notion that monetary policy was unexpectedly tight at that time. The negative shocks persist through 1978–79 and 1980 and become increasingly negative. This too is consistent with the notion that monetary policy in the last years of the 70s and in 1980 is unexpectedly tight.

An *unexpected* policy-induced *rise* in aggregate demand, such as occurred during 1972–73, will lower unemployment and raise both output and the price level. An unexpectedly *tight* monetary policy will raise unemployment and lower output and the price level. If such an unexpected tightening of monetary policy occurs at the same time as *expected* monetary growth is rapid, then inflation will remain high while the economy goes into a recession. This pattern of events is what occurred in the United Kingdom during 1979–1980.

Of course, this exercise is not a scientific one. We could equally well have started with the shocks and worked backwards to figure out what the unexpected policy must have been! As a matter of fact that is not how we proceeded, but such an ungenerous interpretation could easily be placed upon it. The fact of the matter is that what is required to provide a definitive analysis of these issues is a careful, serious, independent establishment of what was known and not known, expected and not expected, based on a detailed historical investigation. Nevertheless, we believe that the more limited exercise conducted here is an interesting one and gives insights into what might have been going on in the 1970s in the United Kingdom.

D. Is the Thatcher Government Pursuing Monetarist Policies?

Although the Thatcher government is a self-advertised Monetarist government, it seems to us that such a description is an inaccurate one. It is certainly not accurate if the term Monetarism is to be used in the way in which we have used it in this book. Recall from Chapter 1 how we defined Monetarism — the use of fixed rules for a limited number of macroeconomic policy instruments. Specifically, as elaborated in Chapters 37–39, a Monetarist policy would set the money supply growing at a constant rate and hold the money stock growth rate fixed indefinitely regardless of the state of the economy. Further, such a policy would put the government's budget into a deficit that was sustainable in the long run with the money supply growing at its pre-announced target rate. There is no sense in which the Thatcher government has embarked upon such a course. As we saw in Chapter 36, the Bank of England has not even adopted a technique of monetary control capable of delivering a growth rate of the money supply that is predictable in advance. Further, the government has not taken steps to cut government spending and/or raise taxes by amounts sufficient to achieve a budget deficit that is compatible with long-run, steady, money growth objectives. In many ways, the Thatcher macroeconomic policies may be seen as a natural extension and continuation of those pursued by the previous Callaghan Labour government. Money growth has been decelerated and sharply so, but that process had begun well over a year before the election of the Thatcher government.

There is another fundamental sense in which the Thatcher government is not pursuing Monetarist policies. This arises from the lack of consensus concerning Monetarism, not only amongst the political parties but even within the Conservative party. To pursue Monetarist policies a course must be set which is held steady not just for a year or two but for decades. To pursue such a policy requires a broadly based political consensus, so that people may form their expectations rationally on the presumption that the policy will be adhered to in all circumstances. In the British political system, either a change of Prime Minister and Chancellor of the Exchequer within a given political party, or a change in the political party in power, are capable of producing policy switches that are triggered by developments in the economy, thus abandoning any previously announced rules. The (unwritten) British constitution which assigns absolute power to parliament and lacks restraints on parliamentary power and legal mechanisms for enforcing those restraints mitigates against Monetarism being employed in the United Kingdom. This line of reasoning, although going well beyond the technical analysis that has been the concern of this book, suggests that the macroeconomy of the United Kingdom is in deep trouble and will not recover easily or quickly from its present painful state. For recovery to occur, a new consensus has to be forged, and that consensus then has to be embodied in statutes and institutions. Until that is done, we can predict (with some confidence) a continued erratic performance with a continuation of high and even possibly accelerating inflation over the longer run. Stopping that course will be a difficult task, but one that will at least not be made any harder as a result of having as thorough an understanding of macroeconomic processes as the current state of knowledge permits. We hope that this book has helped you towards such an understanding.

SUMMARY

A. Fiscal Policy

The patterns in the United Kingdom fiscal policy since 1950 are shown in Figure 41.1. Spending and taxes tended to fall up to 1958. They rose from 1958 to 1968, then dipped briefly to 1972, rose again to 1975 and fell slightly in the final years of the 1970s. The deficit has fluctuated, and swung into surplus briefly in 1961 and more strongly in 1969–71. A persistent deficit emerged in 1973 and remains firmly in place in 1980.

B. Monetary Policy

Up to 1972, the exchange rate of the pound was fixed so that there was, in effect, no independent domestic monetary policy. Money supply growth rates were volatile but reflected fluctuations in world macroeconomic developments. After floating the pound in 1972, United Kingdom money supply growth became volatile and rapid. (Figure 41.2 illustrates.)

C. Policy Patterns and Effects

The Conservative government of the early 1950s aimed to reduce the scale of government spending and taxes and succeeded in doing so. After 1958, regardless of whether the government was Conservative or Labour, the goals and objectives were the same — to expand social welfare and other government programmes, raising government spending as appropriate. Taxes were increased more reluctantly so that, from time to time, budget and balance of payments deficits emerged. With a fixed exchange rate constraint, taxes were always increased eventually to cover the budget and restore balance of payments equilibrium. With the abandonment of a fixed exchange rate in 1972, a more sustained expansionary fiscal and monetary policy was undertaken.

Policy was probably fairly well anticipated during the fixed exchange rate period but, after the adoption of flexible exchange rates, the strength of expansion in 1972–73 was probably underestimated, and the degree of policy tightness in 1974–75 was also probably underestimated. Further, and perhaps more seriously, tight monetary policies combined with a large and persistent deficit are probably best interpreted as implying unexpectedly tight monetary policy. The pattern of shocks estimated (and shown in Figure 7.6, Chapter 7) after 1972 is broadly consistent with this interpretation.

D. Is the Thatcher Government Pursuing Monetarist Policies?

On the definition of Monetarism employed in this book, it is evident that the Thatcher government is not a Monetarist government at all. Indeed, it is difficult to visualise how there could be Monetarist policy in the absence of a broad consensus embodied in appropriate statutory and institutional arrangements.

Appendix

1. *Fiscal Policy*

(a) Government Receipts and Expenditures in Current £s (£ million)

Year	(1) Government Expenditure on Goods and Services	(2) Transfer Payments	(3) Debt Interest	(4) Total Outlays and Receipts	(5) Taxes	(6) Debt Issues	(7) Money Creation
1950	2 509	1 570	510	4 589	4 784	−236	41
1951	3 239	1 697	527	5 463	5 119	278	66
1952	3 693	1 739	575	6 007	5 320	582	105
1953	3 897	1 401	604	5 902	5 235	583	84
1954	3 748	1 499	602	5 849	5 703	43	103
1955	3 826	1 593	653	6 072	6 108	−152	116
1956	4 192	1 693	668	6 553	6 403	74	76
1957	4 363	1 784	666	6 813	6 832	−134	115
1958	4 454	2 014	716	7 184	7 306	−186	64
1959	4 825	2 077	688	7 590	7 606	−153	137
1960	5 091	2 236	774	8 101	7 855	147	99
1961	5 507	2 503	784	8 794	9 589	−882	87
1962	5 952	2 716	693	9 361	9 359	5	−3
1963	6 290	2 942	809	10 041	9 615	293	133
1964	6 911	3 071	807	10 789	10 366	193	230
1965	7 543	3 519	850	11 912	11 684	60	168
1966	8 206	3 753	879	12 838	12 832	−109	115
1967	9 185	4 590	948	14 723	14 312	271	140
1968	9 844	5 447	1 083	16 374	16 155	65	154
1969	10 283	5 798	1 120	17 201	18 182	−1 108	127
1970	11 465	6 187	1 126	18 778	20 289	−1 693	182
1971	12 863	6 836	1 059	20 758	21 544	−992	206
1972	14 452	8 028	1 115	23 595	22 791	155	649
1973	17 089	9 200	1 364	27 653	25 656	1 593	404
1974	21 059	12 293	1 832	35 184	32 019	2 295	870
1975	28 138	15 549	2 184	45 871	40 959	4 238	674
1976	32 262	18 450	3 031	53 743	47 584	5 402	757
1977	34 144	21 039	3 663	58 846	54 207	3 349	1 290
1978	37 675	25 266	4 308	67 249	60 276	5 813	1 160
1979	43 555	29 249	5 497	78 301	72 074	5 176	1 051

(b) Government Receipts and Expenditures in Constant 1975 £s

	(1) Government Expenditure on Goods	(2)	(3)	(4) Total Outlays and	(5)	(6)	(7)
Year	and Services	Transfer Payments	Debt Interest	Receipts	Taxes	Debt Issues	Money Creation
1950	10 806	6 761	2 196	19 764	20 604	−1 016	176
1951	12 980	6 800	2 112	21 893	20 515	1 114	264
1952	13 564	6 387	2 111	22 063	19 540	2 137	385
1953	13 898	4 996	2 154	21 049	18 671	2 079	299
1954	13 110	5 243	2 105	20 459	19 948	150	360
1955	12 935	5 385	2 207	20 529	20 650	−513	392
1956	13 347	5 390	2 126	20 865	20 387	235	241
1957	13 350	5 459	2 037	20 847	20 905	−410	351
1958	13 011	5 883	2 091	20 986	21 343	−543	186
1959	13 865	5 968	1 977	21 811	21 857	−439	393
1960	14 373	6 312	2 185	22 871	22 177	415	279
1961	15 046	6 838	2 142	24 027	26 199	−2 409	237
1962	15 728	7 177	1 831	24 737	24 731	13	−7
1963	16 250	7 600	2 090	25 941	24 841	756	343
1964	17 333	7 702	2 024	27 059	25 998	484	576
1965	18 177	8 480	2 048	28 706	28 157	144	404
1966	19 027	8 702	2 038	29 768	29 754	−252	266
1967	20 721	10 355	2 138	33 214	32 287	611	315
1968	21 567	11 934	2 372	35 875	35 395	142	337
1969	21 732	12 253	2 367	36 352	38 425	−2 341	268
1970	22 492	12 137	2 209	36 839	39 803	−3 321	357
1971	22 783	12 108	1 875	36 766	38 158	−1 757	364
1972	23 195	12 885	1 789	37 870	36 580	248	1 041
1973	25 399	13 673	2 027	41 100	38 132	2 367	600
1974	26 750	15 615	2 327	44 693	40 673	2 915	1 105
1975	28 138	15 549	2 184	45 871	40 959	4 238	674
1976	28 313	16 192	2 660	47 166	41 760	4 740	664
1977	26 711	16 459	2 865	46 035	42 406	2 619	1 009
1978	26 497	17 769	3 029	47 297	42 392	4 088	815
1979	27 257	18 304	3 440	49 002	45 105	3 239	657

(c) Government Receipts and Expenditures in Constant 1975 £s as a Percentage of Trend Real GDP

Year	(1) Government Expenditure on Goods and Services	(2) Transfer Payments	(3) Debt Interest	(4) Total Outlays and Receipts	(5) Taxes	(6) Debt Issues	(7) Money Creation
1950	21.89	13.69	4.45	40.04	41.74	-2.05	.35
1951	25.60	13.41	4.16	43.19	40.47	2.19	.52
1952	26.05	12.26	4.05	42.38	37.53	4.10	.74
1953	25.99	9.34	4.02	39.37	34.92	3.88	.56
1954	23.87	9.55	3.83	37.26	36.33	.27	.65
1955	22.94	9.55	3.91	36.40	36.62	-.91	.69
1956	23.05	9.30	3.67	36.03	35.20	.40	.41
1957	22.45	9.17	3.42	35.05	35.15	-.68	.59
1958	21.30	9.63	3.42	34.36	34.94	-.88	.30
1959	22.10	9.51	3.15	34.77	34.85	-.70	.62
1960	22.31	9.80	3.39	35.50	34.43	.64	.43
1961	22.74	10.33	3.23	36.32	39.60	-3.64	.35
1962	23.15	10.56	2.69	36.41	36.40	.01	-.01
1963	23.29	10.89	2.99	37.18	35.60	1.08	.49
1964	24.19	10.75	2.82	37.76	36.28	.67	.80
1965	24.70	11.52	2.78	39.01	38.26	.19	.55
1966	25.18	11.51	2.69	39.39	39.37	-.33	.35
1967	26.70	13.34	2.75	42.80	41.60	.78	.40
1968	27.06	14.97	2.97	45.01	44.41	.17	.42
1969	26.55	14.97	2.89	44.41	46.94	-2.86	.32
1970	26.76	14.44	2.62	43.82	47.35	-3.95	.42
1971	26.39	14.02	2.17	42.59	44.20	-2.03	.42
1972	26.16	14.53	2.01	42.72	41.26	.28	1.17
1973	27.89	15.01	2.22	45.14	41.88	2.60	.65
1974	28.61	16.70	2.48	47.80	43.50	3.11	1.18
1975	29.30	16.19	2.27	47.77	42.65	4.41	.70
1976	28.71	16.42	2.69	47.83	42.35	4.80	.67
1977	26.37	16.25	2.82	45.46	41.87	2.58	.99
1978	25.47	17.08	2.91	45.47	40.76	3.93	.78
1979	25.52	17.13	3.22	45.88	42.23	3.03	.61

2. *Monetary Policy*

	(1)	(2)	(3)	(4)	(5)	(6)
Year	MB	MB Growth Rate	M1	M1 Growth Rate	£M3	£M3 Growth Rate
1951	1 869	--	--	--	8 212	--
1952	1 974	5.5	--	--	8 447	2.8
1953	2 058	4.2	--	--	8 714	3.1
1954	2 161	4.9	--	--	8 982	3.0
1955	2 277	5.2	--	--	8 734	-2.8
1956	2 353	3.3	--	--	8 815	.9
1957	2 468	4.8	--	--	9 043	2.6
1958	2 532	2.6	--	--	9 317	3.0
1959	2 669	5.3	--	--	9 895	6.0
1960	2 768	3.6	--	--	10 077	1.8
1961	2 869	3.1	--	--	10 339	2.6
1962	2 862	-.2	--	--	10 614	2.6
1963	2 995	4.5	7 860	--	11 420	7.3
1964	3 225	7.4	8 110	3.1	12 080	5.6
1965	3 393	5.1	8 290	2.2	12 870	6.3
1966	3 508	3.3	9 270	11.2	13 300	3.3
1967	3 648	3.9	8 990	-3.1	14 570	9.1
1968	3 802	4.1	9 500	5.5	15 700	7.5
1969	3 929	3.3	9 490	-.1	16 020	2.0
1970	4 111	4.5	10 340	8.6	17 530	9.0
1971	4 317	4.9	11 330	9.1	19 790	12.1
1972	4 966	14.0	12 880	12.8	24 630	21.9
1973	5 370	7.8	13 700	6.2	31 430	24.4
1974	6 240	15.0	15 190	10.3	34 660	9.8
1975	6 914	10.3	17 220	12.5	36 980	6.5
1976	7 671	10.4	18 950	9.6	40 280	8.5
1977	8 961	15.5	23 090	19.8	44 340	9.6
1978	10 121	12.2	26 940	15.4	51 080	14.2
1979	11 172	9.9	29 470	9.0	57 840	12.4
1980	11 785	5.3	30 560	3.6	68 620	17.1

Sources for Tables in Appendix 41:

Fiscal Policy Source for Table 1(a)
1950–1955:

> *Government expenditure on goods and services* is the sum of the expenditures on goods and services by the central government and local authorities on the current account and the capital account.

> *Transfer payments* is the sum of subsidies and grants made by the central government and local authorities on the current account and grants made by central government and local authorities on the capital account, less grants from abroad and transfers from abroad.

> *Debt interest* is the sum of the central government's and local authorities' debt interest, less interest and dividends, etc. made by the central government and local authorities.

> *Total outlays and receipts* is the sum of government expenditure on goods and services, transfer payments and debt interest.

> *Taxes* is the sum of taxes on income, taxes on expenditure collected by the central government and local authorities, gross trading income of the central government and local authorities, gross rental income of the central government and local authorities, and taxes on capital.

> *Debt issues* is total outlays and receipts, less money creation.

> *Money creation* is the change in monetary base.

> 1950   *National Income and Expenditure 1961*, Table 43, pp. 40–1.
> 1951–2 *National Income and Expenditure 1962,* Table 43, pp. 44–5.
> 1953–4 *National Income and Expenditure 1964,* Table 43, pp. 48–9.
> 1955   *National Income and Expenditure 1966*, Table 48, pp. 58–9.

1956–1979:

> *Government expenditure on goods and services* is the sum of current expenditure on goods and services, non-trading capital consumption, gross domestic fixed capital formation and increase in value of stock.

> *Transfer payments* is the sum of subsidies, current grants to personal sector, current grants paid abroad (net), and grants and other transfers.

> *Total outlays and receipts* is the sum of government expenditure on goods and services, transfer payments, and debt interest.

> *Taxes* is the sum of taxes on income, taxes on expenditure, national insurance, etc. contributions, gross trading surplus, rent, imputed charge for consumption of non-trading capital and taxes on capital and other capital receipts.

> *Money creation* is the change in the monetary base.

> *Debt issues* is total outlays and receipts, less taxes and money creation.

> 1956–8 *National Income and Expenditure 1967*, Table 47, pp. 56–7.
> 1959–65 *National Income and Expenditure 1970,* Table 43, pp. 50–1.
> 1966   *National Income and Expenditure 1966–76*, Table 9.1, p. 61.
> 1967   *National Income and Expenditure 1967–77*, Table 9.1, p. 65.
> 1968   *National Income and Expenditure 1979 edition*, Table 9.1, p. 63.
> 1969–79 *National Income and Expenditure 1980 edition*, Table 9.1, p. 59.

Source for Table 1(b)

Government receipts and expenditure in constant 1975 pounds are government receipts and expenditure in current pounds deflated by the GDP Deflator which has the value of 100 in 1975. The Appendix to Chapter 2 gives the GDP Deflator.

Source for Table 1(c)

Government receipts and expenditure in constant 1975 pounds as a percentage of trend real GDP are calculated by dividing government receipts and expenditure in constant 1975 pounds by trend real GDP and multiplying by 100. The Appendix to Chapter 2 gives trend real GDP.

Source for Table 2

Monetary base (MB):

Bank of England Quarterly Bulletin, March 1981, pp. 63–4.
(The figure in the table is the mid-December figure.)

M1:

1963–78 *Quarterly Money Stock Series, 1963I–1979III,* Bank of England, December 1979.
1979–80 *Bank of England Quarterly Bulletin,* Vol. 21, No. 2, June 1981, Table 11.1.
(The figure in the table is the fourth quarter figure.)

Sterling M3 (£M3):

1951–62 *Bank of England Statistical Abstract,* No. 1, 1970, p. 81.
1963–78 *Quarterly Money Stock Series 1963I–1979III,* Bank of England, December 1979.
1979–80 *Bank of England Quarterly Bulletin,* Vol. 21, No. 2, June 1981, Table 11.1.
(The figure in the table is the fourth quarter figure.)

Review Questions

1.   Review the main trends in fiscal policy since 1950:
     (a) during which periods was government expenditure on goods and services expanding (contracting) as a percentage of GDP?
     (b) during which periods did current tax revenues exceed (fall short of) expenditures?

2.   Compare and contrast the fiscal policy patterns (the scale and directions of change in spending, revenue, and deficits) in the three decades since 1950.

3.   Using the latest data available to you (which you will find in *Economic Trends*) update the figures given in Tables 1(a), 1(b) and 1(c) of the Appendix to this chapter to include 1980 (and when possible subsequent years). [The value of trend real GDP in 1975 prices which you should use for Table (c) calculations is, for 1980, £m. 109, 682, and for subsequent years use a growth rate of 2.66% p.a.] Is there any sign that government spending, taxes and the deficit have changed markedly during the years of the Thatcher government?

4.   Review the main patterns in money supply growth since 1950. During which periods was money supply growth rising? During which was it falling? During which periods is there ambiguity (because of divergences in growth rates of different aggregates)?

5.   Compare and contrast money growth in the UK under fixed exchange rates with that under flexible exchange rates.

6.   Has post-war macroeconomic policy in the UK been more nearly like that described in this book as Keynesian or Monetarist?

7.   Examine the monetary and fiscal policies of the self-proclaimed Monetarist government of Mrs Thatcher. Are those policies 'Monetarist' in the sense in which that term is used by macroeconomists and as used in this book?

8.   Is it possible to account for the rise in unemployment in the United Kingdom in 1981 to more than 3 million with existing macroeconomic models? What, according to those models, has been the role of policy in creating this unemployment? What can policy do to create a situation in which more people have jobs?

9.   What have been the major influences on inflation in the United Kingdom in the period since 1950? How could policy have been modified to prevent the strong outburst of inflation in the 1970s?

Index

Notes

Notes

Notes

Notes